KNOW IT AND GROW IT
III

A Guide to the Identification and
Use of Landscape Plants

by

Carl E. Whitcomb, Ph.D.

KNOW IT AND GROW IT

III

Illustrations by
Joyce Gehrke Hughes
Leesburg, Florida

All Photographs by
Carl E. Whitcomb

Library of Congress Catalog Card Number: 83-81600

ISBN 0-9613109-0-1

Lacebark Inc., Publications and Research
P.O. Box 2383
Stillwater, Oklahoma 74076

This book is dedicated to

my wife, LaJean,

whose interest and assistance made

KNOW IT AND GROW IT,

KNOW IT AND GROW IT, 'II',

and now

KNOW IT AND GROW IT, 'III'

realities
and to the many students who struggled through my
plant materials courses without a text,
and students of plant science everywhere.

Their interest and enthusiasm played a major
role in the development of these books.

ACKNOWLEDGMENTS

Many people have influenced the development of this book. Ted Barkley, Professor of Botany, and Ray A. Keen, Professor of Horticulture, Kansas State University, played a major role in developing my interest in plant identification and use. Eliot C. Roberts, former Professor of Plant and Soil Science, University of Rhode Island, and director of the Lawn Institute, further assisted in this interest.

Appreciation is extended to the following for reviewing the original manuscript: Paul J. Mitchell, Extension Horticulturist, Oklahoma State University; Frank R. Carpenter, Associate Dean, College of Agriculture, Kansas State University; Gerald Smith, Extension Horticulturist, University of Georgia; Dwight Hughes, Jr., Hughes Nursery, Cedar Rapids, Iowa; Eleanor Hill, Tulsa, Oklahoma; and Ruth Ann Stuart, Stillwater, Oklahoma.

Cara Beer, Stillwater, Oklahoma, assisted with editing the manuscript of II.

Joyce Gehrke Hughes, The Pen and Ink Design Studio, Leesburg, Florida transformed my crude sketches into illustrations to show key plant features.

My two sons, Andy and Benjamin, served as able assistants in taking many photos. Their fingers appear on numerous pages throughout the text. Their understanding of "Daddy's work" on the original book helped more than they realize. Now that they are grown, their further assistance and understanding greatly aided the completion of this revised and expanded version. Andy, Benjamin, and Pamela Whitcomb were most helpful in editing, typing, and all of the details that go into a major revision of such a large book. Most of all to my wife, LaJean, for the huge number of hours spent on the word processor and in assisting in many ways. Without her help this book would never have become a reality and certainly this major revision would never have gotten done.

Many thanks to all.

Carl E. Whitcomb

TABLE OF CONTENTS

About the Author

Carl E. Whitcomb was born and raised in a rural community in southeast Kansas. Following an assortment of construction work experiences, intermingled with attending Kansas State University, he received the degree, Bachelor of Science in Agriculture, with a major in Horticulture in 1964. He received the Master of Science degree, majoring in Turf Management, and Doctor of Philosophy degree with majors in Horticulture, Plant Ecology, and Agronomy from Iowa State University in 1969. He joined the faculty of the University of Florida, Department of Ornamental Horticulture in 1967. There he taught "Identification of Landscape Plants", "Ground Maintenance", "Nursery Production", "Plant Growth in the Urban Environment" and "Arboriculture". In 1972 he joined the faculty of the Horticulture Department at Oklahoma State University. In addition to studying and teaching the identification and use of landscape plants, he conducted extensive research on the establishment of woody plants in the landscape, effects of grass competition and other factors on growth of woody plants, and factors influencing growth and performance of nursery stock.

He is an avid photographer. All photos in this book were taken by the author. He is author or co-author of over 300 technical and semi-technical publications and is a frequent speaker before various nursery, turf and landscape organizations. The original *Know It & Grow It* began as a dream about 1968, and as an active project in November 1972. The first revised and expanded version consumed much of 1982 and early 1983. Deciding what to add to this latest revision and simply revising and updating each existing page was a huge task. It is a culmination of over 35 years of active interest in the identification and use of woody landscape plants.

Whitcomb is also author of *Plant Production in Containers*, 1984, Revised 1988; *Production of Landscape Plants*, 1987, Revised 1989; *Establishment and Maintenance of Landscape Plants*, 1987, Revised 1991, published by Lacebark Inc., Publications and Research, Stillwater, Oklahoma.

Since retiring from Oklahoma State University in 1985 to pursue personal interests, he has conducted research on products to solve problems for the nursery and landscape businesses and several of those products are on the market. A great deal of time has been devoted to the selection of superior cultivars of crapemyrtle and other landscape plants from large seedling populations.

In 1991 he began working with farmers, nurserymen, and greenhouse operators that could not get their crops to grow normally. The culprit was the contamination of the widely used fungicide, Benlate 50 DF. The key contaminants were sulfonylurea-type herbicides and flusilazole. Continued research into the sulfonylurea-type herbicides has confirmed that they are volatile and damage most broadleaf species and some conifers at low rates beyond the imagination. These volatile herbicides (trade names: Oust, Escort, Telar, Glean, Ally, Finesse, and others) cause a huge array of deformities in flowers, fruits, leaves, stems, and roots of plants. The photographs in this book are of plants the way they should be and used to be, but not necessarily as you will find them at the present time. As one researcher described it: the plants are experiencing metabolic mayhem. As a result of the herbicide damage, the plants cannot tolerate stresses that would normally be considered routine and of little consequence. Research into this problem will continue.

Introduction

This book is intended to assist students, nurserymen, amateur gardeners and others interested in the identification and use of plants in the landscape. Reference books on plant identification without illustrations or photographs are very difficult to use. Even botanists collect and press plant specimens in herbariums to assist in identification so they can see the real thing. Many books use line drawings in an attempt to show leaf forms and other key plant features. In some cases, these can be of assistance; however, enough detail to make a positive identification is generally lacking. Written descriptions of plants play a major role in relating features of each species, but words can only provide a limited description or interpretation of what the writer has seen. Rehder, in his ***Manual of the Cultivated Trees and Shrubs Hardy in North America,*** used an array of terms in an attempt to relate to the reader such features as leaf shape and leaf surface texture. To the professional horticulturist or botanist, many of these terms have meaning, but to the practicing nurseryman, landscape architect, or amateur gardener, many of these terms mean another trip to the glossary and additional confusion.

In this book, photos have been used to complement the written descriptions whenever possible. It is hoped that photographs of bark, leaves, and other features can be used for direct comparison with the plant one wishes to identify. However, even photographs are subject to the author's interpretation of what is normal or typical. In a few instances, several photos of leaves or bark were included to show the variation commonly encountered. In other cases, there was not sufficient space to show all the variations. Photos of entire plants are intended to show the form one might expect of such a plant in the landscape.

The maps in the upper right show where the plant is generally well adapted with the northern limit the top of the hardiness zone. Within the broad black line, the plant will generally do well on most sites, assuming reasonable soil and growing conditions. Extra care must be given to selecting the planting site and/or in preparing the site, watering, or other maintenance beyond the black line. These geographic areas of adaptation are based on the experience and observations of the author. All areas are approximate. Many plants can be extended beyond these general areas of adaptation if sufficient consideration is given to their specific requirements and environmental modification made to meet these requirements. It should be remembered that, as a general rule, **the farther a plant is removed from its native habitat or similar environment, the more care and maintenance it will require in order to do well.**

In some cases, several species are grouped together on one page. This was done to conserve space since cultural requirements and adaptation are similar for the group. Also, plants of minor importance are mentioned only as a closely related species or when distinguishing species is difficult. In some cases, the key features to look for in order to distinguish between two similar plants are listed under **NOTES.**

Plant adaptation lists have been included in the appendix to aid the user in finding a landscape plant adapted to a specific site or condition. In addition, lists give plants with showy flowers, fruits, fall color, fragrance, or other useful landscape features. All plants with confirmed poisonous properties are marked XX-POISON-XX. All plants with suspected poisonous properties if eaten in quantity are marked ??-POISON-??. This information is based on the text by Kingsbury and other references.

I have followed ***Hortus III*** for plant names in nearly all instance. Also, I am not prone to accept the absurd name changes simply some taxonomist has too much time on his hands and/or needs a publication for the resume. Also, I have chosen to stay with the USDA Hardiness Zone Map as a rough approximation of the cold hardiness of a plant.

With best wishes,

Carl Whitcomb

Carl E. Whitcomb

PLANT IDENTIFICATION: SOME SUGGESTIONS

Flowers, fruits, leaves, stems, bark, and overall form are the plant features most commonly used in plant identification. Our present system of plant classification is based primarily on the reproductive parts of plants (flowers and fruits) since these are less subject to alteration by the growing conditions experienced by a particular plant. Flowers may be showy as the rose or nearly obscure as in the case of the hickories and other nut trees.

Carya spp.
Hickory

Rosa spp.
Rose

Likewise, fruits may be large and showy or small and nearly hidden by the leaves as in the case of fragrant sumac and sugar maple.

Rhus aromatica
Fragrant Sumac

Acer saccharum
Sugar Maple

However, much of the time when it is necessary to identify a plant neither flowers nor fruits are available. Therefore, one is dependent on the use of other plant features. Whether leaves and twigs are arranged opposite or alternate on the stem is a basic feature which should always be considered. There are only a few trees with opposite leaves; thus if the specimen you have has opposite leaves, the search can be narrowed a great deal very quickly. Many people have difficulty distinguishing holly, *Ilex*, from the false holly, *Osmanthus*, but since holly have alternate leaves and false holly have opposite leaves, there is no need for confusion. Unlike the trees, many shrubs have opposite leaves and stems, such as the glossy privet.

Ligustrum japonicum
Glossy Privet

Leaves vary a great deal and can be grouped in several ways for ease of identification. Simple leaves consist of one leaf blade or expanded portion as in the case of the dogwood, maple, and sycamore. Note that the dogwood leaf is more or less egg-shaped or oval with a wavy margin or edge, while the maple and sycamore leaves both have three major fingers or lobes. However, there are many teeth on the margin of the sycamore while the sugar maple leaf margin is smooth. On young, vigorous stems, the sycamore also has another unique feature at the base of the leaf. This small leaf-like appendage is called a stipule and, since few woody plants have stipules, it is a good aid to plant identification.

Cornus florida
Flowering Dogwood

Acer saccharum
Sugar Maple

Platanus occidentalis
American Sycamore

Compound leaves have several leaflets or leaf-like blades attached to a central stem or rachis. One of the most difficult tasks for the beginner is to determine what is a simple leaf and what is a group of simple leaflets which comprise a compound leaf. Two features are helpful here: 1) most true leaves are slightly enlarged or swollen where they attach to the stem, and 2) if a true leaf is removed from the stem, it generally breaks clean leaving no "strings" or jagged edges. On the other hand, if a leaflet is removed from the central stalk of a compound leaf, it nearly always tears, leaving a group of "strings" or jagged edges at the base.

Shape, number and arrangement of leaflets on the compound leaf are also useful features in plant identification. The tree photos below show once-compound leaves with similarly shaped leaflets, yet each has unique characteristics. These features are very difficult to describe in words, but can readily be seen in photographs.

Fraxinus americana
White Ash

Carya illinoinensis
Pecan

Rhus glabra
Smooth Sumac

Two leaf features probably account for more errors in plant identification than all others. These are **leaf size** and **leaf color**. One should use leaf size and leaf color for identification **only** after all other plant features have been considered. Leaf size may be influenced by moisture stress, soil fertility, light intensity or shading, and other environmental factors. Leaf color may be due to time of year, cultivar, nutrient deficiencies, insect damage, or herbicide toxicity. For example, the two American elm leaves below were taken from the same plant. Likewise, the three hickory leaves all came from a rapidly growing young tree.

Ulmus americana
American Elm

Carya cordiformis
Bitternut Hickory

The nandina leaves below are yellow because of severe iron and manganese deficiency. Note the green veins. By contrast, the pyracantha leaves are yellowing along the margin and green in the center. This is characteristic of damage from certain herbicides.

Nandina domestica
Heavenly Bamboo

Pyracantha spp.
Pyracantha

It is important to obtain mature leaves or leaves fully expanded when attempting to identify plants. The very young hickory leaves in the photo below do not yet resemble the mature leaves at the top of the page. However, when the odor of crushed foliage is a useful feature, very young leaves are more helpful than older leaves. The odor of crushed leaves can be a useful feature for identification of several plants such as junipers, southern wax myrtle, and Chinese pistache.

Carya cordiformis
Bitternut Hickory

Prunus spp.
Cherry

Young, vigorously growing shoots often have corky growths on the bark called lenticels. Whether the lenticles go around the stem as in the case of the cherry, left, or are diamond-shaped or go up and down the stem, are also useful features for identification. Some plants have only a few lenticels while others have many.

Bark features are often only subtly different, and only with experience can these be of assistance. Also bark on trees may vary due to genetic differences among seedlings. The bark of the two pecan trees below appear rather different.

Carya illinoensis
Pecan

Carya illinoensis
Pecan

The age of the stem may also affect bark appearance. The tuliptree below has a smooth bark when young, yet it begins to furrow and appear quite different with age. By contrast, the bark on the branch of the sweetgum appears quite similar to the main stem.

Liriodendron tulipifera
Tuliptree

Liquidambar styraciflua
Sweetgum

With experience, one can identify many trees and shrubs by their overall form. For example, compare the form of the pin oak or Bradford pear with the pecan, red mulberry, and white poplar. The pin oak is more upright and loose while the Bradford pear is dense and narrowly oval. The pecan, red mulberry, and white poplar have a similar rounded crown in mature form, yet can be easily distinguished.

Quercus palustris
Pin Oak

Pyrus calleryana 'Bradford'
Bradford Pear

Carya illinoensis
Pecan

Morus rubra
Red Mulberry

Populus alba
White Poplar

However, in order to do so, one must **learn to see detail** in every plant feature. One of the best ways is to observe a specimen several times but only for a few minutes each time. Plant features missed on the first visit often become apparent the second or third visit. It is unlikely anyone can "cram" plant features into the brain with any degree of accuracy or detail.

The following two pages of general plant features should be learned in order to relate immediately written descriptions to visual features. This list of representative features has been greatly simplified, compared to those of other authors. These are the most common useful features encountered in identifying most landscape plants.

The binomial system of nomenclature is used here. The scientific name of any plant is in two parts: 1) the name of the genus and 2) the name of the species. For example, the scientific name of white oak is *Quercus alba*. *Quercus* being the genus for all oaks and *alba* the species specifically of white oak. The genus is always a noun and is always written with a capital initial letter. The species name is often descriptive of the plant and is never capitalized. In modern horticulture, many plant selections have been made of a particular genus and species. These plant selections are generally reproduced asexually and may be quite different from the parent, thus the term, cultivar. For example, *Acer palmatum*, Japanese maple, has been grown in cultivation for centuries and many selections have been made with leaf forms different from most seedlings. These selections or cultivars represent a variation of the species. Cultivars may be named for a different leaf or growth form, increased cold tolerance, disease or insect resistance, flower color, or some other feature. In modern landscaping, the cultivar is a major factor. For example, *Ilex vomitoria* is a large shrub or small tree reaching 20 feet in height, whereas *Ilex vomitoria* 'Nana' is a densely compact shrub, rarely reaching more than 3 to 4 feet in height. Cultivars, therefore, are very important in achieving the desired landscape effect. **Cultivar names are always capitalized and in single quotes**. This is done to avoid confusion between the species and cultivar name. However, even with the capital and single quotes, the genus and species names should always be used in writing. The most prominent example is with *Ilex cornuta* 'Rotunda' which is a low, compact shrub. However, if one writes *Ilex* 'Rotunda', it could easily be confused with *Ilex rotunda*, the tree. This would be especially true if the single quotes and/or capital were omitted for the cultivar rotunda.

For more information on cultivars, the reader is encouraged to review *The Concept of the Cultivar* by J.S. Pringle, Vol. 27, no. 3 of the Garden Bulletin, a publication of the Royal Botanical Gardens, Hamilton, Ontario, Canada.

Scientific names in this text are followed by the abbreviation of the name of the person(s) naming the plant. This is important only to the professional horticulturist or botanist who wishes to know where that specific plant name originated. In some cases, a plant name(s) has been given to a specific plant by two or more persons, independent of the other. Thus the complex of names following a few plants. For a complete explanation of this procedure, the reader is encouraged to refer to Porter's *Taxonomy of Flowering Plants* or a similar reference book.

Common leaf shapes.

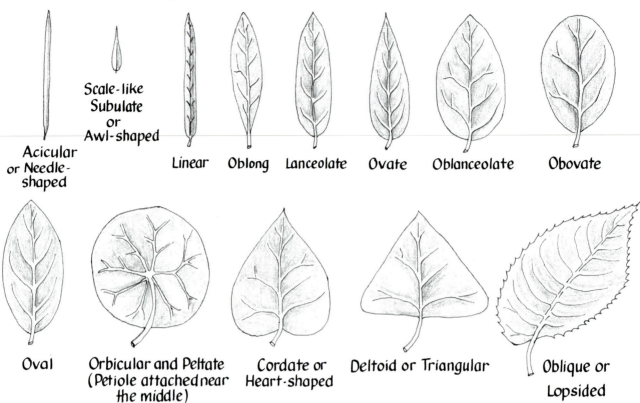

Acicular or Needle-shaped

Scale-like Subulate or Awl-shaped

Linear

Oblong

Lanceolate

Ovate

Oblanceolate

Obovate

Oval

Orbicular and Peltate (Petiole attached near the middle)

Cordate or Heart-shaped

Deltoid or Triangular

Oblique or Lopsided

Leaf tips.

Leaf margins.

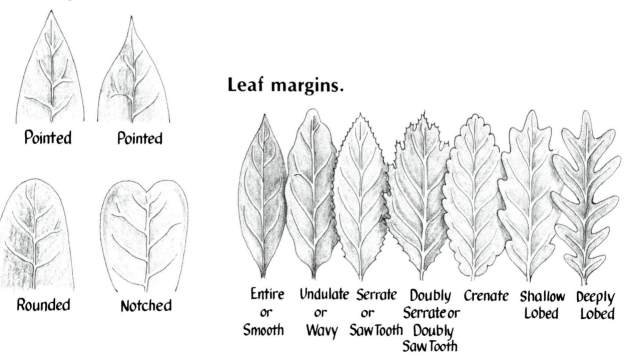

Pointed

Pointed

Rounded

Notched

Entire or Smooth

Undulate or Wavy

Serrate or Saw Tooth

Doubly Serrate or Doubly Saw Tooth

Crenate

Shallow Lobed

Deeply Lobed

Leaf types.

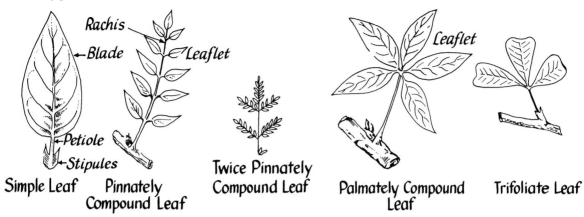

Simple Leaf   Pinnately Compound Leaf   Twice Pinnately Compound Leaf   Palmately Compound Leaf   Trifoliate Leaf

Arrangements of flowers.

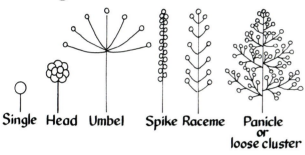

Single   Head   Umbel   Spike   Raceme   Panicle or loose cluster

Leaf arrangements on a stem.

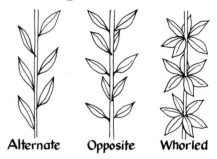

Alternate   Opposite   Whorled

Parts of a flower.

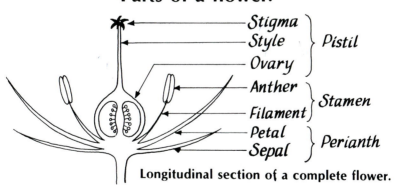

Longitudinal section of a complete flower.

Flower parts individually.

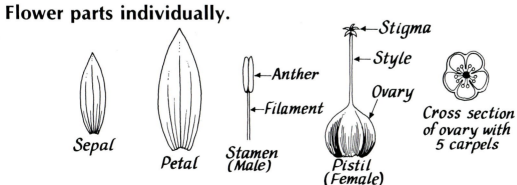

Sepal   Petal   Stamen (Male)   Pistil (Female)   Cross section of ovary with 5 carpels

PLANT SELECTION AND USE: A CAUTION

The question frequently arises, "Why can't I grow an *Egothromia fumblioides*?" Actually, most plants grow in spite of us, not because of us. This is particularly true since the environment of the planting site is often abruptly different from the plant's native habitat. Consider the contrast in the photos below. The woodland understory is "home" to many landscape plants. In such a "home" the plant is cooled by the surrounding trees and shrubs, the sunlight is filtered, and the wind is reduced. The soil is undisturbed by bulldozers and is covered by a thick mat of litter which holds many nutrients, serves to keep the roots cool, and retains often precious moisture.

The dogwood tree is native to such a home yet it is often planted in the city where concrete, asphalt, steel, and pollution are king. In such an environment the dogwood generally does poorly and dies a premature death.

When concrete and asphalt cover the soil surface, oxygen and water are prevented from entering the plant's root zone. Carbon dioxide builds up beneath such pavings. Soil temperatures go up and up because the precious litter is gone and the soil coverings absorb much heat. Air temperatures are much higher than in the cool, humid woodland. The wind speeds through the maze of buildings, often intensifying as it rounds a corner, and drys the plant's leaves excessively.

The once fertile woodland topsoil is probably somewhere beneath a street or parking lot and the plants are left to grow in a maze of compacted and polluted subsoil.

A few trees and shrubs can tolerate such conditions if allowed to adapt and adjust to the site. However, large trees which have over many years developed a fine balance between tops and supporting roots, rarely survive "bulldozer and asphalt blight" and thus die a slow agonizing death (see below). Stress on large trees shows in the uppermost branches first.

A well meaning few occasionally make a half-hearted attempt to aid a large tree in a new development by building a "well" around it. Such efforts and dollars should instead be spent on preparing planting holes with good topsoil for replacement trees.

If beautiful native trees are on a site where homes or other structures are to be located, there are only two choices. The first choice and by far the most desirable, is to keep every bulldozer, tractor, portable toilet, and any other man, machine, or structure totally clear of the dripline of the tree at all times. The dripline is where the outermost branches are vertically above the soil. Do not allow **any** cut or fill, change of grade, or soil disturbance. Even under such circumstances the likelihood of the tree surviving may be from 60% to 90% depending on the site, the tree species, and the health and vigor of the tree. The second choice is to cut the trees down during clearing for construction, enjoy the firewood, and spend the dollars saved in ease of construction and tree removal when the tree finally dies, on good topsoil and good quality nursery stock to replant.

Only the ignorant would do anything in between. Why complicate construction when the trees will all be dead in one to five years and during the "survival period" before death, appear as disgusting gnarled snags. However, if the trees are given the appropriate priority and are considered for their true value to the site, they will be allowed sufficient space and care and will be saved. If the trees are to be saved, remember these five points:

1. **Allow no disturbance of the soil in any way, at least out to the dripline of the tree, or beyond the dripline to increase the chance of survival.**

2. **Allow no cut or fill of any kind where tree roots are located.**

3. **Leave the leaf litter over the soil surface. It also makes a good mulch in which to plant ground covers or shrubs.**

4. **Allow no storing of any materials on the soil beneath the tree.**

5. **Provide for some economic lever ($) if the above requirements are not met by the builder or contractor.**

The most important factor in plant performance in the landscape is matching the requirements and/or tolerances of the plant to the particular site. The farther a plant is removed from its native habitat or similar environment, the more care and maintenance it will require in order to do well. Some plants, such as the azalea tolerate little variation from their native habitat. Others, such as the junipers are very tolerant and can be found in nearly every city across the United States.

One major factor in plant performance in the landscape is hardiness or the ability to withstand cold. Included is a plant hardiness zone map based on data from many sources and compiled by the United States Department of Agriculture (USDA). Plants in this text are given a hardiness zone rating based on this map of average winter low temperatures. For example, hardiness Zone 7 will experience a low temperature between 0 degrees to 10 degrees F most winters.

The ability to withstand cold is, however, only one of several factors which influence plant performance. When one travels from east to west after leaving the western edge of Louisiana, Arkansas, or Missouri, the total annual rainfall, as well as the regularity of rainfall, decreases. In addition, with less rainfall, the soils generally are more alkaline. That is, they contain larger quantities of calcium, magnesium, and/or sodium. Alkaline soils are noted for their ability to tie-up nutrient elements, thus making them unavailable for plant growth. This often shows up as yellow leaves and a general unthrifty appearance. On each right hand page of the major text, there is a map of the eastern United States. Outlined on that map within the solid black line is the area where the plant is well adapted. Beyond the line more care in matching a plant to a planting site is required. It is not recommended that the plant be used very far beyond the solid line. You will note that many plants will not do well in the western region of the Prairie States, while a limited few will grow almost anywhere.

Many texts leave the impression that if a plant is hardy in Zone 5, one should automatically assume it will grow in Zones 6, 7, 8, 9, and 10. This is far from true. For example, turn to page 15 and note the suggested use range for Norway maple. The problem with growing Norway maple in the South is not its ability to withstand cold, but rather an intolerance of the plant for high temperatures.

Plant Hardiness Zone Map

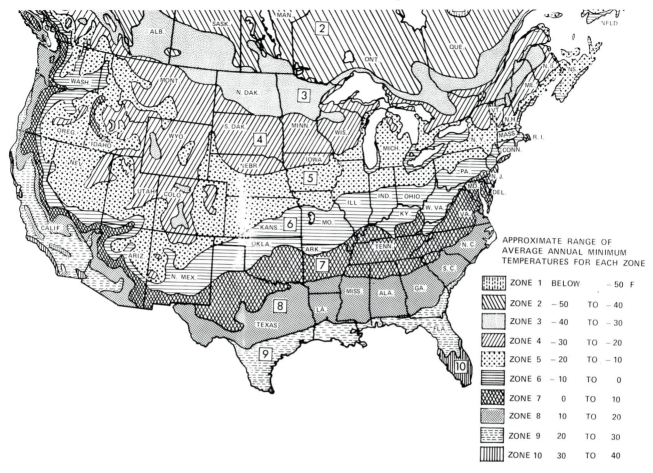

		APPROXIMATE RANGE OF AVERAGE ANNUAL MINIMUM TEMPERATURES FOR EACH ZONE
ZONE 1	BELOW	− 50 F
ZONE 2	− 50	TO − 40
ZONE 3	− 40	TO − 30
ZONE 4	− 30	TO − 20
ZONE 5	− 20	TO − 10
ZONE 6	− 10	TO 0
ZONE 7	0	TO 10
ZONE 8	10	TO 20
ZONE 9	20	TO 30
ZONE 10	30	TO 40

Mulches serve as a replacement for the mat of litter found in most native sites. Many materials work well as mulch, such as pine bark, peanut, cottonseed, pecan hulls, or attractive stones. In addition to conserving moisture and reducing the soil temperature around plant roots, mulches can create an interesting contrast with the landscape plant(s).

When the time comes to purchase landscape plants, the cheapest is often **not** the least expensive. Container-grown plants are more likely to succeed than bare root or ball in burlap plants, under most conditions. This is primarily due to the fact that if the container-grown plants have been treated properly, they have 100% of their roots intact. On the other hand, bare root or ball in burlap plants have had a sizable portion of their roots removed.

This is by no means to say that all container plants are good and all others are less desirable. Container plants that have "rooted out" through the drain hole in the bottom should be avoided (see below).

Likewise, plants that have been allowed to sit on an open parking lot in full sun with little, if any, care should be avoided unless they are obviously fresh and good quality.

Bare root or ball in burlap plants are fine **if** they have received proper care. Your best insurance here is to buy from a reputable nurseryman. Bare root or ball in burlap plants require more care than container plants and therefore deteriorate more rapidly with poor care.

For best results:
1. Select a plant adapted to the site in question.
2. Purchase healthy plants of good quality.
3. Provide water, fertilizer, and other maintenance as needed, giving particular attention to the first full year.

DECIDUOUS TREES

Deciduous trees play a major role in developing a landscape setting. They provide shade during the summer and create interesting line patterns against the sky in winter. Wise placement of deciduous trees can play a significant role in keeping homes, offices, and outdoor use areas cooler in summer and warmer in winter, thus making a more comfortable environment and conserving substantial amounts of energy.

Some deciduous trees have attractive flowers and fruits, interesting foliage patterns, and in a few instances, spectacular fall color. Bark color and texture may add an additional feature to the landscape.

Acer buergerianum Rehder   Trident Maple
Aceraceae or Maple Family   Hardiness Zone 5
Native to China and Japan.
SIZE: 20 to 30 feet tall with a 15- to 25-foot spread. Moderate grower.
FORM: Low, rounded crown tree.
TEXTURE: Medium.   **EXPOSURE:** Sun or some shade.

LEAVES: Opposite, simple; 2 to 3 inches long, distinctly 3-lobed and rounded at the base with a smooth margin. Upper surface in medium to dark green, lighter below; orange-red in the fall.

STEM: Young stems are slender and flexible, green or reddish green turning gray-brown. Old stems are orange-brown, especially where sections have peeled off and contrast with other bark that may be gray-brown to brown. Branches low to the ground, with wider branch angles than some maples. Wood is only moderately stout.

FLOWERS: Small, yellow-green. Not showy.

FRUIT: Typical winged seed in pairs. About 1 inch long.

COLOR; Foliage is medium to dark green; orange-red in the fall.

PROPAGATION: Seed or softwood cuttings.

CULTURE: Attractive, small tree that grows in moist, fertile, and at least somewhat acid soils. In soils over pH 6.0 to 6.5, iron chlorosis may develop. This problem is compounded by the fact that much of the water used is somewhat alkaline which slowly increases the alkalinity of the soil and decreases the availability, especially of iron and manganese. The best defense appears to be annual applications of elemental sulfur at about 3 pounds per 100 square feet. Like most maples, trident maple is only moderately drought-tolerant. However, the specimen in the photograph is growing on a heavy clay soil in Dallas, Texas and receives only occasional supplemental watering during dry periods. Soil conditions, and in turn, root distribution probably influence drought tolerance more than generally realized.

PESTS: None serious.

NOTES: A very attractive, small tree with low, spreading branches and attractive bark. Deserves more attention for use around outdoor living areas, particularly where a small amount of protection from drying summer winds exists and a good layer of leaf litter or mulch can be maintained over the soil surface. Not common in the nursery trade at the present time.

CULTIVARS: None known in this country. Several have been named in China.

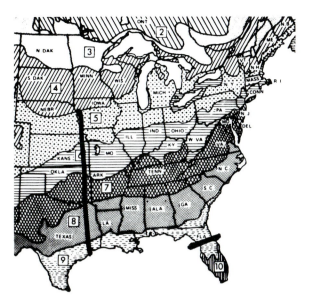

Acer campestre L.   Hedge Maple
Aceraceae or Maple Family   Hardiness Zone 4
Native to Europe and western Asia.
SIZE: 30 to 50 feet tall with a 20- to 30-foot spread. Moderate grower.
FORM: Broad, oval tree.
TEXTURE: Medium.   EXPOSURE: Sun to partial shade.

LEAVES: Simple, opposite, generally 5-lobed with a smooth margin. Leaves may be 3 to 4 inches across; deep dark green above; light green below: somewhat resembling leaves of a sugar maple only with more distinct lobing. Dense foliage prevents light from reaching beneath, thus usually there is bare soil below.

STEM: Main stem is upright, branching profusely near the base and developing strong lower branches. Wood is moderately durable and wind resistant. Young twig is a medium brown turning dark brown to gray with age. Bark becomes a dark gray with only slight furrowing with age.

FLOWERS: Inconspicuous.

FRUIT: Small winged seeds, in pairs.

COLOR: Foliage is deep dark green; orange to red-orange in the fall. Generally a good show of color, but varies among seedlings.

PROPAGATION: Seed, which must be stored slightly moist or in some cases, softwood cuttings.

CULTURE: Tolerant of a wide range of soil conditions, but grows best in a fertile, moist, clay loam soil. Grows well throughout a wide range of the United States as far west as central Kansas and Oklahoma when supplemental water is provided during drought periods or where the tree is located along stream banks, ponds, or other water features. Responds well to fertilizer and good cultural practices. May be planted and/or pruned to make a dense, large hedge but requires considerable horizontal space and maintenance.

PESTS: None serious.

NOTES: An attractive small to medium side tree, quite tolerant to a wide range of growing conditions except for the poorest soils left from urban construction. Works well as an understory tree to other plants and on north sides of buildings where some trees become rather open and spindly due to low light intensity. Not for a dry, wind-swept hill or open, new housing additions with few other plants. Not as tough and adaptable as amur maple, but more adaptable and drought-tolerant than sugar, silver, or Norway maple.

CULTIVARS: 'Queen Elizabeth': a vigorous grower that becomes rather flat-topped with age. Leaves are dark green, glossy, and generally larger than the species. Fall color is yellowish. 'Schwernii': has leaves that are at first wine-red then slowly turn green. Other cultivars may exist.

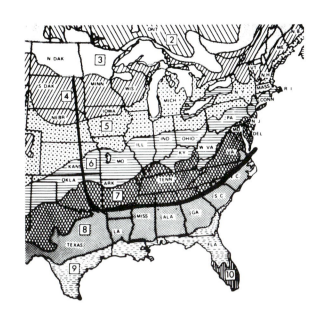

Acer ginnala Maxim.   Amur Maple
Aceraceae or Maple Family   Hardiness Zone 2
Native to central and northern China, Manchuria, and Japan.
SIZE: 15 to 20 feet tall with a 15-foot spread. Moderate grower.
FORM: Round-headed, low, dense, small tree.
TEXTURE: Medium.   EXPOSURE: Sun to partial shade.

LEAVES: Simple, opposite; generally 2 1/2 to 3 1/2 inches long, with 3 lobes and a few coarse, serrated teeth. The 2 basal lobes are much smaller than the terminal leaflet or finger. Medium green above; light green below. Petiole sometimes takes on a red tint on branches in full sun, particularly in the spring. Leaves emerge very early: one of the first trees to leaf out in the spring.

STEM: Generally single-stemmed, branching low to the ground. Develops a broad, oval crown at maturity. Young stems are quite smooth and green, soon turning silver-gray, remaining this color until quite old. Only with much age does a furrowed bark texture develop. Moderately durable wood.

FLOWERS: Yellowish white; slightly fragrant; long-stemmed panicle very early in the spring.

FRUIT: Red or red-orange winged fruit on long stem. Sometimes showy.

COLOR: Foliage is medium green. Fruit is red to red-orange.

PROPAGATION: Seed or softwood to semi-hardwood cuttings, with difficulty.

CULTURE: Will grow in a wide range of soil conditions and exposures from far north-eastern United States throughout most of the Midwest, as far west as central Kansas, Oklahoma, and Texas. Grows best in a good fertile soil but tolerates most soils reasonably well. Responds well to moderate fertilization, supplemental watering during drought periods, and removal of grass competition from the base of the tree, particularly when young.

PESTS: Leaf spot disease, particularly in the South and Southwest, may make leaves unsightly by mid-summer and cause earlier drop in the fall.

NOTES: An excellent small tree because of its form, foliage, and fall color. Can be used as a specimen, screen, or background. Nearly maintenance-free on good sites. The low, broad-spreading crown makes it attractive in many situations. Grows best in full sun but will tolerate some shade from structures or from larger, overhanging trees. Very drought-tolerant, especially in partial shade or somewhat protected locations. A good, small tree beneath large existing trees or on north sides of large structures where light intensity is low. A smaller, more durable tree than *Acer campestre*. Amur maple should be used more where a small, multi-branched tree is required.

CULTIVARS: 'Compactum': a smaller, compact crown; very consistent compared to some-what variable seedlings. Good red fall color north of Zone 7. 'Flame': a dense shrub or small tree with red fruits and excellent fall color. Several other cultivars can be found in localized areas mostly with red fruits in mid summer and good fall color. Otherwise, they appear to be little different from seedlings which tend to be rather uniform.

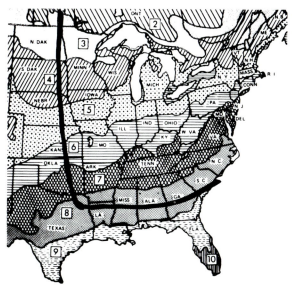

Acer griseum (Franch.) Pax.   Paperbark Maple
Aceraceae or Maple Family   Hardiness Zone 5
Native to China.
SIZE: 20 to 30 feet tall with a 15- to 20-foot spread. Slow grower.
FORM: Small tree with rounded crown.
TEXTURE: Medium.   **EXPOSURE:** Sun or partial shade.

LEAVES: Opposite, compound; trifoliate, with 3 distinct leaflets each 1 1/2 to 2 inches long with irregular lobes or teeth. The entire leaf may be 3 to 5 inches long with a dark green to purplish upper surface, pale greenish white beneath, and red to red-orange fall color, varying among seedlings. Petioles are distinctly hairy.

STEM: Young stems are slender, smooth, reddish brown, with a few hairs at first. The cinnamon brown bark begins peeling on 2-year-old twigs and continues even on large branches. Very attractive bark, perhaps the most showy of any of the temperate zone trees. Wood is moderately stout.

FLOWERS: Yellow-green; inconspicuous.

FRUIT: Flattened, winged seed, typical of the genus.

COLOR: Foliage is dark green to purplish; bark is cinnamon brown; very attractive.

PROPAGATION: Seed, although good seed is difficult to obtain. Softwood cuttings, with difficulty.

CULTURE: Paperbark maple is well adapted to much of the United States as are many of the plants native to northern China. Grows best in a rich, well-drained, moist soil, but will tolerate sandy to clay soils and some drought, if not planted in an exceptionally hot location. East of the border of Kansas and Missouri, full sun is satisfactory. however, in the West and Southwest, planting on the north or east side of structures or under some shade is preferred. A specimen on a good, sandy, loam soil and under shade of large pecan trees in central Oklahoma lived through the extreme heat and drought of the summer of 1980 with no assistance and no ill effects. Needs some pruning to develop a good branch structure and tree form. it would most likely respond to mulching and reduction of weed and grass competition. Very slow growing.

PESTS: None serious.

NOTES: A spectacular, small tree that should be planted more. The foliage is good during the growing season and turns red to red-orange very early in the fall, exposing the attractive bark. Bark quality and attractiveness exceed those of river birch and lacebark elm. Unfortunately, there are few specimens around to be seen, thus promotion of this fine tree is slow. Must be seed to be truly appreciated. A superb patio tree in that not only is the fall color good and the bark outstanding, but the early leaf drop allows outdoor activities later into the fall. The growth is slow, even under ideal conditions making nursery production on a large scale unlikely. On the other hand, if you find a specimen available and have a suitable site, buy it: you will not be disappointed.

CULTIVARS: None known.

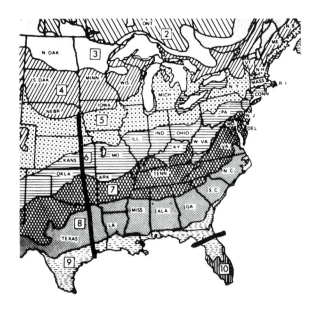

Acer miyabei Maxim.   Miyabe Maple
Aceraceae or Maple Family   Hardiness Zone 4 or 5?
Native to China and Japan.
SIZE: 30- to 50-foot tree, with nearly equal spread. Moderate grower.
FORM: Medium-sized tree with dense foliage and rounded crown.
TEXTURE: Medium.   **EXPOSURE:** Sun or partial shade when young.

LEAVES: Opposite, simple; 3 to 5 inches long; 5 distinct lobes with several smaller lobes or irregular teeth. Upper leaf surface is medium green, only slightly lighter below. Both upper and lower leaf surfaces are hairy when young but soon become smooth or nearly so. Fall color is yellow; however, the leaves remain green late, change color, then quickly fall. Petioles are long, slender, and flexible. When leaves are removed from the stem, a milky sap exudes. Of the other maples in American landscapes, only Norway maple and shantung maple have this feature.

STEM: Young stems are slender and covered with hairs at first, soon becoming smooth and gray-brown. The older bark is slightly corky with irregular, vertical furrows. Wood is moderately stout, not readily damaged by snow or ice.

FLOWERS: Inconspicuous. Small and yellow, among the leaves in early spring.

FRUIT: The winged seeds are 1 to 2 inches long, perpendicular to the seed stalk (see photograph).

COLOR: Foliage is medium green, yellow in the fall.

PROPAGATION: Seed, or softwood cuttings with difficulty.

CULTURE: Not widely planted, thus the cultural requirements are less well known than many other species. However, this tree is very impressive at the Morton Arboretum near Chicago, Illinois, on a clay loam soil and on both well drained and poorly drained sites. Likewise, specimens at the Minnesota Landscape Arboretum and St. Louis Botanical Gardens are on heavy soils and are very thrifty. Best suited to fertile, moist soils but with some tolerance to poor drainage, similar to other maples. All maples need occasional pruning to avoid narrow "V" forks related to the upright, opposite branching.

PESTS: None serious.

NOTES: An impressive, medium-sized tree with dense foliage. The large specimens at the Morton Arboretum stand out among various other specimen trees. Unfortunately, seed availability has been very limited and the few seeds produced by the few plants large enough to fruit in this country have very low viability. A tree for the future. Hopefully, with improved relations with China, seed will be more readily available. This is probably a superior tree to most of the cultivars of Norway maple and red maple currently widely planted. Like most maples, the root system is shallow and fibrous and the shade is dense which eliminates grass from beneath. However, some ground covers are capable of providing an attractive carpet beneath.

CULTIVARS: None known. However, since there is considerable variation among seedlings, some will be developed sooner or later, when a good selection is found that will also root from cuttings.

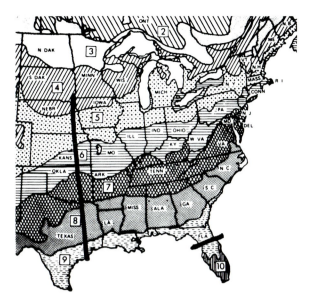

Acer negundo L.   Boxelder
Aceraceae or Maple Family   Hardiness Zone 2
Native to eastern North America.
SIZE: May reach 50 to 80 feet tall with a 40- to 50-foot spread. Very rapid grower.
FORM: Wide-spreading, rather open tree.
TEXTURE: Medium.   **EXPOSURE:** Sun to shade.

LEAVES: Opposite, once-compound; either 3 or 5 leaflets. leaflets are ovate to oblong or slightly lanceolate, coarsely toothed on the margin. Pale green above and light, almost silvery green below when young. The compound leaf may be from 3 to 6 inches long. Leaves of young seedlings or suckers may have 3 leaflets and resemble poison ivy; however, the absence of aerial roots and opposite leaves (vs. alternate leaves for poison ivy) are the best identification features.

STEM: Young twig is green with a chalky white covering, remaining green for 1 to 3 seasons, depending on rate of growth and age of tree. Older stem takes on a corky, irregular bark pattern with a gray to gray-black color. not a well-defined bark pattern; tends to be very irregular, changing throhghout the tree and among seedlings. When the bark is peeled back on a young stem, it has a very pronounced, foul odor. This can be useful in identifying boxelder from other species of maple when they are dormant. Silver maple has a similar odor, but twigs are red-brown.

FLOWERS: Small, greenish; inconspicuous.

FURIT: 1 1/2 inches long, in drooping clusters in summer. The 2-winded seeds nearly touch at the base. Not showy.

COLOR: Foliage is pale green.

PROPAGATION: Seed or cuttings.

CULTURE: Will grow anywhere. Extremely cold hardy and drought-resistant. Grows in the western extremes of the Prairie States, in nearly every kind of soil and environmental conditions. Tolerates the abuse of restricted root space in city conditions and is, in general, a super-tough tree. however, the wood is very weak and brittle. A short-lived tree of questionable merit unless nothing else can be grown on the site. Seeds germinate readily and become weed problems in other landscape areas.

PESTS: Boxelder bugs, aphis, borers; a wilt fungus may cause wilting and death of branches or an entire tree.

NOTES: A short-lived tree of questionable merit. A rapid grower with very brittle wood. Frequently drops twigs and branches or breaks up in wind or ice storms.

CULTIVARS: 'Variegata': has broad white margins on the leaves and is strikingly attractive. Unfortunately, it suffers all of the maladies of the species. 'Aureo-variegatum': Leaves with yellow spots. Many other cultivars exist. Interesting that this species has been cultivated extensively in Europe and to some degree in China, Japan, and Australia and many cultivars have been selected in those areas. On the other hand, it is a tree of nearly zero value in North America...where it is native.

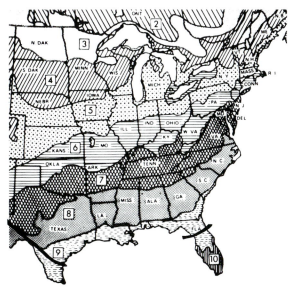

Acer palmatum Thunb. Japanese Maple
Aceraceae or Maple Family Hardiness Zone 5
Native to Japan and Korea.
SIZE: Maximum height of 20 feet with spread of 20 feet.
FORM: Broad, round-headed or mound-like, small tree or large shrub.
TEXTURE: Fine to very fine. **EXPOSURE:** Partial shade to shade.

LEAVES: Opposite, simple; although some cultivars are so deeply lobed it appears the leaf is palmately compound. Fingers of leaves are generally from 2 1/2 to 4 inches long and about 1/2 inch wide, very thin, papery and transparent. Leaf margin is doubly toothed. Some cultivars are red when they first emerge then turn green, others remain purple-red all season if the light intensity is sufficiently high. Others emerge and remain green all season. Fall color is generally red to red-orange and spectacular.

STEM: Very slender and graceful, creating a lacy line effect when leaves are absent. Young stems are green or reddish; older stems are light brown to gray-brown, remaining fairly smooth.

FLOWERS: Nearly inconspicuous. Small, creamy, and cup-like.

FRUIT: Winged seeds, 1 inch long. Stay on the tree throughout the fall.

COLOR: Foliage is green to metallic purple-red depending on cultivar. Red to red-orange in the fall.

PROPAGATION: By seed, but seedlings vary greatly. Selected cultivars are either grafted onto seedling rootstocks or propagated from softwood cuttings.

CULTURE: Needs protection from drying winds and exposure, especially in poor, dry soils. Leaf scorch is common on exposed sites with dry or poor soils. Does best in protected locations or semi-enclosures with considerable moisture and high humidity. Where such conditions can be provided it does well. Responds reasonably well to fertilizer and grows in any good soil as long as it is not extremely dry and has some shade and protection.

PESTS: Aphids on new growth and occasionally chewing insects such as grasshoppers (particularly in more rural areas).

NOTES: Outstanding specimen for formal gardens, around patios, in planters, tubs, or urns, or indoors in sunny locations. One of the most spectacular of the small trees where it can be grown. Purple-leaved cultivars will remain green when shade is excessive. Not for general planting in new subdivisions where no trees exist.

CULTIVARS: 'Bloodgood' : a small tree with new foliage a brilliant red, deepening to dark red in moderate sun. Probably the most brilliant of the red-foliaged cultivars. 'Burgundy Lace': very slender branches with deeply lobed leaves. Leaf appears to be palmately compound. Red leaves are very finely serrated and lacy. 'Disectum': sometimes referred to as thread-leaf. Branching habit is more weeping. The doubly-lobed leaves are a soft green. Very fine, almost fern-like texture. 'Disectum Atropurpureum' is like 'Disectum' except the foliage is bright red in locations with moderate light. 'Oshu-Beni': red-leaved with a very finely serrated margin. Slightly lighter red than 'Bloodgood'. 'Tamukeyama': finely divided leaves which remain purple throuhgout the year in eastern United States. Many other cultivars exist.

Japanese Maples, by J.D. Vertrees is an excellent book giving the history and culture and many, many cultivars. Also, *Maples of the World* by Gelderen, deJong, and Oterdoom, lists hundreds of cultivars.

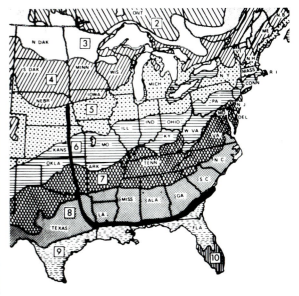

Acer platanoides L.   Norway Maple
Aceraceae or Maple Family   Hardiness Zone 3
Native to Europe and western Asia.
SIZE: 50 to 80 feet tall with a 30- to 40-foot spread.
FORM: Broad, oval-crowned tree.
TEXTURE: Medium.   EXPOSURE: Sun to partial shade.

LEAVES: Opposite, simple; on an exceptionally long petiole; with 5 lobes and a sharply toothed margin. Exceptionally long petiole. Generally 3 to 6 inches long and equally wide. Bright green, medium green below, turning light yellow before dropping in the fall. Foliage is not as spectacular as on sugar maples and is generally later in the season. When the leaves are removed from the stems during the growing season, a milky sap is present, unlike with sugar maple, and is a good identification feature. Several green- and purple-leaved cultivars exist.

STEM: A central leader tree with generally good branch development, but some narrow forks will need attention. Fall and winter buds are rounded and quite large relative to other maples. Young twigs are at first light green, turning light brown, and eventually become a gray-brown; lightly furrowed. Wood is moderately durable, fairly wind- or storm-resistant.

FLOWERS: Inconspicuous; small yellow flowers, very early.

FRUIT: Winged seed about 1 1/2 inches long.

COLOR: Foliage is green to red-purple depending on cultivar, yellow in the fall.

PROPAGATION: Seed or grafting of selected cultivars.

CULTURE: Tolerates low temperatures over a wide range and functions in the eastern 1/3 of the United States and extreme Northwest. In the Prairie States, South, and Southwest, the tree has a severe problem with leaf scorch from drying wind during the summer thus reducing the overall landscape value. Generally questionable west of a line through Tulsa, Topeka, and Omaha. Tolerates a wide range of soil conditions, high pH, and restricted root systems. Does moderately well as a street tree in the East and Northeast; but stem canker is becoming a serious problem. Relatively short-lived in restricted spaces.

PESTS: Aphids in early spring. Stem canker may be severe on trees under stress.

NOTES: Can be a useful landscape tree in the northeastern portion of the United States and throughout the Upper South. Does not belong in the dryer southwest regions of the Prairie States. Has been overly promoted in the landscape trade and overplanted in certain parts of the country, especially the upper Midwest and the Northeast. *A. truncatum* is a much better and tougher tree.

CULTIVARS: 'Schwedleri': slightly smaller than the parent. Leaves are red when they open in spring, gradually becoming green during the growing season, light gold in the fall. 'Crimson King': red leaves in the spring, which remain red to red-purple during the growing season; more orange to red in the fall. A very dominant plant in the landscape. Leaf color is not compatible with other plants in some situations. 'Emerald Queen': a rapid growing, oval-headed tree with green leaves. 'Jade Glen': a rapid grower with straight stems, a spreading habit, and green leaves which turn golden in the fall. 'Superform': a rapid growing selection with dense, dark green leaves. 'Columnare': a compact, narrowly upright tree with dark green foliage. 'Deborah': similar to 'Schwedleri' but has more upright branching. Leaves are light green with a white margin; striking. 'Summer Shade': a rapid grower said to be more heat-resistant than the species. Leaves are dark green and leathery. **Many** other cultivars exist.

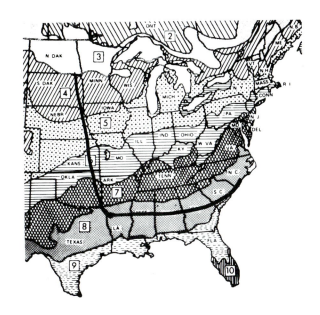

Honeylocust   Norway Maple

'Globosum'

Sugar Maple   Norway Maple

Acer rubrum L.   Red or Swamp Maple
Aceraceae or Maple Family   Hardiness Zone 3
Native to the eastern U.S.
SIZE: 50 to 80 feet tall with a 40- to 60-foot spread, depending on cultivar.
FORM: Round-headed tree, but some cultivars are more upright.
TEXTURE: Medium.   **EXPOSURE:** Sun to shade.

LEAVES: Opposite, simple; ovate to oval, 2 to 4 inches long and 2 to 3 inches wide with generally 3 or 5 lobes, depending on cultivar and varying with seedlings. Generally medium green above; powdery silver-white with hairs below. Margin is generally unequally toothed to nearly smooth. Leaves on many trees have a distinct red to red-purple petiole in the spring, particularly on leaves in full sun, eventually turning green. Foliage in the fall turns red to red-orange.

STEM: Young twigs are generally slender, reddish to red-brown with prominent pale lenticels and have little, if any, odor when scratched. Bark is smooth and light gray at first, becoming darker, furrowed, and flakey on old trees, almost gray-black in some instances. Wood is moderately durable: weaker than sugar maple but stronger than silver maple or boxelder.

FLOWERS: In leaf axils, early in spring, before the leaves, generally red or yellow. Slightly showy.

FRUIT: Generally bright red and showy very early in the spring.

COLOR: Foliage is medium green to red; red-orange in the fall. Flowers are red. Fruit is red.

PROPAGATION: Seed, semi-hardwood cuttings of selected cultivars, or grafting.

CULTURE: Will grow in a wide range of drainage conditions but is only moderately tolerant of drought. Does best in moist or other poorly drained locations and can be used to advantage there. Native to swamp areas in the Gulf Coast states and Southeast. Will also grow in good soil on most reasonable sites in the East and Southeast. A rapid grower. Responds to fertilizer, mulching, and removal of weeds around the base of the young trees.

PESTS: None serious.

NOTES: Particularly useful in areas with excessive soil moisture where many other trees do poorly. Attractive specimen tree with moderately good fall color and in most instances a showy silver-gray stem even in the winter. Can be distinguished from silver maple by the smaller, more shallowly lobed leaves with dense white hairs below and lack of odor when the young stem is scraped.

CULTIVARS: 'Drummondi': 3- to 5-lobed leaves which are wooly white on the undersurface and medium green above, and scarlet fruit generally larger than that of the species. 'Trident': leaves which have three obovate lobes which are sparingly toothed on the margin and may be entire near the base of the leaf. White to silver-white below. 'Columnar': a densely upright growth habit. 'Autumn Flame': a large, globe-headed tree with slightly smaller leaves and early fall color (patent #2377). 'October Glory': a large, globe-headed tree with glossy green leaves which turn scarlet to crimson in the fall. One of the best cultivars for consistent fall color and good form. 'Red Sunset': a vigorously growing, broad, upright form with good fall color. This is an excellent cultivar. Many others exist. Also, *Acer* X *freemani* are considered to be hybrids between *A. saccharinum* the silver maple and *A. ruburm*, the red maple. They are generally more like the red maple parent in adaptation. 'Autumn Blaze': good fall color. 'Autumn Fantasy': attractive crimson fall color. May be bit more drought-tolerant. Others exist.

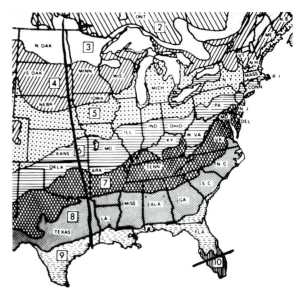

Acer saccharinum L. Silver, Soft, or River Maple
Aceraceae or Maple Family Hardiness Zone 4
Native to the eastern U.S.
SIZE: 60 to 100 feet tall with a 50- to 100-foot spread. Rapid grower
FORM: A broad, oval-topped, spreading tree.
TEXTURE: Medium. **EXPOSURE:** Sun to partial shade.

LEAVES: Opposite, simple; 4 to 7 inches long, generally with 5 deep lobes and sharp teeth on the margin. Medium to light green above, silvery light green below with only a few hairs along the veins. Very soft and pliable leaves. Fall color is a bright yellow briefly before the leaves drop.

STEM: Young stem is green, soon turning a varnished light brown with prominent lenticels and a strong foul odor when scraped. Eventually turning a light, silvery gray and finally developing a red-brown to gray bark which flakes off with age. Some variation among seedlings. The wood is brittle and weak, easily broken by wind or ice storms but the tree can be improved by selective pruning to avoid weak branch forks (note lower right photo).

FLOWERS: Inconspicuous. Red-brown.

FRUIT: Winged; 2 inches long; greenish in early spring.

COLOR: Foliage is medium to light green, yellow in fall.

PROPAGATION: Seed or softwood cuttings.

CULTURE: Grows over a wide range; a very adaptable plant. Does best in areas of good soils with adequate moisture; however, it is also very drought-resistant. Does well around homesteads in small towns in western portions of the prairie states. Quite tolerant of a wide range of soil pH, growing in alkaline or very acid soils. Responds vigorously to fertilizer or supplementary water during moisture stress. Requires pruning to develop sound branches of the young tree and to avoid weak internal branching that may limit the life of the tree. Only if the pruning is done properly should the tree be considered because the wood is brittle.

PESTS: None serious.

NOTES: Commonly sold as a promotional item by chain stores and others and is therefore purchased by the unsuspecting and planted in many sites where it really does not belong. Wood is sufficiently brittle that once the tree reaches considerable size, it becomes a hazard to persons and property during any wind or ice storm. Under good conditions a tree may grow as much as 6 to 8 feet in a single season. Such features have been promoted. Sometimes sold as, "The beautiful silver Acer which grows high as a house in a single season". Should be used only where other trees will not grow and where there is room for its large size. Has a very shallow root system which uproots sidewalks and may crack foundations of houses or basements. Difficult to grow grass or other shrubs nearby. Should be avoided. Not good as a street tree. To be used only as a specimen tree in a large landscape or around water features. Best distinguished from red maple by the larger, more deeply lobed leaves and foul odor from the young bark. Sometimes sold under the incorrect alternative name, *Acer dasycarpum*.

CULTIVARS: None of merit. 'Crispum': deeply lobed leaves and crinkled margins. 'Silver Queen' : dark, glossy leaves and more upright growth habit.

Acer X *freemani* are considered to be hybrids between *A. saccharinum.* and *A. rubrum*. The cultivars generally appear more like the red maple parent and are sold as various cultivars.

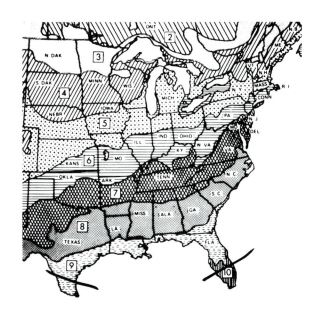

Acer saccharum Marsh.   Sugar, Hard, or Rock Maple
Aceraceae or Maple Family   Hardiness Zone 3
Native to the eastern U.S.
SIZE: May reach 60 to 80 feet tall with a 40- to 60-foot spread. Slow to moderate grower.
FORM: Oval- to rounded-crown tree.
TEXTURE: Medium.   **EXPOSURE:** Sun to partial shade.

LEAVES: Opposite, simple; 3 to 5 inches long and equal width. 5-lobed (occasionally 3) and a smooth margin. Points of lobes are slightly rounded as opposed to very sharp points on *A. rubrum*, *A. saccharinum*, or *A. platanoides*. Dark green above, slightly lighter green below with a few hairs along the veins. Slightly stiffer than those of *A. platanoides*. No milky sap is present when the leaves are broken off the old stem, which distinguishes this from Norway maple. Fall color is brilliant red to red-orange to yellow with much variation among seedlings. One of the showiest of the ornamental trees for fall color.

STEM: Generally single-stemmed with strong secondary branching. Young stems are very slender, light brown, turning dark brown to almost black with age. Lenticels are conspicuous on the young stem. Fall and winter buds are small, red-brown, and shaped like a pencil point.

FLOWERS: Early spring before the leaves. Inconspicuous.

FRUIT: Ripens July through September. Winged seed about 1/2 to 1 inch long.

COLOR: Foliage is dark green in spring; brilliant yellow to red-orange in the fall.

PROPAGATION: Seed collected in early fall, stored over winter and planted in the spring. It should not dry out (as with all maple seeds) or they must soak in warm water overnight before planting. Cuttings are difficult to root. Cultivars are grafted onto seedlings.

CULTURE: Best adapted to the cooler and more humid regions of the eastern and northeastern portion of the U.S. In the South and the southwestern region; seedlings, particularly those from plants in the Northeast, suffer leaf scorch and generally do not do well. 'Caddo' is an exception, produced from seed collected from trees growing in southwest Oklahoma. These trees, apparently an ecological relic, are much more resistant to drying winds and drought and much better adapted to the prairie states. Responds reasonably well to fertilizer and mulching to reduce the soil temperature and conserve moisture. Occasionally needs corrective pruning to avoid weak branching.

PESTS: None serious.

NOTES: The sugar maple of the Northeast, known for its brilliant fall color. The maple from which syrup is extracted in winter and early spring. Spectacular tree where it can be grown. Creates a very dense shade with almost no sun flecks coming through the canopy, making it difficult to grow shrubs, flowers, or grass beneath. Fairly durable wood. Probably the Florida maple, *Acer floridanum* or *A. barbatum* is an ecological race better adapted to the Lower South.

CULTIVARS: 'Caddo': drought-resistant, native to southwest Oklahoma. Leaves, seed, growth form, and other features appear similar to northeastern seedlings. By far the best variety for the Great Plains. R.A. Vines lists this as *Acer grandidentatum* Nutt. 'Sinuosum': a variety of the big tooth maple. 'Newton Sentry' ('Columnare'): a columnar form, fairly adaptable with a moderate growth rate. 'Temples Upright: a strict, narrow upright; slow grower in nearly all conditions. 'Green Mountain': a cultivar resulting from a cross of the black and sugar maples. Leathery, dark green leaves have some resistance to scorch. 'Legacy': grows faster and appears to be more adaptable than other sugar maple cultivars. Fall color is red to orange and some yellow. Very showy. Other cultivars exist.

'Caddo'

Acer truncatum Bunge. Purpleblow or Shantung Maple
Aceraceae or Maple Family Hardiness Zone 6
Native to the Middle East and western China.
SIZE: 30 to 60 feet tall with a 20- to 40-foot spread. Moderate grower.
FORM: Oval-crowned, medium-sized tree.
TEXTURE: Medium. EXPOSURE: Sun or slight shade.

LEAVES: Opposite, simple; 3 to 4 inches long, with mostly 5 (occasionally 7) lobes which are triangular, long, slender, and pointed at the tip. Upper surface is dark glossy green; paler below, with no hairs anywhere. yellow-orange to orange fall color; variable among seedlings. Leaves look like sweet gum leaves except they are smoother and more glossy, opposite instead of alternate on the stems, and exude a milky sap when torn.

STEM: Young stems are slender, smooth, and shiny green with a milky sap when damaged. Some seedlings have a waxy bloom on the new shoots. By the end of the growing season, the shoots have turned a light brown, gradually becoming a bright, medium brown with age. Older branches and the main trunk develop a shallowly furrowed, silvery gray bark, with near-black furrows. Wood is moderately stout, not readily damaged by wind or ice. Branch angles tend to be more open than many maples, thus less breakage in storms.

FLOWERS: Yellowish green among the leaves. Not showy.

FRUIT; A large, winged seed, typical of the maples. However, when the seed coat is removed, the inner seed coat is black and somewhat velvety and sticky. This sticky characteristic appears to prevent the seed from dessication. Only bout 1/3 of the seed will develop in the seed coats, although most remain on the tree all summer.

COLOR: Foliage is dark, glossy green.

PROPAGATION: Seed or softwood cuttings.

CULTURE: This attractive and durable maple is known only in very limited areas and has been regarded in some of the literature as sensitive and intolerant. This is definitely not true. There are several large trees growing in central Oklahoma. Three are on a deep, sandy loam soil along a stream and 2 are on an exposed hill on heavy clay. All have performed very well during both wet and dry years and tolerate drying winds and heat as well or better than any other maple, with the exception of the native 'Caddo' sugar maple of southwest Oklahoma and northern Texas. However, this tree grows much faster than 'Caddo'.

PESTS: None serious. Very sensitive to drift of 2,4-D type herbicides.

NOTES: An attractive tree that has proven itself in a challenging environment in which many trees, especially maples do only fair to poor. Deserves more attention. Seedlings vary in growth rate, form, and fall color. Cultivars can be selected to improve consistency since cuttings can be rooted.

This may be *Acer cappadocium*, Colosseum maple, or *Acer mono*, which are very similar. These 3 species apparently overlap and are very similar in central and western China where they are native, or may actually be ecological races of the same species.

CULTIVARS: *Hortus* lists 'Aureum' with yellow leaves in spring and fall. 'Rubrum': blood-red leaves when young, sprinkled with pink. Some variation in leaf color and growth habit exists with a seedling population.

 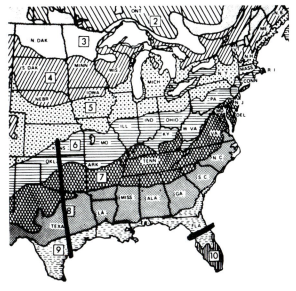

Aesculus arguta Buckl.   Texas Buckeye
Hippocastanaceae or Buckeye Family   Hardiness Zone 5
Native to east Texas through Oklahoma and Missouri.

SIZE: A large shrub or small tree 15 to 25 feet tall with a 10- to 15-foot spread. Moderate grower.

FORM: A large shrub or small tree with stout branches and a rounded crown.

TEXTURE: Medium to coarse.   **EXPOSURE:** Partial shade to shade.

LEAVES: Opposite, palmately compound; with generally 7 and occasionally 9 leaflets. Leaflets radiate in a whorl at the tip of the petiole and are finger-like, 2 1/2 to 5 inches long, 1/2 to 1 1/2 inches wide with a toothed margin. Upper surface is olive green and glossy, lower surface is more pale and somewhat hairy. Fall color is yellow-brown, pleasant but not spectacular.

STEM: Young twigs are stout, light brown and slightly hairy at first, becoming smooth with age. Terminal buds are large, smooth, sharp-pointed and a medium to chocolate brown. Older stems are a corky, ash-gray to gray-brown.

FLOWERS: In the spring after the leaves emerge, yellow clusters standing above the leaves at the tips of the young new shoots. Clusters are generally 4 to 8 inches long, 2 to 3 inches across, with 3 to 15 flowers in a cluster. Pale yellow to yellow-green. Moderately showy.

FRUIT: Matures in June or July. A round or oval capsule, about 1 to 1 1/2 inches in diameter; light brown; armed with short stout warts or prickles or occasionally smooth. Opens to release two flattened, lustrous, dark brown seeds.

COLOR: Foliage is olive green, yellow-brown in the fall. Flowers are yellow.

PROPAGATION: Seed.

CULTURE: Grows well in a wide range of soils over eastern Texas, Oklahoma, Kansas, and moist areas to the east. Does best in areas of undisturbed soil, natural woodland-type conditions. If used directly in a sodded landscape, should be heavily mulched to retain moisture, reduce soil temperature, and keep away competitive vegetation. Best grown as an understory tree or with a slight amount of sun. Will develop a good canopy of leaves and flower and fruit under these circumstances, unlike many other trees. Not for full sun, exposed locations.

PESTS: None serious.

NOTES: A good small tree or large shrub for use in naturalistic plantings over a wide range of the southern United States. Makes an interesting patio tree, tree to complement other landscape plantings, or as an understory tree because of its interesting texture and color. May leaf-scorch in areas of extreme drought or when exposed to a desiccating wind in the lower Great Plains. Closely related to Ohio buckeye. *Hortus III* says they are the same; however, based on the greater adaptability and much smaller size of Texas buckeye than Ohio buckeye, I have serious doubts. All parts are poisonous. XX-POISON-XX

CULTIVARS: None known.

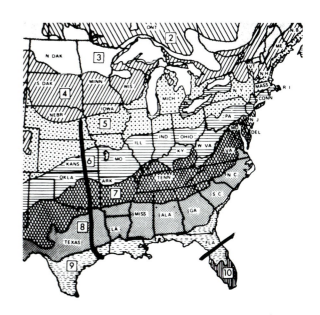

Aesculus glabra Willd.   Ohio Buckeye
Hippocastanaceae or Buckeye Family   Hardiness Zone 4
Native to the Ohio and Mississippi River valleys.
SIZE: Reaches 40 to 60 feet with a 20- to 30-foot spread.
FORM: Tree with oval or round crown.
TEXTURE: Coarse.   **EXPOSURE:** Sun to partial shade.

LEAVES: Opposite, palmately compound; usually 5 leaflets, sessile on the 4 to 6 inches long petiole. Individual leaflets are 4 to 6 inches long, 1 1/2 to 2 inches wide, elliptical to oblong, tapering to a sharp point. Margin is toothed. Upper leaf surface is a smooth, glossy, dark green; undersurface is lighter green. Yellow in early fall. Undesirable odor when crushed. One of the first trees to leaf out in the spring and drop leaves in the fall.

STEM: Young twigs are stout, light brown, and slightly hairy at first, becoming smooth with age. Buds are large, smooth, sharp-pointed, and pinkish to brown. Older stems are ash to dark gray and shallowly furrowed, breaking into large, scaly blocks at maturity.

FLOWERS: Appear in large clusters at the tips of the branches soon after the leaves are fully developed. Yellow-green, moderately showy.

FRUIT: Round capsule, very prickly when young, losing the prickles when mature. Contains one to three nuts, generally dark mahogany in color. Nuts are sometimes carried as a superstition to ward off rheumatism. Nuts are poisonous to cattle. However, squirrels eat them with no ill effect. Very messy on sidewalks or streets

COLOR: Foliage is dark, glossy green turning yellow in fall. Flowers are yellow-green.

PROPAGATION: By seed.

CULTURE: Tolerates a wide range of soil conditions. Does best in areas of moist soil or where irrigated during droughts. In the western portion of its natural range, west of eastern Nebraska, Kansas, and Oklahoma, it exhibits considerable leaf scorch during the summer. Makes a very dense crown, blocking out most of the light below and making it difficult to grow grass or other vegetation. Best suited to naturalistic areas where soil and leaf litter are relatively undisturbed.

PESTS: None serious. However, leaf scorch may make the tree unsightly following a drought. Leaf scorch can be severe in large cities and is therefore probably related to air pollution.

NOTES: Moderately attractive tree when in flower in early spring and as a specimen or background tree. Not a good shade tree because of the small crown. Is disappointing in areas where the soils have been destroyed by construction and supplementary moisture is not available. Sometimes known as "stinking buckeye" because of the disagreeable odor given off by the bark or twigs. All parts are considered poisonous. XX-POISON-XX

CULTIVARS: None known.

RELATED SPECIES: *Aesculus hippocastanum*, the horsechestnut, has large compound leaves generally with seven wedge-shaped leaflets. Leaves are much larger than those of the buckeyes. Used some as a lawn and street tree in the Northeast but is generally of limited landscape value. Frequently leaves scorch severely in mid-summer and appear to be quite sensitive to air pollution. Not recommended for landscape use. All parts are poisonous.

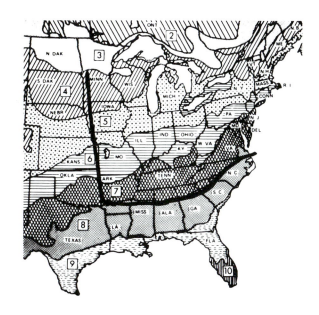

Aesculus hippocastanum L.   Horsechestnut
Hippocastanaceae or Buckeye Family   Hardiness Zone 4
Native to Europe.
SIZE: 60 to 80 feet tall with a 40- to 60-foot spread on good sites. Moderate grower.
FORM: Tree with large, oval crown.
TEXTURE: Coarse.   **EXPOSURE:** Sun or light shade.

LEAVES: Opposite, palmately compound; generally with 7 leaflets (sometimes 5 or 6).
Leaflets are sessile on the petiole which is generally 4 to 6 inches long. Leaflets are generally 8 to 12 inches long; obovate and wedge-shaped with coarse teeth on the margin. Upper
leaf surface is dark green, lighter below. Yellow in the fall.

STEM: Young twigs are very stout and light brown, with very prominent, terminal buds
that are sticky to the touch and bright brown when dormant. Leaf scars are very large and
horseshoe-shaped and still prominent on twigs that are several years old. Mature bark is a
shallowly furrowed, scaly bark generally gray to gray-black. Wood is durable; not readily
broken.

FLOWERS: Appear soon after the leaves are fully expanded. Large clusters above the
leaves, mostly creamy white, tinged in red. 6 to 12 inches long and 3 to 5 inches wide.
Very showy in early May.

FRUIT: Large, spiny, about 2 inches and more or less round. Light brown, maturing in late
summer and splitting to release two seeds. Very messy on sidewalks or streets.

COLOR: Leaves are dark green; yellow in the fall. Flowers are creamy white.

PROPAGATION: By seed, budding, or grafting of cultivars onto seedlings.

CULTURE: Adaptable to a wide range of soils and growing conditions; however, horsechestnut is not drought tolerant and should not be planted in the Great Plains states except
for unique areas with irrigation or other supplemental moisture. Horsechestnut was extensively planted in Europe as a street tree and was similarly planted in America. It tolerates
the restricted root zone space and poor soils, but is not compatible with air pollution. Leaf
scorch and early leaf drop is much more severe in areas with air pollution compared to
similar growing conditions in small towns. This is a limiting factor for what is otherwise a
very adaptable tree.

PESTS: Leaf blotch, anthracnose, and powdery mildew, especially on young trees in shady
locations. Mealy bugs and other problems, which may be at least partly a reflection of the
general weakening of the tree by air pollution.

NOTES: A large, adaptable tree in most respects, except it does not appear to be compatible
with the automobile and related air pollution. Careful consideration should be given
before planting a horsechestnut. XX-POISON-XX

CULTIVARS: 'Alba': pure white flowers. 'Pyramidalis': a narrow, upright and compact
growth habit. 'Umbraculifera': a compact, rounded crown. 'Pendula': weeping branches.
Others probably exist.

Aesculus pavia L.   Red Buckeye
Hippocastanaceae or Buckeye Family   Hardiness Zone 5
Native to Missouri, Arkansas, Texas, Louisiana, and eastward to Florida.

SIZE: Rarely reaches more than 15 to 18 feet tall with a spread of 6 to 10 feet. Slow to moderate grower.

FORM: Large shrub or small, oval-shaped tree developing a dense crown on short crooked branches.

TEXTURE: Medium to coarse.   **EXPOSURE:** Sun to shade.

LEAVES: Opposite, palmately compound; generally with 5 leaflets, but occasionally 3 to 7. Leaflets are oblong to elliptical, or occasionally oval, tapering to a sharp point with a sawtooth margin. Individual leaflets are 3 to 6 inches long, 1 1/2 inches wide, and rather firm or stiff. Upper surface is a deep, dark green; lower surface is pale green. Fall color is yellow.

STEM: Green to gray or brown, rather crooked, stout and smooth. Lenticels are pale brown to orange. Leaf scars are large and prominent. Bark eventually develops a gray or brown color and is smooth on the young branches, becoming roughened into short plates which may flake off on the older stem.

FLOWERS: Generally during April or May in 4- to 8-inch clusters. Individual flowers are red, 1 to 1 1/2 inches long, and quite showy for a short period.

FRUIT: A capsule, 1 1/2 to 2 inches in diameter, globose, light brown; mostly smooth but may be finely pitted. Eventually opens to expose one to three rounded or slightly flattened seeds which are dark brown.

COLOR: Foliage is deep, dark green; yellow in fall. Flowers are red.

PROPAGATION: By seed.

CULTURE: Adapted to moist, fertile soils and woodland conditions. Only moderately tolerant to exposure of the suburbs and the competition from intense turf cover. Best grown as an understory tree with some shade or on north or east sides of structures or other vegetation. Responds fairly well to fertilization. In an urban situation, should be mulched heavily to reduce soil temperature and conserve moisture.

PESTS: None serious.

NOTES: A showy, small tree during early spring. Leaves and flowers emerge very early, giving a show before many other landscape plants. May best be used in a background situation. All parts are poisonous. XX-POISON-XX

CULTIVARS: None known. However, considerable variation exists between seedlings from various areas and leads to some confusion.

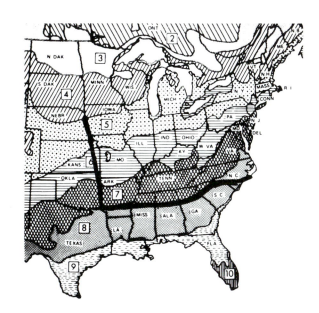

Ailanthus altissima (Mill.) Swingle.   Tree-of-Heaven
Simaraubaceae or Quassia Family   Hardiness Zone 4
Native to China.
SIZE: 30 to 60 feet tall with a 30- to 40-foot spread. Very fast growth rate.
FORM: Flat-topped or oval-topped tree with open branching.
TEXTURE: Medium.   **EXPOSURE:** Sun.

LEAVES: Alternate, compound; 1 to 3 feet long with 11 to 41 leaflets. Terminal leaflet is almost always present. Individual leaflets are 3 to 5 inches long, 1 to 2 inches wide. Margin is smooth or with blunt teeth, mostly near the base. Reddish when young, becoming lighter green when mature. Glands on the basal lobes of leaflets give off a disagreeable odor when crushed. Large compound leaves may give the tree a palm-like appearance.

STEM: Young stems are very stiff, inflexible, and brittle with very large leaf scars. When broken, the large center or pith has a granular texture and reddish or pink color. As the stem ages it becomes smooth and dark gray to tan, finally a dark gray, slightly rough and fissured on a old tree. Wood is weak and brittle, making it susceptible to wind, ice, or vandalism damage.

FLOWERS: Male and female on separate trees (dioecious). Appear in upright clusters, yellow-green, soon after leaves are fully developed in late spring. male flowers have foul odor, thus male trees should be avoided. Females disperse large quantities of seeds that easily germinate.

FRUIT: Large clusters of winged seed, propeller-shaped; twisted with a central seed cavity.

COLOR: Foliage is reddish green becoming green during the growing season. Slightly yellow fall color.

PROPAGATION: Seed or suckers. Often seeds naturally into sidewalks, landscapes, or abandoned areas.

CULTURE: Virtually an indestructible tree. Will grow where most other vegetation will not survive. Tolerates high heat, poor soils, wind, smog, salty soils, and limited soil availability. Often grows between cracks in the sidewalks. Must be considered one of the most durable trees of all. Will grow amazingly fast and if both male and female plants are present, will produce a tremendous amount of seed and become a real pest. In addition, once a tree becomes established, it has a tremendous ability to sprout or send suckers into a wide range of the landscape. Should be avoided.

PESTS: None (unfortunately!)

NOTES: An amazing tree, tolerating every kind of undesirable circumstance that landscape plants can possibly encounter: wet or dry, hot or cold, good or poor soils. if nothing else will grow in a particular location, a tree-of-heaven will.

CULTIVARS: 'Metro': a male tree with fair form. At least it does not produce seeds! Several are available with bright red leaves and purple stems or bright red fruit. However, these are not recommended for planting.

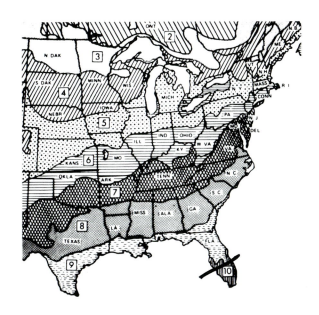

Albizia julibrissin Durazz.   Silktree or Mimosa
Leguminosae or Pea Family   Hardiness Zone 6
Native from the Near East to central China.
SIZE: 30 to 35 feet tall with a 30- to 35-foot spread. Very rapid grower.
FORM: Flat-topped or low, umbrella-like tree.
TEXTURE: Very fine, lacy.   **EXPOSURE:** Sun.

LEAVES: Alternate, generally twice-compound; with numerous small leaflets, about 1/4 to 1/2 inches long. Individual leaflets are attached by a corner, not in the center as with most other legume trees. Leaves fold at night. Generally a medium green with pale yellow fall color; not showy.

STEM: Light brown when young with many prominent lenticels. Tree develops a wide-spreading, low-branching, flat top with relatively few stiff branches. Older bark is smooth and gray, rarely furrowing even with considerable age. Branch angles are often narrow and subject to splitting.

FLOWERS: Fluffy masses of pink stamens in ball-like clusters, 1 1/4 to 2 inches across. Pink or red and very showy. Open consecutively in the summer months, frequently blooming from June to August and intermittently throughout the fall in some locations. Flowers somewhat resemble a pin cushion. Rather messy on a patio or sidewalk. Some trees are very showy.

FRUIT: Large, strap-shaped pod, 5 to 6 inches long. Seed is a smooth, brown bean.

COLOR: Foliage is medium green. Flowers are pink to red.

PROPAGATION: By seed, suckers, or root sprouts.

CULTURE: Very tolerant of adverse exposures and soils in much of the southwestern United States. Grows well as far west as New Mexico. Tolerates alkaline soils moderately well. Severe pruning only hastens the death of the tree and should be avoided. Should be grown as a single stem. Avoid allowing several branches to develop from the same point.

PESTS: Vascular or mimosa wilt occasionally kills, particularly older trees. Mimosa webworm can be a very serious problem, particularly in the South and Southwest.

NOTES: Its soft wood is very easily damaged by wind, ice storms, or vandalism. Generally, it is the last tree to leaf out in the spring. Many times appears as though it is dead, then it finally emerges. Seedlings or suckers can become a nuisance in flower beds or other areas of the landscape. Because of the short-lived nature of the tree, litter from seed pods, and disease, insect, and sucker problems, it is not recommended for general planting. Ordinances have been passed by some cities to prevent further planting of mimosa. However, even with all its weaknesses, it is spectacular when in bloom and develops a low-spreading crown with a light shade not common among trees in the United States.

CULTIVARS: 'Rosea' and/or 'E.H. Wilson': deep pink flowers and more cold hardy than seedlings?. 'Charlotte': said to be resistant to mimosa wilt. Others may exist.

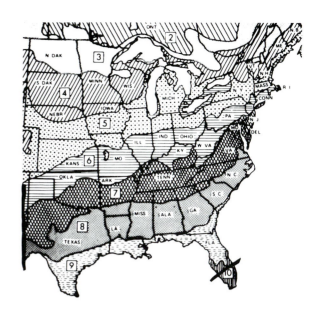

Alnus glutinosa (L.) Gaertn.   Black Alder
Betulaceae or Birch Family   Hardiness Zone 3
Native to Europe, western Asia, Siberia, northern Africa.
SIZE: 60 to 80 feet tall with a 30- to 40-foot spread. Rapid grower.
FORM: Pyramidal tree when young, eventually developing a rounded crown with age.
TEXTURE: Medium to coarse.   **EXPOSURE:** Sun to partial shade.

LEAVES: Alternate, simple; more or less oval, 2 to 5 inches long, 1 to 3 inches wide with irregularly rounded teeth on the margin. Generally very dark green during the growing season, pale green beneath, with a short stout petiole. Little fall color, but leaves remain green late into the fall.

STEM: Young trees have a vigorous-growing central leader with excellent development of young branches along and around the main stem. Develops an attractive triangular form reminiscent of pin oak or sweet gum as a young nursery plant. Young twigs are reddish brown, remaining light brown for several years. Finally the main stem develops a shallow-ly furrowed gray to gray-brown bark. Wood is moderately stout. Suckers readily develop at the base, especially on trees under stress.

FLOWERS: Not showy.

FRUIT: A small, rounded cone-like structure about 1/2 inch in diameter. Looks like a miniature pine cone; red-brown to brown, containing many hard black seeds.

COLOR: Foliage is very dark green. Little or no fall color.

PROPAGATION: Seed.

CULTURE: Grows well in wet swampy soils but is tolerant of a wide range of soil conditions. Heavy soils or soils with poor aeration where they have become compacted due to construction, are suitable, particularly if moderate moisture from irrigation or rainfall is available. Attractive tree through central Nebraska, Kansas, Oklahoma, central Texas, east and northward. One of the better very fast growing trees so commonly requested at nurseries. Requires considerable moisture to become established as the foliage loses considerable water by transpiration. May be difficult to hold as a sizable ball and burlap or container-grown nursery plant because of the large quantity of water lost. Apply plenty of water until established. Alders have nitrogen-fixing bacteria associated with the roots which allows them to grow on very poor soils.

PESTS: None serious.

NOTES: An attractive tree, very tolerant of wet locations, with attractive foliage and good form. Useful for many landscape situations in the Southeast and East, particularly where heavy soils may be wet for long periods during the winter or spring. Foliage remains green late into the fall, thus providing a good green background to accent fall color of other trees and shrubs. Black alder has become naturalized in northeast and north central United States.

CULTIVARS: Numerous selections exist; however, they vary principally in leaf shape and leaf form, and have little additional value in landscaping. Not commonly available in the nursery trade. 'Pyramidalis': a nice, upright, columnar form, resembling lumbardy poplar. This cultivar does merit more attention.

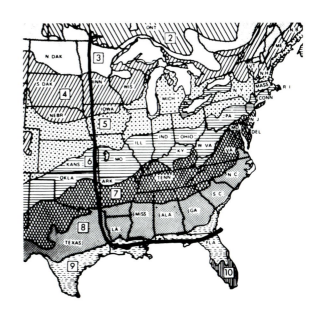

Amelanchier arborea (Michx. F.) Fernald.   Downy Serviceberry or Juneberry
Rosaceae or Rose Family   Hardiness Zone 3
Native to eastern North America.
SIZE: 15 to 30 feet tall. Moderate grower.
FORM: Multiple-stemmed, large shrub or small tree with rounded crown.
TEXTURE: Medium.   **EXPOSURE:** Sun or slight shade.

LEAVES: Alternate, simple; more or less oval, 1 to 3 inches long, with a distinct, saw-toothed margin. Upper leaf surface is gray-green to slightly blue-gray-green; purplish and densely hairy beneath when young, becoming smooth with age. Fall color is orange or sometimes red to red-purple, variable with season and seedlings.

STEM: Slender, smooth, green when young, turning reddish brown and covered with a gray "skin". Older stems and main trunk are gray with vertical darker lines (see photo). Attractive. Wood is stout.

FLOWERS: White; perfect; in clusters 2 to 3 inches long with the leaves. Showy but short-lived.

FRUIT: A small, green, apple-like fruit, turning red with maturity, then purplish. At this point the birds generally have a feast.

COLOR: Foliage is gray-green. Flowers are white. Bark is gray.

PROPAGATION: Seed.

CULTURE: Serviceberries are easily transplanted and grow on most good sites. Of course the better the soil, the more vigorous the growth. During dry periods, growth ceases and some leaves may drop but unlike some species, the trees survive. Slow grower in the Prairie States.

PESTS: Fire blight in areas of poor air movement or near a very susceptible plant. Rust may be a problem in some locations. Occasionally leaf-eating insects.

NOTES: A showy small tree with attractive form, foliage, and bark with good fall color. Used moderately in the Northeast, but rarely seen in Zones 6 and 7. Deserves more use.

CULTIVARS: None? But several hybrids exist.

RELATED SPECIES: *Amelanchier X grandiflora* Rehd., apple serviceberry, is hardy in Zone 3, and is a hybrid between downy serviceberry and Allegheny serviceberry. Young leaves are purplish and hairy, mature leaves are somewhat larger than either of the parents. Flowers are white and showy. 'Robin Hill': flowers buds with a touch of pink but white flowers. 'Rubescens': purplish flower buds and white flowers tinged with pink. Propagated by budding and grafting. 'Autumn Sunset': more heat- and drought-tolerant and has orange fall color.

Amelanchier laevis Wieg., Allegheny serviceberry, is hardy in Zone 3. Fruit is black, the leaves are not hairy and purplish when young, otherwise similar to downy serviceberry in every respect. Cultural conditions are similar.

Differences between these and other species of serviceberry are small, thus considerable confusion exists in the nursery trade. Fortunately, adaptation and general landscape performance of the several species are similar.

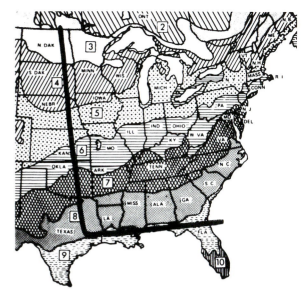

A. grandiflora

A. grandiflora

Betula nigra L.   River Birch
Betulaceae or Birch Family   Hardiness Zone 2
Native to the eastern United States as far west as central Oklahoma.
SIZE: 50 to 60 feet tall in most instances, occasionally larger in native habitat as a single-stemmed tree. Frequently seen as a multiple stem in the landscape; 30 to 40 feet tall with a 20- to 30-foot spread. Moderate to fast grower.
FORM: Upright, oval head or multiple-stemmed tree giving a vase shape.
TEXTURE: Fine to medium.   **EXPOSURE:** Sun or partial shade.

LEAVES: Alternate, simple; ovate or egg-shaped with a sharp point at the tip and a doubly toothed margin. Hairy when young, generally along the veins on the underneath side. Petioles are about 1/2 inch long. Leaves are tapered at the base, not rounded. Dark green and shiny above with a tough, somewhat leathery texture. Fall color is a bright yellow.

STEM: Slender, dark red to red-brown and shiny when young. Buds are red-brown, small, pointed, and slightly fuzzy. Bark is thin and papery on young branches and pinkish or tan on the outer surface, peeling back around the stem to reveal a red-brown inner surface. The most striking feature of the tree is this peeling bark on the 2- to 5-inch diameter branches. Old stems are irregularly furrowed and less attractive.

FLOWERS: Male and female on the same tree (monoecious). Male catkins are in clusters which are 2 to 3 inches long. Female catkins are about 1/4 inch long. Neither is showy.

FRUIT: Cone-like and about one inch long, containing small winged seeds.

COLOR: Foliage is dark green; bright yellow in fall. Bark is pinkish or tan.

PROPAGATION: By seed or softwood cuttings.

CULTURE: Native to stream banks and other moist locations over most of the eastern U.S. Will tolerate a wide range of soil and nutritional conditions and exposure, as long as adequate moisture is provided through either site selection or supplementary irrigation during periods of drought. Responds well to fertilization and good cultural practices. Easy to grow with plenty of water. Short lived as a street tree.

PESTS: None serious although mites may be a problem in hot, dry locations.

NOTES: Two-toned tan and copper-colored young bark stands out in most landscape situations. Grown as a multiple-stemmed tree or as several young trees planted together in a clump, it makes an outstanding landscape specimen for all seasons. Should be located in areas where moisture is present: along streams or around water features or ponds. Native from central Florida to Wisconsin and Michigan, giving a tremendous range of temperatures and soil conditions. In periods of drought, the tree will defoliate and frequently die back on the young branches. A second set of leaves may emerge late in the season under these circumstances and the appearance of the plant decreases. Should be used more in the South. An under-rated tree.

CULTIVARS: 'Heritage': larger leaves and a lighter, more showy bark than most seedlings. It can be easily rooted from softwood cuttings; however, it is patented. The author has a selection that is as yet unnamed with slightly slower and compact growth habit, near-white bark, and large, leathery leaves. More drought-tolerant than the species. It will be patented and released in 1996.

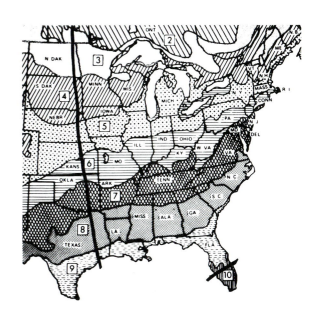

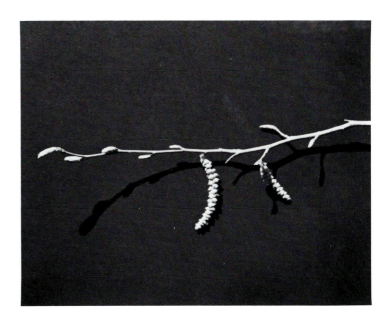

Betula pendula Roth (Syn. *verrucosa, alba*)　　European Birch
Betulaceae or Birch Family　　　　　　　　Hardiness Zone 2
Native to Europe and western Asia.
SIZE: 20- to 60-foot tree depending on growing conditions and geographic locations. Moderate grower.
FORM: Umbrella-crowned, multi-stemmed clump or oval-crowned, single-stemmed specimen.
TEXTURE: Medium.　　　　　　　　　　**EXPOSURE:** Sun to partial shade.

LEAVES: Alternate, simple; unevenly toothed on the margin, about 1 to 2 1/2 inches long, 1 to 1 1/2 inches wide. The base of the leaf is flat, not rounded or V-shaped like other species are. Shiny, bright green above and pale green below, turning bright yellow before dropping in the fall.

STEM: Young twigs are slender and light tan, taking on a characteristic white bark appearance during the second or third season. Trunk is generally straight and tapering. Bark is smooth and white, marked irregularly with dark patches or rings, particularly where branches are attached. Bark on an old tree may be nearly black, with one inch deep furrows. Wood is only moderately durable.

FLOWERS: Male and female on same tree but separate (monoecious). Not showy.

FRUIT: Narrow, woody, brown, cone-like structure about 1 inch long bearing many small, winged seeds.

COLOR: Foliage is bright green; bright yellow in the fall. Bark is white.

PROPAGATION: By seed or softwood cuttings or by grafting of selected cultivars.

CULTURE: Grows best in a moist, loam soil but will tolerate a fairly wide range of soil conditions. Full sun or some shade. Quite cold-resistant but only slight resistant to drought. Needs watering during dry periods, particularly in the Midwest to avoid stress. Responds to fertilizer, supplemental moisture, mulching, and other good cultural practices.

PESTS: Borers are the most damaging pest, attacking weakened trees or trees of some size declining in vigor. Some spider mites and aphids, but rarely are these serious.

NOTES: A beautiful, showy tree because of the white bark and yellow fall color. A stately, attractive tree against a winter sky or background of coniferous evergreens. Generally should not be planted west of a line through Tulsa, Topeka, and Omaha or south of Zone 7. Does not do well in the extreme South or Gulf Coast areas where river birch is well adapted. Sometimes known as European white birch.

CULTIVARS: 'Dalecarlica' or cutleaf weeping birch grows 25 to 35 feet tall with a weeping habit and is very showy, with deeply cut leaves. 'Purple Rain' : wine foliage all season contrasts with the white bark. Other cultivars exist.

RELATED SPECIES: *Betula papyrifera* Marsh., canoe or paper birch, is very similar to European white birch in growth rate, tolerance, and other requirements. It is native to the northeastern United States. Most easily identified by the larger leaves, frequently 2 1/2 to 3 1/2 inches long and 1 1/2 to 2 inches wide. In most conditions it grows to be a taller tree, sometimes reaching 80 to 100 feet with a broad, rounded crown. Somewhat more resistant to birch borer. Sometimes used in landscaping in the Northeast, either singularly or as several plants located together in a clump. Selection of good clones that root well from cuttings could greatly improve the landscape acceptance of this tree in its native range.

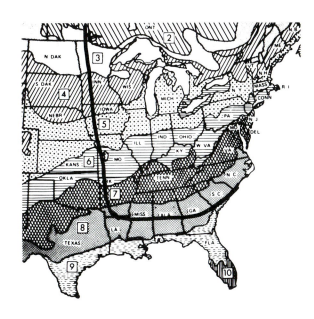

Betula papyrifera

Broussonetia papyrifera (L.) L'Her.   Paper Mulberry
Moraceae or Mulberry Family   Hardiness Zone 5
Native to China and Japan.
SIZE: 30 to 50 feet tall, frequently spreading 30 to 40 feet. Rapid growth rate.
FORM: Broad, oval, spreading tree.
TEXTURE: Coarse.   EXPOSURE: Sun.

LEAVES: Simple and alternate, (occasionally on a young, rapidly growing plant, leaves appear opposite). May reach 8 to 9 inches long, 4 to 5 inches wide. Basically heart-shaped or ovate with a coarsely toothed margin, or it may be lobed with one or more large lobes per leaf. Adjacent leaves may be quite different in terms of lobing. New leaves are light green to gray-green and very sandpapery, with a dense mat of hairs on both upper and lower surfaces. Base of petiole is nearly always accompanied by two small, spine-like stipules. Turn slightly yellow in the fall, not particularly showy. Leaves have a milky sap and wilt very quickly when removed from the tree.

STEM: Young stem is green to green-gray and quite sandpapery with rough, stiff hairs, retaining these for about one season. Later the bark takes on a gray-brown appearance, finally becoming a sandy brown with age. Branching is generally low to the ground resulting in a broad-crowned tree. Wood is soft and brittle; broken easily by wind, ice storms, or vandalism. Has milky sap.

FLOWERS: Inconspicuous. Male and female on separate trees (dioecious).

FRUIT: A globe-shaped ball. Not showy.

COLOR: Foliage is light green to gray-green. Slightly yellow fall color.

PROPAGATION: By seed, suckers, cuttings. Very easy.

CULTURE: Will grow in almost any circumstances: cracks of sidewalks, drain areas, or flower beds. Becomes a weed in some locations and must be frequently removed. Grows in a wide range of soil conditions, is very drought-resistant, and tolerates soils with a high pH, and areas where the root system would be restricted due to soil compaction, structures, or paving. Responds vigorously to fertilization and other good cultural practices. Pruning to prevent narrow branch forks will substantially increase the strength of the tree.

PESTS: None serious.

NOTES: A very tough, rugged tree. Must be included in a class with tree-of-heaven and Siberian elm in terms of ruggedness and durability. It has some merit in areas where other trees do not do well or will not tolerate the adverse conditions. Its broad, spreading canopy provides excellent shade for outdoor recreational areas. The young stem has milky sap which, when broken, is a useful feature for identification. Has merit in terms of producing future cultivars suitable for urban locations. In some instances where soils are very poor following urban development, paper mulberry may be one of the better trees that can be grown without hauling in 6 to 8 inches of topsoil.

CULTIVARS: 'Variegata': variegated white or yellow foliage. Others exist but are of no value.

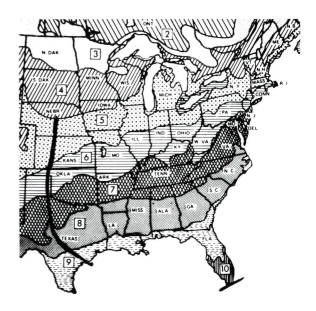

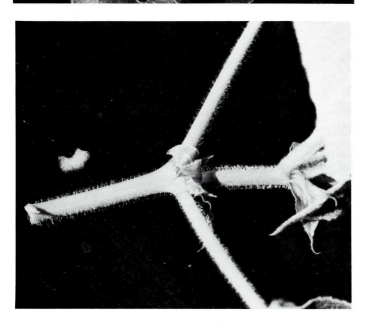

Bumelia lanuginosa Pers.   Chittimwood
Sapotaceae or Sapodilla Family   Hardiness Zone 5
Native to a wide range of the southern and southwestern U.S.
SIZE: 20 to 40 feet tall with a 20- to 25-foot spread. Slower grower.
FORM: Small to medium-sized tree with a round-headed crown.
TEXTURE: Fine.   **EXPOSURE:** Sun to partial shade.

LEAVES: Alternate, simple; often borne in clusters whorled around short, stubby branches. Generally 1 to 3 inches long, 1/2 inch wide, broadest near the tip and tapering to a short stalk; somewhat wedge-shaped. Leathery, shiny green and smooth above, varying from rusty-colored to white to wooly gray beneath. Petioles are short and wooly. Leaves remain green late into the fall and drop from the tree throughout the winter with no fall coloration. Appear early in spring.

STEM: Young twig is gray to red-brown; somewhat zigzag in appearance. Slender yet stiff and hairy at first, then gray or rusty-colored, losing hair and becoming a red-brown to dark gray with age. Bark is dark brown or gray and moderately fissured into narrow ridges. Numerous short, thick, tough thorns resembling those of the hawthorns appear on young branches. Wood is yellow-brown, very hard and tough. Bark texture and the hardness of the wood are reminiscent of *Maclura pomifera,* osage orange.

FLOWERS: Small clusters in June or July; not showy.

FRUIT: Small, shiny, black berries ripening in September or October on slender drooping stems. Not showy.

COLOR: Foliage is deep green, no fall color.

PROPAGATION: By seed or cuttings.

CULTURE: Mostly native to rough, rocky, dry sites with alkaline, shallow soils: in general, undesirable conditions by most standards for growing trees. However, it is occasionally found growing vigorously on a good site and may reach considerable size in height and trunk diameter. Very durable, rugged, small tree that will grow in extremely adverse sites. Does not tolerate disturbance of the root system once it has become established, thus no moving of soil or fill should be done around the tree. Difficult to transplant because of the strong taproot development under natural conditions. Should be grown as a nursery tree if it is going to be transplanted. Slow-growing, taking years to develop a specimen tree; however, growth rate is much faster in good soils.

PESTS: None serious.

NOTES: Outstanding small tree. Where it is growing native, it should be allowed to remain undisturbed as part of the landscape. Should be planted more because of its drought resistance, wind tolerance and virtual immunity to vandalism through spines and strength of wood. Has a great deal of merit in many locations throughout the South and Southwest, being a disease- and insect-free small tree with small fruits that do not make a mess and leaves that are small and cause no difficulty. Has possibilities for improvement through breeding, selection, or mutation. Other common names are wooly bucket bumelia, gum bumelia, and false buckthorn.

CULTIVARS: Some authors have attempted to split chittimwood into several species throughout the southern United States. These are probably only ecological races as the variation is minor.

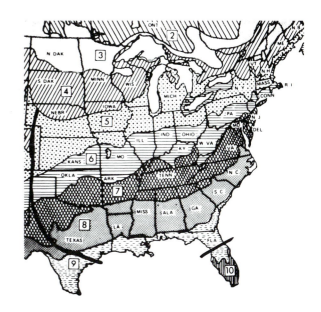

Carpinus betulus L.   European Hornbeam
Betulaceae or Birch Family   Hardiness Zone 4
Native to Europe and southwest Asia.
SIZE: 30 to 50 feet tall with similar spread. Slow to moderate grower.
FORM: Pyramidal when young, becoming more rounded with age.
TEXTURE: Medium.   **EXPOSURE:** Sun or slight shade.

LEAVES: Alternate, simple; distinctly undulating on the upper surface with the veins giving a herringbone effect. Two to 4 inches long with a doubly saw-toothed margin. Dark green upper surface, slightly lighter below with yellow fall color. Leaves are more distinctly veined than on American hornbeam.

STEM: Very slender when young; smooth and brownish-green with distinct, long, tapering buds. Branch development is very orderly, giving a neat and clean appearance in winter. Branches are smooth, steel-gray and muscled or rippled, including the main stem. Attractive. Wood is very strong: wind-, ice-, and vandal-resistant.

FLOWERS: Male and female separate on the same tree (monoecious). Male catkins are about one inch long, female catkins are 2 to 3 inches long; similar to American hornbeam. Noticeable but not showy.

FRUIT: A small nutlet.

COLOR: Foliage is dark green, yellow in the fall. Bark is steel-gray.

PROPAGATION: By seed or grafting of cultivars.

CULTURE: European hornbeam is somewhat difficult to transplant which probably accounts for its limited use in American landscapes. Grows on most soils: wet or dry, clay, or sandy. However, it is only moderately drought tolerant when young, perhaps a bit more with age. Responds to mulching, reduction of grass and weed competition, and watering during droughts. A handsome tree that should be used more.

PESTS: None serious.

NOTES: A most attractive, small to medium tree. Foliage is clean, dense, and dark green during the growing season. During the fall and winter the branch structure and silvery gray bark are very attractive. The two primary limitations are the very dense shade and the difficulty in transplanting. An adaptable tree for many landscape uses including as hedges and screens. A superior tree to the American hornbeam for most landscape uses.

CULTIVARS: 'Columnaris': a dense, upright form that is quite attractive but very formal. 'Fastigiata': dense and similar to 'Columnaris' when young only broader with age. 'Globosa': rounded in outline with little or no central leader, but many stems of similar size. 'Purpurea': wine foliage early, quickly fades to green. Growth habit is like the species. Numerous other cultivars have been identified in Europe; however, most are rare in this country.

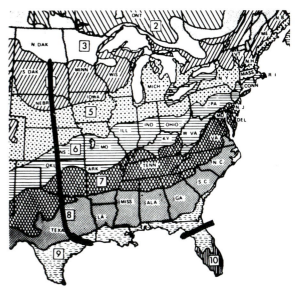

'Columnaris'

'Columnaris'

Carpinus caroliniana Walt.   American Hornbeam or Blue Beech
Betulaceae or Birch Family   Hardiness Zone 3
Native to the eastern United States.
SIZE: 25 to 35 feet tall with a 20- to 25-foot spread. Slow grower.
FORM: Irregular, crooked-stemmed, small tree eventually forming an umbrella-like crown.
TEXTURE: Fine to medium.   **EXPOSURE:** Sun to partial shade.

LEAVES: Alternate, simple; ovate or egg-shaped, 2 to 3 1/2 inches long, 1 to 1 1/2 inches wide, pointed at the tip. Edges of the leaf are doubly toothed. Dull green above and pale green beneath with a few white hairs where the veins intersect. Leaves are elm-like; pale, yellow-orange fall color.

STEM: Young twigs are slender, rough, sandpapery to the touch and dark red-brown with very small buds. Bark is steel-gray with age, quite smooth and irregularly fluted or furrowed on the sides with muscle-like ridges on the vertical stem of the tree. In cross-section, nearly every stem is irregular, not round as would be expected with most trees. Very hard, durable wood. Excellent wide-angle branch development.

FLOWERS: Male and female flowers on the same plant in early spring (monoecious). Male flowers are catkins 1 to 2 inches long; female are almost inconspicuous.

FRUIT: A small nutlet on a 3-lobed, leaf-like structure, develops in clusters in late summer. Green turning brown. Not showy, but noticeable upon close inspection.

COLOR: Foliage is medium green, pale yellow-orange in the fall; only moderately showy.

PROPAGATION: By seed.

CULTURE: Native to stream bottoms and moist, fertile soils throughout the eastern and southern states. However, it tolerates a fairly wide range of soil conditions as long as moisture is not extremely limited. In seepy or wet areas along water features or drainage ways, this small tree has considerable merit. Appears to have some value as a street tree, certainly in the more eastern portion of the United States. Mulching to stabilize soil temperature and moisture increases the growth rate.

PESTS: None serious.

NOTES: An interesting small tree because of overall texture and form, smooth, almost steel-gray bark, and overall line against a wintry sky. Works well as a patio tree or adjacent to single-story dwellings. Makes an excellent tree for kids to climb because of the excellent branch development and wood strength. Adapted to a wide range of the United States. Its slow growth rate and difficulty to transplant from the wild probably account for its limited use as an ornamental tree in this country. Should be used more. Frequently confused with *Ostrya virginiana* but easily distinguished, because *Carpinus* has smooth leaves and bark and *Ostrya* has sandpapery leaves and a rough bark peeling in vertical strips.

CULTIVARS: 'Pyramidalis': somewhat more upright and narrow tree than the species, but still gets quite broad. Not common in the trade. Others may exist.

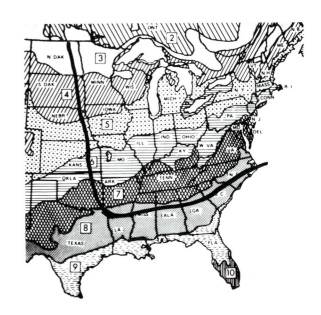

Carpinus caroliniana　　*Ostrya virginiana*

Carya spp.
Juglandaceae or Walnut Family
Native to most of the eastern U.S.
Hickories
Hardiness Zone 3 through 6

SIZE: 60 to 100 feet tall. Slow to moderate growers.
FORM: Generally single-stemmed tree with a slightly spreading ovate to rounded crown.
TEXTURE: Medium. **EXPOSURE:** Sun to partial shade.

LEAVES: Alternate, compound, generally with 5 to 9 leaflets. Depending on species, may reach 10 to 20 inches long and 6 to 10 inches wide, generally with the terminal leaflet the largest. Leaflets going back toward the base of the compound leaf get smaller. Margin is toothed. Upper leaf surface is medium to dark green, lower leaf surface is pale green to yellow-green. Several species have leaves which are pubescent or wooly. Fall color is a dull yellow to yellow-orange.

STEM: Young stems are stout and brown to gray-brown, generally with egg-shaped or somewhat football-shaped terminal and axillary buds. Bark varies from being very smooth and steel gray to very rough, almost black, and peeling in vertical strips, depending on species.

FLOWERS: Male and female on the same tree (monoecious). Not showy.

FRUIT: A nut of varying sizes and shapes, about 1 to 1 1/2 inches in diameter. Very hard nut with thick husk and little meat inside. Edible but not desirable.

COLOR: Foliage is medium to dark green, with fall color of pale yellow to yellow-orange.

CULTURE: Native to upland, generally fairly good soils, where leaf litter is accumulated and moderately good moisture and nutrition exist. As a whole does not tolerate disturbance of the root system, either through compaction, removal of soils or fill soils in urban development. Of moderate landscape value in terms of areas where they are to be planted. Difficult to transplant, either from wild or nurseries. Of most merit when left alone, totally undisturbed, on native sites to be developed. There they can add a great deal for many years.

PESTS: Tent caterpillars are very troublesome; otherwise hickories are fairly resistant to disease and insect pests. Mushroom root rot may play a role in the decline of the tree once the root system has been disturbed and/or the soil compacted.

NOTES: Not a plant for general landscape use, but should be utilized where they exist on sites being developed. Otherwise are generally inferior to many other trees for urban locations. Fruits may be a problem on walks or driveways.

CULTIVARS: None. Several species are native throughout the southeastern United States.

SPECIES: *Cary cordiformis*, bitternut hickory, is a tall slender tree with gold-yellow buds that aid in its identification. *C. glabra*, pignut hickory, probably has the best golden fall color of the various species native to the eastern United States. *C. laciniosa*, shellbark hickory, has an edible fruit and is very similar in appearance to *C. ovata*, including a rather shaggy bark. However, shellbark hickory is native to, and will tolerate wet sites that are not suited to shagbark hickory which is adapted to dryer sites and, in general, needs better drainage. *C. ovata*, shagbark hickory is similar in appearance to shellbark and also has edible nuts but is different in adaptation. *C. glabra* and *C. ovata* are the most common and widely distributed of the species.

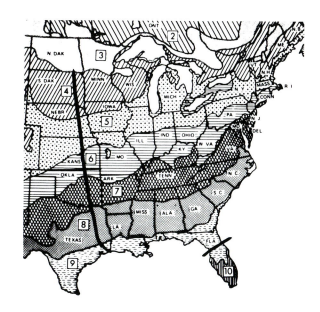

Above *Carya cordiformis*

Above *Carya ovata*

Carya illinoinensis (Wangh.) Koch.   Pecan
Juglandaceae or Walnut Family   Hardiness Zone 5
Native to river bottoms from Texas throughout the South.
SIZE: Large tree: may reach 125 to 150 feet with 100-foot spread.   Slow to moderate grower.
FORM: Large, round-headed tree.
TEXTURE: Medium.   **EXPOSURE:** Sun.

LEAVES: Alternate, compound; 12 to 20 inches long, with 9 to 15 leaflets. Terminal leaflet is always present. Individual leaflets are 4 to 6 inches long, 1 to 1 1/2 inches wide, and generally of uniform size with a slight reduction of those near the base of the compound leaf. Dark green to yellow-green above, pale green below. Margin is doubly toothed. Young leaves are quite hairy and have a very distinctive odor when crushed.

STEMS: Young stems are stout and reddish brown. Buds at the tips are about 1/2 inch long, generally pale yellow to yellow-brown and very fuzzy. When a young stem is cut diagonally, the pith in the center looks like brown sugar. Bark is thick, light to dark reddish brown and relatively smooth or deeply furrowed and scaley. Bark varies a great deal among trees, particularly seedlings. Wood is moderately durable and fairly wind-resistant but somewhat brittle in ice storms. Inferior to the hickories in terms of durability.

FLOWERS: Male and female on the same tree (monoecious). Not showy.

FRUIT: On the common pecan it is generally in clusters of 3 to 8 or more, oblong or football shaped. It has a thin husk and varies a lot in size of nut and kernel, depending on cultivars and within seedlings. Fruit is highly prized for its use in cooking.

COLOR: Foliage is yellow-green to dark green; dull yellow in the fall.

PROPAGATION: By seed; selected cultivars are grafted or budded onto seedlings.

CULTURE: Native along creek bottoms in deep, moist soils throughout the southern United States. Not well adapted to upland or urban sites with no topsoil. Difficult to transplant and slow to regenerate feeder roots. Should be planted only where pest control is assured or it will be disappointing in the landscape.

PESTS: Tent caterpillars are the main pest of the foliage. If not controlled, fruit pests such as weevils, pecan scab, and shuck worms cause considerable loss of the fruit.

NOTES: Where good soils exist, pecans can be desirable shade trees and producers of edible nuts. Leaves, buds, husks of nuts, and perhaps the wood release a material during rain or when damaged that can stain patio furniture, car tops, and sidewalks. This may be an undesirable feature depending on the location of the tree. Should be used only in areas of good growing conditions where pests will be controlled.

CULTIVARS: Many selections available. All are grafted onto seedlings. In addition to nut quality, overall form and crown development vary with selections. 'Gormely' is a small, spreading tree with dense foliage and an early ripening nut. 'Maramec': larger tree, good fruit and tree form. 'San Saba': small tree, open foliage, good fruit. 'Moneymaker': thin foliage, good loose shade, fair fruit. 'Western': rapid grower, needs spraying for scab. 'Stuart': old variety, widely planted: an inferior upright-grower with weak branches. Avoid it for landscpae use. Many many others exist.

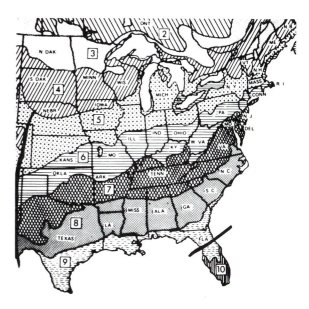

Castanea mollissima Blume.   Chinese Chestnut
Fagaceae or Beech Family   Hardiness Zone 4
Native to China and Korea.
SIZE: 30 to 40 feet tall in most instances with a 30- to 35-foot spread. Moderate grower.
FORM: Small- to medium-sized tree with broad-spreading crown.
TEXTURE: Medium to coarse.   **EXPOSURE:** Sun.

LEAVES: Alternate, simple; oval-oblong to oblong-lanceolate. Rounded at the base, sharply pointed at the tip, 3 1/2 to 6 inches long, about 1 1/2 to 2 inch wide, very coarsely toothed on the margin. Smooth, shining, deep green above; light green, almost pubescent white to velvety white beneath or on old leaves at least along the veins. Short, stiff petiole. Fall color is rusty yellow-brown with leaves remaining into the winter.

STEM: Young stem is moderately slender and glossy light brown, turning darker brown and finally gray-brown on the old stem. Bark pattern is reminiscent of the American elm. Wood is light but moderately durable.

FLOWERS: Female and male on the same tree (monoecious). Not showy.

FRUIT: A prickly husk about 1 to 1 1/2 inch in diameter, with 1 to 5 large brown nuts. Many, many spines on the husk. Edible and quite tasty (if you can beat the squirrels).

COLOR: Foliage is deep green in spring; rusty yellow-brown in fall.

PROPAGATION: By seed with some variation in form and nut quality; also by grafting of cultivars.

CULTURE: Prefers a fertile, well-drained soil but grows in fairly rocky, poor soils as long as they are not alkaline or very dry. Will not stand excessively wet or dry soils. Does best in full sun and open locations. Once established will not tolerate soil compaction or disruption of the root system.

PESTS: Few. Moderately resistant to the chestnut blight which caused the extinction of the American chestnut, *Castanea dentata*.

NOTES: An attractive tree with a low, spreading crown, good leaf texture, fairly good fall color, and good branch structure. However, it does not tolerate disturbance of the root system by machinery, planting, or additional landscape development. Should be planted more where a good shade tree that branches low to the ground is needed. Has good summer shade, but leaves hang on into the winter. Roasted chestnuts are quite tasty.

CULTIVARS: 'Esstate-jap': highly resistant to chestnut blight. 'Sleeping Giant': a larger tree than most seedlings. 'Kelsey': a smaller tree with a spreading crown and good nut quality. Others probably exist.

RELATED SPECIES: *Castanea dentata*, American chestnut, was native to much of northeastern North America. It is nearly extinct as the result of chestnut blight introduced from the orient. A few struggling trees remain, thus some possibility exists for resistance. The American chestnut fruit was edible, the tree was stately, and the woody was sturdy. Hybrids between Chinese, Japanese, and American chestnut trees were made which have yielded trees that are similar to American chestnut in growth and form and produce considerable nuts. Chestnut Hill Nursery in Alachua, Florida is one of the few growers of these hybrid chestnuts.

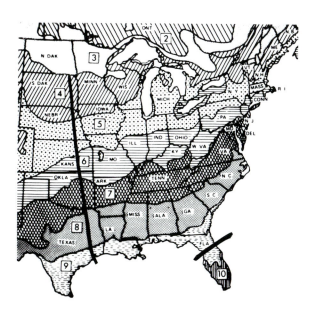

Catalpa bignonioides Walt.   Southern Catalpa
Bignoniaceae or Bignonia Family   Hardiness Zone 6
Native to the southeastern United States.
SIZE: 40- to 60-foot tree frequently attaining a spread of 30 to 40 feet. Moderate to rapid grower.
FORM: Broad, spreading-crowned tree.
TEXTURE: Coarse.   **EXPOSURE:** Sun.

LEAVES: Opposite or whorled, simple; with a smooth margin. Generally 6 to 12 inches long, 4 to 6 inches wide and heart-shaped. Light yellow-green to medium green above, pale green below. Have soft and pliable texture and are velvety pubescent or hairy. Very prominent midrib. Leaves turn black and drop with first severe frost in the fall. No fall color.

STEM: Young branches are green but may have a purple tint when they first appear. Tends to thicken at the nodes during the first winter, taking on a light brown or gray-brown color with age. Bark on an old stem is generally light brown tinted with red, separating into large, thin, irregular scales. Wood is rather coarse-grained, not strong, and fairly brittle, but moderately decay-resistant.

FLOWERS: Large, showy; 2 inches long in loose panicles. White, marked with yellow in the throat and brownish-purple streaks or spots. Very showy in mid-spring.

FRUIT: Elongate, cylindrical, bean-like capsules hanging down from the branches. About 1/4 inch in diameter and 8 to 12 inches long. Seeds have two wings when the pod opens; the tips of the wings are fringed with long hairs. Seeds and wings are about one inch long.

COLOR: Foliage is medium to yellow-green. No fall color. Flowers are white.

PROPAGATION: By seed.

CULTURE: Tolerates a wide range of soils but grows best in a moist, fertile, well-drained soil. Moderately tolerant of high pH soils and drought-resistant. Tolerates some heat, growing in most full sun locations or tolerates some shade, particularly when young.

PESTS: Caterpillars may damage the leaves. Sometimes trees are planted for the caterpillars which are good fish bait.

NOTES: A rather messy tree. Although flowers are very showy when in bloom, they drop and cover the ground and sidewalks and become a slippery, gooey mess. Seed pods are large and somewhat difficult to rake or handle. Leaves are very large and difficult to remove from a lawn or landscape area. A very tough, durable tree which tolerates a wide range of conditions such as poor, dry soils and has some merit in that respect. Moderately good shade tree because of the spreading branch habit. Coarse-textured, tropical-appearing foliage is very striking and distinctive and should not be used indiscriminately. Should be used only in large areas with plenty of space. Picturesque and attractive tree on large sites and when viewed from a distance.

CULTIVARS: None known.

RELATED SPECIES: *Catalpa speciosa* Warder., the western or northern catalpa, is similar in many respects to *C. bignonioides* except that it is more cold hardy. It can be distinguished *C. bignonioides* by the flowers that are in more loose panicles, fewer flowers per cluster, fruits that are stout and thick-walled, and shorter and thicker than on *Catalpa bignonioides*.

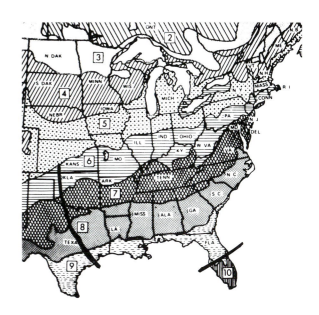

Celtis laevigata Willd.   Sugarberry or Sugar Hackberry
Ulmaceae or Elm Family   Hardiness Zone 5
Native to the southeastern United States.
SIZE: 40 to 60 feet tall and may attain a 40- to 50-foot spread. Medium grower.
FORM: Large, broad-spreading tree.
TEXTURE: Fine to medium.   **EXPOSURE:** Sun to partial shade.

LEAVES: Alternate, simple; ovate to egg-shaped with long, pointed, lance-shaped tip, often hooked left or right. Has a few remote teeth on the margin near the tip, while the remainder of the leaf margin is smooth. Medium green and smooth above, pale green below with three conspicuous veins on the underneath side near the base. Generally 2 1/2 to 3 1/2 inches long, 1 to 2 inches wide. Yellow in the fall, not showy.

STEM: Young stem is slender, somewhat zigzag, and greenish at first turning red-brown, with small buds in the leaf axils. Bark is gray-brown to silver-gray. Young bark in upper branches is smooth. The old stem and oldest branches vary in bark pattern but generally have a few warty projections but never as densely as on hackberry. Main branches are frequently well formed and stout.

FLOWERS: Male and female flowers on the same tree (monoecious). Not showy.

FRUIT: Fleshy, berry-like, 1/2 inch in diameter. Red-purple to black, maturing in fall.

COLOR: Foliage is medium green, slightly yellow in fall. Poor fall color.

PROPAGATION: By seed.

CULTURE: Native to low stream banks, flood plains, and moist, fertile soils throughout the southern United States. Only moderately tolerant of urban conditions. Not as widely adaptable to soils, moisture stress, and dry, exposed locations as is hackberry. Can be a desirable, medium-sized tree in conditions with good soils. Certainly should be preserved if the tree exists on land to be developed.

PESTS: None serious. May be host to mistletoe in the South.

NOTES: An attractive, medium-sized tree with few problems in low areas or areas with fertile soils. Moderately durable wood. Not for general planting in urban conditions where soils are of poor quality. Often confused with hackberry; however, hackberry has a very rough, warty bark overall, limbs two or more inches in diameter, and leaves which are larger and rougher on the upper surface. By contrast, sugar hackberry has a smooth bark except for irregular rough patches mostly on the main stems, and leaves which are smaller and smoother on the upper surface. However, natural hybrids between the two species are not uncommon and may exhibit characteristics of both species.

CULTIVARS: 'All Seasons': a rounded crown, and small, dark green leaves. Well suited to city conditions. 'Magnifica': said to be a hybrid between sugarberry and common hackberry with dark glossy leaves and a rounded crown. Others probably exist.

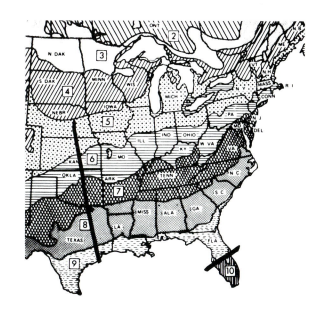

Celtis occidentalis L.   Hackberry
Ulmaceae or Elm Family   Hardiness Zone 3
Native to the eastern United States.
SIZE: 40 to 90 feet tall with a 30- to 40-foot spread. Moderate grower.
FORM: Large, oval-crowned tree.
TEXTURE: Fine to medium.   **EXPOSURE:** Sun.

LEAVES: Alternate, simple; narrowly egg-shaped, ovate to elliptical, tapering to a point at the tip. Medium to dark green above; pale green below. Young leaves are soft with a few hairs on the underneath side. Mature leaves are often sandpapery, 2 1/2 to 4 inches long and 1 1/2 to 2 inches wide, with slender petioles. Leaves are frequently hooked or sickle-shaped, and the margin generally has a few teeth. Fall color is pale yellow.

STEM: Young stems are slender and light brown, becoming gray with maturity. May have a cluster of small branches from a single point on the young stem, commonly referred to as "witches brooms". Older branches are grayish with many rough, warty projections. Generally single-stemmed, upright-growing tree, branching like an American elm. Fairly durable wood is wind- and vandal-resistant.

FLOWERS: Male and female on the same tree (monoecious). Not showy.

FRUIT: Fleshy, berry-like, purple to black when mature. About 1/2 inch long. Edible.

COLOR: Foliage is medium to dark green; pale yellow fall color.

PROPAGATION: Seed.

CULTURE: Common hackberry is native to rich bottomland and stream banks where it becomes a large, vigorously growing tree. However, it is tolerant of a wide range of soils and growing conditions. Will grow in almost any type of soil and is drought- and wind-resistant. A very durable, rugged tree, particularly in the Prairie States. Responds vigorously to fertilization and other good cultural practices. Will also tolerate moist locations fairly well. One of the most well adapted trees to upland soils in urban conditions.

PESTS: "Witches broom" is probably the major pest, causing the proliferation of young branches into clusters: somewhat unsightly, but to some, considered ornamental. Also, nipple gall caused by mites forming a nipple-like projection on leaves. Neither of these problems appears to be particularly detrimental to the overall growth of the tree. Recently a slow decline of unknown origin has killed numerous trees. No known control.

NOTES: Seldom an outstanding specimen tree but a good, tough, durable, shade tree that should be used more often for general landscape purposes. Provides a desirable, light-textured shade, is maintenance- and pest-free, and fits in with other ornamentals in the landscape. Tolerates most growing conditions.
   Hackberry has leaves which are broader in proportion to length, not as long; more taper-pointed at the tip, toothed on the margin and may be sandpapery when mature. This contrasts with *Celtis laevigata* which has narrower and longer leaves with finer teeth on the margins and a smooth surface. The warty appearance of the bark is more widely distributed throughout the stem and branches on hackberry, whereas sugar hackberry has only a few warty projections in irregular patches on the main stems.

CULTIVARS: 'Prairie Pride': upright grower when young, more spreading with age. Said to be more resistant to "witches broom". 'Chicagoland': a central leader tree, which avoids the narrow forks that commonly create structural problems in hackberry. 'Windy City': an upright grower with glossy foliage. Others probably exist.

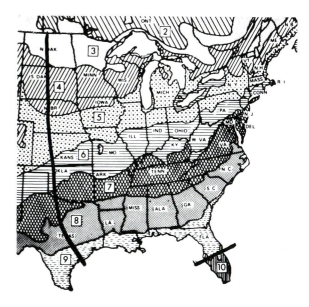

Cercidiphyllum japonicum Siebold & Zucc. Katsuratree
Cercidiophyllaceae or Katsuratree Family Hardiness Zone 5
Native to China and Japan.
SIZE: 50 to 80 feet tall with a 30- to 50-foot spread. Moderate grower.
FORM: Large, pyramidal tree.
TEXTURE: Medium. **EXPOSURE:** Sun or slight shade.

LEAVES: Opposite, simple; distinctly heart-shaped, 2 to 4 inches long, with a wavy margin. Somewhat purplish when very young; bluish green above, lighter below with maturity. Mostly yellow in the fall. Leaves look like redbud leaves, except that they are opposite instead of alternate and the margins are wavy.

STEM: The young stem is brown, smooth and slender, and swolen at the nodes (see photograph). Older bark is shallowly furrowed and light brown to slightly gray-brown. Wood is moderately stout, not readily broken.

FLOWERS: Male and female on separate trees (dioecious). Neither flower is showy.

FRUIT: A small pod; not showy or conspicuous.

COLOR: Foliage is blue-green; yellow to slightly orange in the fall.

PROPAGATION: By seed. Cuttings root poorly if at all.

CULTURE: Katsuratree is very sensitive to drought and drying winds. For example, in Oklahoma, 6- to 8-foot trees in five-gallon containers grow and transplant well in fall or spring. However, when temperatures exceed 95 degrees F and the drying summer winds begin, the leaves scorch and drop even if regularly watered enough to make the soil moist. Even trees planted along a continually moist drainage area live only about two seasons. When grown in the field and balled-in-burlap, it has a reputation for being somewhat difficult to tranplant. However, starting the seedlings in bottomless containers and placing plastic in the bottom of the nursery planting hole can eliminate these transplanting difficulties. Since it is a shallowly rooted tree it grows best in good soils with mulch and supplemental moisture during drought and with the elimination of grass and weed competition.

PESTS: None serious, although an occasional chewing insect will have it for lunch.

NOTES: A large, attractive tree where it can be grown. Trees at the Morton Arboretum near Chicago, Illinois are spectacular (see photograph). It has been proposed in some writings as a street tree; however, this seems questionable since it does not tolerate low soil oxygen. Should not be planted south of Zone 7 and in general, west of the Mississippi River. Should be planted in carefully selected sites only. Useful on golf courses with irrigation as it is a neat and attractive tree with no messy flowers, fruits, or large leaves to complicate maintenance.

CULTIVARS: 'Pendula': gently drooping branches and an attractive contrast to the species. Others probably exist.

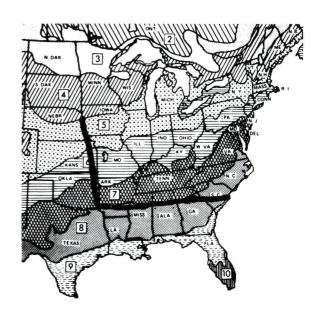

Cercis canadensis L.   Eastern Redbud
Leguminosae or Pea Family   Hardiness Zone 4
Native to the eastern United States from the Gulf Coast to Canada.
SIZE: May reach 20 to 25 feet tall with a 15- to 20-foot spread. Moderate grower when young; slow grower with maturity.
FORM: Flat-topped, widely spreading, single- to multiple-stemmed, small tree.
TEXTURE: Medium to coarse.   **EXPOSURE:** Sun.

LEAVES: Alternate, simple; heart-shaped, 2 to 3 1/2 inches long and wide, with smooth margins and long petioles. The petioles are rather bulbous where they attach to the leaf and to the stem. Dark green in summer, turning a rather attractive yellow in the fall.

STEM: Young stem is zigzag, slender, and rather sandpapery to the touch because of the prominent lenticels. Red to red-black to deep red-brown, darker with maturity. Bark is reddish to reddish-brown with loose scales tinted red with age. Single- or multiple-stemmed small tree with hard, durable wood. Moderately wind-resistant. Needs pruning to prevent weak, narrow branches, especially near the base.

FLOWERS: Purple-red in clusters along the stem before the leaves emerge in very early spring. Very showy. May also be white, depending on the cultivar.

FRUIT: Oblong, flattened pod, 2 to 3 inches long. Reddish to brown, persistent through the winter on most trees.

COLOR: Foliage is dark green; yellow in the fall. Flowers are purple-red or white.

PROPAGATION: By seed or grafting of selected cultivars onto seedlings.

CULTURE: Native to a wide range of growing conditions. Tolerates poor soils, hot dry locations, and rocky outcrops. Responds to better growing conditions but is amazingly tolerant. Flowers best in full sun but tolerates some shade. Needs some corrective pruning when young to develop good strong branches and avoid the weak forks which commonly lead to early death of the tree. Rather difficult to transplant, particularly from the wild.

PESTS: Stem canker, leaf rollers, leaf miners, borers on old trees.

NOTES: Widely adaptable, tough, and durable small tree. Highly prized for the magnificent show of flowers very early in the spring, for its size, and its broad-spreading crown which relates well with many single story dwellings. Extensively planted and of considerable merit. Trees from the wild are difficult to transplant and generally short-lived.

CULTIVARS: 'Alba': white flowers. 'Oklahoma': deep purple flowers, and very lustrous shining leaves. Less susceptible to leaf rollers, probably due to the leaf structure and surface texture. It is also slightly more drought-resistant than most seedlings. 'Forest Pansy': intense purple foliage at first, gradually turning more green. However, 'Forest Pansy' is less drought-tolerant than most seedlings and does best in a somewhat protected location. 'Silver Cloud': leaves are speckled with cream colored blotches. An interesting novelty but generally not as tough as the species, especially in full sun.

RELATED SPECIES: *Cercis chinensis* Bunge., Chinese redbud, is a multiple-stemmed shrub form rarely reaching 15 to 20 feet tall with no distinct central leader or stem. Flowers about the same time in the spring as eastern redbud and usually more profusely along the many upright stems. No particular advantage other than shrub form versus a single-stemmed tree form. About equally tolerant to growing conditions.

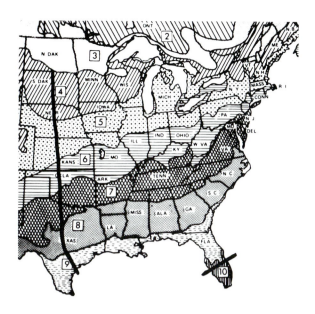

Chilopsis linearis (Cav.) Sweet   Desertwillow
Bignoniaceae or Bignonia Family   Hardiness Zone 7
Native to the southwestern United States.
SIZE: 15 to 30 feet tall with a 15- to 25-foot spread. Moderate grower.
FORM: Irregular, small tree with rounded, umbrella-like crown.
TEXTURE: Fine.   **EXPOSURE:** Sun.

LEAVES: Alternate, simple; long and narrow, willow-like; 4 to 8 inches long, 1/4 inch wide, with a smooth margin and medium green color. No fall color but drop quickly to reveal interesting branch structure. Leaves are thicker and more leathery than true willow.

STEM: Young twigs are slender with distinct lenticels, reddish-brown or slightly purplish brown in winter. Dormant buds are very small and hairy. Bark on older stems and the main trunk is gray-brown, breaking into irregular patches. Wood is moderately stout.

FLOWERS: In clusters, appearing in May or June and continuing at irregular intervals throughout the growing season. Flowers are on new growth. Therefore, with each flush of growth, new flowers appear. May be dark lavender to nearly white, depending on seedling or cultivar. Flowers have a long throat with large, funnel-shaped face. May be 2 to 3 inches long and 1 to 2 inches across the face.

FRUIT: Long, slender, cylinder-shaped pods, 4 to 8 inches long. Open at maturity to release flattened seeds with many hairs on each end.

COLOR: Flowers are lavender to nearly white.

PROPAGATION: By seed or softwood cuttings taken in mid spring.

CULTURE: A rapid-growing tree when young, slowing with age. Responds with vigor to good soils and improved growing conditions, especially to the removal of grass competition. If watered during or after dry spells, it will make another flush of growth with more flowers. Will tolerate poor soils and considerable drought; however, it will not tolerate very heavy clays or wet, swampy conditions.

PESTS: No disease or insect problems under most conditions.

NOTES: An attractive, small tree, much overlooked in the urban landscape. The adaptation of the leaves and crown to desert conditions make it ideal for many urban conditions. The showy flowers which begin in May or June and continue with successive growth flushes make it especially useful for color after the spring bloomers are finished. Not as spectacular as crapemyrtle for flowers but superior in overall form, light-textured shade, and interesting branch structure. Is not common in nurseries or urban landscapes but fits in well with single-story dwellings and should be used a great deal more, especially in open, full sun, and new housing areas in the South and Southwest, where sites are droughty. On such sites, it is superior to flowering dogwood as a small patio or outdoor living area tree.

CULTIVARS: The USDA Soil Conservation Service has released the cultivar, 'Barronco', which has lavender flowers. 'Alba': white flowers, but is otherwise similar to the species.

RELATED SPECIES: A desert willow and catalpa hybrid resulted in an interesting plant, sometimes listed as chitalpa. This is a small to medium tree with open, upright branches and good form. Flowers are mostly white and produced in July or August at the ends of new growth. Flowers are in long clusters and are quite showy. The leaves are longer and broader than desert willow, but much smaller than catalpa. The leaves are tufted near the outer part of the branches. Probably hardy in Zone 6. Well adapted to hot, dry locations as long as the soil drains well. Should be used more.

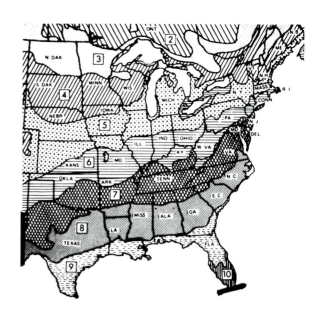

Chitalpa

Chitalpa

Chionanthus virginicus L.　　　　　　　　Fringetree or Old Man's Beard
Oleaceae or Olive Family　　　　　　　　　Hardiness Zone 5
Native to eastern United States.
SIZE: 20 to 25 feet tall with a 15- to 20-foot spread. Slow grower.
FORM: Irregular shrub or small tree with rounded crown.
TEXTURE: Medium to coarse.　　　　　**EXPOSURE:** Partial shade.

LEAVES: Opposite, simple; 4 to 8 inches long, 2 to 4 inches wide. Dark blue-green above, lighter green below with a smooth margin. The base of the petiole is a distinct purple. Fall color is a clear yellow.

STEM: Young branches are gray, stout, and prominent with prominent lenticels. Dormant buds are small and smooth. Old stems are smooth and silver-gray. Wood is moderately stout.

FLOWERS: Very showy in mid spring. Drooping clusters of loose, delicate, white flowers with strap-like petals (thus "fringetree") are very showy against the new leaves that have just emerged. Flower clusters may be 4 to 8 inches long and remain for two weeks or more if a hard rain does not occur. A unique flower show.

FRUIT: An oval fruit about 1/2 inch or less long. Bright blue and showy if present in large quantities. Readily eaten by birds.

COLOR: Flowers are white and very showy. Excellent contrast with the new foliage.

PROPAGATION: By seed. Cuttings root poorly, if at all.

CULTURE: Native to a range of natural conditions as an understory tree. Grows best with good soil, mulching, and removal of grass competition. The ideal site for fringetree has good soil, some supplemental watering during droughts, and sun from early morning until midday. Like dogwood, fringetree does not belong in full sun, or in urban conditions where soils are poor and reflected light and heat may create additional stress. Mulching or ground covers such as English ivy or vinca assist in keeping the soil cool, which aids this attractive, small tree.

PESTS: Occasionally mites in full sun locations, but few, if any, problems, in locations suitable for good growth.

NOTES: A spectacular, small tree that rivals dogwood for a spring show and attractive foliage throughout the season. However, like dogwood, it is best suited to partly shaded conditions. Should be used more but is somewhat difficult to transplant.

CULTIVARS: Some probably exist.

RELATED SPECIES: *Chionanthus retusus* Lindl. and Paxt., Chinese fringetree, grows 20 to 30 feet tall and is similar in adaptation and use. However, leaves are smaller and more leathery with a more distinct petiole. Hardiness Zone 6. Flowers appear on current season's growth, this is a bit more showy than *C. virginicus*. Occasionally offered by nurseries. A good landscape plant; should be used more.

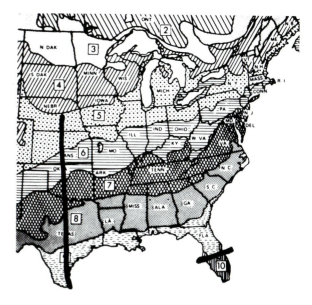

Chionanthus retusus

Cladrastis lutea C. Koch (Kentukea)   American Yellowood
Leguminosae or Legume Family   Hardiness Zone 3
Native to east central United States.
SIZE: 30 to 50 feet tall with a 30- to 50-foot spread. Slow to medium grower.
FORM: Broad, rounded crown, generally with low branching.
TEXTURE: Medium.   **EXPOSURE:** Full sun or partial shade.

LEAVES: Alternate, once-compound; generally with 5 or 7 leaflets, occasionally 11. Upper leaf surface is yellow-green early, changing to bright green, glossy, and smooth; very attractive. Lower leaf surface is dull green. Fall color is yellow. The base of the petiole is swollen which is typical of most legume trees. However, in this case it encloses the bud.

STEM: Upright, central leader trunk, but branches low to the ground (generally). Bark on mature stems is relatively smooth and gray with slightly horizontal ridges (not deeply furrowed like many species). The young stem zigzags, is smooth and bright reddish-brown. Wood is yellow and moderately stout.

FLOWERS: White, very showy. In large clusters 8 to 12 inches long, during May or June. Flowers are somewhat fragrant and contrast with the glossy, green foliage.

FRUIT: Typical legume pod, 2 to 3 inches long; maturing in mid fall.

COLOR: Flowers are white. Foliage is bright green; fall color is a fair yellow.

PROPAGATION: By seed. However, seed must be acid treated in order to germinate.

CULTURE: Native to a wide range of areas from stream banks to upland sites. Tolerates most soils except for the very wet. Moderately drought-tolerant. Good soil improves growth rate; however, performs reasonably well on most urban sites if the slow growth rate is acceptable. Moderately difficult to transplant since the root system is not fibrous. Perhaps best suited to semi-shade or locations where some shade or protection is provided for part of the day.

PESTS: None serious.

NOTES: A desirable, medium-sized tree that stays in scale with single story dwellings. The low, rounded crown provides a pleasant escape from the hot sun, yet most ground covers and some grasses can be grown beneath the canopy, partly because of the loose foliage canopy and the fact that legume trees are not severe competitors with adjacent plants. Should be used more. Growth rate and ease of transplanting can be improved with innovative nursery production techniques, particularly air-root-pruning to stimulate root branching when young.

Recently the name was changed from *C lutea* to *C. kentukea* as a result of too many taxonomists having too much time on their hands. I have chosen to stay with *C. lutea* as this will be the name in the nursery trade for decades to come.

CULTIVARS: *Hortus III* lists 'Rosea' with pinkish flowers; however, I have never seen any cultivars in the nursery trade.

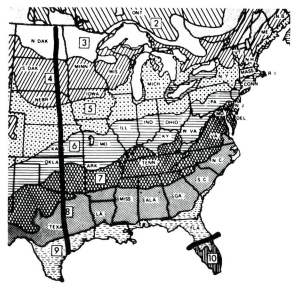

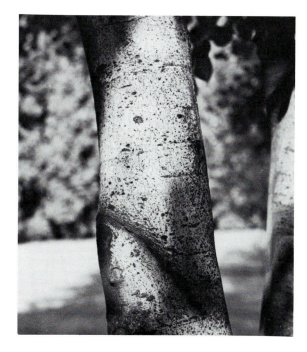

Cornus florida L.   Flowering Dogwood
Cornaceae or Dogwood Family   Hardiness Zone 4 or 5
Native to the eastern United States from the Gulf Coast to Canada.
SIZE: 20 to 30 feet tall with a 20- to 25-foot spread. Slow to moderate grower.
FORM: Broad-crowned, small tree.
TEXTURE: Medium.   EXPOSURE: Sun to shade.

LEAVES: Opposite, simple; 3 to 5 inches long, 1 1/2 to 3 inches wide. Elliptical, pointed at the tip, smooth margin, and a short petiole. Bright green above, pale green below. Veins tend to radiate out and parallel the margin. Fall color is red to red-orange; very showy.

STEM: Young twigs are slender, greenish to greenish-purple, and have a waxy bloom turning greenish gray; until 1 to 1 1/2 inches or more in diameter are rather smooth and steel-gray to gray-brown in color. Old bark is reddish tan to dark brown, and broken into rather uniform square or rounded blocks. May be single- or multiple-stemmed. Wood is very hard and durable; highly prized for making certain furniture items.

FLOWERS: Appearing before the leaves, four petal-like or leaf-like bracts surround a cluster of small, greenish yellow to white flowers. The true flowers are not showy. Bracts may be white or pink, depending on variety, and are shaped somewhat like the leaves except the center of the tip has a rusty looking indentation. Very showy. Blooms about the same time as eastern redbud, frequently making a spectacular combination. Pink-flowered cultivars require more cold chilling of the buds than do the white-flowered cultivars and thus are restricted to more northern areas. The white-flowered cultivars can be found growing all along the Gulf Coast states and into central Florida.

FRUIT: Egg-shaped; in clusters, about 1/2 inch long. Bright red to red-orange.

COLOR: Fall color is red to red-orange. Flowers are white or pink. Fruit is red.

PROPAGATION: By seed, cuttings with difficulty, or grafting of selected cultivars.

CULTURE: Understory tree in moist, fertile woodlands throughout eastern United States. Can be grown in a wide range of soil types from the sandy soils of Florida to heavier clay soils as long as soils are moist but not excessively wet. Mulching reduces soil temperature, retains moisture, and assists in the nutritional balance. Will not tolerate prolonged water-logging of soils. Will tolerate full sun in landscape situations, but does not tolerate hot, dry, exposed locations of parking lots and new urban areas. Under harsh conditions, leaves desiccate on the margins and become very unattractive. Hardiness depends on seed source.

PESTS: Leaf spot is common but control is impractical. Borers attack trees under stress. A stem canker has become a problem in the Upper South, especially in nurseries. Old trees finally die of mushroom or similar root rot organisms, but trees are fairly problem-free if the proper planting site is selected.

NOTES: Very attractive, small tree that is widely planted throughout the eastern United States for its fall color, flowers, and fruit color, and as a small shade tree. Has been abused to a considerable extent by planting in exposed areas of poor soil with little moisture and high heat. Dogwoods are doomed to fail in compacted, poorly drained soils.

CULTIVARS: 'Cherokee Chief', plant patent 1710: dark pink flowers (bracts); very showy. 'Cloud 9', plant patent 2112: heavy-blooming white, heavy-fruiting. 'White Cloud': old, established, heavy-blooming. 'Spring Song': bright rose-red bracts. 'Cherokee Princess': large white bracts, blooms at an early age. 'First Lady': green-yellow variegated foliage. 'Rubra': pink flowers. 'Welch Junior Miss': a pink that does well in the lower South. Many others probably exist.

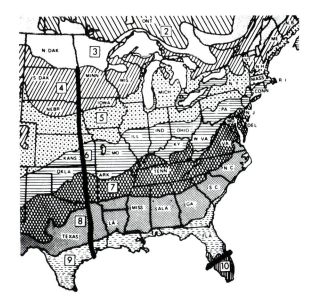

'Cherokee Chief'

'Welchi'

Cornus kousa Hance.   Kousa Dogwood
Cornaceae or Dogwood Family   Hardiness Zone 5
Native to Japan and China.
SIZE: 15 to 20 feet tall with similar spread. Slow to medium grower.
FORM: Irregular, round-topped, small tree.
TEXTURE: Medium.   **EXPOSURE:** Sun or partial shade.

LEAVES: Opposite, simple; 2 to 4 inches long, more or less oval, or oval-elongate, with a wavy margin and short petiole. Upper leaf surface is dark, glossy green, only slightly lighter beneath. Red to red-orange or red-purple in the fall. Showy.

STEM: Young stems are slender and green, soon turning tan and eventually gray-brown with irregular peeling areas. Rather attractive.

FLOWERS: White, very showy. Actually, like the flowering dogwood, the true flowers are small and yellowish in the center of the four large, white bracts or modified leaves that are generally referred to as the "flower". The 4 bracts form a flower that is 2 to 4 inches across; however, the bracts tend to be more separate than on the flowering dogwood. The points of the bracts are long and pointed, not indented, thus creating more of a star shape than flower-like feature. Flowers bloom about 1 month later than flowering dogwood and generally remain showy longer.

FRUIT: An irregular globe, about 1 inch across. Green, turning pinkish red in the fall.

COLOR: Foliage is dark green; red to orange-red in the fall. Flowers are white, and fruits are pinkish red.

PROPAGATION: By seed, or softwood cuttings with difficulty.

CULTURE: Grows best on fertile, moist soils, with an accumulation of leaf litter or mulch to reduce soil temperatures and stabilize moisture. Will not tolerate wet feet or heavy clay soils. Neither drought- nor heat-tolerant. Should not be planted in parking lots or on the west or south sides of buildings that have a lot of glass. Needs some occasional pruning for good branch development.

PESTS: None serious.

NOTES: A very attractive tree when in flower and during fall and winter, when the form adds interest compared to many other trees. Not widely grown, but a bit tougher than flowering dogwood and equally well adapted to the areas where flowering dogwood can grow. Should be planted more. When used with flowering dogwood, the bloom times can complement one another giving an extension to the normally short show of the flowering dogwood. Easily distinguished from other dogwoods by the leaves, flowers, and unusual fruit.

CULTIVARS: 'Milky Way': somewhat smaller in stature but with flower bracts that are 4 to 5 inches long; very showy. 'National': a vase-shaped tree with cream-colored flowers and large fruits. 'Summer Stars': dark foliage, reddish purple in the fall. "Flower" show lasts 4 to 6 weeks. Other cultivars exist.

RELATED SPECIES: Hybrids between *C. kousa* and *C. florida* may be good substitutes for *C. florida*. 'Rutban': upright with cream flowers. 'Rutgan-Steller Pink': light pink flowers. 'Rutdan-Galaxy' : pure white flowers. 'Rutfan-Stardust': branches low and spreads widely with white flowers. Several others have been named.

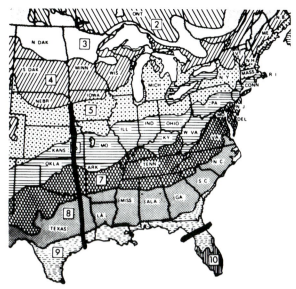

Cornus mas L.   Corneliancherry Dogwood
Cornaceae or Dogwood Family   Hardiness Zone 5
Native to Europe and western Asia.
SIZE: 15 to 25 feet tall with equal spread. Moderate grower.
FORM: Large shrub or small tree with rounded crown.
TEXTURE: Medium.   **EXPOSURE:** Sun or some shade.

LEAVES: Opposite, simple; 2 to 4 inches long, more or less oval, with a smooth margin and distinct veins. Foliage is dense, allowing little light through to the soil below. Upper leaf surface is dark green; lighter below. Fall color is red in the Northeast but may be absent in the central United States.

STEM: Young stems are slender, smooth and green, turning reddish where exposed to the sun and finally gray-brown. Sections of the old bark may be nearly black with irregular tan sections where the bark has peeled off. Rather attractive.

FLOWERS: Yellow. In terminal clusters, very early in the spring before the leaves. Not very showy unless associated with evergreens to provide a contrast.

FRUIT: Elongated, cherry-like, red; 1/2 to 3/4 inches long, maturing in late summer; however, they are partially hidden by the dense foliage and are therefore only moderately showy. Edible; sometimes used for preserves.

COLOR: Foliage is dark green. Flowers are yellow. Fruits are red.

PROPAGATION: By seed.

CULTURE: Like most of the tree dogwoods, prefers a moist, well drained soil with an accumulation of leaf litter or mulch. However, like the flowering dogwood, it will not tolerate heavy clays or very wet soils. Not drought-tolerant, but slightly more tolerant of drought and adverse soil conditions than the popular flowering dogwood. Most often used as a large, rounded shrub; however, if pruned into a multiple-stemmed tree form and used adjacent to outdoor living areas, the attractive bark can be very effective.

PESTS: None serious.

NOTES: As a shrub, it gets too large for many locations and does not contribute enough to the landscape to warrant the space consumed. However, as a small tree, it is much more useful, particularly since the bark is attractive year-round. Sometimes confused with the kousa dogwood because the leaves, overall size, and growth form are similar. The corneliancherry generally has 5 pairs of veins on the leaves, yellow flowers and dark red, cherry-like, elongated fruits, whereas kousa dogwood generally has only three pairs of veins on the leaves, large, white flowers, and pinkish fruits. Not commonly seen in Zones 7 and 8. However, it will grow well in these areas provided soil drainage and moisture conditions are met.

CULTIVARS: 'Alba': white fruits. 'Aureo-elegantissima': leaves edged in gold with a bit of red. 'Flava': yellow fruits. 'Nana': a rounded, medium shrub. 'Aurea': yellow leaves. 'Variegata': leaves with a white edge. Others probably exist.

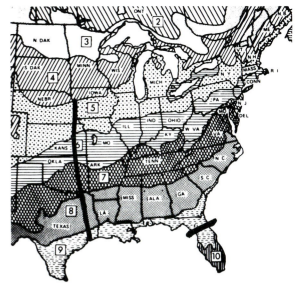

Cotinus coggygria Scop. (Syn. *Rhus cotinus*)   Smoketree
Arnacardaceae or Cashew Family   Hardiness Zone 3
Native to southern Europe and Asia.
SIZE: 12 to 18 feet tall with a 10- to 12-foot spread. Moderate to rapid grower.
FORM: Small tree or large shrub with an oval crown.
TEXTURE: Medium.   **EXPOSURE:** Sun.

LEAVES: Alternate, simple; 2 to 3 inches long, 1 1/4 to 2 inches wide, and rounded at the tip with a smooth margin. More or less ping-pong paddle-shaped on long petioles. Bright green to purple, depending on cultivar, turning a blazing orange or scarlet in the fall.

STEM: Upright, spreading, generally multiple-stemmed. Young stem is rather husky. A new flush of growth in the spring terminates in the flower cluster as the days become longer. Young stem is green, turning greenish brown and finally a dull, smooth brown. Even with age the bark does not become furrowed or patterned. Wood is only moderately strong and sometimes broken by vandals, but rarely does it suffer from wind damage because of its small size.

FLOWERS: Small, yellowish, in multiple-branched terminal clusters generally during May or June. Many flowers are sterile.

FRUIT: Pinkish fruiting clusters on feathery branches, 7 to 10 inches long, consisting of a few seeds on lengthy stalks. Numerous sterile flowers cover the tree in large quantities during June and July and persist, giving the tree a "smoke" appearance.

COLOR: Foliage is bright green to purple, red-orange to scarlet in the fall. Fruit is pinkish.

PROPAGATION: By seed or cuttings of selected cultivars.

CULTURE: A very tough, durable plant. Grows in a wide range of soils: alkaline or acid, infertile, rocky or gravelly. Quite drought-resistant. Does very well throughout the southern Great Plains and other regions of the South. Appears to be well adapted to the abused urban soils so commonly encountered.

PESTS: A stem canker may be troublesome in the Northeast and Southeast; rarely encountered in the Great Plains.

NOTES: An interesting small tree or large shrub. A green or purple cultivar is a real item of interest in a small landscape. Excellent for a small garden as a novelty effect or accent, particularly since it is very tough and tolerant to most growing conditions. Not long-lived under most conditions.

CULTIVARS: 'Purpurea': young leaves are deep red when they first open, gradually darkening and becoming greener. Fruit clusters are more purplish. 'Nordine Red': deep purple-red leaves; good color retention all season. 'Velvet Cloak': intense purple leaves when young. Very striking, holding the purple color well throughout the season as long as light intensity is high. 'Royal Purple': foliage emerges dark purple and tends to darken more to a near black. almost too dark to be attractive. Others probably exist.

RELATED SPECIES: *Cotinus obovatus*, American smoketree, is a small tree of 20 to 25 feet with rounded crown. leaves are larger then *C. coggygria* and bluish green. Fall color is generally yellow-orange to red. A good plant for well drained soils and deserves more attention.

83

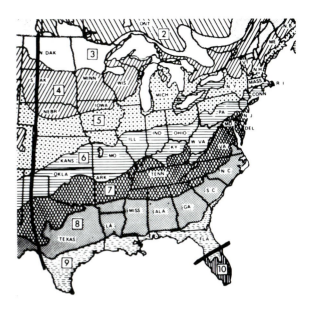

Crataegus spp.   Hawthorn(s)
Rosaceae or Rose Family   Hardiness Zone 6 through 3
Native to the eastern United States, Europe, and North Africa

SIZE: Generally small trees, 15 to 30 feet tall with a spread of 15 to 20 feet. Slow to moderate growers.

FORM: Broad, oval crown; small- to medium-sized tree.

TEXTURE: Medium.   **EXPOSURE:** Sun to partial shade.

LEAVES: Alternate, simple; on slender petioles. Egg-shaped to broadly elliptical with a toothed margin. May have various types of lobing on the side of the leaf. May be hairy when young. Generally deep green above, unless infected with disease; light green below, turning yellow to yellow-orange in the fall.

STEM: Low-branching, very tough, durable wood creating a broad, oval, rugged crown. Young stems are slender and generally thorny. Thorns may be 2 to 3 inches long on some species; or relatively short, 1/3 inch or less, on other species. A few species or cultivars do not have thorns. Young stem is generally a varnished brown, turning gray-brown, taking on various texture patterns on the old bark.

FLOWERS: White to pink and generally in clusters which is typical of many Rosaceae family members. Many flowers are one inch across and quite showy for a brief period when in full bloom in mid to late spring.

FRUIT: Small, apple-like. Red to red-orange; quite showy.

COLOR: Foliage is green. Fall color is orange to yellow-orange. Flowers are white or pink. Fruit is red.

PROPAGATION: By seed or grafting of selected cultivars.

CULTURE: Tolerates a wide range of growing conditions. Moderately drought-resistant and fairly adaptable to a range of soil types. Hawthorns do reasonably well in areas of confined root development and city conditions. Both nursery and wild plants are somewhat difficult to transplant, principally because of the strong taproot.

PESTS: Cedar apple rust is probably the most severe pest of the hawthorn in the lower South. Causes extensive damage to the leaves and stems, reducing fruit to an unsightly, irregular glob. May cause defoliation by mid summer. Much variation in susceptibility among species. The incidence and severity of disease varies with the location of the plant in the landscape. If hawthorns are to be used at all, they should be: 1) planted in open areas with good air circulation, and 2) kept away from eastern red cedars, which are alternate hosts for cedar apple rust. Fire blight may also be a problem on some species.

NOTES: Hawthorns are very difficult to identify with certainty. A very confused genus in terms of identification, either resulting from crosses or hybrids or simply due to a tremendous diversity of species. *Flowering Plants of Missouri* by Palmer and Steyermark lists 79 major species. Many of these species have various cultivars that have been selected. Because of the severity of cedar apple rust on most of the hawthorns throughout the southern the United States, it is recommended that they not be planted except in extreme cases.

RELATED SPECIES: *Crataegus crus-galli* L., the cockspur hawthorn, is a small tree up to 25 to 30 feet with a rounded, broadly spreading crown and many long, slender spines. Hardy in Zone 4. Seedling plants are variable. Leaves are simple, alternate, thick and leathery, 2 to 4 inches long, mostly obovate, not lobed, and broadest above the middle, with irregular teeth along the margin. Upper leaf surface is a dark, glossy green; paler beneath. Fall color is yellow to orange to red, depending on exposure. Flowers are white, appear after the leaves, very showy, with 5 distinct petals and 10 stamens. Fruit is about 1/2 inch, apple-like, deep red, and matures in mid fall. Generally showy. Cockspur hawthorn is native to east central United States, and well-adapted to much of the U. S. and a wide range of soil. The limitations of this beautiful hawthorn is not environment, rainfall, or soils, but rather the host of diseases and insects that plague most hawthorns. 'Inermis': the thornless cockspur hawthorn, is much more resistant than the parent to disease and insect problems. Resistance may be at least partially physical since the leaves are thick and glossy with a heavy cuticle. Flowers are white, fruit is red, and fall color is red-bronze. This is one of the best hawthorns.

Crataegus mollis Scheele., the downy hawthorn, is a round-headed tree, which reaches 25 to 30 feet and is hardy in Zone 4. Thorns are long, pointed and stout. Leaves are 2 to 4 inches long, ovate and doubly sawtooth on the margin, with 4 or 5 pairs of shallow lobes. Upper leaf surface is medium green, densely hairy beneath, thus the common name. Fall color is bronze to red-bronze. Flowers are white, about one inch across and in terminal clusters. Fruit is red, about 1/2 inch across, ripening and falling early. An attractive small tree but quite variable from seed. This unpredictable aspect limits its landscape use even though it is generally less susceptible to disease and insect problems than other species.

Crataegus phaenopyrum (L.) Medic., the Washington hawthorn, is a small, round-headed or somewhat upright tree, reaching 25 to 30 feet, with long, tapering spines. Hardy in Zone 4. Leaves are more or less triangular and two to three inches, with irregular teeth on the margin. Dark, glossy green above, paler below. Fall color is orange to red-orange. Flowers are white in dense terminal clusters; quite showy. Fruit is red, about 1/4 inch long, coloring in early fall and persisting late into the winter. In general, Washington hawthorns are not as susceptible to rust and other diseases as the cockspur hawthorns and its close relatives.

Crataegus X *mordenensis* Boom., 'Toba': a hybrid between *C. oxyacantha* 'Pauls Scarlet' and *C. succulenta* which grows upright, 12 to 15 feet tall. Spines are short. Leaves are three-lobed and bright green. Flowers are double, open white and turn pink. Fruits are bright red and 1/2 inch long.

Crataegus X *lavallei* is a hybrid between *C. stipulacea* X *C. crus-galli*, Lavalle hawthorn. A small tree about 25 feet tall with dark green foliage and good coppery fall color. Flowers are white and fruits are red. Generally free of rust in most situations, making the foliage attractive all season.

Many other species and cultivars exist, but are difficult to identify with certainty. Good luck.

Crataegus crus-galli

C. crus-galli

C. crus-galli

C. crus-galli 'Thornless'

C. mollis

C. phaenopyrum

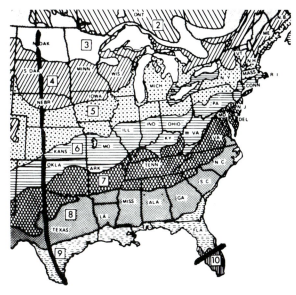

C. phaenopyrum

C. phaenopyrum

C. phaenoyrum

Diospyros kaki L.   Oriental Persimmon
Ebonyaceae or Ebony Family   Hardiness Zone 7
SIZE: 20 to 30 feet tall with a 20- to 30-foot spread. Slow grower.
FORM: Low, round-headed, small tree.
TEXTURE: Coarse.   **EXPOSURE:** Sun to partial shade.

LEAVES: Alternate, simple; 3 to 7 inches long, 2 to 2 1/2 inches wide, and somewhat heart-shaped with a smooth margin. Petiole is short and stout. Generally shiny, dark green above; pale green below, and red-orange in the fall. Quite showy.

STEM: Forms a wide-spreading crown. Young stem is relatively slender with flexible branches easily trained into various shapes or forms. Light brown, eventually turning a medium to dark brown. Irregular bark pattern. Wood is fairly brittle, particularly on young branches, and may break in ice or wind storms or by vandalism, but becomes much stronger with age.

FLOWERS: Inconspicuous.

FRUIT: Large, edible, orange-red in the fall, 2 to 4 inches long. Rounded or somewhat egg-shaped, depending on cultivar. Ripens on the tree after leaves have fallen. Seedless, rather tasty, not as puckery and tart as common persimmon. Some variation with cultivar in fruit size, shape, and quality . Quite showy: somewhat like Christmas ornaments.

COLOR: Foliage is deep green; red-orange in the fall. Very showy. Fruit is orange-red, quite showy.

PROPAGATION: By grafting of selected cultivars onto common persimmon seedlings.

CULTURE: Grows in most well-drained soils. Will not tolerate wet feet or extremely heavy soils where drainage is poor. Responds to fertilization, mulching, and other good cultural practices. Can be pruned and shaped as desired, as a small, ornamental tree. Produces fruit on current season's growth. Somewhat difficult to transplant, but is easiest to establish as a container-grown tree; otherwise fairly easy to grow.

PESTS: None serious.

NOTES: Very showy foliage in the fall, and showy fruit after leaves have fallen. Fruits look like large Christmas tree ornaments hanging over the naked frame. Can be messy over a driveway, walk, or patio. Does tolerate growth in tubs, patios, and other places with confined root system space. Very interesting small tree of some merit across the South. Should be used more, particularly in a large planter or as a patio tub specimen.

CULTIVARS: 'Hachiya', 'Fuyu', 'Tam-o-pan', 'Tane-na-shi', differing primarily in fruit size and quality. 'Chocolate': fruits that are near brown when ripe. 'Eureka': bright orange to near red fruits. Very showy.

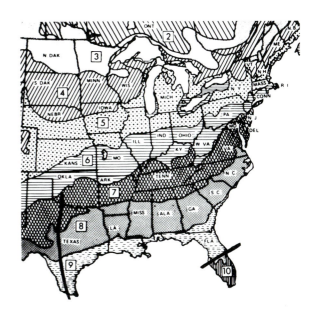

Diospyros virginiana L.   Common Persimmon or Possumwood
Ebonyaceae or Ebony Family   Hardiness Zone 4
Native to the eastern and central United States from the Gulf Coast to Canada.
SIZE: 30 to 60 feet tall with a 20- to 30-foot spread. Moderate to rapid grower.
FORM: Oval-crowned tree or clump of trees.
TEXTURE: Medium.   **EXPOSURE:** Sun.

LEAVES: Alternate, simple; oval or elliptical, 2 to 6 inches long, 1 1/2 to 2 inches wide. Rounded at the base of the leaf blade and tapering to a point at the tip with a smooth margin. Glossy, deep green upper surface, paler green below. Turns a bright yellow very early in the fall; second only to black gum in earliness of fall color.

STEM: Upright, single-stem; but may be clumped either through seedlings that have developed in close proximity to one another or through suckers where a tree has been cut down. Central leader usually persists in each particular tree. Young twigs are slender, and slightly zigzag. Generally many young branches in the crown, giving a thick, bushy appearance. Young stem is varnished brown, eventually turning gray-brown to black. Old bark is brown to near black; broken into many small blocks that are almost square or slightly rectangular, making a very interesting checkerboard pattern.

FLOWERS: Inconspicuous.

FRUIT: A several-seeded, round or slightly ovate berry, 1 to 1 1/2 inches in diameter, varying among seedlings. Green when young; yellow, yellow-orange, then purple or brownish black before falling. Fruit is subtended by five large sepals. Contains several large, flattened seeds. Pulp is very tart when not ripe. Finally, after a frost in early fall, fruit becomes very yellow-orange and quite tasty. Much variation in fruit quality among seedling trees.

COLOR: Foliage is glossy, deep green; yellow very early in the fall. Fruit is yellow-orange.

PROPAGATION: By seed, grafting or digging up of suckers or seedlings in the wild, but difficult to transplant.

CULTURE: An extraordinary plant that grows in a tremendous range of conditions from very dry, sterile, sandy woodlands to river bottoms to rocky hillsides, and moist or very dry locations; just about anywhere. Responds to fertilizer and care when planted as an ornamental; grows vigorously, developing into a full-headed, small tree with very showy, good, dense foliage. Will thrive and compete with any plant in harsh growing conditions. Seedlings or suckers are difficult to transplant.

PESTS: Tent caterpillars are severe pests both in the wild and in cultivation. Must be sprayed or removed and burned soon or they defoliate and severely damage a young plant. A wilt fungus occasionally causes death of a few trees in the wild; not common. Otherwise disease- and insect-free.

NOTES: An excellent small to medium size tree. Limiting factor is generally the problem of tent caterpillars attacking during mid summer. One of the most durable of small trees. Deep green foliage stands out from a mixture of plant materials. Wood is very hard, durable, and wind-resistant. Fruits can be somewhat messy on sidewalks or patios, but are also very showy in the fall, which offsets the negative value. Should be planted more, particularly in the poor soils of many urban areas.

CULTIVARS: Several are available as males or with improved fruit size and quality.

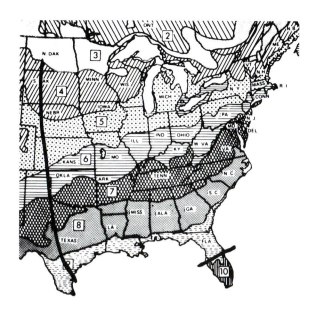

Elaeagnus angustifolia L.   Russian Olive
Elaeagnaceae or Oleaster Family   Hardiness Zone 2
Native to southern Europe and west and central Asia.
SIZE: 20 to 30 feet tall with a 15- to 20-foot spread. Moderate to rapid grower.
FORM: Low-spreading, oval-crowned tree.
TEXTURE: Fine.   **EXPOSURE:** Sun.

LEAVES: Alternate, simple: about 2 to 3 1/2 inches long, 1/2 to 1 inch wide. lanceolate to somewhat oblong-lanceolate, tapering to a blunt point with a smooth margin. Upper surface is generally bright silver-green to green with obscure veins; lower surface is silvery and densely scaly of flaky, with slightly more evident veins. petiole is also covered with silver scales, technically called trichomes, which are flattened, snowflake-like leaf hairs. The density of leaf hairs varies with age and environmental conditions. Very showy foliage but little coloration in the fall.

STEM: Young stem is slender and at first, covered with silver scales. With age becomes red to red-brown and loses the scales, eventually becoming a rough, vertically striped bark: shallowly furrowed. Young branches may or may not have long thorns, depending on growth rate and seedling variation. Spines may be a much as 2 inches long and quite thick on some trees.

FLOWERS: Appear in May, in the leaf axils, along the new growth. Not particularly showy, but very fragrant. Also covered with silvery scales.

FRUIT: Generally matures August through September, is drupe-like, about 1/4 to 1/2 inch long. Oval and silvery gray, eventually becoming yellow to tan with maturity. The seed is hard, oval, and ridge along the long axis. Generally viable.

COLOR: Foliage is bright silver-green; little fall color.

PROPAGATION: Seed, cuttings, or grafting.

CULTURE: Very durable, rugged, small tree that tolerates a wide range of soils. has been found to establish and grow well on roadside banks and in subsoils of very poor quality as long as it drains fairly well. Drought-resistant, moderately wind-resistant and, in general, an extremely durable plant. Responds with vigor to good soils, fertilizers, and watering during drought periods.

PESTS: None serious in the dry areas. A stem canker may be severe in the more humid regions of the east and southeast United States. Verticillium wilt kills most trees planted in wet areas or in heavy soils.

NOTES: A very attractive, fast-growing, large shrub or small tree. If lower branches are allowed to remain, it develops a more dense, shrubby form. If these lower branches are removed, the plant develops a rather broad-spreading attractive tree form, but it may sucker at the base. Of considerable merit, both for foliage contrast and fragrance in the landscape. A good, small tree for the central and southern Great plains and much of the Southeast: particularly in open, exposed urban areas with poor soils. May be short-lived (8 to 10 years) on some sites, but should not be avoided since it will make a major contribution to the landscape during that time.

CULTIVARS: 'Cardinal': red fruit, otherwise similar to the species. 'Red King': also has red fruits. I could not tell the two cultivars apart.

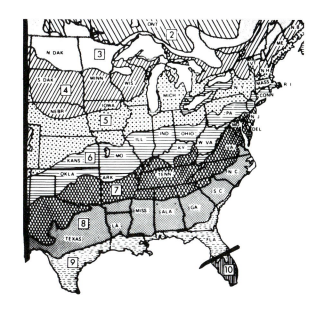

Eucommia ulmoides D. Oliver.   Hardy Rubbertree
Eucommiaceae or Eucommia Family   Hardiness Zone 5
Native to China.
SIZE: 30 to 50 feet tall with similar spread. Moderate grower.
FORM: Tree with a broad, rounded crown.
TEXTURE: Medium.   EXPOSURE: Sun.

LEAVES: Alternate, simple; 3 to 5 inches long. More or less oval, with a distinct, sawtooth margin and tapering to a sharp point at the tip. Upper surface is glossy and dark green, pale green below; little if any fall color. Broken leaves exude a sticky sap somewhat like a that of a mulberry.

STEM: Young stems are slender and light green at first, turning yellowish brown to gray-brown. Old bark is gray-brown with shallow, vertical furrows. Wood is stout and not readily damaged by ice or wind. Exudes a rubbery sap when damaged.

FLOWERS: Inconspicuous. Dioecious.

FRUIT: Small, dry, not showy. Seed is generally not viable in the United States.

COLOR: Foliage is glossy and dark green.

PROPAGATION: By seed or softwood cuttings.

CULTURE: A very adaptable tree, but not widely known or planted. The specimen in the photo is growing on a fair, clay loam soil at the Morton Arboretum west of Chicago, Illinois. Attractive specimens can also be found in Woodward, Oklahoma near the Oklahoma Panhandle on a sandy loam soil and in Will Rogers Park in Oklahoma City on a very heavy clay soil. Trees in central Georgia also look good. This diversity of climatic and soil conditions suggests that the tree is very adaptable and deserving of greater use. Develops a good crown with little, if any, pruning and makes a good shade tree.

PESTS: None known.

NOTES: A very attractive tree during the growing season with very glossy, dark green leaves. Unfortunately, fall color is almost non-existent and the bark and branch form adds little to the landscape in winter. On the other hand, it is a much better tree than some of the soft maple species and sweetgum currently being widely promoted solely for their good fall color. Availability of seed probably limits greater production by the nursery industry. However, since softwood cuttings root fairly well, more need to be grown. Foliage is always glossy and dark green with little insect injury. The foliage looks very elm-like, thus the species name.

CULTIVARS: None known.

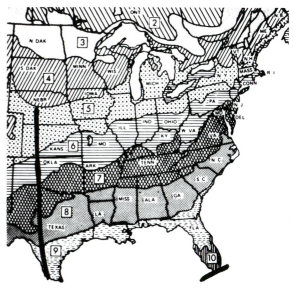

Euonymus bungeana Maxim.   Winterberry Euonymus
Celastraceae or Staff Tree Family   Hardiness Zone 4
Native to northern China and Manchuria
SIZE: 15 to 20 feet tall with a 10- to 12-foot spread. Moderate grower.
FORM: Found to oval-headed, small tree.
TEXTURE: Medium.   **EXPOSURE:** Sun.

LEAVES: Opposite, simple; 3 to 4 inches long and 1 1/2 to 2 inches wide. Oval to slightly ovate-elongate, tapering to an abrupt point at the tip and with a saw-toothed margin. Peas green turning pink to red in the fall.

STEM: Loose, irregular branching habit; some seedlings have a slight weeping habit. Young stems are green and moderately slender, developing a gray to gray-brown bark with age: irregular but not flaking. Wood is moderately stout and durable.

FLOWERS: Yellowish. Not showy but may attract flies. 3 to 7 per cluster.

FRUIT: Deeply 4-lobed, like a bishop's cap. About 1/4 inch across and yellowish to pinkish white, opening to expose the orange seed coating. The fruit remains on the tree following coloration and dropping of the leaves in the fall, and are quite showy.

COLOR: Foliage is pea-green turning pink to red in the fall. Fruit is pink and orange. Foliage and fruit color do not mix well with other red and orange fall colors.

PROPAGATION: Seed or cuttings.

CULTURE: Tolerates a wide range of growing conditions: particularly well-adapted to dry soils in the southern Prairie States. Appears to tolerate most soils and exposures. Sometimes used for windbreaks and screens. Grows with vigor under good moisture and nutritional conditions. In dry land areas, responds to mulching to help conserve moisture and reduce weed competition.

PESTS: None serious. Rarely does euonymus scale become a problem on the deciduous forms, even though it is a severe problem on evergreen euonymus.

NOTES: A widely adaptable, small tree. Tolerates poor soils and drought conditions, is easy to transplant, and is quite insect- and disease-free. moderately easy to grow. Should be used a great deal more, particularly in the he southern Prairie States and the Southwest. Has merit as a patio or specimen tree around a single story dwelling. leaves and fruits may be mildly toxic if eaten in quantity. ??-POISON-??

CULTIVARS: 'Pendula': weeping branches. 'Sempersistens': half evergreen foliage. 'Pink Lady': A seed-propagated cultivar, released by the Soil Conservation Service in 1972 is a prolific fruit producer and the fruits remain after the leaves drop, creating quite a show in the fall.

RELATED SPECIES: *Euonymus europaea* L., European spindle tree, is similar in appearance but is less tolerant of growing conditions and the leaves are more rounded. May reach 15 to 20 feet tall is hardy in Zone 3.

Euonymus americanus, American euonymus or strawberry bush is native to a wide area of North America. In central Oklahoma the plant goes unnoticed until October when the leaves drop and the fruits open to expose the orange-red seeds. it can add quite a show for many weeks. May grow 8 to 10 feet tall with good conditions. Deserves more attention.

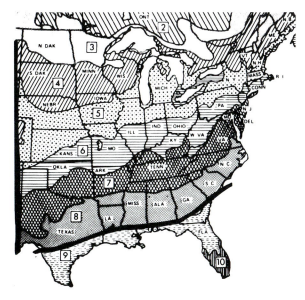

Euonymus europaea

Euonymus europaea

Fagus grandifolia Ehrh.   American Beech
Fagaceae or Beech Family   Hardiness Zone 3
Native to a wide range of the eastern United States.
SIZE: A 50- to 80-foot tree with similar spread. Very slow to slow grower.
FORM: Magnificent, straight stem, with low, wide-spreading branches.
TEXTURE: Medium.   **EXPOSURE:** Sun to partial shade.

LEAVES: Alternate, simple; 3 to 5 inches long, 1 to 2 inches wide. ovate to oblong and toothed on the margin (elm-like). Silvery when first emerging, turning dark, glossy green, then yellow-bronze in the fall; finally drying like parchment and hanging on the trees most of the winter.

STEM: The main stem is smooth and steel gray with distinct markings where branches attach to it. The young twigs are smooth and slender with a slight zigzag pattern; silvery gray. Terminal dormant buds are long, slender, and cigar-shaped. The wood is strong and durable.

FLOWERS: Not showy. male and female are separate on the same tree (monoecious).

FRUIT: A triangled nut, enclosed in a prickly husk.

COLOR: foliage is dark, glossy, green; then yellow-bronze in the fall. Bark is attractive at all times.

PROPAGATION: Seed.

CULTURE: Native to fertile, well-drained, upland sites and does not do well without considerable help in abused and compacted, urban soils. Beech have a very fibrous, but shallow root system that is readily damaged by soil compaction. Likewise, growth is severely restricted by grass competition in the landscape. Consider planting beech only where soils are good and well-drained, the exposure of the site is not unusually harsh, and mulch can be provided to keep grass and weed competition to a minimum, soil temperature low and moisture available without the soil being excessively wet. Although this sounds very restrictive at first, the tree is well worth the effort, and sites with these conditions can often be created with only moderate costs.

PESTS: None serious. However, low soil oxygen (soil compaction) and overwatering may kill or damage the roots.

NOTES: A spectacular tree, much admired and praised. Not common in the nursery trade; however, should be grown and promoted more. Recent advances in nursery practices that accelerate growth and reduce transplant stress make this magnificent tree ready for a comeback. For the tree to do well, the conditions described under culture must be closely adhered to, but the reward is worth the effort.

CULTIVARS: Unlike with European beech, few cultivars exist.

RELATED SPECIES: *Fagus sylvatica* L., European beech, is similar in size, form, adaptation, and overall elegance. In the nursery trade, European beech is more common than the American beech. Cultivars such as 'Asplenifolia": with weeping branches, 'Riversii' and 'Cuprea': with purple foliage are excellent. Many cultivars exist, especially in Europe.

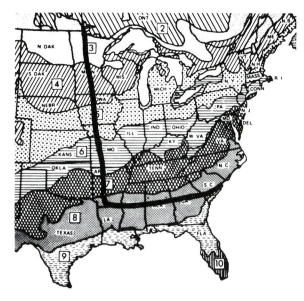

Fagus sylvatica

Ficus carica L.   Common or Edible Fig
Moraceae or Mulberry Family   Hardiness Zone 7b
Native to the Mediterranean Region.
SIZE: 20 to 30 feet tall with a 20-foot spread. Rapid grower.
FORM: Broadly spreading, multiple-trunk, small tree.
TEXTURE: Coarse.   EXPOSURE: Sun to partial shade.

LEAVES: Alternate, simple; usually having 3 to 5 lobes. Rough and hairy above and below. Dark green with no fall color: leaves turn black and drop after a hard freeze. Foliage is dense and shades out most vegetation beneath, unless pruned into a distinct tree form.

STEM: Coarse-textured branches with a distinct, spear-shaped terminal bud. Old leaf scars are prominent. Young shoots are greenish gray, turning gray-brown with maturity. Wood is only moderately stout, especially with young stems of 1 inch of less.

FLOWERS: Inconspicuous.

FRUIT: Pear-shaped, with a small opening in the base; variable in size. Green, turning brown with maturity. Edible; and variable among seedlings and cultivars. Most plants bear fruit after 3 or 4 years. Fruits are produced on new growth.

COLOR: Dark green foliage.

PROPAGATION: Hardwood or softwood cuttings.

CULTURE: Figs are well adapted to all but poorly drained clays or very compacted soils. heat-tolerant and can be grown on southern exposures in the Southwest with limited supplemental moisture. Responds to mulch, grass control, and good cultural practices. With reasonable growing conditions it is a vigorous grower that needs some pruning for good structural development and size control.

PESTS: Nematodes may be a problem on sandy soils.

NOTES: A delicious fruit on a tough, durable plant, with attractive foliage and low, spreading branches. Seems too much to wish for unless you do not like the fruits and the mess they create on sidewalks, patios, pools, or driveways. Rotting fruits attract bees and flies; ripening fruits may attract youngsters. When having planned for it is a good, small tree. May be left to develop branches to the ground or pruned to reveal a tree form with age. All ficus species have a sticky, milky sap that is undesirable on patio furniture.

CULTIVARS: Varying in cold tolerance and fruit quality. 'Brown Turkey', 'Celeste', 'Magnolia', and 'Kodota' are old favorites 'Brown Turkey': may survive as far north s Zone 6b in protected locations or when heavily mulched to prevent damage to the main stem from suckers arising in mid spring to produce more foliage and fruits. Many other cultivars exist in localized areas.

RELATED SPECIES: Many species of *Ficus* are native to tropical regions of the world. Some can be especially vigorous and are prolific seed producers, making many problems in the landscapes. Common fig is not such a plant as it stays put and is not aggressive or troublesome.

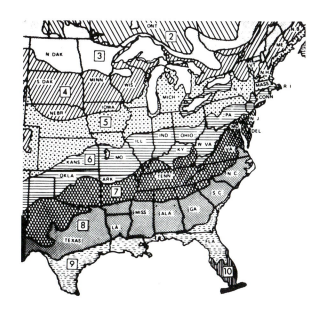

Fraxinus americana L.   White Ash
Oleaceae or Olive Family   Hardiness Zone 2
Native to the eastern United States from the Gulf Coast to Canada.
SIZE: May reach 80 to 100 feet tall with a spread of 60 to 80 feet. Moderate growth rate.
FORM: Oval-crowned, large tree.
TEXTURE: Fine to medium   **EXPOSURE:** Sun.

LEAVES: Opposite, compound; generally 8 to 13 inches long with 5 to 11 (usually 9) ovate to lanceolate leaflets with pointed tips. The terminal leaflet is always present. Individual leaflets are generally 3 to 5 inches long, and 1 1/2 to 2 1/2 inches wide. May have a smooth or a tooth margin. Dark green above; pale whitish below. Fall color is yellow to yellow-orange.

STEM: Young stem is large and green at first, turning brown to gray; stout and smooth with pale lenticels. The old stem is light gray to dark brown with narrow ridges separated by deep furrows in the bark in an interlacing pattern; rather attractive. Wood is fairly light, yet stout and wind-resistant.

FLOWERS: Not showy. There are male and female trees (dioecious).

FRUIT: Ripens August through September. A flattened fruit with winged tip. Body is short and plump, constituting half of the overall length. The wing is terminal generally with notched tips. Shaped like a canoe paddle. Not showy.

COLOR: Foliage is deep, dark green. Fall color is yellow to yellow-orange.

PROPAGATION: Seed or grafting of selected cultivars.

CULTURE: Native to well-drained, rich, upland soils. Tolerates wet feet, but is only moderately tolerant of poor or compacted and abused soils. Responds with vigor to fertilizer, mulch, and good cultural practices. Intolerant of soil compaction or other soil disturbance, once established.

PESTS: Borers on trees that are under stress, recently transplanted, or old. Less subject in rural areas to defoliation by grasshoppers than green ash. Diseases are on the increase in ash. Also, ash seems especially susceptible to injury from herbicide drift which causes a slow decline.

NOTES: Attractive and desirable shade tree in areas with good soil. Less satisfactory in urban areas where no topsoil remains or where soils are heavy clays and/or compacted. Light, lacy texture of the foliage and the general rounded crown of the tree are very useful for numerous landscape purposes. Best distinguished from *Fraxinus pennsylvanica*, green ash, by the 9 to 11 leaflets instead of 7, the whitish lower leaf surface, and the stalks of lateral leaflets that are winged.

CULTIVARS: 'Autumn Purple': male, seedless, turning to a rich purple in the fall that contrasts with most seedlings trees. 'Rose Hill': a very rapid-growing, upright tree; male, good branching structure and bronzy fall color. On good sites, it may grow 4 to 8 feet per year while young. 'Autumn Applause': male and seedless, with dark maroon fall color. 'Champaign County': good growth habit and smaller, dark green leaves. Other cultivars exist.

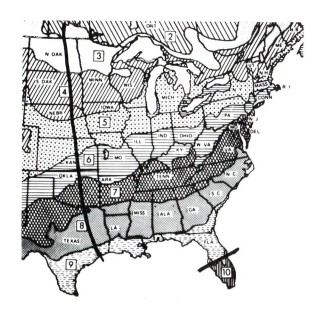

'Rose Hill'

White Ash   Green Ash

Fraxinus excelsior L.   European Ash
Oleaceae or Olive Family   Hardiness Zone 5
Native to Europe and southwest Asia.
SIZE: 40 to 80 feet tall with equal spread in most cases. Moderate to rapid grower.
FORM: Somewhat pyramidal when young but rounded with age.
TEXTURE: Medium.   **EXPOSURE:** Sun.

LEAVES: Opposite, compound; with 7 to 11 ovate or ovate-elongate leaflets 2 to 3 inches long with distinctly sawtooth margin. Leaves are dark green above; lighter green below, with only a fair yellow fall color. Note: 'Hessei': has simple leaves (see photograph), unlike the parent or other ash species.

STEM: Young stems are stout but smooth with distinct, black, dormant buds. Bark is smooth and steel gray on larger limbs, splitting into vertical strips or scales with age, but retaining the steel gray color on the surface of the scales. Very distinct. Wood is stout and not readily broken.

FLOWERS: Both perfect and separate: male and female flowers on the same plant (monoecious). Not showy.

FRUIT: Thin, flattened, strap like; 1 to 1 1/2 inches long.

COLOR: Foliage is dark green.

PROPAGATION: Seed or grafting of cultivars.

CULTURE: Widely grown in Europe, particularly as a lawn and street tree. Many cultivars have been selected from among a variable seedling population. Like green ash, it tolerates poor soil and marginal drainage conditions, but it is slightly less drought-tolerant. Tolerates alkaline soils but grows best in deep, fertile soils with good moisture. Attractive specimens can be found; however, not widely planted, consequently less is known about tolerance and adaptation than with other ash species that are planted extensively in this country. The large, rounded crown should lend itself well to parks, gold courses, and other large, open areas.

PESTS: None serious, although borers will attack weakened trees. Like other ash species, it appears quite susceptible to damage from herbicide drift, thus causing a slow decline.

NOTES: An attractive and different ash in both form and bark characteristics. Specimens at the Morton Arboretum near Chicago, Illinois, on a diversity of soils and exposures are very impressive. Easier to transplant than blue ash. Should be planted more.

CULTIVARS: 'Hessei': simple leaves that at first make it difficult to believe the tree is an ash, but the leaves are opposite and buds are typical of the genus. Leaves are coarsely sawtoothed and glossy, dark green. An attractive tree with a round crown and attractive, gray-black bark. 'Rancho': Selected by Ed Scanlon for its smaller overall size and round form. 'Aurea': yellow stems. Many other cultivars are listed by European nurseries.

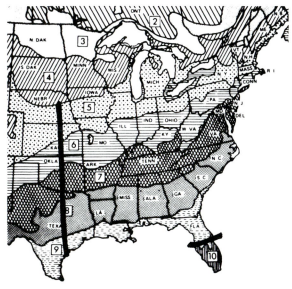

F. excelsior   F. pennsylvanica

'Hessei'

Fraxinus pennsylvanica   Green Ash
Oleaceae or Olive Family   Hardiness Zone 2
Native to the eastern United States from the Gulf Coast to Canada.
SIZE: 60- to 80-foot tree with a 40- to 50-foot spread. Rapid grower.
FORM: Round to oval-headed tree.
TEXTURE: Medium.   **EXPOSURE:** Sun.

LEAVES: Opposite, once-compound; 8 to 12 inches long. With 5 to 9 (usually 7) leaflets that are ovate to oblong-lanceolate. Smooth or irregularly toothed on the margin. Lustrous dark green on both upper and lower surfaces or slightly paler beneath but never silvery. Individual leaflets may be 2 to 6 inches long and 1 to 2 inches wide. Stalks on lateral leaflets are generally winged. Pale yellow to yellow-orange in the fall.

STEM: Upright, central leader. Young twigs are green, eventually turning gray to gray-brown. Fairly stiff, large, and rigid with large terminal buds. Bark is brown to light gray in tight ridges, shallowly furrowed. An attractive, irregular pattern. Wood is only moderately strong, some problem with wind damage or breaking, particularly on old trees.

FLOWERS: Not showy. Male and female on separate trees (dioecious).

FRUIT: In clusters. Individual fruits are winged seeds, 1 to 2 inches long, about 1/4 inch wide; usually 1-celled. Wing is broadest in the middle, tapering back toward the seed and tip. Shaped like a canoe paddle.

COLOR: Foliage is lustrous dark green; yellow in the fall.

PROPAGATION: Seed or grafting of selected cultivars.

CULTURE: Native to wet, swampy areas and stream banks. However, has proven to be a very durable and drought-tolerant tree for wide usage throughout the Great Plains and elsewhere. tolerates many soils found in urban conditions, restricted root systems, some soil compaction, and transplants easily. Is generally a rapid grower, even on alkaline soils. Response to supplemental moisture and fertilization. More tolerant to adverse conditions than white ash but neither do well on heavy clay soils. Easy to grow on most sites.

PESTS: Borers occasionally on newly transplanted, old, or weakened trees. Grasshoppers may damage leaves in rural areas. Aphids may cause leaves to form grotesque clusters, especially near the ends. Very susceptible to herbicide drift which causes a slow decline.

NOTES: Green ash is a desirable large tree for many uses. Can become a very attractive and useful shade tree in a wide range of landscape conditions. Fruits from the female trees can be somewhat messy, but not particularly troublesome. New cultivars are superior in overall form, branch development, and are males which avoid the seed problem. Do not plant on heavy clay soils. Can best be distinguished from white ash in that the leaves have 7 leaflets and are green or a slight yellow-brown on the underneath side. Stalks on the lateral leaflets are generally 1/4 to 1/2 inch long, and somewhat winged whereas white ash leaves generally have 9 leaflets or more, are whitish below, and the stalks of the lateral leaflets are generally 1/2 to 1 inch long and not winged. Sometimes listed as *Fraxinus pennsylvanica* 'Lanceolata' which is incorrect.

CULTIVARS: 'Marshall Seedless': a standard cultivar, selected in Nebraska and used extensively throughout the Great Plains. An excellent tree, tough, and drought-resistant with smooth, glossy foliage. 'Summit': a less vigorous grower than 'Marshall Seedless' but straighter growing with smaller leaflets. The true cultivar is male with no fruit. Numerous others exist.

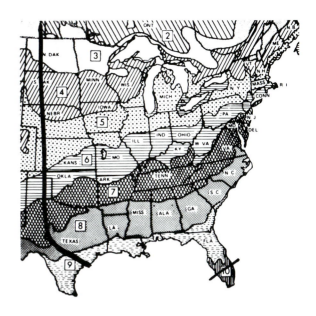

Fraxinum quadrangulata Michx. Blue Ash
Oleaceae or Olive Family Hardiness Zone 4
Native to the eastern United States.
SIZE: 40 to 80 feet tall with equal spread with age. Moderate to fast grower.
FORM: Pyramidal when young; broad, rounded crown with age.
TEXTURE: Medium. **EXPOSURE:** Sun.

LEAVES: Opposite, once-compound; with 7 to 11 leaflets, each 2 to 4 inches long. Oval or oval-elongate with distinct teeth on the margin. Dark green in summer; yellow in the fall.

STEM: 4-angled when young, thus the name, quandrangulata. Stout and green, eventually turning reddish brown. Wood is moderately durable, similar to other ash species. Mature stems have a shallowly furrowed bark with irregular, scaly plates, gray to slightly gray-brown. Bark is distinct from other ash species. When the bark is removed, the exposed sapwood turns slightly blue which probably accounts for the common name.

FLOWERS: Perfect; in short clusters near the tips of branches.

FRUIT: Dry and flattened, in clusters. Oblong, 1 to 2 inches, and often notched at the tip.

COLOR: Foliage is dark green; yellow in the fall.

PROPAGATION: Seed or grafting.

CULTURE: Blue ash is native to upland sites over a moderate range of the central and eastern United States. Prefers a well-drained soil with heavy leaf litter, not the wet, swampy soils frequented by green ash. more sensitive to soil compaction and root restrictions than green ash. Somewhat difficult to transplant unless grown with air-root-pruning as a seedling to stimulate dense root branching. Not for the poor soils sometimes mentioned in conjunction with green ash.

PESTS: Most of the ash species when under stress are subject to borers.

NOTES: Blue ash is an underrated tree in Zones 5, 6, 7, and perhaps 8. Grows more slowly in Zone 4 but still makes a useful and attractive tree. Not widely grown in the nursery trade, perhaps because it is somewhat more difficult to transplant than white or green ash. The broadly rounded crown provides excellent shade for many landscape functions (see photograph). There is moderate variation in growth forms and foliage color of seedlings suggesting that superior cultivars could be selected much like with white and green ash. The square young stem is probably the easiest identification feature to distinguish from other ash. Should be used more.

CULTIVARS: None known but deserves attention and selection.

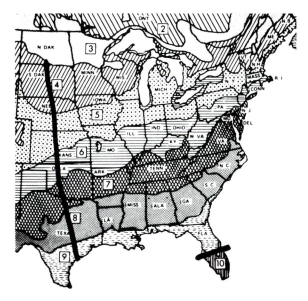

Ginkgo biloba L. Ginkgo or Maidenhair Tree
Ginkgoaceae or Ginkgo Family Hardiness Zone 4
Native to China.
SIZE: 80- to 100-foot tree, variable spread. Slow grower except under the best conditions.
FORM: Upright, and round-headed to columnar tree; much variation among seedlings.
TEXTURE: Medium. **EXPOSURE:** Sun.

LEAVES: alternate, simple; often having 2 to 6 leaves clustered on short branches called spurs, or sometimes singly on new growth. 2 to 4 inches across, wedge- or fan-shaped; outer margin frequently has a cleft in the center and the base gradually narrows. The margin is wavy. petiole is 1 to 4 inches long, slender, and green to yellowish. leaves are medium green. Fall color is a brilliant yellow, but leaves drop quickly.

STEM: The young stem is smooth, stout, and green, turning glossy yellow or brown with age. In some cases, thin vertical strings may develop on young stems. Bark is light tan to medium brown; with age it may become gray or black, and rather smooth at first, then finally roughened by rather deep furrows. Generally a central-leader tree with many branches in the crown. Wood is quite durable: wind- and ice-resistant.

FLOWERS: Not showy. Male and female flowers on separate trees (dioecious).

FRUIT: About 1 inch in diameter and pale yellow at maturity with a disagreeable odor. Female trees should be avoided.

COLOR: Foliage is medium green; yellow in the fall.

PROPAGATION: Seed or grafting of males of selected cultivars.

CULTURE: Tolerates a wide range of city conditions: smoke, air pollution, and confined root system. although this tree has been cultivated for nearly 200 years, it is variable when from seed and thus recommendations for its culture vary widely. Drought-resistant and moderately tolerant of hot, dry winds. however, does best in areas of good to superior soils and moisture where growth will be more rapid. Not for general use.

PESTS: None.

NOTES: Highly acclaimed by some for street tree planting and for urban landscaping; however, growth rate is extremely slow. It is difficult to transplant and to produce in nurseries because growth is slow and it is difficult to graft male trees. Performance in many urban areas has been disappointing due to planting in poor soils.

CULTIVARS: 'Princeton Gold': spreading, upright form; male. 'Princeton Sentry': narrow, columnar form; male. 'Autumn Gold': outstanding fall color; male, grows 30 to 40 feet tall with an oval crown. 'Pendula': has semi-weeping branches. 'Palo Alto': a nice oval form; male. One of the nicer cultivars. Several other cultivars exist. Because of the nasty fruits on the females, only males should be planted in landscapes with close contact with people.

Gleditsia triacanthos L.   Honeylocust
Leguminosae or Pea Family   Hardiness Zone 4
Native to the eastern U.S.
SIZE: 60 to 80 feet tall with a 30- to 50-foot spread. Moderate grower.
FORM: Oval-crowned, large tree.
TEXTURE: Very fine.   **EXPOSURE:** Sun.

LEAVES: Alternate, once- or twice-compound. Leaflets are without stalks, in 7 to 15 pairs per section; narrowly ovate or lanceolate, and rounded at the base and tip. Margin is smooth. Generally medium green above and below. Fall color is pale yellow.

STEM: Young stems are slender, red-brown, and tend to zigzag with the buds embedded in the twigs. All branches are very stiff, inflexible, and somewhat brittle. Bark is silver-gray to almost black and smooth at first, later becoming sandpapery. Breaks into vertical strips which peel from around the stem but rarely slough off, simply peels back. Stems, branches, and trunks of native or seedling trees are generally heavily laden with 1- or 3-pointed spines, anywhere from 2 to 6 inches long and glossy red-brown. The grafted cultivars are all thornless. Stem may sunscald in exposed locations.

FLOWERS: Not showy. Male and female on separate trees (dioecious, at least partially so).

FRUIT: A flattened, twisted pod, 10 to 18 inches long. Green, turning dark red-brown; with seeds encased in yellow pulp. Edible and sweet; thus the name, honeylocust.

COLOR: Foliage is medium green; yellow in the fall.

PROPAGATION: Seed, grafting, or budding of thornless and fruitless cultivars.

CULTURE: Honeylocust is a rapid-growing tree native to rich, moist soils along streams throughout the eastern United States. Tolerates a wide range of soil conditions; responds with vigor when planted in deep fertile soils. However, it survives and may make an acceptable tree in the poorest of soils. Very drought-resistant. Planted throughout the Great Plains in shelterbelts and for windbreaks. Tolerates alkaline or acid soils and extreme conditions.

PESTS: In the early 1970s, mimosa webworm became a serious pest of honeylocust, which was extensively planted as a replacement for American elm. Unless trees are sprayed, webworms make them look very drab by mid summer. Trees may suffer from heavy infestation of spider mites during mid summer. Sometimes weakened or old trees are attacked by borers.

NOTES: An overrated tree. Two of the improved cultivars, 'Skyline' and 'Shademaster', are worthy of consideration. Most others are inferior. Honeylocust has sufficient problems in terms of growth and, more recently, with mimosa webworm to make it questionable for future consideration. Does, however, provide a very light-textured shade and develop a broad-spreading crown, and a mature specimen is very attractive and pleasant in the landscape. Shade is very open and loose and thus, as with many other legume trees, a good stand of turf or other shrubs can be grown beneath.

CULTIVARS: 'Inermis' cultivar name given the first thornless, female trees. More recent cultivars such as 'Skyline' are both thornless and male. 'Inermis Skyline' is incorrect and should be notated as 'Skyline'. 'Skyline': narrowly upright as a young tree, broadening to an umbrella-like tree with age. Dense, small leaflets. 'Shademaster': more open and arching in habit, wineglass-shaped, and somewhat reminiscent of the American elm at maturity. 'Moraine': a rapid grower with upward-growing branches. 'Sunburst': yellow golden new foliage, gradually turning green. 'Ruby Lace': a splash of red-purple when the new leaves emerge, becoming green with age. Several other cultivars exist.

'Shademaster'

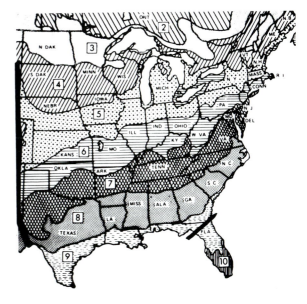

Gymnocladus dioica K.Koch.   Kentucky Coffee Tree
Leguminosae or Pea Family   Hardiness Zone 4
Native to the central United States.
SIZE: 60 to 80 feet tall with irregularly spreading branches. May spread 30 to 50 feet. Moderate grower.
FORM: Large, round-topped tree.
TEXTURE: Fine.   **EXPOSURE:** Sun.

LEAVES: Alternate, twice-compound; 1 to 3 feet long and 1 to 2 feet wide with a long central stalk or stem, swollen at the base. Individual leaflets may be 1 to 3 inches long, 1/2 to 1 inch wide, and oval with a pointed tip. Medium gray-green above; lighter green below and turning yellow in the fall. Both color and texture stand out in a mass planting.

STEM: Young stems are large and very stiff, consisting of few branches in the crown of the tree. Green at first, turning gray to slightly gray-brown; somewhat hairy when very young. leaf scars are very large and conspicuous; somewhat heart-shaped. A young stem, when broken or cut in sections, has a large, salmon-colored pith. With age, stems take on a steel-gray color with a shallowly furrowed, rough bark which is very attractive. Wood is moderately strong; young branches are fairly brittle, but the main stem and branches of the tree are quite durable.

FLOWERS: Not showy. Male and female on separate trees (dioecious).

FRUIT: A large pod, persistent into the winter. Generally 4 to 8 inches long, 1 to 2 inches wide; green, green turning brown at maturity. Quite pulpy and sticky between the seeds. large, flattened, hard, oval seed that requires an acid treatment for germination.

COLOR: Foliage is medium gray-green; yellow in the fall.

PROPAGATION: Seed or grafting of male trees.

CULTURE: Native to rich bottomlands throughout the lower Midwest, but grows in a wide range of soil and moisture conditions. Has amazing tolerance for disturbed or poor, rocky, gravelly soils, either well-drained or poorly drained. Responds vigorously to fertilizer, mulching, and other good cultural practices. Difficult to transplant, but very tolerant once established. Grows much faster than generally recognized.

PESTS: None serious.

NOTES: A very attractive tree, developing a light, very open and loose crown. Lets much light through beneath the tree, which makes it easy to grow shrubs or turf under the canopy. Very attractive in silhouette against wintry skies. Highly underrated. Deserves much more attention than it has received in the past. male trees are desirable due to their lack of seed pods and thus, the potential poisoning from the pulp around the seed. Should be planted a great deal more. XX-POISON-XX

CULTIVARS: 'Variegata': has irregular blotches of cream among the green leaflets. unusual and rarely seen. A male with good form would be a good contribution to the landscape industry.

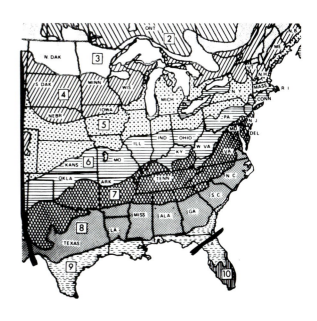

Halesia carolina L.   Carolina Silverbell
Styracaceae or Storax Family   Hardiness Zone 5
Native to the south-central United States.
SIZE: 20- to 40-foot small tree. Slow to moderate grower.
FORM: Small tree with low branches and a narrow crown.
TEXTURE: Medium.   **EXPOSURE:** Slight shade.

LEAVES: Alternate, simple; ovate, and 2 to 4 inches long with very fine teeth on the margin. Covered with hairs when young but the hairs on the upper surface are soon lost. Leaf color is dark green under good growing conditions and partial shade, lighter in color in sunny locations. Fall color is yellow and leaves drop early.

STEM: Young stems are fairly stout and curve upward (see photograph). Hairy when very young, becoming smooth with age. No terminal bud develops, but rather strong, axillary buds do, just behind the terminal. Two-year-old stems have a stringy bark which develops into shallow ridges and turns reddish brown with age. Wood is soft and somewhat brittle, but, since the tree does not grow very large, this is not normally a problem.

FLOWERS: White; somewhat bell-shaped, 1/2 inch long. In drooping clusters, 2 to 5 inches long, in mid spring. Showy.

FRUIT: A 4-winged, more or less oval or bell-shaped fruit; green, turning brown. Rather attractive.

COLOR: Leaves are dark green to yellow-green, depending on exposure and growing conditions. Flowers are white. Fruits are brown.

PROPAGATION: Seed or softwood cuttings.

CULTURE: An understory tree native to the central United States and the Upper South but quite cold hardy. Native to rich, moist, fertile soils where leaf litter is thick and provides good moisture and control of root temperatures. Silverbell is not drought-tolerant and does poorly in new housing areas where soils are poor and compacted and no soil covering exists except for grass. Responds to good soils, mulching, and moisture. Grass competition may be a factor influencing performance in urban areas. Performs best in slight shade or where full sun is received only in the mornings or on the north side of buildings. Not for general planting. Relatively easy to transplant.

PESTS: Normally a pest-free tree.

NOTES: An attractive, useful small tree if given thorough consideration for cultural requirements; otherwise it will be disappointing. Since it is shade-tolerant, consider using it as a small understory tree surrounded by shrubs such as azaleas, where the soil is not disturbed and leaf litter is allowed to accumulate.

CULTIVARS: 'Rosea' has pink flowers. Others probably exist.

RELATED SPECIES: *Halesia monticola* Sarg., mountain silverbell, is virtually identical except that the flowers and the tree are slightly larger. These are probably not separate species but rather ecological races that evolved under slightly different conditions.
  Halesia diptera Ellis., 2-winged silverbell, is native to the Gulf Coast but hardy in Zone 5. A small tree 20 to 30 feet tall, with white flowers and fruit that has only 2 wings instead of 4. Less planted than Carolina silverbell but a very nice, small tree.

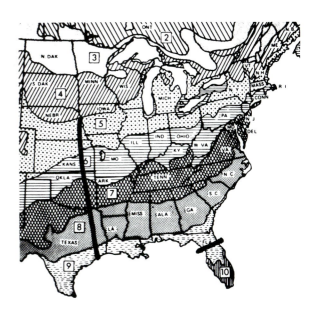

Halesia monticola

Halesia monticola

Hamamelis virginiana L.   Common Witchhazel
Hamamelidaceae or Witchhazel Family   Hardiness Zone 4
Native to eastern North America.
SIZE: 15 to 25 feet tall with a similar spread. Slow to moderate grower.
FORM: Irregular, large shrub or small tree.
TEXTURE: Medium to coarse.   **EXPOSURE:** Sun or shade.

LEAVES: Alternate, simple; 3 to 4 inches long. Oval with an irregularly toothed or wavy margin, mostly near the tip. Leaves are bright green above and only slightly paler below. Yellow to yellow-orange fall color. Some selections have outstanding fall color.

STEM: Young stems are slender and covered with hairs when young, but become smooth by the end of the growing season. Yellow-brown when young, turning dark brown. Vegetative buds have no bud scales but are covered by brown hairs. Bark is thin, light brown, and smooth to slightly scaly. Wood is heavy and stout.

FLOWERS: Yellow and fragrant, with 4 strap-like petals. Clusters of 2 to 4 in the leaf axils in September to November, depending on seedlings, exposure and geographic location. Interesting, more because of the unusual flowering time than real attractiveness. Also, flowering frequently coincides with fall color, which detracts from the flower show.

FRUIT: A small, dry capsule; about 1/2 inch long or less, maturing and throwing the seed one year after flowering. Not showy.

COLOR: Leaves are bright green; yellow in the fall. Flowers are yellow.

PROPAGATION: Seed or cuttings or grafting of selected cultivars.

CULTURE: Witchhazel is native from southeastern Canada to north Florida, along the edges of forests and woodlands and along streams. Grows best in deep, rich, moist soils, but tolerates a variety of soils, but not prolonged drought. Needs some pruning and training to develop a good tree form either single- or multiple-stemmed.

PESTS: None serious.

NOTES: Has merit as a small tree with attractive foliage both during the growing season and the fall. The flowers are unusual in both appearance and time of bloom. On the other hand, there are superior small trees for most situations. As a large shrub, witchhazel consumes more space than can be justified except in very large areas.

CULTIVARS: Some exist in localized areas.

RELATED SPECIES: *Hamamelis vernalis* Sarg., vernal witchhazel, is an upright shrub 6 to 10 feet tall that suckers readily at the base, but as a large shrub is neater in appearance than the common witchhazel. Leaves are similar in shape but slightly larger than those of common witchhazel. Flowers are yellow to reddish and very fragrant and emerge in January to March, remaining 2 to 3 weeks. Of interest mostly because of the unusual flowering time. Fall color is a bright yellow. Adaptation is similar to common witchhazel, and it is equally sensitive to extended drought. Foliage is dense during the growing season, thus it may have use as a screen or barrier.

Several other witchhazel species and hybrids are seen in the nursery trade, but in general they are of limited landscape importance. An oil obtained from the leaves, stems and bark is used in some salves and medicines.

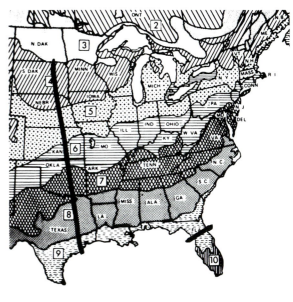

H. vernalis   H. virginiana

H. vernalis

Juglans nigra L.   Black Walnut
Juglandaceae or Walnut Family   Hardiness Zone 4
Native to the eastern United States.
SIZE: May reach 80 to 100 feet tall or more with a 40- to 50-foot spread. Slow grower.
FORM: Large, rounded-crowned tree.
TEXTURE: Medium.   **EXPOSURE:** Sun.

LEAVES: Alternate, compound; may be 12 to 24 inches long, generally with 13 to 23 leaflets. Individual leaflets are 3 to 5 inches long, 1 to 1 1/2 inches wide; ovate to lanceolate, tapering to a sharp point at the tip. Somewhat rounded at the base with a very short petiole. Generally yellowish to medium green; lower surface is fuzzy. Leaves have a distinct odor when crushed. Fall color is dull yellow and not particularly attractive. Leaves generally drop earlier than other species.

STEM: Young stems are stout, brownish or brownish gray and covered with light rust-colored hair, including the large terminal and axillary buds. As the stem gets older, it takes on a steel gray-brown color, later becoming a dark chocolate brown to black; fissured into deep blocks on old trees. When cut diagonally, the pith in a young branch is distinctly chambered. Wood is very tough and durable: highly prized for use in furniture and veneer.

FLOWERS: Male and female on the same tree (monoecious). Male is a 3- to 5-inch long catkin; female is inconspicuous.

FRUIT: A large, round nut with a hard shell covered by a husk that is originally green and quite thick, with a greenish yellow juice. Husk turns black when mature. Nut is very hard, with many ridges on the surface. Meat is edible and highly prized for its use in cooking.

COLOR: Foliage is medium to yellow-green.

PROPAGATION: Seed, or grafting of selected cultivars onto seedlings.

CULTURE: Native to deep, fertile, well-drained, moist soils along river bottoms and flood plains. Will tolerate shallow, poor, or abused soils such as those commonly found in urban areas if planted there when small. Needs good moisture and nutrient supply for best growth, but tolerates drought in good soils. Difficult to transplant and slow to recovere following transplanting.

PESTS: Tent caterpillars, fall webworms, and a leaf spot disease are the main enemies of the foliage. Other diseases attack the fruit and foliage.

NOTES: Attractive, large tree in spring and early summer where it is growing native in lowlands, woodlands, or streambanks. Not suited for most urban landscapes except where good soils exist and space is plentiful. More importantly, it should be left totally undisturbed when growing in areas being developed. Difficult to transplant and slow to grow, but a good tree where it occurs naturally. Releases a chemical (Juglone) from leaves, fruits, and bark, which may severely stunt tomatoes and certain other plants. This chemical does not appear to influence other woody trees or shrubs. The juice from leaves and fruits can stain automobiles and other surfaces, thus location is very important.

CULTIVARS: Numerous; primarily based on nut quality. Form and landscape value vary little in this respect.

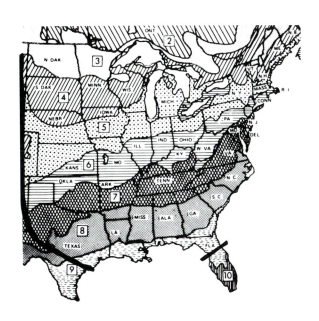

fall webworm

Koelreuteria bipinnata French.   Goldenrain or Chinese Flame Tree
Sapindaceae or Soapberry Family   Hardiness Zone 7
Native to China and Formosa.
SIZE: 40 to 60 feet tall with a 30- to 40-foot spread. Rapid grower.
FORM: Broad, round-headed tree.
TEXTURE: Medium.   **EXPOSURE:** Sun.

LEAVES: Alternate, twice-compound (occasionally 3 times compound, or nearly so), 16 to 24 inches long. Ovate to lanceolate leaflets with irregularly toothed margins. Generally the terminal leaflet is absent, making the leaflets even-numbered; but on young, rapidly growing trees, the terminal leaflet may be very prominent. Secondary branching on the main leaf stalk may be opposite or alternate. medium green above; lighter green below, turning yellow and dropping very early in the fall.

STEM: Young stem is stout in appearance, with many prominent, white, and corky lenticels. Leaf scars are prominent. Young branches are brittle with a large, white pith. With age the stem develops an irregular, sandy brown and a lightly furrowed bark. Wood is only moderately stout, but breakage results from weak "V" branches.

FLOWERS: Brilliant yellow clusters; 15 to 20 inches long, covering the outer portion of the tree. Generally blooms in late July or August, 1 or 2 months later than *Koelreuteria paniculata*. Individual flowers are about 1/2 inch in diameter.

FRUIT: Papery-walled, bladder-like capsule, about 2 to 2 1/2 inches long; appears inflated. Generally contains 2 or 3 black, round seeds. Capsules are salmon-pink to almost pink-orange and retain their color for weeks, finally dropping early to mid fall.

COLOR: Foliage is medium green; yellow in the fall. Flowers are yellow. Fruits are pink.

PROPAGATION: Seed.

CULTURE: A moderately tough plant which grows in a wide range of conditions: from heavy clay soils to the poor, sandy soils of Florida. Responds vigorously to fertilization, reduced weed competition, mulching, and good cultural practices. Needs selective pruning early to develop a good branching system, due to the rather weak wood.

PESTS: None serious. Mushroom root rot may hasten the death of an old tree.

NOTES: Must be in full sun for good flowering. Becomes spindly, open, and unattractive in shade or semi-shade. Very rapid-growing, small to medium size tree. Provides an excellent show of flowers and fruit in late summer, when few other plants are showy. Deserves more attention, particularly in backgrounds, where it blends in with other vegetation, when it does not have flowers or fruit. sometimes called Chinese flame tree. Young seedlings are subject to cold injury the first 1 or 2 years, especially if growing vigorously. However, once established, this species will survive -10 degrees F or lower with no injury. Seedlings can be a weed in some areas.

Can be distinguished from *Koelreuteria paniculata* in that *K. paniculata* has smaller, once-compound leaves, is a smaller tree that flowers in June and has yellow seed pods that turn red-brown to brown in the fall, but never pink. *K. paniculata* is better adapted to Zones 5 and 6, whereas *K. bipinatta* is best adapted to Zones 7, 8, and 9.

CULTIVARS: None known.

RELATED SPECIES: *Koelreuteria elegans* (Seem) A.C. Sm., sometimes listed as *K. formosana*, Formosan goldenrain tree or flamegold, is hardy only in Zones 9 and 10 and is impossible to distinguish from *K. bipinnata* except that it is evergreen.

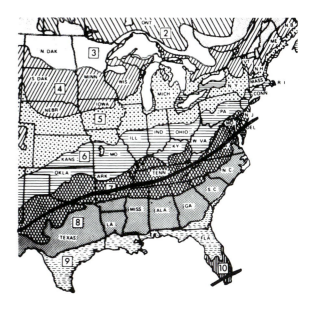

Koelreuteria paniculata Laxm.   Panicled Goldenrain Tree
Sapindaceae or Soapberry Family   Hardiness Zone 5
Native to China, Korea, Japan.
SIZE: 25 to 30 feet tall with a 15- to 20-foot spread. Moderate growth rate.
FORM: Small, compact, round-headed tree.
TEXTURE: Fine to medium.   EXPOSURE: Sun.

LEAVES: Alternate, once-compound; 8 to 14 inches long, composed of 7 to 17 leaflets. Terminal leaflet is nearly always present. Individual leaflets are 1 1/2 to 3 inches long, 1 to 1 1/2 inches wide, ovate, with a pointed tip and an irregularly-toothed margin. May be deeply cut, appearing as though the leaf is twice compound in some instances. Leaflets are on very short, almost non-existent petioles. Deep green to almost blue-green above, light green below. Leaves drop early in the fall after turning a dull yellow to yellow-orange.

STEM: Young stem is stout in appearance, and the crown does not have an abundance of branches. Typical of the soapberry family, the tree will begin a flush of vegetative growth (leaves) in the spring; then triggered by day length, begin producing flowers. Thus, on one flush of growth, about the first half will be vegetative with leaves, while the remainder will be flower clusters. Unlike most trees, in the fall there is no terminal bud. The new flush of growth for the following year comes from a side bud below the flower cluster. The old bark of the tree takes on a shallowly furrowed pattern, generally a silver-gray to gray-brown. Wood is only moderately stout so fairly easily broken by vandalism or ice when young. Fortunately, the tree does not get very large, and it should not be discarded because of the weak wood.

FLOWERS: Bright yellow, in large terminal clusters, appearing in June or late May, covering the tree. Each flower is about 1/2 inch in diameter with orange markings at the base. Very showy.

FRUIT: Papery-walled, bladder-like capsule, 1 to 2 inches long, appearing inflated. Contains 3 round, black seeds about 1/4 inch in diameter. Light yellow-brown at first, changing to light red-brown; persist into winter. Quite showy but less showy than *K. bipinnata*.

COLOR: Foliage is deep green to nearly blue-green; yellow in the fall. Flowers are yellow. Fruit is yellow to red-brown.

PROPAGATION: Seed. Seedlings are quite uniform.

CULTURE: Grows almost anywhere: a very adaptable and tolerant small tree. Tolerates poor soils and alkaline soils. Responds and grows more vigorously in better soils. Quite drought-resistant, but intolerant of poorly drained conditions. Responds to fertilizer and clearing of grass and weeds from around base.

PESTS: Boxelder bugs may be a nuisance.

NOTES: A very attractive small tree, useful in many landscape situations. Multiple color combinations of the foliage, fall color, flowers, and seed pods make it an attractive tree throughout the year. Also attractive as a silhouette against the sky in the winter, when only a few of the seed pods remain. It is planted extensively throughout the Great Plains and is deserving of the attention it has received.

   Can be distinguished from *Koelreuteria bipinnata* in that *K. bipinnata* grows 40 to 60 feet high, has twice-compound leaves, blooms in August and has a salmon-pink to orange-pink colored fruit somewhat larger than that of *K. paniculata*. *Koelreuteria bipinnata* is hardy only into Zone 7, whereas *K. paniculata* is hardy to Zone 5.

CULTIVARS: 'Fastigiata': columnar in habit. 'September': flowers in late summer.

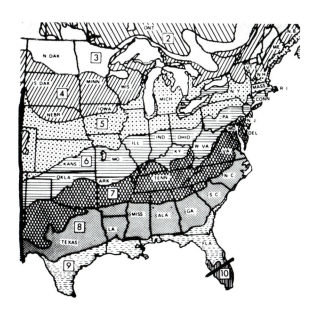

Larix decidua Mill.   European Larch
Pinaceae or Pine Family   Hardiness Zone 3
Native to north and central Europe.
SIZE: 60 to 80 feet tall, variable spread. Moderate to rapid grower.
FORM: Pyramidal when young, becoming open and irregular with age.
TEXTURE: Fine.   **EXPOSURE:** Sun.

LEAVES: Deciduous, with needles about 1 inch long, somewhat flattened; in clusters of 30 to 40 on short spurs, more or less spirally arranged on the stem. Soft blue-green to green in the spring, becoming darker green in summer and turning yellow in the fall. This is one of the few deciduous conifers.

STEM: Young stems are slender, very flexible; smooth, yellowish, often drooping when wet. The two-year-old leaf bases provide a roughened appearance. The short spurs on stout leaf cluster supports begin growth the third year and grow very slowly for many years forming what appears to be a short, stubby tree stump on the branch in winter. Bark is thin and scaly on young stems and deeply furrowed, thick, and dark grayish brown with age, showing a reddish-brown streak in the furrows on rapid growing trees.

FLOWERS: Small. Female and male cones are noticeable in spring before the leaves.

FRUIT: A small, brown cone about 1 inch long, with 40 to 50 scales and soft, brown hairs.

COLOR: Foliage is soft; blue-green to green in the spring.

PROPAGATION: By seed or grafting of cultivars.

CULTURE: Although native to the mountains of eastern and northern Europe, larch grows over a wide range of the upper United States, especially in Zones 3, 4, and 5. More tolerant of poorly drained soils and heavy clays than many conifers, and moderately drought-tolerant as well. European larch has been planted extensively in North and South Dakota as a part of windbreaks. Not for Zones 6 and 7, except for perhaps as a special effect. Grows more slowly and tends to have more problems farther south. This is probably due to the fact that it is sensitive to the length of the day, thus further north where summer days are longer it grows better than further south where summer days are shorter.

PESTS: Many types of insects may feed on foliage and cause problems.

NOTES: Drab and unappealing in winter. However, the emerging leaves are very soft and attractive. Then when the trees reach 15 to 20 years old and begin bearing the small, delicate cones, the spring and summer effect is even greater. Unfortunately the fall color is only fair.

CULTIVARS: 'Pendula': weeping branches; very attractive. Other cultivars probably exist.

RELATED SPECIES: *Larix laricina* C.Koch., American larch or tamarack, is hardy in Zone 1 and is similar in overall appearance to European larch. Growth form is more narrowly columnar and cones only have 15 to 22 scales, making distinction of the species relatively easy. Not as ornamental as European larch.

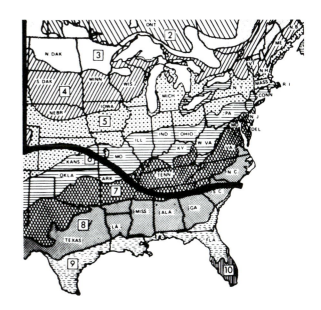

Liquidambar styraciflua L.   Sweetgum
Hamamelidaceae or With Hazel Family   Hardiness Zone 5
Native to the southeastern United States.

SIZE: 80- to 100-foot tree with a 40- to 60-foot spread, varying with individuals, locations and competition from surroundings. Rapid grower in the South, much slower in the North.
FORM: Oval-crowned, large tree.
TEXTURE: Medium to coarse.   **EXPOSURE:** Sun.

LEAVES: Alternate, simple; 3 to 6 inches long, basically star-shaped with 5 lobes or points with a saw-toothed edge. Leaves are deep dark green above; lighter green below, on a long petiole. Actively growing leaves have a pronounced odor when crushed. Leaves resemble those of a maple except that the leaves are alternate instead of opposite on the stem. Brilliant yellow to red; red-orange in the fall, variable among seedlings or cultivars.

STEM: Young stem is rusty red, sometimes with corky wings or appendages, but these are not always present. Winter buds on young stems are very large, glossy, and bright brown. Bark is light gray and smooth on young branches, finally turning a dark brown; fissured and rough on old trunks. Usually a central leader stem with excellent branch development around the tree and good spacing between the branches. Little, if any, pruning required. The form on a young tree is triangular, broad at the base, tapering to a tip, very similar to a young pin oak. Wood is somewhat weak and brittle; may be damaged by wind or ice.

FLOWERS: Male and female on the same tree (monoecious). Not showy.

FRUIT: The globular, spiny fruit is 1 to 1 1/2 inches in diameter, green when young and brown when mature. Appears by mid summer, drops by mid fall. A nuisance when hit by lawn mowers or on patios, sidewalks, driveways, or other places of pedestrian traffic. Very discomforting to a bare foot!

COLOR: Foliage is deep green; yellow to red-orange in the fall.

PROPAGATION: Seed or grafting of selected cultivars.

CULTURE: Sweetgums are native to stream banks and low, swampy bottomlands throughout the southeastern United States. Require an abundance of moisture to grow well. Not for dry land areas or where droughts occur. Should be used only where considerable moisture exists at all times, such as around water features and on stream banks. Sweetgums have no place as a street tree in most cities. Poorly adapted to the most abused urban soils that remain following construction. Difficult to transplant in the fall.

PESTS: Tent caterpillars; occasionally aphids and spider mites, but mostly problem-free.

NOTES: Greatly overplanted. A young tree in the nursery is spectacular in form, foliage, and branch development. However, many urban sites are such that it does very poorly after being transplanted. Should be planted only after careful consideration is given to the features of the site as they relate to the growth habit and requirements of the tree.

CULTIVARS: 'Autumn Glow': red to red-purple fall color; very showy. 'Burgundy': grows 40 to 60 feet tall, deep red to purple fall color, persists on the tree. 'Festival': narrow upright, light fall colors, many shades of red and yellow. 'Palo Alto': pyramidal, deep green foliage; orange-red in the fall. Not well adapted to the Upper South or northward. 'Rotundaloba': is a grafted seedless cultivar. Without the seeds, one negative is removed, but there still are many better trees for most locations. Several others exist.

RELATED SPECIES: *Liquidambar formosana* Hance., Formosan sweetgum, has fuzzy leaves with only 3 lobes. Some seedlings have a broad, spreading form and excellent fall color. Not common but may be a superior tree on some sites. Generally does not get as large.

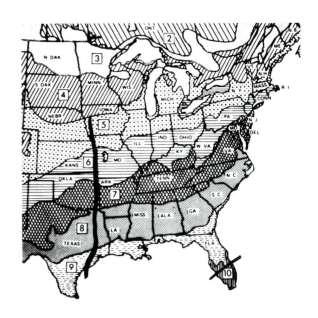

Liquidambar formosana

Liriodendron tulipifera L.   Tulip Tree or Yellow Poplar
Magnoliaceae or Magnolia Family   Hardiness Zone 4
Native to the eastern United States from the Gulf Coast to Canada.
SIZE: 100 feet or more tall with a 60- to 80-foot spread. Rapid grower on good sites.
FORM: Huge, broad, oval tree.
TEXTURE: Coarse.   EXPOSURE: Sun.

LEAVES: Alternate, simple; generally 4 to 6 inches long or more and equally broad. Somewhat tulip-shaped in profile, with 2 large lobes on each side of the center notch of the leaf. Upper surface is dark green and shiny, lower surface is a very pale green. Petioles are generally 3 to 6 inches long, very slender and flexible, allowing leaves to seem to chatter somewhat in the wind like those of a cottonwood or aspen. Fall color is yellow, turning late in the season.

STEM: Young stems are greenish to reddish brown, sometimes with a waxy coating. Dormant bud is long, slender, and duckbill-shaped, with only 2 bud scales exposed. Wood is somewhat brittle: readily broken in wind or ice storms. Young branches are steel gray for several years, with a thin bark; eventually bark becomes moderately furrowed and gray-black in color. Where the major branches attach to the main stem there are distinct lines or connection markings. Only *Tilia spp.* have more pronounced markings where branches attach to the main stem.

FLOWERS: Generally in April or early May; male and female parts in the same flower. Flowers are 3 to 5 inches across, cup-shaped. Green on the outside, with an attractive orange-yellow center. They face upward, therefore are not showy from the ground, but very attractive from a balcony or second story window.

FRUIT: A dry, cone-like structure, ripening in September or October. Composed of numerous woody, brown scales about 2 to 3 inches long, containing the seeds. Neither showy nor particularly troublesome.

COLOR: Foliage is dark green; yellow in the fall. Flowers are orange-yellow.

PROPAGATION: By seed.

CULTURE: Native to fertile, moist soils. Strictly a tree for good growing conditions. Does poorly in most street plantings. Should be used only around water features or other locations where adequate moisture is present and good soils exist. Becomes a huge tree and thus does not lend itself to small properties. Leaves tend to drop sporadically throughout the growing season creating a litter problem.

PESTS: A leaf spot disease is probably most serious, causing leaves to drop early and create litter in the landscape.

NOTES: A huge tree with somewhat brittle wood, adapted only to fertile, moist sites. Should be considered only as a specimen plant or a background plant on locations where there is much space, good soil, and adequate moisture. Not for general planting. When clearing part of the trees from native woods for development, tulip trees are generally more affected by the disturbance than other species and sometimes abruptly die.

CULTIVARS: 'Fastigiatum': an upright grower with good form but may reach 40 feet or more and 20 feet wide. Several other dwarf and/or oddity cultivars exist.

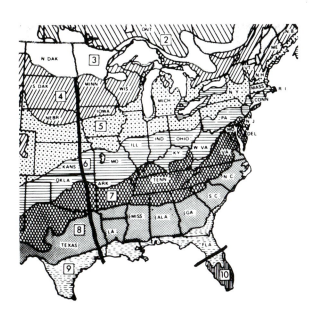

Maclura pomifera Schneid.   Osage Orange
Moraceae or Mulberry Family   Hardiness Zone 5
Native to the lower Mississippi River Valley.
SIZE: 40 to 60 feet tall with a 20- to 40-foot spread. Rapid grower.
FORM: Low-branching, round-headed tree.
TEXTURE: Medium to coarse.   EXPOSURE: Sun.

LEAVES: Alternate, simple; broadly ovate to nearly heart-shaped, with a smooth margin. Rounded at the base, long tapering to a point at the tip. Usually 3 to 6 inches long, 2 to 3 inches wide, with rather slender petioles about 1/2 to 1 1/2 inches long. Deep, dark green, very glossy upper surface; light green below. Clear yellow in the fall in the lower Midwest and Great Plains; may drop early and color less well in the Southeast.

STEM: Stout, zigzag, with leaves appearing either individually or in clusters on spurs (short stout stems). Seedlings develop sharp spines below the spurs and at the leaf axils on rapidly growing branches. Generally light brown at first, turning an orange-brown during the first winter; ultimately becoming a rather irregularly rough, orange-brown. Bark on an old tree furrows deeply and retains the orange cast. Wood is extremely hard and durable: storm-, ice-, vandal-, and decay-resistant.

FLOWERS: Male and female on separate trees (dioecious). Not showy.

FRUIT: Visible during mid summer, remains into the fall. A large, green ball; 4 to 5 inches in diameter, with a rather rough surface with milky juice. Very messy.

COLOR: foliage is deep, dark, glossy green; clear, bright yellow in the fall.

PROPAGATION: Seed, cuttings, or grafting.

CULTURE: Will grow almost anywhere; a remarkably tough plant tolerating disturbed or poor soils, poorly drained or rocky soils, and other conditions common to urban areas. Responds with vigor to improved growing conditions, supplemental fertilization and watering. Extremely wind- and drought-resistant, and virtually pest-free.

PESTS: None serious.

NOTES: a tough, rugged tree with deep, glossy, green foliage. Much overlooked and ignored as a landscape plant for urban areas. Root system is shallow. roots are covered with a brilliant orange, paper-like wrapping, making identification easy. The wood is also an orange color. the root system competes severely with grass and adjacent trees. Only the thornless male cultivars should be planted since fruits are very messy and undesirable. A good, tough tree with durable wood. Cultivars should be planted more. Also known as hedge apple or bois d'arc.

CULTIVARS: 'Pawhuska' and 'Chetopa': thornless and male, thus bear no fruit. Released in 1973 by Kansas State University. Propagated by cuttings from 2 trees found growing in the wild. 'Park' and 'Wichita' are thornless males. 'Wichita': has very few thorns when young and none with age. Should have a bright future in the urban landscape and as a street tree. Unfortunately, young, rapidly growing trees of the thornless cultivars have a few thorns when young, making the public acceptance (sale) of these superior cultivars difficult. As additional thornless male selections are made and evaluated, no doubt some will be found that do not develop thorns at all. Wide acceptance of osage orange as a landscape tree may have to wait until that time.

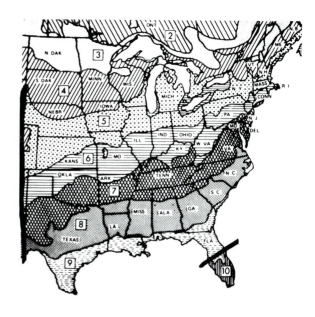

Magnolia acuminata L.   Cucumbertree Magnolia
Magnoliaceae or Magnolia Family   Hardiness Zone 4
Native to the east central and southeastern United States.
SIZE: 60 to 80 feet tall with a 30- to 40-foot spread. Slow to moderate grower.
FORM: Pyramidal to rounded-crown, medium to large tree.
TEXTURE: Coarse.   **EXPOSURE:** Sun to partial shade.

LEAVES: Alternate, simple; 5 to 12 inches long, 2 to 6 inches wide. Elliptical to oblong with a smooth margin. Young leaves are often densely hairy when they first unfold. Later, upper surface is olive to deep green and glossy; lower surface is a pale, dull green. Petiole is short and stout. Fall color is yellow to yellow-brown.

STEM: Young twigs are stout, red to brown, and hairy at first; becoming smooth with numerous prominent lenticels. Winter buds are large, oval-shaped, and densely hairy with only 2 visible bud scales. Older buds are light to medium gray turning dark brown to gray-brown with age, developing a furrowed trunk with thin scales. Wood is only moderately strong: some susceptibility to wind damage.

FLOWERS: Appear in May or June after the leaves. Bell-shaped; greenish yellow, not particularly showy.

FRUIT: A cucumber-shaped cone, oblong to ovoid, 2 to 3 inches long, 1 inch in diameter, often curved. Matures in the summer; not showy.

COLOR: Foliage is olive to deep green; yellow to yellow-brown in the fall.

PROPAGATION: Seed or grafting. Cuttings root poorly, if at all.

CULTURE: Native to rich, moist soils along stream banks and rocky slopes throughout the east central and southeastern United States. Not tolerant of poor or disturbed soils commonly found following construction. Should be used sparingly and only where soil and moisture requirements meet the needs of the plant.

PESTS: None serious.

NOTES: An attractive, medium to large tree with dense foliage where adapted. Does not belong in most urban areas. Should be used more on large estates, golf courses, or parks where soil is undisturbed and adequate moisture is assured.

CULTIVARS: Some may exist. Of limited availability in the trade.

HYBRIDS: *Magnolia acuminata* X *M. lilliflora* = 'Evamaria': has purple unopened flower buds, rose colored when open. *M. acuminata* X *M. denudata* = 'Elizabeth': has yellow flowers and a pyramidal growth habit.

RELATED SPECIES: *Magnolia virginiana* sweetbay or swamp magnolia, grows similarly to cucumbertree magnolia. However, leaves are semi-evergreen, oblong, 3 to 5 inches long, shiny, dark green above, and distinctly whitish below. Flowers appear in June and are creamy white, 2 to3 inches across. Hardy in Zone 5 and native as far south as central Florida. Tolerates wet conditions and shade, and grows more vigorously in the warmer climates. Should be used more in areas with heavy or poorly drained soils. Not drought-tolerant.

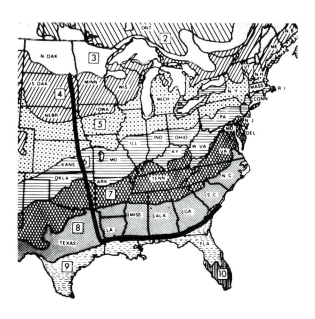

Magnolia soulangiana Soul.-Bod.   Saucer Magnolia
Magnoliaceae or Magnolia Family   Hardiness Zone 5
A hybrid between *Magnolia heptapeta* Buch. and *Magnolia quinquepeta* Buch.
SIZE: 20 to 25 feet tall with a 20- to 30-foot spread. Moderate grower.
FORM: Broad-spreading, small tree.
TEXTURE: Coarse.   **EXPOSURE:** Sun to partial shade.

LEAVES: Alternate, simple; 4 to 7 inches long, 2 to 4 inches wide. Thick and soft with a smooth margin and a point at the tip. Rather woolly when young. Light to medium bright green. Fall color is a pale yellow; not showy.

STEM: Young stem is a glossy, varnished brown; woolly at first becoming smooth with age. Dormant flower buds are very large and fuzzy: leaf buds are smaller, but both have only 2 bud scales showing. Older branches and main trunk are a smooth silver-gray. Bark color stands out in winter. Develops numerous low, stout, spreading branches.

FLOWERS: Appear before the leaves, very early in the spring: one of the first trees to bloom. Purplish pink on the outside of the petals, creamy white on the inside, with a purple center. May be 4 to 6 inches in diameter. Very striking. Even very young plants bloom profusely. Petals fall early, just as the leaves begin to emerge. A short, tremendous burst of color, but frequently damaged by late spring freezes. Cultivars differ mostly in the color of the outside of the petals.

FRUIT: Not showy.

COLOR: Foliage is light to medium, bright green; little fall color. Flowers are pink-rose, to white. Bark is attractive silver-gray.

PROPAGATION: Seed, cuttings, or selected cultivars may be grafted onto seedlings.

CULTURE: Prefers a rich, moist, well-drained soil. Not adapted to poor dry soils. Sites should be selected carefully. Responds to fertilizer and mulching with organic or inorganic materials to assist in conserving moisture. Somewhat difficult to transplant, but transplants best in spring.

PESTS: None serious.

NOTES: Spectacular, small tree when in bloom very early in the spring. Of no specific landscape value the remainder of the growing season. However, bark is rather attractive in silhouette against a wintry sky. Useful, small tree for planting in locations to emphasize the coming of spring. it later blends into the mass of greenery and is mostly obscure until the following spring.

CULTIVARS: 'Alexandrina': blooms somewhat later, purplish pink flowers and rich green foliage. 'Amabilis': flowers are white, leaves are dull green. 'Lilliputian': a smaller, shrublike form with dull, leathery leaves; pink flowers. 'Brozzonii': has huge white flowers. many others exist.

RELATED SPECIES: *Magnolia stellata* Maxim., star magnolia, is a shrub which grows 6 to 12 feet tall. Flowers are white or pink, with many more petals than *M. soulangiana*, but similar in adaptability.
    Magnolias by Neil G. Treseder, 1978, provides an excellent accounting of the many species and hybrids of magnolias along with much detail about their development.

Magnolia stellata

Magnolia virginiana L.
Magnoliaceae or Magnolia Family
Native to the southeastern United States.
SIZE: 20- to 50-foot tree. Moderate grower.
FORM: Irregular tree.
TEXTURE: Medium.

Sweetbay or Swamp Magnolia
Hardiness Zone 5

EXPOSURE: Sun or partial shade.

LEAVES: Alternate, or nearly whorled on the terminal branches, simple; 3 to 6 inches long, oval-elongate, with smooth margins. upper leaf surface is dark, glossy green and distinctly whitish beneath, especially when young; very noticeable when moved by the wind or when viewed from below. Semi-evergreen in the Deep South.

STEM: Young stems are slender, green, smooth, and aromatic when crushed. Older stems are smooth and light gray to greenish brown. Wood is moderately stout.

FLOWERS: Solitary; creamy white, 3 to 4 inches across. Fragrant: lemon-scented. Showy but generally not produced in abundance.

FRUIT: A cone-like fruit, 2 to 3 inches long with red-skinned seeds.

COLOR: Leaves are dark green; white below. Flowers are creamy white.

PROPAGATION: Seed or softwood cuttings.

CULTURE: Native to rich, fertile, moist soils along streams. Moderately adaptable to urban conditions since compacted soils are low in oxygen, like very moist soils are. Not drought-tolerant. heavy mulches are probably a great assist in most urban areas.

PESTS: No serious problems except drought.

CULTIVARS: Some may exist.

RELATED SPECIES: *Magnolia macrophylla* Michx., bigleaf magnolia, is hardy in Zone 5 and native to the southeastern United States. Leaves are 18 to 36 inches long in the tree's native habitat; smaller in most landscape situations. Dark green; unique. Flowers are creamy white, opening after the leaves; 8 to 12 inches across and fragrant. A very coarsely textured, round-headed tree, reaching 25 to 35 feet or more on a good site. Not tolerant to wet, swampy soils like sweetbay magnolia is. A unique tree, very dominating either in the landscape or in natural woodlands. Interesting, but of limited landscape value.

Magnolia tripetala L., umbrella magnolia, is a small to medium size tree with open branching, hardy in Zone 4. Leaves are 8 to 18 inches long, dark green above and whitish below with a smooth margin and herringbone veination pattern (see photograph). The large leaves are crowded on the tips of the branches giving an umbrella effect to the overall tree. Flowers appear after the leaves, are 6 to 10 inches long, and creamy white with an unpleasant odor. Lacks drought tolerance.

Many other deciduous magnolias exist as species and hybrids. For more information, the book, **Magnolias** by Neil G. Treseder, published in 1978 by Faber and Faber Ltd., 3 Queen Square, London, is high recommended. A most comprehensive study of the genus, *Magnolia*.

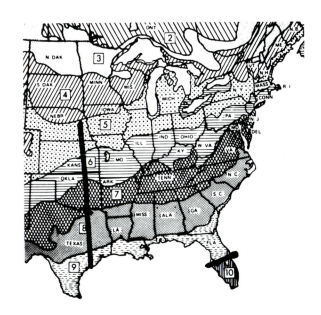

M. macrophylla

M. tripetala

Malus spp. (several species and hybrids)   Flowering Crabapple
Rosaceae or Rose Family   Hardiness Zone 3
Native to Asia.
SIZE: 15 to 30 feet with a 15- to 35-foot spread. Moderate to rapid grower.
FORM: Round-headed, low-branched to irregularly upright, small trees.
TEXTURE: Medium.   **EXPOSURE:** Sun.

LEAVES: Alternate, simple; oval or oblong, 2 to 4 inches long, 1 to 2 inches wide, with a sawtooth margin. Color is variable: bright to dark green, red or purple, depending on cultivar. Fall color is variable but generally not showy.

STEM: Young stems are generally densely wooly and red-purple to red-brown. With age stems become glossy and smooth, becoming gray to gray-brown, finally developing an irregular, shallow-furrowed bark on the main trunk. Wood is moderately stout. Trees are often low-branched; some branches are horizontal or nearly so.

FLOWERS: White, pink or red; slightly fragrant, 1 to 2 inches long, in clusters. Terminal blossoms open first and progress back giving a longer show. Very showy in early spring.

FRUIT: Small, tart, apple-like; green turning yellow, orange, or red. Very showy on some cultivars during late summer and fall. Some make good jelly.

COLOR: Foliage is bright to dark green, red, or purple. Flowers are white, light to dark pink, or red. Fruit is yellow, orange, or red.

PROPAGATION: By cuttings or grafting of cultivars. Seedlings are extremely variable.

CULTURE: A very adaptable tree. Tolerates most soils, but does best in a deep, fertile, moist soil. Needs some pruning to insure good structural development of branches. Blooms and fruits best and is most disease-free in full sun. Excessive fertilization may increase incidence of disease, especially fireblight.

PESTS: Fireblight may be more serious when tree is growing very rapidly. Cedar apple rust, powdery mildew, and apple scab affect many cultivars. Webworms can be a problem.

NOTES: Very showy for a short burst in the spring, generally good foliage during the growing season and showy fruit during late summer and fall. Numerous cultivars develop an irregularly rounded to oval crown and very dense shade. Trees remain in scale with single story dwellings. Only cultivars resistant to disease should be used.

CULTIVARS: Following are only a few of the disease-resistant cultivars. *Malus baccata* 'Jackii': white flowers, glossy red fruits, upright. 'Donald Wyman': single flowers, pink buds open white; fruit is bright red, 1/2 inch. 'Inglis': single flowers, pink buds open white; fruit is scarlet, 1/2 inch. 'Margaret': double pink flowers in clusters; late bloomer, fruit is greenish. 'Mount Arbor Special': carmine buds and flowers fade to dull pink; red fruit. 'Robinson': single, crimson buds and flowers; fruit is red, 1/2 inch. 'Tomiko': single flowers, dark maroon buds open reddish purple. 'Callaway': light pink buds; white single flowers; red, 1 inch fruit. 'Molten Lava': single, white flowers; fruit is red-orange, 1/2 inch.

RELATED SPECIES: *Malus floribunda*: slightly susceptible to scab, powdery mildew and fireblight. Deep pink to red buds, single white flowers; blooms while young; fruit is yellow and red, 1/2 inch. 'Dolga': good disease resistance and flowering and attractive fruit. 'Mary Potter': susceptible to powdery mildew. Single flowers; pink buds open white; fruit is red.

  Malus sargentii: susceptible to scab and fire blight? White, fragrant flowers, dark red fruit; may grow twice as broad high. 'Snowdrift': pink buds then pure white flowers; 1/2 inch long orange-red fruit; lustrous green foliage. Many, many others exist.

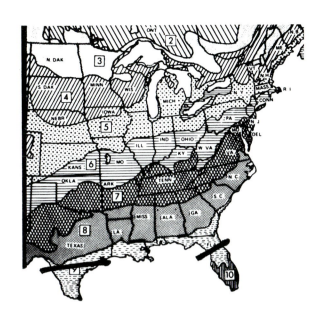

Melia azedarach L.   Chinaberry
Meliaceae or Mahogany Family   Hardiness Zone 7
Native to Asia.
SIZE: 30 to 40 feet tall with a 30- to 35-foot spread. Rapid grower.
FORM: Broad, oval, umbrella-like crowned tree.
TEXTURE: Fine.   **EXPOSURE:** Sun.

LEAVES: Alternate, twice-compound or occasionally appears to be 3 times compound. Entire leaf may be 18 to 24 inches long and 10 to 12 inches wide. Individual leaflets may be 1 1/2 to 2 1/2 inches long, and 1 to 1 1/2 inches wide with an irregular coarsely toothed margin. leaflets may vary in size and shape on the same compound leaf. The leaflets are opposite on the main leaf stalk, and the terminal leaflet is always present.

STEM: Young stems are large and irregularly shaped, with protrusions where the large leaves were attached. leaf scars on the young stem are more or less horseshoe-shaped, with a dormant bud in the center. The wood is weak, very brittle, and soft; particularly on the young stems: easily broken or damaged. Some dieback occurs on the young twigs during most winters in the northern part of its range. The older wood has a steel-gray, smooth bark; later becoming shallowly furrowed and gray to gray-black.

FLOWERS: Generally appears in April or May. Blue to purplish, about 1/2 inch across in large loose clusters. Moderately showy.

FRUITS: Ripen in September or October. About 1/2 inch in diameter, marble-like, generally pale white to yellow, finally shrivel and dry to a light brown and have a foul odor. Eaten by birds and mammals and spread freely.

COLOR: Foliage is medium green. Flowers are blue to purple. Fruits are yellow to dull white.

PROPAGATION: Seed, cuttings, or root suckers.

CULTURE: A weed tree, said to be naturalized in all the warmer climates of the world. Tolerates a wide range of soil conditions, and will grow almost anywhere. The pulp on the fruit is poisonous. A worthless landscape tree which produces many seeds and suckers that become a severe nuisance. Wood is very brittle, readily broken in storms. Should not be planted.

PESTS: None serious, unfortunately.

NOTES: In the Southwest, chinaberry is sometimes confused with soapberry, *Sapindus drummondi*. However, chinaberry leaves are twice-compound with toothed margins on the leaflets and blue flowers. Soapberry leaves are smooth on the margins, and only once-compound, and flowers are creamy yellow. Also in the Southeast, chinaberry is sometimes confused with goldenrain tree, *Koelreuteria bipinnata* or Formosan goldenrain tree, *K. elegans*, particularly in the seedling stage. Goldenrain tree can be identified by the yellow flowers and Japanese lantern-type fruits in late summer or early fall, and by the absence of a terminal leaflet on most of the large, double compound leaves, whereas chinaberry generally has all terminal leaflets present. However, this contrast is true only on trees 12 to 15 feet tall or taller. XX-POISON-XX

CULTIVARS: 'Umbraculiformis', Texas umbrella chinaberry: a slightly smaller tree than the parent with a broad, flattened head. No particular advantage for landscaping purposes except as a slightly smaller tree. Has problems similar to the parent.

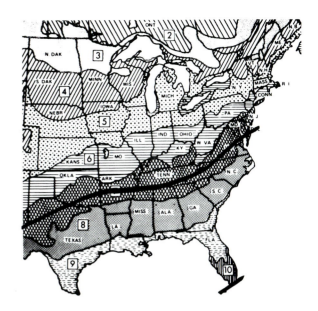

Metasequoia glyptostroboides H.H. Hu & Cheng.   Dawn Redwood
Taxodiaceae or Taxodium Family   Hardiness Zone 5
Native to China.
SIZE: 80 to 100 feet tall. Rapid grower.
FORM: Narrow, pyramidal tree with upright branching.
TEXTURE: Fine.   EXPOSURE: Sun.

LEAVES: A conifer with deciduous, opposite branches. Branchlets are double-ranked (appear flattened) with opposite, simple, needle-like leaves. Each leaf has 2 to 6 lines on the underside. medium green; coppery brown in the fall.

STEM: Branches with needles are deciduous. The woody, persistent branches are slender with opposite buds and branching; bright reddish brown when young. Bark on the main stem is shallowly furrowed, peeling in vertical strips. Trees nearly always have a very distinct central leader that tapers gradually from the soil line to the very tip of the tree, very similar to that of bald cypress. Wood is light weight but stout and decay-resistant.

FLOWERS: Male and female separate but on the same tree (monoecious). Male flowers are in clusters at the ends of branches.

FRUIT: Rounded, hanging down on long stalks. Dark brown; containing 5 to 9 winged seeds.

COLOR: Foliage is medium green; copper-brown in the fall.

PROPAGATION: Seed or softwood cuttings.

CULTURE: Dawn redwood will grow in a variety of soils as long as sufficient moisture is present. Not as drought-tolerant in the Prairie States as bald cypress. Grows best on fertile, moist soils east of the Mississippi River, although attractive trees exist further west.

PESTS: Few. However, a stem canker is becoming more common.

NOTES: Sometimes referred to as a living fossil, since it was first described from fossils in 1941 and the first living trees were not discovered until 1948. Since that time, seedlings have been planted in various parts of the world. it has been promoted as a very fast growing, disease- and insect-free tree. This is only partly true in that it grows fast only if on a good, fertile, moist soil and in full sun and even though few diseases and insect pests have yet been noted; under stress and age, some problems will no doubt develop. The form is similar to bald cypress but more narrow and upright. Trees this author has seen do not have the overall visual quality of a good bald cypress. however, it is useful as a large, deciduous screen or form forming a visual barrier during the growing season. Some of the first trees planted in the United States are now 60 to 70 feet tall and produce cones with viable seed. One of the largest specimens, over 100 feet tall, is on the campus of William and Mary College in Williamsburg, Virginia. The St. Louis Botanical Gardens and National Arboretum in Washington, D.C. also have numerous large specimens.

CULTIVARS: 'National': with a very strict, upright growth habit. 'Sheridan Spire': more upright than the species but only moderately so.

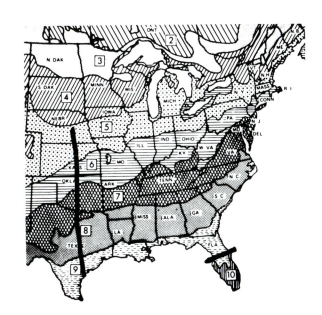

Morus alba L.   White Mulberry
Moraceae or Mulberry Family   Hardiness Zone 3
Native to China?

SIZE: 30 to 40 feet tall with a 25- to 35-foot spread. Rapid grower.
FORM: Medium-sized tree with a broad, spreading crown.
TEXTURE: Medium to coarse.   **EXPOSURE:** Sun.

LEAVES: Alternate, simple: ovate or oval, rather asymmetrical, or somewhat heart-shaped (variable). May be 2 1/2 to 8 inches long, 1 to 5 inches wide, and have 0 to 3 or more lobes. The margin has blunt teeth. Upper surface is olive green, glossy and smooth; petiole is slender and 1/2 to 1 1/2 inches long. Fair yellow fall color.

STEM: Young stems are reddish brown, generally smooth, zigzag, becoming tan with age. Bark on the old stem is brown to gray-brown and broken in narrow, irregular furrows, often twisted ridges. Wood is fairly hard and durable; moderately wind-resistant.

FLOWERS: Male and female flowers on the same tree (monoecious). Not showy.

FRUIT: Generally in late May or June. Oval, about 1/2 inch long and green turning white to pink with maturity. Sweet and edible.

COLOR: Foliage is olive green; yellow in the fall.

PROPAGATION: By seed, cuttings, or grafting.

CULTURE: Grows practically anywhere. An extremely tough, rugged tree, said to be grown in more countries throughout the world than any other species. Tolerates poor, infertile soils; grows with vigor on moist fertile soils. Very drought-tolerant. Was first introduced into the United States for use as windbreaks in the southern Great Plains, and has proven to be a most useful plant for this and other purposes. One of the more successful trees in heavy clay soils or disturbed soils.

PESTS: Borers on old trees or trees under stress; cotton root rot.

NOTES: A most useful tree in areas where selection of plant material is limited. Excels as a shade tree, windbreak or ornamental in the southern Great Plains.

CULTIVARS: 'Fruitless': commonly sold as fruitless mulberry, an excellent round-headed, medium-sized tree with bright green leaves. A rapid grower in most soils. 'Chapparal': a non fruiting, weeping form with cascading branches gives an unusual appearance. 'Hampton': a wide, spreading tree; fruitless. 'Lingan': glossy, leathery leaves; fruitless. 'Mapleleaf': may be several fruitless cultivars sold under this name. 'Stribling': a fast growing, fruitless clone with yellow fall color. Others exist.

RELATED SPECIES: *Morus rubra* L., red mulberry, is native to the central United States. Grows best on fertile, moist, bottomlands and is not as tolerant to poor, thin soils as is white mulberry; likewise it is less drought-resistant. An inferior plant for most uses. The two can best be distinguished by the fact that white mulberry twigs are glossy, not hairy, and its leaves are thin and smooth on upper and lower surfaces. The twigs on red mulberry are fuzzy, and its leaves are sandpapery to the touch, particularly on the upper surface.

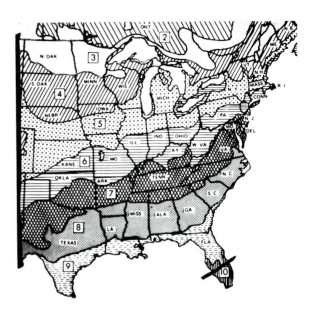

'Fruitless'

'Chapparal'

Nyssa sylvatica Marsh.   Black Gum, Sour Gum, or Black Tupelo
Cornaceae or Dogwood Family   Hardiness Zone 4
Native to the eastern United States.
SIZE: 60 to 100 feet tall with a 30- to 50-foot spread. Moderate grower.
FORM: Pyramidal tree when young, rounded crown when mature.
TEXTURE: Fine to medium.   **EXPOSURE:** Sun to partial shade.

LEAVES: Alternate, simple; 2 to 6 inches long, 1 to 3 inches wide with a smooth margin or a few widely spaced teeth. Shiny, dark green Above, paler and hairy below; brilliant red to red-orange very early in the fall.

STEM: Young stems are slender, gray to gray-black, hairy at first becoming smooth and reddish brown with age. Finally develop into an irregularly check-like bark, deeply furrowed and almost black. Wood is hard, very tough, durable and wind-resistant. The terminal bud is elongated, somewhat like the point on a lead pencil. However, unlike with the bud on an oak, there are only two or three bud scales visible.

FLOWERS: Male and female on separate trees or occasionally on the same tree. Not showy.

FRUIT: Ripens September to October. Small and plum-like, dark blue, on a long fruit stalk. The hard seed is football-shaped, with 10 to 12 ribs on the long axis.

COLOR: Foliage is shiny, dark green above, brilliant red to red-orange in the fall. Generally the first tree to turn color in the fall.

PROPAGATION: By seed.

CULTURE: Native to wet, swampy locations throughout the eastern half of the United States. Commonly found with bald cypress and willow along streams. Grows well in wet locations. However, it also does well on moderately dry soils when given reasonable care. Makes a desirable shade and ornamental tree, with supplemental watering, as far west as Dallas, Oklahoma City, Wichita, and Omaha. Responds to fertilization, mulching, and supplemental watering during dry periods. May need occasional pruning to aid in good branch development. This tree has been by-passed by the nursery industry, probably because of the difficulty of transplanting as a bare root or balled-in-burlap plant. It is also challenging to grow in the nursery as seedlings are variable and death of the terminal bud seems to occur more frequently on trees fertilized and cared for which, in turn requires more pruning. Best transplanted in the spring. Container-grown trees survive very well.

PESTS: None serious but a leaf spot disease may cause early leaf drop.

NOTES: Not commonly sold as an ornamental but should be planted a great deal more. Fall color appears very early: it is generally first to color of all the species and is spectacular. An adaptable species with good form, foliage, and fall color. Appears to tolerate urban conditions particularly areas with compacted soils which may be very wet for extended rainy periods during the spring and fall. Fruits may be somewhat messy over a sidewalk or patio. Should be planted more.

CULTIVARS: None known at the present time.

RELATED SPECIES: *Nyssa aquatica*, water tupelo, is native to areas that are swampy and has longer leaves and fruits than black gum. Seldom used as a landscape tree.

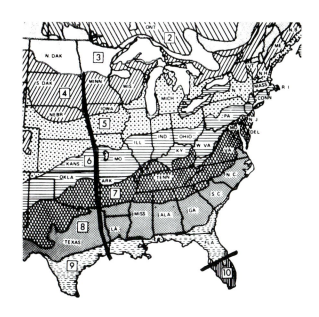

Ostrya virginiana K. Koch.   American or Eastern Hophornbeam
Betulaceae or Birch Family   Hardiness Zone 3
Native to the eastern United States.
SIZE: 20 to 50 feet tall with a 20- to 25-foot spread. Slow to moderate grower.
FORM: An irregular, central leader, small tree; pyramidal when young but more ovate with maturity.
TEXTURE: Medium.   **EXPOSURE:** Sun to shade.

LEAVES: Alternate, simple; ovate, with a pointed tip. Leaf margin is doubly-toothed. Generally 2 1/2 to 3 1/2 inches long, about 1 to 2 inches wide. Very short, hairy petiole, about 1/4 inch long. Upper surface is medium green, lower is a lighter pale green; sandpapery to the touch. Fall color is pale yellow to rust.

STEM: Young twigs are very slender, brown and hairy at first, later becoming smooth. Axillary buds are very small and shiny. Bark is very dark brown, eventually splitting into thin, vertical, shred-like scales. Wood is very hard, strong, tough; branches are usually right-angled to the main stem; very stout and vandal-resistant.

FLOWERS: Male and female separate but on the same tree (monoecious). Males are catkins in groups of two or three, female are on short stalks. Not showy.

FRUIT: A cluster of nutlets in bladder-like sacks combined to form a cone-like cluster resembling the "hops" used in making beer, thus the name, hophornbeam. The sack containing the nutlets is covered with stiff, bristly, spine-like hairs, readily embedded in the skin when handled.

COLOR: Foliage is pale green; pale yellow to rust in the fall.

PROPAGATION: By seed.

CULTURE: Native to upland sites and rocky hillsides; distinctly dryer sites than where *Carpinus* is found. Appears to tolerate a wide range of soils. Fairly drought resistant, tough and durable. Responds favorably to heavy mulching of the root system, similar to what occurs in nature with litter on the woodland floor. This also aids to conserve moisture and reduce competition from grass and weeds. Should be planted much more in urban areas with poor soils.

PESTS: None.

NOTES: A very tough, rugged, small tree. Very vandal- and wind-resistant. Tolerates a wide range of growing conditions and is moderately drought-resistant. Although it does not have a spectacular fall color and does not have deep green leaves, it has merit as a street or landscape tree because of its durability, size and form. Difficult to transplant from the wild. Should be grown as a nursery plant. Frequently confused with *Carpinus caroliniana* but easily distinguished, because *Ostrya* has sandpapery leaves, and a rough bark peeling in vertical strips or shred-like scales, whereas the leaves and bark of *Carpinus caroliniana* are smooth.

CULTIVARS: None known.

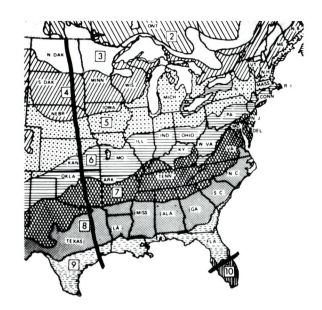

Oxydendrum arboreum (L.) DC.   Sourwood
Ericaceae or Heath Family   Hardiness Zone 5
Native to the eastern United States.

SIZE: 20- to 30-foot tree is most common, occasionally larger. Slow grower.
FORM: Neat, pyramidal tree with rounded crown and drooping branches.
TEXTURE: Medium.   **EXPOSURE:** Sun or partial shade.

LEAVES: Alternate, simple. Shiny dark green in summer, red to red-purple in the fall. Leaves are 4 to 7 inches long with finely saw-toothed margins and few hairs along the veins below. Sour tasting.

STEM: Young stems are slender and drooping; smooth and green to red-brown with age. Axillary buds are small, and nearly inconspicuous. Older stems develop an interesting, furrowed bark: gray with scale ridges. Wood is stout and durable.

FLOWERS: White, in drooping terminal clusters 3 to 10 inches long. Very showy and fragrant during July or August.

FRUIT: A small, dry capsule. Not showy.

COLOR: Flowers are white. Foliage is shiny, dark green; fall color is red to red-purple.

PROPAGATION: By seed or softwood cuttings in late spring with difficulty.

CULTURE: Similar to flowering dogwood in that it **must have** a moist, fertile, well drained soil to do well. In areas of heavy clays, mounds or large raised planters filled with good soil, heavy mulch, and faithful watering during dry periods are required. For example, flowering dogwood will grow well in Tulsa, Oklahoma, with proper site selection, whereas sourwood will struggle on the same site without further mulching, watering, and care. Keeping grass competition away aids considerably, especially when young or in a sunny location.

PESTS: A leaf spot disease may cause early leaf drop and a gradual weakening of the tree in some locations. Few other problems.

NOTES: A refined, high quality, small tree where it can be grown. Rivals flowering dogwood in many respects for form and flower show. The flowers are especially timely in that crapemyrtle is the only other landscape plant that blooms in late July or August. Outside of its native habitat of Pennsylvania, the Carolinas, and the Gulf Coast west to Louisiana, it requires additional planning and consideration to do well in the landscape. Not drought-tolerant. Perhaps the drying summer winds of the Texas, Oklahoma, Kansas corridor are more injurious than generally realized. In these areas, it is an effort to grow but very rewarding if successful.

CULTIVARS: None known. Many individual seedlings are deserving but because of the difficulty in rooting of cuttings, none have made it into the trade.

155

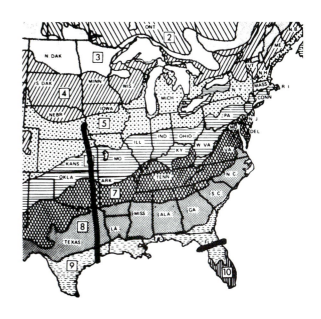

Parkinsonia aculeata L.   Parkinsonia or Jerusalem Thorn
Leguminosae or Legume Family   Hardiness Zone 9
Native to tropical America.
SIZE: 25- to 30-foot tree with a 20- to 25-foot spread. Rapid grower.
FORM: Single-stemmed tree with umbrella-like crown.
TEXTURE: Fine, fern-like.   **EXPOSURE:** Sun.

LEAVES: Alternate, compound; 6 to 12 inches long with 20 to 30 pairs of very small leaflets. Generally 2 long, slender leaves occur at each node and are accompanied by heavy spines. Leaflets drop early, leaving the long, slender, central leaf stock. leaves are dark green with no fall color.

STEM; The young stem zigzags. All stems are heavily armed by two sharp spines at each node. Spines remain on the tree for many years. Young stems are green and remain green for several years, finally turning brown with small, smooth, thin scales. Wood is hard and durable.

FLOWERS: Yellow. Very showy against the fern-like, dark green foliage. Fragrant, in clusters of 4 to 6 inches long; in early spring or with a flush of growth following a dry period. Pea-shaped flowers, persisting for a week or more.

Fruit: Slender pods, 2 to 4 inches long, constricted between seeds, brown at maturity. Seeds are green turning brown at maturity. Seeds require acid or physical scarification treatment to germinate.

COLOR: Flowers are yellow; foliage is dark green and fern-like.

PROPAGATION: By seed. Acid treatment is required for germination unless the seeds are collected before the seed coat matures (while seeds are green) and are planted immediately. Filing or other means of seed coat opening to water will also aid germination.

CULTURE: A very tough, heat- and drought-tolerant, small tree. Does well in all but poorly drained, heavy clay soils. Responds with vigor to fertilizer; a very fast grower when young. This tree defends itself admirable against all but the chain saw. Does not drop branches (and spines) on lawns or patio areas but is short-lived.

PESTS: None serious.

NOTES: A very attractive, tough, and durable, small tree. Functions, very well in public areas when vandalism may otherwise be a problem. The very light-textured shade from the loose, fern-like foliage is very pleasant near a patio or outdoor living area. The wood is very strong for such a fast-growing tree, thus breakage in wind storms is rarely a problem. May occasionally seed itself into unwanted locations, but not a pest tree.

CULTIVARS: None known.

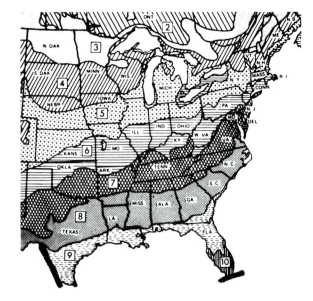

Paulownia tomentosa (Thunb) Steud.
Bignoniaceae or Trumpet Creeper Family
Native to China.

Royal Paulownia or Empress Tree
Hardiness Zone 6b or 7

SIZE: to 50 feet tall with a spread of 40 to 50 feet. Rapid grower.
FORM: Irregular, broad, spreading tree.
TEXTURE: Very coarse.　　　　　　　　　**EXPOSURE:** Sun to partial shade.

LEAVES: Opposite, more or less heart-shaped; 6 to 12 inches long and 4 to 8 inches wide, with a smooth or occasionally gently waving margin. Young leaves are densely wooly, velvety to touch, with the upper surface becoming less wooly with age. petioles are 4 to 6 inches long and are also wooly. medium green, no fall color: they turn black and drop with a hard freeze.

STEM: Young stems are smooth, large, and brittle. Occasionally grows as a central leader tree but more commonly has several large branches developing near the ground due to freezes killing the late fall growth. Bark is rather smooth and gray-black. Wood is weak and brittle.

FLOWERS; Blue-violet flowers appear before the leaves. Very striking and fragrant. Flowers are catalpa-like; 2 inches long, and 1 1/2 to 2 inches across the face.

FRUIT: A rounded capsule about 2 inches in diameter and wooly. Splits into two sections containing many small seeds that are readily scattered and become weeds.

COLOR: Flowers are blue-violet.

PROPAGATION: By seed or cuttings; very easy (unfortunately).

CULTURE: Grows anywhere in Zone 7 and southward, along road cuts, disturbed areas, cracks in sidewalks, etc. The invasive tree-or-heaven of the South. This tree has been sold by unscrupulous promoters to the unsuspecting as "the royal empress tree that grows in any soil and will be as tall as you house in a single season". Sold throughout the United States even though only cold hardy in Zone 7 and southward. Rarely flowers in Zone 7 since the flower buds or flowers are killed by late spring freezes.

PESTS: None (unfortunately).

NOTES: Not a good tree. Is occasionally planted as an oddity in that the blue-violet flowers are very uncommon. However, if it flowers, seeds and seedlings are sure to follow. Paulownia has naturalized over much of the southeastern United States, particularly in disturbed areas and around poorly maintained housing or businesses. A plant to avoid in most cases, yet there has been some interest in growing Paulownia for lumber.

CULTIVARS: None known.

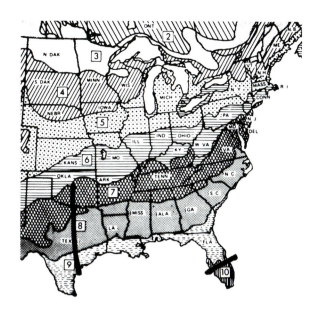

seed pods

Phellodendron amurense Rupr.   Amur Corktree
Rutaceae or Rue Family   Hardiness Zone 4
Native to China and Japan.
SIZE: 30 to 50 feet tall with similar spread. Slow grower.
FORM: Low, umbrella tree with open branching.
TEXTURE: Medium.   **EXPOSURE:** Sun.

LEAVES: Opposite, compound; 4 to 6 inches long with 7 to 13 ovate leaflets that are opposite on the rachis with a distinct, terminal leaflet present. The margins of the leaflets are smooth. leaves are a dark, rich green; very attractive, but only a fair yellow-brown in the fall.

STEM; Young stems are very stout, slightly yellow-brown to brown, and smooth except for distinct lenticels and prominent, horseshoe-shaped leaf scars. Roots are also yellow when scraped. Inner bark of young stems is yellow to yellow-green; very distinct. On rapidly growing limbs of a young tree, the bark develops a shallow, furrowing pattern. However, with age the bark becomes deeply furrowed, soft and corky. Attractive and distinct. Wood is not dense but is quite strong. Breakage is rarely a problem.

FLOWERS: Yellow-green, in 4- to 6-inch clusters during May or June. Not showy. Male and female flowers on separate trees (dioecious).

FRUIT: Black, rounded, about 1/2 inch. Matures in September of October; remaining on the tree until mid to late winter.

COLOR: Foliage is dark, rich green.

PROPAGATION: Seed.

CULTURE: A tough and durable tree once established. However, with conventional nursery practices, it has a reputation of being tough to transplant. On the other hand, a high percentage of trees grown with containers that stimulate root-branching survive when transplanted. Drought-tolerant once established in a good soil; however, is sensitive to drought and drying winds when young. For example, trees in central Oklahoma survive, but grow only a few inches each year and suffer leaf scorch in summer when temperatures reach 100 degrees F and humidity is low, even if they are drip-irrigated. Photoperiod-sensitive as are some of the pines and other conifers. In the South where the photoperiod is shorter during the growing season, growth is restricted whereas in the North with long summer days, the growth is much more rapid.

PESTS: None to very few.

NOTES: A spectacular, low, spreading tree where it can be grown and sufficient space exists. A super tree for climbing or for an outdoor living area in summer. The crown is open and airy, allowing air movement and sun rays to penetrate, yet provides a most pleasant respite from the heat (see photograph). Deserving of more attention in the nursery and landscape trade now that it can be more easily grown for transplanting.

CULTIVARS: 'Macho': thick leathery leaves. A male so does not fruit; otherwise, similar to the species.

RELATED SPECIES: *Phellodendron chinense* C.K. Schneid., Chinese corktree, is similar in all respects except it doe snot grow as tall, rarely exceeds 25 to 40 feet tall and leaflets are slightly wider than those of amur corktree.

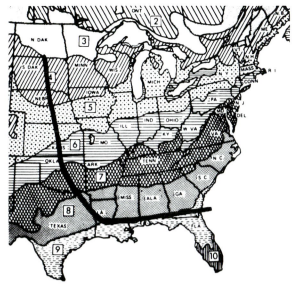

P. chinense   P. amurense

Pistacia chinensis Bunge.   Chinese Pistache
Anacardaceae or Suman Family   Hardiness zone 6
Native to China.
SIZE: 20 to 40 feet tall with a 20- to 30-foot spread. Moderate grower.
FORM: Low, umbrella-like, crowned tree.
TEXTURE: Fine.   **EXPOSURE:** Sun.

LEAVES: Alternate, once-compound; 8 to 10 inches long, 4 to 5 inches wide. Generally 10 to 14 leaflets, lanceolate to slightly ovate, on very short stalks; rarely is a terminal leaflet present. medium to dark green above, paler green below. Leaves have a very pronounced odor when crushed. They remain green late into the fall, finally bursting into a spectacular orange to red-orange, rivaling the show of the sugar maples of the Northeast. A brilliant fall color on most trees most years; however, an occasional seedling may have only moderate fall color.

STEM: Young stem is tan, rugged in appearance, with large, rounded axillary and terminal buds in late summer, fall, and winter. Stem retains tan color as it ages, finally turning gray-brown and developing a shallowly furrowed, irregular, patchy bark. Sometimes takes on a salmon color when pieces of the old bark slough off. Wood is extremely hard, durable, and decay-resistant: so very wind-, ice-, and vandal-resistant.

FLOWERS: Male and female on separate trees (dioecious). Not showy.

FRUIT: Small, round, about 1/4 inch or less in diameter. Green, turning purple-red in the fall. Generally the seed is viable only in the southern United States where the growing season is sufficiently long. Most viable seed comes from California where the tree is also quite successful. Some females set sufficient seed to be attractive.

COLOR: Foliage is medium to dark green; orange to red-orange in the fall. Spectacular.

PROPAGATION: Seed. Cuttings simply do not root and grafting is difficult.

CULTURE: Extremely tough, durable, small tree. Grows best in a deep, well drained soil but tolerates a wide range of conditions and grows in most urban conditions, regardless of soil types. Very drought-resistant: tolerates extreme heat from nearly desert-like atmosphere to low humidity and drying winds. Very deep-rooted. Transplants well in the spring or from containers. An "ugly duckling" when young, but worth the wait and effort. Needs pruning when young to assist in good branch structure and spacing. Sometimes said to be a slow grower but, with good management, it will grow three or more feet a year. I have been working with and promoting this tree since 1970 and have yet to find a serious weakness or drawback. Pistache is quite sensitive to triazine and sulfonylurea-type herbicides.

PESTS: None serious.

NOTES: Excellent medium-sized tree with very durable wood. Develops an oval, umbrella-like crown somewhat reminiscent of the American elm, but much smaller in stature. Excellent light-textured shade during the growing season. Spectacular in the fall. Nearly disease- and insect-free, and the fruit is not a problem. A near perfect tree. Should be planted far more, particularly throughout the South and Southwest.

CULTIVARS: None known.

RELATED SPECIES: *Pistacia vera* is the pistacio nut of commerce. A small tree of about 30 feet high, but tolerates temperatures only to 5 to 10 degrees F, thus a Zone 8 or 9 plant. Sometimes planted across the southern states, but inferior to Chinese pistache in shade and ornamental features.

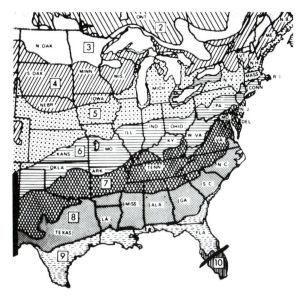

Platanus occidentalis L.　　　　　　　　Sycamore or American Planetree
Platanaceae or Sycamore Family　　　　Hardiness Zone 3
Native to the eastern United States.

SIZE: 150 feet tall or more, may have a 100- to 125-foot spread. Growth rate is rapid when young, slower with age.

FORM: Huge, slightly pyramidal to round-headed tree with immense, spreading branches.

TEXTURE: Coarse.　　　　　　　　　　**EXPOSURE:** Sun.

LEAVES: Alternate, simple. May reach 10 to 12 inches long, 6 to 8 inches wide with 5 main lobes (sometime 3) very coarsely toothed or may be lobed a second time. Papery thin, medium green above, paler green beneath with dense fuzz on the underneath side. The base of the leaf completely covers the axillary or terminal buds so they are not visible until the leaves drop, like removing the cap from a pen. This feature readily identifies the genus *Platanus*. Little fall color, slightly orange-brown, attractive against the whitish bark.

STEM: Young stem is moderately stout and green to slightly gray-brown. Hairy at first, smooth later, slightly zigzag. Axillary and terminal buds are cone-shaped, covered by the base of the leaf. Bark is dark gray when young; however, after the limbs reach one inch or more in diameter, bark is white to grayish white and showy. Old trunks may be very rough and platy with dark brown to gray-brown scales. Wood is moderately durable.

FLOWERS: Male and female flowers are separate on the same tree. Not showy.

FRUIT: Golfball-like, 1 to 1 1/2 inch in diameter, with many seeds. Green when young, brown when mature, hanging on the tree throughout the fall, generally shedding in late spring. Only 1 fruit ball per string-like stalk.

COLOR: Foliage is medium green above; light orange-brown in the fall. Not very showy except as a contrast to the whitish branches. Bark is white to greenish white on branches up to 10 inches in diameter, varying with seedlings and growth rate.

PROPAGATION: Seed collected in late winter or hardwood or softwood cuttings.

CULTURE: Native to river bottoms. Moderately tolerant to a wide range of soil conditions as long as ample moisture is present. Not a drought-tolerant tree. However, will tolerate low humidity and drying winds, as long as roots have moisture. Under good circumstances grows very rapidly when young; slower with age. Needs only slight pruning to assist in good branch development. Easy to transplant.

PESTS: Anthracnose attacks leaves and young twigs. May completely defoliate a young tree one or more times during a wet spring. This causes the death of enough young twigs to cause a litter problem. Lacebug may be a serious problem some seasons.

NOTES: An enormous tree often planted where smaller trees should be. Should be used only where ample space allows for good branch development, such as in parks and large estates. Generally not for the single story dwelling unless plenty of space exists. Creates considerable litter by dropping leaves, twigs and, from a middle-aged tree, bark.

RELATED SPECIES: *Platanus* X *acerifolia* (Ait.) Willd., London planetree, a hybrid between *P. occidentalis* L. and *P. orientalis* L., European sycamore or oriental planetree. Hardy through Zone 5 and resistant to anthracnose. A smaller tree, rarely reaching more than 100 feet tall. Otherwise, branch development, bark color, leaf size, and adaptability are very similar. American planetree has 1 fruit ball per stalk and London and European planetrees have 2 or 3 per stalk.

CULTIVARS: 'Bloodgood': resistant to anthracnose. 'Columbia' and 'Liberty': good pyramidal forms, anthracnose-resistant. From the National Arboretum.

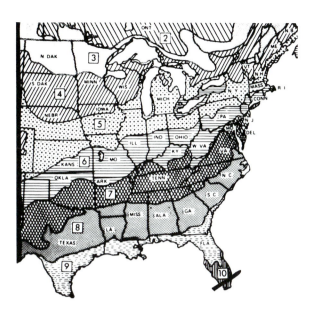

Platanus acerifolia

Populus alba L.   White or Silver-leaved Poplar
Salicaceae or Willow Family   Hardiness Zone 3
Native to southern and central Europe and central Asia to Siberia.
SIZE: 60-80 foot tree with 40-50 foot spread. Rapid grower.
FORM: Broad, oval to low spreading tree.
TEXTURE: Medium.   **EXPOSURE:** Sun.

LEAVES: Alternate, simple; more or less oval with several bluntly pointed tips; quite variable. Upper surface is deep dark green, lower surface and petiole are chalky white. In the wind, leaves take on a two-toned appearance. Generally 2 to 4 inches long, 1 1/2 to 2 inches wide. Fall color is generally a pale yellow: not spectacular, but attractive with the white bark.

STEM: Young stem is slender, chalky white and hairy at first, becoming smooth and gray-green with age. Later the bark develops a smooth, white to whitish green color with prominent diamond-shaped lenticels. Old bark eventually fissures near the base into firm, dark ridges. Very attractive bark. In many instances it rivals the birch or sycamore for bark color and stem interest in the winter. Wood is moderately soft, somewhat brittle, and subject to vandalism.

FLOWERS: Male and female on separate trees (dioecious). Not showy.

FRUIT: Capsule, about 1/4 inch long, fuzzy with two valves. Very small, but contains numerous seeds. Not showy.

COLOR: Foliage is deep green above, chalky white below; pale yellow in the fall. Bark is white until very old, then near black.

PROPAGATION: Cuttings, root sprouts, or suckers. Very easy.

CULTURE: Grows over an unusually wide range. Will grow moderately well in any soil type or conditions. An amazingly durable tree: tolerates wet conditions and extremely dry, droughty sites. Will grow from southern Canada to central Florida and as far west as many areas of the Rocky Mountain regions and California. Wood is only moderately strong, but this should not be considered a serious disadvantage. Suckers profusely when in stress but, as long as the tree is growing vigorously, few suckers occur. Once wind, insect or root damage occurs, the suckers begin and can be a major problem. However, it is a tree of considerable merit, useful in many locations where other trees can not be grown due to poor soils or extreme site conditions.

PESTS: Leaf hoppers occasionally. Poplar canker is less common on white poplar than on other species, although occasionally it does kill a tree. Crown gall is very common. Although it does not appear to limit the growth in many instances, it probably serves as a source of crown gall to spread to other landscape plants.

NOTES: An attractive tree in the landscape: good form, bark color, and texture. A good shade tree that grows in a wide range of conditions: wet or dry, hot or cold, good or poor soils. These are pluses that must be weighed in favor of white poplar. However, the weakness of the wood, the crown gall problem, and the development of suckers with age or stress are considerable disadvantages. Still, it has a great deal of merit for many sites.

CULTIVARS: 'Bolleana' or 'Pyramidalis': a dense, narrow, columnar tree with leaves slightly more disc-shaped than those of the species, but similar in color and size. Similar to *P. nigra* 'Italica', lombardy poplar, in appearance but superior for most uses. 'Globosa': a small tree or large shrub with dense, oval to globe-shaped head; leaves only slightly lobed, slightly pink when very young. 'Pendula': weeping branches.

'Bolleana'

Populus deltoides Marsh.   Eastern Cottonwood
Salicaceae or Willow Family   Hardiness Zone 3
Native to the eastern United States.
SIZE: 80- to 100-foot tree with a 40- to 60-foot spread. Rapid grower.
FORM: Ovate-crowned large tree.
TEXTURE: Medium.   **EXPOSURE:** Sun.

LEAVES: Alternate, simple; 3 to 6 inches long, 3 to 4 inches wide, and more or less triangular with a bluntly toothed margin. Deep, dark green above; shiny, apple green below. Petiole is long and flattened allowing the leaves to flutter in any breeze. Fall color is bright buttery yellow.

STEM: Young twigs are moderately stout, light brown or tan, with large, bold, more or less football-shaped terminal buds during fall and the dormant period. As stems get larger, bark becomes a greenish yellow to gray-green, eventually thickening and deeply furrowing on old trees to become gray to silvery gray to nearly black.

FLOWERS: Male and female on separate trees (dioecious). Not showy.

FRUIT: Long cluster of capsules containing seeds in a cottony mass, thus the common name.

COLOR: Foliage is deep green above; bright yellow in the fall.

PROPAGATION: Seed, cuttings, or transplanting of trees from streambanks and other disturbed locations where they develop naturally.

CULTURE: Native to bottomlands along rivers and streams, generally in rich moist soils. Does not tolerate poor, dry soils. However, it will tolerate a dry climate in areas where soils are moderately good and moisture is present for at least part of the year, such as along small streams, rivers, or water features. Under these conditions it does well throughout most of the Great Plains. Very rapid grower. An old tree is one of 50-70 years. Wood is soft and decays rapidly when the tree becomes mature or when limb damage allows decay organisms to enter.

PESTS: Borers may attack newly transplanted, or old or weakened trees. Wind damage may allow entry of decay organisms that could substantially weaken the tree.

NOTES: A most useful tree in areas where a tree of enormous stature is desired in a short period of time. In many areas of the Great Plains where few trees are well adapted, the eastern cottonwood or other closely related species serves a real need in providing shade and attractive specimens in the landscape. Tends to naturalize along streambanks, disturbed areas, abandoned fields, and other wet locations. A good tree where species are limited. Must be criticized for its weak wood and extremely rapid growth on a good site. A desirable feature is the rustling of leaves with any slight breeze, lending a sound feature to the landscape which is not normally provided by plants. Profuse root development may plug drains, etc. Very bad about developing massive fibrous roots in golf greens, other areas of intensive turf culture or flower beds. Cotton from female trees may plug radiators of autos and air conditioners and become matted on window screens. Many cities have ordinances against planting cottonwood because of the weak wood, large size, massive root system, and heavy seed production.

CULTIVARS: Male trees are commonly propagated as cottonless cottonwoods. These are generally not superior, except that the seed and "cotton" do not develop and create problems as with female trees. Names include 'Souixland', Robusta', 'Lydick' and others. Other extremely fast growing cultivars are being developed for pulpwood production but have no place in landscaping.

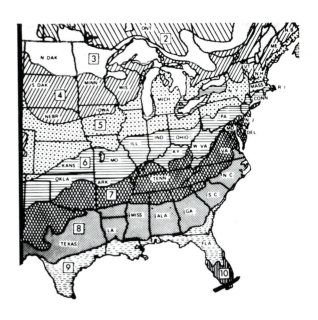

Populus nigra L. 'Italica'
Salicaceae or Willow Family
Native to Europe and Asia.

Lombardy Poplar
Hardiness Zone 3

SIZE: 40 to 80 feet with a spread of 6 to 10 feet. Rapid grower.
FORM: Dense, narrowly upright tree.
TEXTURE: Medium.

EXPOSURE: Sun.

LEAVES: Alternate, simple; with a sawtooth margin. Generally 2 to 3 1/2 inches long and 1 1/2 to 3 inches wide. Shiny, bright green above, dull green below (not white). Petioles are flattened, allowing the leaves to flutter slightly in the wind. Fall color is buttery yellow.

STEM: Young stems are slender, light tan, or slightly reddish, shiny and glossy, with sharply pointed, dark brown buds. As the stem ages, it becomes green, then finally light brown with a rough and irregularly ridged bark. Wood is weak and brittle.

FLOWERS: This cultivar has infertile flowers and no fruit.

FRUIT: None.

COLOR: Foliage is shiny, bright green; buttery yellow in the fall.

PROPAGATION: Cuttings.

CULTURE: Will grow in most soils. Tolerates considerable drought or wet locations, good or poor soils, heat or cold. A very rugged plant in terms of establishment. However, it is a short-lived tree subject to wind damage and stem canker. it suckers profusely when damage to the crown occurs. The root system is shallow and may cause problems in drain tiles or lawns, flower beds, and gardens.

PESTS: The most serious problem is poplar canker which attacks young twigs, trunk, and stem at various locations and often kills half or more of the crown of the tree before it reaches ten years of age. Thrips may be a leaf problem in some instances. Crown gall may also be a problem.

NOTES: A very tough, rugged, young tree. Rises like an exclamation point in the land-scape. For a short-term, quick effect or a screen, it may be useful. However, should be used only with caution and for short-term considerations. Is profuse in developing roots into drains or sewers. Very shallow-rooted: difficult to grow other shrubs or grass in conjunction. Use of this tree should be discouraged. Commonly promoted by chain stores and others as a quick screen (yes: quick to grow, quick to die). Best identified by the green underneath surface of the leaf, the serrate leaf margin, and the green to grayish bark, whereas *Populus alba* 'Bolleana' has irregularly lobed leaf margins, leaves are chalky white below and the bark is white or greenish white.

CULTIVARS: 'Italica' is the most common *Populus nigra* cultivar grown in this country. The parent plant is rarely seen.

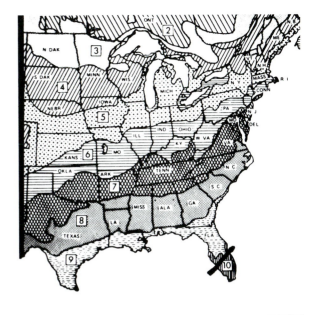

Prosopis juliflora Torr.   Mesquite
Leguminosae or Legume Family   Hardiness Zone 6
Native to the southwestern United States and northern Mexico.
SIZE: 20 to 30 feet tall with variable spread. Moderate grower.
FORM: A small tree or large shrub.
TEXTURE: Fine.   **EXPOSURE:** Sun.

LEAVES: Alternate, deciduous, generally twice compound. Leaflets are long and slender, dark green, about 2 inches long by 1/4 inch wide. The petiole is several inches long, then splits into what appears to be 2 compound leaves. A most unusual leaf arrangement. Leaves emerge late in the spring and drop early with little color change.

STEM: Young twigs zigzag, usually armed with spines from 1/2 to 2 inches long, but sometimes spineless. The old bark is rough, reddish brown to nearly black, split into vertical section.

FLOWERS: May through September. Perfect, in creamy to yellowish green cylindrical clusters. Pleasantly fragrant.

FRUIT: A rough, leathery, brown pod; 5 to 9 inches long. Somewhat constricted between seeds.

COLOR: Foliage is dark green. Flowers are creamy to yellowish green.

PROPAGATION: Seed.

CULTURE: Native to poor, arid soils, especially over-grazed pasture land in the Southwest where it becomes especially troublesome. However, when grown as a single or multiple stemmed tree in the landscape, it is quite attractive and not a problem. Grows in practically any soil as long as it is not poorly drained. It is difficult to transplant from the wild due to the strong tap root. However, it transplants well when grown from seed in containers that provide for air-root-pruning.

PESTS: None serious.

NOTES: When encouraged to grow as a single-stem tree it can provide a fern-like texture and a fragrance to landscapes that are hot, dry, and windswept. As a multiple-stemmed tree, branching low to the ground, it remains in scale with single story dwellings. Unlike on open range land, it is not a problem plant in the landscape, except for the spines.

CULTIVARS: None. However, an ecological race generally referred to as velvet mesquite has leaves with many short, velvety hairs. Otherwise, it is similar in size and adaptation to the species.

RELATED SPECIES: *Prosopis pubescens*, screwbean, is native to the same geographic area and grows to 25 feet tall with even more delicately compound leaves and yellowish flowers. The fruits are coiled like a door spring. Rarely seen in landscapes but has merit.

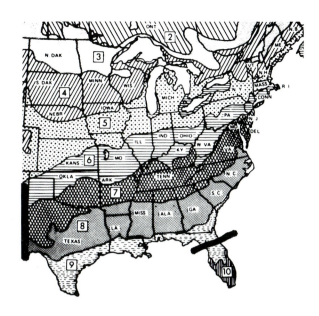

Prunus armeniaca L.   Apricot
Rosaceae or Rose Family   Hardiness Zone 5
Native to western Asia.
SIZE: A small tree reaching a height of 20 to 25 feet with a spread of 20 to 30 feet.
FORM: Broad, oval crown on a distinct tree stem.
TEXTURE: Medium.   **EXPOSURE:** Sun.

LEAVES: Alternate, simple; ovate to round-ovate or almost heart-shaped, 2 to 3 inches long and 2 to 3 inches wide, abruptly pointed at the tip. Variable. Many small teeth on the leaf margin. Medium green above, lighter green below, and fairly soft and pliable to the touch. Veins on the underneath side of the leaf are pubescent. Petiole may be reddish.

STEM: An upright-growing central leader early, generally losing this central leader system after it reaches a height of 6 to 10 feet, developing a multitude of branches that form a broad spreading crown. The young stem is a light cinnamon brown, becoming a dark gray-brown with a slightly rough or flaking bark on the old stem.

FLOWERS: About 1 inch across, pinkish to white, solitary, generally before the leaves appear. Often killed by late spring freezes due to their very early emergence.

FRUIT: From 1 to 2 1/2 inches in diameter, edible, nearly smooth on the outer surface, on a very short stem. The stone in the center of the fruit is nearly smooth and the enclosed seed may be poisonous if eaten in quantity. Apricots are a common tree grown in the garden or in the landscape, particuarly for the edible fruits.

COLOR: Foliage is medium green. Flowers are pinkish to white but not particularly showy. Fruit is green, turning reddish yellow when mature (if you are lucky).

PROPAGATION: Seed or grafting of selected cultivars on seedling understock.

CULTURE: One of the toughest, most durable and drought-resistant of fruit trees. It is commonly found surviving in old windbreaks that are 30 to 40 years old with zero care. Extremely drought-resistant: does well in western Oklahoma and the panhandle of Texas. In the more humid conditions of the eastern and southeastern states, borers may become a problem. A slow to moderate grower.

PESTS: Borers, particularly on old plants under considerable stress; more common in the eastern range of the United States than in the Southwest. Some leaf feeding insects may be a problem at times.

NOTES: A very useful, attractive, and durable small tree. Very dependable, particularly in the West and Southwest where the selection of plant materials is limited. Makes a good shade tree for patios, remains in scale for most single family dwellings, and may be used as a dual-purpose landscape plant and occasional fruit producer. Requires a minimum of care in terms of spraying and attention when compared with other common fruit trees such as apples, peaches, or pears. Seed may be poisonous. A good small tree. XX-POISON-XX

CULTIVARS: Numerous cultivars exist, primarily varying in the size, texture, and quality of the fruit and earliness of flowering.

RELATED SPECIES: *Prunus mume*, Japanese apricot, is a tree 25 to 30 feet tall with a rounded crown, green twigs, and white to red flowers. 'Alba Plena': double white flowers. 'Peggy Clark': near red flowers. Other cultivars exist, especially in the Orient.

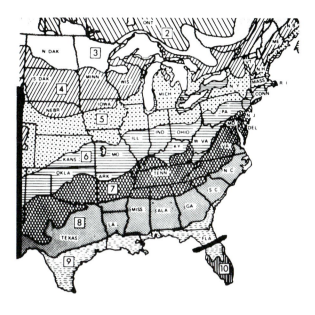

Prunus cerasifera Ehrh.   Purpleleaf or Cherry Plum
Rosaceae or Rose Family   Hardiness Zone 3
Native to western Asia.
SIZE: 15 to 25 feet tall with a 10- to 12-foot spread. Moderate grower.
FORM: Single-stemmed, pyramidal, small tree with vase shape and dense foliage.
TEXTURE: Medium.   **EXPOSURE:** Sun.

LEAVES: Alternate, simple; ovate to obovate, 1 1/2 to 3 inches long, 1-2 inches wide, rounded at the base, tapering to the tip. Leaves have fine teeth with glands on the margin. Most cultivars currently grown have purplish or red-purple leaves, particularly when exposed to full sun; in shade the leaves are more green and less striking. Leaves are soft and pliable.

STEM: Young stems are slender; reddish brown to purple-brown when young, becoming dark, almost purple-black to purple-gray with age. Stems have large, prominent lenticels, particularly on the old stem. Inner bark is pink. Bark on old trunks splits or peels in plates or patches.

FLOWERS: Pink to pinkish white in early April; about one inch in diameter. Flowers open about the time the leaves appear; somewhat showy but not as striking as crabapples.

FRUIT: A plum about one inch long, elongated, obscured by the leaves, ripens in August. Edible but not particularly tasty.

COLOR: Foliage is purplish to red-purple in full sun on most cultivars.

PROPAGATION: Cuttings or grafting of cultivars. Seeds germinate but are quite variable.

CULTURE: Grows well in a moderate range of soils throughout the United States. Tolerates heat and drought moderately well, but does best in a light-textured well-drained soil with good moisture conditions. Not particularly suited to poor, compacted soils, where stress makes it more susceptible to borers. Best suited to full sun conditions, where foliage color will develop to its maximum potential.

PESTS: Peach twig borer is the most serious. Brown rot causes blossoms and twigs to wither and die. Occasionally mites on the foliage, particularly in hot dry locations.

NOTES: Spectacular small- to medium-sized tree in terms of foliage color. Very dominating in the landscape. Retention of foliage color from spring to fall is variable with cultivars. Long in cultivation: probably introduced about the 16th century, with many Selections and hybrids. Some have crossed with other species, thus specific information on parentage of many cultivars is difficult to find. A much confused group. Excellent as a lawn, patio, or tub specimen. Easy to cultivate and tolerates a wide range of growing conditions.

CULTIVARS: 'Atropurpurea': an old selection with purple leaves larger than normal and pink flowers. Fruit is dark, wine-red, often sold incorrectly as 'Pissardi'. 'Thundercloud': very deep purple foliage, single white flower, more upright grower. 'Newport': pink flowers, striking purple foliage. Many other cultivars exist.

RELATED SPECIES: *Prunus* x *cistena* N.E. Hansen, purpleleaf sand cherry, is a cross between *Prunus cerasifera* 'Atropurpurea' and *Prunus pumila*. Rarely grows more than 14 feet tall. Leaves are hairy along the lower midrib, flowers are white/pinkish, fragrant and rarely fruits. Very cold hardy and commonly used in hardiness Zones 5 and 4. 'Minnesota Red': darker purple-red leaves.

Prunus persica (L.) Batsch.   Common Peach
Rosaceae or Rose Family   Hardiness Zone 5
Native to China.
SIZE: 20 to 30 feet tall with equal spread. Rapid grower.
FORM: Small tree with a wide, spreading, oval crown.
TEXTURE: Medium.   **EXPOSURE:** Sun.

LEAVES: Alternate, simple; very elongated or spear-shaped, 3 to 6 inches long. Dark, glossy green with a finely sawtooth margin and with glands on the petiole. Fall color is yellow, not showy, and leaves drop early.

STEM: Young stems are stout, smooth, green turning light reddish brown by the end of the first growing season. Both flower and vegetative buds are covered with dense hairs. Older stems are silvery gray with a black, furrowed bark developing only on very old trees. Wood is moderately stout, but subject to breakage during heavy fruit loads and storms.

FLOWERS: Pink, before the leaves, very showy, either single as on fruiting cultivars or double on flowering selections. Flowers are often damaged by late spring frosts, which limit consistent fruit production in many areas.

FRUIT: The common fuzzy peach. Color, size, and shape vary with cultivar. Delicious: a fresh ripe peach is mouth-watering.

COLOR: Leaves are dark, glossy green. Flowers are pink.

PROPAGATION: Softwood cuttings or grafting of cultivars onto seedlings or dwarfing rootstocks. Grown from seed the fruit size and quality will generally be disappointing.

CULTURE: Peaches will grow on a wide range of soils as long as reasonable fertility and moisture exist. Grow best on deep, fertile, sandy soils with supplemental water during dry periods but serve well as landscape trees in urban areas if mulched, fertilized and watered. In order to obtain good fruit, plant only cultivars adapted for your area since flower buds open in the spring after the required number of chilling hours (temperatures below 40 degrees F) has been met. Along the Gulf Coast, peach trees have short chilling requirements, whereas farther north, the same tree would flower far too early and no fruit would be produced. Likewise, a northern cultivar would flower poorly, if at all, in the Deep South because the required amount of flower bud chilling time would not be met.

PESTS: Many. Do not plant a peach tree without full knowledge of the spraying required for good fruit production. Even the double flowering ornamental cultivars require spraying for aphids, mites, borers, tent caterpillars and other insects. On the other hand, fruit tree sprays with both insecticides and fungicides to control brown rot and other diseases work well, but you must spray 3 to 5 times, beginning with the first show of pink.

NOTES: Peaches require work and attention and are short-lived under most conditions, but are worth the effort. No peach ever tasted better than the one you grew. Dwarf cultivars are grafted onto sand cherries which restrict their size but not their fruit production.

CULTIVARS: Many. Most widely known is 'Alberta', but in most areas, superior cultivars exist. For example, in Oklahoma, the cultivar, 'June Bride', has medium fruits and is one of the more consistent producers since all flowers do not open at the same time. This means the fruit do not ripen together, which is fine for the home gardener but not acceptable to the commercial grower. 'Alba Plena': double white flowers, few fruits. 'Early Double Red': double red flowers, few fruits. Check with your local state university for the best cultivars for your area.

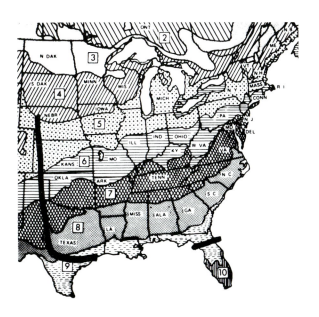

a double flowering cultivar

Prunus serotina Ehrh.　　　　　　　　Black Cherry
Rosaceae or Rose Family　　　　　　　Hardiness Zone 3
Native to a wide range of the eastern United States and Canada.
SIZE: 60- to 80-foot tree with limited spread. Moderate grower.
FORM: Narrow, oval-headed, medium to large tree.
TEXTURE: Medium.　　　　　　　**EXPOSURE**: Sun to partial shade.

LEAVES: Alternate, simple; more or less lance-shaped, and 3 to 6 inches long. Finely saw-toothed margin with one or more glands on the petiole near the base of the leaf (very small but noticeable). Upper leaf surface is dark, glossy green, paler below. Fall color is yellow-orange to red-orange, variable with season and seedlings.

STEM: Very slender and flexible when young; may droop on some trees or when wet with rain. Young stems are green, turning red-brown with age. Old stems develop a unique bark pattern that is irregular, yet distinct, and reddish brown to nearly black. Wood is reddish pink, finely grained and beautiful when used to make furniture. The wood ranks with maple and walnut in beauty and durability.

FLOWERS: White, in elongated terminal clusters with the leaves. Noticeable but not showy.

FRUIT: Black, rounded, about 1/4 inch in diameter. Matures in late summer. Edible, sometimes used to make wine or jelly.

COLOR: Leaves are dark, glossy green. Yellow-orange to red-orange in the fall.

PROPAGATION: Seed and often in areas where it is not desired.

CULTURE: Black cherry is native from north Florida, west to eastern Texas, Oklahoma and Kansas, northward to Minnesota and Ontario, and as far east as New Brunswick on rich, fertile soils with good moisture and deep leaf litter. Somewhat difficult to transplant. Definitely not suited to most urban landscape conditions of poor, compacted soils, exposure to excessive reflected heat and light, and intense competition from turf. The latter may be black cherry's greatest enemy in the urban landscape. If it is to be planted, consider cultural requirements carefully: heavy mulch to provide cool root temperatures, constant moisture availability, good soil aeration, and limited grass and weed competition.

PESTS: Eastern tent caterpillar, fall webworm, and others. Most chewing insects seem to have lunch on the black cherry from time to time, but, if growing conditions are favorable, it survives without interference by man.

NOTES: Since it is native over a wide geographic range, it often is left when native woods are partially cleared for new developments. It almost always dies a slow, lingering death under these circumstances. It is very intolerant to disturbance. If a black cherry is to be left on a new construction site, the root zone should be totally undisturbed. Nothing should be stored, stacked, or disturbed from beyond the dripline to the trunk. Black cherry is a magnificent tree that deserves better than to be abused. With air-root- pruning of seedlings and improved production techniques, the "difficult to transplant" image should slowly disappear, but the rather specific requirements for good growth will remain.

CULTIVARS: 'Spring Sparkel': dense, compact growth with slight weeping at the branch tips and many white flowers. It does produce fruit which can be a nuisance.

Prunus serrulata Lindl.   Japanese Flowering Cherry
Rosaceae or Rose Family   Hardiness Zone 6
Native to China and Japan.
SIZE: 20 to 50 feet tall or more. Rapid grower.
FORM: Tree with rounded crown.
TEXTURE: Medium.   **EXPOSURE:** Sun.

LEAVES: Alternate, simple; 3 to 5 inches long, and ovate or ovate-elongate with a saw-tooth margin, tapering to a distinct point at the tip (see photograph). Upper leaf surface is glossy, dark green, only slight lighter below, but reddish when first emerging. petioles have 2 to 4 prominent glands. Only moderate yellow fall color.

STEM: Slender when young. Green at first, turning reddish brown to nearly purplish brown with age. Lenticels are very prominent, and go around the stem (see photograph). Wood is moderately stout and not readily broken.

FLOWERS: Usually pink and double, but some white and single-flowered cultivars are available. Flower size is from 1 to 2 1/2 inches across, depending on cultivar. Blooms along the stems just below the current flush of growth in late spring. Very showy.

FRUIT: Not showy: small and black. Not present on some cultivars.

COLOR: Foliage is glossy, dark green. Flowers are usually pink; showy.

PROPAGATION: Grafting of selected cultivars onto mazzard cherry or other cherry seedlings or roots of cuttings.

CULTURE: Japanese flowering cherries are adapted to the eastern United States but are marginal west of the Mississippi River except in selected sites, with good cultural conditions and well-drained soils. Do not plant where drainage is marginal Not drought-tolerant. When trees become stressed for any reason, borers and other problems increase. The farther west, the shorter the life expectancy. However, it is a very showy tree and worth the effort, even if for only 10 years or so. Mulch, reduced grass and weed competition, and water during dry periods will assist growth, health, and flowering.

PESTS: Borers, stem canker, mites, and other problems.

NOTES: A spectacular tree when in flower, plus foliage is attractive when first emerging and during the growing season. The bark is a striking reddish brown, smooth, glossy, and marked with distinct lenticels. Before purchasing a Japanese flowering cherry, consider benefits vs. complications. Flowering is best in full sun.

CULTIVARS: 'Kwanzan': probably the most widely grown. Flowers are double, carnation-like, 2 to 2 1/2 inches across and bright pink, appearing after the leaves emerge. May reach 20 to 25 feet or more with rounded crown. 'Mt. Fugi': pink buds, double white flowers and horizontal drooping branches. 'Shirofugen': extremely double white flowers. Very striking and a wide spreading form. Other cultivars exist in local areas. Donald Wyman lists many cultivars in his book, *Trees for American Gardens* .

RELATED SPECIES: *Prunus subhirtella*, autumn flowering cherry, grows to 20 to 30 feet and flowers in November to March on bare stems. 'Autumnalis Rosea' flowers are semi double and pinkish. 'Pendula Plena Rosea': weeping branches and rosette of pink flowers.

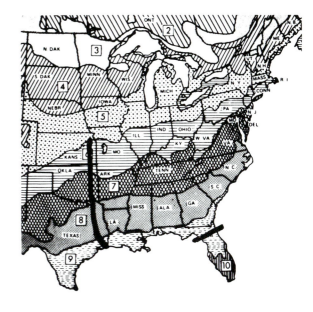

Pyrus calleryana Dcne.   Callery Pear
Rosaceae or Rose Family   Hardiness Zone 4
Native to China.
SIZE: 30 to 60 feet tall with 25- to 35-foot spread. Moderate grower.
FORM: Oval to round-headed medium-sized tree.
TEXTURE: Medium.   **EXPOSURE:** Sun.

LEAVES: Alternate, simple; 2 to 3 inches long, roughly triangular, and mostly rounded at the base with an irregular sawtooth margin. Deep, dark green above, slightly lighter green below, on a flexible petiole. Orange to red-orange fall color, quite showy some seasons, and dropping quickly to reveal an attractive branch structure.

STEM: Stout and stiff, generally with numerous short, stiff, spine-like branches with new growth. Young stem is at first densely wooly, but hairs soon drop to reveal a glossy, brown twig that becomes gray with age, developing a gray-brown, shallowly furrowed, irregular bark pattern. Wood is durable, hard, and wind- and vandal-resistant except at weak forks.

FLOWERS: White. Appearing very early in the spring, moderately showy, but unpleasant odor. Most pears are self-sterile thus planting one cultivar produces little or no fruit. Male and female in the same flower (perfect).

FRUIT: Green turning black, 1/2 inch in diameter. Not showy: rarely seen on some trees.

COLOR: Foliage is deep green; orange to red-orange in the fall. Very showy some seasons. Flowers are white.

PROPAGATION: Seed, grafting or budding of selected cultivars; cuttings with difficulty.

CULTURE: Very tough and tolerant of urban conditions and poor soils. Well adapted to city conditions such as restricted root space and limited water supply. Has considerable drought, wind, and desiccation resistance. Spines on some cultivars may be advantageous in discouraging vandals. Seedlings generally develop a branch structure with little pruning. Some cultivars MUST have corrective pruning while young.

PESTS: None serious. Less susceptible to fire blight and leaf spot than other pears.

NOTES: A very desirable shade and ornamental tree. It performs well in a wide range of circumstances with good foliage and few problems. Good form and crown development. Spines should not discourage planting of the seedling tree. Should be planted more.

CULTIVARS: 'Aristocrat': somewhat similar to 'Bradford', but more broadly ovate in form, with slightly larger leaves, and the branches tend to be borne at more right angles to the stem. 'Bradford': a thornless, rather oval form that reaches 30 to 40 feet tall, is generally fruitless, with good fall color. Highly acclaimed tolerance to city conditions and heavy clay soils. Flowers smell foul and appear very early in the spring. **Terrible** branch structure. Not a good tree. 'Chanticleer' or 'Cleveland Select': pyramidal form, somewhat narrower than 'Bradford', with yellow to red fall color. 'Fauriei': a dwarf selection, grows to about 30 feet with a somewhat rounded head at maturity, and is similar to 'Bradford' but smaller. 'Rancho': good red fall color, white flowers, somewhat similar to others. 'Whitehouse': a columnar form but of little merit. 'Capital': upright form but very susceptible to fire blight. 'Red Spire': pyramidal form with better structure than 'Bradford', a few spines and some problem with fire blight. 'Paradise': develops a central leader more than others and may be the better tree form of the lot. Other cultivars exist.

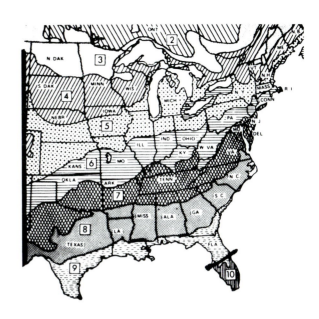

'Bradford'

Pyrus communis L.   Common Pear
Rosaceae or Rose Family   Hardiness Zone 5
Native to Europe and Asia.
SIZE: 30 to 50 feet tall with a 20- to 30-foot spread. Slow to moderate grower.
FORM: Irregularly pyramidal tree, often with drooping lower branches.
TEXTURE: Medium.   **EXPOSURE:** Sun.

LEAVES: Alternate, simple; on short lateral spurs or branches. Ovate to somewhat elliptical, 3 to 4 inches long, 1 1/2 to 2 inches wide. Margin is finely toothed. Leaf tapers to a point at the tip, sometimes abruptly. Deep, dark green above, pale green below. Fall color is brilliant yellow to orange-yellow; generally quite showy.

STEM: Young stems are rather fuzzy at first, later becoming smooth and reddish brown to gray. Older stems are gray to black as the bark develops an irregular but shallowly furrowed plate-like texture. Wood is durable, very hard, and wind-resistant.

FLOWERS: Open just before the leaves in the spring. White, in terminal clusters borne on short twigs. Very showy, but last only a few days. Male and female parts in the same flower (perfect flowers). Mostly self-sterile, thus more than one cultivar should be planted if fruits are wanted.

FRUIT: Ripens late summer to early fall. Pear-shaped, 2 to 4 inches long, depending on cultivar. Edible, but some cultivars are very gritty, having many stone cells.

COLOR: Foliage is deep green above, and yellow to orange-yellow in the fall. Flowers are white. Fruit is green, turning yellow with age.

PROPAGATION: Seed, grafting or budding of selected cultivars.

CULTURE: Grows over a wide range of conditions and soil types: dry or moist, deep or shallow soils, and is tolerant of abused urban soils. Found surviving on abandoned farmsteads throughout the Great Plains. A spectacular show of flowers in the spring and most cultivars produce at least some fruit suitable for eating or canning. Very hard durable wood: wind- and vandal-resistant. Many of the lower branches droop to some extent; the upper branches, being less developed, create an interesting triangular form. Should not be over fertilized as such may increase likelihood of disease. Only disease-resistant cultivars should be planted, and only in open, exposed areas with good air circulation.

PESTS: Fire blight and leaf spot are serious on some cultivars. Occasionally aphids or mites, but these are rarely serious problems. Spoiling fruits can be very messy and attract wasps and honeybees, which may pose a hazard.

NOTES: Old pear trees are spectacular landscape plants when used properly. Very tough, rugged individuals, but rarely planted as ornamentals. However, the form, foliage, fall color, flowers, and fruit are all desirable. Tolerance and adaptability of the plant lend itself to many conditions encountered in present-day urban planting. Should be planted a great deal more, since the rewards are many and troubles few.

CULTIVARS: Because of the severity of fire blight, only resistant cultivars should be planted. 'Kifer': an old cultivar with gritty fruits. Should not be planted. The following four cultivars appear to be most resistant; however, many cultivars exist. 'Magness': a vigorous grower, somewhat spreading, may have a few thorns. It is self-sterile so will not produce fruit unless planted with another cultivar. 'Maxine': very similar to 'Starking Delicious'. A good fruit producer; some fruit when planted alone. 'Moonglow': an upright, vigorous grower, it will produce some fruit when planted alone. Many cultivars exist.

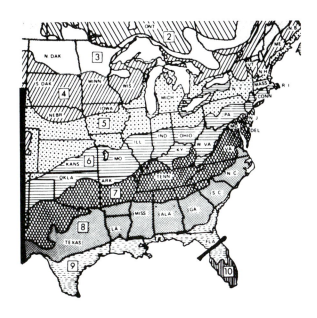

Most authors divide the oaks into two sub-groups, white oaks and red oaks, each containing numerous species. In addition, there are probably numerous hybrids within each of these groups. The genus *Quercus* has several features that aid in identification of both groups. Leaves are simple, alternate, and variously toothed or lobed. Oaks do not develop a separation layer between leaf and stem as do most deciduous trees. Thus, leaves do not drop readily in the fall and may be retained all winter, finally dropping just before the spring flush. Three to six or more terminal buds are generally clustered at the tip of the current season's growth. Buds are quite conspicuous from early August until the spring flush begins. In most cases, not all of these buds develop. Young branches tend to be five-angled with raised podium-like enlargements where the leaves were attached. Seen in cross section, the pith of young branches is five-angled or five-pointed. Distinctness varies with pith size and species but the five points are always there. This can be very useful in identifying oaks among other genera during the dormant season. Oaks are wind-pollinated and frequently the male and female flowers on a tree are not functional at the same time, thus many hybrids occur. Collecting acorns from the same tree each year only insures that one of the parents is known as the other parent varies with the year. Some people are allergic to oak pollen, and asthmatic conditions are aggravated by the abundant pollen.

White oaks

Best characterized by white oak, *Quercus alba.* Leaves are rounded at the tips with no sharp bristles or points; they do not have bristle-tipped lobes or teeth. A light gray or brown bark generally develops and, in most cases, becomes scaly or flaky by the time the trunk is two inches in diameter. Acorns of white oaks mature in a single season and are generally sweet to taste. Seed will germinate as soon as mature, but may be difficult to store over winter. Wood has pores that are plugged with a plastic-like material called tylose. Because of this, the wood is capable of holding water or other liquids, and is used in constructing barrels principally for the liquor industry. Wood is moderately decay-resistant.

Red oaks

A large and variable group. Probably best characterized by the northern red oak, *Quercus rubra.* Many are slightly faster growers than the white oaks. Leaves can be distinguished by their bristle-tipped lobes, or, if there are no lobes, as in the case of *Quercus imbricaria* or *Quercus phellos*, the tip of the leaf terminates in a single bristle. The bark is generally dark gray to gray-black and is smooth when young and hard and ridged with maturity, but not flaky. Acorns take two seasons to mature and are bitter when eaten. Acorns remain small the first season (you must look closely to see the miniature acorns) and grow very rapidly the second season. Seed must be cold-stored over winter or left outdoors before germination will occur with most species. Pores in the wood are open and do not hold water. Wood is much more subject to decay than the white oaks when used as posts or other construction in contact with the soil.

White Oak

Red Oak

White Oak   Red Oak

Quercus acutissima Carruthers. Sawtooth Oak (Red Oak Group)
Fagaceae or Beech Family Hardiness Zone 4
Native to Korea, China, and Japan.
SIZE: 50 to 60 feet tall with a 30- to 40-foot spread. Moderate to rapid grower.
FORM: Pyramidal when young; more rounded crown with maturity.
TEXTURE: Medium. **EXPOSURE:** Sun.

LEAVES: Alternate, simple; oblong to nearly lanceolate, 3 to 7 inches long, 1 1/2 to 2 inches wide, and rounded at the base. Leaves have a distinct sawtooth margin with bristle-like teeth. Leaves are somewhat fuzzy at first, but this persists only for a short period. Little, if any, fall color; leaves generally turn a dull brown and are retained most of the winter. Deep green above during the growing season.

STEM: The young stem is fairly stiff, light brown, and tends to have clusters of prominent, sharply pointed buds at the tip during late summer and throughout the dormant period. Bark takes on an irregular, almost diamond-shaped pattern, and is shallowly furrowed and gray to gray-black in color. Wood is moderately strong, quite wind- and vandal-resistant. Generally a single stem tree with a central leader.

FLOWERS: Male and female separate on the same tree (monoecious). Not showy. Male is a long catkin in early spring.

FRUIT: Acorn about 1 inch in diameter; cap has long, recurved scales and encloses about half of the nut. Takes two seasons to mature.

COLOR: Foliage is deep green; dull brown in the fall and retained on the tree.

PROPAGATION: Seed. Seedlings are somewhat uneven in growth form and rate.

CULTURE: Adapted to a considerable variety of soil types, moisture conditions, and temperature ranges. Relatively untested on many of the poor soils encountered in urban areas or as a street tree. Generally good transplant success. It has not be in use long in this country but deserves more attention. Remember, there is no fall color and leaves remain on the tree.

PESTS: None serious.

NOTES: A widely adaptable and fast-growing oak. Is doing very well on a range of sites from Michigan to central Texas and Oklahoma and eastward. Value of this tree over the long term remains to be determined, but certainly, the present indications are that it should be used more. Fruits may be a problem on sidewalks, driveways, or patios. Seed production tends to be somewhat erratic. Has merit for wildlife plantings. One of the more tolerant of the oaks to alkaline soils. Leaves may be confused with Chinese chestnut; however, the chestnut leaf is broader with longer teeth on the leaf margin and many hairs on the underside.

CULTIVARS: None known.

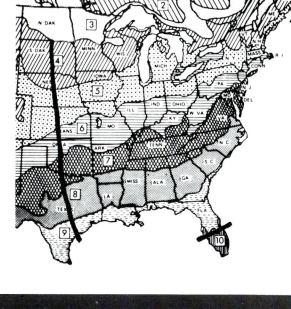

Quercus alba L.   White Oak (White Oak Group)
Fagaceae or Beech Family   Hardiness Zone 3
Native to the eastern United States.
SIZE: 80 to 100 feet tall with a spread of 50 to 60 feet. Slow to moderate grower.
FORM: Round-headed tree.
TEXTURE: Medium to coarse.   **EXPOSURE:** Sun.

LEAVES: Alternate, simple; 4 to 9 inches long, 3 to 5 inches wide on a short stalk. Somewhat wider near the tip of the leaf. Generally with 7 to 11 finger-like lobes. All points on the leaf are rounded. Deep green to slightly blue-green above; pale blue-gray-green below. Fall color is wine-red to red-orange and very showy some seasons.

STEM: Young stems are fairly slender and greenish red early, becoming red-brown by the end of the growing season. Buds are globe-shaped and clustered at the tip of the branch. Leaf scars are shaped like a half-moon. With age, the bark on the young branches becomes a light gray, eventually developing flat ridges separated by shallow fissures and flaky or scaley in appearance. Branch angles are excellent. Wood is hard, strong, durable, and very vandal- and wind-resistant.

FLOWERS: Male and female flowers separate on the same tree (monoecious). Male is a long, hairy catkin in early spring. Not showy.

FRUIT: Acorn is about 1 inch oblong, and shiny tan to dark brown on a very short stalk. The cap is very shallow, covering only about 1/4 of the nut.

COLOR: Foliage is deep green to slightly blue-green, wine-red to orange-red in the fall and very showy some seasons.

PROPAGATION: Seed, which germinate soon after falling, but can be collected and stored dry over winter for spring planting.

CULTURE: Native to rich bottomlands throughout much of the eastern United States. White oaks make spectacular shade and ornamental trees where soils are fair to good and a moderate supply of moisture is present or can be supplied through irrigation. Excellent branch development. Not well adapted to shallow or abused soils of many urban sites or where moisture is particularly limited. Somewhat difficult to transplant unless seedlings are grown with root-branching techniques. Supplemental fertilization, mulching, and removal of grassy weeds aids young trees substantially.

PESTS: None serious in most areas.

NOTES: Spectacular large tree when it is doing well in the landscape. Attains a size that may not be in scale with many single story dwellings. Excellent for parks, golf courses, and other recreational areas where adequate space is present and soils are good and not disturbed. May be criticized for holding its leaves well into the winter, thus blocking winter sun and being a nuisance with the continual dropping of leaves.

CULTIVARS: Several hybrids or closely related species are noted by some authors but for purposes of a shade or ornamental tree, these offer little variation from the species.

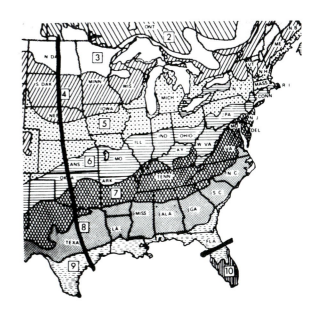

Quercus bicolor Willd. Swamp White Oak (White Oak Group)
Fagaceae or Beech Family Hardiness Zone 3
Native to the eastern United States.
SIZE: 80 to 100 feet tall with a 40- to 50-foot spread. Slow to moderate grower.
FORM: Somewhat pyramidal when young, eventually developing a large, rounded crown with slightly drooping lower branches.
TEXTURE: Coarse. **EXPOSURE:** Sun.

LEAVES: Alternate, simple; 4 to 7 inches long, 3 to 4 inches wide. Basically obovate to oblong, generally widest above the middle. Margin is irregularly, but not deeply, lobed. Bronze-green above and silvery white below when young. Later upper surface is glossy, dark green; fall color is slightly yellow to yellow-brown, only moderately showy.

STEM: Young stems are stout and green when young, becoming orange-brown to reddish brown with age. As they mature they become various shades of gray to dark brown with deepening fissures. Ridges become flattened and curl back loosely to give a rough appearance. Bark color is similar to white oak, except that it is more irregular and more deeply furrowed. Wood is very strong, tough, and wind-resistant. Branch angles are excellent.

FLOWERS: Male and female separate on the same tree (monoecious). Not showy.

FRUIT: Matures in one season, generally in September to October; 1 to 1 1/2 inches long, 1/2 to 1 inch in diameter, and ovate to oblong. Cup is bowl-shaped, covers about 1/2 of the acorn; light brown and fuzzy but sometimes smooth. Looks like a small bur oak acorn.

COLOR: Foliage is glossy, dark green above; yellow to yellow-brown in the fall.

PROPAGATION: Seed.

CULTURE: Native to semi-swampy locations throughout the southeastern United States. Does well on any good fertile soil with a moderate amount of moisture. Is not exceptionally drought-tolerant but is not overly sensitive either. Because of the similarity in appearance, it is sometimes planted in locations where bur oak is intended. Less tough or tolerant to adverse conditions than bur oak. For good soils and moderate moisture only. Moderately difficult to transplant. A good park or estate tree.

PESTS: None serious in most areas.

NOTES: Desirable, large, shade and ornamental tree where soils are good and space and moisture are adequate. Not generally suited to most urban conditions or areas of poor soils. Gets too large with age for many single story dwellings, although it is a slow grower and does not quickly overgrow the site. Fruits are large and may be a problem in some landscape situations. Similar to white oak in terms of holding leaves late into the winter. Should be planted more.

CULTIVARS: None known.

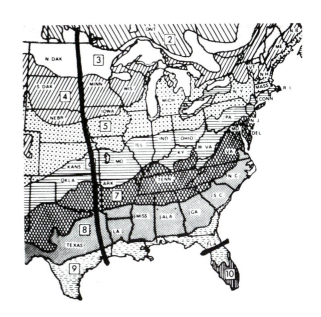

Quercus falcata Michx.   Southern Red Oak (Red Oak Group)
Fagaceae or Beech Family   Hardiness Zone 4
Native to the southeastern United States.
SIZE: 60 to 80 feet tall with a 50- to 60-foot spread. Moderate to rapid grower.
FORM: Broad, oval-topped tree.
TEXTURE: Coarse.   **EXPOSURE:** Sun.

LEAVES: Alternate, simple; 6 to 7 inches long, 4 to 5 inches wide. Somewhat variable in shape and lobing, but generally has 3 to 7 bristle-tipped lobes which may be quite slender. Medium to dark green above, pale yellow to grayish white beneath. A change of color can be noticed in the wind. Fall color is dull brown to slightly yellow-brown.

STEM: Reddish brown, stout, and hairy at first; later becoming smooth. With age, bark becomes steel gray to grayish black, and eventually breaks into deep fissures, but not flakes. Wood is moderately stout and wind-resistant.

FLOWERS: Male and female separate on the same tree (monoecious). Not showy.

FRUIT: Rounded acorn, 1/2 inch long, and orange-brown. One-fourth is enclosed in a shallow, saucer-shaped cup. Matures during the second season.

COLOR: Foliage is medium to dark green, slightly yellow-brown in the fall.

PROPAGATION: Seed.

CULTURE: Native to dry ridges and sandy open flatlands; sites that are generally considered to be adverse. Makes a good shade and ornamental tree. Tolerates poor soils, drought, and some degree of neglect as long as adequate space is provided. Grows fairly well in heavy, poorly drained clays. Responds vigorously to fertilizers and will grow quite rapidly on a good site.

PESTS: None serious in most areas.

NOTES: An attractive large tree. When grown in the open, it will develop a broad, full crown. Should be used more in the South as a shade and ornamental tree. Must be criticized for not dropping leaves early in the fall, but this applies to most oaks. Can best be identified by deeply lobed leaves with yellow to whitish gray lower surface, whereas, *Quercus rubra*, northern red oak, has leaves that are more shallowly lobed with a pale blue-green cast above and a pale green below, never yellow or whitish gray. Slightly less attractive than *Q. rubra* in most instances.

CULTIVARS: None known.

RELATED SPECIES: *Quercus pagodifolia*: cherry bark or swamp Spanish oak, is most likely an ecological race of southern red oak. The variation is slight and inconsistent.

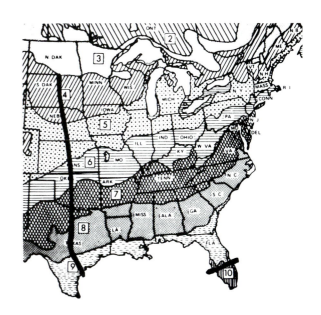

Q. falcata   Q. shumardi

Quercus macrocarpa Michx. Bur Oak (White Oak Group)
Fagaceae or Beech Family Hardiness Zone 3
Native to the eastern United States.
SIZE: 60 to 80 feet tall with a 30- to 50-foot spread. Slow to moderate grower.
FORM: Large, round-headed tree with bold, heavy branches.
TEXTURE: Coarse. EXPOSURE: Sun.

LEAVES: Alternate, simple; 6 to 10 inches long, 4 to 5 inches wide. More or less oval, being broadest above the center, and tapering gradually to the stalk, and with a very short petiole. Generally 5 to 9 lobes separated by deep cuts. The terminal lobe is usually largest. Dark green above, pale green below. Fall color is a dull yellow-brown.

STEM: Young stems are stout and light brown to yellow-brown. Densely hairy at first; smooth when mature. Terminal buds on young shoots are egg-shaped. Occasionally corky wings or ribs develop on the more vigorous twigs of the previous season. Bark is gray to reddish brown when young, developing thick, deep furrows that break into irregular ridges on old trees and are almost black; very rugged appearance. Wood is very strong, durable, and wind- and vandal-resistant.

FLOWERS: Male and female separate on the same tree (monoecious). Not showy.

FRUIT: Very large acorn that is somewhat variable in size and shape, and may be as much as 2 inches in diameter. A deep cup covers about 1/2 or more of the nut. Scales on the cup are thick and have a bushy, fringed appearance on the surface and around the edge around the nut.

COLOR: Foliage is deep green; dull yellow-brown in the fall.

PROPAGATION: Seed.

CULTURE: Grows best in rich, well-drained soils but is found native on dry, exposed slopes in rather open, hostile locations in the Great Plains. Tolerates poor soils and low rainfall best of the various oaks that are used as ornamentals. Can be used successfully as a shade or ornamental tree over the central and southern plains of Nebraska, Kansas, Oklahoma, and Texas, although it will require supplemental watering when young. Eventually will grow into a sizable tree needing considerable room to develop. Not for the small site. Somewhat difficult to transplant balled in burlap but transplants easily with improved root system technology.

PESTS: Aphids and spider mites occasionally but no serious problems.

NOTES: Extremely tough and durable, tolerating dry conditions especially well once established. Very coarse texture makes it somewhat difficult to use in the landscape. Fruits are large (golf ball size) and may create a maintenance problem when landing on golf courses and some other recreational areas or on sidewalks, patios or driveways. May be distinguished from swamp white oak by the more deeply lobed leaves and deeply furrowed bark, whereas swamp white oak has shallowly lobed leaves and gray-black, shallowly furrowed bark.

CULTIVARS: None known.

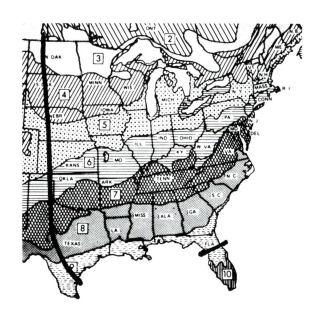

Quercus marilandica Muenchh.　　Blackjack Oak (Red Oak Group)
Fagaceae or Beech Family　　Hardiness Zone 4
Native to the eastern United States.
SIZE: 20 to 50 feet tall with a 15- to 40-foot spread.　Slow to moderate grower.
FORM: Shrubby and twiggy, round-topped, symmetrical, small tree.
TEXTURE: Medium.　　EXPOSURE: Sun.

LEAVES: Alternate, simple; 3 to 6 inches long, and 2 to 5 inches wide.　Paddle or club-shaped; broadest at the outer end, tapering toward the base.　Leaves have three lobes which may have several bristles around the edge.　Deep green above, yellow-green and wooly beneath.　Fall color is red-orange to brown.　Stiff and leathery texture.

STEM: Young stem is gray-brown, stout and stiff, with oval-shaped buds turning nearly black by the second year.　Develops into a dark brown, finally black, rough, block-like or platy bark that is deeply furrowed with age and quite variable.　Wood is very tough, durable, and wind-resistant.　Develops many short, stubby branches.

FLOWERS: Not showy; however, large quantities of pollen are produced which may stain sidewalks and lawn furniture.　Male and female separate on the same tree (monoecious).

FRUIT: Small acorn which ripens in two years, about 1/2 inch long.　A bowl-like cup encloses one-half of the acorn.

COLOR: Foliage is deep green above; red, orange to brown in the fall.　Variable.

PROPAGATION: Seed.

CULTURE: Native to droughty, poor soils.　An extremely tough and durable tree native on very adverse sites with low fertility.　Rarely planted as an ornamental; however, it has merit when left undisturbed in development areas of native trees.　Should be considered for some urban sites where the soils are poor and rainfall is limited.　When grown in a fair to good soil with moderate fertility and good cultural practices, it becomes a dense, round-headed tree with weeping lower branches (see upper left photo) much different in appearance from most trees in their native habitat (right center photo).

PESTS: None serious, although spring canker worm may cause some damage.

NOTES: Interesting, small- to medium-sized tree.　The nearly black bark against a wintry sky can be desirable in appearance.　Tolerates extremely adverse conditions but is difficult to transplant, especially from the wild.　However, when air-root-pruned as a seedling and container grown, transplant survival is near 100%.　Should be planted more in areas of the South and Southwest where plant materials which are well adapted to open urban conditions are limited.　Blackjack holds dead twigs for years whereas post oak twigs die, decay and soon fall.　The dead twigs and branches in a blackjack are very hard and difficult to cut.　Commonly found growing native with post oak, which can be readily distinguished by its smoother, gray bark and more deeply lobed leaves

CULTIVARS: None.

Quercus muehlenbergi Engelm.
Fagaceae or Beech Family
Native to the eastern United States.

Chinquapin Oak or Yellow Chestnut Oak
(White Oak Group)

Hardiness Zone 3

SIZE: 30 to 60 feet tall with a 20- to 40-foot spread. Slow to moderate grower.
FORM: Irregular, asymmetrical, round-topped tree.
TEXTURE: Medium.   **EXPOSURE:** Sun.

LEAVES: Alternate, simple; 2 to 4 inches long, 1 1/2 to 3 inches wide, more or less egg-shaped to elongate-ovate. Broadest slightly above the middle. Tip is pointed with large rounded teeth on the margin (without bristles) and teeth decrease in size toward the tip. Dark green and shiny above, silvery white below. Fall color is crimson to orange-yellow to brown. Attractive most seasons.

STEM: Slender, orange-brown to tan, hairy at first becoming smooth with age. Branches develop a light gray-tan, rough, flakey bark which becomes shallowly fissured and breaks into irregular squarish scales with age. Variable. Bark color is somewhat similar to a white oak. Wood is tough, durable, and very stout.

FLOWERS: Male and female separate on the same tree (monoecious). Not showy.

FRUIT: Acorn about 1/2 inch long, oval, and dark brown. Enclosed about 1/4 by the cup which is thin, bowl-shaped, brown, and somewhat fuzzy. Rodents tend to eat these first and the thin seed coat allows easy entrance for weevils, so good seed is difficult to find.

COLOR: Foliage is deep green; crimson to orange-yellow to brown in the fall.

PROPAGATION: Seed.

CULTURE: Native to dry limestone bluffs and hillsides throughout much of the central and south central United States. Quite drought-resistant and tolerates exposure and windswept hillsides. Not commonly used in urban landscaping but does well as long as soil is moderately well drained. However, where topsoil has been removed and nothing remains at a homesite except subsoil clay, it would not be a wise selection. When planted as a single stem tree in a landscape with moderate to good soils, it develops a short trunk and a broad, low crown. Spectacular. Responds well to nutrition and supplemental watering during drought. Difficult to transplant from the wild. However, with air-root-pruning of the seedling and container production, success rate is very high.

PESTS: None serious.

NOTES: Generally develops a low, spreading crown with low branches, a somewhat unusual form but very attractive. Should be used more in landscaping. Difficulty in transplanting is probably responsible for its near absence in the nursery trade. Modern production techniques such as air-root-pruning to stimulate root branching when very young makes this now an easy tree to grow. The only problem now is beating the squirrels and weevils to the acorns. Should be planted more.

CULTIVARS: None.

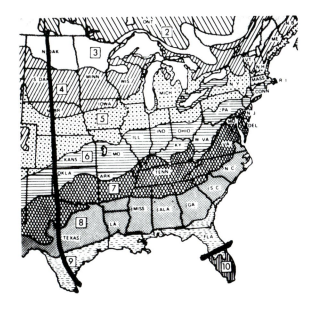

Quercus nigra L.   Water Oak (Red Oak Group)
Fagaceae or Beech Family   Hardiness Zone 6
Native to southeastern United States.
SIZE: 60 to 100 feet tall with a 50- to 60-foot spread. Rapid grower.
FORM: Broad, oval- to round-topped tree.
TEXTURE: Medium.   EXPOSURE: Sun to partial shade.

LEAVES: Alternate, simple; narrowly club-shaped, 2 to 4 inches long, and 1 to 2 inches wide, with the broadest portion near the tip, but **extremely variable**. Edges are smooth or slightly wavy with one or more bristle tips along the margin. Upper leaf surface is a deep green; lower surface is light green. Nearly evergreen in some areas of the South; semi-evergreen farther north. Fall color is green, finally turning brown in winter.

STEM: Young stems are smooth, slender, gray-brown to brown, remaining smooth for several years, finally developing into a brown to grayish black bark. Only slightly furrowed or having irregular patches of smooth bark and furrowing around the stem of a mature tree. Wood is only moderately strong, probably the weakest of the oaks normally grown as ornamentals, but it has acceptable wind and ice resistance.

FLOWERS: Male and female separate on the same tree (monoecious). Not showy.

FRUIT: Ripens in September or October, 1/2 inch in diameter, and more or less globe-shaped with a thin cup covering only about 1/4 of the acorn.

COLOR: Foliage is deep green; green in the fall; brown in the winter.

PROPAGATION: Seed.

CULTURE: Native to wet swampy areas and lowlands throughout the southern states. In areas of good soil and adequate moisture it grows rapidly, becoming a somewhat weak-wooded, rather spindly, undesirable tree. However, in the more northern and western areas where it grows more slowly, it makes a rather desirable, broad-spreading, landscape tree. Tolerates most soil conditions, especially compacted soils.

PESTS: Scale insects, various chewing insects, and occasionally root rot on old trees.

NOTES: Planted some as a landscape tree. Has some merit particularly in the lower Great Plains where it grows more slowly, develops a stronger wood and more rounded crown, and has fewer insect and disease problems. Transplants fairly easily, particularly from nursery stock that has been root-pruned. May be suitable for some locations, particularly where adequate space is available and a semi-evergreen tree is desired.

CULTIVARS: None. Numerous hybrids, probably between water oak and live oak or water oak and laurel oak, exist in nature. Much variation between seedlings in terms of form, branching, and leaf shape.

RELATED SPECIES: *Quercus laurifolia*, Laurel oak, is similar in appearance and adaptability, and often the two are found growing together and may hybridize. Laurel oak is best distinguished from water oak by the long slender leaves that are much like willow oak, only broader and more variable, but it is subject to the same problems as water oak. *Quercus hemisphaerica* is probably an ecological race of laurel oak. The variations in leaves and growth are minor. Since oaks hybridize and are quite variable from seeds, even when the seeds are collected from an isolated group of one species, attempts to separate into more than broad groups in a species seems futile.

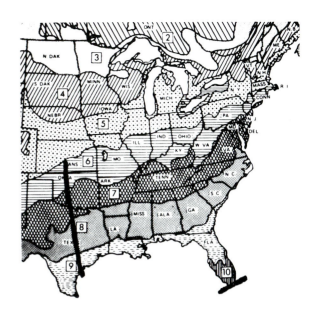

Quercus laurifolia

Quercus palustris Muenchh.   Pin Oak (Red Oak Group)
Fagaceae or Beech Family   Hardiness Zone 3
Native to the eastern United States.
SIZE: 80 to 100 feet tall with a 40- to 50-foot spread. Moderate grower.
FORM: Pyramidal when young, developing a broader, rounded crown, and drooping lower branches with age.
TEXTURE: Medium.   **EXPOSURE:** Sun.

LEAVES: Alternate, simple; 4 to 6 inches long, 2 to 5 inches wide with 5 to 9 variable lobes. Lobes are generally forked and have bristle tips. Leaves are dark green, smooth, and shiny above; paler green below with tufts of hair at the intersections of the veins. Overall shape is oval to slightly oblong, but variable. Leaves often show yellowing during the growing season as a result of iron deficiency. Red to red-orange in the fall.

STEM: Young stems are slender, green to reddish brown, later becoming brown to gray and smooth, remaining smooth for several years. Finally at the base of old trees a shallow-fissured, light brown to gray-brown bark develops. Wood is tough, durable, and wind-resistant. Lower branches have a distinctive droop on both young and old trees.

FLOWERS: Male and female separate on the same tree (monoecious). Not showy.

FRUIT: Small acorn which matures in September or October, about 1/2 inch or less in diameter, more or less rounded. Light brown, about 1/4 enclosed by a broad, thin, saucer-shaped cup. Much smaller acorn than on northern red or shumard oak.

COLOR: Foliage is dark green; red to red-orange in the fall. Generally showy.

PROPAGATION: Seed or grafting of selected cultivars with difficulty.

CULTURE: Native to deep rich soils of bottomlands and streambanks throughout the eastern United States. However, it survives in a wide range of conditions and makes a good ornamental tree except where the soils are extremely poor and the pH of the soil is high (alkaline). Young trees start off well, then if the pH of the soil is high or water is alkaline, varying stages of chlorosis develop, probably due to iron and manganese deficiency. **The most sensitive of the oaks to high pH soils.** A shumard or northern red will grow in the same site and be deep green in color when a pin oak shows severe iron chlorosis. Responds vigorously to fertilization, mulching, or acidifying the soil with sulfur to keep the soil pH below 6. One of the easiest oaks to transplant.

PESTS: None serious.

NOTES: Used extensively in landscaping. Very overplanted. A very formal specimen where it is doing well, yet not really serving as a shade tree because of the upright, pyramidal growth when young. Extreme sensitivity to high pH soils makes it questionable for general use. Even where soils are naturally acid, residues that raise soil pH are left behind following construction create difficulties for pin oak. Holds its leaves all winter. Should be planted where lower branches can remain near the ground.

CULTIVARS: 'Sovereign': a selection with only horizontal or upright branches, making it more desirable for street tree use, and more consistent in form. 'Clownright': similar to 'Sovereign' but more narrow and upright. Difficulty of propagation and graft incompatibility have limited the use of these cultivars.

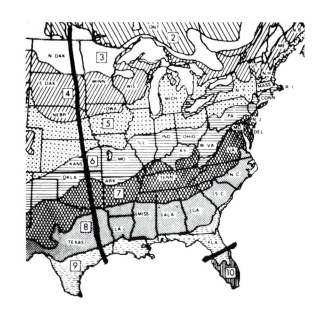

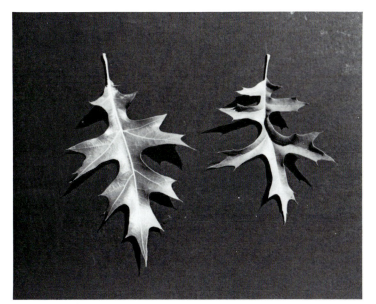

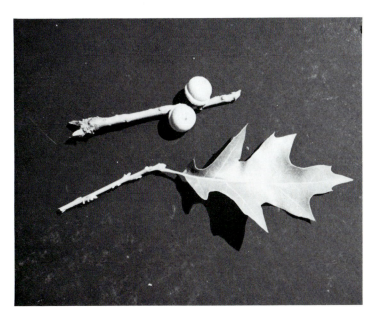

Quercus phellos L.　　　　　　　　　　Willow Oak (Red Oak Group)
Fagaceae or Beech Family　　　　　　　Hardiness Zone 4
Native to the eastern United States.

SIZE: 80 to 100 feet tall with a 40- to 60-foot spread with age. Moderate grower.

FORM: Pyramidal when young; spreading, rounded crown with age. Reminiscent of water oak but with a more refined appearance.

TEXTURE: Fine.　　　　　　　　　　**EXPOSURE:** Sun.

LEAVES: Alternate, simple; narrowly spear or lance-shaped, 3 to 5 inches long, and 1/4 to 1/2 inch wide with a bristle tip. Somewhat reminiscent of a willow, except the leaves are more stiff and rigid. Medium to deep green; yellow to yellow-brown in the fall.

STEM: Slender, green when young, but turning reddish brown, and finally becomes gray and smooth for several years thereafter. Develops a slightly furrowed or fluted bark only with age and at the base of large trees. Wood is fairly durable and tough, similar to other oaks. Lower branches droop, and bark is similar to pin oak.

FLOWERS: Male and female separate on the same tree (monoecious). Not showy.

FRUIT: 1/2 inch long, rounded or slightly flattened, and often striped. Cup covers about 1/4 of the acorn.

COLOR: Foliage is medium to deep green; yellow to yellow-brown in the fall.

PROPAGATION: Seed.

CULTURE: Native to rich bottomlands throughout the eastern United States. Tolerates a moderate range of fair to good soils, as long as reasonable moisture exists and soil pH is **not high. Similar to pin oaks in sensitivity to high pH and iron chlorosis.** Form is similar to pin oak, water or laurel oak, but has a finer texture. Sometimes used in landscaping because of this feature. Transplants reasonably well, more easily than many oaks.

PESTS: None serious.

NOTES: Resembles the pin oak in form but has a much finer texture. Pyramidal when young; does not make a good shade tree until older, but is interestingly ornamental. Should be planted more, particularly in areas where persons object to the coarse texture and large acorns of some oaks. Sometimes confused with shingle oak, *Quercus imbricaria* Michx., which is similar in growth and leaf form, but shingle oak leaves reach 4 to 6 inches long, 1 to 1 1/2 inches wide; are much larger, broader, and more rounded at the base than willow oak. Shingle oak is probably somewhat more drought-resistant and adaptable to poor soils than willow oak but more difficult to transplant.

CULTIVARS: None.

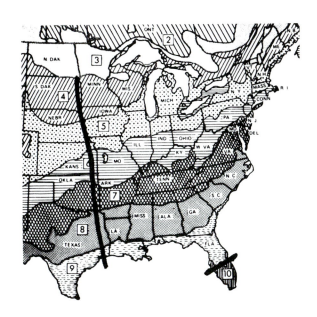

Quercus robur L.   English Oak (White Oak Group)
Fagaceae or Beech Family   Hardiness Zone 4
Native to Europe, northern Africa, western Asia.
SIZE: 60 to 80 feet tall with variable spread. Moderate grower.
FORM: Large tree with a rounded crown at maturity.
TEXTURE: Medium.   EXPOSURE: Sun.

LEAVES: Alternate, simple; elongate to almost strap-like in some instances, 2 to 5 inches long, and 1 to 2 1/2 inches wide, with 3 to 7 pairs of rounded lobes. Variable among seedlings. Quite thick on the tree, giving a very dense canopy. Deep dark green to slightly blue-green above, whitish below, with a dull brown fall color. Leaves are like miniature white oak leaves.

STEM: Young stem is moderately stout, light brown to red-brown, and develops a thin, scaly, gray-brown to gray-black within two years. On old stems, bark is scaly, shallowly furrowed, gray-brown to nearly black. Wood is stout, durable, and wind-resistant.

FLOWERS: Male and female separate on the same tree (monoecious). Not showy.

FRUIT: Elongate acorn, 1 to 1 1/2 inches long and 1/2 inch in diameter. Cup encloses about 1/4 or less of the nut. Light brown to dark cinnamon brown. The stalk is as long as the nut. Matures in one year.

COLOR: Foliage is deep dark green to slightly blue-green; brown in the fall.

PROPAGATION: Seed or grafting of selected cultivars with difficulty.

CULTURE: Tolerant to a moderate range of soil conditions. Acceptable on fair soils with reasonable moisture and drainage. Grows with vigor in good, fertile, moist soils. Responds to fertilizer, supplemental moisture during dry periods, and removal of weed competition, particularly around young plants. Generally develops good branch structure with little or no pruning. Transplants fairly well, particularly when young; easier than many oaks.

PESTS: Powdery mildew can be serious in humid areas or where air circulation is restricted by other vegetation or buildings.

NOTES: Should be planted more. Has a very dense canopy in most cases and a textural feature unlike many of the native oaks. Stands out in the landscape. Spreading forms or seedlings should be given considerable room for development. English oaks in Stillwater, Oklahoma and other areas in the prairie corridor and eastward have performed well, but remember, there is no fall color and the leaves hang on most of the winter, shading sidewalks and preventing the sun from melting ice or snow or otherwise warming the area.

CULTIVARS: 'Fastigata': a very columnar, upright habit. 'Pendula': drooping branches. 'Variegata': leaf margins are white. 'Rosehill': grows like 'Fastigata' but is more resistant to mildew. Numerous other cultivars exist.

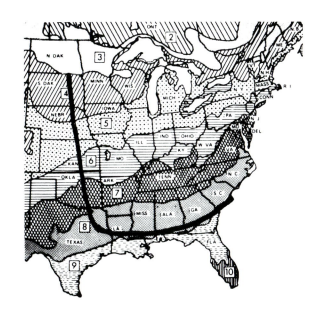

'Fastigata'

Quercus rubra L. (Syn. *Quercus borealis*)   Northern Red Oak (Red Oak Group)
Fagaceae or Beech Family   Hardiness Zone 3
Native to the eastern United States.
SIZE: 80 to 120 feet tall with a 60- to 80-foot spread. Moderate to rapid grower on fertile sites.
FORM: Round- to oval-headed large tree.
TEXTURE: Coarse.   **EXPOSURE:** Sun.

LEAVES: Alternate, simple; 5 to 8 inches long, 4 to 6 inches wide. Oblong to oval, and generally with 7 to 11 lobes of varying sizes that may extend halfway to the middle of the leaf. Tip has 1 to 3 bristles. Deep dark green to slightly blue-green above; light green below. Petiole is red on leaves in the sun. Fall color is red-orange; very showy.

STEM: Young stems are moderately stout, reddish brown, and slightly hairy at first; becoming smooth with age. Buds are reddish, football-shaped, and fringed with hair. Bark remains smooth and steel gray to gray-brown on the young branches for several years. Only with age does the main stem develop a dark reddish brown to black bark with shallow fissures in broad flat ridges. Wood is heavy, strong, and very ice-, wind-, and vandal-resistant.

FLOWERS: Male and female separate on the same tree (monoecious). Not showy.

FRUITS: Mature in October or November of the second year, 1 to 1 1/4 inches long, 1 inch in diameter. Cup encloses about 1/4 of the nut, and generally the nut is scaly below the cup. Nearly identical to shumard oak.

COLOR: Foliage is deep dark green; red-orange in the fall.

PROPAGATION: Seed.

CULTURE: Native to deep moist, well-drained soils. However, it is very tolerant of many urban conditions, particularly where soils are fair to good. Moderately drought-resistant once established and does well as far west as Omaha, Nebraska; Wichita, Kansas; and Tulsa, Oklahoma. Supplemental water will assist a young tree in getting started. Responds vigorously to fertilizer, mulching, and reduction of weed competition, particularly in young. Transplants fairly well in late fall, winter, or early spring.

PESTS: None serious.

NOTES: The round or oval form of a mature tree and the very deep green foliage give it a character which is somewhat unique. Its size is such that it should be planted with care around single story dwellings. Nuts are small enough to be not troublesome in most situations. Very desirable shade tree that should be planted more. Very similar to *Quercus shumardi* in foliage, form, and fruit. Difficult to distinguish, but *Quercus rubra* generally has more lobes on the leaf, a slight blue-green color, a red petiole, and the lobes are not nearly as deep as on *Q. shumardi*. These two trees can be and are used interchangeably by many nurserymen. *Q. shumardi* should be used south of hardiness Zone 7, whereas *Q. rubra* should be used north.

CULTIVARS: None.

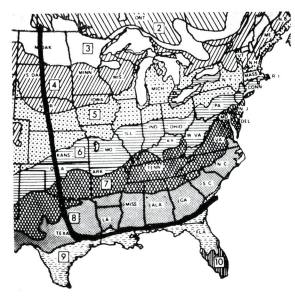

Quercus shumardi Buckl.
Fagaceae or Beech Family
Native to the eastern United States.

Shumard Oak (Red Oak Group)
Hardiness Zone 3

SIZE: 80 to 100 feet tall with a spread of 50 to 60 feet. Moderate to rapid grower.
FORM: Broad, oval tree with stout, spreading branches.
TEXTURE: Coarse.   **EXPOSURE:** Sun.

LEAVES: Alternate, simple; 4 to 8 inches long, 3 to 6 inches wide. Oval to rounded in outline with 7 to 9 bristle-tipped lobes that are more or less symmetrical in placement around the leaf. Considerable variation among leaves on the same tree. Upper surface is dark green and lustrous. Lower surface is a paler green with tufts of hairs where veins connect. Fall color is red-orange to orange.

STEM: Moderately stout, reddish tan becoming grayish brown. Smooth when young, sometimes remaining smooth and almost green-gray for several years before finally developing an irregular, interlacing, shallowly fissured bark that is gray to gray-brown. Lower branches do not droop as in pin oak. Wood is tough, durable, and strong.

FLOWERS: Male and female flowers separate on the same tree (monoecious). Not showy.

FRUIT: About 1 inch long, 1/2 to 1 inch wide, and rounded to slightly flattened. Set in a shallow cup covering only about 1/4 of the nut, and scales are tightly oppressed. Matures the second season. Almost identical to the acorn of northern red oak.

COLOR: Foliage is dark green above; red-orange to orange in the fall.

PROPAGATION: Seed.

CULTURE: Native to rich river bottoms and along the edge of swampy locations. However, it has been found to tolerate urban conditions very well, growing at an exceptional rate in fair to good soils. Does moderately well in poor and abused soils. Appears to be slightly more tolerant of heavy clays than northern red oak. Grows with and appears to tolerate restricted root spaces such as planting between sidewalk and curb. Responds vigorously to good growing conditions such as fertilization, removal of weed competition, and mulching, particularly when young. May need some pruning to assist in good branch development. Transplants fairly easily.

PESTS: None serious.

NOTES: A desirable large shade and ornamental tree. Planted much more in recent years and is deserving of that attention. Difficult to distinguish from *Quercus rubra*, northern red oak, and, in most areas, grows and responds similarly. Fruit, bark characteristics, growth, and form are almost identical. However, northern red oak has more lobes on the leaf but is shallower, and has a slight blue-green leaf color and a red petiole on leaves in the sun. A good tree for large sites.

CULTIVARS: None.

RELATED SPECIES: *Quercus nuttalli*, nuttall oak, is native to acid soils and wet sites in east Texas, Arkansas, and eastward. The appearance is very similar to *Q. shumardi*, but growth in the nursery is generally faster **but** tolerance to alkaline soils is **poor** compared to *shumardi*. A good landscape tree in areas with acid soils and heavy clays or marginal drainage. *Q. texana*, Texas oak or Texas shumard oak, is probably an ecological race of *Q. shumardi* that is even more adapted to alkaline soils and drought than the species. Generally smaller than *Q. shumardi* but otherwise similar in appearance.

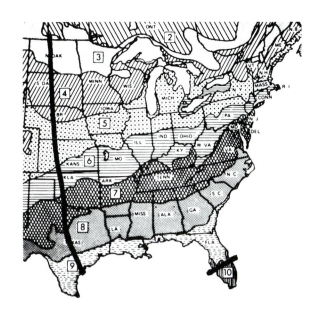

Quercus stellata Wangh.   Post Oak (White Oak Group)
Fagaceae or Beech Family   Hardiness Zone 4
Native to the eastern United States.
SIZE: 40 to 50 feet tall with a 30- to 40-foot spread. Slow grower.
FORM: Round-headed or oval-headed tree.
TEXTURE: Medium to coarse.   **EXPOSURE**: Sun.

LEAVES: Alternate, simple; 4 to 7 inches long, and 3 to 4 inches wide. Broadest above the middle with upper lobes that extend to make somewhat of a cross shape. Dark green above; yellow to dull green below. Fall color is yellow-brown which is not attractive on most trees. However, an occasional tree will color dull red-orange. Fall color varies season to season.

STEM: Young stems are stout, wooly, and green at first, turning light brown, orange, or tan. Buds are globe-shaped and wooly. Bark pattern develops early; brown to gray-brown and divided by deep fissures and scaly ridges, even on a young tree. Wood is dense, hard, and wind-resistant. However, once a branch dies, it decays rapidly. This is a distinct contrast to *Q. maralandica*, the blackjack oak that is commonly found in the same habitat.

FLOWERS: Male and female separate on the same tree (monoecious). Not showy.

FRUIT: Small acorn about 1/2 inch long, matures in one season. A somewhat bowl-shaped cup encloses 1/4 to 1/2 of the nut. Scales on the tip are tightly appressed and smooth.

COLOR: Foliage is dark green above; brown in the fall, with some exceptional trees showing attractive red and orange.

PROPAGATION: Seed.

CULTURE: Generally an indicator of poor soils where native. Can be found on dry sites often associated with blackjack and chinquapin oak and several hickory species. A good oak for planting on dry exposed locations where soils are poor. Difficult to transplant from the wild, but not as a nursery tree. May be advantageous to plant seed rather than to transplant larger trees unless nursery-grown. Amazingly tolerant of poor soils, low fertility, and drought in its native conditions in the lower Prairie States. Responds to water, fertilizer, mulching, and other good cultural practices. Large trees do not tolerate compaction or removal of soil in developments where they should be left alone and maintained in their native condition.

PESTS: None serious.

NOTES: Desirable shade and ornamental tree in many areas where soils are poor and rainfall is limited. Develops an attractive crown with strong horizontal branches. Nursery-grown trees and/or trees that have grown from a small tree with good soils and nutritional conditions are very attractive.
    Post oak can be distinguished from black jack oak by its gray, scaly bark instead of black rigid bark, and by readily decaying dead twigs and limbs instead of hard dead wood that is very slow to decay, and by the distinct leaf shapes.

CULTIVARS: None. However, many hybrids have been named, but they are of no additional value for landscape purposes.

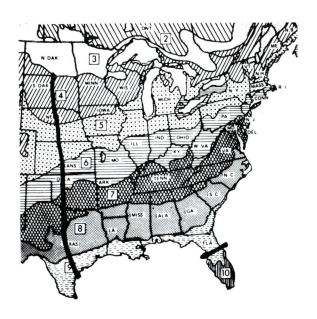

Rhamnus cathartica L.   Common Buckthorn
Rhamnaceae or Buckthorn Family   Hardiness Zone 2
Native to northern Europe and Asia.
SIZE: 15 to 30 feet tall with a 10- to 20-foot spread. Rapid grower.
FORM: Large shrub or small tree with a rounded, irregular crown.
TEXTURE: Medium.   **EXPOSURE:** Sun or some shade.

LEAVES: Opposite or nearly so (see photoograph), simple; oval, and 1 to 3 inches long with a sawtooth margin. Dark, glossy green above and pale green below with very prominent veins. No fall color; however, the leaves stay green and provide a contrast long after other leaves have turned color and dropped.

STEM: Young stems are slender and stout, occasionally terminating in a spine-like tip (like pyracantha), thus the name...buckthorn. Stems are gray and smooth, becoming gray to gray-black with age. Old bark is shallowly furrowed and flaky. Wood is stout and durable.

FLOWERS: Yellowish green, in 2- to 5-flowered clusters. Not showy.

FRUIT: A black, juicy berry, about 1/4 inch in diameter, and containing 3 or 4 seeds. Readily eaten by birds that spread the seed. Very messy fruits over patios, sidewalks or driveways.

COLOR: Foliage is dark, glossy green.

PROPAGATION: Seed, whether wanted or not. Softwood cuttings.

CULTURE: An exceptionally tough and cold-tolerant shrub or small tree. Grows vigorously on most soils: wet or dry, sandy or clay. Transplants easily and tolerates city conditions. Development of a sterile cultivar would be helpful, since the plant has many good qualities and a toughness necessary to survive in many urban locations.

PESTS: Leaf spot, rust, and powdery mildew. Buckthorns are alternate hosts for rust on oats and are therefore banned in grain producing regions.

NOTES: Bucktorns have attractive foliage, but are very weedy due to birds spreading the seeds. Overplanted in many areas.

CULTIVARS: None known.

RELATED SPECIES: *Rhamnus davurica* Pall., Dahurian buckthorn, is a small tree that is 20 to 30 feet tall with stout branches, spines, and dark, glossy green foliage which is spear-shaped or nearly so (see photograph). Hardy in Zone 5. Very tough and durable even in the Prairie States as far south as north Texas. Unfortunately, it is plagued by the same fruit/seed/bird problem as other species.

Rhamnus frangula L., glossy buckthorn, is a large shrub with alternate, oblong leaves and dormant buds without bud scales. Leaves are dark, glossy green with smooth margins, attractive. 'Columnaris' or 'Tall Hedge' is narrowly upright and reaches 12 to 15 feet tall, making a good screen. Overplanted in Zones 4 and 5.

Rhamnus caroliniana, Carolina buckthorn, is native as far west as eastern Kansas. Grows 15 to 20 feet tall, has glossy foliage and red fruits in the fall. A sterile selection would be useful.

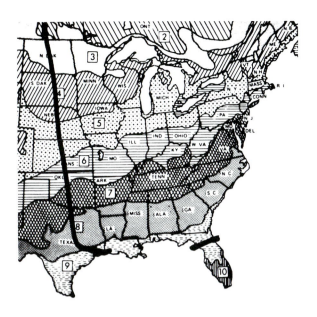

Rhamnus davurica

Robinia pseudoacacia L.   Black Locust
Leguminosae or Legume Family   Hardiness Zone 4
Native to the east central United States.
SIZE: 60 to 80 feet tall with a 30- to 40-foot spread. Extremely rapid grower.
FORM: Umbrella-like, often multiple-stemmed tree.
TEXTURE: Fine.   EXPOSURE: Sun.

LEAVES: Alternate, once-compound; with 9 to 17 leaflets. Overall leaf may be 8 to 14 inches long, and 2 to 3 inches wide. Individual leaflets are 1/2 to 2 inches long and 1/2 to 1 inch wide on a very short stalk. Leaflets are rounded at both ends. Leaves fold on dark cloudy days or at night. Young leaves are silvery gray-green, becoming deep green with maturity. Yellow in the fall.

STEM: Young stem is slender, dull brown, with or without paired rose-like spines on either side of the bud. Young branches are brittle. Buds are embedded in the twigs and are not conspicuous. Spines tend to form only on rapidly growing stems. Bark is gray to reddish brown, rough-ridged, and furrowed; sometimes appearing to be twisted or spiraled around the main trunk or branches. Wood is greenish yellow, stiff, moderately strong, and resistant to decay. Used for fence posts and rough construction.

FLOWERS: Individual flowers are pea-shaped, about 1 inch long; white or pink and showy. In clusters 4 to 5 inches long. Fragrant and attractive in the spring.

FRUIT: Thin brown pod, 2 to 4 inches long and 1/2 inch wide. Each pod contains 4 to 8 flat, kidney-shaped seeds. Pods persist on the tree throughout the winter.

COLOR: Foliage is deep green; yellow in the fall. Flowers are white or pink.

PROPAGATION: Seed, cuttings, or suckers.

CULTURE: Does best on fertile, moist soils. Tolerates and will survive on a wide range of soil conditions including very poor, infertile, and alkaline soils. However, it does not grow profusely under these situations and is frequently short-lived due to the locust borer, an insect which often kills weakened trees. When the tree is doing well, it is moderately attractive and has some merit as an ornamental. However, when it is attacked by borers or when other stressful conditions occur, it frequently sends up numerous suckers or root sprouts that become a terrific nuisance. Rapid growing suckers are generally heavily spined.

PESTS: Locust borer is the most serious, particularly on trees of poor vigor in stressful locations. Leaf miners and several other insects may damage the foliage.

NOTES: Not a desirable ornamental tree. Planting should be considered only where soils are extremely poor but supplemental fertilizer and other growing aids can be supplied. As long as it is growing well, it is rather attractive in form and texture, and flowers in the spring. Dropping of twigs with spines are very undesirable in the landscape. Should be avoided in most instances. Appears to persist best in fence rows and woodlot plantings, or around abandoned farmsteads where soils are fair to good. Bark and seeds are poisonous.
XX-POISON-XX

CULTIVARS: Many have been selected. Most vary in leaf form or overall form of the tree, but none have resistance to the borer or are spineless, which would make them more suitable as landscape trees. 'Decuisneana' has fragrant pink flowers.

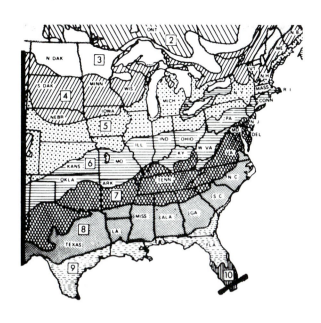

Grafted, globe form

Salix alba L.
Salicaceae or Willow Family
Native to north China.

Weeping or White Willow
Hardiness Zone 3

SIZE: 30 to 50 feet tall with a 30- to 40-foot spread. Very rapid grower.
FORM: Round-headed tree with very long, drooping branches.
TEXTURE: Fine.　　　　　　**EXPOSURE:** Sun.

LEAVES: Alternate, simple; narrowly lanceolate, and somewhat fuzzy at first, but smooth and glossy at maturity. 3 to 5 inches long, 1/4 to 1/2 inch wide, sometimes curling or twisting. Medium to olive green; yellow in the fall.

STEM: Young stems are very slender; green at first, later turning yellowish, and finally brown. Drooping branches may grow 4 to 10 feet or more during a single season and weep from the crown of the tree near to the ground. Buds are flattened against the stem. Branches are a dull brown to gray-brown. Bark finally develops into an irregular, shallowly furrowed pattern which is gray-brown. Wood is soft and easily broken. However, the tree grows so fast that recovery from moderate wind or ice damage is quick.

FLOWERS: Appear in April or May in small catkins. Male and female flowers on separate trees (dioecious). Not showy.

FRUIT: A small capsule; not showy.

COLOR: Foliage is medium to olive green; yellow late in the fall.

PROPAGATION: Seed, or cuttings are very easy any time of the year.

CULTURE: Grows well in a wide range of soils throughout the United States as long as adequate moisture is present. Has extensive, shallow, aggressive root system. Roots can plug sewer lines and drains and severely compete with other plants growing in the immediate vicinity. Needs pruning from time to time to keep it from getting too large and to assist in good structural development. Should not be sheared; branches should be selectively removed from the crown to allow more light to penetrate below and to avoid weak improper branching. Short-lived in most locations, 15 to 30 years.

PESTS: Thrips, aphids, and occasionally borers on old trees but rarely are these serious.

NOTES: Spectacular tree, very dominating in its overall effect in the landscape. Should be used sparingly, since it captivates the viewer. A water-loving tree that suggests moisture to most who view it. Does not fit in a high, dry, arid-type landscape. Good tree for quick growth; makes a dense screen but consumes considerable space.

CULTIVARS: 'Tristis': a good yellow-stemmed weeping cultivar or maybe a hybrid between *Salix alba* and *S. babylonica*. In the trade there is considerable variation in this cultivar. 'Ovalis' has a rounded crown, looking as though it were sheared. Numerous other cultivars exist.

RELATED SPECIES: *Salix babylonica* L., the babylon weeping willow, is very similar and is often sold interchangeably with *S. alba*. However, its root system is not as dense and young stems are more greenish as opposed to the more yellow-green stems of weeping willow. Could be used interchangeably in most locations.
　Salix X 'Blanda',Wisconsin weeping willow, is a cross between *Salix babylonica* and *S. fragilis*, but is not as desirable as *S. babylonica* or *S. alba* 'Tristis' in the landscape but is offered by some nurseries.

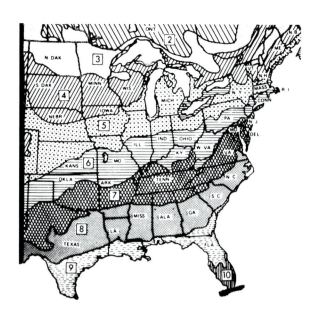

Salix discolor Muhl.   Pussy Willow
Salicaceae or Willow Family   Hardiness Zone 2
Native to northeastearn United States and southeastern Canada.
SIZE: 15- to 25-foot tree or large shrub. Rapid grower.
FORM: Single stem or multiple stem; large shrub or small tree.
TEXTURE: Medium.   EXPOSURE: Sun or slight shade.

LEAVES: Alternate, simple; oblong, and 2 to 4 inches long, with a wavy or toothed margin or occasionally nearly smooth. Leaves are bright green above and silvery white below and very striking. Generally with stipules at the base of the petiole.

STEM: Young stem appears fairly stout, partly because of the large axillary and flower buds. Buds are more or less football-shaped, a conspicuous reddish brown to reddish purple, and shiny. Young branches are dark red-brown and very hairy at first, but losing most of the hairs to the rain and battery by other branches and leaves in the wind. Bark is thin, light brown, and smooth, except for prominent lenticels, until very old. Wood is weak, brittle, and subject to decay.

FLOWERS: Male and female on separate trees (dioecious), appearing before the leaves. The pussy willow flowers used in floral arrangements and seen in paintings are the male flowers or catkins with their golden pollen.

FRUIT: A small, cone-shape capsule that is seen mostly in the wild.

COLOR: Male flowers are golden and very showy. Foliage is bright green.

PROPAGATION: Cuttings anytime, even in a glass of water.

CULTURE: Pussy willow is one of many, many willow species that play an important part in soil stabilization and erosion control. Native to wet areas and amazingly tolerant to flooding and poorly drained soils. With sustained flooding, roots may form in the water above the soil line, much like a stem of coleus in a glass of water. Because of the tolerance of flooding, they are sometimes useful on compacted and heavy clay soils where oxygen is also lacking. Easy to propagate and grow, but short-lived. Like most willow and poplar species, keep away from drain lines or sewers since the root system is very aggressive.

PESTS: Various leaf-eating insects damage the foliage, but are rarely a serious problem.

NOTES: A pussy willow is nice to have somewhere nearby for forcing the male flower buds throughout the winter for flower arrangements. They are short-lived and have an aggressive enough root system, such that they should not be planted near desirable, long-lived shrubs. Attractive around water features and can double in assisting with erosion control. May be propagated by simply sticking cut limbs into the moist bank of a water feature. Several willow species have similar male flowers that are showy and useful in floral arrangements.

CULTIVARS: Several exist, most have been selected for the florist trade since slight variations in male flower size and color are more important there than in the landscape. Some have strikingly flattened stems.

RELATED SPECIES: *Salix gracilistyla* Miq., the rosegold pussywillow, is a shrub up to 6 feet tall that is hardy in Zone 6 and has similar flowers. Not common in the nursery trade, but has merit because of the grayish foliage and more desirable size. Similar to pussy willow in adaptation.

Salix matsudana G.Koidz. 'Tortuosa'   Corkscrew Willow
Salicaceae or Willow Family   Hardiness zone 4
Native to China.
SIZE: 20 to 50 feet tall with a 10- to 30-foot spread. Rapid grower.
FORM: Irregular, oval, small tree with upright branching.
TEXTURE: Fine.   **EXPOSURE:** Sun.

LEAVES: Alternate, simple; 2 to 4 inches long and narrow; tapering to a distinct point at the tip and slightly rounded at the base. Leaves may or may not be curled or twisted, as the cultivar name implies. Glossy, dark green under good growing conditions, but may be pale green on a tree under stress, especially from lack of moisture. Yellow in the fall.

STEM: Young stems are upright, green, smooth, slender, and twisted or contorted in various ways. Stems 1 inch or more in diameter retain their twisted and unusual growth characteristics with the main stem and branches becoming more round and "normal" only with considerable age. Bark on an old stem develops a gray-brown color and becomes shallowly furrowed. Wood is soft and brittle and is very subject to decay.

FLOWERS: None.

FRUIT: None.

COLOR: Leaves are dark green; twisted young stems are green.

PROPAGATION: Cuttings anytime.

CULTURE: Grows well anywhere that moisture exists. Grows on practically any soil as long as it is moist. A very rapid-growing, short-lived willow with typical weak wood and decay susceptibility. The root system is aggressive and frequently causes problems in drain or sewer lines. If one is to plant this tree, choose a site with plenty of moisture or around a water feature but out of the primary viewing area.

PESTS: Leaf-eating insects frequently damage foliage, but rarely is it serious. Mites occasionally on a very hot site such as on the west side of a building with glass.

NOTES: Praised by some, scorned by others, but sold in large quantities by the nursery trade. Very easy to grow and short-lived. it is a real eye-catcher, more because of the bizarre than the beautiful. Should be located discreetly among other plants to avoid over emphasis or distraction among other plants. Moisture is a must. Grows well even in the heavy clays of Dallas and alkaline soils of San Antonio, Texas, if moisture is present. Useful in creating a quick diversionary effect away from some adjacent area. Plant at your own risk.

CULTIVARS: 'Navajo': a round-headed tree of about 20 feet; quite formal. Not at all twisting and contorted like 'Tortuosa'.

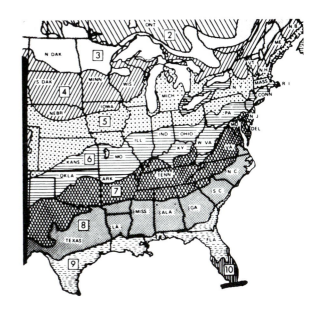

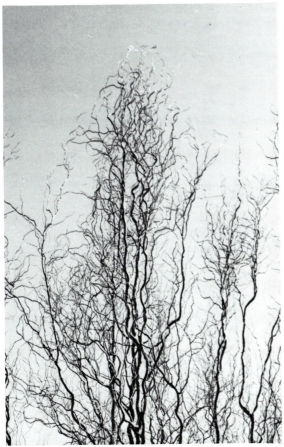

Salix nigra Muhl.   Black Willow
Salicaceae or Willow Family   Hardiness Zone 3
Native to the eastern United States.
SIZE: 40 to 80 feet tall with a 30- to 50-foot spread. Growth rate is very rapid.
FORM: Broad-crowned, often multi-stemmed tree.
TEXTURE: Fine.   **EXPOSURE:** Sun.

LEAVES: Alternate, simple; narrowly lanceolate or spear-shaped, 3 to 6 inches long, and 1/4 to 1/2 inch wide. Rounded at the base and long pointed. Edges are finely toothed. Medium to dark green above, pale green below; yellow in the fall.

STEM: Young stem is very slender and green at first, becoming smooth and red-brown with age. Young stems stand upright (no weeping). Eventually develops a light brown to black rough bark that is deeply fissured into thick shaggy scales. Bark often appears to be spiraling up the stem.

FLOWERS: Male and female flowers on separate trees (dioecious). Flowers (catkins) appear about the time the leaves emerge or slightly before.

FRUIT: Small capsule; inconspicuous.

COLOR: Foliage is medium to dark green; yellow in the fall.

PROPAGATION: Seed or cuttings; very easy.

CULTURE: Like most willows, it is moisture-loving. Any moist location is likely to contain some native willows. Plays an important role in stabilizing streambanks and riverbeds. Tolerates a wide range of soil conditions as long as sufficient moisture is present. Good for use around water features and in seepy or moist areas. Responds vigorously to supplemental fertilization. Very easy to grow. Short-lived on most sites. Needs some pruning while young to assist in strong branch development. By cutting out the female (seed-producing) trees the problem of seedlings everywhere can be reduced somewhat, but since the seeds travel for miles in the wind, it is not the total solution.

PESTS: Borers and stem canker on stressed trees.

NOTES: An attractive and interesting small to medium-sized tree, particularly around water features. Similar texture but contrasting form with weeping willow, in that black willow branches are mostly upright. No weeping. The umbrella-like crown of foliage is very light-textured, allowing considerable light to penetrate, making a desirable shade or shadow effect. Wood is soft and weak and readily broken in wind or ice storms, creating some maintenance problems. Grown as a single stem or several trees planted together. It can be a useful landscape tree with interesting form and light texture. However, only male trees should be planted to reduce the seedling problem. Numerous other species of willow can be found in various parts of the world. Most have somewhat similar leaf form and growth habit and are rather difficult to distinguish.

CULTIVARS: None known.

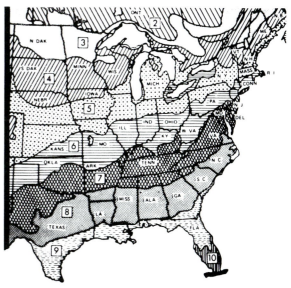

Sapindus drummondi Hook and Arn.   Western Soapberry
Sapindaceae or Soapberry Family   Hardiness Zone 5
Native to the south central United States.

SIZE: 30 to 40 feet tall with a 25- to 35-foot spread as a single-stem specimen. Slow grower.

FORM: Broad, oval, small to medium size tree with slightly weeping branches.

TEXTURE: Fine.   **EXPOSURE:** Sun.

LEAVES: Alternate, compound; 5 to 12 inches long, with 4 to 11 pairs of leaflets. Individual leaflets are 1 to 2 1/2 inches long, 1/2 to 1 inch wide; slightly curved or sickle-shaped, and asymmetrical at the base. Medium to yellow-green; yellow-gold in the fall.

STEM: In the spring, a new flush of growth begins developing leaves. As the length of the days gets longer, the same flush becomes reproductive and sets numerous flowers. In the following year, the new shoot arises from one of the small axillary buds behind where the flowers and fruits were produced the previous season. This unusual process gives the stem a very unusual zigzag effect. Young stems are yellowish green to gray. With age, stems become smooth and gray-brown, eventually developing a shallowly furrowed, platy or scaly bark that is salmon-brown to orange-brown. Wood is strong, durable, and wind-resistant.

FLOWERS: Small, dense clusters at the tips of the current season's growth. Yellow-green to white; not showy.

FRUIT: In clusters at the tips of the new growth, about 1/2 inch round, and translucent yellow-orange when ripe. Attractive. Seed is black, 1/4 to 1/2 inch diameter. Soapberries derive their common name from the berries which, when crushed in water, develop a lather like soap. Fruit has a mildly poisonous property.

COLOR: Foliage is yellow-green to medium green; brilliant yellow-gold in the fall. Fruit is yellow-orange and showy.

PROPAGATION: Seed or softwood cuttings.

CULTURE: Native to dry, poor soils throughout much of the southern prairie states. Extremely tough and tolerant of poor soils with little moisture and low fertility. Should be planted much more on urban sites, particularly where the soil has been greatly disturbed and is poor to fair at best. Easy to transplant and generally adjusts quickly to a new site. Wood is hard and durable. Form is umbrella-like, making an excellent shade or patio tree, and it retains a size relative to single story dwellings. Fruit remains showy throughout the winter until early spring. Seeds do sprout and become a nuisance in flower beds, ground covers, and other landscape areas. However, if soapberry is placed in an open yard where the young seedlings are mowed with the grass, seedlings are not a problem. Must be one of the best and yet most overlooked of the small or medium-sized native trees that could be utilized in urban landscaping. DO NOT confuse this with Chinaberry, *Melia azedarach*.

PESTS: None serious.

NOTES: Far superior to many of the questionable species being sold. Has a great deal of merit as a shade and ornamental tree. Has good shade, form, color, and durability, is relatively pest-free, and will grow on most sites. Long overlooked and should be planted more. Although the fruit pulp is mildly poisonous, it is also very bitter, making it highly unlikely anyone would eat enough to cause more than a mild stomach ache. ??-POISON-??

CULTIVARS: None.

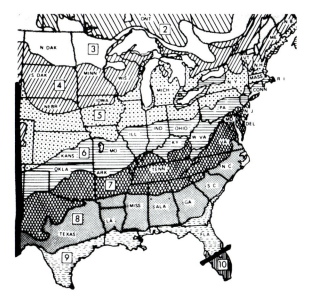

Sapium sebiferum (L.) Roxb.   Chinese Tallow Tree
Euphorbiaceae or Euphorbia Family   Hardiness Zone 8
Native to China and Japan.
SIZE: 30- to 50-foot tree with a 20- to 40-foot spread. Rapid grower.
FORM: Tree with rounded crown and loose, open branching.
TEXTURE: Medium.   **EXPOSURE:** Sun.

LEAVES: Alternate, simple; ovate with a long, tapering point at the tip, 2 to 3 inches long overall with a smooth margin and medium green color. Fall color is very strikingly red-orange to yellow. Very showy.

STEM: Young stems are slender and smooth. Bark is brown and becomes rough and flaky with age.

FLOWERS: Small clusters of yellow flowers at the tips of branches in the spring. Not showy.

FRUIT: White, waxy seeds hang on the tree throughout the fall and winter. Rather showy.

COLOR: Fall color is spectacular, even in the Deep South.

PROPAGATION: Seed.

CULTURE: A very adaptable species, restricted only by temperatures that drop below zero degrees F. It is very drought-tolerant and will grow on virtually any soil: good or poor, wet or dry. Serves well as a street tree where soils are often compacted and root space is limited. Easy to grow as a nursery tree with good straight trunk and transplants easily. In situations where a very fast-growing tree is needed, this is a better choice than some of the weeds such as silver maple, box elder, royal paulownia, and varnish tree.

PESTS: None.

NOTES: A very adaptable and tolerant tree. However, it is short-lived, geneaally only 15 to 25 years. In the Houston, Texas area, and similarly across the Deep South, Chinese tallow tree has escaped to become a nuisance in many areas, much like tree-of-heaven in the North. On the other hand, it functions very well as a street tree or in locations of reflected heat and light, poor soils, and/or drought where few other trees will grow. Fall color is superb, rivaled in the South only by Chinese pistache, since few plants in Zone 9 color well in the fall. It is called popcorn tree in some areas because of the popcorn-like fruits that persist throughout the winter. Virtually insect- and disease-free. Plagued only by lawnmower and vehicle blight, as are all trees, particularly in public areas. Transplants easily. There is much need for a sterile cultivar that can be propagated from cuttings so as to take advantage of the strengths and avoid the weaknesses (seedlings). ??-POISON-??

CULTIVARS: None known.

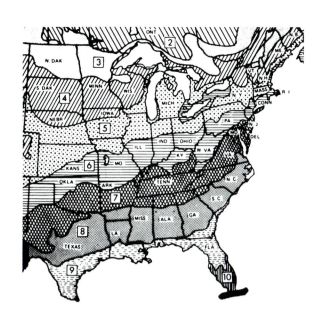

Sassafras albidum (Nutt.) Nees.   Sassafras
Lauraceae or Laurel Family   Hardiness Zone 5
Native to the eastern United States.
SIZE: 30 to 50 feet tall tree. Fast grower.
FORM: An irregular tree in clumps or with narrow, rounded crown as a single stem.
TEXTURE: Medium.   **EXPOSURE:** Sun or partial shade.

LEAVES: Alternate, simple; ovate or with 1 to 3 lobes, and smooth margin. Some leaves are shaped like mittens. Bright green above and hairy when young; later, the hairs on the upper surface are lost. Emit a pleasant, spicy odor when crushed. Fall color is orange to red-orange.

STEM: Young twigs are yellow-green, slender and hairy, becoming smooth with age, and have a spicy odor when scraped or broken. The bark becomes thicker, rough, deeply furrowed, and red-brown to brown as it ages. Wood is orange-brown, weak, and brittle.

FLOWERS: Male and female on separate trees (dioecious). Female flowers are yellow, fragrant, and in small terminal clusters before the leaves. Not showy. Male flowers are not conspicuous.

FRUIT: Small, oval, blue-black fruits on reddish stalks (pedicels). Fruit is readily eaten by wildlife.

COLOR: Foliage is bright green; orange to red-orange in fall.

PROPAGATION: Seed, root cuttings, or suckers.

CULTURE: Occurs in mixed stands over a wide range of the eastern U.S. from near the Gulf Coast to the Canadian border. Readily invades disturbed sites in its native range, but grows more slowly and is less aggressive west of the Mississippi River. Responds to good soils, moisture, mulching, and fertilizer. Difficult to transplant from the wild, probably due to a strong taproot, slow regeneration of roots, and high water loss from the leaves. Best when grown from root cuttings or seeds.

PESTS: The foliage is frequently damaged by leaf-eating insects, but normally not devoured. Occasionally root rot on wet, heavy, clay soils.

NOTES: The light, bright green foliage contrasts with leaves of most other plants. A thicket of sassafras is spectacular in the fall. Useful in slightly out-of-the-way areas as a filler plant that waves a delightful farewell to summer. It is more dense and attractive when grown as a single-stem specimen tree. Not common in the nursery trade, probably due to the difficulty in transplanting field-grown trees and the strong taproot which is not compatible with container production. Best propagated by planting seed on the site or by root cuttings planted on the landscape site, if practical. The bark of the roots is sometimes used to make sassafras tea. Not tolerant of drought or drying winds. Leaves lose water quickly and may drop during droughts. West of its normal range, heavy mulches of leaves or other organic matter aid the tree.

CULTIVARS: None known although the potential is there.

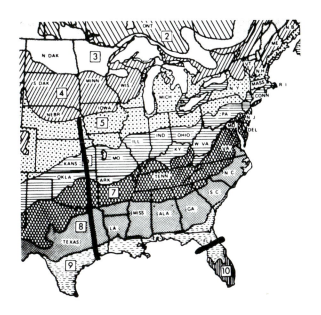

Sophora japonica L.   Japanese Pagoda Tree/Chinese Scholar Tree
Leguminosae or Legume Family   Hardiness Zone 4
Native to China and Korea.
SIZE: 40 to 80 feet tall with a 20- to 40-foot spread. Rapid grower on most sites.
FORM: Round-headed tree with spreading branches; variable.
TEXTURE: Fine.   EXPOSURE: Sun.

LEAVES: Alternate, compound; 6 to 10 inches long, composed of 7 to 17 ovate leaflets that are 1 to 2 inches long with smooth margins. Leaves are rounded at the base and taper to a point at the tip. Medium to dark green above and only slightly lighter green below; some yellow fall color.

STEM: Young stem is green and moderately slender. Young branches remain a dark, shiny green for several years before finally becoming a medium to dark brown. Bark on a mature tree is shallowly furrowed and medium brown. Wood is moderately strong and sufficiently flexible, so wind or ice damage is minimal.

FLOWERS: Cream colored, pea-like, 1 to 1 1/2 inches in diameter, in loose clusters 10 to 12 inches long, appearing in June or July. Male and female in the same flower (perfect). Moderately showy.

FRUIT: A 2- to 4-inch long, yellow-green pod, which is constricted between each of its numerous seeds. Can be rather messy over a sidewalk or patio.

COLOR: Foliage is medium to dark green. Flowers are cream-colored.

PROPAGATION: Seed or grafting of selected cultivars.

CULTURE: Tolerates a wide range of moisture and atmospheric conditions as long as soils are fair to good. Does not tolerate extremely poor soils. Where soils are fair to good, it will tolerate considerable drought. Considerable variation among seedlings in form, branch development, and crown type, thus the selection of improved cultivars. Used some in the Northeast for planting in areas of restricted root systems and city conditions. Tolerates smoke and atmospheric pollution well. Likewise, on the west coast it is considered a desirable shade and ornamental tree.

PESTS: Occasionally spider mites.

NOTES: A desirable, textured, shade tree. May have good form, spreads horizontally to cover patios and outdoor recreation areas well. Often said to be a small to medium-sized tree. On good sites this is not true, since it can reach 40 to 60 feet in a relatively short period of time. Leaves and seeds may have a mildly toxic property.   ??-POISON-??

CULTIVARS: 'Regent': a rapid grower with straight trunk. Flowers heavily. 'Fastigiata' or 'Columnaris': a more strict, upright grower of fair appearance. 'Pendula': a weeping form, propagated by seed. Other cultivars probably exist.

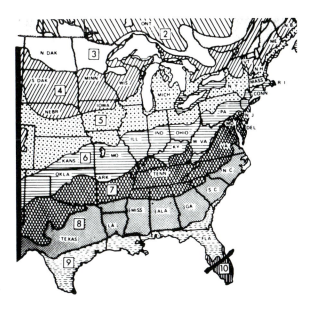

Sophora secundiflora   Texas Mountain Laurel, Mescal Bean, Coral Bean
Leguminosae or Legume Family   Hardiness Zone 7B
Native to west Texas and southward into Mexico.
SIZE: 15 to 30 feet tall, 12 to 15 feet wide; variable. Slow grower.
FORM: Irregular, small tree; either single- or multiple-stemmed as a clump.
TEXTURE: Fine.   **EXPOSURE:** Sun.

LEAVES: Alternate, compound; with 7 to 13 leaflets, each more or less oval, rounded, or notched at the tip and gradually tapering to the base and with a smooth margin. Leaflets are sessile or nearly so. Glossy, dark green upper leaf surface with a few hairs when young; paler below with more hairs.

STEM: Green; slender and covered with fine hairs when young, later becomes smooth and gradually changes to orange-brown. The old bark is dark gray to nearly black, broken into shallow furrows with thin scales. The wood is orange to nearly red; quite tough and durable.

FLOWER: In dense clusters with the young leaves in March or April; 4 to 6 inches long or more. The violet to lavender flowers are quite striking and fragrant.

FRUIT: A green pod which turns brown in late fall and stays on the tree. The hard, woody pod is 2 to 5 inches long and covered with dense brown hairs and is slightly to severely constricted between seeds. Seeds are red and about 1/2 inch in diameter with very hard seed coat, typical of the family.

COLOR: Flowers are violet to lavender. Foliage is dark, glossy green.

PROPAGATION: Seed. After scarification or acid treatment to break down the hard seed coat germination proceeds rapidly. Cuttings root with difficulty, if at all.

CULTURE: Native to limestone soils in central and west Texas. Once established it tolerates drought and reflected light and heat. Must have drainage in order to thrive. It is difficult to transplant from the wild, but if grown in air-root-pruning containers, which force the tap root to branch, it can be moved without difficulty as a nursery plant. Planting the seeds directly in conventional containers is an error as the tap root will spiral and provide poor anchorage, if the plant survives.

PESTS: None serious in its native habitat.

NOTES: A spectacular small tree when in flower and the attractive glossy, green foliage adds to the landscape the remainder of the growing season. Once established, it requires little care and can survive severe drought, reflected light, and heat. Seedlings are variable in terms of flower color, tree form, and other features. This unique tree is generally not known outside of its native range. In warm climates and where soils or large raised planters drain well, this could add a unique benefit elsewhere.

CULTIVARS: None known.

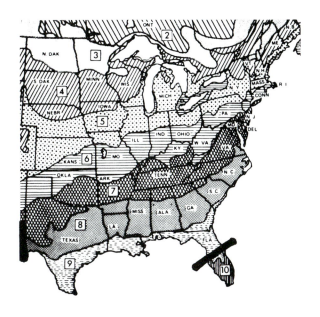

Sorbus aucuparia L.   European Mountainash
Rosaceae or Rose Family   Hardiness Zone 3
Native to Europe and western Asia.
SIZE: 15 to 30 feet tall with a 10- to 20-foot spread. Rapid grower under good conditions.
FORM: Upright, columnar or spreading-crowned, small tree. Variable.
TEXTURE: Fine.   **EXPOSURE:** Sun to shade.

LEAVES: Alternate, compound; fern-like, and 5 to 7 inches long. Composed of 9 to 15 leaflets that are 1 to 2 inches long with toothed margins. Dull green to gray-green above, paler below. Brilliant orange to red in the fall.

STEM: Red to red-brown and straight with limited branching. Bark develops a gray cast with age, finally becoming a gray-brown but remains relatively smooth and does not furrow. Wood is only moderately strong. Branches tend to develop narrow forks if not properly pruned.

FLOWERS: White. About 1/2 inch in diameter, in large flat clusters that appear in late spring.

FRUIT: Shiny red to orange; 1/4 to 1/2 inch in diameter, in large flat clusters; very attractive during late summer and fall. Similar to pyracantha berries.

COLOR: Foliage is dull green to gray-green; red to red-orange in the fall. Flowers are white. Fruit is red to orange, depending on cultivar.

PROPAGATION: Seed or grafting of cultivars.

CULTURE: Grows in a wide range of soils. Very tolerant to cold. However, it does not tolerate drought or sustained heat which might be encountered in city locations with a lot of paving. Does best in areas where nights are cool and days are sunny such as Rocky Mountain areas and northeastern United States. However, for a short, quick effect in many areas of the upper South, it is a spectacular, rapidly growing small tree which is short-lived but very showy. Perhaps best suited to light, shifting shade. Needs pruning when young to aid in strong branch development.

PESTS: Borers on trees under stress or on poor sites. Occasionally spider mites or aphids. Fire blight may be serious in humid locations with poor air movement.

NOTES: A spectacular tree where it can be grown. Assisted by mulching to conserve moisture and reduce soil temperatures in areas of the South and Southwest. Should be considered a short-term landscape plant with a maximum duration of 6 to 10 years. By that time, vigor will decline and it will become susceptible to borers.

CULTIVARS: Many exist, mostly variable in fruit color and growth form. 'Fastigiata': very upright growth habit. 'Pendula': weeping branches. 'Xanthocarpa': a round-headed tree with yellow fruit. 'Cardinal Royal': rich green leaves with red fruits; very striking.

RELATED SPECIES: *Sorbus alnifolia*, Korean mountainash, is hardy in Zone 3, grows to 40 feet, and has leaves that are ovate (not compound), flowers are white and fruits are reddish in Ocotber. Very showy. May do well as far south as Zone 7?

Sorbus tianshanica, Tianshanica mountainash 'Red Cascade' grows only to 15 feet or so but is quite showy with dark green foliage, white flowers, and red fruits.

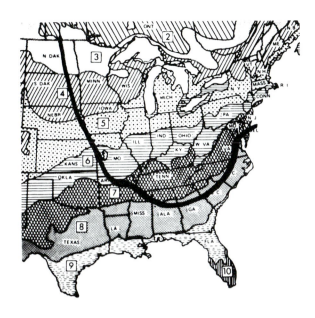

Stewartia pseudocamellia   Japanese Stewartia
Theaceae or Tea Family   Hardiness Zone 5
Native to Japan
SIZE: 20 to 40 feet or more. Moderate grower.
FORM: Pyramidal to oval, small tree.
TEXTURE: Medium.   **EXPOSURE:** Sun to partial shade.

LEAVES: Simple, alternate; oval to elliptical; 2 to 3 1/2 inches long, 1 to 2 inches wide with a serrate margin. Dark green to slightly pale green above; light green below and with a few long hairs. The petiole is quite short. Fall color is orange to red-orange.

STEM: Mostly a central leader to somewhat irregularly branched tree. The young twigs are green, soon turning an orange light brown. Limbs about one inch or more in diameter begin the striking peeling bark revealing the orange-brown bark beneath. The bark is very showy and remains so, even with the trunks of old plants.

FLOWERS: White; about 2 inches across, with many yellow anthers and appears much like a camellia. The flower buds have a red-tipped bract on each side. Flowers generally appear in July or August. Very showy.

FRUIT: A capsule about 1 inch long and hairy; splits into 5 sections. Not showy.

COLOR: Foliage is dark green; orange to red-orange in the fall. Flowers are white. Bark is orange-brown and spectacular.

PROPAGATION: Seeds which require two winters before germination occurs. Roots poorly from cuttings, if at all.

CULTURE: Needs good soils, drainage, and fairly uniform moisture to do well. Appears to be sensitive to drought and definitely not for areas with poor soil drainage or where reflected light and heat add to the environmental stress. This plant is quite tolerant to cold but not to prolonged heat and drought. Also, it does not appear to be the stress of transplanting, as with some species. In Stillwater, Oklahoma, plants watered and cared for during their first two summers either died or severely died back the third summer when no supplemental water was applied. From this experience, lots of mulch and supplemental summer watering may be the key.

PESTS: None serious.

NOTES: This is a truly spectacular tree and is worth all the effort required to get it established and keep it growing well. Perhaps the best of the various *Stewartias*.

CULTIVARS: None.

RELATED SPECIES: *Stewartia sinensis*, Chinese Stewartia, grows to 15 to 25 feet tall as a small tree or large shrub. Fragrant white flowers in July. Leaves are generally larger than *S. pseudocamellia* on stems that are hairy and nearly red. Outer bark is coppery brown revealing the cream-colored stem.

Stewartia ovata, Mountain Stewartia, is a small tree or large shrub, 10 to 15 feet tall. Good fall color but the bark is not as attractive as *S. pseudocamellia* or *S. sinensis*, but the flowers are larger, sometimes 3 to 4 inches across.

Several other *Stewartia* species exist.

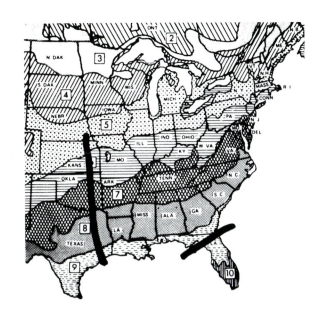

S. ovata

Syringa reticulata (Blume) Hara. Japanese Tree Lilac
     (Syn. *Syringa amurensis*)
Oleaceae or Olive Family Hardiness Zone 3
Native to northern China.
SIZE: 20 to 30 feet tall with a 10- to 15-foot spread. Slow to moderate grower.
FORM: Upright, small tree with rounded crown.
TEXTURE: Medium. **EXPOSURE:** Sun or slight shade.

LEAVES: Opposite, simple; broadly ovate to nearly heart-shaped with a smooth margin, 3 to 5 inches long, and 2 to 4 inches wide. Rather dull, dark green above; lighter green below. Foliage on a healthy tree is quite dense.

STEM: Young branches are stout and bright brown with large, prominent, horizontal lenticels, much like cherry. Wood is stout and durable. Older stems are red-brown to brown and smooth, except for the lenticels.

FLOWERS: White, in large, dense clusters, 4 to 8 inches long or more. Appear after the leaves are fully mature, generally in June. Very showy for 1 to 2 weeks. Flower clusters are on the outer surface of the foliage. Very striking.

FRUIT: In loose clusters all over the tree. Each seed pod is oblong and 1/2 to 1 inch long.

COLOR: Flowers are white and very showy. Foliage is dark green and dense.

PROPAGATION: Seed or softwood cuttings.

CULTURE: Japanese tree lilac is more adaptable than generally realized. Mature trees are very attractive at the Bartlett Arboretum near Wichita, Kansas, and young trees growing in a poor, heavy clay in central Oklahoma survive but grow very slowly. Flowering is best in full sun. Probably should not be planted below Zone 7 due to chilling requirement of the flower buds and the shorter photoperiod. Grows best in Zones 5, 4, and 3 where the days are long during the May/June/July period.

PESTS: Lilac borer in trees under stress; occasionally scale and mites. However, on a good site, this excellent tree has few problems.

NOTES: A very showy tree that is quite adaptable to a range of soils and growing conditions. Deserves to be used much more. Because of the time of bloom (June), frosts do not damage flower buds as they do with other lilac species and cultivars.

CULTIVARS: 'Ivory Silk': more flowers and glossier foliage. 'Regent': a vigorous upright grower. 'Summer Snow': a prolific bloomer and has a lighter, more attractive bark. Others probably exist.

RELATED SPECIES: *Syringa pekinensis* Rupr., Chinese tree lilac or Pekin lilac, is hardy in Zone 4 and grows 15 to 20 feet tall. May be grown as a large, multiple-stem shrub or small tree. Leaves are 2 to 3 inches long, ovate, and dark green. Flowers are creamy yellow, in large clusters and appear in June. Even less well-known than the Japanese tree lilac, but is an excellent large shrub or multiple stem, small tree. Somewhat neater and more refined in appearance than the larger Japanese tree lilac. Deserves much more attention. Softwood cuttings can be rooted and respond well to nursery conditions and care in the landscape. 'Summer Charm': has smaller leaves and many cream-colored flowers. Others probably exist.

245

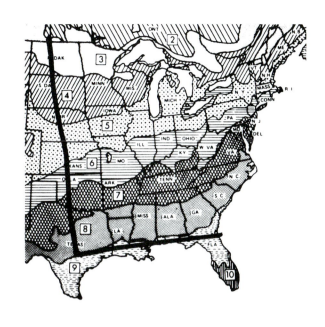

Taxodium distichum (L.) A. Rich.   Bald Cypress
Taxodiaceae or Bald Cypress Family   Hardiness Zone 4
Native to the southeastern United States.

SIZE: 60 to 100 feet tall with variable spread. Moderate to rapid grower, depending on site.

FORM: Pyramidal to moderate-spreading tree, varying with seedlings and seed sources.

TEXTURE: Very fine, fern-like.   **EXPOSURE:** Full sun only.

LEAVES: Needle-like, 1/2 to 1 inch long, and very delicate. Arranged in two ranks in a feather-like fashion along very small branchlets. Leaves are flat with pointed tips. In the fall the entire branchlet consisting of many leaves drops as one unit. Also unusual in that this conifer drops whole twigs of leaves, whereas most are evergreen. A soft, medium green; coppery bronze in the fall.

STEM: Light green at first, but becomes reddish brown and rough-surfaced by the end of the first season. Very flexible. Branches are mostly at near-right angles to the trunk. Bark develops a cinnamon brown by the end of the second or third season. Fairly smooth, yet finely divided into vertical strips that are separated by shallow furrows. The main stem tapers gradually from the base to the tip. In wet locations, the trees develop numerous knees, which are stump-like projections sticking up around the base of the tree, sometimes in great numbers. These do not develop when the tree is planted on a dry to only moderately moist site. Wood is light weight, but very durable and decay-resistant.

FLOWERS: Male and female separate on the same tree (monoecious). Males are in long, drooping clusters; females are small globe-shaped units on the ends of branches.

FRUIT: Globe-shaped, woody cone, about 1 to 1 1/2 inches in diameter, with thick, irregular scales that contain seeds. The cones have numerous oil glands and can be rather messy.

COLOR: Foliage is soft, medium green; coppery bronze in the fall.

PROPAGATION: Seed, or softwood cuttings with difficulty.

CULTURE: Native to swampy areas throughout the southeastern United States. Grows profusely in a wide range of soil types: heavy clay, silt, or muck, or wherever considerable moisture is present. Will grow quite rapidly with fertilization, as long as adequate moisture is present, either surface or subsoil. Does well around ponds, water features, or seepy areas in almost any location. Will tolerate dry periods without difficulty. May shed its foliage and appear to be dead during a long drought. However, the tree is rarely damaged.

PESTS: None serious.

NOTES: A spectacular, fern-like tree. The lacy foliage and fall color make bald cypress a highly prized landscape plant. Far more adaptable than is generally realized. Is very intolerant of shade and must be planted where all parts of the plant receive full sun for good development.

CULTIVARS: 'Pendens': droops at the tips of branches and produces many male flowers.

RELATED SPECIES: *Taxodium ascendens* Brong., pond cypress, is much more upright and narrow with string-like leaves. Similar in adaptability and fall color. A very striking, desirable tree.

Taxodium mucronatum, Montezuma cypress, is native to west Texas and much of Mexico. The leaves are more gray, but otherwise similar to bald cypress. More tolerant of alkaline soils. This is probably an ecological race that evolved in a different climate.

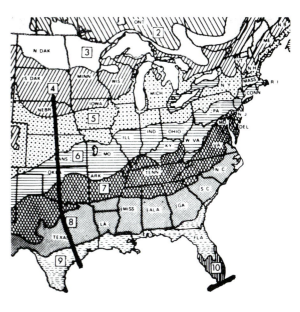

Taxodium ascendens

Tilia americana L.   American Linden or Basswood
Tiliaceae or Basswood Family   Hardiness Zone 3
Native to the eastern United States.
SIZE: 40 to 80 feet tall with a 40- to 50-foot spread. Moderate to rapid grower.
FORM: Broad, rounded-crown tree.
TEXTURE: Medium   **EXPOSURE**: Sun to partial shade.

LEAVES: Alternate, simple; basically heart-shaped but lopsided, tapering to a point at the tip, 2 to 6 inches long, 2 to 4 inches wide, on slender petioles. Leaves are variable even within the same tree. Margin is coarsely toothed. Generally dark green above, paler green below; bright yellow in the fall.

STEM: Young stem is moderately stout, red to red-green at first and zigzags. Later takes on a smooth, silvery gray color for several years and finally becomes a gray-brown to black, narrowly ridged, moderately fissured bark when mature. Ridges extend unbroken for great lengths up the trunk. There is a distinct "attachment scar" where branches are attached to the main stem. Buds are egg-shaped with 2 visible bud scales shiny red to red-brown. Wood is light, soft, only moderately wind-, ice-, or vandal-resistant. However, this is rarely a problem unless weak branch angles are allowed to develop.

FLOWERS: Individual flowers are yellow to white, very fragrant, full of nectar, and attract many bees. In clusters on the ends of a long stalk. Each stalk is borne with a narrow, leaf-like wing. Not showy, but interesting.

FRUIT: Round, gray-green, nut-like, about 1/4 inch in diameter, hanging from the underside of the leaf-like ribbon; very distinct. Matures in the fall.

COLOR: Foliage is deep green; yellow in the fall.

PROPAGATION: Seed or grafting of cultivars.

CULTURE: Grows best in fertile soils where adequate moisture is present. Is moderately tolerant to heat, extreme conditions, and low humidity, but not drought-resistant, and should not be used where soils are only fair to poor. Has a desirable form and is a good landscape tree for many uses where soils are good and moisture is adequate. Leaf scorch may occur in the lower mid-plains states during drought period. Needs some corrective pruning to assure good branch development and avoid weak narrow branching.

PESTS: None serious, occasionally borers on a weakened tree growing on an ill-suited site.

NOTES: More broadly spreading and round-headed than the European linden and thus more desirable as a shade tree. When doing well, foliage gets quite dense, making it difficult to grow plant materials beneath it. Fragrance of the flowers must be listed as a plus in the landscape. However, may be troublesome to people because of the high population of bees when flowers are open in the spring. Good for a moderately moist location where willow and bald cypress are not wanted.

CULTIVARS: 'Redmond' is now considered a cultivar rather than a hybrid as listed in some references. In the past, it was listed as *Tilia* X *euchlora* 'Redmond'. Leaves are more leathery and heat scorch-resistant. Similar in form to most seedlings. 'Douglas': broad, pyramidal form with deep green foliage. 'Legend': pyramidal growth, good form, leathery leaves are less prone to tatter. Others exist.

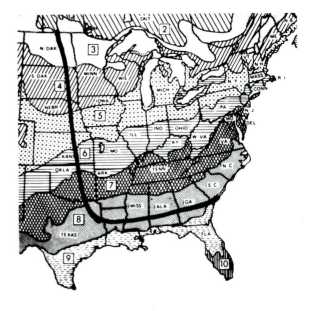

'Redmond'

Tilia cordata Mill.   European Littleleaf Linden
Tiliaceae or Basswood Family   Hardiness Zone 3
Native to Europe.
SIZE: 40 to 80 feet tall with a 20- to 40-foot spread. Rapid grower.
FORM: Densely pyramidal when young, spreading slightly with age.
TEXTURE: Medium.   **EXPOSURE:** Sun.

LEAVES: Alternate, simple; 1 1/2 to 2 inches wide, more or less heart-shaped but lopsided. Distinctly heart-shaped at the base. Irregularly toothed margin. Medium to dark green above, much lighter below; fall color is yellow.

STEM: Young stem is slender, reddish brown, slightly zigzag. Buds are much smaller than on American linden. Buds are egg-shaped with only two visible bud scales. Branches remain steel gray for several years, finally developing a gray to gray-black, shallowly furrowed bark. Wood is soft and rather brittle. Extremely variable with seedlings (some are strong, some very weak), thus the importance of selected cultivars that have superior wood strength and strong branch development.

FLOWERS: Individual flowers are yellow to white, very fragrant, in clusters at the end of a long stalk. Each stalk is borne with a narrow, leaf-like wing. Flowers are full of nectar and attract many bees. Not showy but very noticeable due to the fragrance.

FRUIT: Round, gray-green, nut-like, 1/4 inch in diameter, and hanging from the underside of the leaf-like ribbon. Very distinct. Matures in the fall.

COLOR: Foliage is deep green; yellow in the fall.

PROPAGATION: Seed or grafting of cultivars.

CULTURE: Tolerates a wide range of soil conditions. Very adaptable as long as moisture is not particularly limiting. Withstands some moisture stress, but is not for the southwestern states, where drought may be severe at times, unless planted around a water feature, moist area, or where irrigation can supply moisture during times of limited rainfall. May require occasional pruning to avoid weak branch development or double leaders.

PESTS: Japanese beetle in areas of the Upper South and northeastern United States. Other insects may defoliate portions of leaves at times. No serious diseases.

NOTES: An attractive, densely pyramidal tree, particularly when young. Reminiscent of a pin oak but much more tolerant of alkaline and poor soils as long as moisture is present. Interesting texture contrast with pin oak. Cultivars should be used more, but only where consideration is given to the moisture requirement. When it is in flower, bees can be a hazard.

CULTIVARS: 'Chancellor': characterized by a straight trunk, dense foliage, and a compact, narrow, upright growth habit. 'Greenspire': a rapid-growing selection with a narrow oval form, straight trunk, dense foliage, and many small fragrant flowers in the spring. 'June Bride': narrow and upright with glossy green foliage. 'Glenleven': very dark green foliage, with strong central leader and narrow, pyramidal form. 'Rancho': narrow upright selection with very small foliage; a vigorous grower. Several others exist.

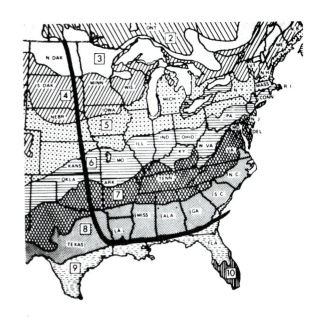

Tilia tomentosa Moench.   Silver Linden
Tiliaceae or Basswood Family   Hardiness Zone 4
Native to southeastern Europe and southwestern Asia.
SIZE: 40 to 70 feet tall with a 30- to 50-foot spread. Moderate grower.
FORM: Pyramidal when young, becoming broader and more rounded with age.
TEXTURE: Medium to coarse.   **EXPOSURE**: Sun or slight shade.

LEAVES: Alternate, simple; 3 to 4 inches long, and more or less heart-shaped but lopsided, with a doubly saw-toothed margin. Shiny, dark green above; hairy, nearly white beneath. Very attractive when viewed from beneath or during a moderate breeze. Fall color is yellow but not especially attractive.

STEM: A strong, central leader tree with light gray bark that is smooth and attractive and becomes furrowed only with age. Wood is not particularly strong, which is typical of all lindens, but since branch angles are generally wide and young limbs are flexible, breakage is not a serious problem. Young stems are green and covered with hairs at first, becoming silvery gray with age.

FLOWERS: Yellow, fragrant, appear in clusters on a papery modified leaf in early summer. Bees love them, so they should not be planted near outdoor living areas.

FRUIT: A nut-like structure, 5-angled; suspended from a papery, modified leaf.

COLOR: Leaves are glossy, dark green above, nearly white below. Bark is silvery gray.

PROPAGATION: Seed or grafting.

CULTURE: Grows in a range of soils, but prefers deep, fertile soils with adequate moisture. Like most lindens, it is not especially drought-tolerant. Rather slow to establish following transplanting, thus some additional attention to watering may be required, especially in the Prairie states. Mulching, supplemental watering during droughts, and eliminating grass and weed competition will increase the growth and appearance following the transplanting of this magnificent tree.

PESTS: Various leaf-eating insects may damage foliage.

NOTES: A spectacular tree in overall form. Likewise, the glossy green foliage is eye-catching when viewed from a distance. The white underside of the leaves provide an unusual effect when viewed from below. The silvery bark is attractive anytime of the year. It is surprising that this tree has not been planted more, since it has so many outstanding visual qualities. Special care in site selection and assistance during establishment is needed especially west of the Mississippi River and south of Zone 7, but this tree is well worth the effort. The specimen in the photograph is in a home landscape with many other trees in west central Illinois. It stands out (without being gaudy like a crimson king Norway maple). Refined elegance might be the most appropriate description.

CULTIVARS: 'Green Mountain': a more rapid grower with rounded crown and very dark leaves. 'Sterling': more upright grower with dark foliage. Very attractive. Said to be somewhat resistant to beetle damage. Others exist.

Ulmus americana L.   American Elm
Ulmaceae or Elm Family   Hardiness Zone 2
Native to the eastern United States.

SIZE: 80 to 100 feet tall with a 60- to 80-foot spread. Rapid grower when young, slower with age.

FORM: Large tree with broad, umbrella-like crown and vase-shaped branching.

TEXTURE: Medium.   **EXPOSURE:** Sun.

LEAVES: Alternate, simple; 4 to 6 inches long, 1 to 3 inches wide. More or less oval but uneven or lopsided. Tip is drawn out to a narrow point, base is rounded and margin is doubly toothed. Rough and sandpapery on the upper surface. Bright medium green above, slightly paler green below; golden in the fall.

STEM: Slender, reddish brown, turning gray with age. Eventually forms an irregular, gray to gray-black bark that is deeply furrowed and covered with irregular, thin scales. Wood is strong and stout, making it wind-, ice-, and vandal-resistant.

FLOWERS: Borne in clusters along the stem in late winter. Not showy.

FRUIT: Not showy; 1/4 to 1/2 inch long with a single seed in a circular, papery wing that is notched at the tip. Matures in early spring.

COLOR: Foliage is bright medium green; yellow in the fall.

PROPAGATION: Seed, softwood cuttings, or root cuttings.

CULTURE: Will grow in virtually any site: wet or dry, good or poor soils, exposed or protected locations. Because of diversity, tolerance, beauty, and form as a shade tree, it was vastly overplanted throughout much of the United States. In many cities, most of the shade and ornamental trees were American elm. Thus, when Dutch elm disease began to take a very high toll, cities were left with very few trees. This should serve as a drastic illustration of why one species should not be planted in such large numbers. A diversity of plant materials is less susceptible to any ravaging disease. In terms of adaptability, size, and ease of maintenance, it was one of the most desirable trees for much of the Prairie States. Develops a tremendous, wide-spreading root system, making it somewhat difficult to grow turf or other ornamentals beneath. A fierce competitor for water and nutrients.

PESTS: Dutch elm disease has been devastating and accounts for the greatest losses of American elms in the United States, particularly in the northeast. Phloem necrosis is severe, although not as rampant as Dutch elm disease, but has a similar effect on the tree. Elm leaf beetles occasionally damage a specific tree. Elm scale is subtle and may further weaken the tree, making it more susceptible to disease.

NOTES: Because of the high incidence of disease in the Midwest and Upper South, planting of American elm should not continue. However, as long as a tree is growing rapidly on a good site, it appears to have some resistance. Considering the form and adaptability of American elm, it may still be superior to planting silver maple and other less desirable species for a short-term landscape plant. For a period of 15 to 20 years, it may function well with less problems than many other trees.

CULTIVARS: 'Washington': some resistance to Dutch elm disease. 'Liberty': released as Dutch elm disease-resistant. 'Princeton': resistant to elm leaf beetle. Others exist. However, my advise is to wait and see as I doubt that they will be Dutch elm disease-resistant in the long run and/or under stress.

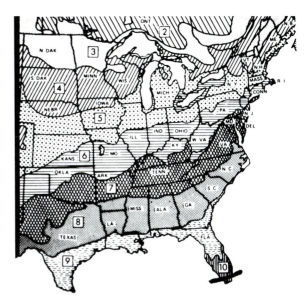

prairie form

Ulmus crassifolia Nutt.   Cedar Elm
Ulmaceae or Elm Family   Hardiness Zone 6
Native to the south central United States.
SIZE: 60 to 80 feet tall with a 40- to 50-foot spread.
FORM: Oval-crowned, medium to large tree.
TEXTURE: Fine.   **EXPOSURE:** Sun to partial shade.

LEAVES: Alternate, simple; about 1 to 2 inches long, 1/2 to 1 inch wide, elliptical to ovate. Gently tapers to a point and is somewhat rounded at the base with a double saw-tooth margin. Leaves are glossy green above, especially in the spring; paler green below. Somewhat hairy, rough on the upper surface; very stiff. Petioles are very short and stout and may be hairy.

STEM: Young stem is reddish brown, slightly hairy. May have small corky wings on either side, but the wings are never as extensive as on *Ulmus alata*, winged elm. Bark on the old stem is brown to gray with shallow ridges and thin, loose scales. Wood is moderately stout, hard, and heavy.

FLOWERS: Small, inconspicuous, appear in late September or early October.

FRUIT; Small, winged seed. More or less oval or horseshoe-shaped with a notch in the end, typical of the elm family. Hairy; matures in the fall.

COLOR: Foliage is glossy green. Only fair yellow to yellow brown in fall.

PROPAGATION: From seed collected in the fall, cold-stored over winter, and planted in the spring; or softwood cuttings.

CULTURE: A very adaptable, tough, tolerant tree for the Southwest and other areas of the South, especially where poor or heavy soils exist. This tree does very well in central Texas on heavy, poorly drained, clay soils. Drought-resistant, moderately wind-resistant, and moderately tolerant to soil compaction or disturbance of the root system, as are more elms. Native to rocky hillsides and along stream beds. Well adapted to the Southwest. Should be used more throughout other regions of the South.

PESTS: Cedar elm has considerable resistance to Dutch elm disease. Dutch elm disease has only recently reached the native habitat of cedar elm where it has been planted and used extensively. Elm leaf beetles may cause slight damage some season, but rarely as severe as on Siberian elm, *Ulmus pumila*.

NOTES: A mature cedar elm with glossy green leaves, slightly weeping branches, and rounded crown, is a very attractive landscape plant. The new leaves in the spring are extremely glossy green, creating an almost glistening effect in contrast to other dull green leaves in the landscape. Well adapted to Oklahoma, Texas, and eastward across the South and should be considered for other landscape uses. its greatest asset after its form and beauty probably lies in its tolerance to heavy clay soils which may be very wet for extended periods of time during spring or fall rains. A most attractive tree that should be planted much more. Sometimes confused with winged elm, *Ulmus alata* Michx. However, winged elm has larger, more obvious corky wings on the young branches and flowers in the spring with fruits maturing in May or June. On the other hand, cedar elm has much less wing on the young twig, flowers in late summer, and has fruits that mature in the fall like lacebark elm, *Ulmus parvifolia*. Of the elms commonly grown in the United States, only cedar elm and lacebark elm produce fruits which mature in the fall. Other elms produce fruits that mature in spring or early summer.

CULTIVARS: None known.

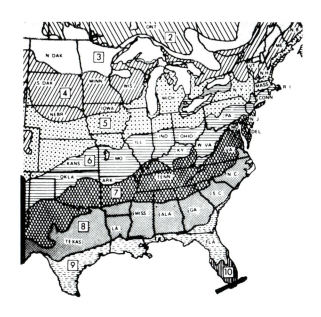

Ulmus alata

Ulmus parvifolia Jacq. (Syn. *U. sempervirens*)   Lacebark Elm (true Chinese elm)
Ulmaceae or Elm Family   Hardiness Zone 4 or 5
Native to China.
SIZE: 40 to 60 feet tall; spread of 30 to 40 feet. Rapid grower south; slower in the north.
FORM: Medium size tree with oval crown, generally without a central leader.
TEXTURE: Fine.   **EXPOSURE:** Sun to partial shade.

LEAVES: Alternate, simple, ovate. About 1 to 1 1/2 inches long, 1/2 to 1 inch wide with a sawtooth margin. Tapering to a point at the tip, rather lopsided at the base. Leaves may hang in dense clusters; however, the entire canopy of the tree is generally open with leaves throughout. Medium to dark green above; pale yellow in the fall.

STEM: Very slender, nearly threadlike, reddish brown turning gray-brown with age. Finally develops a bark that is gray-brown with irregular, almost circular plated which flake off the large stems and trunk, giving it a flaky or lacy appearance. Where flakes peel off, a sandy salmon inner bark is exposed. Wood is strong and durable: quite wind- and ice-resistant. Far superior to *Ulmus pumila*, Siberian elm, which is sometimes incorrectly called Chinese elm.

FLOWERS: Borne in clusters in the leaf axils in October. Not showy.

FRUIT: Profuse clusters among the leaves developing in October or November. Green when young, maroon on some trees when seeds are exposed to full sun. Somewhat showy.

COLOR: Foliage is medium to dark green; pale yellow in the fall.

PROPAGATION: Seed or softwood cuttings.

CULTURE: Extremely tough and durable. Will grow virtually anywhere. Tolerates parking lots, poor soils, restricted root systems, and soil compaction. Must be considered one of the toughest and adaptable of all trees. Highly resistant to disease and insect attack. Responds vigorously to fertilizer, good soils, and good cultural practices.

PESTS: Highly resistant to Dutch elm disease, phloem necrosis, and elm leaf beetle. Some seedlings may develop anthracnose leaf spot disease under nursery conditions.

NOTES: Often confused with Siberian elm, which is much less desirable tree. Siberian elm has leaves that are larger, a bark which deeply furrows, does not develop a flaky pattern, and flowers and fruits in the spring. Lacebark elm has smaller leaves; flowers and fruits in the fall. The confusion has led to lacebark elm being condemned as an inferior tree. Nothing could be more wrong. This tree does well in any soil or location. Extremely drought- and wind-resistant. Enough cannot be said about this very desirable medium-sized tree. Should be planted much more. Grows more slowly in Zones 5 and 6.

CULTIVARS: 'Sempervirens' selected because of striking bark, a low, rounded crown and greater retention of foliage. Almost evergreen in California and some areas of the Deep South. Sometimes listed as *Ulmus sempervirens* or *Ulmus sempervirens* 'Drake'. 'Drake' is semi-evergreen in southern California and the Deep South with low, rounded crown. Beautiful bark. 'True Green': more evergreen, retaining its leaves well into the fall. Very glossy deep green; makes a graceful, round-headed, small tree. The more evergreen cultivars are not as cold hardy as the species. 'Allee': more upright and narrow in form with beautiful bark. 'Athena': has a broad, rounded-crown and beautiful bark. 'Emerald Vase': a broad, oval, wider than tall, good bark pattern and very dark leaves. 'Kings Choice': a vigorous growing selection but does not develop the attractive bark. Other cultivars exist.

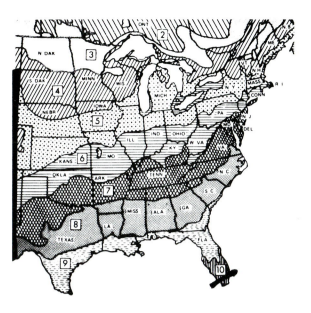

Ulmus pumila L.   Siberian Elm
Ulmaceae or Elm Family   Hardiness Zone 3
Native to Siberia and northern China.
SIZE: 30 to 50 feet tall with a 20- to 40-foot spread. Rapid grower on nearly all sites.
FORM: Round-topped, open-headed tree.
TEXTURE: Fine.   **EXPOSURE:** Sun.

LEAVES: Alternate, simple; ovate, 1 to 3 inches long, 1/2 to 1 inch wide with a sawtooth margin. Semi glossy green above, paler beneath. Pale yellow in the fall, not showy.

STEM: Young stems have large, round, black buds during the fall and winter. Young stems are slender and smooth. Red-brown, becoming gray with age but remaining smooth until finally developing a deeply furrowed, gray to gray-black bark with age. Wood is moderately stout on healthy trees. Young twigs frequently die, creating some litter.

FLOWERS: Small clusters among the leaves in early spring. Not showy.

FRUIT: In clusters among the leaves. Maturing in May or June. Not showy.

COLOR: Foliage is semi glossy green above.

PROPAGATION: Seed or softwood cuttings.

CULTURE: A very tough, durable, and rugged tree. Will grow virtually anywhere. Tolerates drought, poor soils, and adverse conditions. Siberian elm was planted extensively throughout the Prairie States as part of the windbreak program of the 1930s following the "Dust Bowl" and has persisted in spite of its problems. However, it has proven to be an inferior tree to *U. parvifolia* and *U. crassifolia* for all but the most inhospitable sites. Do not plant if other suitable choices exist.

PESTS: The elm leaf beetle is the most serious problem. Wetwood disease is also very common because of the many dead branches in the crown.

NOTES: Often confused with the lacebark elm (true Chinese elm); however, they can be easily distinguished. Siberian elm has deeply furrowed gray to gray-black bark, flowers and fruits in the spring, and has larger leaves. During the dormant period, the buds on Siberian elm are black and rounded like a basketball. Lacebark elm bark has irregular platelets that flake off on most trees: not furrowed, flowers and fruits in the fall, and has smaller leaves. During the dormant period, buds on lacebark elm are oval and pointed much like a football. Siberian elm is inferior to lacebark elm for use in most cases. Many seedlings develop in undesirable locations such as flower beds and shrubs. Should not be planted except where no other choice exists. In spite of all of the condemnation, one must admire the toughness and durability of this tree, especially on terrible sites. if a selection could be found that was resistant to elm leaf beetle and was sterile so as to stop the nuisance seedling problem, my evaluation of this tree would change dramatically.

CULTIVARS: 'Chinkota': a cold hardy selection from S. Dakota State University. 'Mr. Buzz': a vigorous grower with dark green leaves. Very attractive. Others exist.

HYBRIDS: 'Sapparo Autumn Gold' (a release from the University of Wisconsin) is a hybrid between *Ulmus japonica* and *Ulmus pumila* and said to have form and vigor similar to American elm and highly resistant to Dutch elm disease. however, it is extremely susceptible to elm leaf beetle. Likewise, the 'Urban' elm, released by the National Shade Tree Laboratory is devastated by elm leaf beetle. 'Homestead' (a *U. pumila* X *U. hollandica* hybrid) has good form and is Dutch elm disease-resistant but is also susceptible to elm leaf beetle.

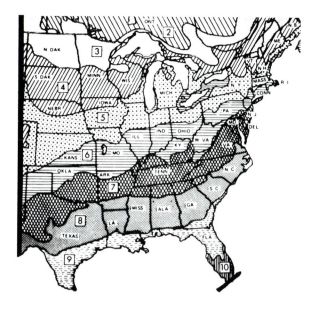

Zelkova serrata (Thunb.) Makino.   Japanese Zelkova
Ulmaceae or Elm Family   Hardiness Zone 4
Native to Japan.
SIZE: 40 to 80 feet tall with a 40- to 60-foot spread. Moderate to rapid grower.
FORM: Broad, rounded-crown tree reminiscent of the American elm.
TEXTURE: Fine to medium.   **EXPOSURE:** Sun.

LEAVES: Alternate, simple; oval to oblong, 3 to 5 inches long, 1 to 1 1/2 inches wide, with a sawtooth margin. Very similar in appearance to many elms only more long and narrow and **not** double-toothed. Medium to dark green during the growing season, yellow to slightly yellow-red in the fall.

STEM: Young stems are slender, brown, becoming reddish brown and mottled. With age, develops into a bark texture similar to young rapidly growing American elm, but more patchy and irregular. Brown or orange-brown when mature and with large lenticels. Wood is durable and wind resistant.

FLOWERS: Among the leaves in late spring; small, not showy. Female flowers are near the branch ends, male flowers are farther back.

FRUIT: A small drupe about 1/8 inch long.

COLOR: Foliage is dark green; yellow to slightly yellow-red in the fall. Variable with seedling.

PROPAGATION: Seed or grafting of cultivars, or rooting of softwood cuttings.

CULTURE: Tolerates a range of growing conditions and is moderately drought-resistant. has received attention as a street tree in the Northeast were root systems are restricted and the American elms are gone. Grows quite rapidly under good conditions but may need some assistance in developing a good crown structure.

PESTS: Elm leaf beetle may be a problem in some areas of the Midwest and Southwest. A leaf spot disease may cause some leaves to drop early. Stem canker may be a problem in some areas.

NOTES: Sometimes planted as a substitute for the American elm. Foliage size, tolerance of conditions, and rapid growth make it suitable for many locations. However, leaf shape and margin, fruit and bark pattern are probably the best features to distinguish Japanese zelkova from the elms.

CULTIVARS: 'Village Green' has longer, more slender leaves that the species and bark is nearly a purple-brown when growing rapidly. A rapid grower with vase form and graceful arching crown, said to have disease- and insect-free foliage in the eastern United States. Does only fair in the hot, droughty locations of the Southwest. 'Parkview': a selection with good vase shape; height is similar to the species. 'Green Vase': vase form and vigorous grower with dark green foliage and bronze-red fall color. Said to grow much faster than seedlings or most other cultivars. 'Halka': similar to 'Green Vase' in form and vigor. 'Green Vase' and 'Halka' may give the best vase form of those available. Others may exist.

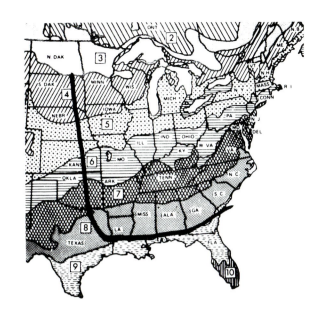

'Village Green'

Ziziphus jujuba Mill.   Jujube or False Date

Rhamnaceae or Buckthorn Family   Hardiness Zone 7

Native to Syria and adjacent areas of the Middle East.

SIZE: 20 to 50 feet tall with spread of 20 to 30 feet as a single stem. Slow to moderate grower.

FORM: Small to medium-sized tree with rounded irregular crown.

TEXTURE: Fine.   **EXPOSURE:** Sun to partial shade.

LEAVES: Alternate, simple; 1 to 2 1/2 inches long, 1/2 to 1 1/2 inches wide, on branchlets arising from short, thickened, spur-like twigs. Leaves and branchlets appear as once-compound leaves instead of simple leaves. Leaves are bluntly toothed on the margins. Upper surface is dark waxy green and shiny, lower surface is pale green. Slightly yellow fall color.

STEM: Young twigs are stout, green to gray-green or black, and zigzag. Young rapidly growing shoots have spine-like stipules, 1/4 to 1/2 inch long, either straight or curved and rose-like. With age, branches become a mottled gray or black, smooth on younger branches, developing a roughly furrowed and peeling bark in loose shaggy strips on the old stems. Wood is very tough, durable, and wind resistant.

FLOWERS: Yellowish green during April or May in axils of leaves, singly or in clusters, male and female in the same flower, not showy.

FRUIT: Ripens late summer to early fall. Slender, round-elongate, variable in size and shape, may be 1/2 to 1 1/4 inches long, 1/4 to 1 inch in diameter. Green turning yellowish then reddish brown to black at maturity. Pulp is sweet, edible, date-like, often grown for the fruit, either eaten fresh or made into preserves. Young tree bears fruit when about two years old.

COLOR: Foliage is dark waxy green; slightly yellow in the fall.

PROPAGATION: Seed, suckers, or grafting of selected cultivars.

CULTURE: Tolerates most soils except very heavy clays or wet swampy locations. Is well adapted to the southwestern United States and thrives in hot and dry sites. Tolerates high pH soils (alkaline) very well. Grows best in a good, moist, but well-drained soil. May need some pruning to assist good branch development when grown as a single-stemmed tree.

PESTS: None serious.

NOTES: Not often planted but should be considered as an ornamental and fruit tree for much of the southern Great Plains and other areas of the South. Interesting bark pattern and good foliage color. Should not be planted over sidewalks or patios as the fruit can become messy in late fall. Fruits are edible, date-like, and quite tasty when ripe. Seedlings rarely become a problem. A trouble-free small tree, tolerant of a wide range of soil and site conditions. Should be used a great deal more.

CULTIVARS: 'Enermis' a thornless variety. 'Lang' and 'Lye' have improved fruit size and quality. Fruits may reach 2 inches long and 1 inch in diameter. Others exist.

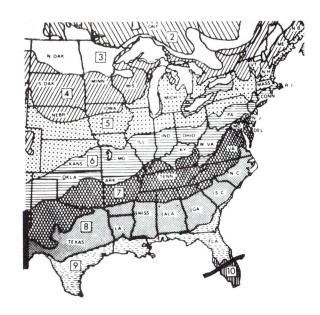

DECIDUOUS SHRUBS AND VINES

Deciduous shrubs and vines create a spectacular color show in early spring. Flowering quince, forsythia and the spiraeas have long been considered the signal of the beginning of spring. However, after their short burst of color, most deciduous shrubs add little to the landscape until the following year. They perhaps best serve as fillers or background for other trees and shrubs. When planted in perimeter areas in groups they attract much attention when in bloom then "disappear" until the following spring.

The major exception is crapemyrtle. Crapemyrtle begins flowering in early summer and under good growing conditions and full sun continues to flower until fall. Thus it fills a gap when few other plants produce landscape color.

Aesculus parviflora Walt.

Bottlebrush Buckeye

Hippocastanaceae or Horsechestnut Family

Hardiness Zone 5

Native to the southeastern United States.

SIZE: 8 to 10 feet tall, with equal or greater spread. Moderate grower.

FORM: Mounding large shrub.

TEXTURE: Coarse.

EXPOSURE: Sun or partial shade.

LEAVES: Opposite, palmately compound; most often with 5, occasionally 7 leaflets. Mostly oblong, tapering to a sharp point and slightly drooping. Overall leaf may be 6 to 8 inches long, and medium to dark green with a finely sawtooth margin. Yellow in the fall.

STEM: Branches are stout, stiff, gray-brown to nearly black on some plants with large, dormant, terminal buds. Some suckers arise from the base, thickening the clump. Horizontal branches are fairly stout creating a layered or tiered effect.

FLOWERS: White. In 8- to 10-inch clusters above the foliage in early summer; very showy.

FRUIT: A rounded capsule, 1 inch or more across. Light brown, containing 2 to 4 hard, brown seeds. Not commonly seen in Zones 5 and 6, but noticeable and more common in Zones 7 and 8.

COLOR: Foliage is medium to dark green. Flowers are white.

PROPAGATION: Seed or root cuttings.

CULTURE: Native to, and best adapted to, partial shade: beneath large trees or where full sun is received for only a few hours each day. Perhaps most showy and dense in full sun but protected, such as on the north or east side of buildings or large plantings. Accumulation of leaf litter or mulching assists growth and drought tolerance. Not for hot, dry, exposed locations or extremely heavy soils that are poorly drained. Occasionally needs a little pruning to keep it neat.

PESTS: None serious.

NOTES: An eye-catching, coarse-textured shrub with a neat, mounding form (see photograph). The early summer flowers add to the overall beauty of the shrub and the landscape at a time when few other plants are flowering especially in Zones 5 and 6 where crapemyrtle is not cold hardy. Not attractive in winter, but it more than makes up for this deficiency in summer. Unlike its relatives, Ohio buckeye and horsechestnut, it does not have the myriad of foliar diseases and problems, thus deserves consideration for many uses as long as some protection is provided. Useful around outdoor living areas since its attractive period coincides with outdoor activities. Because of its considerable shade tolerance, it retains foliage to the ground and rarely gets leggy or open at the base as do many medium to large shrubs.

CULTIVARS: 'Rogers': flowers later than the species and flower clusters may reach 15 to 30 inches long. **WOW.** Not common in the trade but well worth the hunt. Others may exist in localized areas.

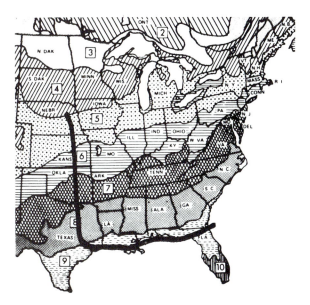

Amorpha glabra Desf.   Mountain Indigo
Leguminosae or Legume Family   Hardiness Zone 6
Native to the United States, south of the Mason-Dixon Line.
SIZE: 3 to 6 feet tall with irregular spread.
FORM: Irregular, mounding shrub.
TEXTURE: Fine.   EXPOSURE: Sun.

LEAVES: Alternate, deciduous, once-compound; 4 to 8 inches long. Individual leaflets number 9 to 19, more or less oval; 3/4 to 1 1/2 inches long, 1/2 to 3/4 inch wide. Smooth margin. Upper surface is dark green and smooth, lower surface is much lighter.

STEMS: Slender and smooth, green turning yellowish brown and finally dark brown to gray. Stems are semi-upright initially but tend to droop with age. No spines are present and stems are quite tough.

FLOWERS: Long, compact spikes may be 6 to 8 inches long, extending beyond the foliage. Blue to lavender; striking. Generally appear April or May.

FRUIT: A brown pod about 1/3 inch long generally contains 1 or 2 seeds. Not showy.

COLOR: Foliage is dark green. Flowers are blue to lavender.

PROPAGATION: Seed or cuttings in early summer.

CULTURE: Native to the open prairie and riverbanks where light intensity is high. Quite tolerant to all but severely water-logged soils. Transplants easily when grown in a nursery, less well fro the wild. Responds to fertilizer and reduced weed competition.

PESTS: Rust can be serious and cause defoliation, but plants generally recover.

NOTES: The unique blue to lavender flowers provide sufficient contrast to be noticed, unlike some plants with very pale blue flowers. This is an attractive deciduous shrub that requires little to no care once established and produces flowers that are showy for several weeds as the spikes develop from bottom to top. Should be used more, especially where maintenance is low and irrigation is not available.

CULTIVARS: None known.

RELATED SPECIES: *Amorpha fruticosa* L., false indigo, is similar in adaptation only it is much more cold-tolerant, Zone 4, and may reach a height of 6 to 8 feet. Leaves are similar in appearance to *A glabra* except more gray-green and densely hairy below. Flowers are spikes, 3 to 6 inches long, dark purple to near blue or occasionally white. Generally in May or June. False indigo is a larger and more irregular and open shrub than mountain indigo, but deserves consideration as it is spine-free but tough and durable with early summer flowers. A cultivar, 'Dark Lance' is a rapid grower with purple flowers in especially long spikes.

Amorpha canescens Pursh., lead plant, has compound, gray leaves covered with dense hairs throughout. Grows only about 30 inches tall. An attractive shrub with purple flower clusters in June that contrast with the gray foliage. Deserves more attention as a landscape plant.

271

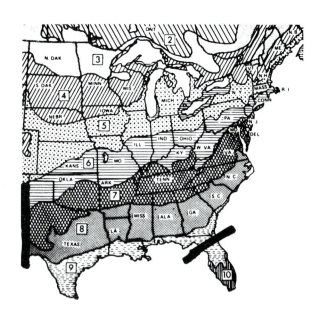

Arundo donax   Giant Reed Grass
Poaceae or Grass Family   Hardiness Zone 6
Native to the Mediterranean Region.
SIZE: 10 to 15 feet tall or more, spreading as a clump. Rapid grower.
FORM: A tall grass clump.
TEXTURE: Medium.   **EXPOSURE:** Sun to partial shade.

LEAVES: Elongated, strap-like. May reach 2 feet long and 2 and 1/2 inches wide. Many leaves occur along the stems in 2 ranks that are mostly alternate. The color is medium green to nearly blue-green but brown with the first frost. Margins are rough and finely saw-toothed.

STEM: Perennial. The erect stems emerge from rhizomes at the soil surface each spring and grow rapidly, generally reaching their full height by July or August. The stems are about 3/4 to 1 inch in diameter and flexible, thus ready movement in any breeze.

FLOWERS: Large, dense panicles, 18 to 24 inches long. Whitish; generally in August and remaining all winter. The flowers are most attractive in late summer and early fall, then become a dull brown. Can be collected and dried and hold up well.

FRUIT: A small seed with associated glimes and awns. The seeds are viable in some areas of the South.

COLOR: Foliage is green to blue-green. Flowers are white.

PROPAGATION: Division or in some areas, seed.

CULTURE: Grows best in moist, well drained soil. This plant gets large and spreads by rhizomes at a modest rate, creating a dense clump or thicket. Sometimes used for erosion control. The old tops should be removed before growth begins in the spring. Once a hard freeze has occurred, the mass becomes a bit of a fire hazard if adjacent to wooden structures.

PESTS: None.

NOTES: Will grow so large and thick as to create a visual barrier that will hide many things. However, unless the old dead tops are removed each winter, the mass becomes unattractive. It is too invasive for many uses, although Roundup will keep it in check. Best used in the landscape where it can be seen in the distance. Sometimes referred to as reed bamboo. It does look somewhat like bamboo, but the stems are much less durable, plus bamboos do not flower in this country.

CULTIVARS: 'Variegata': called striped giant reed grass, has striped green and near white leaves. Very striking, especially when young stems begin emerging in late spring. Some leaves will be nearly all creamy white. This plant rarely grows more then 6 to 8 feet tall and is not such a vigorous spread. Sometimes listed as cultivar, 'Versicolor'.

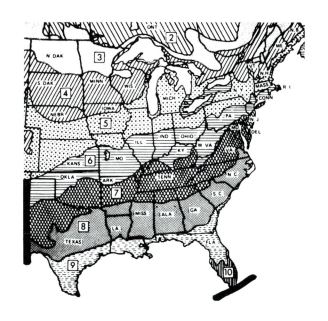

Berberis thunbergi L.   Japanese Barberry
Berberidaceae or Barberry Family   Hardiness Zone 3
Native to Japan.
SIZE: 5 to 8 feet tall with a 4- to 6-foot spread. Moderate grower.
FORM: Dense, round-headed, medium-sized shrub.
TEXTURE: Fine.   **EXPOSURE:** Sun to partial shade.

LEAVES: Simple, alternate; obovate to oblong, 1/2 to 1 inch long, narrowing at the base into a distinct petiole. The margin is smooth except for a single sharp prickle at the tip. Leaves are often clustered on short spurs which are alternately arranged making the leaves appear to be whorled in these clusters. May be bright green, purplish red to purple-black, depending on cultivar and exposure. Cultivars with red or purple leaves turn green when grown in moderate to dense shade. Fall color is generally red to red-maroon.

STEM: Young stems are slender, often weeping, with a 1- to 3-pronged spine at each leaf axil. Young stems are purple-brown to red-brown in color becoming reddish gray with age. Inner bark is buttery yellow, typical of the family. Wood is hard and durable.

FLOWERS: Yellow in the center, reddish on the outside, about 1/4 inch across. Solitary or 2 to 4 in a cluster. Noticeable, but not showy.

FRUIT: Oval elongate, about 1/4 inch long. Bright red, on a long slender stalk. Remains after the leaves drop. Showy, especially in Zones 4, 5 and 6 where fruit set is heavier.

COLOR: Foliage is green to purplish; fall color is red. Flowers are yellow. Fruit is red.

PROPAGATION: Cuttings, softwood in early summer, or semi-hardwood in early fall.

CULTURE: Quite tough and tolerant of soil conditions; however, it is only moderately tolerant of drought. Often drops a substantial portion of its leaves during prolonged dry periods, making the plant unsightly with perhaps some dieback in the crown. This happens less on good soils than on poor soils. At the same time, it is not tolerant of excessive moisture. Needs a fertile, moist, well-drained soil for best performance. Can be sheared or trimmed into a hedge or various forms as desired. Makes a very desirable hedge plant in that it is not easily penetrated by pets or people, retains its form well and is moderately attractive with fruit set in the winter. Fruit set is less heavy in the South.

PESTS: Sometimes aphids on new growth and root rot on old plants in wet locations.

NOTES: A most useful deciduous shrub for various locations in the landscape, particularly where accent or color is desired during the growing season. The show of color can be spectacular, particularly with the red leaf forms. For the red pigment to develop in the leaves, the plant must be in full or nearly full sun. In shade locations, even the purple cultivars become a green or green-purple and much less attractive.

CULTIVARS: 'Atropurpurea' reddish leaves throughout the season in full sun. 'Atropurpurea nana': a dwarf cultivar with reddish leaves and dense growth habit. Many other cultivars are listed as 'Atropurpurea'...such as 'Crimson Pigmy' which grows only to about 2 feet; 'Erecta' which is more upright; 'Rose Glow' has mottled purple and cream leaves. Many others exist.

RELATED SPECIES: *Berberis mentorensis* L.M. Ames., mentor barberry, is a hybrid between *B. julianae* and *B. thunbergi* and grows to 7 feet tall with a 6- to 7-foot spread. Leaves are 1 inch long, oval to elongate, and semi-evergreen. Leaves have several prickles or spines on the margin which is the easiest way to distinguish it from *B. thunbergi* cultivars. A large, dense shrub, perhaps more vigorous than Japanese barberry cultivars. Appears to be more drought-resistant.

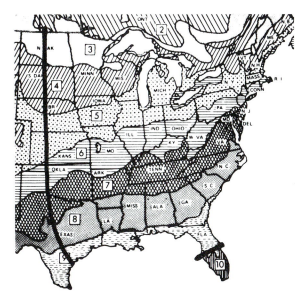

'Atropurpurea Nana'

B. mentorensis

'Erecta'

Buddleia davidii Franch.   Butterfly Bush, Summer Lilac
Loganiaceae or Logania Family   Hardiness Zone 5
Native to China.
SIZE: 6 to 12 feet tall with greater spread; variable with cultivar. Rapid grower.
FORM: Irregular, mounding shrub.
TEXTURE: Medium.   **EXPOSURE:** Sun to partial shade.

LEAVES: Opposite, simple, deciduous. Ovate-elongate to lanceolate, 3 to 8 inches long, 1 to 3 inches wide with a finely sawtooth margin. Color ranges from gray-green to dark green above, depending on cultivar or seedling. Nearly white with fine hairs beneath. Petiole is very short. Leaves appear late in the spring but are held late into the fall.

STEM: Stout and multi branched; covered with fine hairs when young, smooth with age. In cross-section, the young stems are 4- to 6-sided, occasionally 8-sided. Branches on some cultivars grow up, then arch rather gracefully but can be loose and open.

FLOWERS: In terminal, spike-like panicles; 4 to 8 inches long on the new growth. Striking and fragrant. Colors range from near white to purple and pink. Because of the long spike-like flower cluster and opening from the base to the tip, flowering extends from early summer to late fall with some cultivars. Can be used for cut flowers.

FRUIT: A 2-valved capsule about 1/3 inch long. Not showy.

COLOR: Foliage is gray-green to dark green. Flowers are white to purple or pink.

PROPAGATION: Seeds germinate easily. Cuttings root easily anytime during the summer.

CULTURE: A very tough, durable shrub that will survive on most sites. However, since flowering is on new growth, more growth and extended growth throughout the season yields more flowers. Responds to fertilizer, supplemental water, mulching, and a reduction in grassy weed competition. Transplants easily.

PESTS: None serious.

NOTES: As the name implies, the butterflies love this plant, adding another item of interest. Should be planted in a mass for best appearance and ease of maintenance as a single plant is not neat. Can be pruned back slightly to severely and comes back with vigor. Bloom time can be extended by cutting off early maturing seed heads.

CULTIVARS: Many, many. 'African Queen': dark violet flowers. 'Black Night': very dark purple flowers. "Pink Delight': a light near-pink. 'White Bouquet': near-white flowers. 'Peace': a smaller plant with white flowers with an orange throat. Many others exist.

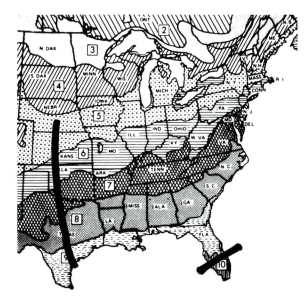

Callicarpa americana L.   American Beautyberry
Verbenaceae or Verbena Family   Hardiness Zone 6
Native to the southeastern North America.
SIZE: 6 to 8 feet tall with 8- to 12-foot spread. Rapid grower.
FORM: Irregular, mounding shrub.
TEXTURE: Coarse.   **EXPOSURE:** Sun to shade.

LEAVES: Simple, opposite or mostly so; aromatic, more or less oval or ovate to elongate, with a sawtooth margin. The petiole is slender, yet generally holds the leaves out from the stem like wings of a bird. Leaves are generally dark green, 4 to 8 or more inches long. Sand papery to the touch and generally with stiff hairs below.

STEM: Young twigs are more or less 4-sided, slender; gray to reddish brown and covered with fine hairs. Older stems are smooth and gray. Easily broken.

FLOWERS: Generally in June through October, borne in clusters surrounding the stem at the base of the leaves. Generally pine to bluish but not particularly showy.

FRUIT: August through November, the berry-like fruits appear in clusters around the stems. Each fruit is about 1/8 to nearly 1/4 inch long, containing four seeds. Color ranges from white, blue, violet, to rose.

COLOR: Foliage is dark green. Fruits are white, blue, violet, to rose.

PROPAGATION: Seeds or cuttings nearly anytime, even hardwood cuttings under a jar in early spring.

CULTURE: Native to rich woods and thickets from the east coast westward to eastern Kansas, Oklahoma and Texas. Grows best in deep, moist soils with an accumulation of leaf litter and debris on the soil surface and in partial shade to shade. However, it flowers and fruits well in full sun as long as moisture is not severely limiting and the plant is generally more compact in full sun or at least with full sun for part of the day. Responds with vigor to fertilizer, water, mulching, and control of grassy weed competition.

PESTS: None serious.

NOTES: A striking plant in late summer, fall, or early winter when the fruits are in full color. Because of the leaf/flower/fruit arrangement, the fruits are generally noticeable even before leaf drop in the fall. The clusters of fruit are especially eye-catching after the leaves have dropped. The fruits are eaten by quail and song birds as well as various wild life. The seeds germinate readily when planted, but generally do not become weedy and troublesome.

CULTIVARS: 'Lactea' is white-fruited. Other cultivars probably exist.

RELATED SPECIES: *Callicarpa dichotoma*, purple beautyberry, is native to China but has naturalized in the eastern United States and is hardy to Zone 5. In general, the leaves are much smaller, (about 1 to 3 inches long) and more coarsely serrate and with fewer hairs below than *C. americana*. Height is about 3 to 4 feet, somewhat greater in spread, and with slender, arching branches. Fruits are lavender or white. Other aspects of growth and adaptation are similar.

 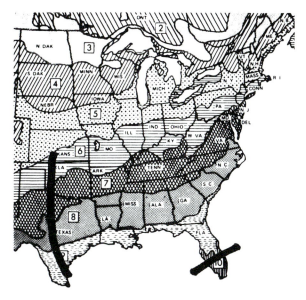

Calycanthus floridus L.   Sweetshrub or Carolina Allspice
Calycanthaceae or Calycanthus Family   Hardiness Zone 5
Native from Virginia to Florida
SIZE: 4 to 8 feet tall with an equal or greater spread. Slow to moderate grower.
FORM: Rounded, irregular shrub.
TEXTURE: Coarse.   EXPOSURE: Sun or shade.

LEAVES: Opposite, simple; 3 to 5 inches long, more or less oval with a smooth margin.
Upper surface is dull gray-green, lighter below with dense hairs. No fall color.

STEM: Upright, with limited secondary branching. Young stems are somewhat flattened,
stout, aromatic and camphor-like when crushed or scraped. Subject to winter die back in
Zone 5; however, regrowth from lower stems occurs with minor consequences.

FLOWERS: Reddish to red-brown and 1 1/2 to 2 inches across. Unusual color and form
(see photograph). Borne singly in the leaf axils in early summer. Pleasant, somewhat
strawberry-like fragrance.

FRUIT: A small, cup-shaped capsule. Not showy.

COLOR: Foliage is gray-green. Flowers are red-brown.

PROPAGATION: Seed or softwood cuttings.

CULTURE: A very adaptable and tolerant shrub. Grows in full sun or fairly heavy shade,
but stays more compact in sunny locations. Tolerant to most soils except for very poorly
drained locations. Prune after flowering to stimulate branching and neatness of form.
May be cut back severely from time to time to keep it in scale with surroundings. Gets
rather scraggly if left unpruned. Only moderately drought-tolerant, thus the farther west,
the more important it is to plant sweetshrub in shade.

PESTS: None serious.

NOTES: Also known as Carolina allspice or strawberry shrub in some areas. A shrub that
is better detected with the nose than the eye since overall appearance is rather scraggly or
weedy even with some pruning. On the other hand, when in flower, contributes a dimension not often considered in modern landscapes, since appeal to the sense of smell is equally important. Because sweetshrub will grow in sun or shade, it is best used as a background or filler plant out of primary view, but near outdoor living areas. Well adapted to
the South, especially Zones 7 and 8, although not often used because of the many broadleaf
evergreens available. However, behind a group of broadleaf evergreens a sweetshrub
would grow well and be noticed without ever being seen.

CULTIVARS: 'Athens' (Katherine) has yellow fllowers. 'Urbana': said to be especially
fragrant but otherwise like the species. Others may exist.

 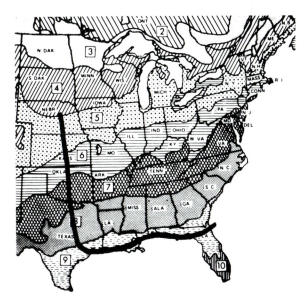

Campsis radicans (L.) Seem. ex Bur.   Trumpet Creeper
Bignoniaceae or Bignonia Family   Hardiness Zone 5
Native to the eastern U.S.
SIZE: 30 to 40 feet tall. Rapid grower.
FORM: Twining vine or dense thicket.
TEXTURE: Medium.   EXPOSURE: Sun to partial shade.

LEAVES: Opposite, once-compound; with 9 to 11 oval leaflets. Leaflets have a sawtooth margin with a variable number of teeth. Medium to dark green; yellow in the fall.

STEM: A twining vine with aerial roots that attach to almost everything. Young stems are a very light tan, becoming slightly darker with age. If nothing is nearby to climb, a dense thicket develops as stems root when they touch the ground and send up further stems.

FLOWERS: In clusters at the tips of shoots. Orange, bladder-like, and rounded on the end before opening. Funnel-form, 3 to 4 inches long and 2 inches across when open. Flowers begin in mid summer and continue through September.

FRUIT: A green pod, 3 to 6 inches long and nearly 1 inch in diameter. Turning brown with maturity, finally opening to release many small seeds with velvety white hairs. Unfortunately the seeds are viable and germinate everywhere.

COLOR: Foliage is medium to dark green. Flowers are orange.

PROPAGATION: Seed, division, or cuttings.

CULTURE: An extremely tough plant that will grow practically anywhere. Can be found growing in cracks in sidewalks or on abandoned piles of rubble. It is very weedy and, more often than not, becomes a pest. The flowers are attractive and the hummingbirds love them, but the problems outweigh the benefits in nearly all cases.

PESTS: Leaf-eating insects, but none serious.

NOTES: A showy, flowering vine that generally escapes and becomes a nuisance. The aerial roots attach to trees, buildings, masonry, and window screens and are difficult to remove. Too aggressive for nearly all landscape uses. The flowers are attractive in mail order catalogs, but the best advice is to resist.

CULTIVARS: 'Flava': flowers are orange-yellow. 'Praecox': red flowers. 'Crimson Trumpet': red flowers. Others probably exist.

RELATED SPECIES: *Campsis grandiflora* (Thunb.) K. Schum., Chinese trumpet creeper, has 7 to 9 leaflets of similar size but flowers that are slightly larger and more orange-scarlet. Hardy only in Zone 7 and southward. The Chinese trumpet creeper is equally as adaptable and aggressive and should be planted with care. Perhaps the best choice is on a fence away from other other vegetation. When it flowers in mid summer, it will be very noticeable and if it gets out of bounds, Roundup weed killer will solve the problem. 'Thunbergi' has orange flowers.

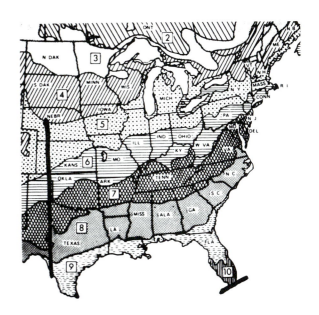

Caragana arborescens Lam.　　　　　Siberian Peashrub
Leguminosae or Pea Family　　　　　Hardiness Zone 2
Native to Siberia and Manchuria.
SIZE: 10 to 15 feet tall with nearly equal spread. Rapid grower.
FORM: Upright growing shrub with an oval crown.
TEXTURE: Fine.　　　　　　　**EXPOSURE:** Sun.

LEAVES: Alternate, pinnately compound; 3 to 6 inches long with 8 to 12 leaflets, occasionally more. Each leaflet is ovate and about 1 inch long with a smooth margin. Pale, medium green above, paler below, and only slightly yellow in the fall.

STEM: Young stems are green, stout, and hairy at first; remaining green for several years, and have prominent horizontal lenticels. Main stems are upright and fairly stout. Can be grown as an interesting small tree. The gray-green bark is somewhat attractive.

FLOWERS: Yellow and pea-like, among the terminal leaves in late spring. Noticeable but not particularly showy.

FRUIT: A yellow-green pod maturing in late summer, turning brown.

COLOR: Foliage is medium green. Flowers are yellow.

PROPAGATION: Seed or softwood cuttings.

CULTURE: A very tough, durable shrub. Tolerates heat, drought, and exposure even on poor, sandy soils. Extensively planted as the first row of many windbreaks following the dust bowl era, and it still persists in many old plantings across the Prairie States. Needs some pruning to maintain attractiveness. Useful primarily in Zones 2, 3, 4, and 5 where shrub selection is limited.

PESTS: Spider mites on very hot, dry sites, especially with reflected heat.

NOTES: As a large shrub, Siberian peashrub is of limited landscape value compared to other large shrubs of similar toughness and durability. On the other hand, although seldom used in this manner, as a small tree it is quite attractive. Since the branches remain green for several years, and the older bark is a green-tan, this small tree adds landscape interest in winter and summer. However, as a large shrub, the twiggy upper branches are not nearly as attractive.

CULTIVARS: 'Lorbergi': pale yellow flowers and narrow leaflets. 'Pendula': weeping branches and when grafted onto a single stem, the plant makes an interesting specimen. 'Tidy': a broad, spreading grower with light yellow flowers. 'Walker': a low growing plant with small leaves. 'Sutherland': an upright grower that makes a good screen.

RELATED SPECIES: *Caragana frutex* (L.) C. Koch., Russian peashrub, is hardy in Zone 2 and grows 6 to 8 feet tall, generally with dense branches and an oval form. There are usually four dull green leaflets. Flowers are bright yellow in late spring or early summer. Spreads by suckers and may crowd out adjacent plants, but is useful for erosion control. 'Globosa': a compact, globe form that grows 3 to 4 feet tall and does not sucker.

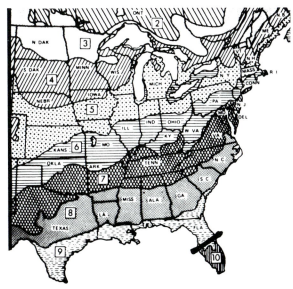

Caragana frutex 'Globosa'

Celastrus orbiculatus Thumb.   Oriental Bittersweet
Celastraceae or Staff Tree Family   Hardiness Zone 5
native to China and Japan
SIZE: Climbs 20 to 30 feet high. Rapid grower
FORM: Irregular, twining vine,
TEXTURE: Medium.   **EXPOSURE**: Sun or shade.

LEAVES: Alternate (although at the very tip they may appear opposite or nearly so), simple; 2 to 4 inches long, rounded to oblong. More or less ping-pong paddle-shaped with a sawtooth margin. Upper leaf surface is medium green, only slightly lighter below. Fall color is yellow.

STEM: A vigorous, twining vine. Smooth and green when young, turning gray-brown and remaining rather smooth with age.

FLOWERS: Male and female are on separate plants (dioecious), therefore both sexes must be present for fruit production. One male pollinator will suffice for several female plants. Flowers are in the leaf axils on oriental bittersweet, whereas they are in terminal clusters on American bittersweet. Neither species has showy flowers.

FRUIT: Yellow, about the size of an English pea. It splits in late September or October to reveal the orange-red, fleshy coated seed. Seeds persist on the vine throughout most of the winter and are showy.

COLOR: Foliage is medium green. Fruits are yellow. Seeds are orange-red.

PROPAGATION: Seed or softwood cuttings.

CULTURE: Very tough and adaptable, grows in practically any soil and is moderately drought-resistant. Will grow in very shady locations; however, fruits best in sunny locations or when the vine reaches the top of a tree or structure, thus getting sufficient sunlight for flowers and fruit production. Container production has made production and transplanting of bittersweet easier.

PESTS: None serious, although some are usually present.

NOTES: A very showy vine during the fall and winter when landscape color is decreasing. The fruits are attractive and contrast with evergreens and snow, creating some attractive scenes. A moderately aggressive vine; therefore, the planting site should be selected carefully such as a section of fence away from other landscape plants and that gets several hours of sun. Will grow on trees, trellises, or arbors. Drops leaves cleanly in the fall, letting in winter sun through the attractive fruits.

CULTIVARS: None known.

RELATED SPECIES: *Celastrus scandens* L., American bittersweet, is native to a wide range of North America and hardy in Zone 4. Adaptation, tolerance and performance of the two species are similar. Both species need a male plant along with the female plant(s) for fruit production. American bittersweet has fruits in clusters at the ends of branches, whereas oriental bittersweet fruits are dispersed along the stems. American bittersweet generally has fewer branches and less dense foliage than does oriental bittersweet. Foliage and stems otherwise are similar. Bittersweet is generally inconspicuous in the landscape until fall when the yellow fruits open to expose the striking orange-red fruits.

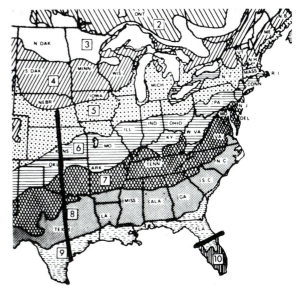

Celastrus scandens

Chaenomeles speciosa Nakai. (Syn. *laginaria*)   Flowering Quince
Rosaceae or Rose Family   Hardiness Zone 4
Native to Asia.
SIZE: 4 to 8 feet tall with a 4- to 6-foot spread. Rapid grower.
FORM: Densely twiggy, round-headed shrub.
TEXTURE: Medium.   **EXPOSURE:** Sun to partial shade.

LEAVES: Alternate, simple; 1 to 3 inches long, 1/2 to 1 inch wide, ovate to oblong with a sharply sawtooth margin. Leaves may be clustered on short stalks or spurs on older, slow-growing branches. Often accompanied by two irregularly rounded or sawtooth stipules at the base of leaves on young rapidly growing shoots. Deep, often glossy green above, sometimes reddish purple when new. No fall color.

STEM: Young stems are shiny, light brown, and slender. A multi-stemmed shrub with stems rarely reaching more than 1/2 inch in diameter, often with long tapering spines, particularly on older branches. Wood is moderately stout.

FLOWERS: Red, pink, or white, depending on cultivar. One to 2 inches across and rose-like. Quite showy on the the old wood in the spring before foliage appears.

FRUIT: Apple-like; 1 to 2 1/2 inches in diameter. Green or yellowish green.

COLOR: Foliage is glossy green. Flowers are red, pink, or white.

PROPAGATION: Hardwood cuttings during fall or winter, softwood cuttings during the growing season, or seed, but seed is extremely variable.

CULTURE: A tough, durable shrub that tolerates most soils except where pH is very high (alkaline), where it suffers from iron cholorsis. Responds vigorously to fertilization, good soil and moisture conditions. A showy shrub early in the spring, especially in full sun.

PESTS: Rarely serious; however, San Jose scale may be a problem in some portions of the country. Other scale insects sometimes attack in the South. Aphids, particularly on new foliage. Occasionally spider mites in hot, dry locations. Rabbit damage may be serious in rural areas.

NOTES: A showy shrub early in the spring; one of the first showing red or red-orange blooms. A good Great Plains and Southwest substitute for azaleas. Generally a low-maintenance plant, requiring little attention and making a contribution to the landscape early in the spring; the rest of the year the contribution is minimal. Does well as a sheared hedge and is sufficiently spined to stop pets and people from trampling. Spreads or thickens at the crown. In some instances, it may become a pest due to sprouts or suckers arising further out from the base of the plant causing it to creep or spread.

CULTIVARS: Many have been named, only a few will be listed here. 'Snow': white, single flowers. 'Apple Blossom': single pink flowers. 'Crimson Beauty': single red flowers. 'Coral Beauty' single red-orange flowers. 'Glowing Amber': single red-orange flower. 'Sunset': double red-orange flower. Many other cultivars exist.

RELATED SPECIES: *Chaenomeles japonica* Lindl., Japanese flowering quince, is a much smaller shrub, rarely reaching a height of more than 3 feet. Very similar to flowering quince in all respects except size: leaves, stem, form, and tolerance to soils and moisture. Sometimes preferred because of its smaller size, requiring less pruning and remaining more compact. Flowers are more reddish purple. A distinctly different flower color than the red, red-orange of the common flowering quince. *Chaenomeles* X *superba* Rehd. is a hybrid between the two species of intermediate size. 'Cameo' is salmon pink, 'Jet Trail' is white, 'Texas Scarlet' is scarlet red. Many others exist.

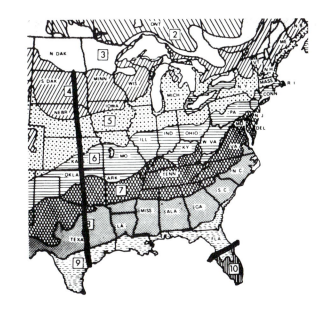

C. japonica   C. speciosa

C. japonica   C. speciosa

Clematis spp.   Clematis
Ranunculaceae or Buttercup Family   Hardiness Zone 4
Native to northern North America and Asia (see species).
SIZE: 3 to 20 feet, depending on support and species.
FORM: Irregular vine. Moderate grower.
TEXTURE: Medium.   EXPOSURE: Slight shade.

LEAVES: Deciduous, opposite, simple or compound; generally with smooth margins. Foliage is generally dark green.

STEM: Slender, twining vine; green at first, turning brown.

FLOWERS: Spectacular, perfect flowers. Red-lavender to white, depending on species and cultivar. Very showy with open, flat faces.

FRUIT: Small seeds with persistent hairs.

COLOR: Foliage is dark green. Flowers are red-lavender to white. Very showy.

PROPAGATION: Softwood cuttings.

CULTURE: Clematis are considered by some to have very specific cultural requirements. However, this may not be true. A good soil is an asset often not recognized in the planting success and growth of most landscape plants. With good soil, mulching, and reasonable management of fertilizer, clematis can be grown in most semi-shade locations. Not for an exposed, southwest wall or sites with poorly drained, heavy clay soils. Should be watered during droughts. Container-grown plants are generally easier to transplant.

PESTS: More common on weakened plants in poor locations. Leaf spot, as well as mites, scale insects, and white fly: may require spraying some seasons.

NOTES: The magnificent, large flowers are so striking that clematis are worth the extra effort normally required. Container grown plants establish more quickly and generally out-perform bare root plants. Should be grown on a trellis or fence for best results. There are over 200 species of clematis.

RELATED SPECIES: *Clematis* X Jackmani T.Moore, a hybrid between *Clematis lanuginosa* and *C. viticella*, Jackman clematis: flowers on new growth during summer and early fall. Flowers are violet-purple, 4 to 6 inches across. 'Gypsyqueen' has dark, velvety purple flowers. 'Madame Edouard Andre' has purplish red flowers. 'Mrs. Cholmondeley' has light blue flowers. 'Henryi' has creamy white flowers, 6 inches across. 'Rubra' flowers are deep red. Many other cultivars exist of this hybrid group, some limited to localized areas.
    Clematis paniculata J.F. Gmel., sweetautumn clematis, has dark green compound leaves that are opposite with three, occasionally five, broadly ovate leaflets 2 to 4 inches long with smooth margins. Stems are tan with vertical ridges. Flowers are prolific, white, about 1 inch long, appearing in late summer; very fragrant. The plume-like, silvery seed head clumps are attractive after the petals have fallen. A vigorous, aggressive vine. Should be planted with care.
    Clematis virginiana L., woodbine or virginsbower, is native to the northeast United States. A climbing vine, its leaves are compound with three ovate leaflets. Somewhat similar to sweetautumn clematis with white flowers, but the flowers are earlier and not fragrant. Seed heads are gray.
    In general, much confusion exists with clematis and the many species, hybrids and cultivars. The Jackmani types are probably best for the beginner. Donald Wyman's book, *Shrubs and Vines for American Gardens*, discusses the group in detail.

291

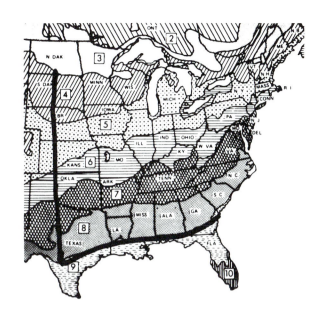

Cornus stolonifera Michx.   Red-Osier Dogwood
      (Syn. *C. sericea* L.)
Cornaceae or Dogwood Family   Hardiness Zone 2
Native to most of the United States.
SIZE: 4 to 8 feet tall; sprouting and spreading considerable distances. Rapid grower.
FORM: Multi-stemmed, upright shrub with few secondary branches.
TEXTURE: Medium.   **EXPOSURE:** Sun to partial shade.

LEAVES: Opposite, simple; oblong or lanceolate, 2 to 5 inches long, 1 to 2 1/2 inches wide, tapering to a point, rounded at the base with a smooth margin. Veins are in 5 to 7 pairs. Medium green upper leaf surface, lighter gray-green below. Little fall color.

STEM: The main stems are strictly upright but spread by underground stems. Young stems are slender, red, very smooth with a large white pith. Bark remains red for some time, finally developing a gray-brown, rough, sandpapery texture. Seedlings vary in the attractiveness of the red stems.

FLOWERS: Mid to late spring, dull white, in flat-topped clusters, 1 to 3 inches across, at the tip of the new growth. Somewhat showy.

FRUIT: Maturing mid to late summer, oval-elongate, white or lead colored, about 1/4 inch long with a hard seed inside.

COLOR: Foliage is medium green. Young twigs are red.

PROPAGATION: Hardwood or softwood cuttings or division of a clump.

CULTURE: Native to wet swamp lands and moist, seepy areas or shady areas beneath large trees. Tolerates most soil conditions as long as they are not excessively dry. Tolerates alkaline or acid soils and most poor soils. A tough, rugged plant. Responds vigorously to good growing conditions and fertilizer. Horizontal spread is slow, thus it does not become a "weed".

PESTS: None serious.

NOTES: A tough, durable, deciduous shrub which spreads at a moderate rate on a moist site, thus has some use in erosion control on banks or slopes. Most showy in the winter time with a low, evergreen ground cover to contrast with the red twigs or when snow is present on the ground. Provides good cover for birds and wildlife.

CULTIVARS: 'Flaviramea': yellow twigs. 'Nitida': green twigs. 'Kelseyi': very dwarf, rarely exceeding 2 feet tall. 'Cardinal': striking cherry red stems. Other cultivars probably exist.

RELATED SPECIES: *Cornus alba* L., tatarian dogwood, has very showy, variegated foliage in some cultivars, but is less drought-tolerant than many other species of dogwood. 'Argento-marginata' has white-bordered leaves that are 5 inches long; very showy. 'Gouchulti' has variegated yellowish and pink, 5-inch-long leaves.

Cornus drummondi C.A. Mey., roughleaf dogwood, is native to many of the Prairie States. Commonly found growing in dense thickets on rocky, dry soils. Good for wildlife and naturalistic plantings, but not showy as an ornamental.

Cornus stolonifera

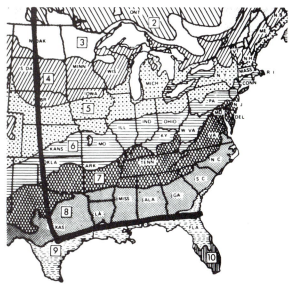

Cornus stolonifera

Cornus alba 'Argento-marginata'

Cornus drummondi

Cortaderia selloana Aschers. and Graebn.　　Pampas Grass
Graminae or Grass Family　　　　　　　　Hardiness Zone 7
Native to Argentina and southern Brazil.
SIZE: 6 to 8 feet tall with an equal spread. Rapid grower.
FORM: Large, fountain-like, grass clump.
TEXTURE: Fine.　　　　　　　　　　EXPOSURE: Sun to partial shade.

LEAVES: Arising from a basal clump, about 1/2 inch wide, tapering to a slender point, often reaching 5 to 7 feet long. The margin is sharply saw-toothed when going toward the base of the leaf and can cause a cut when brushed the wrong way. Leaves often rise 6 feet or more in the air, then cascade to the ground in a fountain-like clump. Generally dark or medium green, no fall color. Nearly evergreen in Zones 8, 9 and 10.

STEM: Dense clumps of grass-like stems near the ground. The only tall stems develop when the plant begins to develop flowers. No bark.

FLOWERS: Female plant has silvery, cotton candy-like, white plumes; 12 to 24 inches long, 4 to 8 inches in diameter. Silky-hairy, rising well above the foliage of the plant, often 1 to 3 feet taller. Very showy; generally emerge late August and remain showy until December or January. Often used in dry flower arrangements. Male flowers are much less attractive.

FRUIT: Small, grass-like seed on female plants. Not showy. Generally of limited viability in the southern states. Does not become weedy.

COLOR: Foliage is dark to medium green. Flowers are silky white or pinkish.

PROPAGATION: Seed or division of a clump.

CULTURE: Tough and drought-resistant. Tolerates all growing conditions except those that are extremely wet or shady. Does best in full sun with any reasonable soil conditions. Responds vigorously to fertilization during the growing season but should be allowed to slow down in growth prior to cold weather. It will turn brown in late fall or early winter after some hard freezes. Dead foliage should be left on the plant until sometime in March, then cut back to within about 18 inches of the ground and allowed to come back from the crown. Cutting the plant down in early or mid-winter may reduce the cold hardiness of the plant. Mulching the soil surface helps the crown of the plant survive in Zone 7. Best to propagate by division, thus avoiding male plants with less attractive flowers.

PESTS: None serious in most areas. However, in the Gulf Coast States and southern Florida, sugar cane borer may become a problem. Extremely sensitive to some herbicides.

NOTES: A very large, showy, grass-like clump that stands out in the landscape because of its fine texture and unusual form. Plume-like flowers are spectacular during most of the fall, particularly when allowed to contrast with or complement other plants in the landscape. Must have full sun for good development and flowering. A drought-resistant, desirable shrub that should be used more.

CULTIVARS: 'Rosea': similar to the parent except that the flower plumes are pinkish.

RELATED SPECIES: Plume grass, *Erianthus ravennae*, has a smaller, grassy mound of leaves but taller flower stalks than *C. selloana*. It is also more cold hardy and serves as a good substitute in Zones 5 or 6 where pampas grass will not survive the winter.

Fountain grass, *Pennisetum alopecuroides*, is an attractive, smaller, ornamental grass rarely exceeding 3 feet in height and is cold hardy in Zones 5 and 6.

Pennisetum ruppeli has crimson foliage.

Cotoneaster spp.   Cotoneaster
Rosaceae or Rose Family   Hardiness Zones 5-7
Native to the Orient
SIZE: 1 to 8 feet tall, depending on species and cultivar. Moderate grower.
FORM: Ground cover or medium shrub, depending on species.
TEXTURE: Medium.   **EXPOSURE:** Sun.

LEAVES: Alternate, simple; with a smooth margin. Deciduous or nearly evergreen.

STEM: Upright or weeping, depending on species and cultivar.

FLOWERS: White or pink; single or in small clusters.

FRUIT: A small red berry that may be quite showy.

COLOR: Green foliage and red fruits.

PROPAGATION: Cuttings or seed.

CULTURE: Cotoneasters are tough and adaptable in terms of soils, moisture, and sunlight. However, most cotoneaster species and cultivars are **very susceptible to fire blight**. This bacterial disease is impractical to control with sprays; therefore the only control is to locate cotoneasters in sunny locations with good air movement. Cotoneasters are very attractive when healthy but because of this disease, they go in popularity cycles.

PESTS: Fire blight, mites, webworms.

NOTES: Tend to become very popular and widely planted, then, perhaps tied to the increase in susceptible plant population and a particularly favorable season for fire blight, many plants are killed or damaged and the market for cotoneasters in the nursery industry sharply drops. In a few years the cycle occurs again. Plant with caution. Perhaps it is more appropriate to add, "Enjoy them while they last".

RELATED SPECIES: *Cotoneaster horizontalis* Decne., rockspray cotoneaster, is hardy in Zone 4 and grows 2 to 3 feet tall while spreading 5 feet or more. Branches are flattened and leaves are dark, glossy green (see photo), about 1/2 inch long with a very short petiole. Stems form an irregular, layered effect. Small, pink flowers are showy among the leaves in late spring. Fruit is small; bright red in late summer. Nearly evergreen in Zones 7 and 8 and semi-evergreen in Zones 5 and 6. 'Little Gem' is a smaller, slow-growing form. 'Variegata' has leaves edged in white. Other cultivars exist.

Cotoneaster lucidus Schlechtend., hedge cotoneaster, is hardy in Zone 5 and grows 6 to 10 feet tall. Leaves are ovate and shiny dark green with a few hairs when young; later only a few hairs remain on the underside of the leaf along the veins. Stems are upright with much branching. Flowers are pinkish white, attractive. Fruit is black. Useful as a hedge plant because of the upright growth habit and dense branches; however, unsheared it also forms a good screen.

Cotoneaster multiflorus Bunge., the many-flowered cotoneaster, is similar to hedge cotoneaster except that the flowers are white and fruits are red. Useful and attractive.

Cotoneaster divaricatus Rehd. and E.H. Wils., spreading cotoneaster, hardy in Zone 5. Grows 4 to 6 feet tall with drooping outer branches. Leaves are ovate, very glossy and dark, nearly blue-green; very showy. Flowers are pink and fruit is red.

Cotoneaster dammeri C.K. Schneid., bearberry cotoneaster, is hardy in Zone 6 and grows about 1 foot tall and spreads 4 to 6 feet. Leaves are about 1 inch long, oval and dark green. Flowers are white; fruit is bright red. In general, rockspray cotoneaster is superior.

Many additional species and cultivars of cotoneaster exist; however, most share the problems discussed here.

297

C. lucidus

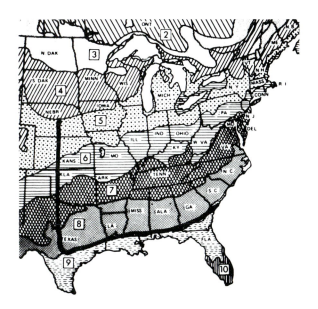

C. lucidus

C. dammeri

C. horizontalis

Deutzia X *lemoinei* Lemoine   Lemoine Deutzia
Saxifragaceae or Saxifrage Family   Hardiness Zone 4
A hybrid between *Deutizia parviflora* and *Deutzia gracilis*.
SIZE: 4 to 5 feet tall with a similar spread. Moderate grower.
FORM: Upright growing, round-topped, twiggy shrub.
TEXTURE: Medium.   EXPOSURE: Sun.

LEAVES: Opposite, simple; 1 1/2 to 3 inches long, lanceolate, with a sawtooth margin and a very short petiole. Upper and lower surfaces are medium to dark green. Leaves drop early with no fall color.

STEM: Upright growing shrub with smooth, slender, green stems when young, soon turning brown. Older stems are brown with peeling bark and are hollow.

FLOWERS: White; about 1/2 to 1 inch across, in terminal clusters in late spring or early summer. Moderately showy.

FRUIT: A small, dry capsule. Not showy.

COLOR: Foliage is medium to dark green. Flowers are white.

PROPAGATION: Softwood or hardwood cuttings.

CULTURE: An attractive shrub especially in full sun, where it remains more compact and produces more flowers. Grows in most soils of reasonable fertility and moisture. Should be pruned following flowering to assist in shaping and/or size control.

PESTS: None serious.

NOTES: Quite attractive as a late spring or early summer flowering shrub, but not outstanding. The flowers are nice but two weeks of showy blooms do not make up for 50 weeks of mediocre foliage and bare stems. Can be sheared to make an acceptable hedge.

CULTIVARS: 'Compacta': grows 3 to 4 feet tall and is more compact. Others may exist.

RELATED SPECIES: *Deutzia gracilis* Sieb. & Zucc., slender deutzia, is hardy in Zone 5, grows 3 to 4 feet tall and has white flowers in terminal clusters. Leaves and stems are more slender than those of lemoine deutzia and the overall plant is smaller, finer textured, and more compact and flowers earlier.

Many other species and hybrids exist but are generally less attractive and less cold-tolerant. Only a few are in the nursery trade and in most areas there are much better choices of deciduous shrubs for the landscape.

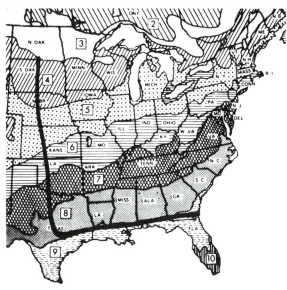

'Compacta'

Erianthus ravennae L. Plume Grass
Poaceae or Grass Family Hardiness Zone 5
Native to Europe.
SIZE: Foliage is 4 to 6 feet tall. Flower spikes up to 10 feet. Fast grower.
FORM: Foliage is rounded mound with tall flower spikes.
TEXTURE: Fine. **EXPOSURE:** Sun.

LEAVES: Medium green. Long and narrow and flat, growing off the upright stem and arching to the ground. Leaves turn an orangey brown in the fall. The leaf margin is finely serrate but poses little hazard.

STEM: Perennial. Upright, in a clump from tillering at the crown. Fairly stiff and only moderately subject to movement in the wind.

FLOWERS: On tall, slender stalks that extend far above the mound of stems and leaves. Individual flower spikes of 18 to 20 inches are silvery white long in September. However, with cool weather, the flowers turn brown. Very showy and often collected and dried for use indoors.

FRUIT: Small seed. Not showy.

COLOR: Foliage is green. Flowers are white.

PROPAGATION: Seeds or division.

CULTURE: A very tough grass. In sunny locations on good soils with adequate moisture, it grows faster, thicker, and taller. However, on terrible and droughty soils, it still performs but does not get as large. Likewise, in northern areas with the shorter growing season, it does not get as large as in the South.

PESTS: None.

NOTES: Sometimes referred to as hardy pampas grass. The two species do grow similarly but the flower plumes of plume grass do not get as white, large and fluffy, as pampas grass. This makes a good landscape grass in climates where pampas grass (Zone 7B) will not survive. The growth form is distinctly different from *Miscanthus, Arundo, Penniselum* and most other ornamental grasses, in that the flowers extend far above the foliage. In the southwest United States, and perhaps elsewhere, the plant produces viable seed and can be a pest. However, in Zones 8, 7, 6 and 5, viable seeds are rarely produced.

CULTIVARS: None.

RELATED SPECIES: *Erianthus alopecuroides*, silver plume grass, is native to the southeastern United States, grows only 4 to 7 feet tall and produces silvery flower spikes in late summer. Although not commonly seen; this, and other native species of *Erianthus* could make useful ornamentals with some selections of seedlings.

Euonymus alata Sieb.   Winged Euonymus or Burning Bush
Celastraceae or Staff Tree Family   Hardiness Zone 3
Native to northeast Asia.
SIZE: 8 to 10 feet tall with a 8- to 12-foot spread. Moderate to slow grower.
FORM: Densely branching medium to large shrub.
TEXTURE: Medium.   **EXPOSURE:** Sun to partial shade.

LEAVES: Opposite, simple; oval to slightly oval-elongate, 2 to 3 inches long, 1 to 1 1/2 inches wide, on a very short petiole. Generally deep green during the growing season and brilliant red early in the fall. Leaf margin is finely saw-toothed. Leaf texture is moderately soft and flexible; not hard.

STEM: Stiff, spreading branches, generally with 2 or 4 broad, brown to tan, corky wings on each stem: very prominent. Branches give the plant interesting character in winter after the leaves have dropped. Bark is green on young stems, gray to gray-brown on older stems, but not prominent because of the development of the brown wings on the branches.

FLOWERS: Yellowish, not showy; usually 3 on a short stalk.

FRUIT: Showy in the fall. One to 3, sometimes 4 purplish, Bishop's cap-shaped pods opening to expose an orange-red seed coating.

COLOR: Foliage is deep green during the growing season; brilliant red in the fall. Fruit is orange-red.

PROPAGATION: Cuttings or seed, but seedlings are variable.

CULTURE: Grows in a wide range of soil conditions: moderately moist to moderately dry soils. A useful, very adaptable deciduous shrub. Spectacular fall color, relatively early. Rather slow to develop following propagation from seed or cuttings, but once established in the landscape it is adaptable and tolerant. Easy to transplant because of the very fibrous root system. Most showy in full or nearly full sun, less spectacular in the shade. Can be sheared into a dense hedge or other form because of the many lateral buds.

PESTS: None serious. Unlike the evergreen euonymus species, it rarely has euonymus scale. Spider mites may be a problem in hot, dry locations.

NOTES: A most spectacular deciduous shrub in terms of fall color. Striking when planted in front of dark evergreens. Could be used as a multiple-stemmed small tree for tub or patio use. Leaves and fruits may be toxic if eaten in quantity. XX-POISON-XX

CULTIVARS: 'Compacta': slower growing, compact, densely branching form with slightly smaller leaves, easier to maintain in many instances. Slightly less brilliant fall color. 'Nordine Strain': branches low to the ground, is semi dwarf, and colors well. 'October Glory': slightly smaller than the species and very dense with excellent fall color. 'Rudy Hoag': very compact form, more compact than 'Compacta'. Relatively new and not yet well known.

 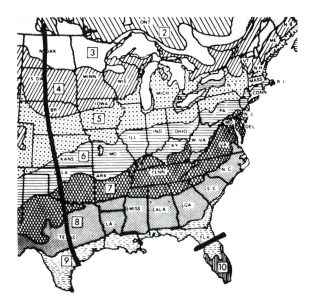

Exochorda racemosa (Lindl.) Rehd. Pearlbush
Rosaceae or Rose Family Hardiness Zone 5
Native to China
SIZE: 10 to 12 feet tall with an equal or greater spread. Rapid grower.
FORM: Large, rounded shrub.
TEXTURE: Medium. **EXPOSURE:** Sun to slight shade.

LEAVES: Alternate, simple; 1 to 2 inches long, more or less oblong, with a wavy, crenate margin, or occasionally with a few teeth near the tip. Leaf surface is glossy blue-green to medium green and distinctly gray-white beneath. No fall color.

STEM: Primary stems are upright with strong, secondary branching creating a rounded form. Young stems are slender, smooth and green, turning brown. Wood is only moderately stout, and if the shrub is allowed to become too large with no pruning or care, it may droop open, greatly reducing the attractiveness.

FLOWERS: White; 1 1/2 to 2 inches across, with distinct petals on a cup and with 5 to 10 flowers in a terminal cluster. Showy, but no fragrance in late spring.

FRUIT: A dry capsule; not showy.

COLOR: Foliage is glossy blue-green. Flowers are white.

PROPAGATION: Softwood cuttings.

CULTURE: Pearlbush is a very tough, durable and adaptable shrub that mostly needs an occasional pruning to retain the large, rounded form and contain the size somewhat. Should be pruned in spring after flowering to avoid loss of flower buds the following year. Will grow in shady locations; however, becomes loose and open and flowers poorly.

PESTS: None serious.

NOTES: A large shrub both in height and spread. Needs room, even when used as a hedge or screen unless pruned severely. On the other hand, it gets large enough to screen unwanted views during the growing season as well as partially during the winter. The plant in the photo is part of a row screening a parking lot. The flowers are nice but not spectacular. It is the sort of plant that has some uses but nothing outstanding. Pearlbush is one of those large shrubs that is seen and enjoyed when in flower but rarely noticed the rest of the year. On the other hand, a tough, widely adapted shrub with no serious disease or insect problems deserves consideration over some of the more showy but problem plants such as cotoneasters, rhododendrons and roses **unless** the person doing the maintenance is willing to pay the price. Donald Wymann in *Shrubs and Vines for American Gardens* notes that *Exochorda geraldi* Hesse. especially 'Wilsoni' has larger and more attractive flowers. However, this plant is rarely, if ever, seen in the nursery trade.

CULTIVARS: Some may exist. Certainly worthy of selections with improved flowering and form.

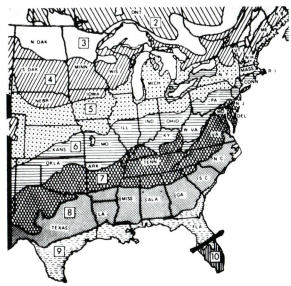

Forsythia spp.
Oleaceae or Olive Family
Native to China.

Forsythia or Goldenbell
Hardiness Zone 5

SIZE: 4 to 10 feet tall, depending on species and cultivar. Rapid grower.
FORM: Upright to spreading shrubs.
TEXTURE: Medium.   **EXPOSURE:** Sun.

LEAVES: Opposite, simple or occasionally compound; 3 to 4 inches long. Ovate-elongate or lanceolate, generally coarsely toothed on the margin and medium to light green above. For species information see notes.

STEM: Green when young, turning light brown or tan; with prominent lenticels. Branches are more or less upright or weeping and spreading depending on species or cultivar.

FLOWERS: Bright yellow and bell-shaped. Very early in the spring: March or April before the leaves, making the plant very showy. No odor.

FRUIT: Dry capsule. Not showy.

COLOR: Foliage is medium green. Little or no fall color except *Forsythia viridissima* has purple-red fall color. Flowers are yellow.

PROPAGATION: Cuttings.

CULTURE: It is easy to grow and does well in almost any soil except those exceptionally dry and poor. Often grows too large for limited space locations. Should be pruned back after the spring blooms since flower buds develop during the summer and fall. Fall pruning would remove flower buds. A vigorous growing shrub that needs plenty of room to develop to be of maximum usefulness.

PESTS: None serious.

NOTES: An old established garden shrub, very showy in the spring but of limited landscape value during the remainder of the season. Often grows rather rank and irregular, and needs pruning and moderate maintenance after a period of time. Two species are commonly found.

RELATED SPECIES: *Forsythia suspensa* Vahl., weeping forsythia, has leaves that are deeply lobed or divided into 3 parts and twigs that are hollow except where the leaves are attached at the nodes. Characterized by drooping or trailing branches. Cultivar 'Sieboldi' has vigorously trailing branches which will hang down over rock walls or ledges.
    Forsythis viridissima Lindl., has long, narrow leaves with teeth only on the outer margin. Mature branches are greenish or brownish; pith is usually divided into partitions between the nodes and fall color is purple-red.
    Forsythia intermedia is a hybrid between *F. suspensa* and *F. viridissima* and in most cases is considered superior to the parents. Many cultivars have been selected from this cross. 'Linwood Gold': flowers are more fully opened than those of the parent; and very heavily distributed along the stems. Upright habit and slightly stiff branching. 'Nana' or 'Dwarf' may be several plants grown under these names by nurseries around the country. Small, more compact, slower grower, with generally good flowering. A 10- to 12-year-old plant may be 5 feet tall and 8 feet in diameter. 'Spring Glory': pale primrose yellow flowers, and generally a greater mass of blooms than the parent. Numerous other cultivars selected from this cross probably exist. 'Arnold Dwarf' is a hybrid between *F. intermedia* and *F. japonica* selected at the Arnold Arboretum. A low dwarf form: six-year-old plant may be 3 to 4 feet tall and 6 feet in diameter with arching branches. Good for erosion control or back slopes. Not recommended for its greenish yellow flowers. Many cultivars exist and seem to excel in localized areas.

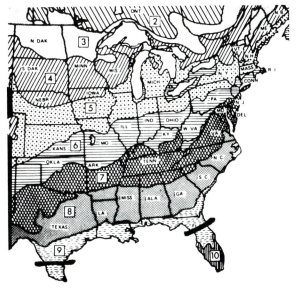

Hibiscus syriacus L. Rose-of-Sharon or Shrub Althea
Malvaceae or Mallow Family Hardiness Zone 5
Native to China and India.

SIZE: 8 to 10 feet tall with a 3- to 5-foot spread. Rapid grower.
FORM: Upright, bushy shrub.
TEXTURE: Medium. **EXPOSURE:** Sun.

LEAVES: Alternate, simple; 2 to 4 inches long, 2 to 3 inches wide. Palmate main veins, generally with 3 lobes and a coarsely toothed margin. Medium to dark green with no fall color.

STEM: A strictly upright, densely branching shrub. Young stems are green during the growing season, later turning light brown and developing a slightly irregular bark; not showy. Wood is only moderately stout. Develops into an acceptable deciduous hedge.

FLOWERS: White, red to almost blue; single or double, 3 to 4 inches across. Very showy. Beginning in mid summer and continuing until mid fall. Flowers are produced on new growth and as long as the plant is actively growing it will continue to bloom during the summer period. Herein lies the value of the plant.

FRUIT: Small; 5-celled, dry capsule. Not showy.

COLOR: Foliage is medium to dark green. Flowers are white, red, to almost blue.

PROPAGATION: Cuttings or seed.

CULTURE: Easily grown; tolerates a wide range of soils and moisture conditions as long as it is in full to nearly full sun. Responds vigorously to fertilizer but may need pruning to keep the plant in check in terms of size, particularly height. Should be pruned in the fall or very early spring since the flowers develop on new growth beginning in early summer. Old flowers and dropping leaves may be somewhat messy in a very formal area.

PESTS: Aphids occasionally on new growth; spider mites may become serious in hot, dry locations.

NOTES: Useful because of its upright growth form, flower color, and time of bloom. Few other plants bloom at the same time of year. In many areas of the South, it is inferior to many of the broadleaf evergreens. It is the only hardy hibiscus. Rose-of-sharon has merit as a tree form near a patio or outdoor living area, especially in hardiness Zones 7 or 6, where crapemyrtle, *Lagerstroemia indica* is not reliably cold- hardy as a tree form.

CULTIVARS: Many. 'Admiral Dewy': pure white single flowers. 'Ardens': light purple, semi-double flowers. 'Bluebird': large, pale blue, single flowers and a compact growth habit. 'Hamabo': pale pink, single flowers with reddish strips. 'Diana': large white flowers and dark green foliage but not very vigorous. 'Helene': pure white with red eye, also lack vigor. 'Blushing Bride': double pink flowers. 'Red Heart': single flowers, white with red center. 'Pink Giant': large single flowers, very prolific bloomer.

RELATED SPECIES: *Hibiscus rosa-sinensis* L., Chinese hibiscus, is hardy only in Zone 10. However, it is sometimes grown as an annual for summer flowering beds farther north. Many, many cultivars. Best distinguished from *Hibiscus syriacus* by the dark, glossy green leaves which are generally not lobed and by the more showy red and yellow flowers.

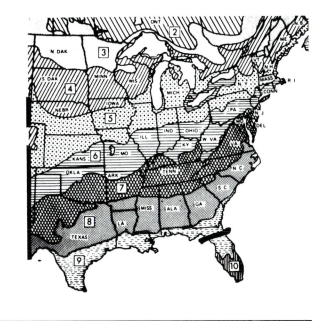

Hydrangea quercifolia Bart.　　　　　　　　Oakleaf Hydrangea
Saxifragaceae or Saxifrage Family　　　　Hardiness Zone 4
Native to Georgia, Florida, and west to Mississippi.
SIZE: 6 to 7 feet tall with a 6- to 8-foot spread. Moderate grower.
FORM: Broad, spreading, loosely branched shrub.
TEXTURE: Coarse.　　　　　　　　　　**EXPOSURE:** Partial to full shade.

LEAVES: Deciduous, opposite, simple; 4 to 8 inches long and nearly as broad. Oval to oblong with 3 to 7 lobes. Lobes have saw-like teeth on the margins. Overall form resembles that of a red oak leaf only larger. The leaf base is rounded. Upper surface is a dull dark green with a few long, white hairs; lower surface is nearly white and densely wooly.

STEM: Young stems are reddish brown or with white wooly hairs. Older stems have a thin, reddish brown bark peeling in shaggy strips. Wood is not stout and is easily broken.

FLOWERS: White. Appearing in May or June in large terminal clusters 4 to 12 inches long. Dense, reddish brown hairs cover the flower stalks. Flowers are of two types: seed bearing and sterile. Sterile flowers are on the outer fringe of the cluster, while the greenish white fertile flowers with 5 petals are near the center of the cluster. Quite showy.

FRUIT: A small, urn-shaped capsule. Not showy.

COLOR: Foliage is dull, dark green. Flowers are greenish white to white.

PROPAGATION: Cuttings or root suckers.

CULTURE: A widely adaptable shrub, which does best in moist, rich soil in partial shade to shade, such as on the north or east side of a structure. Fall pruning allows for thickening of the branches and good spring growth. Moderately tolerant of soil and cultural conditions. Should be planted a great deal more.

PESTS: None serious. Aphids occasionally on new growth.

NOTES: Not commonly planted, but it is a very showy, coarse-textured shrub that grows with little maintenance. Very interesting; should be used a great deal more throughout the South. Leaves of all *Hydrangea* species may be mildly toxic. XX-POISON-XX

CULTIVARS: 'Harmony': spectacular white flowers. 'Snowflake': very showy, pure white flowers. 'Snow Queen': heavy bloomer, fades to pinkish with age. Perhaps more vigorous. 'Peewee': grows only to 3 feet tall but flowers well. Nice for small areas. Other cultivars probably exist.

RELATED SPECIES: *Hydrangea paniculata* Sieb. 'Grandiflora', panicle or peegee hydrangea, is a large, coarse-textured, easily grown shrub, generally flowers in June. Much overplanted in the North and Northeast. Not a good shrub for many locations. It is hardy to Zone 4 and may grow 15 to 20 feet tall. Can be unique when trained as a small tree. 'Tardiva': smaller, reaching 10 feet finally, and much wider. Flowers in late summer.

Hydrangea macrophylla Ser. Hortensiz., garden hydrangea, the houseplant hydrangea, is hardy in Zone 6 but best suited to Zones 7, 8, and 9. Grows 6 to 8 feet tall. Has large, sterile flowers of pink or blue, generally in mid summer. Not a desirable landscape plant for many locations. 'Nikko Blue': grows to 4 or 5 feet with blue flowers on acid soils. 'Pia': a dwarf form with pink flowers and dark foliage. Many others exist.

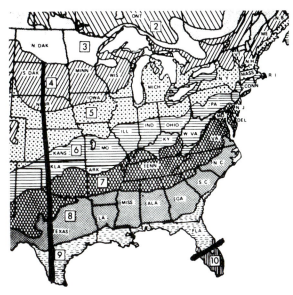

H. paniculata 'Grandiflora'

H. paniculata 'Grandiflora'

Hypericum prolificum L.   Shrubby St. Johnswort
Guttiferae or Garcinium Family   Hardiness Zone 4
Native to the east central United States.
SIZE: 2 to 4 feet tall with a similar spread. Slow grower.
FORM: A rounded shrub with stiff, upright branches.
TEXTURE: Medium.   **EXPOSURE:** Sun or slight shade.

LEAVES: Opposite, simple; 1 to 3 inches long, elongate, with no distinct veins. Has various glandular dots and a smooth margin. Upper leaf surface is dark, glossy green to blue-green, very attractive; pale green below. No fall color but leaves remain green late in the season.

STEM: Young stems are 2-angled, moderately stout; with distinct, opposite, axillary buds. Green turning brown. Older stems have peeling bark; slightly attractive. Branches are stiff, upright and stout, relative to their size.

FLOWERS: Yellow, perfect, about 2 inches across, with many long stamens, giving a pin-cushion effect. Very showy during July and August.

FRUIT: A small, dry capsule. Not showy.

COLOR: Foliage is blue-green. Flowers are yellow.

PROPAGATION: Softwood cuttings.

CULTURE: In the Northeast and Zones 4, 5, and 6, St. Johnswort does well in a wide array of soils and growing conditions. In the southern Prairie States and below Zone 7 it does not do well, with a few exceptions. Should be pruned in early spring since flowers form on new growth, as with most summer-flowering shrubs.

PESTS: None serious.

NOTES: A showy, summer shrub for Zones 4, 5, and to some degree 6, but marginal farther south and west. The flowers are especially bright and attractive. Because the plant size does not exceed 4 feet, it stays in scale with single story dwellings better than many shrubs. It is especially useful where little maintenance is provided or desired.

CULTIVARS: Some probably exist.

RELATED SPECIES: *Hypericum kalmianum* L., Kalm's St. Johnswort, grows about 3 feet tall, has leaves which are slightly shorter and stamens of flowers make them appear like a feathery ball. Very attractive. Hardiness Zone 4. One of the most cold tolerant species of the genus.

Hypericum patulum Thunb., goldcup St. Johnswort, grows 3 feet tall and is hardy in Zone 5. Flowers are larger and more flat, with 5 distinct petals and may be 2 to 2 1/2 inches across. This species is native to China. The leaves stay bluish green late into the fall and are more pointed at the tip. Semi-evergreen in Zone 7. 'Sungold' is a popular cultivar with 2 1/2-inch flowers from June to September and attractive form.

Hypericum calycinum, Aaronsbeard St. Johnswort, is hardy in Zone 5 and does okay in Zones 7 and 8 where other species and cultivars fail or perform poorly. Grows only about 18 inches tall but perhaps 24 inches across with spectacular yellow flowers. Flowers on new growth.

There are about 200 species in this genus with only slightly differing flowers and foliage.

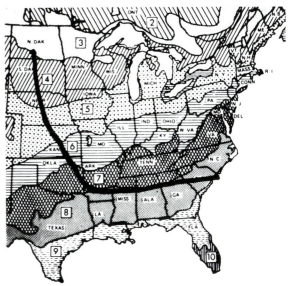

Hypericum kalmianum

H. patulum 'Sungold'

H. patulum 'Sungold'

Ilex decidua Walt.   Possumhaw or Deciduous Holly
Aquifoliaceae of Holly Family   Hardiness Zone 5
Native to the southeastern United States.
SIZE: Large shrub or small tree, may reach 20 feet. Moderate grower.
FORM: Irregular, round-headed shrub or small tree.
TEXTURE: Fine.   **EXPOSURE:** Sun to shade.

LEAVES: Alternate, simple; ovate to ovate-oblong, 1 1/2 to 2 inches long. Either dull or glossy dark green, with a wavy margin. Much variability among seedlings. Somewhat resemble leaves of yaupon holly, *Ilex vomitoria*, only these are more obovate, soft, flexible, and deciduous whereas yaupon leaves are thick and leathery and evergreen.

STEM: Generally stiff, multi-stemmed. New shoots are slender, green turning gray; old bark and twigs are generally a light gray to silvery gray.

FLOWERS: Inconspicuous. Male and female on separate plants (dioecious). A male is needed somewhere in the vicinity for good fruit set.

FRUIT: Borne singly or in small clusters on short spurs. Color varies from yellow-orange to glossy red. A few yellow-fruited cultivars exist. Produced during late summer and early fall. Not a spectacular show until after the leaves drop, exposing the fruit.

COLOR: Foliage is medium to dark green. Fruit is yellow-orange to red.

PROPAGATION: Hardwood cuttings or grafting. Seeds are very slow to germinate and seedlings are quite variable.

CULTURE: Tolerates a wide range of soil conditions. Is native to wet swampy conditions from Florida west to east Texas and Oklahoma. Appears to do best with adequate moisture although it will tolerate considerable drought. Does well in most landscape situations. Fruits best in partial shade to full sun.

PESTS: None serious although spittle bugs can make foliage unsightly.

NOTES: The most attractive deciduous holly. Frequently overlooked in many landscape plantings throughout the South. Should be planted a great deal more. Holds fruit into the late winter and sometimes early spring. Frequently at that time, fruits are eaten by cedar waxwings which in themselves make a spectacular show. When used with an evergreen background or against a blue sky, the dense, showy, red fruits are spectacular. Some fall color; the leaves generally turn a bronze or bronze-tan before they drop. Similar to *Ilex verticillata*, Michigan holly. However, the leaves of deciduous holly are smooth and glossy, whereas leaves of Michigan holly are dull and rough-textured on the upper surface.

CULTIVARS: 'Warren': a seedling selected by Warren Nursery, Oklahoma City. Deep glossy red fruit; dark, glossy green leaves which are retained late into the fall and which turn a spectacular purple-bronze about mid-November. 'Byers Gold': has yellow fruit. 'Council Fire': bright red fruit persist on the plant well into winter. 'Pocahontas', 'Sundance', and 'Walton' are similar with red fruit. 'Red Cascade': a large, rounded shrub with slight weeping habit and good red fruits. 'Red Escort': male with good form and dark foliage. Works well as a pollinator. Other cultivars probably exist in localized areas. Much variation among seedlings.

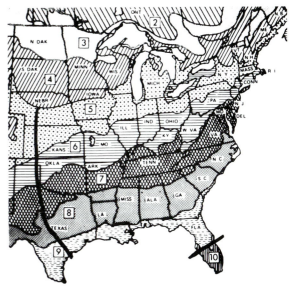

Ilex verticillata   *Ilex decidua*

Ilex verticillata (L.) Gray   Winterberry, Black Alder, Michigan Holly
Aquifoliaceae or Holly Family   Hardiness Zone 2
Native to the east central United States, north into Canada.
SIZE: 6 to 8 feet tall with similar spread. Slow to moderate grower.
FORM: Spreading shrub with many branches.
TEXTURE: Medium.   **EXPOSURE:** Sun or partial shade.

LEAVES: Alternate, simple; 2 to 3 inches long, more or less oval or oblong with a sawtooth margin. Upper leaf surface is dull, medium green; lighter beneath with a few hairs. Little or no fall color as leaves turn black after a hard freeze, but some variation among seedlings and cultivars.

STEM: Primary branches are upright with strong horizontal branches creating a rounded spreading shrub. Young twigs are smooth and green, soon turning gray-green then gray-brown. Wood is strong and durable.

FLOWERS: Male and female on separate plants (dioecious). Both sexes must be present for fruiting although only one male per neighborhood is enough since pollination is by bees. Not showy.

FRUIT: Bright red, about 1/4 inch long, maturing before the leaves, creating an attractive contrast, then remaining on the plant most of the winter. Very showy, particularly with evergreen conifers as a background.

COLOR: Foliage is a dull medium green. Fruits are bright red.

PROPAGATION: Seed or softwood cuttings of cultivars.

CULTURE: Native to wet, swampy areas over a wide area from Missouri, Tennessee, and northward into southern Ontario. However, winterberry does not require swampy areas to grow well but does require a moist soil, since it is not very drought tolerant. Moist, acid soils with a good leaf litter cover or mulch are preferred. Subject to iron chlorosis on alkaline soils or where alkaline debris remains following construction. It is easily transplanted and responds to pruning by branching more. Should be pruned in very early spring or fruit production will be reduced.

PESTS: None serious.

NOTES: A very attractive shrub in late summer when both red fruits and leaves are present and during the fall and winter after the leaves have fallen, especially with an evergreen background. The foliage is not nearly as glossy and attractive as that of its close relative *Ilex decidua*, deciduous holly, which is hardy in Zone 5. Deciduous holly can be distinguished by the glossy leaves and the wavy leaf margin instead of teeth (see photograph). Otherwise, the form, branching, and branch color are similar. However, deciduous holly is much more drought tolerant and does well on alkaline soils.

CULTIVARS: Many exist, but most are used only in localized areas. 'Winter Red', also called 'Red Sprite': grows to 8 feet tall and produces many red fruits. A real show-off and the fruits remain most of the winter. 'Nana': a dwarf form rarely reaches more than 4 feet and has red fruits. 'Chrysocarpa' and 'Winter Gold': yellow fruits; different but not as attractive as the red fruited plants. 'Sunset' is also a red-fruited plant with good form.

HYBRIDS: *Ilex verticillata* X *I. serrata* 'Apollo': grows to 10 feet tall with red fruits. 'Sparkleberry': grows to 10 feet tall or more with striking red fruits. 'Bonfire': may be simply *Iex serrata* but grows to 10 feet tall and has good red fruits which fade with cold weather.

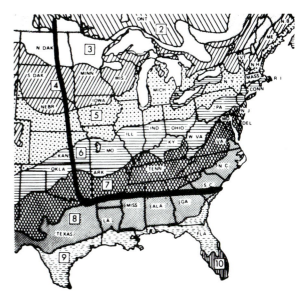

Ilex verticillata   *Ilex decidua*

Itea virginica L.   Sweetspire
Saxifragaceae or saxifrage Family   Hardiness Zone 6
Native to the southeastern United States.
SIZE: 3 to 8 feet tall with greater spread. Moderate to rapid grower.
FORM: Irregular, mounded shrub.
TEXTURE: Medium.   **EXPOSURE:** Sun to shade.

LEAVES: Simple, alternate, deciduous to nearly evergreen along the Gulf Coast. Oblong to near linear and willow-like, but variable depending on seedling or cultivar. One to 4 inches long, 1/2 to 1 1/2 inches wide, with a fine-toothed margin and short petiole. Upper surface is dark green and smooth, lower surface is generally covered with fine hairs when young. Fall color is red to red-orange.

STEM: Young twigs are slender and upright, smooth; green and covered with hairs when young, smooth and brown to gray and broken into small scales with age. Slowly spreads, creating a thicket.

FLOWERS: April through July; white; in terminal clusters 2 to 5 inches long. Somewhat drooping; hairy at first, later smooth. Fragrant and moderately showy.

FRUIT: A capsule, 1/4 to 1/2 inch long. Brown when mature; somewhat horn-like.

COLOR: Foliage is dark green, red to red-orange in fall. Flowers are white.

PROPAGATION: Seeds or hardwood or softwood cuttings.

CULTURE: Native to sandy, acid soils along streams and other moist areas from Virginia to East Texas and southward, generally in partial shade to shade. However, plants in Stillwater, Oklahoma in full sun and fairly heavy clay soils performed well with no supplemental water after the first year. Grows in many soils but does best with moisture and reduced weed and grass competition. Grows well in containers. Also, a shrub can be divided and successfully moved bare root in early spring. Needs water the first year but thereafter is quite drought-tolerant.

PESTS: None serious.

NOTES: A tough, tolerant shrub that in only recent years has begun to receive attention as a desirable landscape plant. In hardiness Zones 8 and 9 some cultivars or seedling sources hold their red leaves for months, including most of the winter. In Zone 9, few plants give good fall color but sweetspire is a striking exception. In its native habitat of moist soils and shady conditions, the plant can be loose and open; marginally attractive. However, when grown with good fertility, some pruning and in partial shade to full sun, the plant is more dense and attractive. Think of this shrub as having the color qualities of nyssa or black gum in the fall, only instead of a week of color, the color lasts for several months.

CULTIVARS: 'Henry's Garnet': selected for the reddish purple fall color and 6-inch long, white flower clusters. Grows only about 3 to 4 feet tall and slightly wider. 'Long Spire': longer than normal flower clusters and more yellow-orange fall color. 'Little Henry': a dwarf form. Other cultivars probably exist.

Jasminum nudiflorum Lindl.   Winter Jasmine
Oleaceae or Olive Family   Hardiness Zone 6
Native to China.
SIZE: 3 to 4 feet tall with a 4- to 6-foot spread. Moderate to rapid grower.
FORM: A rounded mound with arching branches.
TEXTURE: Medium.   **EXPOSURE:** Sun to partial shade.

LEAVES: Opposite, compound; with 3 leaflets.   Individual leaflets are oval or ovate to elongate and about 1 to 1 1/2 inches long, with a smooth margin. Medium green with no fall color.

STEM: Many stems arise from a central crown making a dense mass of arching stems, rooting where they contact the soil. Generally 4-angled or 4-ridged, and remains green giving the plant an evergreen appearance even after the leaves have dropped.

FLOWERS: Before the leaves, very early in the spring along the arching branches. Flowers are yellow, solitary and about one inch across, in leaf axils on 1-year-old wood. An irregular bloomer: rarely a heavy, consistent bloom. Generally blooms sporadically from late February to mid-March.

FRUIT: None.

COLOR: Foliage is medium green. Stems are green. Flowers are yellow but sporadic.

PROPAGATION: Cuttings or divisions.

CULTURE: A very tough, rugged, low shrub. Tolerates poor soil conditions and is moderately drought-resistant. Responds with vigor to improved soils and fertilizers. May need some pruning to assist the arching branches for neatness. Has a slight tendency to creep, rooting where the branches touch the ground, becoming a thick, dense mat. May also be troublesome to remove.

PESTS: Crown gall, bacterial stem gall; rarely any other serious problems.

NOTES: An interesting and unusual growth form among woody plants. The arching branches are useful for certain landscape effects. Can be used to complement round or arching lines. May be used for hanging down over a wall, covering a bank, or simply for a massing effect. Its greatest weakness is the inconsistency of its flowering in the spring. May also have use for erosion control or providing wildlife cover.

CULTIVARS: None known.

RELATED SPECIES: *Jasminum floridum* Bunge., showy jasmine, is a semi-evergreen shrub with spreading branches, hardy in Zone 7. A prolific bloomer throughout the growing season, but becomes irregular and difficult to manage with age.

Jasminum mesnyi Hance., the primrose jasmine, is an evergreen shrub hardy in Zone 8, with long, cascading branches and irregular, yellow flowers in the spring. Primarily useful for the long cascading branches to cover a wall or a bank.

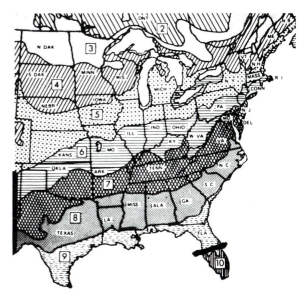

Jasminum mesnyi

Jasminum mesnyi

Jasminum mesnyi

Kerria japonica (L.) D.C.   Japanese Kerria
Rosaceae or Rose Family   Hardiness Zone 4
Native to central China.
SIZE: 3 to 5 feet tall, 4- to 6-foot spread with age. Moderate grower.
FORM: Shrub with many vertical stems forming an irregular clump.
TEXTURE: Medium.   **EXPOSURE:** Sun or partial shade.

LEAVES: Alternate, simple; oval, 1 to 2 inches long with a doubly-toothed margin and distinct stipules. Bright green and smooth above with very prominent veins; lighter in color and hairy beneath.

STEM: Young stems are green, slender and smooth, remain green for several years, then become striped with tan. Spreads slowly by a weak rhizome, therefore the shrub is a dense mass of vertical green stems, the outer stems arch to give an overall rounded effect. Wood is stout but flexible; not easily broken.

FLOWERS: Solitary, yellow flowers in April or May for 2 to 3 weeks. May be single or double, depending on cultivar, and 1 to 2 inches across. Flower buds are formed on last year's growth therefore should be pruned after flowering. Also flowers some during the growing season but not as heavily nor as showy.

FRUIT: A small, dry seed. Not commonly seen.

COLOR: Yellow, in spring; green stems throughout the winter. Good foliage during the growing season and sporadic flowering.

PROPAGATION: Softwood cuttings or division of a clump.

CULTURE: A very adaptable shrub, deserving of more attention. Flowers rival forsythia or any of the common spring flowering shrubs and last for 2 to 3 weeks. Grows in about any soil except for very heavy, poorly drained clays. Responds to fertilizers, and if watered during dry periods, may produce another burst of flowers. May be left unpruned or pruned severely. Heavy pruning will encourage more lateral spread by the weak rhizome. Remember to prune after the spring blooms or immediately after the last, weaker blooms in August or early September so that flower buds again form for spring. Individual old stems may be removed anytime.

PESTS: Few, if any.

NOTES: Adds interest to the landscape throughout the year from flowers, foliage, or green stems. Superior to many deciduous flowering shrubs that contribute to the landscape for no more than a week in early spring. Deserves to be used more, especially in borders, as filler in and around other plants, or in low-maintenance areas. Occasionally found around abandoned farmsteads growing well and flowering profusely with no care. Such independence and durability is shared only with a few of the common lilacs. 'Plentiflora' with profuse double flowers is the preferred cultivar.

CULTIVARS: 'Plentiflora': with double yellow flowers, shaped like a marigold or small carnation; very showy but gets 5 feet tall or more and slowly spreads. 'Picta': single yellow flowers and leaves edged with white; quite striking but only a fair flower producer. 'Shannon': large single yellow flowers. Others probably exist.

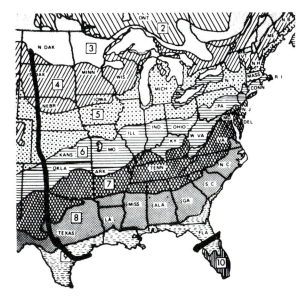

Kolkwitzia amabilis Graebn. Beautybush
Caprifoliaceae or Honeysuckle Family Hardiness Zone 5
Native to China.
SIZE: 10 to 15 feet tall with a 5- to 8-foot spread. Rapid grower.
FORM: Large, upright, vase-shaped shrub.
TEXTURE: Medium. **EXPOSURE:** Sun or slight shade.

LEAVES: Opposite, simple; 1 to 3 inches long. More or less ovate with a long, tapering tip and a smooth margin, or an occasional shallow sawtooth mostly near the tip. Dull green upper leaf surface and lighter green below; both leaf surfaces are covered with hairs when the leaves are young. No fall color.

STEM: Young stems are hairy and light green, eventually turning a light tan. The main stems are strictly upright with an attractive, bright brown bark that splits and peels back (see photograph). Wood is fairly stout.

FLOWERS: Pink, like an elongated balloon at first, becoming bell-shaped when open and having a yellow throat. In dense clusters at the tips of the current season's shoots. Very showy in mid-spring. The base of the flower (recepticle) is densely hairy.

FRUIT: Dry capsules surrounded by dense hairs, on the perimeter of the foliage, remaining into the fall.

COLOR: Foliage is dull green. Flowers are pink and showy.

PROPAGATION: Seed, softwood or hardwood cuttings.

CULTURE: Beautybush will grow in most any sunny location on a variety of soils. This is a large shrub that does not appreciate pruning. Do not shear as a hedge plant. However, if left alone, does make a good tall screen or barrier.

PESTS: None serious.

NOTES: A magnificent show of flowers for about three weeks. Bloom period is longer than that of many spring flowering shrubs since not all the flowers open at once. With beautybush two choices exist: a) leave it alone entirely, thus allowing the lower branches to arch or droop creating an attractive loose mound (see photograph) or b) prune off the lower limbs, select 5 to 7 main stems and train it as a small, multiple-trunk tree. When used in this manner adjacent to a patio or outdoor living area, not only can the attractive flowers be enjoyed in spring but the attractive bark will add interest all year long. In Zones 6 and 7 beautybush may be effectively used as a small tree in tubs or planters. A third alternative, if adequate space exists, is to plant several beautybushes in a clump in an out-of-the-way corner. When it flowers it is very showy, while the rest of the year it blends in with other more or less naturalized vegetation.

CULTIVARS: 'Pink Cloud': probably the same as 'Rosea', heavy producer of dark pink to near reddish flowers. Others may exist in local areas.

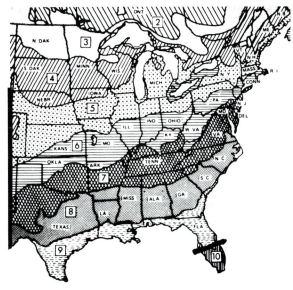

Lagerstroemia indica L. Crapemyrtle
Lathraceae or Loose Strife Family Hardiness Zone 7
Native to China.
SIZE: Ranges from a few inches to 25 feet or more. Growth rate is moderate to rapid.
FORM: Multi-stemmed shrub or small tree.
TEXTURE: Fine to medium. **EXPOSURE:** Sun.

LEAVES: Opposite, or on rapidly growing branches, may appear alternate, simple. Elliptical to ovate, 2 to 4 inches long, 1 to 2 inches wide. Rounded at the base and at the tip with a very short petiole and a smooth margin. Medium to dark green above, paler green below. Fall color is red, red-orange, or yellow, variable with cultivars and seedlings.

STEM: Slender when young, 4-angled or ribbed, becoming smooth with age. Stems that are larger than 1 inch diameter are light tan, appear varnished and smooth but muscled or irregular in cross-section. Very attractive. Wood is moderately durable.

FLOWERS: White, pink, red, or purple, and a few are variegated. In large, showy panicles 4 to 12 inches long; spectacular. Individual petals of the flowers are crepe paper-like, irregularly wrinkled and constricted at the base so the petal appears to have a leaf-like petiole. Generally the blooms begin by mid-July and continue until frost.

FRUIT: A round, tan, capsule, generally splitting into 6 parts.

COLOR: Foliage is medium to dark green; fall color is red or orange. Flowers are white, pink, red, or purple.

PROPAGATION: Cuttings. Hardwood in December, or softwood cuttings in May or June under mist. Seedlings are quite variable.

CULTURE: A widely adaptable shrub or small tree. Easy to grow and transplant. Grows in most soils and performs admirably. Very drought-resistant. A trouble-free shrub or small tree in exposed locations where mildew does not become serious. Because it blooms on new growth during long days, improved growing conditions that stimulate new growth, including fertilization, will stimulate additional flowering.

PESTS: Powdery mildew may be serious, but can be avoided by planting in open, full sun locations with good air circulation. Aphids on soft new growth can be a problem.

NOTES: May be grown as a shrub using dwarf cultivars. These should be severely pruned each winter. If allowed to develop, most cultivars will reach considerable size, being densely bushy. Occasionally grown as a multiple or single-stemmed small tree. Suckers at the base must be removed to show the very attractive bark. A spectacular landscape plant for most of the South, Southwest, and West Coast where it is hardy. Otto Spring introduced several very dwarf forms, commonly referred to as petites or midgets. When cut to the ground each winter, these rarely reach more than 12 to 24 inches tall during the growing season and bloom profusely. One of the problems of crapemyrtle cultivars is the difficulty in maintaining identity as they come and go in popularity.

CULTIVARS: 'Prairie Lace': deep rose flowers with white edges, gives a candy-striped effect. 'Centennial Spirit': upright; dark wine red flowers. 'Raspberry Sunday': pink-red flowers, upright, vigorous. 'Royal Velvet': wine foliage and pink flowers. 'Dynamite': super red flowers on very upright stems. Many cultivars exist in localized areas.

RELATED SPECIES: *Lagerstroemia fauriei* Koehne. is a large shrub or small tree reaching 20 to 25 feet with very attractive red-brown bark, but its flowers are white and only moderately showy. Leaves are dull green; less attractive than those of the common crapemyrtle. This makes an excellent multiple-stemmed tree and is hardy in Zone 7.

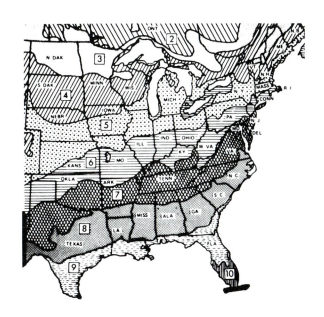

Ligustrum spp.   Privet
Oleaceae or Olive Family   Hardiness Zone 7 through 3 depending on
Native to the Orient.   species and cultivar.
SIZE: 3 to 10 feet tall, spread is variable with species and cultivars. Rapid growers.
FORM: Loose, upright-growing shrubs.
TEXTURE: Fine.   EXPOSURE: Sun to partial shade.

LEAVES: Opposite, simple; small, oval, with short petioles and smooth margins. Medium to dark green or variegated, depending on species and cultivar. No fall color.

STEM: Young stems are slender, light tan or light green, and hairy or occasionally smooth, with small buds in the leaf axils. Wood is flexible and not easily broken. Shears well into a hedge.

FLOWERS: Small, white, in terminal clusters or from axillary buds. Generally fragrant, sometimes repulsively so. Pollen may bother people with hay fever or other allergies. Not showy.

FRUIT: Black, about 1/4 inch in diameter, 1- to 4-celled.

COLOR: Foliage is medium to dark green to yellow-green, depending on species and cultivar.

PROPAGATION: Very easy from softwood or hardwood cuttings. Seed is variable.

CULTURE: Extremely tough, durable shrubs. Will grow in almost any soil in hot locations in full sun or with partial shade. Probably most useful as a sheared hedge or screen, because they branch profusely developing a good, dense hedge of fine texture.

PESTS: None serious.

NOTES: A large group of shrubs which are botanically divided into several species; however, for landscape use, several can be used interchangeably. Therefore, they are considered here as a common unit. Old garden landscape plants not used as extensively in current times as in the past. Leaves and fruits may be toxic if eaten in quantity.

SPECIES AND CULTIVARS: Differences between species and cultivars are small. *Ligustrum obtusifolium* Sieb. and Zucc., border privet, is hardy to Zone 3, grows 9 feet tall with a 5 to 7 foot spread, slightly purplish fall color. 'Regalianum', regal privet, is a low-branching, almost horizontal shrub not growing more than 4 to 5 feet tall. An interesting variation in form.
    Ligustrum ovalifolium Hassk., California privet, hardiness Zone 5, grows 12 to 15 feet tall, with an 8- to 10-foot spread with half evergreen foliage. 'Aureum': each leaf has a green spot in the center surrounded by yellow-gold; fair retention of variegated color during the growing season.
    Ligustrum sinense Lour., Chinese privet, is hardy through Zone 7, grows 10 to 12 feet tall with an 8- to 10-foot spread, may also have some merit as a small tree. 'Variegata' has brilliant yellow-green foliage and is nearly evergreen through Zone 8 and 9. A very useful hedge plant particularly where the variegated foliage is desired.
    Ligustrum vicaryi Rehd., golden vicary privet, a hybrid between *L. ovalifolium* and *L. vulgare* is hardy through Zone 4, grows 6 to 10 feet high and 4 to 8 feet wide with variegated yellow-orange foliage throughout the growing season. Attractive.
    Ligustrum vulgare, common privet, is hardy through Zone 4 and may reach 15 to 20 feet tall. Avoid because of disease in the humid South but useful in the North.

Ligustrum vulgaris

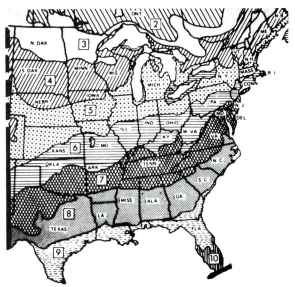

Ligustrum vulgaris

Ligustrum vulgaris

Ligustrum vulgaris

Ligustrum obtusifolium 'Regalianum'

Ligustrum obtusifolium 'Regalianum'

Ligustrum sinense

Ligustrum sinense

Ligustrum vicaryi

Lonicera fragrantissima Lindl. and Paxt.　　Winter Honeysuckle
Caprifoliaceae or Honeysuckle Family　　Hardiness Zone 5
Native to eastern China
SIZE: 10 to 15 feet tall with a 6- to 8-foot spread. Moderate to rapid grower.
FORM: Multi-stemmed large shrub with wide arching branches and rounded head.
TEXTURE: Medium.　　　　　　　　**EXPOSURE:** Sun to partial shade.

LEAVES: Opposite, simple; round to slightly oblong, 1 1/2 to 2 1/2 inches long with a very short petiole and smooth margin. Deep green to slightly blue-green above, gray-green below; thick and leathery. Semi-evergreen in Zones 7, 8, and 9, less evergreen farther north.

STEM: Young stems are purple to purple-green becoming a light sandy brown to dark brown with age. Branches tend to arch out, developing an umbrella-like crown on the shrub if it is left unpruned. Some suckers do develop at the base but seldom become a problem.

FLOWERS: During late winter or very early in spring; not showy but small and creamy white, in the leaf axils. Very fragrant, providing a pleasant aroma to a sizeable area when in flower. Flowering continues for 2 to 3 weeks.

FRUIT: Very pulpy, small red berry, developing in May or June. Not common.

COLOR: Foliage is deep green to slightly blue-green. Flowers are white and fragrant.

PROPAGATION: Softwood or hardwood cuttings, or division of a clump.

CULTURE: A tough, tolerant shrub, adaptable to a wide range of soils, moisture conditions, and light intensity. More compact and dense in sunny locations, but remains acceptably compact in moderate shade. Continues to flower in moderate shade. Responds well to pruning into hedges or forms. Drought-resistant and free of serious pests.

PESTS: None serious.

NOTES: Attractive, semi-evergreen shrub with very fragrant flowers. Will grow in about any location and makes a good background for other plantings. Among the best of the deciduous shrubs for a hedge or screen.

CULTIVARS: None known.

RELATED SPECIES: Several other species of honeysuckle exist and have some potential in the landscape. However, both tatarian and morrow honeysuckle produce lots of viable seeds and as a result, have beomc prolific weeds in the Northeast. use with caution. By contrast, winter honeysuckle is not at all weedy.

Lonicera tatarica L., tatarian honeysuckle, hardy through Zone 3, grows 8 to 12 feet tall, with pink to white flowers in May and a profusion of red berries in mid summer. Numerous cultivars exist. 'Arnold Red' has dark red flowers. 'Lutea' has pink flowers and yellow fruit. 'Virginalis': large, pink flowers. 'Parvifolia': showy white flowers.

Lonicera morrowi A. Grey, morrow honeysuckle, very similar to tatarian honeysuckle. Hardy through Zone 4, grows 4 to 6 feet tall with a 6- to 8-foot spread, and has a more spreading, broad-mound habit. 'Xanthocarpa': white flowers and yellow fruits.

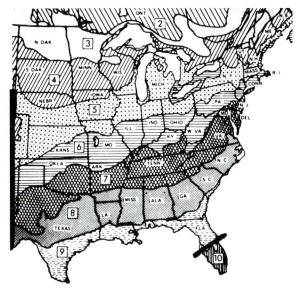

Lonicera tatarica L. Tatarian Honeysuckle
Caprifoliaceae or Honeysuckle Family Hardiness Zone 3
Native to Central Asia.
SIZE: 8 to 12 feet tall with a similar spread. Rapid grower.
FORM: Large, upright, but irregular shrub.
TEXTURE: Medium. EXPOSURE: Full sun to partial shade.

LEAVES: Opposite, simple; more or less oval with a smooth margin, 1 to 2 inches long and nearly as wide. Leaves are bluish green and attractive but have little or no fall color.

STEM: Pronounced opposite buds and leaf scars. Young twigs are very slender but stiff and strong. Green, eventually turning a light tan, then brown and finally gray.

FLOWERS: Pink to white, depending on cultivar. In the leaf axils over the entire shrub in May or June. Showy and fragrant.

FRUIT: Orange to red fruits, about 1/4 inch in diameter, in mid summer. May be showy.

COLOR: Foliage is blue-green. Flowers are pink to white. Fruits are orange to red.

PROPAGATION: Very easy with with either softwood or hardwood cuttings or seed.

CULTURE: A very tough, adaptable, large shrub. Grows in most soils unless they are swampy. Few problems and good branching, make it a widely used hedge. Tends to get leggy at its base, but this can be prevented if it is allowed to branch low when young or if space allows, low compact plants should be planted along its base. Can be a weed.

PESTS: Few in most locations, but Russian aphid is becoming a greater problem.

NOTES: A widely used shrub, particularly the many cultivars. The more compact cultivars and hybrids are easier to maintain, and function for a longer period of time without overgrowing the site. Several related species and hybrids function similarly.

CULTIVARS: 'Alba': grows 6 to 8 feet with white flowers and red fruits. An upright grower with heavy flowering characteristics. 'Arnold Red': very striking, deep red flowers, and red fruit. 'Grandiflora' and 'Parviflora': have large white flowers. 'Morden Orange': pink flowers and orange fruits. 'Nana': several growth forms are sold under this name. More dwarf and compact, generally with pink flowers. 'Zabeli': red flowers and compact, upright growth; makes an especially good hedge bud severe aphid problems. Many other cultivars exist.

RELATED SPECIES: *Lonicera morrowi* A. Gray, morrow honeysuckle, Zone 4, is similar in all respects except the flowers are white at first, changing to yellow, and the fruits are shiny, bright red. Morrow honeysuckle tends to retain low branches better than tatarian honeysuckle. 'Xanthocarpa' has white flowers and yellow fruits.
Lonicera maaki Maxim., amur honeysuckle, is similar in size and adaptation to tatarian honeysuckle. Leaves are more elongate and flowers are white, changing to yellow, and fruit is red. Very similar to morrow honeysuckle but larger and more weedy; less desirable. 'Erubescens' has glossy, green leaves with long, tapering tips. More compact growth.
Lonicera alpigena L., alps honeysuckle, is similar in adaptation. The cultivar 'Nana' is a low shrub, 2 to 3 feet tall; with dark green, crinkled leaves, red flowers in summer, red fruits, and yellow fall color. A very attractive and useful landscape shrub.
A hybrid between *Lonicera tatarica* and *L. xylosteum* L., generally listed as *Lonicera* X *xylosteoides* Tausch. 'Clavey's Dwarf' is a low shrub, rarely growing more than 4 to 5 feet tall; leaves are bluish green. Flowers are yellow in summer and fruits are red. A useful shrub requiring little pruning. Many other species of honeysuckle exist, but these are the most useful in landscaping.

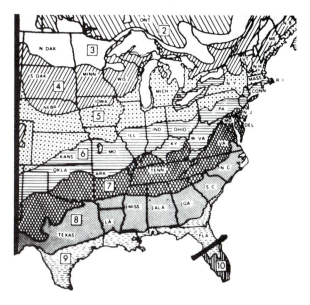

Lonicera x *xylosteoides* 'Clavey's Dwarf'

Lonicera macki

Lonicera macki 'Erubescens'

Lonicera morrowi

Lonicera morrowi

Lonicera morrowi

Miscanthus sinensis   Japanese Silver Grass or Eulalia
Poaceae or Grass Family   Hardiness Zone 4 or 5
Native to eastern Asia or Japan.
SIZE: 6 to 12 feet tall or less, with some cultivars. Rapid grower.
FORM: Upright grass clump
TEXTURE: Fine.   EXPOSURE: Sun.

LEAVES: 1 1/2 to 3 feet long, 1/2 to 1 1/2 inches wide, tapering to a slender tip. Plant and leaf size are variable with cultivar. Flat and green to slightly silvery green. Sharply serrate on the margin.

STEM: Perennial. Vigorous growing, upright stems are stout but flexible and bend freely in any breeze. A weak rhizome or heavy tillering allows the plant to spread at a slow pace.

FLOWERS: White to silvery; in fluffy fan-like clusters at the tip of the stems in late summer and fall. Very showy and keep well for dried arrangements.

FRUIT: A small seed. Not attractive. Seedlings can be a problem in some areas of the Southwest and Deep South.

COLOR: Foliage ranges from green to silvery green. Flowers are white to silvery.

PROPAGATION: Division.

CULTURE: Can be grown practically anywhere and on any soil as long as the site is sunny. Responds vigorously to fertilization and supplemental watering. It does spread and can become a pest in some cases, but Roundup will keep it in check. Transplants easily, either from containers or from division of a clump.

PESTS: None.

NOTES: A spectacular grass clump in late summer and fall when the flowers are present. Leaves turn brown with the first frost, but the flowers remain attractive into the winter. Some cultivars are more showy than others. Needs to be cut off near the soil surface before spring growth begins.

CULTIVARS: 'Giganteus', giant miscanthus (sometimes listed as *M. sacchariflorus*) grows 10 to 12 feet tall and develops a huge clump by slowly spreading. 'Gracillimus': very narrow leaf blades and grows 3 to 5 feet tall. a less vigorous spreader than the species. Flowers are silvery white and up to 10 inches long. 'Yakushima': probably the same as 'Gracillimus'. 'Silver Feather': grows 6 to 8 feet tall and flowers profusely and somewhat earlier than other cultivars. Pale pink flower clusters. 'Purpurascens': reddish purple foliage in sunny locations and reddish flower plumes slowly changing to white. 'Variegatus', striped miscanthus: green and near white strips parallel with the leaf margins. Foliage is quite attractive but flowers are generally more sparse. 'Zebrinus': yellow horizontal bands across the green leaf blade. Sometimes listed as 'Strictus' and called porcupine grass. Interesting and unusual coloration but only noticeable up close. Others probably exist.

 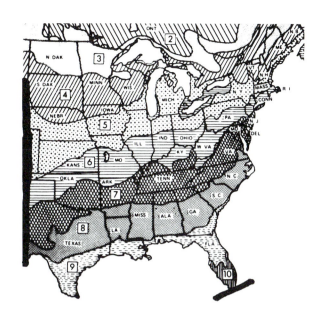

Myrica pensylvanica Loisel.   Bayberry
Myricaceae or Sweet Gale Family   Hardiness Zone 5
Native to northeastern United States and southeastern Canada.
SIZE: 4- to 8-foot shrub. Moderate grower.
FORM: Irregular shrub.
TEXTURE: Medium.   **EXPOSURE:** Sun or partial shade.

LEAVES: Alternate, simple; oblong, 1 to 3 inches long, deep green in most cases, covered with fine hairs above and below. Aromatic when crushed. Margin is irregularly toothed, mostly near the tip, and the petioles are very short. No fall color, as leaves simply drop after extended cold weather in the North; however, in Zones 7 and 8, some plants may be nearly evergreen.

STEM: Young stems are slender, green, turning gray with age; rather stiff. Branching is moderate, forming a dense shrub.

FLOWERS: Inconspicuous. Male and female on separate plants (dioecious). A male must be present for good fruit development.

FRUIT: A small, gray-white fruit about the size of a BB, remains on the stem most of the winter.

COLOR: Foliage is deep green. Fruits are gray-white.

PROPAGATION: Seed or softwood cuttings with difficulty.

CULTURE: Native to sandy soils with low fertility along the northern Atlantic Coast and inland. Does well on poor, sandy, or gravelly soils where other species suffer. Moderate drought tolerance. However, it is not heat-tolerant, particularly in the Prairie states. Generally should not be planted south of Zone 7 and west of Iowa and Missouri. Can be pruned to reduce size and increase overall foliage density. Somewhat difficult to transplant unless grown in containers. On alkaline soils, may develop iron chlorosis which can be corrected by applying elemental sulfur at the rate of about 4 pounds/100 square feet once each year for 3 years. The benefit is a gradual increase in available iron and a slow reduction in the pH of the top few inches of soil.

PESTS: None serious.

NOTES: An attractive, semi-evergreen shrub for Zones 5 and 6, where the number of broadleaf evergreens is limited. The adaptation to poor, sandy soils makes it useful for highway plantings and as a screen in low maintenance areas. With pruning, it makes a dense screen and sound barrier for outdoor living areas. The leaves will be retained long after cold weather limits the use of the patio. Bayberry and related species have the capacity to fix nitrogen like legumes, via a symbiotic nitrogen fixing bacteria, which probably accounts for their tolerance to poor soils. May naturalize on a site and develop thick clumps from the germinating seeds.

CULTIVARS: None known.

Parthenocissus quinquefolia (L.) Planch.   Virginia Creeper
Vitaceae or Grape Family   Hardiness Zone 2
Native to most of the United States.
SIZE: May reach 40 to 50 feet, climbing on a tree or structure. Rapid grower.
FORM: Climbing vine; occasionally a ground cover in shady places.
TEXTURE: Medium.   **EXPOSURE:** Partial shade to shade.

LEAVES: Alternate, palmately compound with 5 leaflets. Individual leaflets are obovate to egg-shaped and slightly wider near the outer end, tapering to a sharp point at the tip. Generally 3 to 6 inches long, 1 to 2 inches wide. The margin is coarsely toothed. Generally a dull, dark green above and pale green with a few hairs below. Brilliant fall color: bright red early in the fall while leaves on most trees are still green.

STEM: Young twigs are light brown, slender, and flexible with very prominent lenticels. Numerous short, spur-like branches develop on older stems. Most branches are sparingly covered with branched tendrils for climbing. These are finger-like projections with flattened, suction cup-like discs at the end. Buds are small, red-brown, and basketball-shaped, whereas leaf scars are saucer-shaped and very prominent. Bark on older stems is light brown becoming deeply furrowed with age.

FLOWERS: Small, white clusters; not showy.

FRUIT: Dark purple with a whitish film, in long clusters on red stalks, matures in summer.

COLOR: Foliage is dull dark green; brilliant red in the fall.

PROPAGATION: Cuttings, seed, or layering.

CULTURE: Best adapted to shady, moist, woodland conditions but will tolerate a wide range of soil conditions, as long as it is not extremely dry during the establishment period. Performs best when mulched or planted in a shady out-of-the-way place where some leaf litter or compost is present. Occasionally used as a ground cover where an occasional mowing encourages thickening of the stems. Responds to fertilization, grows vigorously up deciduous trees, and makes a spectacular show in the fall. Has use on arbors, trellises, or screens where a deciduous vine is acceptable.

PESTS: None serious.

NOTES: Spectacular for a 2 to 3 week period in early fall. Leaves turn color before most trees, creating a contrast between the red of the Virginia creeper, the bark of the tree, and the foliage on the outer branches of the tree. Often confused with poison ivy, which has three leaflets and dense aerial roots with no tendrils, whereas Virginia creeper has five leaflets, no aerial roots, and attaches itself by tendrils on irregular finger-like projections. Disc-like tendrils sometimes remain on the bark of the tree, thus one must look closely to determine if the projections on the stem are tendrils or roots.

CULTIVARS: 'Saint Pauli' and 'Engelmanni' are said to have smaller leaves.

RELATED SPECIES: *Parthenocissus tricuspidata* Planch., Boston ivy, is similar to Virginia creeper. It has a simple, 3-lobed leaf, grows similarly in rate and overall appearance but is much less tolerant to drought and more sensitive to heat and high light intensity. Best adapted to northern or eastern exposures of buildings, on trees, or as a ground cover. Foliage turns brilliant orange or scarlet in the fall. Sometimes preferred for covering walls on the north or east exposures because of the more dense, glossy green foliage. May be more susceptible to spider mites than is Virginia creeper. 'Green Showers': large green leaves. 'Purpurea': purplish leaves all season. Others exist.

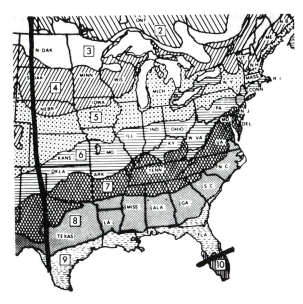

P. tricuspidata, Boston ivy

P. tricuspidata

Pennisetum alopecuroides L.
Poaceae or Grass Family
Native to Asia

Fountain Grass
Hardiness Zone 5

SIZE: 3 to 4 feet tall with similar spread. Rapid grower.

FORM: Graceful, mounded grass.

TEXTURE: EXPOSURE: Sun to partial shade.

LEAVES: Long and slender, arching over to touch the ground. Medium green; sandpapery to touch. Quite tough and tatter-resistant, even in the most challenging environments.

STEM: Perennial. A grassy clump that tillers (very short stems) slowly from the crown.

FLOWERS: Elongated, 6- to 8-inch long, bottle brush-like spikes. Coppery tan and stickery to the touch. The bloom period is roughly August through October. As the flowers mature, the seeds and associated glumes are easily dislodged by wind or any contact. By late fall, only the foliage remains, which is yellow after a frost.

FRUIT; A spiny appearing group of bristles and glumes surround each seed.

COLOR: Foliage is green. Flowers are coppery tan.

PROPAGATION: Seed or division.

CULTURE: An attractive grass clump that will grow almost anywhere except in shade or with very poorly drained soils. The plant needs room as it will spread as much as the height, creating the fountain-like effect of the foliage. Slowly spreads by tillers, eventually becoming a sizable clump and will eventually die out in the center if not divided.

PESTS: None serious.

NOTES: At some point each winter or very early spring, the old foliage should be removed. This improves the appearance of the plant and causes no harm. This is one of the toughest and showiest of the medium-sized perennial grasses.

CULTIVARS: 'Hameln': a smaller plant generally no more than 2 to 3 feet tall. Otherwise, like the species.

RELATED SPECIES: *Pennisetum setaceum* Chiov., crimson fountain grass, is hardy as a perennial only in Zone 8. However, further north it works well as an annual. Overall form and adaptation is similar to *P. alopecuroides* except the foliage is a dark purple and it grows 2 to 4 feet tall. The flower spikes are also distinctly purplish. The flowers spikes may reach 9 to 12 inches and are very showy July through October. In Zones 8 or 9 the seeds are viable and the plant can become a weed.

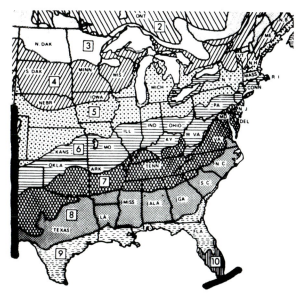

Philadelphis coronarius L.   Sweet Mockorange
Saxifragaceae or Saxifrage Family   Hardiness Zone 4
Native to southern Europe.
SIZE: 6 to 10 feet tall with a 4- to 6-foot spread. Rapid grower.
FORM: Large, upright shrub.
TEXTURE: Medium.   EXPOSURE: Sun or slight shade.

LEAVES: Opposite, simple; 2 to 3 inches long, ovate. Dark green above, much lighter green below with very shallow teeth on the margin, mostly near the tip but occasionally throughout. Slightly yellow or no fall color.

STEM: Slender when young, smooth or with a few hairs. Green, turning reddish brown. Bark on old stems splits and peels. Somewhat attractive.

FLOWERS: White; about 1 to 1 1/2 inches across in terminal clusters and in the leaf axils in mid spring. Showy and very pleasantly fragrant. Unfortunately, the flower show is short-lived: only 7 to 10 days with ideal weather.

FRUIT: A small, dry capsule.

COLOR: Leaves are dark green. Flowers are white.

PROPAGATION: Softwood or hardwood cuttings.

CULTURE: Mockorange will grow on most sites with little care, but responds to good soils and cultural practices. Can be sheared after flowering to develop a dense hedge; however, as the flowers are formed in the late summer and fall, fall pruning will reduce flowers the following spring.

PESTS: None serious.

NOTES: One fragrant mockorange in the landscape is a must, especially adjacent to outdoor living areas. A very pleasant aroma. Branches may be cut and brought indoors to flower early. Makes a good hedge of reasonable density with few problems, and is adaptable to most soils. Can be grown as a tree form which is very nice. The common name, mockorange, leads to confusion since *Pittosporum tobira* and *Poncirus trifoliata* are also called mockorange. Many species and hybrids of mockorange exist.

CULTIVARS: 'Aureus': yellow foliage not readily compatible with other landscape plants. 'Minnesota Snowflake': in an oval form 6 to 8 feet tall with white, fragrant flowers. 'Miniature Snowflake': grows as a globe only 2 to 3 feet tall with fragrant white flowers. 'Snowgoose': dense, white, double flowers on a frame about 5 feet tall with dark green foliage. Nice. Many others exist.

RELATED SPECIES: *Philadelphis* X *lemoinei*, Lemoine, the Lemoine mockorange, is a hybrid between *Philadelphis coronarius* and *P. microphyllus*. A compact shrub with smaller leaves and more prolific, white flowers later in spring than those of sweet mockorange. 'Boule d'Argent' grows 4 to 5 feet tall and is a prolific bloomer with double white flowers about 2 inches across. 'Avalanche' reaches only 4 to 5 feet in height with arching branches and prolific fragrance; white flowers about 1 inch across. 'Girandole': double white flowers and a mature height of about 5 feet. Many other cultivars exist.

Physocarpus opulifolius (L.) Maxim.   Common Ninebark
Rosaceae or Rose Family   Hardiness Zone 2
Native to the northcentral United States.
SIZE: 4 to 8 feet tall with a 4- to 8-foot spread. Moderate grower.
FORM: Irregular, upright, twiggy shrub.
TEXTURE: Medium.   EXPOSURE: Sun or some shade.

LEAVES: Alternate, simple; 1 to 2 inches long. Usually 3-lobed, occasionally 5, with 3 veins intersecting at the base and an irregular, saw-toothed margin. Upper leaf surface is medium green; yellow in the fall.

STEM: Upright, widely spreading shrub with many slender branches. Young stems are bright red-brown and smooth while the old bark peels off in thin, vertical strips exposing a brown inner bark. Very twiggy or brushy without leaves.

FLOWERS: White or pinkish; in terminal clusters after foliage in mid spring. Attractive.

FRUIT: Small, red fruits in the fall. Not commonly seen.

COLOR: Foliage is medium green. Flowers are white to pinkish.

PROPAGATION: Softwood or hardwood cuttings.

CULTURE: Very tough and durable. Grows in dry, sandy soils as well as in heavy clays. Very drought-tolerant and will grow in full sun or moderate shade. Can be pruned or sheared to retain desired size. Slowly spreads but is not a pest in the landscape.

PESTS: None serious.

NOTES: A very tough, durable shrub for most any location. Unfortunately, it does not do anything striking. The flowers are okay but nothing to get excited about, consequently ninebark is not used much except in very cold climates where the list of possible plants is very short. Frequently confused with the spiraeas. Overall growth form, size, and leaf characteristics are similar to those of Vanhoutte spiraea. However, leaves of ninebark are larger, its flowers bloom much later, and the old stems peel in vertical strips, thus easily separating the two genera.

CULTIVARS: 'Luteus', the golden ninebark, has pinkish white flowers and yellow leaves that change to yellow-green. Sometimes called 'Aureus' in error. 'Dart's Gold': grows only 3 to 4 feet tall with green foliage, pinkish white flowers, and yellow fall color. 'Nanus': grows 4 to 6 feet tall and has pinkish flowers. 'Intermedius': a low-growing form (4 to 5 feet) with smaller, darker leaves. Sometimes listed incorrectly as *Physocarpus intermedius*. Other cultivars probably exist.

RELATED SPECIES: *Physocarpus mongynus* (Torr.) Coult., the mountain ninebark, is hardy in Zone 4, grows only about 3 to 4 feet tall, has smaller but similar leaves and pinkish flowers. This is a smaller plant with a more dense growth habit, thus it makes a better low hedge.

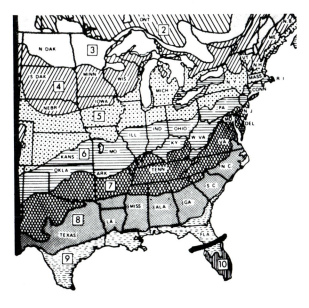

P. *monogynus*, mountain ninebark

Poncirus trifoliata Raf.   Trifoliate Orange
Rutaceae or Citrus Family   Hardiness Zone 7
Native to China and Korea.
SIZE: 15 to 25 feet tall with a 10- to 15-foot spread. Slow to moderate grower.
FORM: A multiple-stemmed, irregular, large shrub or small tree.
TEXTURE: Medium to fine.   **EXPOSURE:** Sun or partial shade.

LEAVES: Alternate, trifoliate (with 3 leaflets), and a winged petiole. Leaves are 2 to 3 inches long, glossy; aromatic when crushed. Leaflets are oval with a round-toothed margin; olive-green above and slightly lighter below.

STEM: Stems up to 1/2 inch or more are dark green, flattened at the nodes and armed with hairy, green, sharp, flattened spines, 1 to 3 inches long. Wood is hard and stiff. Older stems are tan-green and streaked, eventually becoming entirely tan to light brown.

FLOWERS: White; fragrant, 1 to 2 inches across. Appear in mid spring at the base of the spines. Interesting, not particularly showy but the fragrance is pleasant.

FRUIT: A berry, 1 to 2 inches in diameter, aromatic, green when young; yellow when ripe and covered with dense, fine hairs. Fruits are very tart, sour, and filled with many seeds. Somewhat showy but drop by mid winter and provide food for wildlife.

COLOR: Green twigs and stems are interesting in winter. Foliage is olive-green.

PROPAGATION: Seed, grafting or cuttings.

CULTURE: Trifoliate orange is very tough, drought-tolerant, and adaptable. However, like most members of the citrus family, it grows poorly, if at all, in poorly drained, heavy clay soils. Grows well in full sun; however, hot locations should be avoided due to high susceptibility to mites.

PESTS: Mites are a recuring problem on plants in hot locations, particularly where air movement is limited.

NOTES: An interesting, large shrub or small tree as long as human contact is limited. The very sharp spines are unforgiving. However, it makes an ideal bird sanctuary since even cats can not penetrate the spiny web. The flowers are fragrant and pleasant and the fruits are attractive and hang on until mid-winter. Fruits can be somewhat messy over a walk or patio; however, the tree **should not** be in that location. Strictly a background plant. If sheared, it makes an impenetrable living hedge for keeping in or out, dogs, horses, etc. Sheared hedges are sometimes walked on by "brave" but foolish pranksters. Far more cold hardy than other citrus family members. Useful as a conversation piece and for wildlife but not a priority plant except for those that wish to feel "stuck up". Often used as an understock for various citrus species. Is said to impart cold and disease resistance to citrus.

CULTIVARS: 'Monstruosa': especially heavy flowering and fruiting. 'Flying Dragon': has striking twisted stems, but that's it. Other cultivars probably exist.

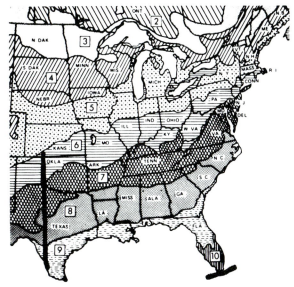

Potentilla fruticosa L.   Potentilla or Bush Cinquefoil
Rosaceae or Rose Family   Hardiness Zone 2
Native to Canada and northeastern United States.
SIZE: 2 to 4 feet tall, spreading about 2 to 4 feet. Moderate grower.
FORM: A rounding shrub with dense branching.
TEXTURE: Fine.   **EXPOSURE:** Sun.

LEAVES: Alternate, compound. With 3 to 7 leaflets which have no stalk and are strap-like or slightly ovate. One-half to 1 inch long with a recurved, or folded under, smooth margin and covered with silky hairs. Leaves are gray-green with no fall color.

STEM: Slender green stems with dense branching, turning shiny brown, with the bark on old stems peeling in vertical, narrow strips.

FLOWERS: Simple, perfect flowers, like a single rose (see photograph) unless semi-double or double. Most cultivars are yellow or yellow-white and flower in the summer.

FRUIT: A small, dry fruit. Not showy.

COLOR: Foliage is gray-green. Flowers are mostly yellow.

PROPAGATION: Softwood cuttings.

CULTURE: Attractive, useful landscape plant, roughly north of the Mason-Dixon Line. In the humid South, they do poorly and in Oklahoma they struggle to survive, given what should be ideal growing conditions. Very good plant for hardiness Zones 3 to 5 but questionable farther south. As with most plants, they grow best in a deep, fertile soil, but in the North, they do well on a wide variety of soils. Full sun for half or more of the day is needed for good flowering. Very fibrous roots and easy to transplant.

PESTS: None serious in the North.

NOTES: A confused group of plants. Many cultivars and species appear similar in growth, flowering and adaptation. In any case, a very adaptable shrub for the North, and it remains in scale with little or no pruning over many years. Not for Zones 7, 8, and 9.

CULTIVARS: 'Abbotswood': grows 2 to 3 feet and has white flowers. 'Coronation Triumph': grows 2 to 3 feet in an oval form and has bright yellow flowers. Nice. 'Gold Drop' or 'Farreri': grows about 2 feet with lemon yellow flowers. 'Goldfinger': a compact shrub reaching about 3 feet with golden yellow flowers. 'Jackmani': grows 3 to 4 feet tall with golden yellow flowers. 'Katherine Dykes': grows 2 to 3 feet and has soft yellow flowers. 'Primrose Beauty': grows 2 to 3 feet tall, has excellent foliage and pale yellow flowers. 'Grandiflora': may reach 5 to 6 feet with bright yellow flowers. Many other cultivars and related species exist.

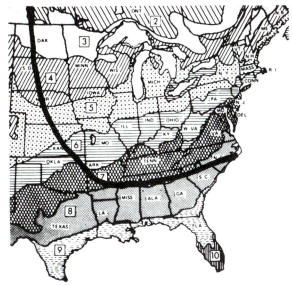

Prunus glandulosa Thunb. Flowering Almond
Rosaceae or Rose Family Hardiness Zone 4
Native to China and Japan.
SIZE: 3 to 5 feet tall with equal or greater spread. Moderate grower.
FORM: Irregular shrub with upright stems.
TEXTURE: Fine to medium. **EXPOSURE:** Sun.

LEAVES: Alternate, simple; oblong to lanceolate, medium green, 1 1/2 to 3 inches long with a saw-toothed margin. Slight red fall color.

STEM: Slender and mostly upright with limited branching. Smooth or slightly hairy on very young stems. Plants thicken from a slowly spreading crown.

FLOWERS: Single or double, pink or white, about 1/2 inch in diameter; in the leaf axils, densely covering the plant. Very showy, very early in spring.

FRUIT: Red. Rarely seen on the double-flowering cultivars that are most widely planted.

COLOR: White or pink flowers in early spring.

PROPAGATION: Cuttings or division of a clump.

CULTURE: A very tough, ornamental shrub that rarely, if ever, fails to attractively mark the coming of spring. Flowers best in full sun and develops a thicker, more attractive form on good soils. A tough, inexpensive, and problem-free shrub.

PESTS: Stem borers and aphids, occasionally.

NOTES: Sometimes relegated to the list of undesirables but such is an error. Not for front-row-center; however, when used wisely in the background or in slightly out-of-the-way filler spots, it glowingly marks the coming of spring. Particularly showy if planted in front of evergreens for contrast. May be short-lived on some sites but it is a very low-cost shrub when purchased bareroot, so it should be enjoyed while it lasts. The size is desirable in that it does not overgrow smaller plants and "bury" buildings as do some shrubs. A good value if used cautiously.

CULTIVARS: 'Rosea': double pink flowers in early spring. 'Alba Plena': has double white flowers. 'Sinensis': double pink flowers, but slightly less cold hardy than the other two cultivars. Other cultivars probably exist.

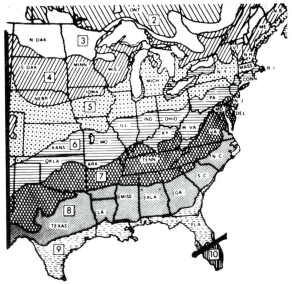

Punica granatum L.   Pomegranate
Punicaceae or Pomegranate Family   Hardiness Zone 7b
Native to southeast Asia.

SIZE: 15 to 20 feet tall with a 12- to 20-foot spread. Dwarf cultivars exist. Moderate grower.

FORM: Multiple-stemmed, large shrub or small tree with an irregular crown.

TEXTURE: Fine.   **EXPOSURE:** Sun.

LEAVES: Deciduous, alternate, simple; opposite or clustered, depending on the growth rate of the stem. Leaves are 1 to 3 inches long, generally strap-like or lanceolate, about 1/4 to 1/2 inch wide with a smooth margin. Upper surface is a bright medium green.

STEM: Young stems are very slender, reddish brown to green at first, somewhat angular or ribbed. Older stems are smooth at first, become gray to gray-brown, finally breaking into small, thin, more or less rectangular scales. May have some short sharp spines, especially on new growth. Wood is fairly hard and durable.

FLOWERS: Spectacular, singly or in clusters; 2 to 2 1/2 inches across, usually red, or red-orange, white, or pink, depending on cultivar. Looks somewhat like a carnation. Blooms from late spring or early summer until mid fall. A prolific bloomer.

FRUIT: A large, round berry with a thick rind and many seeds, maturing in September or October, becoming pink or red. May reach as much as 2 1/2 to 3 inches in diameter. Retains a large bump or pore-like section on the blossom end.

COLOR: Foliage is bright medium green. Flowers are red, red-orange, pink, or white. Fruit is pink or red.

PROPAGATION: Semi-hardwood cuttings in late summer work well. Seedlings are extremely variable.

CULTURE: Native to poor soils and waste areas throughout southeast Asia. Tolerates a wide range of soils in the southern states from moderately dry, heavy clay soils to fertile, moist soils. Responds vigorously to fertilizing, mulching, and good cultural practices. Best adapted to full sun where flowering is best, but will tolerate moderate shade with decreased flowering. Plants may die to the ground during a severe winter but will generally sprout back in spring. Mulching aids winter survival in northern areas.

PESTS: None serious on the foliage; however, mealy bugs are often found on the developing fruits.

NOTES: A spectacularly blooming deciduous shrub, flowering from early summer to early fall in most conditions. Requires full sun for best performance: limited bloom in shade. Dwarf cultivars are very useful.

CULTIVARS: 'Albescens': white flowers. 'Chico': a dwarf shrub with dense, slender branches, glossy green leaves, and double, bright orange-red flowers. 'Chico' has done well in north central Oklahoma and is a real show-off in a sunny location. Killed to the ground at -5 degrees F but bounced back with vigor. 'Flavescens': yellow flowers. 'Nana': dwarf, very compact, rarely more than 12 to 14 inches tall with single red-orange flowers. 'Plentiflora': double scarlet flowers. 'Wonderful': a good fruit producer, medium-sized, 8 to 12 feet tall with a fountain-like branching habit, red-orange blossoms, and large fruits. Others probably exist.

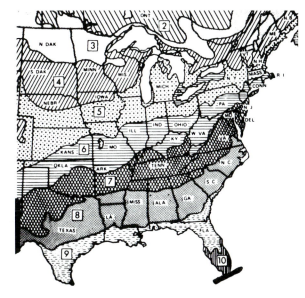

'Chico'

Rhodotypos scandens Sieb. & Zucc.   Black Jetbead
Rosaceae or Rose Family   Hardiness Zone 5
Native to central China and Japan.
SIZE: 3 to 5 feet tall with 3 to 6 feet of spread. Moderate grower.
FORM: Loose, irregular shrub unless pruned regularly.
TEXTURE: Medium.   **EXPOSURE:** Sun or shade.

LEAVES: Opposite, simple; 2 to 3 inches long, more or less ovate, with very distinct veins and a doubly saw-toothed margin. Upper leaf surface is medium green, light green below. No fall color. Leaves resemble those of Japanese kerria.

STEMS: Green, eventually turning brown and then gray, smooth and very slender when young. Branches are flexible and resilient, sometimes drooping at the ends. Black jetbead does not branch readily; thus, when sheared as a hedge, it remains somewhat loose and informal.

FLOWERS: Borne singly at the tips of branches, 1 to 2 inches across; with 4 white, showy petals, in late spring or early summer and sporadically throughout the growing season.

FRUIT: A small, shiny, black fruit about 1/4 inch long.

COLOR: Foliage is medium green. Flowers are white.

PROPAGATION: Seed or cuttings.

CULTURE: Easy to grow on most sites. Transplants easily and responds with vigor to fertilization and good cultural practices. Needs pruning to develop a good, dense mass as a specimen shrub or hedge. Sometimes used in shady locations where many shrubs become open and leggy and flower poorly, if at all. May suffer some winter tip dieback, probably from stem and bud desiccation in the drier areas of Zones 5 and 6.

PESTS: None serious.

NOTES: Interesting leaf veination pattern which adds further contrast to the attractive white flowers. Leaves and stems are sometimes confused with Japanese kerria; however kerria leaves are alternate and flowers are yellow, whereas black jetbead leaves are alternate and flowers are white. An interesting shrub because the lighter foliage color and leaf surface texture contrast with those of many other shrub species. The loose, open habit, even when sheared as a hedge, does not give a stiff, formal look. Black jetbead is a bit like the common hackberry tree: it does a lot of things well but nothing really striking or outstanding so it frequently gets passed by. Easy to grow as a bare root nursery plant and consequently, like many of the deciduous shrubs, it is inexpensive to buy and is rarely bothered by diseases or insects. These features must be weighed relative to the visual effect desired in the landscape. Generally should not be planted below Zone 7.

CULTIVARS: None known.

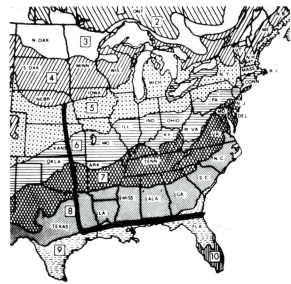

Rhus aromatica Ait.   Fragrant Sumac
Anacardiaceae or Sumac Family   Hardiness Zone 4
Native to Eastern United States as far west as the Rocky Mountains.
SIZE: 3 to 6 feet tall with equal or greater spread. Moderate grower.
FORM: Irregular shrub with upright and horizontal branching.
TEXTURE: Medium.   **EXPOSURE:** Full sun to partial shade.

LEAVES: Alternate, compound; with 3 distinct leaflets with the center one slightly larger. Margins are smooth near the base, shallowly lobed or toothed on the outer portion. The entire compound leaf may be 2 to 4 inches long and covered with dense hairs when young, becoming smooth and glossy, dark green to nearly blue-green with age (the hairs wear off by rubbing of the leaves and by wind and rain). Fall color is excellent in most areas: orange to orange-red to purple, depending on season, exposure and seedlings. Leaves have a distinct odor when crushed. Sometimes confused with poison ivy in general appearance.

STEM: Slender and covered with dense hairs when young, which are lost with exposure to the elements and age, exposing a light brown bark. Older stems remain light to medium brown and are stout but flexible. The outer ends of horizontal branches turn up at the tip. Stems are aromatic when scraped.

FLOWERS: Yellow; in small, terminal clusters, 1 to 2 inches long, in early spring before or with the leaves. Plants are mostly dioecious (male and female flowers on separate plants) with both male and female flowers covered with dense hairs. Male flowers remain visible throughout the growing season.

FRUIT: Red clusters at the tips of the branches at the end of summer. Fruits are about 1/4 inch and densely woolly, falling in October or November. Readily eaten by birds and many species of wildlife.

COLOR: Foliage is dark green to blue-green, fall color is red-orange. Fruit is red.

PROPAGATION: Cuttings, softwood or hardwood, or separation of branches that have rooted where they touch the soil (natural layering).

CULTURE: A very drought-tolerant and useful shrub. Native to limestone hills in areas with rainfall of only 12 to 15 inches. Potentially very useful around structures where alkaline soils are suspected or assured and where many other landscape shrubs would suffer from iron chlorosis. It spreads slowly by horizontal branches that sometimes develop roots when in contact with the soil, but it is easily contained by pruning. This is not a weedy, aggressive shrub but rather an attractive plant of useful size with an attractive growth habit and foliage color during both the growing season and fall. Roots are fibrous, making transplanting easy.

PESTS: None serious.

NOTES: A very attractive and useful deciduous shrub. In locations with only slight shade or shade only in late afternoon, leaves tend to be nearly blue-green and very attractive. Useful for naturalizing: attracting birds and wildlife that eat the fruit. Used more in the North and Northeast than in the Plains States and South, but deserves more consideration. When the site is exposed and alkaline soils are known or suspected, fragrant sumac is as tough or tougher than the junipers with which it combines well. This plant should be screened for improved cultivars with more specific growth forms or fall color. Few shrubs are as tough and adaptable, yet remain of an acceptable size without pruning and without becoming "weedy". Sometimes referred to as "skunk bush", but this is inappropriate as the odor is not particularly offensive and occurs only when the leaves or stems are crushed.

CULTIVARS: 'Gro-Low': a dense, compact selection, only 2 to 3 feet tall. Others may exist.

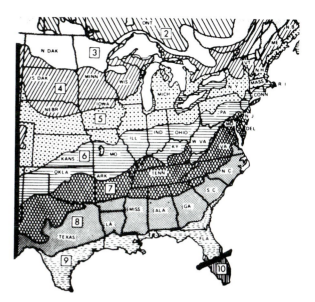

Rhus glabra L.   Smooth Sumac
Anacardaceae or Sumac Family   Hardiness Zone 2
Native to the eastern United States.

SIZE: 6 to 20 feet or more in height, with equal or greater spread as a clump. Moderate to rapid grower.

FORM: An irregular, shrubby clump or occasionally a small tree.

TEXTURE: Fine.   **EXPOSURE:** Sun or partial shade.

LEAVES: Alternate, pinnately compound. With 15 to 21 leaflets, each 2 to 4 inches long, 1 to 1 1/2 inches wide, somewhat elongate; widest at the base, tapering toward the tip, and coarsely toothed on the margin. Glossy green above, greenish white below, bright red or purplish early in the fall, but showy for only a brief period before dropping.

STEM: Young stems are large in diameter, rigid, red-brown to purplish, smooth, and covered by a waxy coating. Buds are football-shaped and covered with gray hairs. Leaf scars are narrow, completely surrounding the bud. Old stems are gray-brown with many corky lenticels. Wood is soft and yellow-brown; not durable or vandal-resistant.

FLOWERS: Male and female on separate plants (dioecious). Blooms appear in May or early June in terminal clusters. Both male and female flowers are yellowish; not showy.

FRUIT: Appears in July or August in dense, triangular clusters near tops of the plants and remains throughout the fall and winter. Seeds are dark red, round, coarsely hairy; showy.

COLOR: Foliage is glossy green; brilliant red to red-purple early in the fall. Fruit is red.

PROPAGATION: Seed, cuttings, or division.

CULTURE: An extremely tough, durable, native plant, growing in a wide range of conditions from roadside ditches to fertile, moist pasture lands. Plants of any size are difficult to transplant from the wild, thus small suckers or small seedlings or direct-seed into the landscape are best. Useful as a small single-stemmed tree for a patio or formal garden but somewhat short-lived. Not commonly used in this manner, but where soils are poor and conditions are dry and exposed, it has merit.

PESTS: None serious, although occasionally chewing insects do damage foliage.

NOTES: Spectacular plant in the fall. Red clusters of fruit and the long graceful leaves which are brilliant red to red-purple are the most outstanding features, particularly when used in front of evergreens or in conjunction with plants that are still green at the time sumac turns color.

CULTIVARS: 'Laciniata', cutleaf smooth sumac: has finely divided, fern-like leaves.

RELATED SPECIES: *Rhus copallina* L. called shining, winged, or planeleaf sumac. A smaller plant, reaching only 6 to 12 feet tall. The principal difference is a more lacey foliage which has only 9 to 15 leaflets, which appear to be connected by a wing or papery leaf-like section between the individual leaflets.

    Rhus aromatica Ait., fragrant sumac, is a low, compact shrub rarely growing more than 5 feet tall. The common name arises from the unpleasant odor of the crushed leaves. Generally wider than it is high, and provides good cover for wildlife. Leaves are alternate, compound, with three leaflets, the terminal leaflet being largest. Dull, deep green, turning brilliant red; red-orange in the fall. Sometimes destroyed because it looks like poison ivy, when young. A very drought-resistant, deep-rooted shrub often found tolerating poor soils and rocky, dry sites. Sometimes planted for erosion control, shelterbelts, or for wildlife. An attractive, low, compact, landscape shrub with no pests or problems. Should be planted a great deal more.

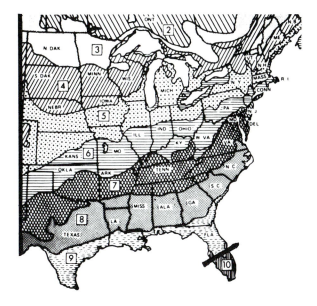

'Laciniata'

Rhus radicans L. (Syn. *Toxicodendron radicans*) Poison Ivy
Anacardaceae or Sumac Family Hardiness Zone 2
Native to most of the United States.
SIZE: Often 30 to 40 feet up a tree or, as a shrub, 4 to 10 feet tall. Rapid grower.
FORM: Vine or multiple-stemmed, shrub-like clump.
TEXTURE: Medium. **EXPOSURE:** Sun to shade.

LEAVES: Deciduous, alternate, compound. Usually with 3 leaflets variable in size and shape but generally egg-shaped, with coarse teeth on the margin, tapering to the tip and more or less rounded at the base. Individual leaflets may be 3 to 6 inches long, 2 to 3 inches wide, green to yellow-green and dull above, and pale green and fuzzy below. Dull scarlet and orange in the fall. Often collected by mistake for fall arrangements in the home. All parts are poisonous to most people and can create a nasty skin irritation.

STEM: A vigorously growing woody vine which develops a profusion of aerial roots when growing up a tree, fence post, or other structure. Young twigs are light brown, slender and hairy. Buds are flattened or rather blunt-pointed with tan hairs. Leaf scars are broad and cresent-shaped. On an older stem, bark is gray to gray-brown, and roughened with tiny raised spots. Bright red-brown, young aerial roots along the climbing stems are very prominent. Wood is quite soft.

FLOWERS: Male and female on separate plants (dioecious); small and yellow-green in grape-like clusters. Appear in late May. Not showy.

FRUIT: Creamy white, about 1/4 inch round; in grape-like clusters, in September.

COLOR: Foliage is green to yellow-green; dull scarlet to orange in the fall.

PROPAGATION: Seed or division. Fruits are often eaten by birds and seeds are scattered throughout the landscape, especially beneath fences and trees.

CULTURE: Poison ivy will grow anywhere but is most troublesome in wooded areas, along small streams or in the shade of various other plants. Best controlled by 2,4-D type brush killers. Care must be taken when using brush killers around desirable plants.

PESTS: None (unfortunately).

NOTES: A most prolific and troublesome pest in landscapes, parks, recreational areas and campgrounds. Commonly encountered by the unsuspecting individual who does not realize the severity of the reaction. May have severe effects on some people: swelling, open sores, discomforting rashes, etc. Some claim to be immune to poison ivy; however, this is variable, and one who may be immune at first contact, may find he is quite susceptible later. Burning of the stems or leaves is not recommended since the toxic principle can be disseminated on blowing ashes. Sometimes found as a shrub or clump in various woodland conditions. Any portion of the plant that is broken or damaged may release a toxic principle. Likewise it is toxic all year. It is doubtful if one can contract poison ivy "out of the air". Direct contact with the chemical can come from handling shoes, clothing or gardening equipment. Washing with soap after contact is advisable but probably does not completely remove the material since it reacts very quickly with the skin. No known cures exist although many have been proposed. Varieties with different growth habits have been identified. Virginia creeper is often confused with poison ivy. However, Virginia creeper has 5 leaflets and does not have aerial roots but tendrils instead, with disc-like suction cups where it attaches to various structures. Leaf scars on Virginia creeper are saucer-like. XX-POISON-XX

CULTIVARS: None.

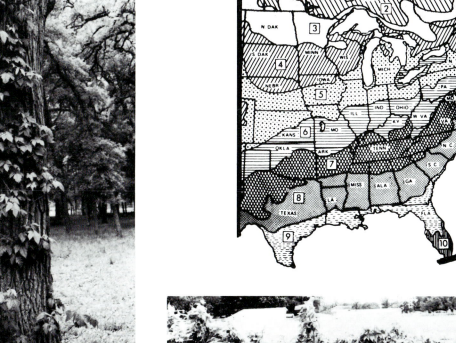

Rhus typhina L.   Staghorn or Velvet Sumac
Anacardaceae or Sumac Family   Hardiness Zone 2
Native to the northeast one-third of the United States and southeast Canada.
SIZE: 15 to 25 feet tall with equal or greater spread as a clump. Rapid grower.
FORM: A large, open, loose shrub or often a clump.
TEXTURE: Fine.   **EXPOSURE:** Sun or partial shade.

LEAVES: Alternate, pinnately compound; with 11 to 19 lanceolate leaflets with a sawtooth margin. Densely hairy when young, dark green in summer, orange to orange-red to red in the fall. The popular cultivars have finely cut leaflets that appear to be twice-compound and fern-like.

STEM: Large and densely wooly when young; velvety to the touch. Hairs are lost by the second season. Old bark is gray to gray-black. Wood is soft and brittle and easily damaged, particularly when grown as a tree form.

FLOWERS: Greenish: not showy. Male and female on separate plants (dioecious).

FRUIT: Red to crimson but eventually fades to a dull red-brown. In dense clusters at the tips of branches on female plants in late summer and hang on most of the winter. Densely hairy.

COLOR: Foliage is green; orange to red in fall. Fruits are red.

PROPAGATION: Seed or root cuttings.

CULTURE: Staghorn sumac is tough and durable, growing well on most sites except for those with poorly drained areas. Suckers badly from the underground stem and often forms large, irregular clumps. However, mowing will keep the suckers in check, unless mowing is not possible because of positions of other shrubs, etc. Sometimes grown as a tree form; however, smooth sumac is superior for this purpose since suckering is not as troublesome. Gets large and frequently overgrows many sites. On the other hand, the lacey-leaved forms make an attractive background or screen during the growing season if sufficient room exists.

PESTS: None serious.

NOTES: Attractive as a large clump, especially on large sites or where they can be naturalized. In the upper Midwest and Northeast, staghorn sumac is somewhat overplanted. However, a large shrub with few problems, attractive foliage, good fall color and fine foliage texture can't be too bad.

CULTIVARS: 'Laciniata': leaves are dissected into what appears to be fern-like sections or twice-compound leaves. Often sold as cutleaf staghorn sumac. 'Dissecta': leaves are more deeply dissected than those of 'Laciniata'. Others probably exist.

 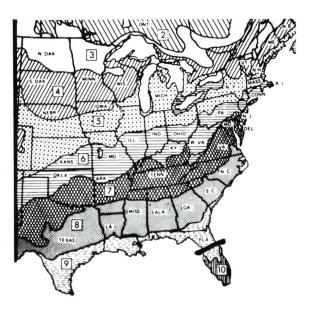

'Dissecta'

Ribes alpinum L.   Alpine Currant
Saxifragaceae or Saxifrage Family   Hardiness Zone 3
Native to eastern Europe.
SIZE: 4 to 6 feet tall with equal or greater spread. Moderate grower.
FORM: Mound-shaped shrub.
TEXTURE: Fine to medium.   EXPOSURE: Sun or shade.

LEAVES: Alternate, simple; 1 to 2 inches long. Palmately lobed with 3, or occasionally 5
lobes, with irregular teeth on the margin. Upper leaf surface is bright green, lower surface
is lighter; yellow in the fall. Leaves emerge very early in the spring.

STEM: Young stems are slender, much branched; brown and smooth, without spines. Old
bark shreds into vertical brown strips. Winter buds are large. Wood is stout but flexible.

FLOWERS: Male and female on separate plants (dioecious). Female are yellow to greenish
yellow, in clusters, in early spring after the leaves, thus are not showy. Male flowers are
slightly larger.

FRUIT: Not normally seen, since male plants are more commonly grown.

COLOR: Foliage is bright green.

PROPAGATION: Softwood cuttings.

CULTURE: A very adaptable shrub in sun or shade as long as soils do not remain excessively wet for long periods. Few plants make a good hedge through both sun and shade,
but alpine currant is an exception. It branches prolifically when pruned.

PESTS: White pine blister rust is an alternate host on several currants. Although this does
little damage to the currant, it is a serious disease on white pine. Male plants are generally
considered more resistant than female, thus male plants are most common. A leaf spot
disease may occasionally be a problem, particularly in cool, shady locations. Mites appear
in hot locations.

NOTES: An attractive shrub often used as a hedge. The bright green foliage is pleasant all
growing season; however, the yellow fall color is only fair.

CULTIVARS: 'Green Mound': a low shrub, generally only 2 to 3 feet tall, with attractive
foliage. 'Aureum': has yellowish leaves nearly all season and grows to 3 to 4 feet tall.

RELATED SPECIES: *Ribes hirtellum* Michx. is the common gooseberry, hardy in Zone 2,
native over much of the upper United States. May have spines although spineless cultivars
exist. Grows 3 to 4 feet tall with attractive green foliage and yellow flowers. Fruits are
tart and green, turning purple or black at maturity. 'Pixwell' has small fruits but no
spines. 'Welcome' has larger fruits. Many other cultivars and hybrids exist.

Ribes cynosbati L., the prickly gooseberry, is hardy in Zone 2 and grows 4 to 5 feet tall.
Flowers are green; fruits are green turning wine-purple when mature. Leaves are similar
to those of alpine currant but many spines are present. Native over a wide area of the
United States and, although it is not often planted, the fruits are frequently harvested for
pies.

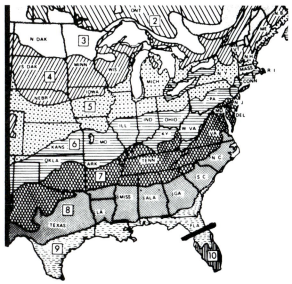

Rosa spp.   Garden Roses
Rosaceae or Rose Family   Hardiness Zone 4
Native--many hybrids and species.
SIZE: 2 to 10 feet tall, depending on species and cultivar. Moderate to rapid grower.
FORM: Irregular, upright, or semi-climbing shrubs.
TEXTURE: Medium.   **EXPOSURE:** Sun.

LEAVES: Alternate, compound; generally with 3 or 5 but occasionally 7 leaflets. Leaflets are 2 to 3 inches long, 1 to 1 1/2 inches wide, and ovate, with a sawtooth margin. Foliage is deep green; variable with cultivar and growing conditions. Two small stipules are present on some selctions where the leaf attaches to the stem.

STEM: Generally stout, upright, green turning light brown to red-brown with age. Stems are covered with hard, stiff, often hook-like spines. Wood is fairly stout.

FLOWERS: At the tips of new growth. Roses may be single or double; white, red, yellow, pink, or nearly purple; and one flower per stem or many per stem, depending on type and cultivar. Very showy. Many cultivars are fragrant.

FRUIT: Large and rounded at the base of the petals. May reach 1/2 to 1 inch in diameter, containing many seeds. Not attractive. Remove to encourage more flowering.

COLOR: Flowers are white, red, yellow, pink, or nearly purple. Very showy.

PROPAGATION: Cuttings or grafting of selected cultivars.

CULTURE: Roses should only be planted in full sun with good soils and air drainage. Sunken rose gardens or gardens surrounded by hedges should be avoided due to the restricted air movement and the disease problems. For best performance, roses should only be planted in good soil. However, raised beds of good soil 10 to 12 inches deep over poor soils work well. Mulch roses heavily to aid root growth and prevent splashing of soil onto the foliage during rains or when watering.

PESTS: Black spot and powdery mildew are most serious and are encouraged by shady locations with poor air movement. Black spot control requires spraying at 7-14 day intervals. Aphids may attack new growth and flowers. Thrips often damage flowers. Crown gall often reduces the vigor of the plant. Mites can also be a problem.

NOTES: Roses should be planted **only** where the requirements of good soil, full sun, and good air drainage can be met. The environment immediately around the plants plays a major role in the disease problem with roses. NOT FOR GENERAL LANDSCAPE USE. Most roses require a high degree of maintenance throughout the growing season. Over 125 species of roses have been described.

CULTIVARS: *Rosa* hybrids, garden roses, are divided into 2 major groups: hybrid tea and floribunda. Hundreds of cultivars exist with new ones introduced each year. The reader is encouraged to refer to a favorite nursery catalog or one of the many books written on rose selections and cultural requirements. The meidiland series are quite disease-free and deserve attention.
RELATED SPECIES: *Rosa rugosa* is hardy in Zone 2, grows 4 to 6 feet tall and blooms heavily only in spring. Flowers are single or double, white or pink, and about 2 inches across. Unlike garden roses, *R. rugosa* is virtually disease-free in most locations. An attractive shrub needing little care. Should be planted more.
   Rosa spp. climbing rose. Several cultivars are desirable, trouble-free, vine-like landscape shrubs. 'Blaze': a vigorous grower that blooms most of the growing season, with scarlet red flowers. 'Pauls Scarlet': scarlet flowers; blooms most of the growing season. 'Golden Showers': yellow flowers. Many others exist.

'Blaze' climbing rose

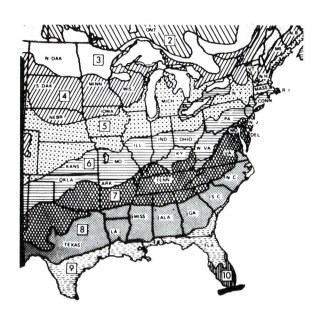

Rosa rugosa

'Peace' hybrid tea

Rosa rugosa

Salvia gregii Grey   Autumn Salvia or Autumn Sage
Labiatae or Mint Family   Hardiness Zone 7
Native to southwestern United States and northern Mexico.
SIZE: 2 to 3 feet tall with 3- to 4-foot spread. Moderate grower.
FORM: Irregular, upright shrub.
TEXTURE: Fine.   **EXPOSURE:** Sun

LEAVES: Opposite, or occasionally slightly not. Narrowly oblong, 1/2 to 1 1/2 inches long, 1/4 to 1/2 inch wide. Dull pale green or grayish green with a smooth margin and mostly smooth leaf surface or with fine hairs. Leaves often cup upward slightly. Petiole is very short to nonexistent. Leaves have a distinct odor when crushed.

STEM: Slender, squarish (typical of the mint family) and much branched. Green to reddish brown, later brown with a scaly bark. When young the stems often are covered with fine hairs. It is fairly tough and flexible. Not easily broken.

FLOWERS: Very showy throughout the summer and fall. In terminal clusters. Flowers are two-lipped, typical of the mint family (see photograph). Colors range from white to blue, pink, red, and nearly orange. Very striking.

FRUIT: A small papery capsule surrounding a small dark seed. Not showy.

Color: Foliage is pale green to grayish green. Flowers are white, blue, pink, or red.

PROPAGATION: Seeds or cuttings, either softwood or semi-hardwood.

CULTURE: Autumn salvia is very tolerant of drought, heat, and exposure. It grows well in a variety of soils, including alkaline and rocky mounds as long as it is well drained. Salvia is intolerant of shade and flowers well only where light intensity is high. Some references note that salvia should not be fertilized; however in container nurseries it responds to fertilizer just as other species. Since the plant flowers on new growth, any assistance in growth translates into more flowers. If the plant gets too tall or leggy it can be cut back to a few inches above the ground in winter or before spring growth begins and it will regrow vigorously and still flower during the summer.

PESTS: None serious.

NOTES: *Salvia gregii* is a spectacular small flowering shrub during the heat of summer and early fall when few other plants are blooming, especially in hot, dry, full sun locations. These attributes, plus the fact that little, if any, irrigation is needed once the plant is established and being nearly pest-free, are rivaled by few flowering shrubs except crapemyrtle. The array of flower colors currently available is quite striking. Cultivars can now be selected that complement or contrast with other flowers or vegetation. Stems with flowers also hold up fairly well indoors.

CULTIVARS: Most cultivars are simply listed as the flower color such as white, coral, maroon, blue, pink, or red.

RELATED SPECIES: *Salvia ballotaeflora*, blue sage, is also native to West Texas, grows two to six feet tall and has bluish to purple flowers.

Salvia regla, mountain sage or royal sage is also native to West Texas, grows 2 to 6 feet tall and produces many off-red flowers.

Many other species of shrubby, drought-tolerant salvias exist.

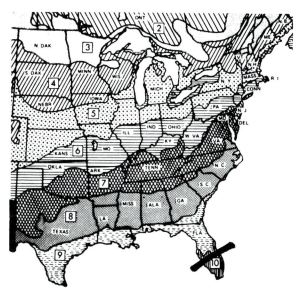

Spiraea X *vanhouttei* Zabel.   Vanhoutte Spiraea
Rosaceae or Rose Family   Hardiness Zone 3
Native: a hybrid between *Spiraea cantoniensis* and *Spiraea trilobata*
SIZE: 4 to 6 feet tall with a 3- to 5-foot spread. Rapid grower.
FORM: Densely twiggy; irregular, upright shrub.
TEXTURE: Medium to fine.   **EXPOSURE:** Sun to partial shade.

LEAVES: Alternate, simple; oval or ovate, 1 to 2 inches long, 1/2 to 1 inch wide with coarse teeth: usually only 3 to 5, near the outer portion of the leaf. Blue-green above, pale blue-green below; slightly yellow-bronze in the fall.

STEM: Very slender, arching, sometimes nearly to the ground. Young stems are smooth and green, soon turning light brown. None develop more than 1/2 inch in diameter.

FLOWERS: Small and white, in many flowered clusters (umbels). Early in the spring. Drooping branches with many flower clusters are very showy.

FRUIT: Small; not showy.

COLOR: Foliage is blue-green. Flowers are white.

PROPAGATION: Softwood or hardwood cuttings or division of a clump.

CULTURE: A vigorously growing shrub with many slender branches arising from the base of the plant. Very tolerant to soil conditions, exposures, and other environmental conditions. Will grow almost anywhere. Widely planted and common throughout the United States. Blooms most profusely in full sun. Some pruning is required immediately following blooming to keep the plant neat and to encourage more profuse flowering the following year.

PESTS: None serious.

NOTES: A very showy, widely planted, spring-flowering shrub. Over 100 different species and cultivars of spiraea exist. Many have similar growth habits and blooming times.

RELATED SPECIES: *Spiraea* X *bumalda* Burv., a hybrid between *Spiraea japonica* and *Spiraea albiflora* (Miq.) Zabel. hardy in Zone 2. 'Anthony Waterer': rarely grows more than 2 1/2 feet tall, blooms intermittently with reddish pink flowers in large flat clusters during June or July. 'Frobell': 2 to 2 1/2 feet tall, dense, low shrub. Blooms in mid July with bright crimson flowers. Very showy. 'Goldflame': new growth is mottled red, copper and gold. 'Atrosanquinea': grows to 3 feet tall and has near-red flowers. 'Flaming Mound': has near-red foliage and red flower buds and pink flowers. Grows to about 2 feet tall. 'Sparkling Carpet': only grows a few inches tall and has reddish foliage but few flowers. many others exist.
    Spiraea prunifolia Sieb. & Zucc., bridal wreath, is hardy through Zone 4. Has lustrous green foliage, white double flowers, 1/2 inch diameter, in long clusters at the tips of the new growth in early May.
    Spiraea thunbergi Sieb., thunberg spiraea, grows 5 feet tall and has small white flowers just as the leaves appear in late April or early May. Fine texture. Slight orange fall color, variable with the season.
    Spiraea X *arguta* Zab., garland spiraea, is a hybrid between *Spiraea thunbergi* and *Spiraea* X *multiflora*. An irregular, upright shrub with long, slender leaves and pure white flowers in clusters after the leaves. Flowers earlier than other spiraeas.
    Spiraea japonica L., Japanese spiraea. The cultivar, 'Alpina', is hardy in Zone 5 and grows 3 feet tall. Flowers are white and much later than those of most other species.

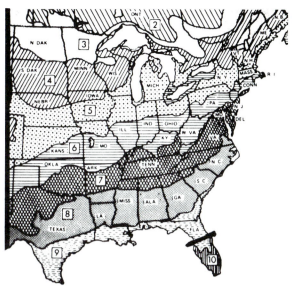

S. x *bumalda*

S. x *bumalda* 'Anthony Waterer'

S. thunbergi

S. thunbergi

Spiraea japonica 'Alpina'

Spiraea japonica 'Alpina'

S. x arguta

S. x arguta

S. prunifolia

S. prunifolia

Syringa vulgaris L.
Oleaceae or Olive Family
Native to southeastern Europe.

Common Lilac
Hardiness Zone 3

SIZE: 6 to 10 feet tall with a 6- to 10-foot spread. Moderate grower.
FORM: Multiple-stemmed, round-headed, large shrub.
TEXTURE: Medium to coarse.   EXPOSURE: Sun.

LEAVES: Opposite, broad ovate; 2 to 4 inches long, 1 1/2 to 3 inches wide, and heart-shaped, on stout petioles. The leaf margin is smooth. Deep, dark green above, pale green below, with no fall color.

STEM: Young stems are stout. During the dormant period, large, rounded buds are prominent in the opposite leaf axils and near the tips. Wood is strong and with age develops a dark gray to gray-brown bark. A multitude of stems develop from the crown giving a dense, twiggy clump.

FLOWERS: Spectacular terminal clusters in May. A wide range of colors: white, violet, blue, pinkish, or purple. Flowers are produced on new growth over the outer periphery of the plant after the leaves appear. Most cultivars are very fragrant.

FRUIT: Small, dry capsule. Not showy.

COLOR: Foliage is deep dark green. Flowers are white, pink, blue, or purple.

PROPAGATION: Cuttings, division of a clump, or grafting.

CULTURE: Extremely tough, durable, adaptable shrub. One of the few survivors on abandoned farmsteads. Long outlives the person who planted it. Very cold-tolerant and drought-tolerant on all soils except those wet for long periods of time. For best flowering and growth, it must be in full sun. Occasionally a young plant will grow very vigorously and not produce flowers for several years after planting. Most cultivars have poor flowering in Zone 8 and southward due to insufficient chilling of flower buds in winter.

PESTS: Lilac scale can be serious, particularly in the Northeast. Lilac borer sometimes attacks the largest stems in an old clump, but rarely does it kill the plant. Mildew may be severe on plants in cool, shady locations.

NOTES: An old garden favorite. First thought to have been cultivated about 1560. Many cultivars have been developed since that time. Most of the lilacs in the nursery trade today, called French hybrids, are really cultivars of common lilacs. Many originated in Lemoine Nursery in France about the turn of the 20th century. Should not be overlooked in modern landscaping, for they add a superb aroma and visual "plus" to the coming of spring. A good cut flower to force for indoor use. Lilacs serve as a good biological clock, because they flower about the time crabgrass begins to germinate in the spring. Thus the crabgrass control chemical should be applied before the lilacs bloom.

CULTIVARS: Many. Wyman's book, **Shrubs and Vines for American Gardens**, has one of the best lists available of the various colored cultivars. Professor Owen Rogers at the University of New Hampshire, Durham, NH, 03824, has done extensive work with lilacs for the Northeast. Check with your local nurseryman for good lilac cultivars for your area.

RELATED SPECIES: *Syringa persica* L., Persian lilac, hardy to Zone 5, is a smaller, more compact plant, generally 4 to 6 feet tall. It originated from a hybrid between *Syringa afghinaea* Schneid. and *S. lacaniata* Mill., about 1750. It is most easily distinguished by the leaves which are more elongate, slightly softer, pliable, and smaller. Also young twigs are more slender and flexible. Distribution of flowers over Persian lilac is broader across the whole plant, but clusters are not as large and showy as on common lilac. Many cultivars.

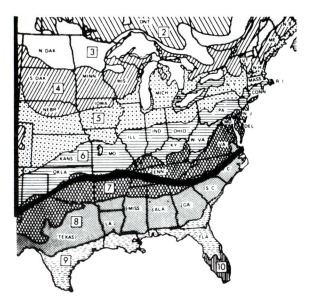

S. persica

S. persica

S. persica   S. vulgaris

Syringa meyeri, Meyer lilac

Syringa meyeri

Syringa X chinensis

Syringa X chinensis

Syringa X *meyeri* Schneid., meyer lilac, is hardy in Zone 3 and grows 3 to 4 feet tall. A dense, small to medium shrub that suckers freely and produces large numbers of small flower clusters in mid spring. Flowers are dark violet to purple. Native to northern China. Not commonly seen in the trade. Some cultivars probably exist.

Syringa X *chinensis* Willd., Chinese lilac, is hardy in Zone 3 and grows 10 to12 feet tall. A large shrub resulting from *Syringa persica* and *S. vulgaris* parents. Purple flowers are very showy in mid spring.

Uniola latifolia Michx.
Poaceae or Grass Family
Native to the eastern and southeastern United States.
SIZE: 3 to 4 feet tall. Moderate grower.
FORM: A narrowly upright clump, arching out at the top.
TEXTURE: Fine.

Northern Sea Oats
Hardiness Zone 5

EXPOSURE: Sun to shade.

LEAVES: Dark green in shade locations; lighter in the sun. Narrowly lanceolate; 4 to 8 inches long, 1/2 to 3/4 inch wide. Arising at intervals up the stems.

STEM: Perennial. Slowly spreads by tillering or a weak rhizome, creating a clump. Stems are flexible and allow the leaves and flower heads to move with the slightest breeze.

FLOWERS: In terminal clusters 10 to 12 inches long, gracefully arching with the maturing seeds. The seeds are arranged in spikelets that appear as if pressed and each one is nestled into the one below. Very showy and persist from mid summer into winter. Green when young, turning a bright yellow-brown at maturity.

FRUIT: A small, brown seed. Not showy.

COLOR: Foliage is green. Flowers and fruits are brown.

PROPAGATION: Seed or division.

CULTURE: This is one of the few grasses that does best in partial shade to shade conditions. It will grow in full sun, but the leaf color and leaf and flower/seed contrast is not as good. Prefers a moist area at the edge of woods or even **in** the woods. Very slowly spreads but it not a problem to keep in check.

PESTS: None.

NOTES: One of the best grasses for ornamental use because it is easy to transplant and establish, not aggressive. Remains a desirable size, grows in practically any light and is very showy for the summer, fall, and winter. Flowers can be picked anytime for use indoors, green or brown, and are not prone to shattering. This plant is not often seen in the landscape but certainly deserves more attention. In north central Oklahoma the plant is native along streams in the shade, yet does well in full sun with no supplemental water, once established. The old tops should be cut off before spring growth, which begins early.

CULTIVARS: None known.

RELATED SPECIES: *Uniola paniculata* L., the sea oats of the Gulf Coast and eastern United States shoreline, is similar in appearance to northern sea oats. It is hardy in Zone 7 but spreads by a vigorous rhizome, which is an asset in its role in stabilizing beach fronts; however, this same rhizome makes it undesirable as an ornamental. Most states restrict the collection of seeds of this plant as it plays a very important role in beach front stabilization. In this case, that is not a problem as northern sea oats is a **much** superior landscape plant.

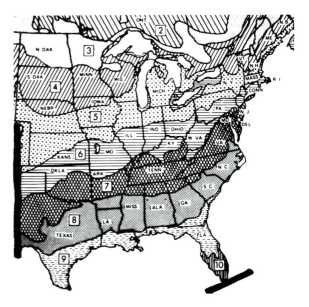

Viburnum spp.   Deciduous Viburnums
Caprifoliaceae or Honeysuckle Family   Hardiness Zone 4 and 5
Native to North America or Asia.
SIZE: Medium to large shrub. Moderate to rapid growers.
FORM: Rounded, irregular shrubs if left untrimmed.
TEXTURE: Medium.   **EXPOSURE:** Sun or partial shade.

LEAVES: Distinctly opposite and most are simple with large axillary buds during the dormant period. Most have dark green foliage. Many have excellent fall color.

STEMS: More or less upright, medium strong but flexible: not easily broken. Light to medium brown on most species.

FLOWERS: Small and white to pinkish, in showy terminal clusters.

FRUITS: May be black, blue-black, or red and very showy.

COLOR: Foliage is attractive with excellent fall color on many species. Flowers are white or pinkish and fruits may be black or red.

PROPAGATION: Softwood or hardwood cuttings, or seed.

CULTURE: Durable and adaptable shrubs, growing in most soils and exposures. Flowering and fruiting is heavier in locations receiving sun for at least 1/2 of the day. Very heavy, poorly drained soils may be a problem.

PESTS: Few are serious. A durable, adaptable group.

NOTES: Showy shrubs that flower in the spring. Some have excellent fall color and showy red fruits that persist well into winter. Widely used in Zones 5 and 4, but sparingly used in Zones 8, 7, and 6. They deserve more attention in these areas since they do well.

RELATED SPECIES: *Viburnum* X 'Burkwoodi' Hort. Burkw. & Skipw., Burkwood viburnum, Zone 5. A hybrid between *V. carlesi* and *V. utile.* Nearly evergreen, up to 6 to 8 feet tall. Leaves are ovate, 2 to 3 inches long, glossy green, and slightly serrated. Underside of leaves, young shoots and buds are densely wooly. Flowers are pinkish, opening white, showy, with a distinct pleasant, spicy odor. Fruits are not showy. A useful hedge or screen plant or used in groups. 'Mohawk': a compact cultivar with red flower buds, opens to white with red spots. The glossy green leaves turn orange-red in the fall.

Viburnum carlesi Hemsl., Koreanspice or mayflower viburnum, Zone 5. A dense shrub with upright branches. Leaves are ovate, 2 to 3 inches long, dull green and wooly above and beneath with a toothed margin. Wine-red some falls. Flowers are white, very fragrant, in dense clusters 2 to 3 inches across. Fruit is not showy. A very showy, fragrant and attractive shrub. The wooly leaves create a contrast with those of other landscape plants. 'Compactum': more dense and compact than the parent. 'Cayuga': compact grower to 5 feet tall with pink buds, white flowers.

Virburnum dentatum L., arrowwood viburnum, Zone 3. An attractive, large shrub with a loose, mounding habit. May reach 8 to 10 feet or more in height and a similar spread. Leaves are ovate to nearly rounded with distinct teeth on the margin. Dark green in summer and yellow to red in the fall, depending on exposure, growing conditions, and seedling differences. Flowers are white, in terminal clusters over the entire plant. Fruits are not showy. One of the more shade-tolerant viburnums. Useful for screening or as a filler. Quite durable and drought-tolerant.

Viburnum lantana L., wayfaringtree viburnum. Zone 3. An 8- to 12-foot shrub with a similar spread: needs room! Leaves are ovate, 2 to 4 inches long with a finely sawtooth margin and rough-textured surface (see photograph). Young leaves and stems are wooly; however, the hairs are not persistent. Leaf color is bluish green, dull, purplish in the fall. Flowers are creamy white in 3 to 4 inch clusters over the surface of the plant. Very showy but has no fragrance. Fruits are yellow at first, turning red then black with maturity: very showy since all colors may be present at one time. A useful and attractive large shrub **IF** sufficient room is available. 'Mohican': grows to about 8 feet with whitish flowers, orange-red fruits which occur in July and are showy for several weeks. The leaves are especially thick and leathery. 'Rugosum': darker green, more attractive foliage. Other cultivars exist.

Viburnum lentago L. nannyberry viburnum. Zone 3. A large shrub or small tree 15 to 30 feet tall. Leaves are ovate, 2 to 4 inches long with a distinct, tapering tip and a finely serrate margin. Leaf surface is glossy green and attractive but fall color is purplish red and erratic. Flowers are creamy white in clusters 4 to 8 inches across: very showy but no fragrance. Fruit is blue-black: not showy. Useful as a large shrub or small tree in dry areas where other small trees might not do well. A consistent plant for good foliage and flowers.

Viburnum opulus L. European cranberrybush viburnum. Zone 3. A shrub 8 to 12 feet tall with an irregular, mounding habit. Leaves are distinctly 3-lobed, maple-like, 3 to 4 inches long and irregularly serrate. Hairy when young, especially below. Foliage color is dark green and sometimes red-purple in the fall. Flowers are white in 3- to 4-inch, rounded clusters over the surface of the shrub. Fruits are red, showy and persist most of the winter since the birds prefer other fruits. A most useful and attractive shrub. 'Roseum': large, sterile flowers; extremely showy (see photograph). Other cultivars exist.

Viburnum trilobum Marsh., American cranberrybush viburnum. Zone 2. Similar in most respects to the European cranberrybush viburnum. Leaves are similar yet distinct (see photographs), flowers are white, and fruits are shiny, bright red. A most useful and attractive large shrub with fewer aphid problems than the European cranberrybush viburnum.

Viburnum plicatum Thunb., doublefile viburnum. Zone 5. A large shrub, 6 to 10 feet tall and with an equal spread. Leaves are oval to nearly round, 2 to 4 inches long with a uniformly sawtooth margin. Dark green above, hairy beneath, especially when young. Veination pattern is distinct (see photographs). Flowers are both fertile and sterile (large) in distinct, horizontal rows (thus the name, doublefile); white with no fragrance. Fall color is often a deep wine-red. A very showy and useful viburnum but which needs a few hours of sun to remain compact and flower well. Often sold as *V. tomentosum* instead of *V. plicatum* 'Tomentosum', which is the more doublefile and heavily flowering cultivar. 'Shasta': grows to 6 feet with nearly horizontal branches, white flowers, red fruits which turn black. Very nice. 'Shoshoni': grows to 5 feet and more compact than 'Shasta', white flowers and red fruits that finally turn black.

Viburnum sieboldi Miq., Siebold viburnum. Zone 5. A large shrub with ovate-elongate, shiny leaves with deep veins and serrate margin. Prolific creamy white flowers and red fruits which the birds love. 'Seneca': grows to 15 feet or more with creamy flowers and refd fruits. Spectacular if trained as a tree form.

Many, many more species and cultivars of viburnum exist. These are only a few of the more useful and adaptable.

V. x 'Burkwoodi'

V. carlesi

V. dantatum

V. dentatum

V. dantatum 'Pubescens'

V. lantana

V. lantana

V. lantana

V. lantana

V. lentago

V. lentago

V. opulus 'Roseum'

V. opulus 'Roseum'

V. trilobum

V. trilobum

V. trilobum

V. plicatum

V. plicatum

V. plicatum

V. sieboldi

Vitex agnus-castus L.   Chaste Tree
Verbenaceae or Verbena Family   Hardiness Zone 6
Native to western Asia.

SIZE: Large shrub or small tree, 12 to 20 feet tall with a 15- to 20-foot spread. Rapid grower.

FORM: Multiple-stemmed large shrub or small tree with an umbrella-like crown.

TEXTURE: Fine.   **EXPOSURE:** Sun.

LEAVES: Opposite, compound; generally with 5 to 7 leaflets, occasionally 3 or 9. The central leaflet is usually longest, linear or lanceolate, tapering to a sharp point at the tip. Individual leaflets may be 2 to 4 inches long. Margin may be smooth or have numerous teeth. Foliage is gray-green to dull green, lower surface is pale green to almost white. No fall color. Leaves have a distinct spicy odor when crushed.

STEM: Young stems are slender, more or less squarish, green to reddish brown or gray. Old bark is smooth, dark gray with broad ridges; not showy but durable.

FLOWERS: Generally in June or July but may bloom erratically until September on new growth. Terminal spikes of dense clusters of flowers are blue to purplish and slightly fragrant. Spikes may be 4 to 8 inches long, covering the outer perimeter of the plant. Showy, but the contrast between flowers and foliage is not great. White-flowered cultivars are the more noticeable.

FRUIT: Small, brown or black seeds, about 1/8 inch. Not showy.

COLOR: Foliage is gray-green to dull green. Flowers are blue to purple.

PROPAGATION: Seed, cuttings, or removal of sprouts from old plants.

CULTURE: Tolerates any soil condition. Particularly adaptable to dry, sunny locations and especially tolerant of poor soils. Responds vigorously to fertilizer and good growing conditions. Sometimes managed as an annual top, and thus is cut back to the ground every year and allowed to re-grow from the root system in the spring. Very tough.

PESTS: None serious.

NOTES: A most interesting flower color and aroma to add to the landscape. The odor of any plant part is rather pleasant and quite distinctive when crushed. Some odor is emitted from the plant even when not disturbed. Gets too large as a shrub for most situations. Has more merit as a multiple-stemmed, small deciduous tree where it is cold hardy. Could be desirable as a patio specimen. Fine-textured, lacey foliage makes a pleasant light pattern against structures or in outdoor living areas. A very tough, durable shrub, commonly found in old landscape situations: not widely planted currently but should be used more as a small tree. Sometimes young plants are mistaken for *Cannabis sativa*, marijuana, and destroyed but *Cannabis* has almost no odor when crushed.

CULTIVARS: 'Alba': white flowers. 'Rosea': pink flowers. 'Serrata': very serrate leaflets. 'Silver Spire': has white flowers. Others probably exist.

RELATED SPECIES: *Vitex negundo* L. is very similar in all respects but grows slightly larger, 15 to 20 feet tall. Leaflets tend to be in threes or fives instead of fives or sevens. Flowers are less compact and less showy. If blue flowers are of landscape value, use *Vitex agnus-castus*. If a larger, deciduous tree form is desired, *V. negundo* may be superior. Very similar in durability and toughness. The two species are often confused in the nursery trade.

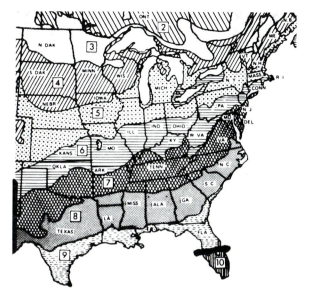

Weigela florida (Bunge) A. DC. Weigela
Caprifoliaceae or Honeysuckle Family Hardiness Zone 4 or 5
Native to China.
SIZE: 4 to 8 feet, depending on cultivar; similar spread. Rapid grower.
FORM: Irregular, spreading shrub.
TEXTURE: Medium. **EXPOSURE:** Sun or slight shade.

LEAVES: Opposite, simple; 2 to 4 inches long, with a sawtooth margin, distinct veins and very short petioles. Upper leaf surface is medium to dark green, lighter below, with hairs on the veins. No fall color.

STEM: More or less upright and arching. Young stems are medium green, soon turning brown, with prominent lenticels. Stems have two rows of hairs. Wood is rather brittle.

FLOWERS: Funnel-shaped and white, red, pink or purple. Very attractive.

FRUIT: An oblong capsule. Not showy.

COLOR: Foliage is medium to dark green. Flowers are white, pink, red, or purple.

PROPAGATION: Softwood or hardwood cuttings.

CULTURE: Weigela will grow on most sites with minimal care and flowers best in full or nearly full sun. In Zones 4 and 5, some dieback occurs most winters leaving a rather unthrifty appearance unless pruned. Flower buds are formed in the fall, so all pruning should be done immediately following flowering to control size.

PESTS: None serious.

NOTES: A spectacular show when in bloom. Unfortunately, the flowers do not last more than 10 to 14 days and the rest of the year the plant is not particularly attractive. Useful as a background or distant screen. When in flower, it won't be overlooked, then it will disappear in with a mass of vegetation. Flowers well in Zones 7 and 8; however, with the additional plants available in the milder climates, weigela is seldom used in Zones 8 or 9.

CULTIVARS: Many. 'Java Red': deep red flowers, grows 3 to 4 feet tall and has a reddish fall color. 'Variegata': grows 4 to 6 feet tall with leaves more elongate and banded with a narrow strip of yellow and has pink flowers. 'Bristol Snowflake': grows 6 to 8 feet tall, with white to pinkish flowers. 'Vanicek': thought to be a hybrid that is cold hardy in Zone 4. Height is 5 to 6 feet and flowers are red. 'Conquerant': grows 8 to 10 feet tall and has pale red flowers. 'Minuet': grows only to about 3 feet tall with dark red flowers. 'Pink Princess': grows to about 6 feet tall with pinkish flowers. 'Red Prince': grows to about 6 feet tall and has striking red flowers in spring and a modest show in late summer. 'Tango': grows to 2 feet tall with red flowers with yellow center. A good, compact dwarf. 'Rumba': flowers most of the summer with red flowers and grows to 3 feet tall. Many other cultivars exist. Check with your local nurseryman for the best cultivars for your area.

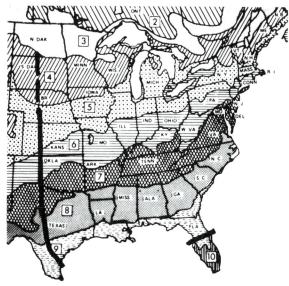

'Variegata'

Wisteria sinensis Sweet.
Leguminosae or Legume Family
Native to China.

Chinese Wisteria
Hardiness Zone 5

SIZE: Vine, growing to 30 to 40 feet or more. Rapid grower.
FORM: Irregular twining vine.
TEXTURE: Fine to medium.   **EXPOSURE:** Sun to shade.

LEAVES: Deciduous, alternate, compound; generally with 7 to 13 leaflets, medium to dark green. Leaflets are ovate to slightly oblong, tapering to a point at the tip, and very fuzzy at first, becoming smooth with age; only a slight yellow fall color. Leaf margin is smooth. New leaves may have a pinkish red color.

STEM: Young stems are covered with dense hairs and are very slender, twining and twisting around any available object. Young stems elongate considerably before the leaves develop. No aerial roots or tendrils are present. Old stem finally becomes a dark gray-brown, almost shrub-like or tree-like, quite woody and stiff.

FLOWERS: Spectacular blue-violet, or white in dense, grape-like clusters, 8 to 12 inches long, before the leaves; fragrant. Very early in the spring. Few blooms in shady locations.

FRUIT: A stiff pod, 3 to 5 inches long with hard brown seeds. Not showy.

COLOR: Foliage is medium to dark green. Flowers are blue-violet or white.

PROPAGATION: Seed, but selected cultivars with defined flowering characteristics and colors must be rooted from cuttings or grafted.

CULTURE: A vigorously growing vine, tolerant of a wide range of soil conditions from acid, more or less poorly drained soils, to dry compacted soils, particularly after the plant becomes established. May become yellow (chlorotic) in alkaline soils. May become a weed and be rather difficult to eradicate particlarly in moist, shady areas where it is not kept confined to a tree or other structure.

PESTS: None serious.

NOTES: Spectacular, spring-blooming deciduous vine. Often used in the South on arbors or allowed to climb up either pines or deciduous trees. Flowers occur in the spring before leaves emerge on the trees, making a spectacular show. An old garden favorite. Needs to be where it can receive at least moderate light intensity for good foliage development and good flowering. Is occasionally grown as a shrub but is difficult to maintain in this fashion, but quite showy when it blooms.

CULTIVARS: 'Alba': white flowers. 'Jako': white flowers, very fragrant. 'Caroline': blue-violet flowers all opening about the same time. A prolific flower producer. 'Black Dragon': dark purple, double flowers. Many other cultivars exist.

RELATED SPECIES: *Wisteria floribunda* (Willd.) DC., Japanese wisteria, is similar in tolerance, durability and adaptation to Chinese wisteria. Can be readily distinguished due to the flowers of Japanese wisteria being very fragrant, much longer, often reaching 12 to 30 inches in length, and the leaflets are smaller; generally 13 to 19 per compound leaf. Flowers appear about the same time as the leaves. 'Longissima Alba': pure white flowers that cascade in spikes up to 3 feet and has long, bright green foliage. 'Rosea': long clusters of pink flowers. 'Royal Purple': violet-purple clusters of flowers. 'Macrobortyrs': a prolific producer of showy, violet-blue clusters up to 3 feet long. Many other cultivars probably exist.

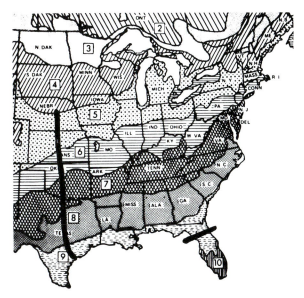

More photographs page 399

Xanthoceras sorbifolium Bunge.   Popcorn Shrub
Sapindaceae or Soapberry Family   Hardiness Zone 6
Native to northern China.
SIZE: 8 to 12 feet tall with a 4- to 10-foot spread. Moderate grower.
FORM: Upright shrub with a rounded crown.
TEXTURE: Fine.   **EXPOSURE:** Sun.

LEAVES: Alternate, pinnately compound; 10 to 14 inches long, with 11 to 17 lanceolate leaflets with sawtooth margins. Dark, shiny green above and pale green below; little or no fall color. Foliage resembles the mountain ash in form and texture, thus the species name.

STEM: Young stems are mostly upright, very stout, gray-green, turning gray-brown with age. The main stems are upright with a smooth or slightly furrowed gray-black bark. Wood is somewhat weak and easily broken.

FLOWERS: White, in terminal clusters before the foliage, about 1 inch across with white petals and a yellow throat. Very showy in early spring, right after forsythia. The white flowers with the yellow throat look somewhat like popcorn; thus the common name.

FRUIT: Large, green seed pods, more or less rounded, 2 to 3 inches across, turning black with maturity and opening to release several irregular, marble-sized seeds. The seeds must be collected in the fall and cold-stratified for easy germination in the spring. Interestingly, about 30 to 40% of the seedlings will be albinos that may grow 4 to 6 inches tall before depleting the stored energy in the endosperm and dying.

COLOR: Foliage is dark, glossy green. Flowers are white.

PROPAGATION: Seed.

CULTURE: Popcorn shrub quickly develops a very strong taproot and is therefore difficult to transplant from a field or landscape situation. However, seeds germinated in raised, bottomless containers with air-root-pruning and grown in containers, transplant easily. Needs full sun for best flowering and compact growth. Grows in very sandy soils and tolerates clays fairly well. Tolerant of drought and heat. Grows well in western and central Oklahoma and retains the attractive, fine-textured foliage all season.

PESTS: None serious.

NOTES: A very attractive shrub in early spring. The flower clusters are large and remain for 2 to 3 weeks. Not a neat shrub, somewhat leggy, but sufficiently showy to deserve consideration for an out-of-the-way corner. The foliage stands out during the growing season because of the fine texture and glossy, dark green color. Particularly useful on exposed droughty sites or as a large, fine-textured screen. A specimen grown as a single-stemmed, small tree is especially attractive. Deserves more attention.

CULTIVARS: None known.

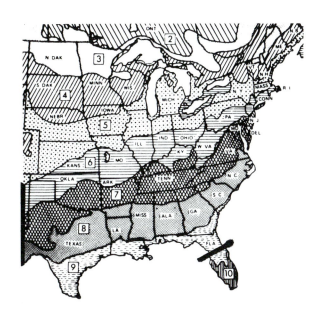

Wisteria floribunda, Japanese wisteria

BROADLEAF EVERGREEN TREES AND SHRUBS

Broadleaf evergreens are "the cake and the frosting" particularly of southern landscapes since many are not hardy north of zone 7. The spectacular flowers of azaleas and camellias, the fragrance of false holly, silverberry, and confederate jasmine and showy fruits of the hollies, create a magnificent show the year around. Most broad leaf evergreens have some shade tolerance and work well as understory plants to pines and other trees. By mixing broadleaf evergreens with other landscape plants, the landscape designer has a vast array of forms, colors, and textures at his disposal. However, one must use caution and avoid a green monotony. Remember that plant growth may be paid and must be given the utmost consideration in plant placement to avoid crowding.

Abelia grandiflora (Andre.) Rehd.   Glossy Abelia
Caprifoliaceae or Honeysuckle Family   Hardiness Zone 6
Native: A hybrid between *Abelia chinensis* and *Abelia uniflora*.
SIZE: 6 to 10 feet tall with a 4- to 6-foot spread. Moderate to rapid grower.
FORM: A graceful, oval shrub.
TEXTURE: Fine.   EXPOSURE: Sun to partial shade.

LEAVES: Opposite, simple, or occasionally in 3's; ovate to oval, 1 to 1 1/2 inches long, 1/2 inch wide with a sawtooth margin on the outer portion and tapering to a point at the tip. Deep green to slight purple-green during the growing season, becoming a green-bronze in the fall and early winter, depending on severity of the weather.

STEM: Basically upright, fairly stiff and erect with very slender young stems. Some stems droop or arch, giving an umbrella-like crown. The young stem is generally a purple to purple-brown and is hollow except at the nodes. Old stems become more or less striped with vertical strips of light and dark peeling bark; appears papery.

FLOWERS: In loose terminal panicles, white to pink. Bell-shaped, about 1 inch long on new growth. After the petals fall, sepals, (generally 5) remain on the plant for the rest of the season and into the winter, looking like miniature dry flowers. A healthy plant will bloom from May throughout August on new wood. An excellent bloom period.

FRUIT: None.

COLOR: Foliage is deep green to purple-green. Flowers are white to pink.

PROPAGATION: Semi-hardwood to hardwood cuttings.

CULTURE: Grows in a wide range of circumstance. Tolerates sun to shade, any reasonable soil, and moist to fairly droughty locations. Responds to fertility and supplemental moisture during drought periods by additional blooms during the summer. May be pruned or sheared into a dense hedge and, unlike many other shrubs under these conditions, will continue to flower. Flowers on new wood, thus may be pruned any time. Flowers best in full sun but has moderate flower production in partial shade locations. Unfortunately, the compact cultivars are less tough and durable.

PESTS: None serious.

NOTES: A very tough, durable shrub for most landscapes. May get too large for many residential plantings unless it is pruned with vigor several times during the growing season. makes an excellent large hedge or screen. The long blooming period makes it especially useful. This hybrid is more durable and adaptable than the parents and other species of abelia.

CULTIVARS: 'Edward Goucher': grows 3 to 4 feet tall with graceful, slender branches. Quite compact with clear pink flowers. A prolific bloomer all summer. 'Prostrata': more like a ground cover with spreading, low branches rarely reaching more than 2 feet tall. new leaves have a red tinge. Flowers are white. 'Sherwoodi': a more dwarf form rarely reaching more than 3 feet tall, with slightly smaller leaves and flowers. Other cultivars may exist.

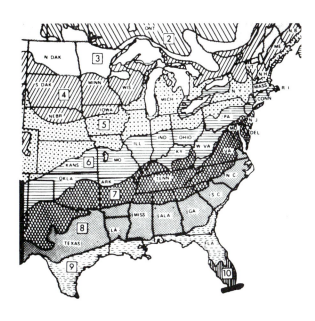

Aucuba japonica Thunb.   Japanese Aucuba or Gold Dust Plant
Cornaceae or Dogwood Family   Hardiness Zone 7
Native to Japan
SIZE: 4 to 12 feet tall with a 4- to 6-foot spread. Slow to moderate grower.
FORM: Upright to oval shrub with dense foliage.
TEXTURE: Coarse.   **EXPOSURE:** Partial shade to shade.

LEAVES: Opposite, simple; elliptical to elliptical-lanceolate, 3 to 7 inches long, 1 to 3 inches wide, depending on cultivar. The leaf margin is smooth near the base but has coarse teeth on the outer half of the leaf. Deep, dark green above or variegated with some cultivars. Veins are generally inconspicuous. Petiole is green and stout.

STEM: Upright, round and smooth, remaining green for several seasons, with a large terminal bud during late summer and the rest of the dormant season: very conspicuous.

FLOWERS: Nearly inconspicuous. Both male and female plants exist. Both are needed if fruits are to be formed.

FRUIT: Bright red, attractive berries; oblong or football-shaped, about 1 inch long with a single seed.

COLOR: Foliage is deep green to mottled yellow-green, variegated. Fruit is red.

PROPAGATION: Very easy from cuttings or seed.

CULTURE: Does best in shady locations or the north sides of structures. The most shade-tolerant of any of the broadleaf evergreens. Will grow in any soil but is assisted by mulching to retain moisture. Very drought-tolerant. Can be pruned but it should be done judiciously because pruning scars show for a considerable period of time. Responds reasonably well to light applications of fertilizer, mulching, and other good cultural practices. Also does well as a house plant.

PESTS: Occasionally scale but rarely does it become a serious problem.

NOTES: Japanese aucuba is a very attractive, coarse-textured, broadleaf evergreen which works very well in many small courtyards or patio locations where it gets protection from desiccating winds, high heat, or direct sunlight. Large, old plants 6 to 8 feet tall with considerable spread make an interesting background for other landscape features or plant materials. Frequently used as a substitute for croton, *Codiaeum variegatum*, in the Gulf Coast states where it is hardy but crotons are not. Hardy as far north as central Tennessee. Does well as far west as central Oklahoma if given some protection. Very drought-tolerant as long as it is shaded. Foliage will wilt and droop whenever the temperature gets below freezing; however, no damage occurs and as temperature rises, the plant assumes normal appearance. Fruits are uncommon in the landscape because most cultivars are females and without a male, no fruit develops. A male should be included with aucuba plantings as the large red fruits are a plus during late fall and winter.

CULTIVARS: 'Picturata': has a bright yellow-gold center in deep green leaves. A slow-growing, compact plant. 'Seratafolia': a more vigorous, bushy grower with dark green leaves and serrate margins. More elongate leaves than normal. Female, and a heavy fruit producer. 'Sulfur': wide, golden edges on the leaves with dark green centers: striking contrast. 'Variegata': a more compact shrub with glossy green leaves speckled with gold. Female. 'Nana': a slow-growing variety; heavy berry producer on female plants. Other cultivars undoubtedly exist.

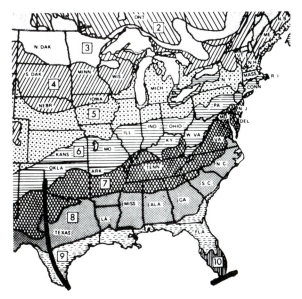

'Picturata'

Bambusa spp.

Graminae or Grass Family

Native to southeast Asia.

Bamboo

Hardiness Zone 7 to 6 depending on species

SIZE: Variable, from 2 feet to 30 feet or more. Rapid growers.

FORM: Many upright, vertical, grass-like stems.

TEXTURE: Medium.   EXPOSURE: Sun to shade.

LEAVES: Long and slender, tapering to a long point at the tip; vary from 2 to 4 inches long with some, to 6 to 12 inches long with others. All have distinct, parallel leaf veins. Foliage color ranges from deep green to yellow-green.

STEM: Upright, with leaves arising from each node or section, rarely with secondary branching. Stems are used as cane or bamboo fishing poles when the leaf stalks are removed. Many bamboo genera and species have strong horizontal stems at or slightly below the soil surface, thus creating a problem as they spread with vigor.

FLOWERS: Not showy and rarely seen in this country.

FRUIT: Not showy; rarely seen in this country.

COLOR: Foliage is a deep green to yellow-green, depending on genus and species.

PROPAGATION: Division of clumps.

CULTURE: Bamboos are native to the tropical and sub-tropical regions of southeast Asia and grow with vigor in moist soils in warm climates. Bamboos will grow in nearly any kind of soil, particularly wet soils, and, to a degree, poorly drained soils. Moderate to good drought tolerance. Most bamboos can be easily propagated and transplanted; however, they must be cut back severely to reduce the leaf surface area until established as they dehydrate quickly once disturbed. With fertilizer and moisture they may become pests.

PESTS: None serious.

NOTES: Several hundred bamboos exist in the world. Grown mostly in the tropical or sub-tropical regions. However, a few species are hardy as far north as Zone 6 and several are hardy in Zone 7. Use with caution unless planting in buried or raised containers which will prevent spreading. The less vigorous bamboos are preferred. Because the bamboos do not flower and fruit in this country, there is a great deal of confusion in identifying genera and species. *Sasa palmata* is sometimes sold as *Bambusa multiplex*, hedge bamboo, and grows 6 to 8 feet tall. A clump-like bamboo which remains confined to an area fairly well. It is hardy in Zone 6 and southward.

RELATED SPECIES: (No cultivars) *Arundinaria variegata*, dwarf white striped bamboo, native to Japan, hardy in Zone 6, grows 3 to 4 feet tall, has leaves striped with white, hairy on both sides, and spreads rapidly in good soil.

    Phyllostachys aureosulcata, yellowgroove bamboo, native to China, grows to 30 feet tall, hardy in Zone 7, spreads vigorously with a strong horizontal stolon or below-ground stem. Frequently used for fishing poles.

    Arundinaria piamaea, dwarf bamboo, rarely grows more than 2 feet tall, hardy in Zone 7, and makes a good dense ground cover with a dark green foliage, particularly in partial shade. Spreads moderately but rarely becomes a pest as do some of the larger bamboos.

    Sasa palmata, palmate bamboo, may grow 6 to 8 feet and is hardy as far north as Zone 6 in moist areas. The hardiest and toughest of the bamboos commonly grown in this country. Leaves are 6 to 12 inches long, 1 1/2 to 3 inches wide, bright green above, rather silver beneath. A vigorous spreader which should be planted only in a confined area or in a buried container or barrel to confine horizontal spread.

'Yellowgroove'

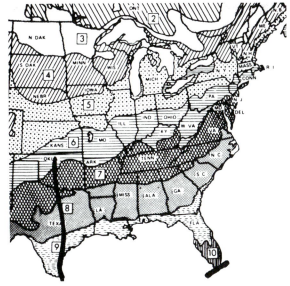

'Yellowgroove'

dwarf bamboo

Berberis julianae Schneid.   Wintergreen Barberry
Berberidaceae or Barberry Family   Hardiness Zone 6
Native to central China.
SIZE: 6 to 8 feet tall with a 5- to 7-foot spread. Slow to moderate grower.
FORM: Graceful, oval, mounded shrub.
TEXTURE: Medium.   EXPOSURE: Sun to shade.

LEAVES: Alternate and simple, in clusters. Generally flat, lanceolate, 1 to 3 inches long, about 1/2 inch wide with many stiff, spiny teeth on the margin. Plants have been selected for dense foliage and no longer is the original alternate leaf pattern detectable. However, they are alternate in clusters. That is, instead of 1 leaf in each alternate location, there will be 3 to 7 leaves in a cluster. Generally a deep dark green to metallic blue-green color in the shade on upper surface, slightly lighter green below. May turn a slight purple in full sun or during a severe winter. New growth appears a bright purple-green.

STEM: Semi-upright, spreading both upright and horizontally. Somewhat weeping with fairly dense branching and moderately stiff, slender stems. Stems are green at an early age, later turning purple-brown. Inner bark is yellow, typical of the family. Has spines, generally at each cluster of leaves, mostly in 3's, about 1 to 1 1/2 inches long.

FLOWERS: Lemon yellow, in clusters; generally late April to mid May. Moderately showy and fragrant.

FRUIT: Bluish black, developing in late summer or fall and hanging on into the winter.

COLOR: Foliage is dark green to blue-green in shade, purple-green in sun. Flowers are yellow. Fruit is black.

PROPAGATION: Semi-hardwood to hardwood cuttings.

CULTURE: Grows in full sun to semi-shade locations with moderate to good soil and moisture conditions. Will tolerate full or nearly full sun only if attention is given to an establishment period of 1 1/2 to 2 years. Grows in most soils if moisture and fertility are closely controlled. Requires little care once established but responds to mulching, removal of competing grass or weeds, and other good cultural practices. A common error is planting too close to structures: 5 to 6 feet should be a minimum. Some pruning is required for best form.

PESTS: None serious.

NOTES: An attractive, broadleaf evergreen. Keep away from direct contact with people because of the sharp teeth on leaves and spines on stems. Moderately durable on good sites but does not belong in the fully exposed new suburb with little or no topsoil.

CULTIVARS: 'Nana' a semi-dwarf form; similar to the parent in other respects. 'Spring Glory': blooms profusely with yellow flowers.

RELATED SPECIES: *Berberis mentorensis* is a hybrid between *Berberis thunbergi* and *B. julianae*. May reach 5 to 6 feet tall with semi-evergreen, spiny-toothed, ovate to elliptical leaves about one inch long. An intermediate between the 2 parents in size and adaptation.

Berberis X *gladwynensis* 'William Penn' (a hybrid between *Berberis julianae* and *B. verruculosa*) is a deep green to blue-green, compact cultivar. New foliage is reddish purple to purple-green, depending on light intensity. A very showy, useful shrub for full sun to semi-shade locations and superior to wintergreen barberry for most uses.

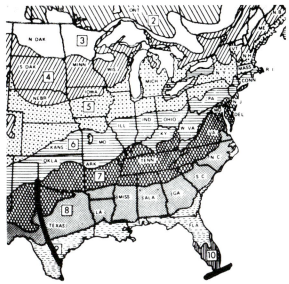

Buxus microphylla Sieb. and Zucc.
Buxaceae or Boxwood Family
Native to Japan.

Japanese Boxwood, Littleleaf Box
Hardiness Zone 5

SIZE: 3 to 4 feet tall with a 1 1/2- to 2-foot spread. Slow grower.
FORM: Compact, oval shrub.
TEXTURE: Fine.　　　　　　　　　　　　**EXPOSURE:** Sun to shade.

LEAVES: Opposite, simple; entire, about 1/2 inch long. Obovate to lanceolate, broadest slightly above the middle and sometimes with a cleft at the tip. Smooth leaf margin, very glossy, deep green upper surface, and a very short petiole. The mid-rib on the underneath side of the leaf is a cottony white. Leaves turn slightly brown in winter in full sun.

STEM: New growth is green, soon turning a light tan. Very slender yet stiff; many branches develop making a dense compact shrub. Easily sheared into various forms. Terminal buds are prominent during late summer, fall, and winter.

FLOWERS: Small, not showy. In clusters in the leaf axil.

FRUIT: Small, 3-pointed capsule. Inconspicuous.

COLOR: Foliage is glossy, deep green.

PROPAGATION: Seed or from cuttings.

CULTURE: Contrary to common belief, boxwoods are very tough, durable plants if given reasonable growing conditions. They do well with little or no attention in areas of good soil and moderate sunlight and moisture. They will grow in all but the poorest soil as long as it is well-drained. Most tolerant of heavy shade of the broadleaf evergreen shrubs, next to aucuba. Boxwoods have a very fibrous shallow root system, thus any hoeing or weeding directly at the base of the plant should be avoided. Fertilizer applications should be light and frequent. Can be sheared to create various forms or shapes; easily manipulated. Not for hot, dry, full sun locations where leaf bronzing in winter is a problem.

PESTS: Occasionally mites. Nematodes may be a problem, particularly in the sandy soils of the lower South. Dogs' urine may kill branches or leaves.

NOTES: Unlike many plants, boxwoods do not appear to respond to mulching. Mulching around the plant may cause a stem rot. Boxwoods make excellent borders and hedges, for a variety of situations. In the extreme western range for boxwood, they do better on the north or east side of structures or with considerable shade, unlike in the East where they will take full sun. All plant parts may be mildly toxic if eaten in quantity. ??-POISON-??

CULTIVARS: 'Compacta': very small, compact form reaching 12 to 24 inches tall after several years' growth. 'Japonica': may get to be 6 feet tall, with leaves up to 1 1/2 inches long. A larger, more robust plant. 'Kingsville Dwarf': very low and compact, rarely getting more than 10 to 12 inches tall. Excellent for edging. 'Koreana': grows to 2 feet tall; probably the hardiest of the various cultivars.

RELATED SPECIES: *Buxus microphylla* leaves are broadest at or above the middle and the tip is generally indented, whereas *Buxus sempervirens* has leaves broadest below the middle and a tip which is rounded or slightly pointed.

　　Buxus harlandi Hance., Korean box, is hardy in Zone 7b with leaves that are 1 to 1 1/2 inches long, gradually increasing in width from the petiole to the tip. Somewhat squarish at the tip, may or may not be indented at the mid vein. Rarely grows more than 3 feet. Similar to *Buxus microphylla* in growing conditions and uses but more susceptible to stem rot.

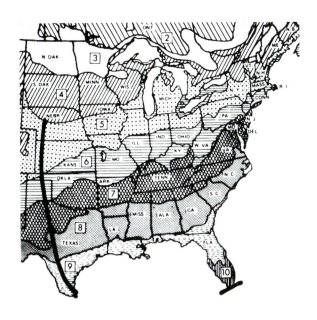

Buxus sempervirens L.　　　　　　　English or Common Box
Buxaceae or Boxwood Family　　　　　Hardiness Zone 5
Native to southern Europe, western Asia, and northern Africa.
SIZE: 3 to 4 feet tall to 20 feet or more, depending on cultivar. Slow growers.
FORM: Somewhat variable, but a round or oval-mounded, small to large shrub.
TEXTURE: Fine.　　　　　　　　　　**EXPOSURE:** Sun to shade.

LEAVES: Opposite, simple; elliptical to obovate to oblong, generally broader at the base, tapering to a point near the tip. Leaves may reach 1 to 1 1/4 inches long, and are dark green above and light green below with a smooth margin. The tip of the leaf is always pointed or rounded, never with the indentation typical of *Buxus harlandi* or *B. microphylla*.

STEM: Medium to light brown when young but with age may take on a gray-brown color. Slender young stems are multi-branched, yet fairly stiff, holding the foliage well in position except in heavy shade. Young stems are squarish on some cultivars. Axillary buds are quite bold during fall and winter.

FLOWERS: Inconspicuous.

FRUIT: Inconspicuous.

COLOR: Foliage is dark green.

PROPAGATION: Seed or cuttings of selected cultivars.

CULTURE: Full sun in the eastern United States, partial shade to shade in the South and Southwest. Any good, fertile soil with good drainage is suitable. In most instances, it can be planted and left alone with only an occasional pruning or spraying for control of leaf miners. The root system is quite compact and shallow, thus hoeing or other disturbance around the base of the plant should be avoided. Shears well into various forms or shapes.

PESTS: Leaf miners, spider mites, nematodes, and root rot, particularly in poorly drained areas or where heavily mulched and excessive moisture remains in the soil. Dogs' urine may burn foliage and, in some cases, kill entire branches.

NOTES: An elegant shrub attaining considerable size with a very fine texture. Good retention of foliage color in winter, thus making an excellent plant for specimens, screen, or accent. Leaves and stems may be mildly toxic. Can best be distinguished from *Buxus harlandi* or *B. microphylla* in that leaves tend to be broader at the base and tapering to a rounded point at the tip, not indented, whereas *B. harlandi* and *B. microphylla* leaves are broadest near the center and often have an indentation at the tip. *Buxus sempervirens* is a larger plant in most instances than the other two common species.

CULTIVARS: No doubt hundreds of cultivars exist since this plant has been in cultivation since the early days of the English and French. 'Arborescens' or 'Angustifolia': 10 to 12 feet tall and may reach 20 feet in the East or Southeast with a spread of 10 to 12 feet. Leaves tend to be more broad in the center, more pointed near the tip; very prominent buds in the leaf axils. Leaves frequently reach 1 to 1 1/2 inches long. 'Suffruticosa' or 'Dwarf Boxwood' rarely reaches a height of more than 2 to 3 feet with a spread of 2 to 3 feet. Somewhat globular shaped shrub with a billowy outline as it ages. Foliage is about 1 inch long.

HYBRIDS: 'Green Gem', 'Green Mountain', Green Mound', and 'Green Velvet' are *Buxus sempervirens* X *B. microphylla* hybrids. All are dark green, compact forms with 'Green Gem' the smallest, about 2 feet tall and 'Green Mountain' about 5 feet tall.

B. harlandi

Callistemon rigidus R.   Bottlebrush
Myrtaceae or Myrtle Family   Hardiness Zone 8 to 9
Native to Australia.
SIZE: 10 to 15 feet tall, irregular. Moderate to rapid grower.
FORM: Upright growing, medium to large shrub.
TEXTURE: Fine.   **EXPOSURE:** Sun.

LEAVES: More or less alternate, simple; 1 to 2 inches long. Linear, stiff and sharp-pointed at the tip with prominent, lateral mid-veins. Aromatic when crushed. Dark green above and only slightly lighter below. Foliage is somewhat willow-like.

STEM: Young stems are slender but stiff, not flexible or drooping, and red-brown, with prominent round terminal buds between flushes and during the dormant period in cooler regions. Growth is stiffly upright. Old stems are reddish brown to tan. Wood is stout.

FLOWERS: Terminal spikes, 3 to 4 inches long, and red with long stamens creating a bottlebrush effect. Spectacular. Each flower is sessile (no stalk). Blooms in spring and summer with occasional flowers in the fall.

FRUIT: Small, hard capsules surrounding the stem.

COLOR: Foliage is dark green. Flowers are red and spectacular.

PROPAGATION: Seed or cuttings.

CULTURE: A very tough, durable, heat- and drought-tolerant shrub which is sensitive to poorly drained soils and/or overwatering, probably due to root rot organisms. It is worthwhile to try a bottlebrush in a protected location in Zone 8 even if it means some special protection during the winter in order to have this added dimension in the landscape in spring and summer. Somewhat difficult to transplant as a large specimen. However, it transplants easily from containers when small.

PESTS: Generally none serious, although mites may be a problem in hot, dry locations.

NOTES: An attractive shrub with spectacular flowers. Useful as a tub or patio specimen even where it is not cold hardy. However, it needs lots of sunshine, thus it cannot be used as a conventional houseplant.

CULTIVARS: 'Nana': a dwarf form remaining more compact and growing more slowly than the parent. Others exist in localized areas.

RELATED SPECIES: *Callistemon citrinus* Stapf., the citrus-leaved bottlebrush, grows to 20 feet or more but is hardy only in Zones 9b or 10. Leaves smell like citrus when crushed and are soft, flexible, and expecially fuzzy when young. Flowers are similar in size and color; very showy. Flowery stems often droop, giving the plant a weeping appearance. Several cultivars have been named in localized areas.

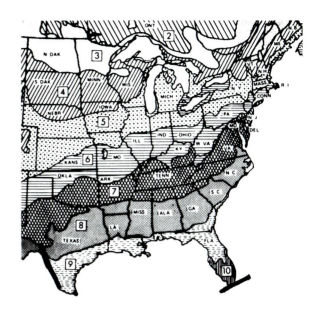

Camellia japonica L.   Japanese Camellia
Theaeceae or Tea Family   Hardiness Zone 7b (flower buds are less hardy)
Native to China and Japan.
SIZE: Commonly found as shrubs 4 to 6 feet tall but may reach as much as 20 to 30 feet as extremely old plants. Generally slow to moderate growers.
FORM: Generally broadly pyramidal with loose, arching branches. Considerable variation between the many cultivars.
TEXTURE: Medium.   **EXPOSURE**: Partial shade to shade.

LEAVES: Alternate, simple; and ovate on short, stiff petioles. Generally 3 to 4 inches long, 1 1/2 to two inches wide. Bluntly pointed at the tip and with a finely sawtooth margin. The upper surface is deep, glossy green; lower surface is light dull green.

STEM: Generally upright with multiple leaders and medium to slender secondary branches which are roughly parallel to the ground. Older stems are smooth and frequently take on a rather mottled green to gray-green appearance due to the growth of lichens. Wood is fairly strong and durable.

FLOWERS: Brilliant colors: pink, reds, white and various shades. Single or double, up to 5 inches in diameter. Selected and hybridized by both professional and amateur gardeners for many years. Many, many cultivars available with variation in flower color, size, and time of bloom. Several cultivars have variegated flowers.

FRUIT: Only occasionally seen. Round or ovate, may reach as much as 1 to 1 1/2 inches in diameter, generally remaining green until dropping from the plant.

COLOR: Foliage is deep green and very attractive under most circumstances. Flowers are white, pink, or red; very showy.

PROPAGATION: Cuttings, air layers, or grafting of cultivars onto seedlings.

CULTURE: Camellias do best in fertile acid soil with adequate moisture. This can be assisted by modifying or amending the soils and mulching heavily. Where soils are very heavy clays, it may be necessary to grow the plant upon a mound of superior light fill soil, then heavily mulch with pine bark, straw, or other material to assist moisture retention. They grow best in partial shade. In full sun, the plants become less attractive and may flower less. In very dense shade, likewise, flowering may be suppressed and plants may become more open and spindly. In upper portions of Zone 8 and Zone 7, camellias may be used as broadleaf evergreen shrubs where the foliage does very well with little, if any, discoloration; however, the flowers are generally killed by early fall freezes.

PESTS: Tea scale is probably the most severe problem in the South. Look for white cottony scales on the underneath side of the older leaves.

NOTES: Grown for many years both as outdoor plants throughout the South and as pot plants in more northern areas. The time of bloom is late fall to winter for many cultivars and is rather unusual in the flowering period of most other landscape plants. By selecting cultivars carefully, a succession of blooms can be developed that begins in early November and continues through early spring. May be used as specimen plants, hedges, foundation plantings, or in other ways depending on the choice of the designer. In more northern areas, camellias do make an excellent broadleaf evergreen shrub, even though the flowers are generally lost. Some cultivars reportedly are hardy in Zone 5 in the Northeast United States. *C. japonica* can best be distinguished from *C. sasanqua* by the leaves of *C. japonica* which are larger and more leathery and are ovate instead of oblong to lanceolate.

CULTIVARS: Many, many exist. Readers are referred to one of the many reference books exclusively on camellias for the many cultivars.

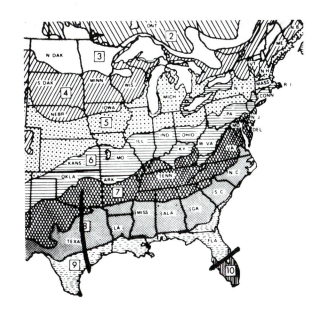

'Pink Perfection'

'Snow Queen'

Camellia sasanqua Thunb.　　　　　　Sasanqua Camellia
Theaceae or Tea Family　　　　　　Hardiness Zone 7 (flower buds are less hardy)
Native to China and Japan.

SIZE: Commonly found as shrubs 4 to 6 feet tall but may reach as much as 10 to 15 feet tall in extremely old plants. Slow to moderate growers.

FORM: Generally pyramidal with loosely arching branches.

TEXTURE: Medium.　　　　　　**EXPOSURE:** Sun to shade.

LEAVES: Alternate, simple; ovate to lanceolate on short, stiff petioles. Leaves are 1 1/2 to 2 1/2 inches long and 1 to 1 1/2 inches wide with a finely sawtooth margin. The upper surface is deep, glossy green, and the lower surface is light dull green.

STEM: Generally upright with multiple leaders and medium to slender secondary branching. Older stems are smooth and frequently take on a mottled green to gray-green appearance due to the growth of lichens. The wood is fairly strong and durable.

FLOWERS: Single or double, up to 3 inches in diameter. Brilliant colors: pinks, reds, lavenders, or white. Selected and hybridized by both professional and amateur gardeners for many years. Many, many cultivars available with variation in flower color, size, and time of bloom. Several cultivars have variegated flowers. Flowers are generally slightly smaller and more open than on Japanese camellia.

FRUIT: Only occasionally seen. Round or ovate, sometimes reaches as much as 1 inch in diameter, generally remaining green until dropping from the plant.

COLOR: Foliage is deep green and very attractive under most circumstances. Flowers are white, pinks, reds, or lavenders. Very showy.

PROPAGATION: Cuttings with difficulty, air layers, or grafting.

CULTURE: Camellias do best in moist acid soils. This can be assisted by modifying or amending the soils and mulching heavily. Where soils are very heavy clays, it may be necessary to grow the plant on a mound of good fill soil, then mulch heavily with pine bark, straw, or other material to assist moisture retention and insure drainage for the root system. They grow best in partial shade or in full sun as long as the site is not excessively hot. In very dense shade, flowering may be suppressed and plants become spindly and open. In the upper portions of Zone 8 and Zone 7, they may be used as a broadleaf evergreen shrubs where the foliage does very well, but the flowers are often killed by early freezes. Slightly less rugged and cold hardy than most cultivars of Japanese camellia.

PESTS: Tea scale is probably the most severe problem in the lower South. Look for white cottony scales on the underneath side of older leaves.

NOTES: Grown for many years both as outdoor plants throughout the South and as pot plants in more northern areas. Their early to late fall bloom time is rather unusual compared to the flowering period of most other ornamental landscape plants. By selecting cultivars carefully, a succession of blooms can be developed that begins in early November and continues through early spring. May be used as specimen plants, hedges, or foundation plantings in a number of ways depending on the choice of the designer. In more northern areas, camellias make an excellent broadleaf evergreen shrub even though the flowers are generally lost. Some cultivars are reportedly hardy in Zone 6 in the northeastern United States. Sasanqua camellia can best be distinguished from Japanese camellia in that the leaves of sasanqua are smaller and less leathery, are ovate to lanceolate instead of ovate to oblong, and the flowers are generally smaller and more open.

CULTIVARS: Many, many exist. Readers are referred to one of the many reference books exclusively on camellias for the many cultivars.

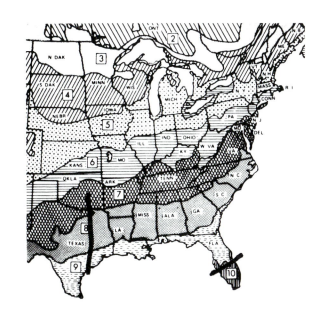

C. sasanqua   C. japonica

Carissa grandiflora A.DC.   Natal Plum or Carissa
Apocynaceae or Dogbane Family   Hardiness Zone 9
Native to South Africa.
SIZE: 3 to 8 feet tall, depending on cultivar; wider spread. Moderate grower.
FORM: Dense, mounded shrub.
TEXTURE: Medium.   **EXPOSURE:** Sun to some shade.

LEAVES: Evergreen. Opposite, simple; about 1 1/2 to 2 inches long and 1 to 1/2 inches wide. More or less oval with a prickle at the tip. Very dark green. The leaves are thick and leathery and exude a white, milky sap when damaged.

STEM: Stiff and stout. Green at first turning brown with age. The stem has a stiff, branched spine at intervals throughout.

FLOWERS: White and fragrant; about 2 inches in diameter. The petals overlap to the left. Very symmetrical, appearing star-like or almost like a fan such that if you blew on it, it would turn.

FRUIT: Red, plum-like; matures throughout the year; about 2 inches long. Attractive and edible.

COLOR: Leaves are dark green. Flowers are white. Fruits are red.

PROPAGATION: Cuttings of selected cultivars root easily.

CULTURE: A very tough, tolerant shrub, **but**, it cannot stand poor drainage. It grows well in near sterile sands along the coast and with some salt spray and considerable salt in the soil as long as drainage is good. The spines are sharp yet the hazard is minimal since the spines are back in among the leaves. Grows well in deep containers and with a mix that drains well. Will tolerate only moderate frosts, thus must be moved indoors in winter in all but central and south Florida. However, its tolerance to heat, salts, and drought makes it a good choice for large containers that can be moved indoors or protected in winter. The specimen at right is in a movable container in a hot, sunny locations but in an area where it would be killed by winter temperatures.

PESTS: Few; occasionally scale insects.

NOTES: Carissa is a beautiful shrub where it can be grown out-of-doors or when used in large containers. The white flowers and red fruits against the dark green foliage make it appear as if decorated for Christmas. The spines clearly suggest "keep your hands off", but not a hazard to life and limb like a few species are.

CULTIVARS: 'Boxwood Beauty': probably the most widely grown. A dwarf, rarely obtaining more than 3 feet in height, but quite dense. The plant in the photograph was probably this cultivar. Other cultivar names appear but to this author's eye, they do not differ significantly from 'Boxwood Beauty'.

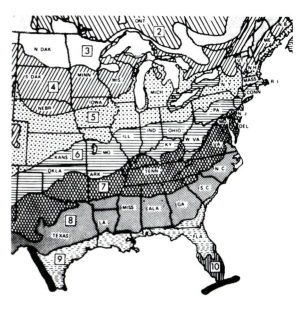

Cinnamomum camphora (L.) Nees & Eberm.   Camphor Tree
Lauraceae or Laurel Family   Hardiness Zone 9
Native to China and Japan
SIZE: 30 to 50 feet tall with a 40- to 60-foot spread. Rapid grower.
FORM: Tree with single or multiple stem; low-branching and rounded crown.
TEXTURE: Medium.   **EXPOSURE:** Sun.

LEAVES: Alternate (but sometimes appear opposite), simple; ovate, 2 to 4 inches long with a smooth but wavy margin. Leaves are glossy, dark green above, very attractive, and light green below. Give off a distinct camphor odor when crushed.

STEM: Young stems up to 2 inches in diameter are green and smooth, with distinct circular lines at each node. Young stems are slender and flexible. Old stems turn an ash gray with irregular vertical furrows adding interest to the bark. Wood is moderately stout, but not readily damaged by wind.

FLOWERS: Green and inconspicuous in the leaf axils on slender stalks.

FRUIT: Black and glossy on slender stalks. Appear a bit like a baseball sitting on a wine glass. About 1/4 inch in diameter with a single seed. Seeds are readily viable and germinate everywhere becoming a maintenance problem.

COLOR: Leaves are dark, glossy green; especially striking when young.

PROPAGATION: By seed or softwood cuttings.

CULTURE: Grows on most soils but is most vigorous on a moist, sandy loam with high fertilizer. Develops a dense shade and with the low, spreading crown and shallow roots, few plants or grasses grow beneath it. May develop iron chlorosis on alkaline soils.

PESTS: Few, if any, perhaps because of the oils in the leaves.

NOTES: A very attractive, broadly spreading tree with glossy, green foliage. Very adaptable. Makes a good street tree except for the messy fruits. Has escaped along the Gulf Coast and Florida. A weed tree of sorts, but has better qualities than some of the other weed trees it has replaced. Useful in parks and open public places where a tree with broadly spreading characteristics and low limbs can develop and be appreciated. A great tree for climbing. Too big for most urban lots and single story dwellings. Sustained cold below 20 degrees F will damage the new growth and cause most leaves to drop, but it generally recovers quickly. Camphor is extracted from the wood and used to ease aching muscles and for other medicinal purposes.

CULTIVARS: 'Majestic Beauty': dark green leaves and more uniform growth habit. Otherwise, like the species.

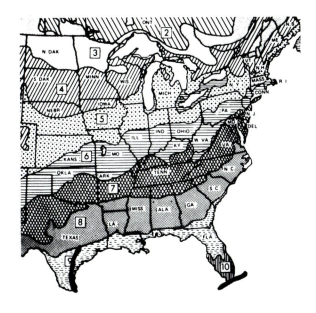

Cleyera japonica Thunb. (Syn. see below)　　　Cleyera
Theaceae or Tea Family　　　Hardiness Zone 7
Native from Japan to India.
SIZE: May reach 20 feet tall with a spread of 6 to 8 feet. Slow to moderate grower.
FORM: Upright-growing small tree or large shrub.
TEXTURE: Medium.　　　　　　　　　**EXPOSURE:** Sun to shade.

LEAVES: Alternate, simple; oblong to lanceolate, about 3 inches long, and 1/2 inch wide. Generally few veins visible on the upper leaf surface. The underneath leaf color is generally a light green; upper leaf surface is generally a deep, almost blue-green color in the shade, lighter green in full sun. The petiole is very short, stout, and nearly always red or purple-red in color, making it very distinct.

STEM: Branches are slender, generally dark gray, and moderately dense with pruning: may be rather open and loose if left unattended. Leaves are generally clustered at the tips of the young branches giving it a tufted appearance.

FLOWERS: Pale yellow, about 1/2 inch in diameter, hanging down from the slender stems. Generally occurring late spring or early summer. Not showy or fragrant.

FRUIT: May reach 1/2 inch in diameter and 1 inch long: egg-shaped. Green when young, becoming red to purple with maturity in late summer or early fall.

COLOR: Foliage is deep metallic blue-green in shady locations; medium green in full sun.

PROPAGATION: Seed. Readily germinates if collected in the fall and planted the following spring. Moderate variability among seedlings. Semi-hardwood or hardwood cuttings can also be successful with very small quantities of mist and auxin.

CULTURE: Moderate tolerance to soil conditions; however, it appears to do best in partial shade to shade or on the east or north side of structures. It does not tolerate heat, high light intensity, exposure, or poorly drained soils. Responds reasonably well to pruning.

PESTS: None serious.

NOTES: A rather unique foliage color and texture combination. Can be easily maintained as a 3- to 5-foot shrub in shady locations with moderate pruning. It is commonly propagated by seed and thus variation does exist among available plants. In the Southwest, it takes on a bronze color in winter but generally retains its leaves well. Because of adaptability to shade and unique foliage color, it should be used more.

　　For some reason the name was changed from *Cleyera japonica* to *Ternstroemia japonica* to *Ternstroemia gymnanthera* to what's next? By whatever name, it is a useful and attractive broadleaf evergreen. The name, cleyera, is firmly entrenched in the industry...at least as a common name.

CULTIVARS: 'Variegata' (sometimes listed as 'Tricolor'): has yellow mottled leaves. Similar to the parent in growth and adaptability.

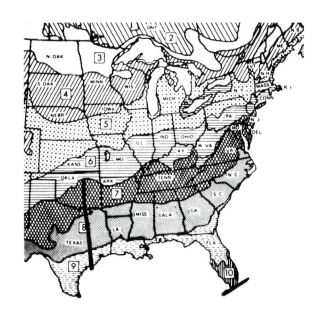

'Variegata'

Dasylirion texanum Scheele   Sotol or Bear Grass
Agavaceae or Agave Family   Hardiness Zone 8
Native to Texas, New Mexico, and Mexico.
SIZE: 2 to 3 feet tall, 5 to 6 feet across. Flowers may reach 12 to 15 feet.
FORM: A rounding mound of sword-like leaves.
TEXTURE: Medium.   **EXPOSURE:** Sun.

LEAVES: Sword-like, 2 to 3 feet long, 1/2 to 1 inch wide with many yellow-green spines on the margin. Radiate out from the stem or crown of the plant, making an attractive clump. Dark to medium green. Leaves do not have a rib which helps distinguish sotol from yucca species.

STEM: Below ground and rarely seen, or just a few inches above ground and covered by the leaf mass.

FLOWERS: On long, slender stalks up to 15 feet tall. Individual flowers are in "worm-like" clusters on the main stalk (see photograph). Golden yellow or white and remain for several weeks.

FRUIT: Small, dry capsule containing a single seed. Not showy.

COLOR: Dark to medium green foliage. Golden yellow or white flowers.

PROPAGATION: Seed.

CULTURE: Native to the desert areas of west Texas, New Mexico, and Mexico and will not tolerate heavy clay soils and poor drainage. Very drought- and heat-tolerant, including reflected heat and drought caused by porous soils in raised planters. Roots will not survive in raised planters at temperatures much below freezing.

PESTS: Few to none.

NOTES: An attractive, low shrub to be used with or in place of yucca or agave species. Especially useful in parking lots and near street corners where heat and desert-like conditions exist, but plants must be low enough for visual access. Should be used more, particularly when full sun to reflected light and heat conditions limit use of other landscape plants. Because of the low growth habit, it may be used in front of plantings of yucca or agave which grow taller. An excellent low-maintenance shrub, well-adapted to the city desert. however, avoid planting in areas where water drains from surrounding pavement onto the soil. Old flower stalks should be removed. Dasylirion means tufted lily.

CULTIVARS: 'Claucum': has bluish foliage.

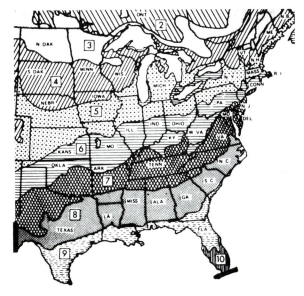

Elaeagnus pungens Thunb.   Thorny Elaeagnus
Elaeagnaceae or Elaeagnus Family   Hardiness Zone 6b
Native to Japan.
SIZE: 8 to 12 feet tall with an 8- to 10-foot spread. Moderate to rapid grower.
FORM: An irregular, semi-upright, large, spreading shrub.
TEXTURE: Medium.   **EXPOSURE:** Sun to partial shade.

LEAVES: Alternate, simple; silver-gray-green. Oval to oblong, 1 1/2 to 2 1/2 inches long and 1 to 1 1/2 inches wide, with a smooth but wavy margin. Underside of older leaves and both upper and lower surfaces of new leaves are covered with irregular scales, giving a flaky, silver appearance. Petioles are short and stout.

STEM: Grows irregularly. Frequently long suckers develop from he crown of the plant, reaching 6 to 8 feet tall in a very short time. Requires frequent pruning. The stems, buds, and twigs are all covered with silver scales. The young bud is irregular but somewhat bulbous. Irregular, long, slender thorns are found on most vigorous new shoots. Thorns are not especially stout, but could be hazardous under certain circumstances.

FLOWERS: Silver-brown; funnelform, about 1/2 inch long. Not showy but very fragrant. Generally appear in mid to late fall.

FRUIT: A 1/2-inch berry, short-stalked; silver-green, turns red when ripe in late fall.

COLOR: Foliage is silver-gray-green. Flowers are silver-brown. Fruit is red.

PROPAGATION: Semi-hardwood cuttings.

CULTURE: Grows well in many difficult situation. Tolerates high heat, drought, some-what wet locations, full sun, partial shade, and a wide range of soil conditions. Requires frequent pruning. Probably the greatest limitation is the rapid regrowth from suckers in the crown following even moderate pruning. needs plenty of space. Elaeagnus has a symbiotic nitrogen-fixing bacteria associated with the roots. This allows the plant to do well on poor soils and very sandy soils which have very limited nitrogen.

PESTS: Spider mites can occasionally become a problem and are difficult to detect be-cause of the scale-like leaf hairs. Sensitive to some herbicides in the landscape.

NOTES: An unusual growth habit is due to the production of vigorous suckers at the crown. The production of trichomes which are the snowflake-like modified hairs that cover the leaves, stems, bud and fruits, give the plant a silvery sheen. makes an excellent screen where ample space is available. Attracts birds.

CULTIVARS: 'Aurea': leaves with yellow margins. 'Fruitlandi': rounded leaves with wavy margins and may be more densely branched than the parent. 'Maculata': leaves with yellow blotch in the center. 'Nana': a dwarf form. Several localized cultivars of this type are available, named or unnamed. Generally considered to sucker less and retain a more dense, compact growth form than that of other cultivars or the species. 'Simonii': leaves are variegated yellow and pinkish white.

RELATED SPECIES: *Elaeagnus macrophylla*: Thun., silverberry, is hardy in Zone 6b, has larger leaves than thorny elaeagnus and no spines on the stem. Silverbeery is a more compact grower with less tendency to sucker at the base than thorny elaeagnus. A superior plant for most uses. 'Ebbengi': more upright and attractive than *Elaeagnus pungens* 'Fruit-landi' and has dark green foliage. Perhaps a hybrid with *E. pungens*. Confusion exists in the nursery trade as to the identity of the two species and their cultivars. However, sil-verberry has considerably larger leaves, no spines on the stems, and stays thick and full to the ground. A superior plant for most landscape uses.

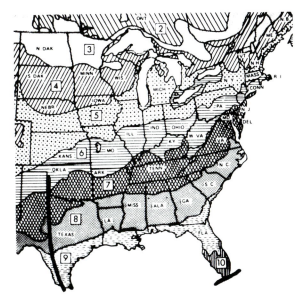

E. macrophylla   E. pungens

E. macrophylla

Eriobotrya japonica Lindl.   Loquat
Rosaceae or Rose Family   Hardiness Zone 8
Native to China and Japan.
SIZE: 20 to 25 feet tall with a spread of 20 to 25 feet. Moderate grower.
FORM: Small tree with a rounded crown.
TEXTURE: Coarse.   **EXPOSURE:** Sun to partial shade.

LEAVES: Alternate, simple; on a very short petiole, crowded on the terminal shoots which gives a rosette or clustered appearance. Individual leaves may be 4 to 12 inches long, 2 to 4 inches wide, are stiff and firm, and oval or oblong with prominent teeth on the margin. Leaf veins are prominent on the upper surface. Leaves are dark green above, underneath is pale green covered with dense, rusty colored hairs. Young leaves contrast with older leaves, from a distance appearing more like flowers.

STEM: Stout; green at first, but soon turning brown. Young stems are densely wooly, but the hair is lost with age. Older stems are brown to dark gray, become smooth, and finally develop a shallowly flaking bark. Not showy.

FLOWERS: Generally appear from August through early fall. Slightly fragrant and in terminal clusters. Yellow to white. Not showy.

FRUIT: Develops in spring or late winter. A small, pear-shaped, yellow fruit that is 1 1/2 to 2 inches long; edible and tasty. May not mature north of Zone 9.

COLOR: Foliage is dark green. Fruit is yellow.

PROPAGATION: Seed or grafting of selected cultivars.

CULTURE: Hardiest of the tropical fruits. Grows in a wide range of circumstances across the southern states and as far west as San Antonio and El Paso, Texas, if irrigated. Does reasonably well on poor soils and tolerates alkaline soils. Moderately drought-resistant. Responds well to fertilization. However, one of the major problems is fire blight, and excessive fertilization tends to increase this problem. Should be planted in open areas with good air drainage to assist in suppressing this disease problem.

PESTS: Fire blight is most serious. Some cultivars are said to have some resistance to fire blight. However, this is doubtful. Best resistance is a healthy plant in an exposed location with good air movement and away from other fire blight susceptible plants such as crabapples, apples, pears, and some pyracanthas.

NOTES: An attractive, small tree with coarse-textured foliage. Reminiscent of southern magnolia but with a low, spreading, umbrella-like crown. More suitable as a shade tree or landscape specimen. Keep in full sun and away from structures where air movement may be restricted. Fruits are tasty, and some cultivars are more prolific fruit producers than others. Widely planted throughout the warmer areas of the South.

CULTIVARS: 'Golden Nugget': large, pear-shaped yellow fruit; particularly desirable. Many others exist.

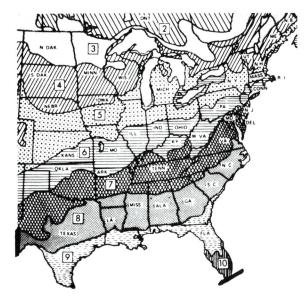

fireblight

Euonymus japonica Thunb. Evergreen Euonymus
Celastraceae or Euonymus Family Hardiness Zone 7
Native to Japan.

SIZE: 10 to 12 feet in height with a 4- to 5-foot spread. Moderate to rapid grower.

FORM: An erect-growing, compact, evergreen shrub. If left unpruned, it will develop an oval form. Frequently used as a sheared shrub or as a hedge plant.

TEXTURE: Medium. **EXPOSURE:** Sun to shade.

LEAVES: Opposite, simple; 1 1/2 to 3 inches long, and 1 to 1 1/2 inches wide. Ovate to elliptical with a slightly sawtooth margin. Glossy deep green above, light green below. Leaves are nearly always upright, at about a 45-degree angle with the vertical stem and never drooping.

STEM: Remains green for several years. Between growth flushes or during the dormant period, large axillary buds are very prominent, particularly on the young wood. With some age, the wood becomes a light gray or light tan. Moderately durable and flexible and makes a good hedge because of the many branches. Generally no aerial roots.

FLOWERS: Small, white clusters from the leaf axils. Not showy.

FRUIT: Small, about 1/4 inch in diameter, with 3 to 5 rounded sections, and gray-tan. Eventually splits to expose several pink, fleshy, coated seeds. Rarely in large numbers.

COLOR: Foliage is deep green and glossy.

PROPAGATION: Semi-hardwood or hardwood cuttings. Very easy.

CULTURE: A very tough, durable landscape shrub. Tolerates pruning exceptionally well to make a dense hedge or irregular mound, whichever feature is desired. Grows well in moist soil and tolerates considerable drought. Will survive in poor soil with poor nutrition, but responds to fertilizer with an enormous flush of growth. Grows in full sun or will do well in partial or very dense shade. A versatile plant, sometimes used as a house plant.

PESTS: The principle pest is euonymus scale. This insect becomes so serious as to limit the use of evergreen euonymus in most landscape situations. The damage from the pest, besides making the plant unsightly, affects the winter hardiness. Mildew may be a problem on new growth on sites with poor air drainage.

NOTES: An extremely useful landscape plant because of its tolerance to soils, moisture, sunlight, and pruning. The serious weakness in the plant is its susceptibility to euonymus scale. It is probably the most susceptible species to euonymus scale, followed by creeping euonymus, and then spreading euonymus. Rarely is scale seen on deciduous species of euonymus. Foliage and fruits may be mildly poisonous. Sometimes confused with spreading euonymus or creeping euonymus. Evergreen euonymus stems are very upright and no aerial roots are present. The leaves are all angled upright, never drooping, whereas spreading euonymus stems are at various angles, many at 60-degree angles and the leaves generally droop or hang from the stem. Creeping euonymus is principally a vine or vine-like ground cover with somewhat drooping leaves and a more prostrate habit of growth, and aerial roots generally are present on the stems. ??-POISON-??

CULTIVARS: 'Aureo-marginata', golden euonymus, has dark green leaves with a bright gold margin. 'Aureo-varigata': medium green leaves with yellow blotches. Quite compact. 'Microphyllus': dwarf, extremely compact form with leaves generally 1/2 to 1 inch long, rarely reaching more than 12 to 15 inches in overall height. 'Silver King': leaves are pale green and blotched with creamy white of varying intensities. Many other cultivars exist.

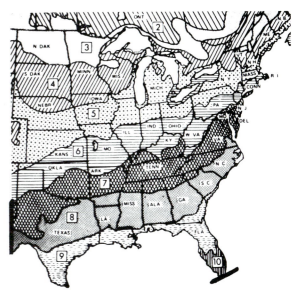

'Aureo-marginata'

'Silver King'

'Microphyllus'

Euonymus kiautschovica Loes. (Syn. *E. patens*)   Spreading Euonymus
Celastraceae or Euonymus Family   Hardiness Zone 6
Native to eastern and central China.
SIZE: 8 to 10 feet tall with a spread of 8 to 10 feet.   Rapid grower.
FORM: Broadly spreading, somewhat irregular shrub.
TEXTURE: Medium.   EXPOSURE: Sun to shade.

LEAVES: Opposite, simple; 1 to 2 inches long, and broadly elliptical to oblong with a sawtooth margin. Tend to droop or weep. Upper leaf surface is a light pale green, much lighter in color and less plastic-like in appearance than leaves of evergreen euonymus.

STEM: Spreading irregularly, some branches will be low to the ground, others at varying angles, making a broadly spreading, dense shrub. Generally with large buds in the leaf axils and moderate branch production along the stems. Stems remain green for several years, eventually turning gray-brown. Aerial roots may form on stems in humid locations.

FLOWERS: In small, greenish white clusters among the leaves. Not showy.

FRUIT: A 3- to 5-celled capsule that is pale gray-green. Eventually splits to expose the orange, fleshy coating of the seed by early October. May be as many as 8 in a cluster. Fruit production is variable with site and cultivar.

COLOR: Foliage is light green. Fruit is orange.

PROPAGATION: Semi-hardwood or hardwood cuttings. Very easy.

CULTURE: A tough, rapid-growing shrub. Tolerates a wide range of soil conditions and full sun to moderate shade. Does not respond to pruning as well as evergreen euonymus and is a less prolific brancher. Responds well to fertilizer and is moderately drought-resistant.

PESTS: Scale, but spreading euonymus is the least susceptible to scale of the evergreen euonymus species. However, under certain circumstances, scale may become serious. Rabbits and pack rats may be a serious problem on young plants in rural areas.

NOTES: A good shrub for screens, massing, borders, foundations, and background plantings. Foliage and fruits may be mildly poisonous. Frequently confused with some cultivars of creeping euonymus and evergreen euonymus. By comparison, spreading euonymus is a broadly spreading shrub with somewhat large, drooping, medium green leaves, whereas evergreen euonymus is an erect-growing shrub, with erect, deep green leaves. Creeping euonymus is a low, spreading shrub or ground cover with somewhat drooping leaves and nearly always has aerial roots present somewhere on the stem. However, spreading euonymus and creeping euonymus cultivars will sometimes confuse even the experienced plantsman. ??-POISON-??

CULTIVARS: 'Manhattan': hardiest of the cultivars (Zone 5). Leaves are 1 1/2 to 2 1/2 inches long. More evergreen than the other cultivars and perhaps slightly more compact. A vigorous grower and tolerant of a wide range of conditions. 'Vincafolia': slightly smaller leaves than the species. Moderately compact-growing shrub. Should be used only in the lower portion of Zone 7 and southward due to less winter hardiness. Other cultivars exist but with only minor variations.

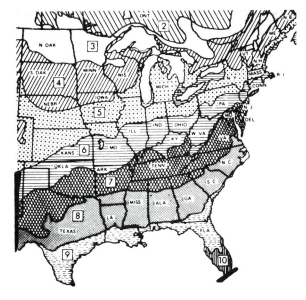

E. japonica   E. kiautschovica

E. japonica   E. kiautschovica

Euonymus scale

Fatsia japonica (Thunb.) Decne. & Planch.   Japanese Fatsia
         (Syn. *Aralia japonica*)   Hardiness Zone 8
Araliaceae or Aralia Family
Native to Japan.
SIZE: 5- to 7-foot shrub with 4- to 6-foot spread. Moderate to rapid grower.
FORM: Irregular, rounded to semi-upright shrub.
TEXTURE: Coarse.   **EXPOSURE:** Partial shade to shade.

LEAVES: Alternate or spirally arranged on the stem, palmately compound with 7 to 9 leaflets or fingers fused together at the base on a long, moderately stout, petiole. The central vein in each finger or leaflet is very prominent. margin of the leaf is smooth or irregularly coarsely toothed. One compound leaf may be as much as 12 to 16 inches long and 8 to 12 inches wide, including the petiole or leaf stalk. Glossy, deep green above; pale green below. Very showy. Retains good color throughout the winter with in partial shade to shady locations.

STEM: Large and coarse. May reach a diameter of 1/2 inch or more at the tip and several inches at the base. Remains green. Not stout and is easily damaged by vandalism or physical abuse.

FLOWERS: Small, white; in rounded clusters above the foliage.

FRUIT: Small, rounded, blue berries in clusters.

COLOR: Foliage is deep, dark green.

PROPAGATION: Seed or cuttings.

CULTURE: Tolerant to a wide range of soil conditions from light sandy to heavy clay soils with moderate to poor drainage. Responds with vigor to fertilization, mulching, reduction of weed competition, and partial shade to shady exposure. Does not do well in full sun or hot, dry, southern, or western exposures.

PESTS: None serious.

NOTES: A foliage plant with very coarse texture. Gives the effect of a tropical foliage plant. Sometimes used in combination with *Aucuba japonica*, Japanese aucuba, to create a tropical effect. Once established in the landscape, it needs little additional attention. Japanese fatsia may also be used as a house plant or a plant for indoor landscaping, since it tolerates low humidity and low light intensity very well. Tolerates cold to about 10 degrees F.

CULTIVARS: 'Moseri': a more compact-growing form. 'Variegata': leaves are bordered with golden yellow. Others probably exist.

RELATED SPECIES: *Fatshedera lizei* is a hybrid between *Hedera helix*, English ivy, and *Fatsia japonica*. It is a semi-climbing shrub or vine with glossy evergreen leaves with 5 to 7 lobes. Hardy in Zone 8 but often used for indoor landscaping. *Fatshedera lizei* 'Variegata': has white leaf margins.

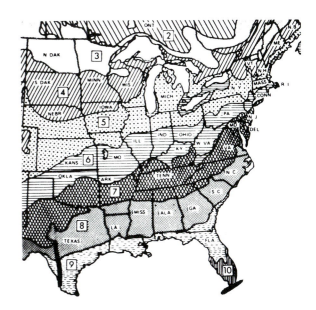

Fatshedera lizei

Fatshedera lizei

Feijoa Sellowiana O.Berg.   Pineapple Guava or Feijoa
Myrtaceae or Myrtle Family   Hardiness Zone 8
Native to Brazil and Argentina
SIZE: 10 to 20 feet tall with a 8- to 12-foot spread. Fast grower.
FORM: Rounded or mounding large shrub or small tree.
TEXTURE: Medium.   **EXPOSURE:** Sun or partial shade.

LEAVES: Opposite, simple; elliptical, ping-pong paddle-shaped. Light to medium green above, and silvery white below due to dense, fine hairs. Margins are smooth and petioles are very short. Leaves may be 2 to 3 inches long and 1 to 2 inches wide.

STEMS: Young stems are nearly white and covered with dense hairs at first, later dropping to expose a smooth, light tan stem. The wood is stout and old stems develop a cinnamon red color: very attractive.

FLOWERS: Very attractive. Fragrant, peppermint-like in that the outside 4 petals are white, while the stamens (internal flower parts) are bright red. Flowers in April or May, depending on geographic locations.

FRUIT: Edible. Round, 1 1/2 to 2 1/2 inches in diameter, with protruding old flower parts. Greenish white, turning yellow at maturity. Flesh is creamy and jelly-like. Generally several plants are needed for fruit production. Plants fruit best in full sun. Fruit production is not common in the southeastern United States.

COLOR: Attractive foliage and bark, especially on tree form. Flowers are colored like peppermints.

PROPAGATION: Seed or grafting of fruit selections; difficult to root from cuttings.

CULTURE: Best adapted to drier sites or well drained soils. Grows very well on the sands of Florida but performs poorly on heavy, poorly drained clay. Plants are more dense and compact in full sun and in more northern locations. Can be sheared or heavily pruned to form a dense hedge or visual screen. Very effective in stopping noise in the urban landscape due to dense, hairy leaves.

PESTS: None serious, except root rot diseases on poorly drained soils.

NOTES: An attractive, useful, large shrub or small tree. Dense leaves create a good screen or sound barrier. has potential as a multiple-stemmed small tree for planters or around patios and outdoor living areas. The attractive bark, flowers, and underside of the leaves provide a unique blend of landscape quality. The fragrance of the flowers is an additional plus. the fruits are tasty but do not commonly form and mature in the southeastern states.

CULTIVARS; 'Coolidge' and 'Pineapple Gem' are self fruiting and are said to be superior fruit producers. Numerous other cultivars have been named, primarily for fruit quality. However, because seed propagation is the only practical means of propagation, more cultivars for the southern United States are not likely.

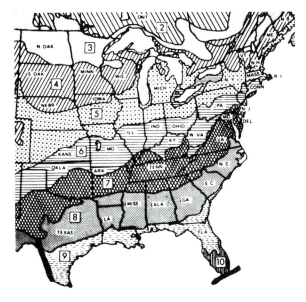

Gardenia jasminoides Ellis.　　　　　　　　　Gardenia, or Cape Jamine
Rubiaceae or Madder Family　　　　　　　　　Hardiness Zone 8
Native to China.
SIZE: 5- to 8-foot shrub. Rapid grower.
FORM: Irregular shrub.
TEXTURE: Medium to coarse.　　　　　　　**EXPOSURE:** Sun or partial shade.

LEAVES: Opposite, or in whorls of 3 and simple. Leathery, 3 to 4 inches long, 1 to 2 inches wide, with a smooth margin. Upper leaf surface is glossy, dark green with prominent folds or undulations at the veins. Stipules are usually present at the base of the petiole. Leaves frequently are yellow or an off-green due to iron chlorosis in Florida.

STEM; Young stems are smooth and green, eventually turning tan or brown. Wood is not stout, but flexible and not readily broken.

FLOWERS; White. Up to 3 inches across, single or double, **extremely fragrant**: in some cases, too much of a good thing. Appear sporadically in early summer and until cool weather, or in early spring in a greenhouse.

FRUIT: A single-seeded berry; not commonly seen.

COLOR: Foliage is dark, glossy green. Flowers are white, showy, and extremely fragrant.

PROPAGATION: Semi-hardwood cuttings.

CULTURE: Gardenias are easy to grow in s sunny location with good soils, drainage, and fertility. However, in many urban locations, they do not do well, especially where soils are poor, are poorly drained heavy clays. Very much subject to iron chlorosis where construction debris has increased pH and decreased iron availability. Several applications of elemental sulfur at 3 pounds per 100 square feet every 6 months will slowly lower the pH and release the iron in most soil. In extreme cases, other treatments or excavation and replacement of the soil is the only solution. Mulching also assists moisture control and aids soil acidity.

PESTS: Many. Very susceptible to aphids, mites, white flies, scale insects, and nematodes. Anyone planting gardenias should be well aware of the maintenance required to keep them healthy. Nearly require as much maintenance as roses.

NOTES: An Old South favorite. Commonly planted without consideration for the pest control problem. Sooty mold growing on debris of aphids destroys the visual quality of an otherwise spectacular plant. The aroma from the flowers is powerful and lasts for three or four weeks. Do not plant near a bedrrom window because the flowers bloom during warm weather when windows may be open.

CULTIVARS: 'August Beauty': dense, glossy foliage and large double flowers. Veitchi': an early bloomer with medium-sized flowers. 'Glazeri', 'Miami Supreme', and 'Mystery' are similar, with flowers 3 to 4 inches across, and later blooming than 'Veitchi'. Probably the best cultivars. 'Belmont': has many large flowers and good foliage. 'Radicans': the same as 'Prostrata', a low-growing cultivar, generally not exceeding 2 feet in height but spreading horizontally several feet. Can be used as a ground cover or to trail over a retaining wall. Subject to all the insect and soil problems of the parent. Flowers are white, fragrant, and about 2 inches across; leaves are shorter and more slender and the veins are not prominent like those of the parent (see photographs).

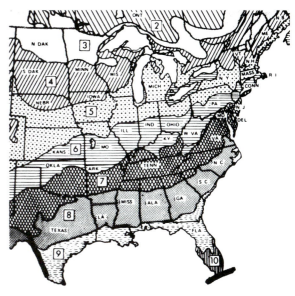

'Vetchi'

'Radicans'

'Radicans'

Gelsemium sempervirens (L.)Air.f.   Carolina Yellow Jessamine
Loganiaceae or Logania Family   Hardiness Zone 7b
Native to the southeastern United States.

SIZE: 3 to 4 feet as a shrub; 10 to 20 feet as a vine climbing on trees, arbors, or other structures. Rapid grower.

FORM: A twining vine or irregular, mounded shrub if not supported.

TEXTURE: Medium.   **EXPOSURE:** Sun to shade.

LEAVES: Opposite, ovate to lanceolate, tapering to a sharp point at the tip; 1 to 2 inches long, 1/2 to 1 inch wide, with a smooth margin and a very short petiole. Deep glossy green above; light pale green below.

STEM: Slender, tough and wiry, becomes sandy brown when very young and retains that color throughout. The plant has no aerial roots or other attachment mechanism but grows by twining or wrapping.

FLOWERS: Bright yellow. Funnel form, 1 to 1 1/2 inches across, and about 1 inch long. Often in a dense cluster, very early in the spring, and very showy. One of the first plants to bloom and continues blooming for several weeks.

FRUIT: An elliptical capsule. Not showy.

COLOR: Foliage is deep, glossy green. Flowers are bright yellow.

PROPAGATION: Seed, semi-hardwood, or hardwood cuttings in the fall or winter.

CULTURE: Grows well in sun or shade. Will grow at the base of a tree, up into the tree, and, unlike many plants under these shade conditions, will retain its foliage and flower well. Grows in any good soil and tolerates wet swampy conditions or moderate drought. In Zones 7b and 8 it may be defoliated by temperatures below 10 degrees F. However, the stems generally survive and only the spring show of flowers is lost.

PESTS: None serious.

NOTES: A very attractive vine or mounded shrub. Can be used near other plants without excessive maintenance to keep them separate. The prolific flower production makes it a very nice show in the spring. The lustrous evergreen foliage makes it showy throughput the winter. An excellent vine for use on a trellis, arbor, or screen. All plant parts are very poisonous, thus one should have some reservations for its use in high-contact-by-children areas. Can be used as a ground cover with repeated mowing; however, few flowers occur under these conditions. XX-POISON-XX

CULTIVARS: 'Pride of Augusta': has double flowers but otherwise, like the species.

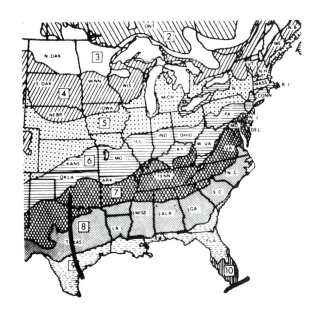

Gordonia lasianthus (L.) Ellis.
Theaceae or Tea Family
Native from North Carolina to Florida.

Gordonia or Loblolly Bay
Hardiness Zone 7b

SIZE: 30 to 50 feet tall, 20- to 30-foot spread. Slow to moderate grower.
FORM: Upright-oval, small tree.
TEXTURE: Medium.

EXPOSURE: Sun or partial shade.

LEAVES: Alternate, simple; 3 to 5 inches long. Thick and leathery with teeth on the margin near the tip. Dark, glossy green above; very pale green below. Petiole is short and stout. Old leaves turn red before dropping.

STEM: Young stems are smooth, medium stout; and green, soon turning tan. Wood is fairly stout. Old bark is gray and shallowly furrowed.

FLOWERS: White. Fragrant, 2 to 3 inches across with many prominent stamens and 5 petals. Single, although occasionally 2 or 3 flowers occur at the same location. Flower buds are large, oval, and very noticeable long before the flowers open. Blooms from May to July across the South. Never has a heavy show of flowers but some occur for 2 months or more, especially in north and central Florida.

FRUIT: A small, woody, 5-parted capsule. Not showy.

COLOR: Foliage is dark, glossy green. Flowers are white.

PROPAGATION: Seed or cuttings.

CULTURE: Gordonia is native to wet swampy areas with acid soils. Can be grown in various landscape locations as long as moisture is consistently present and soils do not become too alkaline. Mulches assist moisture management. Iron chlorosis is common where soils are above pH 6.5. Roots are shallow and easily disturbed, furthering the need for a good mulch. Trees from the wild are very difficult to transplant; however, container-grown trees transplant readily. Winter Haven Nurseries, Winter Haven, Florida was one of the few nurseries growing this excellent tree in quantity for years. Slowly, it has gained in favor elsewhere.

PESTS: None serious.

NOTES: A very attractive small to medium tree. The foliage and lengthy bloom time are very useful in any landscape where soil and moisture conditions are appropriate.

CULTIVARS: None known.

RELATED SPECIES: *Franklinia alatamaha* Marsh., the Franklin tree, is closely related to gordonia and is similar in nearly all respects except that it is deciduous, whereas gordonia is evergreen. This is a small tree, 15 to 30 feet tall; with open, upright branches. Hardiness Zone 6. This is the tree that John Bartram supposedly found in Georgia in 1770 and dug from the wild for his garden in Philadelphia. The plant no longer can be found in the wild and the trees grown today are decedents of those first trees. Leaves are simple, alternate, 4 to 5 inches long, and oblong with a serrate margin. Virtually identical to gordonia except that its leaves are less thick and leathery, and veins on the upper surface are more prominent. Flowers are white, single, 2 1/2 to 3 inches across, and fragrant; blooming in July and August. Fall color is orange-red; very showy. An attractive and unique tree, with attractive foliage and summer flowers.

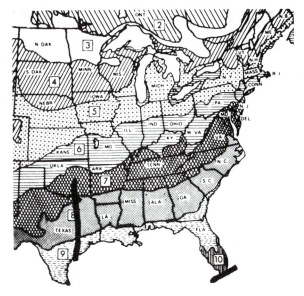

Hesperaloe parviflora (Torr.) Coult.   Red Yucca
      (Syn. *Yucca parviflora*)
Agavaceae or Agave Family   Hardiness Zone 7
SIZE: 2 to 4 feet tall with a spread of 2 to 3 feet. Slow grower.
FORM: A loose, oval mound of leaves with an erect flower stalk.
TEXTURE: Medium to coarse.   **EXPOSURE:** Sun only.

LEAVES: 2 to 4 feet long and folded or rolled in cross-section, making them distinctly different from the flat leaves of the true yuccas. The leaf has white or pinkish threads curling back along the margin. No marginal teeth or spine at the tip, making it distinct from those of the yuccas or agave species. Takes on a blue-green to purple-green color once established in a sunny location.

STEM: No above-ground stem is visible, simply the clustering of leaves in a more or less whorled arrangement at the crown. It does, however, develop a slender, weak rhizome that causes some thickening and can be used for propagation.

FLOWERS: Rose to coral. In large clusters on stalks rising 4 to 6 feet above the whorl of foliage. Individual flowers are about 1 inch long and 1 inch wide at the face and somewhat funnelform or egg-shaped and drooping. Spectacular color generally begins in early June and lasts through July or August, but rarely are enough flower stalks present at one time to make a good show from a distance.

FRUIT: Generally does not develop except in the Southwest.

COLOR: Foliage is blue-green to purple-green. Flowers are rose to coral.

PROPAGATION: Seed or division.

CULTURE: Best in hot, dry locations. Full sun, for at least a portion of the day, is necessary for good color and flower development. Tolerates high heat conditions, reflected light, parking lot situations, and numerous other growing conditions usually not tolerated by most landscape plants. Responds well to fertilization. Makes an attractive show during mid summer. Old flower stalks need to be removed, which generally is the only maintenance necessary. Does not tolerate wet feet, poorly drained soils, or shady, damp locations.

PESTS: None.

NOTES: A small, durable, maintenance-free plant for sunny locations. Use carefully in the landscape. Works well with yuccas, cacti, and other plants indigenous to arid to semi-arid regions.

CULTIVARS: A yellow-flowered cultivar was found by Paul Goodwin, Kingfisher, Oklahoma but is very limited in availability. Others may exist.

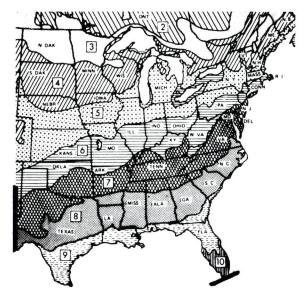

Ilex altaclarensis (Loud.) Dallim.   English Holly Hybrids
Aquifoliaceae or Holly Family   Hardiness Zone 6
Native: a hybrid between *Ilex aquifolium* and *Ilex perado*.
SIZE: Large mounded shrubs; varying depending on cultivar. Moderate growth rate.
FORM: Oval or mounded shrubs with dense branches. Varies with cultivar.
TEXTURE: Medium to coarse.   **EXPOSURE:** Sun to shade.

LEAVES: Generally ovate or oval, 3 to 4 inches long and 1 1/2 to 2 inches wide. Dull to glossy green above; lighter below. Leaf size and number of spines vary with cultivar.

STEM: Irregular, multi-stemmed shrubs. Stems are green or purple for several years, finally turning a medium brown. Young stems are large in diameter compared to other species of *Ilex* except for *I. aquifolium*, which has even larger stems.

FLOWERS: Male and female on separate plants (dioecious). Both are small, yellow-green, and inconspicuous.

FRUIT: About 1/4 inch round, bright red, on female plants, and retained throughout the winter in most areas. A male cultivar or male English holly is necessary for good fruit production.

COLOR: Foliage is dull to glossy green. Fruits are bright red and showy.

PROPAGATION: Cuttings or grafting. Most seeds are sterile although a few have been reported to be viable.

CULTURE: Appear to be slightly more vigorous and durable over a wider range of soil conditions, exposures, and climatic conditions than most English holly cultivars. They do, however, respond to mulching, partial shade, or somewhat protected locations and supplemental moisture in times of stress, typical of most hollies. Several cultivars do well over a moderate range of the Upper South.

PESTS: Spittle bugs may damage foliage during summer.

NOTES: *Ilex perado* is native to the Azores and Canary Islands, as opposed to the more European habitat of the apparently closely related *Ilex aquifolium*. Numerous cultivars have been named from these crosses, either controlled or natural. Very difficult to identify from *I. aquifolium* cultivars. Mostly used as specimen plants, but they also work well as screens, hedges, or backgrounds.

CULTIVARS: 'Altaclarensis': a male holly with vigorous growth, and a dense habit whose young bark is purplish. Leaves are deep green, round to ovate or oval, 3 to 4 inches long, 2 1/2 to 3 inches wide. Spines are numerous on some leaves; others have few or none. 'Camilliaefolia': female, one of the most ornamental. Large, dark red fruit, vigorous habit, growing naturally into a shapely pyramid, retaining dense foliage at all seasons. Bark of young wood is purple. Leaves are oblong or elliptic, dark olive green, very glossy, 3 1/2 to 5 inches long, 1 1/2 to 2 inches wide. Margins are either smooth or have an occasional spine. 'James G. Esson': vigorous habit and rapid growth. Produces an abundance of large, shiny red berries in clusters along the branches. The leaves are a glossy, rich green with 4 to 5 well developed spines along each side. 'Laurifolia' is male; called the smooth-leaved holly. Upright habit with somewhat open, irregular growth. Bark is dark purple when young. Leaves are dark green, very glossy, 2 to 3 inches long, and from ovate to oblong-lanceolate or elliptical, usually with a smooth margin or rarely with 1 to 2 marginal spines. 'Wilsonii': vigorous-growing green-barked female; one of the most ornamental of the green-leaved cultivars. Leaves are sometimes 5 inches long, 2 1/2 inches wide, oval, and armed with numerous, evenly developed 1/4-inch long spines. In shade, leaves are dark green: very distinct due to the well-defined veins. Other cultivars exist.

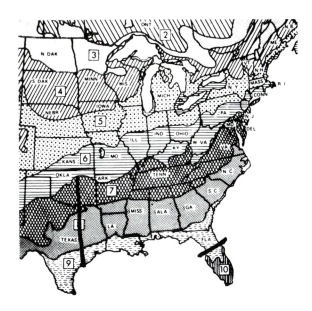

Ilex aquifolium L.   English Holly
Aquifoliaceae or Holly Family   Hardiness Zone 6
Native to England, central and southern Europe, northern Africa, and China.
SIZE: Variable: from shrubs 4 to 6 feet to trees 40 to 60 feet tall. Slow to moderate growth rate.
FORM: From low-spreading to rounded shrubs to pyramidal trees of considerable size with dense branches.
TEXTURE: Medium.   **EXPOSURE:** Sun to shade.

LEAVES: 1 1/2 to 4 inches long, 1 to 2 inches wide, depending on cultivar. More or less oval outline with a short petiole; generally wavy and toothed on the margin. However, teeth may be absent on the leaves of older trees. Leaves are generally glossy, deep green and leathery to the touch. The cultivar, 'Furos', has teeth on the surface of the leaf. Several cultivars have leaves with silver or yellow margins.

STEM: Generally a central leader if a tree form, or irregularly multi-branched if a shrub form. Young stems are very thick and heavy in comparison with those of other hollies, remaining green for one to two seasons and frequently turning purple in fall and winter. Bark is smooth and gray on older stems, with occasional gray patches (lichens).

FLOWERS: Male and female on separate plants (dioecious). Small, yellow-green; not showy.

FRUIT: Red; 1/2 inch or more, round. Appears on previous season's growth and lasts through winter. Similar in size and appearance to *Ilex cornuta* cultivars. A male English holly must be present for good fruit production.

COLOR: Foliage is deep green to green with silver or yellow margins, depending on cultivar. Fruit is red and showy.

PROPAGATION: Cuttings or grafting. Seedlings are extremely variable.

CULTURE: Grows best in a rich, well-drained soil. However, contrary to popular belief, some cultivars of English holly will tolerate heavy clay soils and considerable drought. Also, some are hardy into the upper regions of Zone 6 and are quite rugged. Most cultivars appear to do best in partial shade. West of the Mississippi River, plants do best on northern or eastern exposures, although exceptions can be found. Hollies respond to mulching, light but frequent applications of fertilizer, and irrigation during dry periods. English hollies do not do well on the sandy soils of the Florida peninsula.

PESTS: None serious, although spittle bugs may occasionally damage new leaves.

NOTES: Because of the variability within the species, hybridization with other species, and extensive lists of cultivars, much confusion exists concerning English holly. *Ilex aquifolium* X *Ilex perado* hybrids are now generally listed as *Ilex altaclarensis*. Hybrids between *I. aquifolium* and *I. platyphylla* are probably confused with both of the above species. The English holly probably has contributed more cultivars than any other *Ilex* species. Cultivars with solid green leaves are generally more cold tolerant than variegated forms. Mostly used as specimen plants, but they also work well for massing, screens, and hedges. The attractive foliage, with or without the bright red fruits, is commonly used in holiday arrangements. English holly is grown commercially for this purpose in the Pacific Northwest and along the mid Atlantic coast.

CULTIVARS: 'Angustifolia': narrow, pyramidal habit. Bark is green or purplish. leaves are shining green, about 1 1/2 inches long, 1/2 inch wide with weak, narrow regular spines. 'Argenteo-marginata': a group of silver, variegated hollies, varying somewhat in appearance. Bark of young wood is green. Leaves are broadly ovate, 2 to 2 1/2 inches long, dark green, irregular, narrow, and with a silvery margin. Leaf spines are usually numerous but irregular. names in the trade include 'Silver Queen', 'Silver Prince', 'Silvary' and 'Teufel's Silver Variegated'. 'Argenteo Medio-picta': a group with white variegated leaves; ovate, 1 1/2 to 1 inch long, about 1 inch wide, dark green at the edge with a large central blotch of creamy white, irregular in shape, size, and position; frequently confined to basal half of the leaf. Leaf spines are very strong. Male and female trees available: 'Silver Milkmaid', 'Silver Milkboy'. 'Aurea-marginata' in its widest sense, this name includes a large proportion of the variegated-leaved female hollies with golden margins. Some showing slight variations have been selected and named, so there is considerable latitude. Typically, bark is green, leaves are large, about 2 1/2 to 3 inches long, 1 1/2 inches wide with golden edges, unequal but rather strongly developed about the tip. leaves sometimes are entirely golden. Leaf spines are stout and unequally distributed. 'Aurea Medio-picta' frequently occurs as sports on solid green-leaved English hollies with variations in leaf size, coloration, and spines. Recognized by irregularly marked leaves by a large deep golden blotch, often occupying more than half the surface, while the irregular margin is glossy, dark green. 'Golden Butterfly', 'Harlequin', 'Golden Milkboy'. 'Balkans': female clone hardy at the Missouri Botanical Garden. grown from seed collected in Yugoslavia in 1934. 'Boulder Creek': leaves are very large, glossy, almost black-green; fruit is brilliant red. 'Cilliata Major': free-growing, vigorous plant woth red fruits. Bark and leaves of young shoots are purplish. Leaves are ovate to ovate-oblong, flat with long, broad-based spines mostly near the tip.

HYBRIDS: *Ilex* X *meserveae*, referred to as the blue hollies, are hybrids between *Ilex aquifolium* and *Ilex rugosa*. These hybrids are more cold hardy than many species and cultivars, hardy in Zone 6 or perhaps further north in protected locations. all have foliage that is slightly blue or perhaps more accurately, blue-purple, and females have red fruits. 'Blue Prince' (male) and 'Blue Princess' (female with red fruits): are probably best for general landscape use with an oval-upright form reaching 5 to 7 feet tall or more with good growing conditions. 'Blue Maid' (female) and 'Blue Stallion' (male) are recent introductions with oval forms. The landscape value of these remains to be determined as they can reach 10 feet or more with age. 'Blue Angle' is a slightly smaller, mounding form rarely reaching more than 5 to 6 feet tall.

OTHER MESERVE HYBRIDS: The China series may tolerate winters better that the blue series. 'China Boy': a good pollinator with glossy green leaves. 'China Girl': may reach 8 to 10 feet and produces large, red fruits that are very showy. May be one of the more heat-tolerant cultivars as well. Remember that pollinators are essential to good fruit set and in the landscape the species generally do **NOT** cross-pollinate.

'Cilliata Major'

'Cilliata Major'

'Nellie R. Stevens'

'Nellie R. Stevens'

'Nellie R. Stevens'

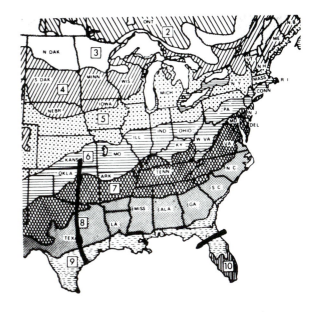

'Boulder Creek'

'Aureo-marginata'

Ilex cornuta Lindl.   Chinese or Horned Holly
Aquifoliaceae or Holly Family   Hardiness Zone 7
Native to eastern China.

SIZE: 4 to 20 feet tall with a spread of 4 to 10 feet depending on cultivar. Moderate growth rate.

FORM: Compact, pyramidal tree or somewhat round-headed shrub or small tree, depending on cultivar.

TEXTURE: Medium.   **EXPOSURE:** Sun to shade.

LEAVES: Shiny, deep green above, dull green below, plastic-like in appearance and to the touch; brittle when crushed. Normally 2 to 3 inches long, 1 to 1 1/2 inches wide, with 5 or 7 tapering, somewhat opaque, spines. Size and number of spines vary with cultivars.

STEM: Central leader or irregularly branched main stem. Young stem is slender and green for most of the growing season, finally turning a light tan with age but remaining smooth.

FLOWERS: Small and yellow-green, appear in clusters in the leaf axils; not showy. Male and female flowers on separate plants; some fragrance. The first holly to bloom in the spring.

FRUIT: Largest fruits of the commonly cultivated holly. Generally bright red, 1/4 to 1/2 inch long, on long stalks, in clusters of 5 to 8. Very showy.

COLOR: Foliage is shiny, deep green except on 'Variegata'. Fruit is bright red or yellow on 'Avery Island' and 'D'or'.

PROPAGATION: Semi-hardwood to hardwood cuttings in fall or early winter. Seedlings are extremely variable.

CULTURE: Chinese holly tolerate a wide range of soil conditions from poor sands in northern and central Florida to heavy, poorly drained clays throughout the cotton belt as far west as central Texas and Oklahoma. Maximum growth and fruiting is generally obtained on rich, well-drained soils with plants in part shade to full sun. Unless soil conditions are exceptionally poor, on a very exposed site, Chinese holly will function well in full sun. In dense shade, most cultivars tend to become open and spindly, and fruit poorly, if at all. As with most hollies, they respond to light and frequent applications of fertilizer, mulching, and supplemental moisture during drought periods.

PESTS: Tea scale in the Lower South may become serious; particularly in cool, shady areas with poor air drainage. Probably the most susceptible holly to scale. Grasshoppers may be a problem in rural areas.

NOTES: Chinese holly cultivars are popular landscape plants wherever they can be grown. For heavy fruiting, male plants must be nearby. Sometimes a male branch is grafted onto the back of a female plant to insure heavy fruiting. Chinese holly can be readily distinguished from other species by the long, tapering, more or less opaque spines on the leaves and the plastic-like leaf texture. Over-fertilization by a quick release chemical fertilizer may cause stunting and marginal leaf scorch or, in severe cases, leaf drop and death. This sensitivity probably relates to the fine, almost watery, feeder roots. Several hybrids between *Ilex cornuta* and other species have been made.

CULTIVARS: 'Burfordi': dark, glossy green leaves, 1 1/2 to 3 inches long; obovate to ovate, with a recurved, smooth margin or rarely with marginal teeth, and a strong spine at the tip. Fruits are in clusters of 4 to 8. Twigs are green, slender, and irregular. May reach a height of 12 to 20 feet. A rapid grower. Excellent plant for a large hedge or as a small tree. 'Burfordi Nana': dark, glossy green leaves, 1 to 2 inches long, more elongated than 'Burfordi'. A more compact, slower grower than regular Burford holly. Moderate fruit producer. May grow 6 to 10 feet tall. 'Rotunda': a superior, compact, low-growing, round or dome-shaped shrub with dense branching. Leaves are very similar to the parent in size, teeth, and shape. May reach a height of 4 to 5 feet with age. Fruit is rarely seen, not to be confused with the tree, *Ilex rotunda*. 'Carissa': sport of 'Rotunda': with similar growth habit but only 1 spine per leaf. 'Willowleaf': a low, mounding form with no spines except for the tip, and no fruit. 'Dazzler': more oval-upright, with large leaves. Compact growth, reaching 5 to 6 feet with red fruit. 'D'or' and 'Avery Island': oval forms with yellow fruit. 'National': an oval form reaching 12 to 15 feet with very large, red fruits. Numerous other cultivars exist.

HYBRIDS: 'Nellie R. Stevens': female hybrid between *Ilex aquifolium* and *Ilex cornuta* with deep green leaves and 3 terminal spines. An amazingly durable and tolerant holly that thrives under a wide range of conditions. Especially drought-resistant and a prolific producer of bright red berries. 'John T. Morris' (male) and 'Lydia Morris' (female) are hybrids between *Ilex cornuta* and *Ilex pernyi*. Attractive shrubs with deep green foliage. Good drought resistance when established. Similar hybrids include 'Red Robe' and 'Atlas'.

'Rotunda'

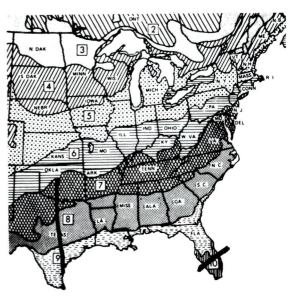

'Rotunda'

'Burfordi Nana'

'Burfordi'   'Burfordi Nana'

'Burfordi'

'Carissa'

'Nellie R. Stevens'

Ilex vomitoria

I. vomitoria 'Nana'

I. vomitoria   I. crenata 'Hetzi'

Ilex crenata Thunb.   Japanese Holly
Aquifoliaceae or Holly Family   Hardiness Zone 6b
Native to Japan.
SIZE: 3 to 6 feet tall with a 2- to 5-foot spread. Old plants of several cultivars may be found 15 to 20 feet tall. Size and growth rate depend on cultivar.
FORM: Generally a compact dome or somewhat oval-shaped shrub, depending on cultivar.
TEXTURE: Fine.   **EXPOSURE:** Sun to shade.

LEAVES: 1/2 to 1 inch long, 1/4 to 1/2 inch wide, obovate; shiny, deep green with crenate or slightly sawtooth margin and a very short petiole. Petioles may have a purple cast, particularly in full sun. leaves on some cultivars are somewhat convex or cupped.

STEM: Plants are dense and twiggy with slender, stiff, somewhat brittle branches. Branches are easily broken where they attach to the main stem. Stems are green or on some cultivars a deep purple in full sun, in late summer and hold that color until spring. Stems eventually turn light brown.

FLOWERS: Very small and creamy white, generally hidden by the foliage.

FRUIT: Green turning black when ripe. In the leaf axils, hidden by the foliage.

COLOR: Foliage is shiny, deep green.

PROPAGATION: Semi-hardwood to hardwood cuttings.

CULTURE: Full sun in all but the most exposed and hot locations, but also does well in shade. Moderate drought tolerance. Appears to do best in clay soils, but will grow in a wide range of soil types, except that nematodes become a serious problem in light sandy soils. Responds well to pruning and fertilization.

PESTS: Scale, spider mites, and in light sandy soils, nematodes. Unsatisfactory in nearly all of the Florida peninsula, probably because of the nematode susceptibility.

NOTES: A very useful species for landscaping, hedges, foundation plantings, topiary, and as a background for annual or perennial beds. Very popular throughout the South. Several cultivars are compact, low-growing forms, requiring little pruning.
    Frequently confused with dwarf cultivars of yaupon holly. However, they can be distinguished since yaupon holly have flat leaves with larger serrations on the margins, twigs turn light gray about 1 year old, and seldom turn purple in fall or winter. Yaupon holly have a small, metallic red fruit, which is seldom seen on dwarf cultivars. Japanese holly leaves may be cupped, twigs and petioles often turn purple, and fruits are black.

CULTIVARS: 'Compacta': superior to older 'Rotundifolia' and 'Convexa' in compactness and foliage color. 'Convexa': sometimes listed as 'Bullata'. Leaves are convex or cupped, deep green, and shiny. May reach 3 to 5 feet tall with a 4- to 6-foot spread. 'Helleri': a very dwarf, compact form. Leaves about 1/2 inch long, elliptical with 2 to 4 teeth on each side. Rarely grows more than 3 feet tall with a 3- to 4-foot spread. Good substitute for boxwood. Not for wet locations. 'Hetzi': leaves are dark green, obovate, slightly convex, about 1 inch long, 1/4 to 1/2 inch wide, rounded at the tip. Generally 7 to 10 teeth on each margin. May reach 5 to 6 feet tall with spread of 5 to 7 feet. 'Kingsville Dwarf': a dwarf form with lanceolate leaves about 1 inch long and 1/4 inch wide. Grows in loose, open mounds and may reach 3 feet tall with a spread of 4 to 5 feet. Leaf is longer and leaf tip is more pointed than on 'Helleri'. 'Rotundifolia': leaves are shiny dark green, flat, obovate to oblong, 1 to 1 1/2 inches long and 1/2 inch wide with 11 to 16 teeth per side. Largest leaf of Japanese holly cultivars. May reach 5 to 6 feet tall with 5- to 6-foot spread. Responds to trimming to make a good hedge. Old plants tend to have stem blight. many cultivars are available in the trade.

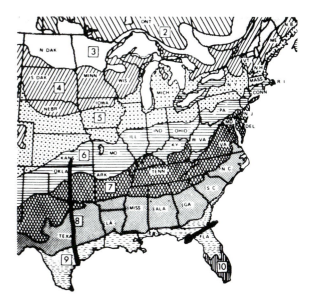

'Hetzi'   'Helleri'

I. crenata   I. vomitoria

Ilex latifolia Thunb.　　　　　　Luster Leaf Holly
Aquifoliaceae or Holly Family　　　Hardiness Zone 7
Native to eastern China and Japan.
SIZE: 40 to 60 feet tall with a 20- to 30-foot spread. Moderate growth rate.
FORM: Pyramidal evergreen tree with stout branches.
TEXTURE: Coarse.　　　　　　　**EXPOSURE:** Sun to partial shade.

LEAVES: Alternate; thick and leathery, with a glossy upper surface and dull green below. Shape is oblong, 4 to 9 inches long, 2 to 3 inches wide, very uniform with a coarse saw-tooth margin. Size and arrangement of leaves on the plant make it somewhat resemble southern magnolia.

STEM: Generally a stout, erect, central leader, with stout secondary branches, which remain green for 1 to 2 years before taking on a gray-brown appearance. Older bark is smooth and often covered with various lichens, giving it an irregular, patchy or blotchy appearance.

FLOWERS: Creamy white. Male and female on different plants (dioecious). Not showy.

FRUIT: Dull red. In axillary clusters, globose, about 1/4 inch in diameter and 1/2 inch long. Fruits are held throughout the winter. A nearby male plant is necessary for good fruit production.

COLOR: Foliage is dark green and lustrous. Fruit is dull red.

PROPAGATION: Hardwood cuttings in the fall or early winter.

CULTURE: Moderately durable: tolerates a fair range of soil conditions and moisture levels. Grows best in full sun but not in extremely hot, dry, exposed conditions. In most cases, it responds to mulching to conserve moisture, and the removal of grass and weeds away from the young plant.

PESTS: None serious; although spittle bug and various scale insects can be problems.

NOTES: An elegant plant. Very attractive. Probably the most coarse-leaved and among the largest of the hollies found in the United States. Not commonly grown but should be used considerably more. In the coastal area of China and Japan, the leaves are used as a substitute for tea. Leaves are somewhat aromatic when crushed, unlike those of most other holly species and so is a good feature for identification. A good "magnolia-appearing" plant for a restricted area, and creates less litter than a magnolia. If a male branch is grafted onto an out-of-view area of the plant, the red fruits and glossy leaves make an excellent show in the fall and winter. The overall photograph at right is not representative of the excellent form of the tree. It was used because the good specimens were all nestled among other plants and could not be photographed in black and white.

CULTIVARS: 'Variegata' has yellow, variegated leaves, less common than the species. 'Mary Nell': has dark green foliage and sets many red fruits. Other cultivars probably exist.

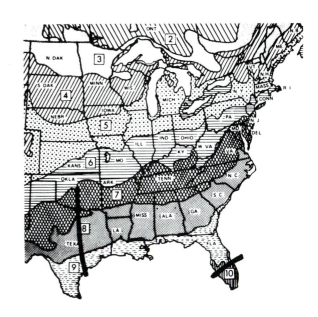

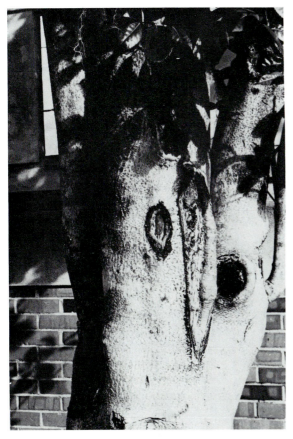

Ilex opaca Ait.   American Holly
Aquifoliaceae or Holly Family   Hardiness Zone 6
Native to the southeastern United States.
SIZE: 40 to 50 feet tall with 15- to 30-foot spread, but variable with cultivars. Slow to medium growth.
FORM: Pyramidal, evergreen trees, with slight variations among cultivars.
TEXTURE: Medium.   **EXPOSURE:** Sun to shade.

LEAVES: Alternate; 2 to 4 inches long, and 1 to 1 1/2 inches wide, depending on cultivar. Leaf margins are usually spiny-toothed and flat to wavy. Dull to glossy surface and medium to deep green color. Leaves are more pliable or flexible than cultivars of Chinese holly or English holly. Two common cultivars, 'East Palatka' and 'Hume #2' have few, if any, teeth on the margin.

STEM: Usually a central-leader tree. Older bark is smooth, light gray, and often mottled in appearance due to numerous lichens. Young stems are slender, remaining green for 4 to 8 months. Wood is hard and durable, not easily broken when bigger than 1 inch in diameter.

FLOWERS: Small, yellow-green, not showy. Male and female on different plants (dioecious). A male is needed within 300 feet of females for good fruit production.

FRUIT: Round, 1/4 inch in diameter. Red, yellow, or orange, depending on cultivar.

COLOR: Foliage is medium to dark green. Fruit is red, yellow, or orange.

PROPAGATION: Softwood or semi-hardwood cuttings or grafting onto seedling root stocks. Seed may take up to 2 years to germinate and seedlings are quite variable.

CULTURE: In its native range, American holly is found on swampy to well-drained sites. North and west of the native range most cultivars appear to do best in well-drained soils. Soil pH should be 6.5 or lower. Where soil pH is higher, due to natural conditions, alkaline irrigation water, or construction residue, iron chlorosis and poor growth frequently occur. In most cases, plants respond to mulching and keeping grass and weeds away from the root zone. Responds best to light but frequent applications of chemical fertilizer or larger and less frequent application of organic fertilizer. Hollies are quite susceptible to fertilizer damage and/or high soluble salts.

PESTS: Several leaf spot diseases may be serious enough to cause leaf drop in humid, shady locations. Leaf miners, scale insects, bud moth, and mites may be serious in some locations. Spittle bugs frequently damage leaves emerging in mid to late season.

NOTES: American hollies are old favorites of southern landscapers. Mostly used as specimen plants. However, they also work well for background, massing, or large hedges. The classical holly wreaths seen during the holiday season are American holly. Mostly magnificent trees. Female plants are laden with red fruit by mid fall and until early spring.

CULTIVARS: 'Croonenburg': a compact, columnar tree with stiff, curved, dark green leaves with prominent teeth. Dark red fruit. An "ugly duckling" when young but handsome with age. 'Greenleaf': a narrow, pyramidal form; very hardy. Leaves are many-toothed, slightly curved, and medium to dark green. A moderate fruit producer. 'Clarendon Spreading': orange fruit and 'Maryland Dwarf' with yellow fruit are slow growing forms remaining under 6 feet for many years. 'Arden': a semi-upright tree with open branches; red fruit. 'Howard': a compact, pyramidal grower, smaller than many American holly cultivars; red fruit. 'Jersey Princess': a pyramidal form with dark, glossy leaves; red fruit. 'Carolina #2: good fruit producer with dark foliage. There are many cultivars of American holly that reach 30 feet or more. Some of the better forms are: 'Bountiful', 'Cumberland', 'Edith May', 'Jersey Knight', 'Lady Alive', 'Merry Christmas', 'Old Heavy Berry', and 'Red Velvet'.

HYBRIDS: The following are now considered hybrids between *Ilex opaca* and *I. attenuata*. 'East Palatka': upright, pyramidal tree with stiff, flat, dark green leaves, typically with a single tooth at the tip. Leaves are 1 1/2 to 2 inches long and about 1 inch wide (considerably shorter than 'Hume #2'). A rapid grower which produces an abundance of red fruits, slightly smaller than the species. 'Hume #2': dense pyramidal form with flat, shiny, leathery leaves typically 3 to 3 1/2 inches long with a single tooth at the tip. (Leaves like 'East Palatka' but much longer). A moderate to heavy fruit producer. 'Savannah': pyramidal tree with curved, dull green leaves which are 3 to 4 inches long, and 1 1/2 inches wide with numerous teeth on the margin. Many are deep red and very prominent fruit.

'Fosteri#2': hybrid between *Ilex opaca* and *I. cassine*. Originally 1 of 5 seedlings known as 'Fosteri #1' to '#5' selected by E.E. Foster of Bessemer, Alabama. Probably only #2 and #3 still exist in the trade. 'Fosteri #2' is a moderate growing, pyramidal form that may reach 20 feet tall with deep, blue-green leaves. Leaves are more narrow and elongated than American holly cultivars, with numerous shallow marginal teeth. Fruits are borne singly or in clusters, are bright red and slightly smaller than *Ilex opaca*. 'Fosteri #2' is superior to most American holly cultivars in foliage color, fruiting, and tolerance of a wide range of light, soils, and moisture conditions. The foliage and fruit is very showy during the Christmas season, but does not hold up well indoors.

'Croonenburg'

'Fosteri #2'

'Greenleaf' 'Fosteri #2'

'Hume #2' 'East Palatka'

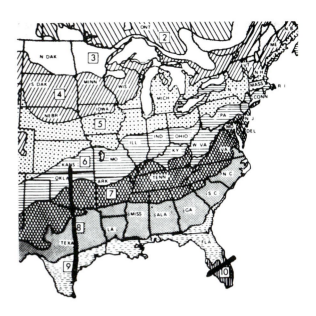

Lichens on stem

'Fosteri #2'

Ilex pernyi French.   Pernyi Holly
Aquifoliaceae or Holly Family   Hardiness Zone 6
Native to central China.
SIZE: With age, 12 to 20 feet tall with a 6- to 10-foot spread. Moderate grower.
FORM: Upright, irregularly pyramidal shrub or small tree, generally with a central leader.
TEXTURE: Medium to fine.   **EXPOSURE:** Sun to shade.

LEAVES: Alternate, simple; ovate, 1/2 to 1 1/2 inches long, generally less than 1 inch wide. Generally has 5 spines about equal in size, 1 very prominent at the tip, 2 on each side of the midrib, about equal in size. The terminal spine tends to be in the same plane as the main leaf blade as contrasted with Chinese holly where the terminal spine frequently points downward and at an angle to the main leaf blade. Leaves are medium to dark green. Petiole is very short; almost absent.

STEM: Moderately heavy, larger in size and structure than Chinese holly. The young branchlets are pubescent or wooly. Generally a central leader shrub or small tree but branching irregularly.

FLOWERS: Small, creamy white; not showy. Male and female are on separate plants (dioecious).

FRUIT: Scarlet. Generally in pairs, globose, and about 1/2 inch in diameter.

COLOR: Foliage is medium to dark green. Fruits are scarlet.

PROPAGATION: Hardwood cuttings in fall or winter.

CULTURE: Tolerates a moderate range of soil conditions. Moderately drought-resistant, and responds well to fertilization. With age the plant may become somewhat open and scraggly but this can be overcome by pruning. Formal specimens need some pruning annually.

PESTS: None serious.

NOTES: Female plants are generally heavy fruiters to the point that the foliage may become unsightly in fall or winter from the transfer of material from the leaves and stems into the maturing fruit. Occasionally an especially heavy-fruited plant may succumb to winter kill because it has been so depleted of nutrients in the leaves and stems. Not widely planted but it does have merit in some landscape locations. Frequently confused with Chinese holly but it can best be distinguished by the young twigs that are pubescent on pernyi holly and the leaves that tend to be in one plane, including the terminal spine, whereas Chinese holly twigs are smooth and the terminal spine is at an angle to the main leaf blade.

CULTIVARS: 'Peryni': smaller, more ovate leaves than those of the species, and red fruits on very short stalks. 'Vetchi': larger leaves than the parent, generally 1 1/2 inches long and larger fruits.

HYBRIDS: 'Aquipernyi': thought to be a cross between English holly and pernyi holly. Has larger leaves than the pernyi parent; with small, round fruits and a very compact growth habit. 'John T. Morris' (male) and 'Lydia Morris' (female) are hybrids between *Ilex cornuta* 'Burfordi' and *Ilex pernyi*. Attractive specimen shrubs with dark green leaves. Moderately drought-resistant. Numerous other cultivars and hybrids probably exist.

Ilex rotunda Thunb.   Round Holly
Aquifoliaceae or Holly Family   Hardiness Zone 8
Native to eastern Asia.

SIZE: A tree reaching 30 to 40 feet tall under very good conditions. More commonly 20 to 25 feet tall with a 12- to 15-foot spread. Slow to moderate grower.

FORM: Somewhat irregular, asymmetrical tree, developing a rounded crown with age.

TEXTURE: Medium.   **EXPOSURE:** Sun to partial shade.

LEAVES: Alternate, simple; 2 to 3 inches long, about 1 inch wide, ovate to broadly elliptical with a smooth margin. Medium to dark green and very glossy above. A very soft and pliable leaf, unlike the commonly grown hollies which have more hard and rigid leaves. Leaves are similar to those of *Ligustrum lucidum* only smaller.

STEM: Generally a tree with a central leader, irregularly branched with somewhat brittle wood. Bark is very light gray to almost white with age. Young shoots are green (purple during fall and winter) turning white after the first season.

FLOWERS: Female flowers are small, creamy white, and inconspicuous. Male and female are on separate trees (dioecious).

FRUIT: Small, about 1/8 inch in diameter. Deep metallic red; very showy, and in clusters of 3 to 7 in the leaf axil on current year's growth. A male must be nearby for good fruit production.

COLOR: Foliage is glossy and medium to dark green. Fruits are deep metallic red.

PROPAGATION: Is very difficult which is probably the reason why it is not well known or more widely planted. Stem cuttings are rarely successful, seed is difficult to germinate, and grafting is a real challenge.

CULTURE: Although not widely planted, it does well in north Florida on poor, sandy soils. Appears to be well adapted farther north on heavy clay soils. Is assisted by mulching for moisture retention and for keeping away grass competition. Fruits best in full sun. Tolerates full sun very well in exposed conditions, but also tolerates partial shade. Should not be fertilized late in the growing season to stimulate late growth. Occasionally defoliated by severe winters in north Florida.

PESTS: None have been observed.

NOTES: Not to be confused with *Ilex cornuta* 'Rotunda'. Round holly is a spectacular tree, particularly in late summer, fall, and early winter when the females are heavily laden with fruits. Very effective as a specimen in the landscape. Few other plants equal round holly for overall form and beauty. Excellent specimens can be found on the campuses of Florida State University (Tallahassee) and the University of Florida (Gainesville).

CULTIVARS: 'Lord' (female): somewhat narrowly upright and pyramidal. Leaves are dark, glossy green. No spines are present on any leaves. Fruits are small and bright, shining red, in dense clusters on the current season's wood. A spectacular plant. Apparently the flowers are not pollinated by any other holly, thus a male round holly must be planted nearby. 'Romal' (male): dark, glossy green leaves with a broadly spreading head. An elegant specimen tree, even without the fruit.

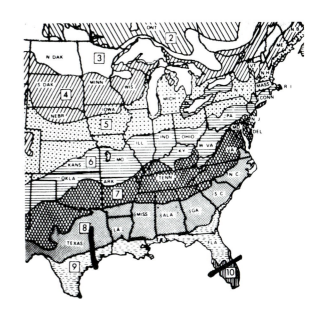

Ilex vomitoria Ait.   Yaupon Holly
Aquifoliaceae or Holly Family   Hardiness Zone 7
Native throughout the Southeast, from Florida to Oklahoma.
SIZE: Small tree, up to 25 feet tall although some cultivars are compact oval shrubs. Slow to moderate grower.
FORM: Most plants in the wild or grown from seed are irregular, multi-stemmed, small trees. Several dwarf cultivars exist which are dense, mounded shrubs.
TEXTURE: Fine.   **EXPOSURE:** Sun to shade.

LEAVES: Alternate, simple; evergreen, oval to elliptical. Vary from 1/2 inch or less, to nearly 2 inches long; nearly always flat. Generally the larger leaves are on the larger tree forms. Glossy green with a crenate or very slightly sawtooth margin. Very new leaves have red veins.

STEM: Young shoots are green, although occasionally they take on a very light brown cast in the fall and winter; sometimes purple. Stems are generally light gray after one or more years. Plants tend to be densely twiggy either in the crowns of the tree form or the entire shrub of the compact, low-growing cultivars.

FLOWERS: Small, creamy white; inconspicuous. Male and female flowers are on separate plants (dioecious).

FRUIT: Opaque, metallic red.

COLOR: Foliage is medium to dark, glossy green. Fruits are opaque, metallic red.

PROPAGATION: Semi-hardwood to hardwood cuttings or seed for the tree forms.

CULTURE: Tolerates full sun, exposed conditions, and considerable heat and drought. One of the toughest of the hollies. Frequently found growing native in wet swampy locations. Grows in nearly all soil types, from very wet to very dry and sand to clay. Responds moderately well to mulching and light but frequent applications of fertilizer.

PESTS: A leaf minor is becoming serious in certain areas of the South and is somewhat difficult to control. Particularly prevalent on the dwarf cultivars. Rarely is scale a problem. Is resistant to the nematode injury which plagues Japanese hollies in light, sandy soils. Leaf phylloxera may be a problem in some areas.

NOTES: Either the tree form, which is very asymmetrical and informal unless severely pruned, or the compact forms, make excellent landscape plants. Sometimes confused with Japanese holly cultivars which have black fruit, young twigs are generally green turning purple in the fall or winter and remain green for several years, and new leaves are green, whereas yaupon holly twigs rarely have a purple cast and turn a light gray after one or more seasons of growth, new leaves always have red-purple veins, and fruits are red.

CULTIVARS: 'Nana': dwarf, compact form with small, shiny leaves: very desirable in planters, as a ground cover, or for general landscape use. Reaches a height of 4 to 5 feet with considerable age. Remains a low dome or oval shape for many years. Should not be planted near foot traffic since the limbs are very brittle. Very little fruiting. 'Pendula': weeping tree form with drooping outer branches. Generally leaves are smaller than regular tree forms. 'Stokes': slightly smaller and more compact cultivar than 'Nana'. Has rich dark green leaves, is a very dwarf, tightly branched form. Probably same as 'Schillings'. Very similar to 'Helleri' Japanese holly but is superior in drought, nematode, and excess water tolerance. 'Soft Touch': growth habit like 'Nana' only the new growth is soft and flexible vs. stiff and rigid. Appears to be somewhat less cold-tolerant. Others probably exist.

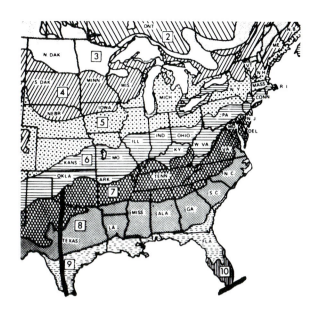

'Nana'

'Nana'

More photographs page 456

Illicium floridanum Ellis   Florida or Purple Anise
Illiciaceae or Illicium Family   Hardiness Zone 9
Native to the United States Gulf Coast and Florida.
SIZE: 10 to 15 feet tall with a 6- to 10-foot spread. Moderate grower.
FORM: Irregular, medium shrub; can be sheared into a dense hedge.
TEXTURE: Coarse.   **EXPOSURE:** Partial shade.

LEAVES: Evergreen, alternate, simple; 4 to 8 inches long with a smooth, glossy upper surface and a smooth and dull underside, clustered near the ends of the branches. Margin is smooth. Crushed leaves have an unpleasant odor. Said to contain a poisonous property that could cause violent stomach reaction or worse, if eaten in large quantities.

STEM: Medium, straight and upright. Green at first, turning red-brown and finally gray. Wood is somewhat brittle.

FLOWERS: Singular or a few together in leaf axils; red-brown to purple with many slender petals separated except at the base. A bit like a spider chrysanthemum. Not showy.

FRUIT: A dry capsule.

COLOR: Leaves are glossy, dark green.

PROPAGATION: Cuttings or seed.

CULTURE: Native to moist, sandy soils along wet areas, but adapted to many urban conditions except for dry, full sun locations. Sufficiently shade-tolerant to retain internal leaves and create a good, dense hedge.

PESTS: Few, if any.

NOTES: Florida anise will tolerate soils that are poorly drained much better than Japanese anise, which requires at least moderately well drained soils. Both species are easy to grow and have few pests. In recent years, both have received more attention in the nursery industry and are becoming more common. XX-POISON-XX

CULTIVARS: 'Alba': has white flowers that provide a striking contrast to the evergreen foliage.

RELATED SPECIES: *Illicium anisatum* L., Japanese anise, native to Japan, has white to yellow fragrant flowers, elongate, and glossy leaves which when crushed have the pleasant aroma of root beer. Japanese anise grows larger and may reach 15 to 25 feet tall, but makes a superior hedge (see photograph) or screen. Even though the branches are upright, secondary branching develops low and leaves are sufficiently shade-tolerant to maintain a visual barrier as well as noise barrier, to some degree. However, plants with large, dense, hairy leaves are more effective in stopping sound. Both anise species have merit as hedges or large screens in semi-shade to shady locations.

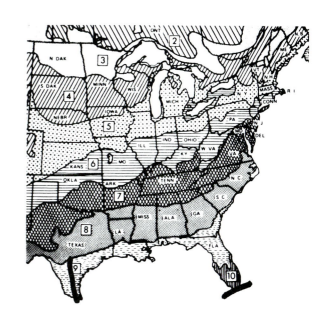

Illicium anisatum

Illicium anisatum

Illicium anisatum

Leucophyllum frutescens I.M. Johst.   Texas Sage
Scrophulariaceae or Figwort Family   Hardiness Zone 8
Native to Texas and the Southwest.
SIZE: 6 to 8 feet tall with a 4- to 6-foot spread. Moderate grower.
FORM: Irregular, medium to large shrub if unpruned; a dense hedge in full sun.
TEXTURE: Medium.   **EXPOSURE:** Sun.

LEAVES: Alternate, simple; ovate, about 1 inch long with very short petioles. Leaves are mostly in clusters at the tips of slender branches. Leaves are densely hairy with short, fine hairs that give the leaves a distinct silver-gray to gray color. Margins are smooth. Foliage contrasts with most other landscape plants, thus creating year round color.

STEM: Slender and covered with dense gray hairs when young. Older stems are grayish black, stiff, and somewhat brittle. Branches readily with pruning, thus develops a good hedge **if** in full sun.

FLOWERS: Lavender to pink; bell-shaped, in leaf axils. Very showy in contrast with the distinct gray foliage. Flowers well only in full sun during early summer. It sometimes flowers profusely following the first rain after a drought.

FRUIT: A small, hard seed; not commonly seen in landscapes, .

COLOR: Foliage is silver-gray. Flowers are lavender or pink.

PROPAGATION: Seed or semi-hardwood cuttings with limited mist.

CULTURE: Very drought- and heat-tolerant and grows well on droughty, sandy soils. Does not tolerate heavy clays or poor soil aeration or drainage. Requires full sun in order to grow well and develop a dense foliage canopy. Foliage is shallow over the branch skeleton and, with low light, the plant becomes unattractive (see photogaph). Likewise, full sun is required for good flowering.

PESTS: Nematodes may be a problem on warm, sandy soils. Also, root rot organisms on poorly drained sites.

NOTES: A most unusual and attractive foliage and bloom combination contrasting with other foliage when planted on an appropriate site. May tend to dominate a landscape if not used carefully. The lavender flowers may clash with reds, oranges or yellows of either structures or of other plants. A handsome plant sometimes avoided because it is so distinct. It deserves to be used more but carefully in well-designed plantings. Fills a real need in southern and southwestern locations, particularly where reflected light and heat are involved and sotol, yucca, and agave are not acceptable. Rather short-lived; however, its value far exceeds the occasional replacement cost. Other common names include: Texas sage, purple sage, barometer plant, and wild lilac.

CULTIVARS: 'Alba': white flowers; however, the limited foliage contrast reduces its attractiveness. 'Floribunda': may produce more flowers than most seedlings. 'Green Cloud': leaves are distinctly more green but flowers are purple-violet. 'White Cloud': silvery foliage and large white flowers. 'Thundercloud': has silvery foliage and many dark purple flowers. Other cultivars may exist.

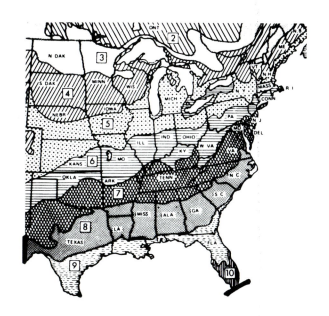

Ligustrum japonicum Thunb.   Japanese or Wax Leaf Ligustrum
Oleaceae or Olive Family   Hardiness Zone 7b
Native to Japan and Korea.

SIZE: 10 to 15 feet tall with a 6- to 12-foot spread. Very rapid grower.

FORM: Medium to large, erect shrub; frequently multiple-stemmed with an umbrella-like crown. Can be used successfully as a small tree.

TEXTURE: Medium to coarse.   **EXPOSURE:** Sun to shade.

LEAVES: Opposite, simple; ovate, about 2 inches wide and 3 to 4 inches long with a smooth margin. Dark green and very glossy or waxy on the upper surface; dull green below and much lighter.

STEM: Generally upright, multiple-stemmed with an umbrella-like crown when mature. Wood is moderately durable and rigid. Young bark is gray-green becoming medium gray-brown with age and has many prominent lenticels on all but the oldest stems.

FLOWERS: White clusters at the tips of new growth during May to early June. Showy; very fragrant, offensive to some people. Pollen and/or fragrance may be troublesome to persons with hay fever or other allergies.

FRUIT: Green, turning black in the fall; about 1/4 inch in diameter. Occasionally escapes and becomes a weed in the lower South.

COLOR: Foliage is dark green and very glossy. Flowers are white. Fruits are black.

PROPAGATION: Semi-hardwood to hardwood cuttings.

CULTURE: A very tough, rapid-growing shrub or small tree. Transplants easily, tolerates drought, poor soils, sun or shade, and exposed sites. Responds well to pruning and is occasionally used for topiary work and formal hedges but is not a good choice because it requires frequent pruning. Wax leaf ligustrum is very susceptible to copper deficiency. Symptoms consist of stunting, leaf distortion, and sometimes tip dieback; but no chlorosis develops.

PESTS: None serious but may be a "carrier" of white fly to other landscape plants.

NOTES: Best used as a small, multiple-stemmed tree. Grows too vigorously to make a good hedge. Leaves and fruits may be poisonous and flowers may be annoying to some. Frequently confused with *Ligustrum lucidum* which has larger leaves with a distinct clear or translucent margin surrounding the leaf blade. *Ligustrum lucidum* frequently attains a height of 20 to 25 feet and sets large, profuse clusters of grape-like black fruits. Otherwise, toughness and durability of the two species is similar. Wax leaf ligustrum may be the same as *L. texanum* in the trade, thus should probably be *L. japonicum* 'Texanum'. ??-POISON-??

CULTIVARS: 'Coreaceum': strict upright grower with leaves appearing folded or rolled. Slow grower so good for Japanese effect. 'Howardi' and 'Frasieri': new growth is yellow to yellow-green, turning green with maturity. Sometimes sold as 'Variegata'. 'Lake Tresca': the lower branches droop to make a mound. Has smaller leaves than the species. As a specimen shrub or low, rounded hedge, it is superb; but quite susceptible to a leaf spot disease in some locations. 'Suwanee River': more compact erect branches and is said to be more cold hardy. Other cultivars probably exist.

RELATED SPECIES: *Ligustrum sinense* Lour., Chinese privet, has leaves approximately 1/4 as large with small wiry stems and a compact, irregular growth habit. 'Variegata': near yellow/white leaves.

475

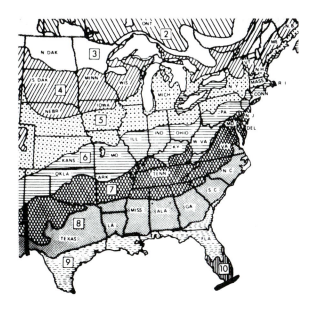

L. lucidum

L. lucidum

'Howardi'

Lonicera japonica Thunb.   Japanese Honeysuckle
Caprifoliaceae or Honeysuckle Family   Hardiness Zone 4
Native to a wide range of eastern Asia.

SIZE: 24 to 30 inches tall without support, but may climb 15 to 20 feet over other vegetation or on a trellis. Rapid grower.

FORM: A twining, tangled, dense mass, particularly in full sun.

TEXTURE: Medium.   **EXPOSURE:** Sun to shade.

LEAVES: Opposite, on a short petiole, ovate to oblong with a pointed tip and rounded base. Somewhat pubescent beneath or almost without hair, dark green to purple above. Generally 1 1/2 to 3 inches long, 1/2 to 1 inch wide. Semi-evergreen in the northern range with bronze leaves in winter; evergreen from the lower Zone 7 and southward.

STEM: A slender, hairy, twining, wrapping vine. Has no attachment mechanism, only the wrapping. Stems are stout and tough. Bark shreds in long vertical strips on old stems.

FLOWERS: Bloom on new growth; white fading to yellow, generally during the same day. Two-lipped, and 1 1/2 inches long with a long funnel-shaped throat. Very fragrant so attracts many bees and other insects. Blooms generally from mid May to September or October if the plant is in full sun and growing.

FRUIT: A small, black berry; not particularly showy or distracting.

COLOR: Foliage is green to purple, depending on cultivar. Flowers are white turning yellow in most cases. Fruit is black.

PROPAGATION: Seed or softwood, semi-hardwood or hardwood cuttings.

CULTURE: Grows in nearly any soil condition under any moisture regime. Responds rapidly to fertilization or good soils. Grows and flowers best in full sun. Becomes spindly, less attractive, less dense and has fewer blooms in partial shade or shady locations. Many times it becomes too vigorous for the site in which it is planted. Needs to be located in an area where it can be confined, as it will grow into and consume other shrubs that have low branches. Responds fairly well to pruning.

PESTS: None serious.

NOTES: Works well for erosion control on road banks or slopes. Covers fences to make an excellent screen. The fragrant flowers are highly prized and lend a very desirable aroma to any landscape. The primary concern should be how to control its growth. Has escaped cultivation in the eastern and southern portions of the United States and has become a weed which is difficult to eradicate.

CULTIVARS: 'Halliana': vigorous growing vine with green leaves and yellow and white flowers. This is the most common form and should be avoided. 'Pollyanna': dull green leaves with a purple tint. Slightly more shrub-like. 'Purpurea': vigorous growing shrub-vine with rich, purple-tinted, dark green leaves and coral red flowers which turn yellow. The best cultivar for most landscape situations. Probably the same as *L. japonica* 'Chinensis'. 'Variegata': leaf is striped irregularly with yellow. Generally an inferior plant. Other cultivars probably exist.

RELATED SPECIES: *Lonicera sempervirens* L., trumpet honeysuckle, is a semi-evergreen vine with long tubular, trumpet-like red or yellow flowers; showy but not fragrant. Before flowering, leaves are opposite, simple, and oval, medium green to blue-green. However, after the plant begins to bloom, the upper pairs of leaves are joined together at the bases. Generally easier to contain than *L. japonica*. 'Magnifica': has bright red flowers. 'Flava' or 'Sulphurea': yellow flowers.

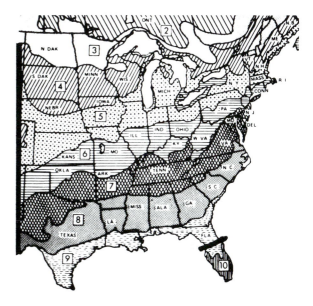

L. sempervirens

Loropetalum chinense D.Oliver   Loropetalum
Hamamelidaceae or Witch Hazel Family   Hardiness Zone 7
Native to China
SIZE: 6 to 8 feet tall with similar spread. Fast grower.
FORM: Irregular, rounded, evergreen shrub.
TEXTURE: Medium to fine.   **EXPOSURE:** Sun to partial shade.

LEAVES: Alternate, simple; evergreen. Ovate to nearly rounded, 1 to 2 inches long, 3/4 to 1 1/2 inch wide. Dark green to wine above, with a smooth margin. The leaves, young stems and receptacles of the fruit are covered by fine hairs.

STEM: Slender; greenish, quickly turning brown. Densely hairy. On old stems the bark exfoliates in long strips of a rich brown. Attractive.

FLOWERS: Cream to white to pinkish. Fragrant. The petals are strap-like and 3 to 5 or more flowers generally are in a cluster on the stem. The effect is unusual and striking. Appear in March, April, or early May.

FRUIT: A woody, rounded capsule appearing like a ball in a stemmed glass. Not showy.

COLOR: Foliage is dark green to wine. Flower are white to pink.

PROPAGATION: Seed or cuttings.

CULTURE: Grows well in many soils, even the pure sands of central Florida and heavy clays of North Carolina. Moderate drought tolerance, once established. Transplants easily from containers or B & B. May be a bit intolerant of alkaline soils, but there are attractive specimens in San Antonio, Texas.

PESTS: None serious.

NOTES: For years the green leaf, white flower forms were all that was known. Recently, cultivars with pink flowers and wine foliage were discovered and have greatly increased the interest in this plant. Plants in Stillwater, Oklahoma were killed in 1982 when the temperature dropped to -10 degrees F in December. However, for a number of previous winters the plant had performed well with winter temperatures near zero degrees F. It deserves more use as it makes a good hedge or just left alone as an irregular evergreen shrub.

CULTIVARS: 'Roseum' has rose-colored flowers and wine foliage. 'Rubrum razzleberri': wine foliage and pink flowers; grows approximately 4 to 6 feet tall. Other cultivars exist.

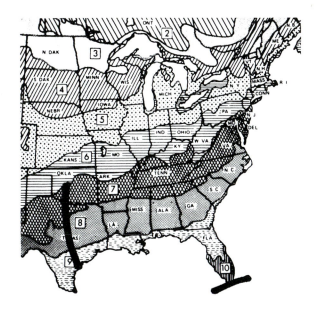

Magnolia grandiflora L.   Southern Magnolia or Bullbay
Magnoliaceae or Magnolia Family   Hardiness Zone 7
Native to the southern United States.

SIZE: 60- to 100-foot tree with a 30- to 50-foot spread. Slow to moderate grower.
FORM: Pyramidal when young, becoming more round-headed with age.
TEXTURE: Coarse.   **EXPOSURE:** Sun to shade.

LEAVES: Alternate, simple; 6 to 12 inches long, 2 to 4 inches wide. Thick and leathery, very durable. Oval with a smooth margin. Shiny dark green above; rusty and hairy below; however, some leaves may be smooth below. Petioles are stout and hairy.

STEM: Young stems are green to pale green, large in diameter, covered with rusty hairs, later becoming smooth but remaining green until finally turning grayish brown. Bark on older limbs is aromatic, finally breaking into thin, small scales. Young stems are very brittle. Old wood is white and hard but not durable. Easily broken by ice storms.

FLOWERS: Single, on short terminal stalks, cup-shaped; 6 to 9 inches across with 6 to 16 rounded petals which are white or slightly white-purple at the base. Very fragrant. Appear late spring to mid summer. Useful as a cut flower.

FRUIT: Ripens July to October. A pinecone-like structure, 2 to 4 inches long, 1 1/2 to 2 inches in diameter. Rusty, hairy, splits to expose seeds covered with red flesh and attached by a thin thread. Forty to sixty seeds per cone.

COLOR: Foliage is shiny dark green. Flowers are white. Fruits are red.

PROPAGATION: Seed, grafting, or cuttings as some cultivars root well.

CULTURE: Native to rich moist soils throughout the southeastern states where it is at its prime. Tolerates a moderate range of soil conditions as long as moisture does not become extremely limited and soils are at least moderately fertile. A very sensitive plant to magnesium deficiency. Young, newly planted trees should be given a heavy dose of magnesium sulfate (Epsom salts) to help insure sufficient magnesium. Somewhat difficult to transplant from the field but transplants best in early spring. The root system is somewhat coarse, not fibrous, and slow to re-establish. The wood is weak, thus narrow forks and weak branching habits should be prevented.

PESTS: None serious.

NOTES: A magnificent large tree which dominates the landscape in most situations. Should be planted only after careful consideration of moisture and soil conditions and landscape effect. Allow sufficient room for development. Most attractive when branches are allowed to remain near the soil surface.

CULTIVARS: 'Majestic Beauty': large, deep green foliage and many flowers. Pyramidal shape when young and large, fragrant, white flowers in summer. 'St. Mary': an old selection with bright, glistening green leaves above and bronze below. Very compact with early, large, white flowers. 'Bracken's Brown Beauty': a pyramidal tree when young with good flowers and heavy, rusty brown hairs on leaf backs. 'Little Gem': leaves smaller than the species and remains more compact with dense foliage, at least until quite old. Prolific bloomer all season. 'Claudia Wannamaker': a vigorous grower with open, pyramidal form and dark foliage. 'D.D. Blancher': an upright grower with dark foliage and orange underside. Many other cultivars exist.

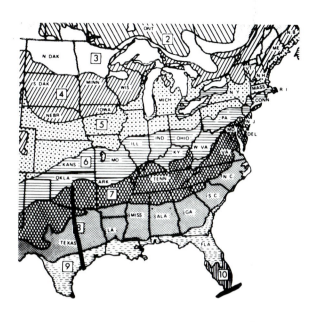

Mahonia aquifolium (Pursh.) Nutt.   Oregon Grape Mahonia or Holly Grape
    (Syn. *Berberis aquifolium*)
Berberidaceae or Barberry Family   Hardiness Zone 5
Native to the northwest coast of the United States.
SIZE: 3 to 6 feet tall with a spread of 6 to 8 feet with age. Moderate grower.
FORM: Irregular clustering of upright stems with little branching.
TEXTURE: Medium.   EXPOSURE: Partial shade to shade.

LEAVES: Alternate, compound; generally 6 to 12 inches long, with 5 to 9 ovate leaflets. Individual leaflets may be as much as 3 inches long and 1 to 1 1/2 inches wide with numerous long tapering points on the margin of the leaflets, making them resemble English or Chinese holly. Generally a deep dark green above, light green below, and taking on a purple-bronze cast in the winter.

STEM: Upright with little branching. Most stems arise from a weak rhizome and only occasionally after damage or pruning does secondary branching occur on the main stems. The color of the inner bark is a brilliant yellow, typical of members of the Berberidaceae family.

FLOWERS: Bright yellow. In dense terminal clusters during late April or early May. Moderately showy.

FRUIT: Bluish black; egg-shaped; during mid summer to early fall. Generally about 1/4 inch long.

COLOR: Foliage is green during summer; purple to purple-bronze in the winter. Flowers are yellow. Fruit is blue-black.

PROPAGATION: Semi-hardwood to hardwood cuttings in the fall or winter, or from seed.

CULTURE: Tolerates a moderate range of soil conditions, as long as it is not excessively wet or hot. Generally responds best to shade or part shade situations, north or east sides of buildings, with moderate moisture and moderate to cool temperatures. Does not tolerate hot, dry situations. May desiccate during fall and winter, turning brown on the margins and becoming unsightly, particularly in exposed and/or windy locations.

PESTS: None serious.

NOTES: An attractive, useful, broadleaf evergreen in scale with many urban landscape uses. A major criticism would be the loose openness of many plants, particularly in poor growing conditions or if they have not been pruned. Best distinguished from the hollies (*Ilex spp.*) by the compound leaves as opposed to the simple leaves of the hollies. Oregon grape mahonia has the fewest leaflets (5 to 9) of the *Mahonia* species encountered in the United States.

CULTIVARS: 'Compacta': a compact, semi-dwarf form with glossy leaves and a bronze winter color. Stays lower, more of a compact oval shrub, rarely reaching more than 2 to 2 1/2 feet in height. Superior to the parent for most situations. 'Golden Abundance': a heavy bloomer and fruit producer. Rather upright form. 'Kings Ransom': upright grower with bluish foliage and wine winter color. 'Orange Flame': new growth is purplish bronze, then fades to dark green. More upright than most. 'Apollo' (may be *Mahonia repens* or a hybrid) only grows 10 inches or so in height to make a ground cover, but flowers well. Others exist.

'Compacta'

Mahonia bealei (Fort.) Carr.   Leatherleaf Mahonia
Berberidaceae or Barberry Family   Hardiness Zone 6b
Native to China.

SIZE: Height of 6 to 8 feet, occasionally more if a very old plant; little horizontal spread. Moderate grower.

FORM: Stiff, upright stem with few, if any, branches. The leaves are clustered at the tops of the stem.

TEXTURE: Medium to coarse.   **EXPOSURE:** Full sun to shade.

LEAVES: Alternate, compound; clustered at the tips of the individual stems. Rarely do the stems branch. Leaves are 12 to 16 inches long with 9 to 15 hard, leathery, ovate leaflets. Each individual leaflet may be up to 5 inches long and 2 1/2 inches wide with 3 to 7 teeth. Each pair of leaflets generally is a different shape from all others. The entire leaf unit and the leaflets are very stiff and rigid, almost plastic-like in appearance and texture. Generally a deep, dark green color above, lighter below.

STEM: Strict, upright, and unbranched. Does develop a weak rhizome which gives rise to the individual stems. Stems frequently reach 1 to 1 1/2 inches in diameter. When the bark is peeled, it has the characteristic golden color of the barberry family.

FLOWERS: Appear in early spring: January or February in the lower South, early to late March in the more northern regions. The flowers are lemon yellow, in dense terminal clusters; quite showy.

FRUIT: Dark blue with a powdery bloom, extremely showy against the coarsely textured, deep green leaves.

COLOR: Foliage is deep dark green. Flowers are lemon yellow. Fruit is dark blue.

PROPAGATION: Hardwood cuttings from the terminal shoots will root, but generally propagated from seed.

CULTURE: Grows well in a wide range of soil types, from light sandy to heavy clays, as long as they are not excessively wet. Responds to fertilization. Best adapted to partial shade locations such as the north or east side of structures. Moderately drought-resistant. If tallest stems on old plants are pruned in winter, more stems form.

PESTS: None serious.

NOTES: A most interesting form in that the plant can be manipulated to give a series of step- or tier-like sections of leaves. Taller plants in back, shorter ones in front, particularly with night lighting effects and complementary mulches beneath, makes a most pleasing landscape effect. When it blooms in February or March the yellow flowers are quite attractive, then are followed by the large blue fruits. Many blue colors are really blue-gray or blue-green and tend to disappear in the landscape, but not the fruits of leatherleaf mahonia. An easy to manage and problem-free shrub. Should be used more. To identify *Mahonia* species, compare number of leaflets, number of teeth per leaflet and leaflet texture.

CULTIVARS: None known.

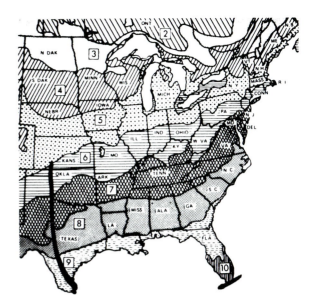

Mahonia fortunei Fedde.   Fernleaf Mahonia
Berberidaceae or Barberry Family   Hardiness Zone 8
Native to China.
SIZE: 4 to 6 feet tall and may spread 4 to 6 feet. A moderate grower.
FORM: A mounding shrub composed of individual vertical stems, rarely branching.
TEXTURE: Fine to medium.   **EXPOSURE:** Partial shade to shade.

LEAVES: Alternate, compound; with 5 to 9 lanceolate leaflets frequently reaching 5 inches long and 1/4 to 1/2 inch wide, with 20 to 30 teeth per leaflet. Very soft and flexible, not stiff and hazardous as are other species of *Mahonia*. Generally very deep, almost blackish green, giving a distinct contrast to many pale green or lighter green shrubs.

STEM: Upright and seldom branching, fairly slender, generally 1/4 inch or more in diameter. A rhizome does exist and accounts for the slowly spreading clump of stems. Like all Berberidaceae, the inner stem is a golden color.

FLOWERS: Yellow. In terminal clusters in early spring. Moderately showy, particularly against the very deep green foliage.

FRUIT: Small, purple-black berry; not particularly showy.

COLOR: Foliage is deep black-green. Flowers are lemon yellow.

PROPAGATION: Semi-hardwood to hardwood cuttings or seed.

CULTURE: Grows reasonably well in a wide range of soil conditions as long as it is not excessively wet or hot (both soil and foliage temperature). Responds well to fertilization, mulching, and other good cultural practices. Is best grown in part shade to shady locations. Flourishes and is most attractive in part shade or on the north or east side of a structure where it attains the very deep foliage color which is an excellent contrast to other lighter colored plants. Responds reasonably well to pruning by producing more stems. Although it does not branch well on the vertical stems, pruning will stimulate further rhizome development and thus cause a thickening in the plant.

PESTS: None serious.

NOTES: A very desirable foliage color in many shade locations because of the contrast year round to most other foliage. Unlike leatherleaf mahonia, this foliage, although tufted at the tips of the stems, does not give a tiered or layered effect. By contrast, *Mahonia fortunei* has an almost fern-like texture and gives a densely mounded or oval shrub form with very little pruning or maintenance problems. Should be used a great deal more. To identify *Mahonia* species, compare number of leaflets, number of teeth per leaflet, and leaflet texture.

CULTIVARS: None known.

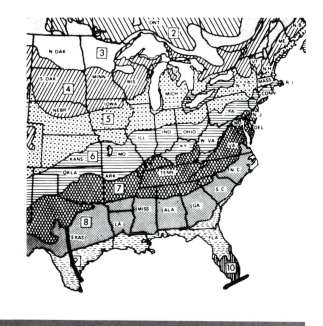

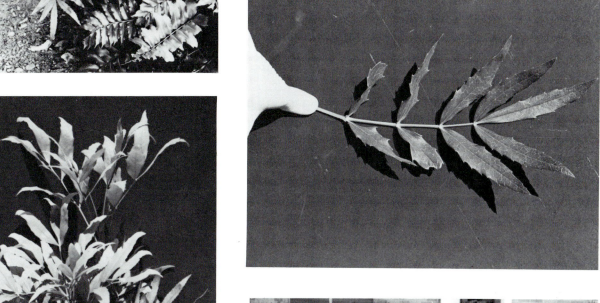

Mahonia lomariifolia Takeda. 　　　　　Chinese Hollygrape
Berberidaceae or Barberry Family 　　　Hardiness Zone 8
Native to China.

SIZE: May grow to 10 to 12 feet tall but rarely spreads more than 3 to 4 feet, developing 10 to 15 vertical stems. Moderate grower.

FORM: Single, unbranched stems with a tufting or layering of the foliage at the top. Much like leatherleaf mahonia.

TEXTURE: Medium. 　　　　　　　**EXPOSURE:** Partial shade to shade.

LEAVES: Alternate, compound; with 15 to 31 leaflets that are generally lanceolate to oblong with 5 to 7 spines per leaflet. Generally a medium green. The overall compound leaf may be as much as 18 to 20 inches long.

STEM: Vertical stems, generally unbranched, with foliage tufting at the tip, appearing to be in a whorled arrangement but really is closely alternate. Stems may reach as much as 1 inch in diameter with a rather rough scaly bark. As with all Berberidaceae, the inner bark is a golden color. A very slight rhizome development is present that gives rise to multiple vertical stems. Pruning rarely develops branching on the main stem but does stimulate further rhizome devlopment and thickening of the clump.

FLOWERS: Yellow. In terminal clusters. Moderately showy, generally in early spring.

FRUIT: Small, oval, blue-purple berry.

COLOR: Foliage is medium green. Flowers are yellow.

PROPAGATION: Semi-hardwood to hardwood cuttings or seed.

CULTURE: Grows well in most moderately fertile soils. Does not appear to be well adapted to light, sandy soils such as on the Florida peninsula or to excessively wet locations. Does, however, have a moderate degree of drought tolerance. Best adapted to partial shade or shady locations on north or east sides of structures, where it performs very well.

PESTS: None serious.

NOTES: A rarely used but very attractive shrub that gives a tiered or layered effect. The texture is very useful in many landscape situations particularly small formal gardens or where a portion or all of the garden is viewed from above. The terminal whorl of leaves is most interesting, particularly when contrasted against a ground cover. Can best be distinguished from leatherleaf mahonia in that Chinese hollygrape frequently has twice as many leaflets which are lighter green and less hard and plastic-like. Can be distinguished from *Mahonia bealei* in that Chinese hollygrape generally has 2 to 3 times as many leaflets which are much more harsh to touch and more plastic-like in texture. In leaf rigidity, Chinese hollygrape is intermediate between the very hard leatherleaf mahonia and the soft and flexible *M. fortunei*. The number of leaflets, number of teeth per leaflet, and texture of the leaflets are probably the best identification features for various species of *Mahonia*.

CULTIVARS: None known.

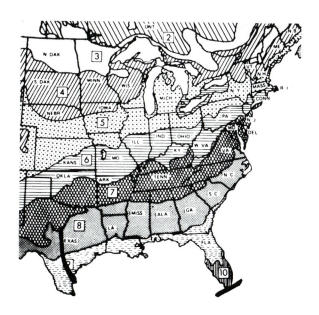

Myrica cerifera L. Southern Wax Myrtle
Myracaceae or Sweetgale Family Hardiness Zone 7
Native to the southeastern United States.
SIZE: 15 to 25 feet tall with a 15- to 20-foot spread. Moderate grower.
FORM: A broadly spreading, small tree or large shrub.
TEXTURE: Fine to medium. **EXPOSURE:** Sun to shade.

LEAVES: Alternate, simple; strap-like, twisted or ruffled with irregular teeth on the margin. About 2 to 4 inches long, 1/2 inch wide, becoming reduced in size toward the tips of branches. Medium to dark green above and pale green below. Both leaf surfaces are covered with yellowish or brownish dots. All leaves have a distinct odor when crushed. Leaves are somewhat similar in appearance to those of laurel oak only much softer and more flexible.

STEM: Young stems are hairy and light green to gray, becoming a light gray with irregular gray patches with age. Commonly heavily coated with lichens, which are small, green or gray, moss-like plants.

FLOWERS: Male and female are on separate plants (dioecious). Not showy.

FRUIT: Round; about 1/8 inch in diameter, in dense clusters. At maturity they are heavily coated with wax, giving a bluish white or gray cast.

COLOR: Foliage is medium yellow green to dark green.

PROPAGATION: Seed, cuttings, or removal of suckers.

CULTURE: Native to sandy swamplands and acid, wet, poorly drained soils throughout the southern states as far west as eastern Texas and southeastern Oklahoma. Tolerates a wide range of soil conditions in moderate shade or full sun. Some plants are dug in the wild and transported to landscape sites. However, it is difficult to transplant them from the wild. Container or field nursery material will greatly increase survival and performance. Responds well to fertilizer and mulching. Especially useful in wet and/or shady locations where an evergreen, multiple-stemmed small tree is desired. Grows too large for many shrub uses except as a large screen or background.

PESTS: None serious, although occasionally webworms will defoliate some branches.

NOTES: A very attractive and useful small evergreen tree or large shrub with an open, loose crown. Suitable for a wide range of landscape situations throughout the southern states. Has an attractive bark and a tendency to develop multiple stems. Must be criticized for its tendency to develop suckers at the base, but these can be kept in check. Female trees produce large quantities of fruit but they do not become a weed in the landscape. Has a symbiotic nitrogen fixing bacterium associated with the roots which allows the plant to grow in low fertility soils.

CULTIVARS: 'Pumila': grows only to about 4 feet tall. 'Fairfax': grows to about 5 or 6 feet, quite compact, and slowly spreads as a clump. 'Georgia Gem': only grows to about 2 feet tall and has small leaves. Others may exist.

RELATED SPECIES: *Myrica pensylvanica* Lois., bayberry, is a deciduous shrub sometimes reaching 6 to 8 feet tall. Leaves fall late and are very aromatic. Grayish white fruit, showy in the winter. Does well in sterile, dry soils in the Upper South and northern states due to the nitrogen-fixing bacteria. Hardy in Zone 5.

 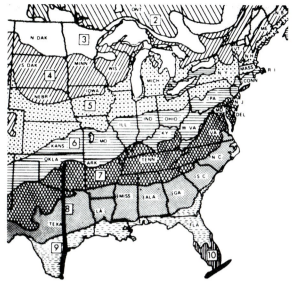

Nandina domestica Thunb.   Heavenly Bamboo or Nandina
Berberidaceae or Barberry Family   Hardiness Zone 6
Native to China.
SIZE: 5 to 7 feet tall with a 3- to 5-foot spread. Moderate to rapid grower.
FORM: Numerous, unbranched stems with flat-topped layers of foliage.
TEXTURE: Fine.   **EXPOSURE:** Sun to shade.

LEAVES: Alternate, 2 to 3 times compound. Leaflets are 1 to 2 inches long and 1/2 to 1 inch wide and are usually ovate and smooth on the margins. An entire compound leaf may be as much as 30 inches long. The supporting stem-like structure (rachis) has the appearance of being glued together at the intersections with small bulbous-like swellings. Deep green to metallic blue-green in shade, or a light green to red-purple in sun.

STEM: Upright and unbranched. Rough, dark brown bark has vertical lines. Plants spread by slow-growing rhizomes, thus pruning of old stems stimulates rhizome development and thickening of the plant. As with all Berberidaceae, the inner bark is golden.

FLOWERS: White. In terminal clusters in mid spring. Moderately showy.

FRUIT: Round; about 1/4 inch diameter, in large grape-like clusters hanging down on top of the foliage. Green, turning bright red by early fall. Spectacular. They remain through most of the fall and winter under good growing conditions. Fruit and foliage contrast is greatest under partial shade to shade conditions.

COLOR: Foliage is green to blue-green in shade; light green to red-purple in sun. Flowers are white. Fruits are bright red.

PROPAGATION: Cultivars are propagated by semi-hardwood cuttings in the fall from rhizomes or may also be propagated from seed collected and planted before red pigment develops. Seedlings are relatively uniform, unlike those of many species.

CULTURE: One of the most durable and tolerant of all shrubs. Very drought-resistant and does well under harsh growing conditions, even in poor soil, as long as soil temperature is not exceedingly high. thus locations such as parking lots or planting strips between curbs and sidewalks should be avoided. Very responsive to fertility, mulching, and other good cultural practices. Grow vigorously and has dense, terminal clusters of foliage and fruits. Although it willsurvive in full sun, it will lose one of its most spectacular aspects, the contrast of the deep red fruits durig the fall and most of the winter with the deep metallic blue-green foliage. unlike many shrubs, it will grow in very dense shade and still flower and fruit. Thin out old stems annually to increase the number of stems.

PESTS: One of the most disease- and insect-free broadleaf evergreen shrubs.

NOTES: An under rated plant, which is as versatile as any landscape shrub. Widely planted in the Lower South as a foundation planting in front of red brick homes which minimizes effectiveness. Should be used more in the proper locations. XX-POISON-XX

CULTIVARS: 'Compacta': more dwarf and compact growing than the parent: 4 to 5 feet tall. Foliage is lighter green, leaflets are slightly smaller and the stem is more slender. 'Nana' or 'Dwarf': a dwarf plant rarely reaching more than 3 feet tall. Unlike the parent or cultivar, 'Compacta', it does branch on the stem giving it a much more dense, oval form. leaves and leaflets are much smaller than those of the parent, making it a smaller, finer-textured plant. Often takes on a red to scarlet fall and winter color, particularly in partial shade to sun. 'Harbour Dwarf': smaller, dark green leaves and more branches. a very nice plant. 'Gulf Stream': dwarf with dense smaller leaves. 'Fire Power', 'Atropurpurea Nana', 'Okame', and 'Woodsdwarf': are all very compact, dwarf forms with reddish to reddish purple foliage.

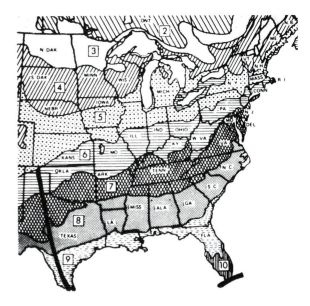

'Nana'

Nerium oleander L.   Oleander
Apocynaceae or Dogbane Family   Hardiness Zone 8
Native to southern Asia.
SIZE: 6 to 16 feet tall in clumps 6 to 12 feet across. Rapid grower.
FORM: Large, multiple-stemmed shrub.
TEXTURE: Fine to medium.   EXPOSURE: Sun to shade.

LEAVES: Opposite or in whorls of 3 or 4. Long, slender, 3 to 5 inches long and 1/2 inch wide, tapers to a point at the tip and has a smooth margin. Smooth and leathery, deep green above and slightly lighter green below. Delicate veins are almost parallel.

STEM: Young stems are upright with few branches. Green at first, finally becoming gray-brown with age. Stems exude a clear sap when damaged.

FLOWERS: During the summer, in terminal clusters. Various colors: pinks, whites, rose or lavender. Generally 5 petals with a funnel-like base. Very showy; odorless.

FRUIT: Small capsule; not showy.

COLOR: Foliage is deep dark green. Flowers are red, white, rose, or lavender.

PROPAGATION: Cuttings or division of a clump.

CULTURE: An extremely tough, durable shrub. Very drought-resistant and salt-tolerant. Tolerates brackish waters and wet or dry locations. One of the most durable and widely adaptable landscape shrubs. In some areas it has been used in highway median plantings as a screen. Responds vigorously to fertilizer. Occasionally grown as a standard or single-stemmed specimen shrub. Flowers best in full sun, but some flowers will be produced in moderate to dense shade.

PESTS: Oleander caterpillar is the most serious pest. This is a stinging caterpillar that should be avoided. May severely defoliate the plant if left unchecked, but is relatively easy to control with sprays.

NOTES: An amazingly durable, showy shrub in terms of both foliage and flowers. All parts of the plants are poisonous if eaten by humans or livestock. Extracts of stems and leaves have been used for rat poisons in Europe for centuries. Numerous cases have been reported of stems being cut and used for roasting hot dogs over a fire and thereby contacting the poisonous principle. Extremely toxic; green or dry. A single leaf is said to be deadly to a 150-pound man. XX-POISON-XX

CULTIVARS: 'Cherry Ripe': brilliant rose-red, single flowers. 'Calypso': single, very showy, bright pink flowers. 'Hardy Pink': single, salmon-pink flowers. 'Hawaii': single, salmon-pink flowers with yellow throats. 'Isle of Capri': single, light yellow flowers. 'Missus Roeding': salmon-pink flowers. 'Sister Agnes': single, pure white flowers. 'Ruby-lace': has large, red flowers. Many others probably exist.

 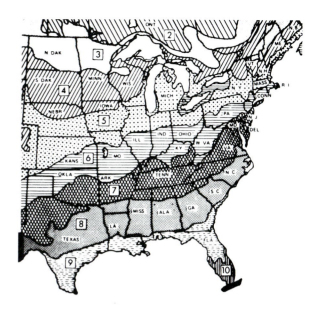

Opuntia spp.   Prickly Pear and Cholla Cactus
Cactaceae or Cactus Family   Hardiness Zone 6
Native to the south central and southwestern United States.
SIZE: Variable, 2 to 12 feet tall, depending on species. Generally slow growers.
FORM: Irregular clumps or shrub-like mounds.
TEXTURE: Coarse.   EXPOSURE: Sun.

LEAVES: Inconspicuous; although the plate-like sections are sometimes viewed as leaves. These more or less leaf-like structures are really modified stems.

STEM: Upright or spreading, often lots of branching with broad, flat joints or pads in the prickly pears. However, the cholla cactus has cylindrical joints or branches. These flat or cylindrical stem sections remain green even with considerable age and are often covered with many tufts of spines. They give rise to the flowers and fruits. Stems are stout but may be broken by vehicles or foot traffic.

FLOWERS: Numerous during mid spring to early summer on the outermost joints or plate-like stem sections. Generally shallowly bowl- or tulip-shaped with many petals. Yellow to orange or red; very showy. Individual flowers last only about 1 day. However, a vigorously growing plant can produce many flowers and thus bloom over a period of several weeks and create an attractive landscape show.

FRUIT: Generally ripen mid to late summer. A large berry; variable in size and shape but may reach as much as 2 to 3 inches long and 1 to 2 inches in diameter. Green at first, red to purple at maturity. Edible, but often covered with clumps of spines.

COLOR: Foliage is green. Flowers are yellow, orange, or red. Fruit is red to purple.

PROPAGATION: Seed or cuttings: plate-like stem sections root readily in most soils.

CULTURE: Native throughout the south central and southwestern United States. Very tolerant of hot, dry conditions and poor, alkaline soils. They lend themselves to the growing conditions of parking lots, paved areas and other hot, dry conditions often encountered in urban or city landscaping. Will not, however, tolerate excessive water or very wet, soggy locations, except for very short periods of time.

PESTS: None serious.

NOTES: Not commonly used in landscaping; however, in combination with *Agave spp.*, *Yucca spp.*, or extensive rock work in the landscape, they can be very pleasant and useful. Virtually maintenance-free. The show of flowers in mid spring to mid summer is spectacular. Some plants produce many flowers over a period of several weeks. An excellent choice for areas where vandalism is high as they have a very effective defense mechanism. However, there are spineless species and/or cultivars available if the spines are not wanted. Should be used more, particularly in hot, dry locations where reflected light or heat from buildings and air conditioner exhaust may kill other plants. Bailey states that more than 250 species of *Opuntia* are known.

SPECIES: *O. imbricata* (Haworth.) D.C., walking stick cholla: 6 to 10 feet tall, sometimes forming dense thickets. Flowers are 2 to 3 inches in diameter, purple, very showy. Hardy in Zone 6 and southward. *O. engelmanni* Salm-Dyck., Engelman prickly pear, is a bushy cactus up to 6 feet tall, generally without a definite trunk. Flowers are yellow, 3 inches in diameter, generally in April or May. Very showy. Fruits are large, red-purple, 2 to 3 inches long, also showy and appear mid summer to fall. *O. lindheimeri* Engelm., Lindheimer prickly pear, may grow 6 to 12 feet tall, generally with a definite trunk though sometimes growing horizontal. Flowers are yellow to orange or red, very showy. There is a spineless form with a distinct bluish green color. Many other species and cultivars exist.

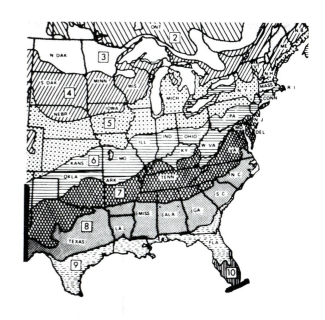

Opuntia imbricata

Opuntia imbricata

Osmanthus heterophyllus   False Holly, Holly Osmanthus
        (Syn. *O. Ilicifolius*)
Oleaceae or Olive Family   Hardiness Zone 7b
Native to Japan.
SIZE: 4 to 15 feet tall with a 3- to 10-foot spread, depending on the cultivar. Moderate to rapid grower.
FORM: A densely growing, upright, broadleaf, evergreen shrub.
TEXTURE: Medium   **EXPOSURE:** Sun to shade

LEAVES: Oval to oblong, 2 to 3 inches long, 1/2 to 1 1/2 inches wide with a few large, spiny teeth on the margin making them look like holly leaves. However, the leaves on all *Osmanthus* species are opposite, whereas the leaves on all *Ilex* species or hollies are alternate and thus can be distinguished. Foliage is generally dark green and very attractive. Petiole is short and stout.

STEM: Very young stems are green, but turn a light sandy brown with some age; moderately slender and branch profusely. Older stems are medium brown and fairly smooth. Wood is slightly less subject to splitting than wood of the hollies.

FLOWERS: Small and white, at the leaf bases. Very fragrant, not showy, appear in early fall.

FRUIT: Not commonly seen.

PROPAGATION: Semi-hardwood cuttings.

CULTURE: Tolerant of a moderate range of soil conditions, but grows best in a good, fertile, moist, soil. Vigorously responds to fertilization, mulching, and control of grassy weeds around the base. Grows best in partial shade locations or where it receives full sun for no more than 4 or 5 hours a day. Shears well into a dense hedge or screen.

PESTS: None serious.

NOTES: Commonly grown throughout the southern states as a hedge or specimen shrub. In many locations, it is not superior to various species of holly for landscape use, except for the very fragrant flowers during the early fall. Sometimes grown as a greenhouse or house plant where it does moderately well in low light.

CULTIVARS: 'Variegatus': leaves are dark green, edged in creamy white, slightly smaller than those of the parent. Sometimes half or more of the leaf may be creamy white. Makes a very striking variegated landscape plant. As with most variegated plants, the variegated cultivars are slightly less cold hardy than the green forms. A rather upright, compact-grower. 'Gulftide': upright-growing, compact shrub with glossy green foliage with twisted spiny margins. More compact and a better hedge or shrub plant than the parent.

RELATED SPECIES: *Osmanthus fragrans* (Thunb.) Lour., the fragrant tea olive, may reach a height of 20 to 30 feet and has leaves up to four inches long and 1 to 2 inches wide, much less coarsely toothed on the margin than those of false holly. Fragrant tea olive gets too large for many shrub uses; however, it is hardy in the lower portion of Zone 7 and southeward and the flowers which appear in the fall have a most delightful fragrance and readily can be detected throughout the landscape. Worthy of planting as a small tree.

Osmanthus X *fortunei* Carriere. is a hybrid between fragrant tea olive and false holly. Intermediate in size between the two parents but no other particular advantages exist. Foliage generally looks similar to that of false holly and may be difficult to distinguish.

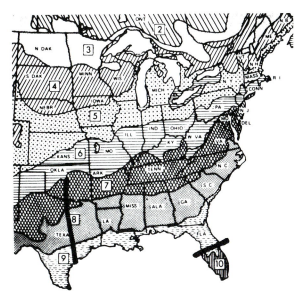

O. fragrans

'Gulftide'

'Gulftide'

Photinia X 'Fraseri' Dress.   Fraser's Photinia or Red Tip
Rosaceae or Rose Family   Hardiness Zone 7
Native: a hybrid between *Photinia serrulata* and *Photinia glabra* Maxim.
SIZE: 12 to 15 feet tall and may spread as much as 8 to 10 feet. Moderate to rapid grower.
FORM: A multi-stemmed, upright, oval, large shrub or small tree.
TEXTURE: Medium to coarse.   **EXPOSURE:** Sun to partial shade.

LEAVES: Alternate, simple; brilliant red at first, finally turning a deep green after several weeks. A new flush of growth on a hedge is striking. Texture of the leaf is fairly soft and pliable which is a useful distinguishing feature between this and Chinese photinia (*Photinia serrulata*) which has a stiffer and more leathery leaf. Most of the teeth on the leaf margin are on the outer half of the leaf.

STEM: Upright, with only moderate branching. A young stem is brilliant red, much like the foliage, later becoming a green-brown and finally a dark brown to gray with age. Responds only fairly well to pruning. Each time a terminal branch is pruned it may produce 2 new shoots, thus photinia does not thicken readily like many shrubs.

FLOWERS: Generally do not develop.

FRUIT: Does not develop, probably because it is a hybrid.

COLOR: Foliage is brilliant red when young becoming a deep dark green with age.

PROPAGATION: Semi-hardwood cuttings.

CULTURE: Grows in a moderate range of conditions as long as soil is not excessively wet. Does best in sun or partial shade. Does not do well in high heat locations or above-ground planters surrounded by concrete. However, in a landscape setting (among other plants or in partial shade) it is very drought-tolerant once established. Responds well to fertilizer. It may take repeated pruning to get the desired density and form. Once the form is obtained it is reasonably easy to retain. May suffer occasionally from late spring freezes in Zones 7 or 8.

PESTS: Twig blight or mildew occasionally in shady areas with poor air drainage. Leaf spot is often found in the nursery, and in the landscape. Where irrigation contacts the foliage a major problem occurs. Problems are generally least in a sunny location with good growing conditions and air movement. However, the leaf spot problem and leaf drop as a result is enough to stop using the plant.

NOTES: Fraser's photinia is probably the most spectacular of the photinias in terms of a hedge or shrub during spring or later in the summer whenever flushes of growth occur. The hedge is fairly durable and rugged from the standpoint of vandalism, abuse, or people contact. Plants get large enough to make a good screen, border, or sound barrier. The foliage is shallow on the periphery of the branches but is thick enough to be effective in stopping noise. This, combined with the color of the new growth, makes a very useful, showy, large shrub. The common error of planting it too close to structures should, by all means, be avoided. Minimum distance to a building should be 5 to 6 feet. Makes a good small tree in conjunction with a deck or patio, especially if viewed from above.
XX-POISON-XX

CULTIVARS: 'Red Robin': has intense red new growth but otherwise about the same.

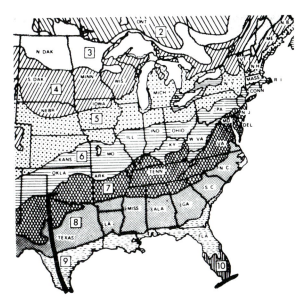

Photinia serrulata Lindl.　　　　　　　Chinese Photinia
Rosaceae or Rose Family　　　　　　　Hardiness Zone 7
Native to China.

SIZE: Frequently reaching 20 to 30 feet tall and may spread as much as 15 to 20 feet. A moderate to rapid grower.

FORM: Generally a multi-stemmed, umbrella-crowned, large shrub or small tree.

TEXTURE: Coarse.　　　　　　　　**EXPOSURE:** Sun to partial shade.

LEAVES: Alternate, oblong; up to 8 inches long, 2 to 2 1/2 inches wide. Dark green and glossy above, pale green below. Stiff and leathery, with many fine yet stiff teeth, principally on the outer half of the leaf margin. When the new leaves first emerge in the spring, they have a red-purple cast, but soon turn a solid green, less showy than Fraser's photinia.

STEM: Generally branching near the soil line, developing a multi-stemmed structure, fanning out to give support to an umbrella-like crown. Although pruning can increase the density of the shrub or small tree, it is not a prolific brancher. The terminal buds in fall and winter are very bold and a green to green-brown. The young twig is red to red-brown. The older bark develops a light, scaly texture and becomes almost black with age.

FLOWERS: Creamy white and quite showy in mid to late spring; generally quite dense across the canopy surface.

FRUIT: About 1/4 inch in diameter, in terminal clusters. Turns red in the fall, finally drying and becoming an unsightly black by early winter.

PROPAGATION: Seed; relatively difficult to propagate by semi-hardwood cuttings.

CULTURE: Grows best in well-drained soils and sunny locations. Will not tolerate wet, poorly drained locations. Responds vigorously to fertilization. Assisted by mulching in the dryer western regions such as Oklahoma and Texas, but is quite drought-tolerant.

PESTS: Mildew in shady locations with poor air drainage. Tip blight, larva of various fruit moths, and a leaf spot disease. However, in a full sun to partial shade locations with good air drainage and growing conditions, Chinese photinia should not be avoided especially as a tree form.

NOTES: Commonly used as a shrub and planted within a few feet of a building where it overgrows the site in a very short period of time. May have a great deal more merit when used as a small tree around patios or other outdoor living areas than as a shrub. It does make an excellent dense, large hedge for privacy or for reducing sound. Chinese photinia is best distinguished from the hybrid, Fraser's photinia, in that the leaves of Fraser's photinia are more soft and pliable, slightly more broad, brilliant red when they first emerge, and have fewer teeth on the tip of the leaf. XX-POISON-XX

CULTIVARS: Some may exist.

RELATED SPECIES: *Photinia glabra* (Thunb.), Japanese photinia, is similar in overall appearance and flowering to Chinese photinia, thus can be used similarly in the landscape. Generally does not grow more than 6 to 12 feet tall. Leaves are 3 to 6 inches long and finely toothed on the margin, as opposed to the longer and more coarsely toothed leaves of Chinese photinia. A useful shrub, but not as showy as Fraser's photinia.

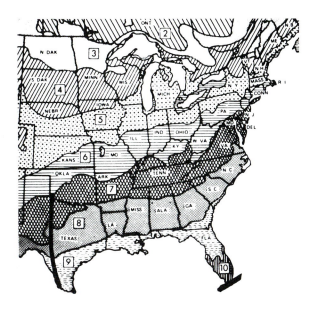

P. glabra

Pieris japonica D. Don.　　　　　　　　　　　　Japanese Pieris, Lily-of-the Valley Shrub
Ericaceae or Heath Family　　　　　　　　　　　Hardiness Zone 6
Native to Japan.
SIZE: 8 to 12 feet or more tall, generally narrow. Slow grower.
FORM: Irregular, upright shrub or small tree.
TEXTURE: Medium.　　　　　　　　　　　　**EXPOSURE:** Sun to partial shade.

LEAVES: Alternate, simple; evergreen, 1 1/2 to 3 inches long and 1/2 to 1 inch wide. Oblong to oblanceolate with a distinctly serrate margin. Glossy, dark green above and much lighter green below. New growth is reddish to reddish brown, slowly becoming dark green. The contrast between new growth and old leaves is nearly as striking as the flowers and occurs over much of the season. Leaves are mostly clustered near the tips of twigs.

STEM: Generally multiple, stiffly upright stems with spreading branches and the foliage is tufted near the tip.

FLOWERS: White. In drooping clusters 4 to 6 inches or more long, generally in March or April. Very showy for two to three weeks against the dark green foliage. The individual flowers are slightly fragrant and shaped like the tops of miniature wine glasses.

FRUIT: A small, dry capsule about 1/4 inch long that remains a long time.

COLOR: Foliage is reddish when new, becoming glossy, dark green with age. Flowers are white.

PROPAGATION: Seed or cuttings of selected cultivars.

CULTURE: Like most members of the heath family, pieris is not very tolerant of heat, drought, or alkaline soils. Prefers well drained, acid soils, supplemental water during droughts, and is aided by organic mulches over the soil surface to further buffer against change. Transplants easily from either containers or field-grown balled-in-burlap.

PESTS: Many. Lacebug, mites, various scale insects, nematodes, and an assortment of leaf spot diseases.

NOTES: A showy, large shrub (eventually). The contrast between new growth and old foliage is striking and persists much of the growing season. The white flowers are also attractive. The evergreen foliage makes a good contrast with structures and the absence of spines or prickles make it a choice over many hollies where people occasionally make contact. Pests are a problem, especially in the eastern United States where it has been planted extensively, but is probably worth the effort. Plants in Stillwater, Oklahoma definitely do not like the summers, but heavy oak leaf and pine straw mulch aids their tolerance. Growth is very slow.

CULTIVARS: Many, and more each year. One of the most striking is 'Mountain Fire' which has red new growth and especially white and attractive flowers. 'Compacta: an old cultivar that does stay more dense, has smaller leaves and flowers extensively. 'Pink Delight': pink buds and white flowers and bronze new growth. 'Valley Valentine': maroon flower buds, long lasting pink flowers, and dark foliage. 'Valley Rose': flower clusters are striking pinkish red against the dark green foliage. There are many more to choose from.

Pittosporum tobira Ait.   Japanese Pittosporum or Mockorange
Pittosporaceae or Pittosporum Family   Hardiness Zone 8
Native to China and Japan.
SIZE: A shrub up to 10 feet tall with a 12- to 24-foot spread. Moderate to rapid grower.
FORM: A densely mounded, ovate to rounded shrub.
TEXTURE: Medium.   EXPOSURE: Sun to shade.

LEAVES: Alternate, although appearing whorled because they are clustered at the tips of the current growth. Generally ovate to obovate in form, 3 to 4 inches long, 1/2 to 1 inch wide and rounded at the tip. Somewhat thick and leathery with a smooth margin slightly folded under or revolute. Deep green and glossy upper surface, pale green below. The petiole is very short, almost inconspicuous.

STEM: Much branching. Pittosporum will frequently set a cluster of 3 to 5 or more terminal buds. These buds break with the next growth flush, making the plant very dense and compact without pruning. The young stem is green, turning a light brown which remains even with considerable age.

FLOWERS: About 1/2 inch across, pale yellow, quite fragrant, but not particularly showy. Attract bees and other insects. Flowers are nestled in the leaves and are inconspicuous.

FRUIT: About 1/2 inch in diameter, more or less shaped like a bishop's cap. Green, turning brown to expose the seed.

COLOR: Foliage is deep green. Flowers are light yellow.

PROPAGATION: Semi-hardwood to hardwood cuttings.

CULTURE: Pittosporum must be considered one of the toughest and most durable of all broadleaf evergreen shrubs. Tolerates moderately heavy clay yet does exceptionally well in the sandy soils of Florida. Will grow in parking lots, street planting strips and other hot, dry locations, but the leaves frequently curl, particularly from the side inward, giving the plant a somewhat different texture from when it is in a lawn atmosphere or has a slight amount of shade. Will tolerate considerable shade and remain moderately compact. Responds well to fertilizer and mulching. Can be grown on any side of a structure, shears well as a hedge and can be easily contained, although if not contained it will reach considerable size. Tolerant to salt spray.

PESTS: A leaf spot disease may become serious in rainy seasons or where there is shade and poor air drainage, but rarely sufficient to limit planting in the landscape. Mealy bugs occasionally.

NOTES: Used extensively across the Lower South in a wide range of conditions. May be over-used in some areas to the point that a high plant population complicates the disease problem. Has long been a mainstay in landscapes as a foundation plant, hedge, border, and for numerous other uses.

CULTIVARS: 'Variegata': growth is like the parent, only the leaf is mottled white, very showy, and attractive. A good contrast with the green parent. 'Wheeler's Dwarf': very compact evergreen shrub with glossy, dark green leaves; smaller leaves and stems than the parent. Rarely reaches more then 3 to 4 feet tall. Requires little maintenance but appears to be more susceptible to leaf spot disease than the parent and less tolerant to adverse growing conditions as a whole. 'Laura Lee': a patented cultivar with dense foliage and slight variegation.

507

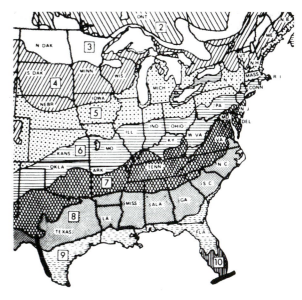

'Wheeler's Dwarf'

P. tobira 'Variegata'

P. tobira

Prunus caroliniana (Mill.) Ait.　　　　　Carolina Cherry Laurel
Rosaceae or Rose Family　　　　　　　　Hardiness Zone 7
Native from North Carolina to Texas, mostly along the Gulf Coast.
SIZE: May reach a height of 30 to 40 feet with a 20- to 25-foot spread. Rapid grower.
FORM: Ovate tree with very dense foliage.
TEXTURE: Medium.　　　　　　　　　**EXPOSURE:** Sun to partial shade.

LEAVES: Oblong to oblong-lanceolate, 1 1/2 to 3 inches long, about 1 inch wide, with a sharp point at the tip. Generally without spines on the margin or with several fine, prickly teeth near the tip of the leaf. Both leaf forms may be present on the same plant. Upper surface of the leaf is deep, dark green; below is light pale green. On the underneath side, near the petiole, there are nearly always 2 small glands visible. New leaves have an odor resembling crushed cherries or cherry foliage. The petiole is slender and red in full sun, green in the shade.

STEM: Light tan the first season, becoming dark gray to almost black with age and acquiring a rough sandpaper-like surface texture. Rarely develops a furrowing bark like many deciduous trees. Young twigs are slender and flexible for the first 2 to 3 seasons.

FLOWERS: Small, creamy white, and about 1/4 inch across in clusters (racemes). Flower clusters are noticeable but not particularly showy in the landscape.

FRUIT: Less than 1/2 inch in diameter, round, and green at first, turning a shining black in late summer or early fall. Seeds are viable under most circumstances and seedlings can become a pest in the landscape from birds eating the fruit and depositing the seeds in a variety of locations.

COLOR: Foliage is deep, dark green.

PROPAGATION: Seeds or cuttings.

CULTURE: Grows in most conditions. Responds vigorously to fertilizer, supplemental water, and good soil conditions. Does not tolerate high temperature conditions or hot, dry locations. May be pruned severely and shaped into various forms or hedges. However, to retain a form requires continual rigorous pruning due to its natural size and vigorous growth.

PESTS: Occasionally grasshoppers and other chewing insects damage the leaves. Likewise, a leaf spot disease is noticed but rarely is severe enough to warrant control. Older plants in wet locations may be killed by one of several root rot organisms. Borers may attack plants under stress.

NOTES: Very rapid-growing, small to medium-sized evergreen tree. Produces a tremendous amount of seeds in many areas of the lower South and becomes a weed or nuisance plant. Commonly a substitution plant in that what once was a hedge of ligustrum, pittosporum, or some other broadleaf evergreen, gradually is transformed into a hedge of cherry laurel from birds depositing the seed in the hedge and the cherry laurel replacing the original plants. In some locations a cherry laurel hedge can be maintained at practically any height and may be a useful feature. Rarely flowers and sets fruit where it is severely pruned. Leaves and fruits may be poisonous. Also known as wild orange or mockorange in some areas of the South. ??-POISON-??

CULTIVARS: 'Bright 'N Tight': an upright, compact shrub or small tree. Leaves are smaller than those of the parent and only rarely have teeth on the leaf margin. Superior to the parent for most uses.

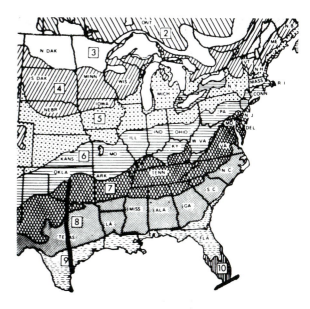

'Bright-N-Tight'

Prunus laurocerasus L.   Cherry Laurel or English Laurel
Rosaceae or Rose Family   Hardiness Zone 7
Native from southeastern Europe to the Near East.
SIZE: May reach 20 to 25 feet tall with a 15- to 18-foot spread, or much smaller, depending on cultivar. A rapid-grower under most conditions.
FORM: Shrub or small tree, basically oval form if left unpruned. Cultivar, 'Zabeliana' is a low, spreading shrub.
TEXTURE: Medium.   **EXPOSURE:** Sun to shade.

LEAVES: Alternate, simple; 3 to 5 inches long, 1/2 to 1 inch wide, oblong to elongate-oblong with either a smooth leaf margin or a few small teeth mostly near the leaf tip. Deep green and glossy above, pale green below. Two prominent glands can be seen on the underside of the leaf near the petiole. Petiole is short and stiff and light green.

STEM: Multiple stems in shrub forms or single or multiple leader in tree form. The young stem is light green for one season, turning light brown and later gray-brown. The bark remains rather smooth. Wood is moderately durable with age.

FLOWERS: White. About 1/4 inch long, in clusters 2 to 3 inches long; fragrant; showy.

FRUIT: About 1/2 inch long, basically round or ovate. Green turning dark purple.

COLOR: Foliage is deep green and glossy.

PROPAGATION: Semi-hardwood to hardwood cuttings of selected cultivars or seed.

CULTURE: Grows in a wide range of soil as long as drainage is good. In heavy clays, root rot diseases are often a problem. Responds with vigor to improved growing conditions or soils. Not particularly sensitive to moisture stress and general exposure conditions. Responds well to pruning but growth is generally fast, making frequent pruning necessary.

PESTS: Grasshoppers during mid summer to early fall damage the foliage. A leaf spot disease is sometimes seen but rarely warrants protection measures in the landscape. On wet sites, mushroom root rot or similar organisms can decrease the life expectancy of the plant.

NOTES: Very attractive foliage and form with some cultivars. Cultivars can be used as a foundation planting and for various other landscape uses requiring either a low-spreading, broadleaf evergreen, or more upright, compact, larger shrub or small tree. Tolerance to a range of conditions makes it desirable for some urban locations. One drawback in certain areas is that the seed is viable and can become a nuisance. May leaf scorch in Zone 7 during severe winters. Most easily distinguished from Carolina cherry laurel by the thicker and more leathery leaves which are longer and have little odor when crushed and by the two prominent glands near the base of the underside of the leaf. ??-POISON-??

CULTIVARS: 'Otto Luykens': compact, low, broadly spreading shrub with dark green, glossy leaves: very attractive. May reach 4 to5 feet tall. White flower spikes along the branches in early spring. 'Zabeliana': low, spreading growth form like a pfitzer juniper. May be 4 feet tall and 12 feet wide. Leaves are more elongate than those of the species, reaching 4 to 5 inches long and about 1 inch wide. Very deep green foliage, particularly in partial shade. Appears to do well in full sun if not an extremely hot location. Easily propagated from cuttings in the fall. Generally no fruit or seed. Has considerable merit and should be planted more. 'Schipkaensis': grows to about 6 feet tall with leaves 3 to 4 inches long and 1 1/2 inches wide, with a few teeth near the tip. Bailey lists approximately 12 cultivars. Numerous others exist, indicating that the seedling population is rather diverse.

'Zabeliana'

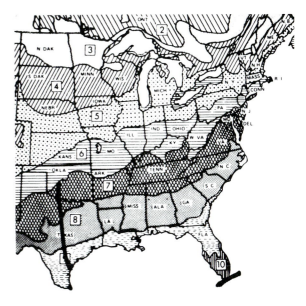

'Zabeliana'

'Zabeliana'

'Zabeliana'

'Otto Luykens'

Pyracantha coccinea Roem.　　　　　　Pyracantha or Firethorn
Rosaceae or Rose Family　　　　　　Hardiness Zone 5 to 6, depending on cultivar.
Native to southern Europe and western Asia.
SIZE: 6 to 10 feet tall with a 6- to 10-foot spread. Rapid grower.
FORM: Irregular, mounding to semi-upright, shrub. Old plants may become tree-like.
TEXTURE: Fine to medium.　　　　**EXPOSURE:** Sun.

LEAVES: Alternate, simple; 1 to 1 1/2 inches long, 1/4 to 1/2 inch wide, narrowly elliptical. Margin is generally smooth or with a few teeth. Medium to deep green above, light green below. Leaves are slightly fuzzy when they first emerge. Evergreen in the South, semi-evergreen to deciduous in the North.

STEM: Semi-upright to spreading with stiff, rigid stems and twigs. Generally gives an irregular, mounding effect. The young stem is green for part of a season and very fuzzy, finally turning a light brown, then medium brown with age. Instead of the young stem terminating in a bud or additional shoot, the tip of the stem appears to die and wither, developing a spine-like point which is very stiff and can produce a painful sore.

FLOWERS: White; in small clusters. Individual flowers are about 1/4 inch in diameter, by April or May. A plant in full bloom is rather attractive.

FRUIT: Yellow, orange to orange-red. Various shades depending on species and cultivar, generally about 1/4 inch in diameter. Apple-like in structure. Generally becoming colorful in September or October and hanging on until December or January.

COLOR: Foliage is dark green. Flowers are white. Fruit is yellow, orange or red.

PROPAGATION: Seed germinates well if the pulp is removed, but seedlings are extremely variable. Semi-hardwood to hardwood cuttings.

CULTURE: Grows best in full sun in a fertile well-drained soil. Will tolerate most soil conditions as long as not excessively wet. Responds vigorously to fertilizers and good growing conditions to the point it may become too large and difficult to manage. Use caution in applying fertilizer, particularly in the Lower South as a second flush of growth may be stimulated which will cover up the fruit in late summer and fall, thus negating one of the most attractive characteristics. Can be pruned into a hedge or various forms, but is not generally recommended because of the irregularity of growth. Plants grown in the field are difficult to transplant.

PESTS: Fire blight in very humid locations, but susceptibility varies with cultivar. Lace bug, particularly in the Southwest. Spider mites, particularly under overhangs or eaves of houses where direct rainfall does not contact the plant. Scale occasionally, particularly in a shady location. Scab or leaf rollers in some areas.

NOTES: A very attractive shrub on sites where it is allowed to develop considerable size with large masses of showy fruits against the evergreen to semi-evergreen foliage. May be used to espalier against a wall, but this should only be undertaken with full knowledge that it will take effort to keep it attractive. Not generally recommended for corner plantings or foundation plantings of single story dwellings as it rapidly grows too big and becomes a maintenance problem with many pest problems under these circumstances. Most red-berried plants are cultivars of *Pyracantha koidzumi* Rehd., generally hardy only as far north as Zone 8, whereas orange to yellow-berried cultivars are hardy through Zone 6, some cultivars go as far north as Zone 4.

CULTIVARS: 'Lalandi': upright growth habit with orange fruit, Zone 5. 'Kasan': red-orange fruit and a compact, mounded shrub, Zone 5. 'Wyatti': a heavy producer of red-orange fruits. Develops into a dense shrub with a minimum of pruning, Zone 5.

'Kasan'

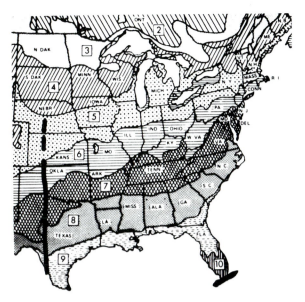

'Lalandi'

'Kasan'

'Lalandi'

Pyracantha koidzumii Rehd.
Rosaceae or Rose Family
Native to Japan and Formosa.

Formosa Pyracantha
Hardiness Zone 8 depending on cultivar

SIZE: 10 to 20 feet tall with a 6- to 12-foot spread. Rapid grower.
FORM: Irregular, mounding to semi-upright shrub. Old plants become tree-like.
TEXTURE: Fine to medium.   **EXPOSURE:** Sun.

LEAVES: Alternate, simple; 1 to 2 inches long, about 1/2 inch wide, narrowly elliptical. The margin is generally smooth. Medium to deep green above, light green below. Leaves are slightly fuzzy when they first emerge. Evergreen in the South, semi-evergreen in the North.

STEM: Semi-upright to spreading or mounding with stiff, rigid stems and twigs. The young stem is green for part of a season and fuzzy, turning a light brown, then medium brown with age. Instead of the young stem terminating in a bud or additional shoot, the tip of the stem appears to die and wither developing a spine-like point which is very stiff and when encountered, produces a painful sore.

FLOWERS: White, in small clusters, in May. Individual flowers are about 1/4 inch in diameter. A vigorously growing plant in full bloom is rather attractive.

FRUIT: Mostly red. Various shades, depending on cultivar, generally about 1/4 inch in diameter. Apple-like in structure. Colorful September through January.

COLOR: Foliage is medium to dark green. Flowers are white. Fruit is red.

PROPAGATION: Seed germinates well if the pulp is removed but seedlings are extremely variable. Semi-hardwood to hardwood cuttings of cultivars.

CULTURE: Grows best in full sun in fertile well-drained soils. Will tolerate most soil conditions as long as it is not excessively wet. Responds vigorously to fertilizers and good growing conditions and may become large and difficult to manage. Use caution in applying fertilizer as a second flush of growth will cover the fruit in late summer thus negating one of the most attractive characteristics of the plant. Can be pruned into a hedge or various forms but is not recommended because of the difficulty and frequency of pruning. Should not be planted under overhangs of structures due to pest problems. Plants in the field are difficult to transplant.

PESTS: Fire blight in very humid locations, but susceptibility varies with cultivar. Lace bug particularly in the Southwest. Spider mites, particularly under overhangs or eaves of houses where direct rainfall does not contact the plant. Scale occasionally, particularly in a shady location. Scab or leaf rollers in some areas.

NOTES: A very attractive shrub on sites where it is allowed to develop considerable size with large masses of showy red fruits against the evergreen foliage. May be used as an espalier against a wall, but should only be undertaken with full knowledge that it will take considerable effort to keep it attractive. Not recommended for foundation plantings of single story dwellings due to maintenance and pest problems. Frequently misused in the landscape. The least hardy of the species grown in the United States.

CULTIVARS: 'Victory': large plant with dark red fruit, Zone 7b. 'Santa Cruz': dark green leaves and red berries, Zone 7b, a more prostrate grower.

HYBRIDS: 'Mojave' has dark green leaves and orange-red fruits. Grows 6-10 feet tall. Hardy in Zone 6. 'Red Elf': a dwarf form with small, dark green leaves and bright red fruits. Hardy in Zone 7b. 'Watereri': hardy in Zone 7, hardiest of the red-fruited cultivars. Many other cultivars and hybrids exist.

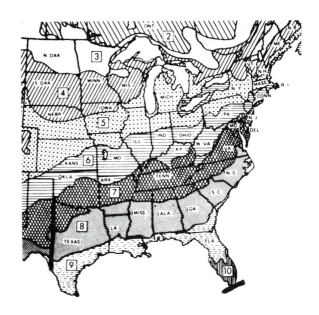

Quercus virginiana Mill.   Live Oak
Fagaceae or Beech Family   Hardiness Zone 7
Native to the southern United States.

SIZE: 40 to 80 feet tall with a spread of 60 to 100 feet in some instances. It is smaller in the extreme western range and likewise in extreme southern Florida. Some authorities consider these as separate species. Slow to moderate grower.

FORM: Broad, oval-crowned tree.

TEXTURE: Fine.   **EXPOSURE:** Sun.

LEAVES: Alternate, simple; leathery, oblong to elliptical, or narrowly obovate. 1 1/2 to 4 inches long, 1/2 to 2 inches wide, quite variable. Leaf margins are generally smooth and unlobed on the mature twigs; however, on twigs produced in summer and young trees, leaves may have 3 or more rounded terminal lobes. On vigorous shoots or sprouts may have sharply toothed margins resembling those of American holly. Leaf blades are generally flat with the margins slightly revolute or rolled under. Leaves are dark green above and generally a distinct gray-green below. Leaves are almost plastic-like in texture and break crisply when bent sharply.

STEM: Generally a single-stemmed tree with many large, horizontal branches. Bark is very dark and furrowed, becoming blocky on some older trees. Wood is extremely strong and durable, one of the most resistant trees to wind and vandalism damage. Unlike most other oaks, the axillary and terminal buds are very small, nearly inconspicuous. The central pith on young stems is 5-sided, a feature of all oaks.

FLOWERS: Male and female are separate on the same tree (monoecious). Female flowers are inconspicuous, males are in long, slender, yellowish clusters in early spring.

FRUIT: An acorn about 1 inch long, football-shaped. Generally medium to dark brown with a pronounced barb at the tip. Cap of the acorn encloses about 1/4 of the nut, scales are tan and closely appressed. Acorns are borne singly or in clusters on short stalks.

COLOR: Foliage is dark green.

PROPAGATION: Seed; however, a few selections have been propagated from cuttings.

CULTURE: Grows in a wide range of conditions. Found native in moist locations throughout much of the Gulf Coast region. Other ecological races tolerate considerable moisture stress and drought throughout central Texas and on the sandhills of central Florida. Contrary to popular belief, live oaks will respond quite readily to a good nutritional program, growing several feet per year. Young trees may need some corrective pruning early to assist in the development of primary branches. Extremely tough and tolerant to poor soils, abused soils and to trampling or compaction of the soil containing the root system of an established tree.

PESTS: Gall-forming insects in the southern Great Plains are unsightly but not particularly harmful. Mushroom root rot on old trees in wet locations.

NOTES: One of the most spectacular trees. Although it does not attain tremendous heights, it is magnificent in stature and proportions. One of the most picturesque of trees. Amazingly tolerant to city conditions, soil compaction and to disturbing of the soil around the root system. Probably the toughest of trees normally encountered in the southeastern United States. Commonly laden with Spanish moss in the South giving it a degree of mystique and grandeur. Fairly easily tranplanted when young, more difficult with age.

CULTIVARS: Several varieties or subspecies exist, these vary principally in leaf size, leaf form, and height. It is questionable if these are different species as they are probably ecological races or ecotypes having evolved in a specific region.

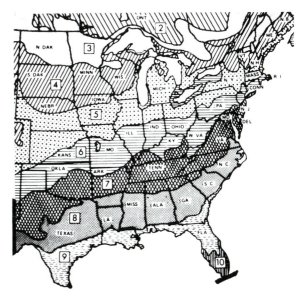

Raphiolepis indica Lindl.   Indian Hawthorn
Rosaceae or Rose Family   Hardiness Zone 7b
Native to southern China.
SIZE: 5 to 7 feet in height with a 4- to 6- foot spread. Slow to moderate grower.
FORM: Irregular, spreading to semi-upright shrub.
TEXTURE: Medium.   **EXPOSURE:** Sun to partial shade.

LEAVES: Alternate, simple; obovate to oblong-lanceolate, pointed or somewhat rounded at the tip, gradually narrowing to the base. Generally 1 1/2 to 2 1/2 inches long and about 1 inch wide. Margin has a few teeth, mostly near the tip of the leaf. Medium to dark, glossy green or may be slightly wooly above and below, particularly when young.

STEM: Spreading to semi-upright, fairly stiff and rigid with some variability among plants. Green when very young and covered with fine red hairs, becoming gray-green and smooth and finally a deep, gray-brown with age. Leaves tend to be tufted at the tips of the young branches rather than evenly distributed.

FLOWERS: White to pinkish, about 1/2 inch across, may be slightly wooly. In loose panicles on the outer and upper perimeter of the plant in late spring.

FRUIT: A bright bluish berry, about 1/4 inch diameter. Appears in mid to late summer.

COLOR: Foliage is medium to dark, glossy green. Flowers are white to pink.

PROPAGATION: Semi-hardwood to hardwood cuttings of cultivars or seed.

CULTURE: Growth response is variable depending on geographic region and soil type. In some areas it is considered an excellent plant, in other areas it is avoided because of poor performance. The reason(s) for this growth response remains unknown. However, it should do well in good, well-drained soils in either full sun or partial shade. In nursery conditions it appears to respond reasonably well to fertilizer and supplementary water. Is moderately drought-resistant once established.

PESTS: A leaf spot disease causes dropping of the foliage and makes the plant less dense and attractive, particularly in moist, shady locations. Susceptibility varies with seasons and cultivars.

NOTES: An attractive shrub when doing well. Resembles pittosporum in some locations, primarily due to the tufting of the leaves at the tip of the branches and overall leaf shape. However, it can readily be distinguished from pittosporum in that the leaves are more leathery in texture and in most instances there is some hair on the underneath side of the leaves, whereas pittosporum has none. Certain cultivars have flowers that are very showy in the spring and early summer.

CULTIVARS: 'Fascination': rose-colored petals with a white center giving a star-like flower. Compact, small mound with dense branching habit; dark green foliage. 'Enchantress': rose-pink flowers in large clusters, blooming from late winter through late spring to mid spring depending on geographic location. More dwarf and compact than the parent. 'Snowhite': pure white flowers in early spring to early summer, foliage remains lighter green than other cultivars or the parent. 'Springtime': bronzy green foliage, rather thick and leathery. Pink blooms, generally late winter to early spring. More vigorous grower than some of the compact forms. Other cultivars exist.

RELATED SPECIES: *Raphiolepis umbellata* Makino., round leaf raphiolepis, has leaves more broad and rounded, but similar to Indian hawthorn in leaf texture and leaf arrangement on the stem. No particular landscape advantage.

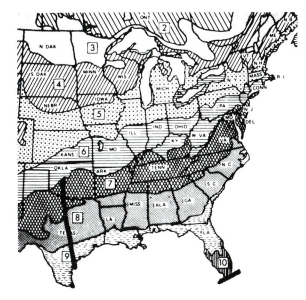

R. umbellata

Rhododendron spp.   Evergreen Rhododendrons
Ericaceae or Heath Family   Hardiness Zone 5
Native to Japan, China, and North America.
SIZE: Medium to large shrubs. Slow to moderate growers.
FORM: Generally rounding mounds.
TEXTURE: Medium to coarse.   EXPOSURE: Light shade.

LEAVES: Evergreen, alternate, simple; mostly ovate-elongate with smooth margins and upper leaf surfaces on most species and cultivars. Petioles are generally short and stout, pale green, and distinct due to the contrasting color with the dark green leaf surface.

STEM: Young stems appear stout but are somewhat brittle. Vegetative buds on young stems are small, whereas flower buds are large and rounded (see photographs). Older stems are tan to brown, loosely branching unless pruned.

FLOWERS: Spectacular. White, pink, lavender to red, depending on species and cultivar. Mostly bell-shaped and in large terminal clusters. Very beautiful in late spring. Flower buds are large and prominent on the ends of branches.

FRUIT: Small, dry capsule.

COLOR: Leaves are dark green. Flowers are spectacular: red, white, pink, lavender.

PROPAGATION: Cuttings of cultivars or seed.

CULTURE: Rhododendrons are among the most "fussy" or specific of the landscape shrubs. Widely planted because of the spectacular flower show on healthy plants. Unfortunately, many plants are placed on sites unsuitable and quickly die. Light shade or shade in the afternoon after morning exposure is ideal. If shade is excessive, flowering will be sparse. Soils must be loose, well-drained, and well aerated with a constant moisture supply. In areas of heavy clay soils, the only practical approach is to construct raised beds filled with good, light-textured soils. Mulches aid in keeping soil temperature and moisture moderated. If soils are above pH 5.5, elemental sulfur should be added at about three pounds per 100 square feet once each year. This will prevent the soil from increasing in pH as nearly all treated water contains some calcium and over time will accumulate and tie-up iron and manganese in the soil. Sounds like a lot of work but most gardeners agree it is worth the effort.

PESTS: Phytopthora root and stem rot is the number one enemy. It is favored by poorly drained soils, overwatering, iron chlorosis or other nutrient stress or a combination of these factors. Mites, mealy bugs, scale insects and various leaf and flower diseases are common. Good growing conditions are the best defense.

NOTES: Spectacular plants. For serious and dedicated gardeners only. XX-POISON-XX

RELATED SPECIES: *Rhododendron catawbiense* Michx., catawba rhodendron, is native from Virginia to Georgia on very specific sites. May reach 6 to 8 feet tall with an equal spread with dark green, attractive foliage and lilac flowers in large, terminal clusters in late spring. Beautiful. Many hybrids and cultivars exist. 'Album' has pink buds and pure white flowers. 'America' has bright red flowers. 'Nova Zembla' has red flowers and may be more heat tolerant than 'America'. 'Roseum Elegans': an old reliable with lavender flowers. Many others exist. Many other Rhododendron species deserve consideration by the dedicated gardeners. ***Rhododendrons and Azaleas*** by Clement Bowers, 1960 McMillan Co., New York, and ***Rhododendrons of the World*** by David Leach, 1961, Charles Scribners and Sons, New York, are excellent books worthy of purchase by any rhododendron fancier. They provide details on these magnificent plants, far beyond the scope of this book.

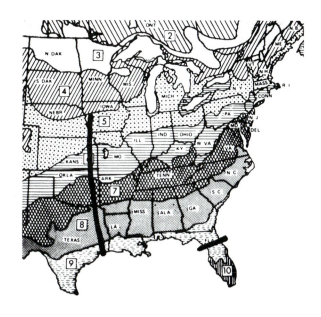

vegetative bud

flower bud

Rhododendron indicum (L.) Sweet.   Southern or Indica Azalea
          (Syn. *Rhododendron simsii*)
Ericaceae or Heath Family   Hardiness Zone 7
Native to China and Formosa.
SIZE: May reach a height of 10 to 12 feet with a spread of 8 to 10 feet in very old plants. Slow to moderate grower.
FORM: Irregular, mounded shrub.
TEXTURE: Medium.   **EXPOSURE:** Sun to shade.

LEAVES: Alternate, simple; 2 to 2 1/2 inches long by 1 1/4 inches wide. Quite hairy on both upper and lower leaf surfaces, petiole, and young stems. Ovate to ovate-oblong. A medium to dark dull green, with a smooth but hairy margin.

STEM: Much-branched, stiff, rigid and slender. Generally green turning a medium sandy brown with age. Covered with a dense mat of hairs at all ages.

FLOWERS: Many colors: whites, reds, lavenders and both singles and doubles. Spectacular. May be 2 to 2 1/2 inches across, funnel-shaped. Generally flowers from April through May, earlier in the Deep South.

FRUIT: A small, dry capsule.

COLOR: Foliage is medium to dark, dull green. Flowers are whites, lavenders, reds.

PROPAGATION: Semi-hardwood cuttings.

CULTURE: Azaleas grow best in shade to semi-shade locations where soil is well-drained, fertile, moist and acid. Iron chlorosis is very common. Incorporation of peat moss, large quantities of leaves, or elemental sulfur can make the soil more acid. In areas where soils are poorly drained azaleas should be grown in mounds or beds on top of the soil and mulched with peat, compost, pine bark pecan hulls or other organic materials. They are very sensitive to drought and injury from excessive fertilizer. Should not be planted too deep and a slow-release or organic fertilizer several times during the growing season helps.

PESTS: Petal blight during wet, rainy seasons, particularly in areas of poor air movement. Mushroom root rot on plants in moist locations. Lace bugs, mites, and scale.

NOTES: Larger plants with larger leaves and flowers than Kurume azalea. However, there are numerous hybrids, making it difficult to tell the parentage of a particular cultivar. Azaleas and rhododendrons probably compose the most confused and poorly understood group of ornamental plants. Over 750 species of rhododendron are known. Plants commonly called azaleas, as well as rhododendron, belong to the genus, *Rhododendron*. There is no definite difference between the two groups, but in general, the rhododendrons are evergreen, whereas azaleas lose some or all of their leaves. Rhododendrons have large leaves with dots or scales on the underneath surface, azaleas usually have small leaves, often with hairs. Rhododendrons have flowers with 10 or more stamens, azaleas usually have 5 stamens. Azaleas require considerable maintenance in terms of soil amendments, frequent irrigation during drought, mulching, replacement of mulch from season to season, fertilization, some pruning and spraying. A high-maintenance plant. XX-POISON-XX

CULTIVARS: 'Brilliant': single flower, watermelon red, mid season. 'Duc du Rohan': single, salmon ink, blooms mid season. 'Fielder's White': large, single, white. 'George L. Taber': larger, single, light orchid with variegations of white in the flower. 'Prince of Wales': single, cherry red. 'Southern Charm': larger, single, rose. Many other hybrids and cultivars exist. The true rhododendrons are adapted only to the cooler regions of the Upper South and the north central United States. Serious azalea enthusiasts should have a copy of **Azaleas** by Fred Galle, 1974, Oxmoor House, Inc.

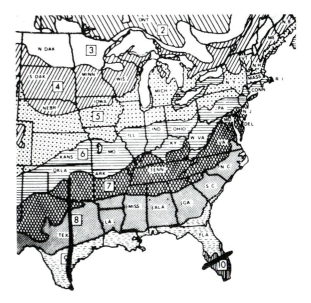

Rhododendron obtusum (Lindl.) Planch.   Kurume Azalea
                (Syn. *Azalea obtusum*)
Ericaceae or Heath Family   Hardiness Zone 6 but variable with
Native to Japan.   cultivars and hybrids.
SIZE: 3 to 4 feet tall with a 3-foot spread. Slow to moderate grower.
FORM: A dense, twiggy, mound with small leaves.
TEXTURE: Medium to fine.   **EXPOSURE:** Partial shade to shade.

LEAVES: Alternate, simple; about 1 inch long and 1/2 inch wide. Ovate or oval. Shiny, dull green above, paler green below with numerous stiff hairs on the surfaces of the leaf, margin, petiole, and young stem. Semi-evergreen in Zones 6 and 7.

STEM: Stiff, slender, and wiry. Green turning light sandy brown, covered with dense, stiff hairs. Profuse branch development.

FLOWERS: Many colors: light pink, white, scarlet or red; single or double. Generally 1 1/4 to 1 1/2 inches across. Appearing in April or May.

FRUIT: A small, dry pod. Not commonly seen.

COLOR: Foliage is dull green. Flowers are spectacular: many colors.

PROPAGATION: Semi-hardwood cuttings work best. Some success with hardwood cuttings.

CULTURE: Azaleas grow best in shade to semi-shade locations where the soil is well drained, fertile, moist, and acid. iron cholorosis is very common where residues from building construction have increased soil pH. Peat moss, leaves, or elemental sulfur can be used to make the soil more acid. Where soils are poorly drained, plant on mounds heavily mulched with pine bark, pecan hulls, or other organic materials. Very sensitive to drought due to fine, almost watery, thread-like roots. Likewise, they are very sensitive to injury from excessive fertilizer. it is safest to use a slow-release or organic fertilizer several times during the growing season. Avoid planting too deep as root suffocation may occur.

PESTS: Petal blight in humid, poorly air-drained locations. Mushroom root rot is fairly common on older plants that have decreased in vigor, particularly when planted among oaks or pines. Lacebugs and mites may occasionally be a problem.

NOTES: Azaleas and rhododendrons are probably the most confused and poorly understood group of ornamental plants. Over 750 species of rhododendron are known. Over 75% of these are evergreen. Plants commonly called azalea as well as those known as rhododendron, belong to the genus, Rhododendron. There is no definite difference between the 2 groups, but in general, the rhododendrons are evergreen, whereas azaleas lose some of all of their leaves. Rhododendrons have large leaves with dots or scales on the underneath surface; azaleas usually have small leaves, often with hairs. Rhododendrons have flowers with 10 or more stamens; azaleas usually have 5 stamens. Azaleas require considerable maintenance in terms of soil amendments, irrigation during any drought period, mulching, replacement of mulch from season to season, fertilization, and some pruning. A high maintenance plant. Use only where maintenance is supplied. leaves may be mildly toxic if eaten in quantity. ??-POISON-??

CULTIVARS: Over 100 cultivars have been named. A few of the more common are: 'Coral Bell': clear, bright pink flowers; low, spreading growth. 'Hino-crimson': deep, dark red. 'Hinodegiri': bright, red flowers; very cold hardy. 'Snow': pure white flowers; slightly later than most cultivars. Many, many others. In addition, numerous hybrids have been made between *Rhododendron obtusum*, *Rhododendron indicum*, and other *Rhododendron* species which vary in growth form, size of flowers, hardiness, and tolerance to growing conditions.

Rosa banksiae Ait.   Banks Rose
Rosaceae or Rose Family   Hardiness Zone 7
Native to China.
SIZE: 15 to 20 feet tall and equally wide. Rapid grower.
FORM: Irregular, mound, large shrub.
TEXTURE: Fine.   EXPOSURE: Sun to slight shade.

LEAVES: Evergreen, alternate, compound; 3 to 5 leaflets per compound leaf. Leaflets are dark green and glossy; elliptical to oblong-lanceolate, 1 1/2 to 2 1/2 inches long with a sawtooth margin. A few hairs may be present on the rachis.

STEM: Green, long and slender when young; modestly branching and thornless or nearly so. The stems tend to grow up, then arch over, creating an irregular mound. The old stems are reddish to reddish brown.

FLOWERS: White or yellow, about 1 1/2 to 2 inches across. In clusters generally from April through June. Slightly fragrant.

FRUIT: Rarely seen.

COLOR: Foliage is dark green. Flowers are white or yellow.

PROPAGATION: Cuttings root easily from softwood, even under a glass jar in the garden.

CULTURE: One of the toughest of the rose family members and similar in adaptability to *Rose rugosa*. By contrast to the hybrid tea, grandifloras and floribunda roses, banks rose, like rugosa rose is at the opposite end of the spectrum. This plant has few problems and is extremely adaptable. The occasional encounter with chewing insects such as Japanese beetles, which feed on practically anything, would be the only reason to spray. Grows well in a container and transplants easily.

PESTS: None serious.

NOTES: An Old South favorite that is little used in current landscapes. Banks rose needs room as the plant gets large. If space is available with sun to partial shade conditions, the show of flowers for 3 to 4 weeks in the spring is excellent. It can provide a good evergreen screen with little maintenance. The absence of spines is also a plus. The long stems will cascade over a wall or down a slope creating an eye-catching effect the year around but especially when in flower. It is an error to plant in small spaces as it is not practical to try to keep it in check by pruning. Can be attached to walls or allowed to clamber over structures that are to be obscured from view. This is a vigorous growing rose but not at all the weedy rose such as *Rosa multiflora*.

CULTIVARS: 'Lutea': a double, yellow-flowered form. 'Lutescens': a single yellow. 'Albo-plena': a double, white, and more fragrant. Others probably exist.

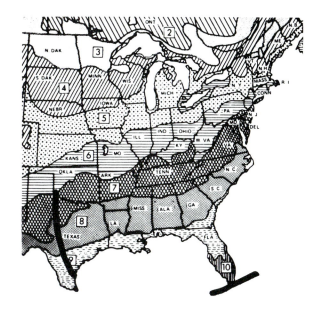

Sarcococca hookerana Baill.
Buxaceae or Boxwood Family
Native to western China, northern India to Afghanistan.

Sweetbox
Hardiness Zone 7

SIZE: 4 to 6 feet tall; width is variable as it slowly spreads. Slow to moderate grower.
FORM: Irregular, mounding, evergreen shrub.
TEXTURE: Medium.

EXPOSURE: Partial shade to shade.

LEAVES: Evergreen, simple, alternate, oblong, to nearly lanceolate; 2 to 4 inches long, 3/4 to one inch wide. The petiole is short and margin is smooth. The leaf surface is dark, glossy green.

STEM: Green and slender; finely hairy when young. Often grows upward, then bends over in a graceful arch but with no consistent pattern. Makes a dense shrub due to underground stems which slowly thicken the shrub and provide a very modest spread. Gives off an unpleasant odor when damaged.

FLOWERS: Off-white, about 1/2 inch long, formed in leaf axils. Fragrant. Mostly appear March or April. Monoecious. Not showy but noticed because of fragrance.

FRUIT: A shiny, black fruit about 1/3 inch long. Not commonly seen.

COLOR: Evergreen, dark, glossy foliage.

PROPAGATION: Cuttings, division, or seeds when available.

CULTURE: A good evergreen for partial shade or shade locations and as a contrast to structures or flowering plants. Grows best in moist but well drained soils, but appears to tolerate a considerable range of soils and at least moderate drought. Plants in Oklahoma have performed well on good soils and with no supplemental watering during the summer.

PESTS: None serious.

NOTES: A good, broadleaf, evergreen which provides contrast. The low, mounding, and slightly spreading habit is attractive, yet requires little maintenance. The spreading habit is not aggressive or a problem. Worth planting just for the fragrant flowers. This plant will cascade a bit over a retaining wall which adds contrast. No spines or prickles.

CULTIVARS: 'Digyna': a shorter plant, but otherwise similar to the species. 'Humilis': grows only 20 to 24 inches tall and is slightly more cold-tolerant. A good plant for small spaces.

RELATED SPECIES: *Sarcococca ruscifolia*, fragrant sarcococca, has simple, alternate, evergreen, glossy leaves much like *S. hookerana*; however the leaves are about one-half the size and the overall plant height is only about 3 feet but spreads with age. The flowers are very fragrant. Hardiness Zone 8. Other species exist but are rarely seen in the nursery trade.

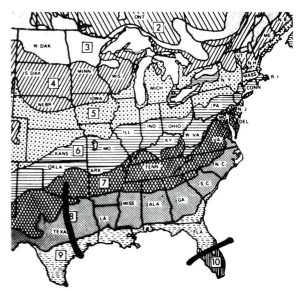

Tillandsia usneoides   Spanish Moss
Bromeliaceae or Pineapple Family   Hardiness Zone 8
Native to South America and southeastern United States.
SIZE: Hanging clumps to 20 feet or more. Slow grower.
FORM: Irregular clumps hanging from trees.
TEXTURE: Fine.   EXPOSURE: Sun to shade.

LEAVES: Long and narrow, 1 to 2 inches long; scattered along silvery gray, thread-like masses. Densely covered with gray scales.

STEM: Essentially none, although the long, thread-like units are technically stems.

FLOWERS: Small, yellowish green to nearly blue with about 1/4 inch long petals. In the leaf axils.

FRUIT: Very small seed.

COLOR: Foliage is silvery gray.

PROPAGATION: Seed or division of existing plants.

CULTURE: Spanish moss is a rootless epiphyte or "air plant" that grows on trees, wires, or other structures for support. The leaves and dense scales collect moisture from the air allowing the plant to dispense with roots. It is not parasitic as it manufactures its own food and has no structural relationship with the plants on which it grows. It obtains the essential requirements for growth from rain water and dust. Outside its native habitat it can be grown in greenhouses or as part of indoor landscaping as long as the moisture is supplied, which may be merely an occasional hand watering.

PESTS: None serious. However, it appears to be sensitive to air pollution including herbicides in the atmosphere.

NOTES: Spanish moss adds a dimension to large trees in the southeastern United States that is difficult to describe. Perhaps the most striking display is when Spanish moss hangs from the horizontal branches of large live oaks. The long gray masses dance with the slightest breeze. The general feeling seems to be that people either like it or hate it. As one northerner exclaimed, "It will be nice when it greens up in the spring", but it never turns green. Like it or not, it is part of the landscape of the deep South and removal can be a challenge.

Spanish moss has long been collected for packaging and stuffing material. More recently it has been used in floral arrangements or among groups of plants in dish gardens as a contrasting filler and to provide support.

CULTIVARS: None.

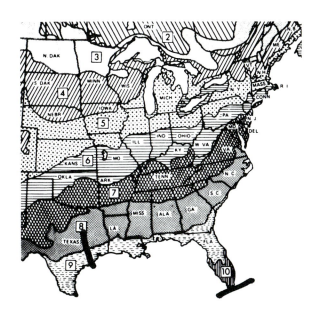

Viburnum rhytidophyllum Hemsl.   Leatherleaf Viburnum
Caprifoliaceae or Honeysuckle Family   Hardiness Zone 5
Native to China.
SIZE: 8 to 10 feet tall with a spread of 4 to 6 feet. Slow to moderate grower.
FORM: A loosely branched, upright-growing shrub.
TEXTURE: Coarse.   EXPOSURE: Partial shade to shade.

LEAVES: Opposite; thick and leathery, ovate to oblong to oblong-lanceolate. To 7 inches long, 1 1/4 to 2 inches wide; deeply wrinkled above with a dull, deep green color. Leaves are very pale green to white below with very prominent veins. Underside of the leaves, petioles, and young stems are densely woolly.

STEM: Basically upright with a few secondary branches off the main stems. Moderately thick, densely woolly when young, becoming less hairy with age but generally retaining some of the woolliness. Opposite buds are very prominent and are easily parted to expose another pair of leaves enclosed, typical of the genus.

FLOWERS: Small and creamy white, about 1/4 inch across, in terminal clusters 4 to 8 inches across. Formed in the fall and open in the spring. Not particularly showy.

FRUIT: A berry: red, turning black with maturity. Not particularly showy.

COLOR: Foliage is dull, deep green.

PROPAGATION: Hardwood cuttings.

CULTURE: Best grown in part shade to shady locations. Does best in well-drained, fertile soils and is only slightly tolerant of poor soil conditions. Needs to be protected from sun or reflected heat and winds. Is best suited to northern exposures of buildings, small enclosures, or nestled in the shade of trees.

PESTS: None serious.

NOTES: A very coarsely textured shrub which does very well in shady locations where many other plants fail. Can make an excellent contrast with buildings or backgrounds or can serve as a background for other plants. Should be used sparingly. Hardiest of the evergreen viburnums.

CULTIVARS: None of merit.

RELATED SPECIES: *Viburnum* X *rhytidophylloides* 'Willowwood' is a hybrid between *V. lantana* and *Viburnum rhytidophyllum.* A more compact shrub. Leaves are as on leatherleaf viburnum except slightly broader and shorter. Appears to be much more tolerant of exposure and high light intensity when in a good soil. May be grown in full sun. Also, 'Allegheny': grows 6 to 8 feet tall, globe-shaped, with dark green leaves and yellowish flowers in May. Red fruit in the fall. Much better than the *V. lantana* parent.
     There are many deciduous species of viburnum which, in hardiness Zone 6 and northward, where few broadleaf evergreen shrubs can be grown, are useful landscape plants. Most of these can be grown in Zones 7 and 8; however, they are generally avoided in favor of azaleas, hollies, and other broadleaf evergreens.

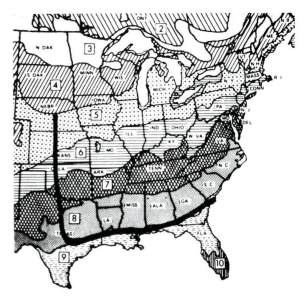

'Willowwood'

'Willowwood'

Viburnum suspensum Lindl.   Sandanqua Viburnum
Caprifoliaceae or Honeysuckle Family   Hardiness Zone 8
Native to islands off the coast of southeast Asia.
SIZE: 4 to 8 feet tall with a spread of 4 to 6 feet. Moderate to rapid grower.
FORM: A compact, oval, or mounding shrub.
TEXTURE: Medium.   EXPOSURE: Sun to shade.

LEAVES: Opposite, simple; basically oval in form. Generally medium to pale green above, pale to light green below. May reach 3 1/2 to 4 inches long, 2 to 2 1/2 inches wide. Slightly rough upper leaf surface as though eroded or furrowed. Margin is slightly sawtooth near the tip. The margin of the leaf may be rolled downward.

STEM: Multi-branched, spreading and upright. Young stems are green, finally maturing to a light brown, very rough, almost pock-marked with very large lenticels, sand-papery to the touch. Occasionally a very robust sprout will develop from the crown with larger leaves than normal. Terminal and axillary buds are nearly always visible like "rabbit ears", however, this is typical of all viburnums.

FLOWERS: Creamy white. Not particularly showy, with a rather undesirable aroma.

FRUIT: Small, football-shaped, about 1/4 inch long. Green finally turning red, moderately showy in some cases.

COLOR: Foliage is medium to pale green. Flowers are creamy white. Fruit is red.

PROPAGATION: Semi-hardwood to hardwood cuttings.

CULTURE: Grows in most soils, does reasonably well even under the most adverse conditions of abused soils common to urban sites. An extremely tough, durable, and adaptable species where it can tolerate the winters. Shears well into various forms, mounds, and hedges. Will tolerate full sun and some heat but is not suited to parking lot conditions or hot, exposed locations, but with any degree of protection, will do very well. Well adapted to partial shade locations where it becomes a deeper green and a more attractive plant. Used extensively throughout the Lower South.

PESTS: None serious, although aphids are common on new growth.

NOTES: A very rugged, adaptable species. Tolerates a wide range of conditions and generally functions well.

CULTIVARS: None known; however, some nurseries sell selections which have superior foliage color and branching and are thus somewhat superior landscape plants.

RELATED SPECIES: *Viburnum odoratissimum* Ker., sweet viburnum, grows much larger, reaching 20 feet, has leaves that are generally larger and very smooth on the upper surface and with only a few teeth on the margin. Grows quite large in both height and wide. Better suited as a multiple stem tree form.

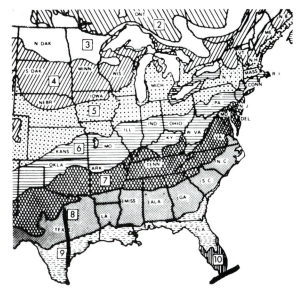

V. odoritissimum

V. odoritissimum

Viburnum tinus L. Laurestinus
Caprifoliaceae or Honeysuckle Family Hardiness Zone 8
Native to the Mediterranean Region.
SIZE: 8 to 10 feet tall with rarely more than a 2- to 3-foot spread. Moderate grower.
FORM: A strict, upright-growing shrub with dense, compact foliage.
TEXTURE: Fine to medium. **EXPOSURE:** Sun to shade.

LEAVES: Opposite, simple; ovate to oblong, 2 to 3 inches long, 1 1/2 inches wide, with a smooth margin. Deep, dark green above, sometimes a metallic blue-green in moderate shade, slightly lighter green below. Generally with some hairs present on both leaf surfaces and the petiole.

STEM: Strict, upright grower, fairly slender, moderately stout, remains erect. A young shoot is green, turning green-black with age. Terminal and axillary buds are prominent on the plant at nearly all times giving a "rabbit ear" effect. Young stems are quite hairy.

FLOWERS: White to slightly pinkish, in clusters 2 to 3 inches across, generally in the summer. Slightly fragrant.

FRUIT: Green, turning metallic blue, finally turning black in late fall. A heavily fruited plant is quite showy for several weeks.

COLOR: Foliage is deep, dark green. Flowers are white. Fruit is metallic blue, finally turning black.

PROPAGATION: Semi-hardwood to hardwood cuttings.

CULTURE: Does well in any good, well-drained soil. Sensitive to root rot problems in areas remaining wet or poorly drained. Responds to modest applications of fertilizer and other good cultural practices. Very little pruning is required because of the dense, compact, upright growth habit. Makes an excellent hedge 6 to 8 feet in height where space is limited.

PESTS: None serious. However, root rot or root suffocation in heavy soils or where plants are repeatedly over watered may be a problem.

NOTES: A desirable, upright-growing, broadleaf evergreen. Extremely useful for vertical line effects or as a slender hedge. When grown in moderate shade with good cultural practices, the blue-green metallic leaves are very attractive and contrast with the green of other plants. Like most viburnums, it does not tolerate high heat or prolonged drought.

CULTIVARS: 'Compacta': a smaller, compact form with deep green foliage. Makes an excellent hedge. 'Robustum': medium-sized plant with very dense evergreen foliage. A heavy bloomer. Flowers are white with a touch of pink. 'Variegatum': variegated leaves, in other respects, much like the parent. 'Eve Price': grows to about 5 feet tall and has small leaves. Other cultivars probably exist.

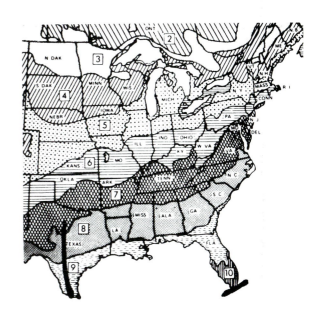

Yucca aloifolia L.   Spanish Bayonet
Agavaceae or Agave Family   Hardiness Zone 6
Native to the southern U.S.
SIZE: 10 to 15 feet tall and may develop a large clump. Rapid grower.
FORM: Irregular, upright-spiraling of leaves generally on unbranched stems.
TEXTURE: Coarse.   **EXPOSURE:** Sun to partial shade.

LEAVES: Dagger-like, closely spiraling on the stem, very stiff, spreading; young leaves point upwards. With some age, leaves lie flat and finally hang down around the old stem. Generally medium green, 12 to 20 inches long, 1 1/2 to 2 inches wide. Widest at the middle or slightly below, gradually narrowing toward the tip and base. The tip is very hard and stiff, terminating in a very sharp brown spine. Margin is sharp with minute teeth and no threads are present.

STEM: Simple or occasionally branched, 3 to 4 inches in diameter, remaining green for several years, finally turning brown. A weak rhizome is present and accounts for the clumping and slow spreading of the plant.

FLOWERS: In large, showy panicles, 12 to 18 inches above the uppermost foliage, 6- to 10-inch diameter clusters. Showy, white, individual flowers are 1/2 to 1 inch long. May occasionally have a tint of pink. Flowers irregularly during late spring and early summer.

FRUIT: A capsule, 1 1/2 to 2 inches oblong. Light green, turning black to purplish at maturity. Pulpy when green, dry and hard at maturity.

COLOR: Foliage is medium green. Flowers are white. Fruit is green turning black.

PROPAGATION: By seed, cuttings or division of a clump.

CULTURE: Best in hot, dry locations. Generally full sun at least for a portion of the day is necessary for good color and flower development. Tolerates high heat conditions, reflected light, parking lot situations, and numerous other growing conditions usually not tolerated by landscape plants. Responds very well to fertilization. Makes an attractive show during early to mid season. Old flower stalks should be removed which generally is the only maintenance necessary. Does not tolerate wet feet, poorly drained soils, or shady, damp locations.

PESTS: A leaf spot in moist areas with poor air drainage. Likewise, scale insects may become a problem in humid, poorly air-drained courtyards.

NOTES: Leaves are sharp, stiff, and dangerous. Keep away from people, especially children. Yuccas make up some of the most durable and maintenance-free broadleaf evergreens available. They need to be planned to fit in with other plants that complement their form and texture and general desert-like atmosphere. Yuccas generally do not blend in with many temperate zone plants. By selecting several species of yucca, a mass of vegetation may be developed ranging from 3 to 4 feet to 12 to 15 feet with a long bloom period. Especially appropriate for parking lots and where vandalism may be a problem.

CULTIVARS: 'Marginata': yellow margin leaf. 'Tricolor': yellow or white stripes in the leaf center and yellow-mottled. Other cultivars may exist.

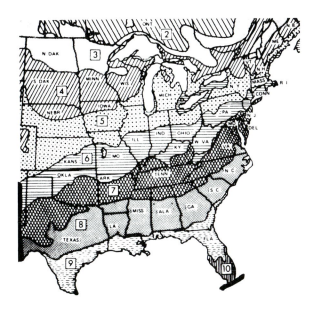

Yucca filamentosa L.   Adam's Needle Yucca
Agavaceae or Agave Family   Hardiness Zone 4
Native from North Carolina to Florida and west through Oklahoma.
SIZE: 3 to 4 feet tall, sometimes making a clump 3 to 4 feet in diameter. Moderate grower.
FORM: A whorling of leaves in a mound.
TEXTURE: Coarse.   EXPOSURE: Sun to partial shade.

LEAVES: About 1 to 1 1/2 inches wide, 24 to 30 inches long, with long, curling, white threads on the margin. Generally medium to dark green above; pale green below, or may have a slight blue cast above and/or below. The tip is fairly sharp to the touch, however, the leaf is moderately flexible and is not dangerous as is Spanish bayonet.

STEM: Rarely exposed above ground. Plant is a mound of leaves without a conspicuous stem. May reach 3 to 4 feet tall with some age. Generally round with tightly attached spiraling leaves.

FLOWERS: Showy, creamy white. In clusters 1 to 4 feet above the top of the foliage, generally in late May to mid June. Somewhat fragrant.

FRUIT: A dry capsule, 1 1/2 to 2 inches long; unattractive. The entire flower stalk should be removed as soon as the blooms have fallen.

COLOR: Foliage is medium to dark green. Flowers are creamy white and showy.

PROPAGATION: Seed, cuttings, or division of the clumps (rhizomes).

CULTURE: Best in hot, dry locations. Generally full sun for at least a portion of the day is necessary for good color and flower development. Tolerates high heat conditions, reflected light, parking lot situations, and numerous other growing conditions usually not tolerated by most landscape plants. Responds very well to fertilization. Makes an attractive show during early to mid season. Old flower stalks should be removed which generally is the only maintenance necessary. Does not tolerate wet feet, poorly drained soils, or shady, damp locations.

PESTS: Leaf spot in moist areas with poor air drainage. Likewise, scale insects may become a problem in humid, poorly air-drained courtyard situations.

NOTES: Yuccas make up some of the most durable and maintenance-free broadleaf evergreens available. Should be used a great deal more. Need to be planned to fit in with other plants that complement their form and texture and general desert-like atmosphere. Often do not blend in with many temperate zone plants. A good plant to use as a buffer to protect people from Spanish bayonet and screen the older basal stems.

CULTIVARS: 'Ivory Tower': has ivory flowers and especially clean, slight bluish green foliage. 'Golden Sword': has white flowers and leaves with a yellow strip down the center. Several others have been named but it is questionable if they are superior to seedlings.

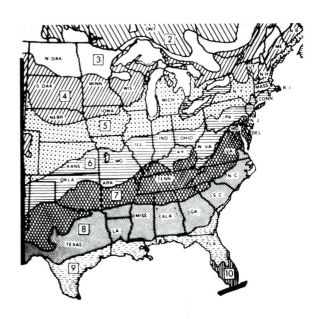

Yucca gloriosa L.   Mound Lily Yucca
Agavaceae or Agave Family   Hardiness Zone 6
Native to the Gulf Coast region of the United States.
SIZE: 6 to 8 feet tall, single-stemmed or multiple-stemmed. Moderate to rapid grower.
FORM: Upright with whorls of leaves.
TEXTURE: Coarse.   EXPOSURE: Sun to partial shade.

LEAVES: Numerous, stiff, straight; spiraling up the stem. Generally broadly linear, broadest at the middle, tapering toward the tip and base with a hardened spine-like tip. Numerous teeth are present on the leaf margin but are inconspicuous. A powdery green to blue-gray-green, except on very old leaves, very showy and a contrast with most green foliage. Softer and more flexible than most yuccas, does not penetrate the skin when contacted.

STEM: May reach 3 to 5 inches in diameter, usually with a few dead leaves at the base. Leaves spiraling up the stem, rarely branching, but there is a weak rhizome present which accounts for the thickening or clumping of older plants. Many times pruning is required to stimulate rhizome development to make an attractive clump.

FLOWERS: Early to mid summer, in showy panicles above the foliage 2 to 4 feet. Individual flowers are 2 to 3 inches long. White or occasionally with a tint of purple, with 3 petals and 3 sepals, generally oblong. Very showy.

FRUIT: A dry capsule, weeping, 2 to 3 1/2 inches long, somewhat constricted in the middle. Green, evenutally turning black. Not showy.

COLOR: Foliage is powdery green to blue-gray-green. Flowers are white. Fruit is black.

PROPAGATION: By seed or division of clumps.

CULTURE: Best in hot, dry locations, generally full sun for at least a portion of the day is necessary for good color and flower development. Tolerates high heat conditions, reflected light, parking lot situations, and numerous other growing conditions usually not tolerated by most landscape plants. Responds to fertilization and makes an attractive show of both flowers and foliage. Old flower stalks should be removed which generally is the only maintenance necessary. Does not tolerate wet feet, poorly drained soils, or shady, damp locations.

PESTS: Leaf spot in moist areas with poor air drainage. Likewise, scale insects may become a problem in humid, poorly air-drained courtyard. The sugar cane borer may be a problem in some areas.

NOTES: Yuccas make up some of the most durable and maintenance-free broadleaf evergreens available. Should be used a great deal more, however, they need to be planned to fit in with other plants that complement their form and texture and general desert-like atmosphere. Often do not blend in with many temperate zone plants. Many yucca species exist and can be very useful in landscaping. Many are not cold hardy and are only seen in the Southwest and indoors.

CULTIVARS: Several cultivars have been named; however, they are generally not superior to seedlings of the species.

RELATED SPECIES: *Yucca elephantiopes* Regel., is an attractive plant with no spines but is only hardy in Zones 9b and 10.

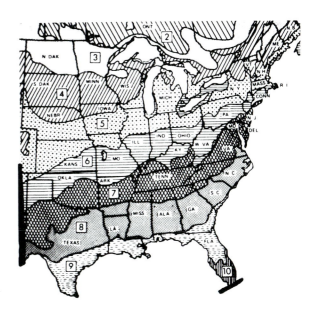

Palms and Cycads

Palms and the cycads which have palm-like appearances add a unique tropical effect to any landscape. Palms are noted to be tropical and many will only grow in hardiness Zone 10 where frosts rarely, if ever, occur. On the other hand there are many palms that are quite hardy and do well in Zones 9 and 8 and a few even into the warmer nitches of Zone 7. Thus a tropical effect can be created in many areas of the southern USA that are not truly tropical. The tropics can be quite wet or extremely dry. As a result, some of the palms and cycads make excellent plants for indoor landscaping. Interiors, especially in the more northern areas, can be very low in humidity and light intensity. Plants native to shade areas in a dry tropical region are therefore well suited to these challenging environments. In addition, since the growth is often slow, once the interior landscape is installed it is visually relatively stable.

Acoelorrhaphe wrightii Wendl.   Paurotis or Everglades Palm
   (Syn. *Paurotis wrightii*)   Hardiness Zone 9-
Palmaceae or Palm Family
Native to Florida and the Caribbean
SIZE: 15 to 30 feet tall in a clump. Slow grower.
FORM: A large irregular clump or multiple stem palm.
TEXTURE: Medium   **EXPOSURE:** Partial shade to sun

LEAVES: Palmate, nearly circular in outline, deeply cut between segments. Individual leaves may be 2 to 3 feet in diameter, usually medium green above and almost silvery beneath. Petioles are armed with sharp orange teeth.

STEM: Slender but stout and covered with a dense mat of well organized fiber which is red-brown when young to near black with age. Stems appear even more slender if the old leaf bases and fiber is removed. Suckers freely at the base and will create a large, dense, forbidding clump if left unattended.

FLOWERS: White; in clusters extending above the leaves then drooping with the maturing fruit. The flowers are perfect.

FRUIT: Black and shiny; about 1/3 inch long.

COLOR: Foliage is medium green.

PROPAGATION: Seed or division

CULTURE: Native to swampy areas in the Florida Everglades but is moderately drought tolerant and will grow in most soils. When soils are extremely alkaline, manganese, iron, and magnesium deficiencies can become severe and make the plant unattractive. Grows well in a container when small, but soon needs more room.

PESTS: None serious.

NOTES: Makes a spectacular clump palm in the general landscape, in raised planters and if space allows, in large interior landscapes. The slender stems (if exposed) and attractive foliage

make for a neater appearing clump than *Phoenix reclinata*. Because of its tolerance to poorly drained sites, it will do well in areas not suited to *Phoenix* and other palm species. That same tolerance make it a good choice for large planters which are often poorly drained if sufficient light is present. Needs room to grow, even though growth is slow, do not underestimate its ultimate size. Of the large clump palms, paurotis is the only true native in South Florida and as such, is getting more attention. If freezing temperatures briefly occur, generally only the current leaves are damaged and regrowth quickly occurs from the terminal buds. The petioles do have sharp teeth, cut they are much less hazardous than the spines on *Phoenix* species.

CULTIVARS: None known. However, some variation occurs among seedlings and with propagation by division, some seedlings may be worthy.

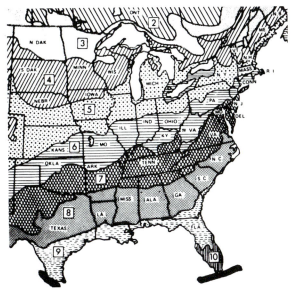

Arecastrum romanzoffiana Becc.   Queen Palm
   (Syn. *Syagrus r.* or *Cocos plumosa*)
Native to Brazil and Argentina   Hardiness Zone 9
SIZE: 25 to 40 feet tall, 1 to 1 1/2 feet in stem diameter. Moderate to fast grower.
FORM: Fine textured clustering of leaves at the tip of a clean vertical stem.
TEXTURE: Fine.   EXPOSURE: Sun to partial shade.

LEAVES: Pinnately compound, 8 to 15 feet long with many long, narrow, drooping leaflets. The leaflets are attached to the primary rachis (central leaf stalk) in groups of two to seven in a cluster and are arranged so that when the leaf is viewed from the end various positioned leaflets form various lines or rankings down the primary leaf stalk. The leaflets are folded with the "V" opened toward the tip of the leaf. Leaflets are generally less than one inch wide and are long, soft, often drooping from the middle out. The base of the primary leaf stalk is densely covered with a burlap-like fiber. The lower portion of the leaf base is often covered with a silvery, flaky material. No spines.

STEM: Roughly 12 to 18 inches in diameter, and stout and smooth. The stem is marked with a series of rings but without projections or striking regular leaf scars giving a smooth appearance somewhat like the royal palm. The stem is often covered with silvery-gray flaking material when young. The leaf bases are broadly attached to the stem and form a long, tapering, inverted "V" where they attach.

FLOWERS: Monoecious. Individual flowers are small and creamy yellow but are in clusters up to 6 feet long. Dropping flowers may create considerable mess on sidewalk, patio or other outdoor living areas. Large flower clusters are moderately showy.

FRUITS: In large clusters up to 6 feet long and 12 to 14 inches in diameter with individual fruits about one inch long and one inch wide; more or less rounded. Yellow when mature, fleshy and can be rather messy on outdoor living areas. Generally one-seeded or occasionally two-seeded. The flowers and fruit are partially covered by a large, woody bract.

COLOR: Foliage is dark green. Flowers are creamy yellow. Fruits are yellow.

PROPAGATION: Seed, which requires 2 to 5 months to germinate.

CULTURE: A tough, tolerant palm which grows fairly rapidly in most soils and transplants easily. Tolerates considerable drought and some salt in coastal conditions. Responds vigorously and develops a heavier crown when fertilized at moderate to heavy rates. Is sensitive to manganese deficiency on very alkaline soils. This is most commonly found in the marl type soils of extreme southern Florida. Requires removal of old leaves from time to time in order to keep the plant attractive. The flowers and fruits can be particularly messy in formal, well manicured lawns or around sidewalks, driveways or patios. Queen palm is an excellent, tough palm with fine texture, often planted as a substitute for the royal palm in cooler areas.

PESTS: Few serious.

NOTES: The genus *Syagrus* and *Arecastrum* were originally included in the genus *Cocos* with *Butia* and the true coconut, *Cocos nucifera.* The old original name, *Cocos plumosa,* is still widely known and used to some degree in the nursery trade.
   Queen palm is occasionally used for indoor landscaping where moderate light intensity can be provided. It must also be kept in mind that even in moderate light intensity and indoors it will grow to considerable size and thus space considerations are important.

CULTIVARS: Probably none, although some seedling variation exists.

549

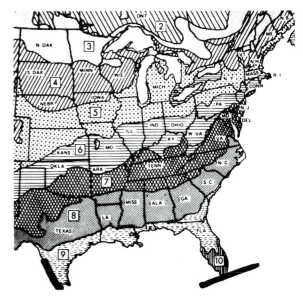

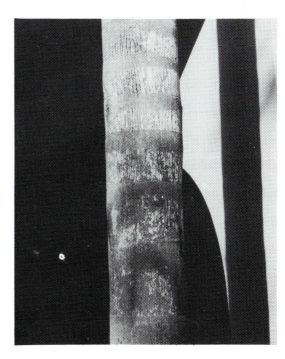

Butia capitata (Mart.) Becc.   Pindo or Jelly Palm
Palmaceae or Palm Family   Hardiness Zone 8b
Native to South America.
SIZE: 10 to 20 feet tall. Slow to moderate grower.
FORM: Lollipop-like crown of fern-like leaves on a single stem on a single stem.
TEXTURE: Coarse   EXPOSURE: Full sun to some shade.

LEAVES: Pinnately compound, 6 to 10 feet long, generally 1 1/2 to 2 1/2 feet wide, arching or curving sometimes almost to the ground or back to the trunk. Leaves are a distinct gray-green or blue-gray-green, very much in contrast to other green foliage in the landscape. The base of the petiole has distinct, hard, brown, often blunt, teeth along the margin. These may be interlaced with fibers at the very base and may be non-existent near where the leaflets begin to develop on the outer portion of the leaf. Leaflets are folded downwards and attach to the main stalk in one plane, forming a broad "V" when viewed from the end.

STEM: Moderately thick, generally 12 to 18 inches in diameter, and stout, but never reaching the size or height of the Washington or sabal palms. Old dead leaves are retained on the base of the stem if not removed, and even after removal the leaf bases remain, giving the basal stem of the palm a very distinct patchwork texture.

FLOWERS: Small, creamy white to yellow, rather showy; on a stalk 4 to 5 feet long which arises from among the lower leaves.

FRUIT: Oblong to nearly round, about 1 inch long; yellow to red. Pulpy, fibrous, and edible. Sometimes used in making jellies or preserves.

COLOR: Foliage is gray-green to blue-gray-green. Fruit is yellow to red.

PROPAGATION: Seed.

CULTURE: An extremely tough, tolerant palm. One of the most durable in the palm family. Pindo palm will grow in virtually any soil, in full sun to moderate shade, or on hot, windy exposed locations, containers, and other environments unsuitable for most other plant materials. Often seen along the Gulf Coast states in small urns, tubs, or barrels around gas stations and other establishments with acres of asphalt or concrete. These conditions are truly the deserts of America and any plant that can survive under these circumstances is awesome.

PESTS: None serious.

NOTES: The genus *Butia* was originally grouped with *Cocos*, the coconut, and *Arecastrum*, the queen palm and was named *Cocos australis*, then later changed to *Butis capitata* as a separate genus and species. Other species of jelly palm have been described but it is questionable if these are indeed different species or just variations in the seedling population. A very showy ornamental palm with few problems or difficulties. However, planting it near sidewalks or patios where the fruit can fall on paved surfaces is undesirable. It is probably the hardiest of the pinnately leaved palms. Because of its adaptability, it should be used more for indoor landscaping farther north where moderate light intensities exist.

CULTIVARS: None known.

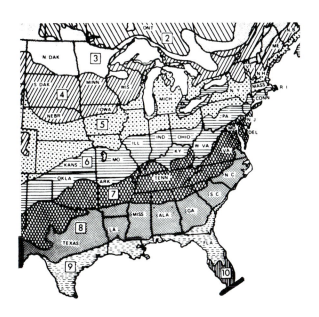

Caryota mitis Lour. Fishtail Palm
Palmaceae or Palm Family Hardiness Zone 10
Native to southeast Asia
SIZE: 15 to 30 feet tall with multiple stems. Moderate grower.
FORM: A multiple-stem, clump palm with no distinct head.
TEXTURE: Medium. **EXPOSURE:** Shade to full sun.

LEAVES: The only palm with bipinnately compound leaves. Leaves may be from 4 to 10 feet long with a 1- to 2-foot long petiole. Individual leaflets resemble the fin or tail of a fish in outline. The leaflets have prominent parallel veins and the outer margin is irregularly saw toothed. Usually dark green. No spines on the leaflets or petiole.

STEM: Multiple stems create a shrub-like cluster when young and an irregular crown clump with age. The long pointed leaf bases are persistent and covered with black fiber.

FLOWER: White; in drooping, mop-like clusters. Monoecious.

FRUIT: Green turning dark red to nearly black when ripe. The fruit pulp contains a skin irritant.

COLOR: Foliage is dark green.

PROPAGATION: Seeds which require several months to germinate.

CULTURE: Very tolerant to a wide range of soils and is fairly tolerant of drought and low humidity. Because of its tolerance to low light intensity and low humidity and restricted spaces, it works well in indoor plantings. Out-of-doors, when the plant gets large, it eventually flowers at the top of a cane progressing downward. When the fruit matures on the lowest flowers, the cane dies. Fortunately, new canes are produced as the plant grows and the visual quality remains after removal of the dead cane.

PESTS: None serious.

NOTES: A most unusual and striking foliage. Quite eye-catching in large, indoor planters or in the landscape, where it is cold-hardy. Well suited to containers and indoor use where its size remains in check and flowering rarely occurs.

CULTIVARS: None known.

RELATED SPECIES: *Caryota urens*, L., solitary fishtail palm, grows taller and may reach 40 feet or more tall. Without the multiple stems the crown appears taller and less attractive than *C. mitis*. Similarly adaptable to soils and indoor use; however, when flowering occurs the plant dies, so it is not commonly planted in outdoor landscapes.

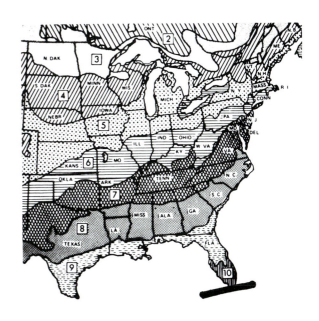

Chamaedorea erumpens H.E. Moore   Bamboo Palm
Palmaceae or Palm Family   Hardiness Zone 10
Native to Mexico and South America
SIZE: 6 to 10 feet tall, depending on age. Moderate to fast grower.
FORM: Generally multiple-stemmed; dense, bamboo-like clump, depending on age and growing conditions.
TEXTURE: Fine.   EXPOSURE: Partial shade to shade.

LEAVES: Pinnately compound; 18 to 24 inches long, generally with 15 to 20 leaflets and the leaflets lie in a single plane, rather broad and flattened. The two terminal leaflets are generally the largest. Color is a medium to dark green.

STEM: Bamboo-like; rarely reaching more than 1 inch in diameter. The base of the leaves encircle the stem and are quite short.

FLOWERS: Dioecious. Creamy yellow; in clusters, moderately attractive.

FRUIT: Black.

COLOR: Foliage is medium to dark green. Flowers are creamy yellow. Fruits are black.

PROPAGATION: From seed or division of a clump.

CULTURE: Especially tolerant of low light conditions. A widely used palm in indoor landscaping. Very sensitive to drought and is often found with browning or burning of the leaf margin caused by excess fertilizer, excess salts in the soil or lack of water or a combination of these factors. Particularly in indoor use where humidity may be very low in the wintertime moisture must be supplied regularly to avoid marginal burn. Responds well to moderate fertilizer applications.

PESTS: Nematodes when grown out of doors. Spider mites are a frequent and can be a serious problem on indoor plants.

NOTES: A very attractive, small palm for indoor landscape use. Perhaps best suited to a large container with other plants, such that moisture is more even, which helps avoid leaflet tip burn and perhaps the mite problem.

Plants treated here as species of the genus *Chamaedorea* have been grouped or split by various individuals in many cases. Hortus III presents the group as species in the genus *Chamaedorea*. This is the format followed here.

Chamaedorea elegans Mart, grown widely under the common name Neanthe bella, commonly called the parlor palm or Neanthe bella palm. Has a solitary stem which may reach 3 to 4 feet tall. Individual leaves may reach 2 to 3 feet long with 10 to 20 leaflets on each side. Foliage is generally deep green unless suffering from high light intensity or spider mite injury when it would be a mottled and more yellow pale green.

C. seifrizii Burret, is very similar to *C. erumpens* in growth form and development of multiple stems and is similar in size, adaptability to shade, and indoor use. However, the leaflets are much more narrow giving the palm a finer texture and neater appearance.

C. microspadix is also of similar size and growth habit and shade tolerance to *C. seifrizii* and *C. erumpens*. However, its strikingly orange-red fruits make it more showy. It is also more cold-tolerant than the other species in this genus, and is hardy in Zone 9 with some protection. Various other species of *Chamaedoea* exist but are not common.

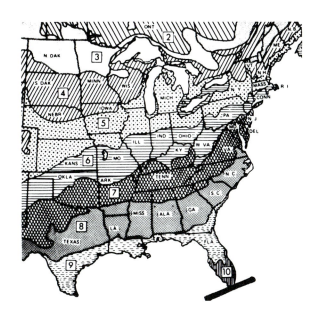

Chamaerops humilis L.   European Fan Palm
Palmaceae or Palm Family   Hardiness Zone 8
Native to the Mediterranean Region.
SIZE: 6 to 20 feet, depending on age and growing conditions; with a crown spread of 6 to 8 feet. Slow grower.
FORM: Mounded or globe-shaped shrub.
TEXTURE: Medium.   **EXPOSURE:** Sun to partial shade.

LEAVES: Spiraling around the main stem, the leaves are palmately compound with many long, slender leaflets. Upper surface is a bright, medium green; under surface is covered with silvery white scales, especially when young. The petiole is heavily laden with long needle-like spines, particularly near the base.

STEM: Often not seen, rising only a short distance above the soil line except on very old plants where it may reach a height of 10 to 15 feet. Stem is densely covered with coarse brown hair, appears to be wrapped in burlap. Unlike many palms, European fan palm develops suckers or offshoots at the bases of older plants. However, the main above-ground stem does not branch.

FLOWERS: Short, yellow clusters among the bases of the leaves. Not showy.

FRUIT: Not common in the United States.

COLOR: Foliage is a bright, medium green.

PROPAGATION: Seed or separation of young plants (suckers) from the base of older plants.

CULTURE: A very tough, tolerant palm. Grows in a wide range of soils, exposures, and temperature ranges, tolerating cold down to about 10 degrees F if not for prolonged periods. Does well as a patio pot plant or for indoor landscaping farther north. The very slow rate of growth makes it expensive to produce in the nursery. However, once established in the landscape, it requires very little further maintenance.

PESTS: None serious.

NOTES: One of the most attractive slow-growing, clump-like or shrub-like palms. Very useful for giving a tropical effect in landscaping. A good palm for solariums or other areas of indoor landscaping in the North. European fan palm is sometimes confused with windmill palm. However, these can be readily distinguished since the windmill palm has drooping tips on the palmate leaves, a dull green underneath of the leaf, very minute saw-like teeth on the base of the petiole, and no suckers on the base. European fan palm leaves do not droop on the tip, are silvery gray on the underneath side, and have long needle-like spines covering the petiole and numerous suckers at the base.

CULTIVARS: 'Macrocarpa': big fruited fan palm, not commonly seen in this country but said to have larger, more showy fruits. Other cultivars may exist.

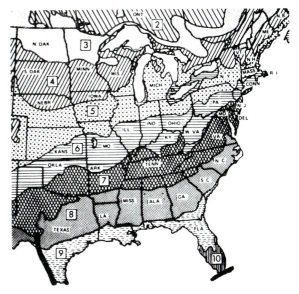
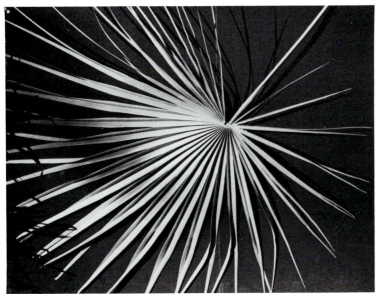

Chrysalidocarpus lutescens H.Wendl.　　　Cane, Yellow, Butterfly, or　Areca Palm
Palmaceae or Palm Family
Native to Madagascar　　　　　　　　　Hardiness Zone 9B
SIZE:　15 to 20 feet tall.　Moderate grower.
FORM:　A multiple stem, large, umbrella crowned, clump palm.
TEXTURE:　Medium to fine.　　　　　　EXPOSURE:　Sun to shade.

LEAVES:　Pinnately compound, 6 to 8 feet long, up to 2 1/2 feet wide, and arching.　The leaflets are bright green; however, in full sun leaves on some plants may have a distinct yellow cast, which is probably a magnesium deficiency.　The leaf stems and mid ribs are a yellow to yellow gold.　All of the leaflets are in a single plane, as if flattened.　Leaflets may be opposite from one another on the central stalk or staggered depending on rate of growth and position on the stalk.　The petiole enclasps the stem.　The leaflets do not droop but are held in a fairly rigid plane.　A distinct crown shaft is present.　No spines.

STEM:　May reach 4 to 6 inches in diameter; however, in a dense clump stems rarely reach more than 3 inches.　A distinct circular ring is visible where each leaf was attached to the stem.　The stems have a distinct yellowish color and are smooth except for the leaf scars or rings.　A very flexible leaf and stem rarely damaged by wind.

FLOWERS:　Not showy; hidden by the dense mass of leaves.　Dioecious.

FRUIT:　About 3/4 inch long; shiny black.

COLOR:　Foliage is medium green to yellow-green, depending on nutritional condition of the plant.　Stem and petiole are yellow to yellow-gold.

PROPAGATION:　Seed.

CULTURE:　A very adaptable palm.　Grows well out of doors in central and south Florida, but likewise thrives in moderate to low light intensity in indoor landscapes throughout the world.　Like most palms it requires a moderate moisture supply and responds with vigor to good soil and fertilization.　Plants grown in containers with adequate supplies of micronutrients and magnesium do not develop the off-yellow color of the leaves that is makes many plants in South Florida unattractive.　Applications of Epson salts to supply magnesium will assist the plants on some soils.　On very alkaline soils, elemental sulfur at the rate of about 6 pounds per 100 square feet around the plants will reduce the pH in the surface few inches of the soil and thus increase the availability of iron, manganese, and other micronutrients and assist good foliage color.　It is moderate to good in tolerance of salt spray.
　　This is one of the most versatile palms and one of the best palms for indoor use or in tubs or containers on a patio.　It may be grown with full foliage to the ground or with lower leaves removed to show the yellow-ringed, smooth trunks.　With leaves and sprouts allowed to develop near the base it can be an effective large hedge or screen in the landscape.

PESTS:　None serious.

NOTES:　This species was originally known in this country as *Areca lutescens* which is incorrect.　The common name, Areca palm is widely used in the nursery trade.　Cane or yellow palm are probably more appropriate and descriptive common names.　The absence of spines anywhere on the plant and the leaflets being in a single plane give it a texture and grandeur unequaled by most other palms of similar size and growth habit.

CULTIVARS:　None.

OTHER SPECIES:　*C. lucubensis* and *C. madagascariensis*.　Both species are relatively unknown in the United States.

Cocos nucifera L.   Coconut Palm
Palmaceae or Palm Family   Hardiness Zone 10
Native to the tropics, worldwide.
SIZE: 30 to 80 feet tall, depending on variety. Moderate grower.
FORM: Tall palms with large crowns and often arching stems.
TEXTURE: Medium   **EXPOSURE:** Sun.

LEAVES: Pinnately compound; often 12 to 15 feet long or more and covered with dark green leaflets which are three feet or more in length and about 1 1/2 to 2 inches wide. All leaflets are in one plane along the petiole. The petiole may be 3 to 4 feet long and wrapped with broad bands of tan fiber. There are no spines or sawtooth margins.

STEM: Trunks are solitary, stout, and straight or gently arching out and upward. The base is often swollen at or just above the soil line. The trunk is ringed but not prominently, often has vertical cracks and is gray to gray-black.

FLOWERS: White, on a 3- to 4-foot long inflorescence. Monoecious.

FRUIT: The common coconut of commerce. Depending on variety, may be from 3 to 12 inches or more with the husk and somewhat triangular. Green turning yellowish then brown when ripe.

COLOR: Foliage is dark green. Trunk is gray.

PROPAGATION: Seed, but six months may be required for germination.

CULTURE: Very tolerant of soils types, moisture, and salt. Grows well in pure sand, marl, or seashells and rock. May be grown in containers but gets too large for interior use and requires high light intensity to remain attractive.

PESTS: Potassium deficiency is common in South Florida. Lethal yellows disease has killed large plantings, yet some varieties are resistant.

NOTES: The coconut provides the ultimate tropical island, wind-dancing foliage effect, even in just a slight breeze. A spectacular palm where it can be grown, yet it has one complication: the falling huge fruit can be hazardous to health and property, especially during high winds. The fruits are edible and widely used for food and oils. In tropical climates a single tree may produce 50 to 75 nuts per year. The coir or fiber from the nut has been used in manufacturing and as a substitute for peat moss in soil mixes for growing plants in containers.

CULTIVARS: Many varieties or ecological races exist. The dwarf Malayan variety is somewhat smaller, produces striking golden yellow nuts and is quite resistant to the lethal yellows disease. This variety has some landscape advantages in terms of size and more color and has become the coconut of choice in most of South Florida.

Cycas circinalis L.
Cycadaceae or Cycad Family
Native to southwest Asia and Africa.

Queen Sago or Fern Palm
Hardiness Zone 10

SIZE: 10 to 15 feet or more tall, with spread of 10 to 16 feet.   Slow grower.
FORM: Symmetrical, fern or palm-like shrub.
TEXTURE: Fine.   **EXPOSURE:** Sun to shade.

LEAVES: Pinnately compound, in a rosette around the bud and stem. Leaves appear like those of a palm, thus the common name. Leaf and leaflets are somewhat stiff and rigid, but much less so than with *C. revoluta*. Leaflets are dark green and glossy but are flat in cross-section and pointed at the tip. Individual leaflets may be 10 to 12 inches long. The petiole is lined with modified leaflets that are spine-like.

STEM: A young queen sago with a stem about 2 to 4 feet tall appears like a near perfect sphere if left unpruned (see photograph). An old stem may be 15 to 20 inches or more in diameter with the leaf bases attached. Very tough and durable.

FLOWERS: Dioecious. Female flower is a flattened structure at the terminal bud. Male flower is a large cone-like structure that at the top and is quite striking.

FRUIT: Orange. More or less egg-shaped, about 1 1/2 inches long.

COLOR: Foliage is dark green.

PROPAGATION: Seed or division.

CULTURE: Grows in almost any warm climate and soil. With the nitrogen-fixing bacteria associated with the roots, the plant grows even in nearly sterile sands. Grows well in containers but gets large--horizontally--even when relatively young, because of the length of the leaves and the circular distribution. Old plants that have a well developed stem transplant easily and are prized as landscape plants in Zone 10 or occasionally indoors elsewhere where space is available. Will grow in full sun but is more attractive in partial shade. Retains leaf color and density even in fairly low light situations.

PESTS: Scale insects, mealy bugs, and occasionally a leaf spot disease.

NOTES: Growth, adaptation, and form are very similar between *C. circinalis* and *C. revoluta*, except for size. Is best grown where it can be left alone to reach the full lollipop-like crown. Where old leaves are removed the plant is much less attractive (see photograph). Makes a very good indoor plant if space is available. The pulp on the seed and the sap are said to be poisonous. XX-POISON-XX

CULTIVARS: None.

RELATED SPECIES: *Cycas media*, commonly called the nut palm because of the nut-like seeds, is native to Australia and appears much like queen sago. Several other related genera exist with similar appearance and most, if not all, are intolerant of cold but do well indoors.

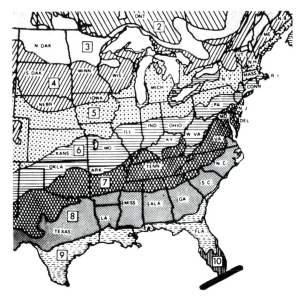

Cycas revoluta Thunb.   Sago Palm
Cycadaceae or Cycad Family   Hardiness Zone 8B
Native to southeast Asia tropics
SIZE: 2 to 10 feet tall or more with age, 5 to 8 feet across. Very slow grower.
FORM: Symmetrical, fern-like or palm-like shrub.
TEXTURE: Fine.   **EXPOSURE:** Sun to shade.

LEAVES: Pinnately compound in a rosette around the bud and stem. Leaves appear like those of a palm, thus the common name. However, the leaf and leaflets are quite stiff and rigid and feel as though they are made of plastic. Very dark green and glossy. The margins of the leaflets distinctly roll under and terminate in a spine-like tip. The petiole is lined with modified leaflets that function like sharp spines.

STEM: Generally a single stem, but may branch with age. The stem is stout and tough, 6 to 12 inches or more in diameter and covered with old leaf bases. The terminal vegetative bud is huge. When the bud expands a proliferation of leaves quickly extend up and out around the entire circumference, creating a circular array that contrasts with the old leaves for a time.

FLOWERS: Dioecious. Female flower is a flattened structure at the top of the plant. Male flower appears also at the top of the plant like a large pine cone that is densely hairy.

FRUITS: Bright red to red-orange, about 1 1/2 inches long and 50 to 100 or more generally are in the inflorescence.

COLOR: Foliage is very dark green.

PROPAGATION: Seed or division.

CULTURE: Amazingly tough. Will grow practically anywhere except very wet conditions. Part of its adaptability to poor soils is the nitrogen-fixing bacteria associated with the roots. Grows well in containers, planters indoors, or out-of-doors or in the soil where it is hardy. Because of the extremely slow growth, it rarely overgrows a site. Likewise, because it generally makes only one new rosette of leaves per season, if the foliage is damaged by cold or other factors, it remains unattractive until the next flush of growth.

PESTS: Anthracnose disease of the leaves. Sometimes scale insects.

NOTES: Cycads are very primitive gymnosperms, thus are more closely related to a pine tree than a palm. The sago palm common name is strictly because of its outward appearance. Sago palm makes an excellent indoor plant because it will tolerate low light intensity and low humidity. Unlike many tropical plants used indoors, its very slow growth means it stays about the same size and form as when installed. It was commonly planted around plantations in the Old South and an occasional specimen can be found 10 feet tall and with several younger off-shoot plants around the base. The pulp on the seeds and the sap are said to be poisonous. XX-POISON-XX

CULTIVARS: None known.

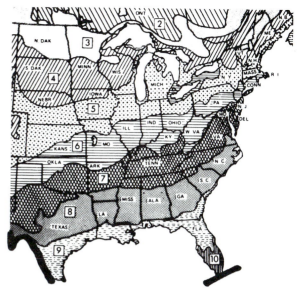

Livistona chinensis R.Br.　　　　　　　　　Chinese Fan Palm
Palmaceae or Palm Family　　　　　　　　　Hardiness Zone 9
Native to central China.
SIZE: 20 to 25 feet tall with round crown. Slow grower.
FORM: A large lollipop-like crown on a single stem.
TEXTURE: Coarse　　　　　　　　　　**EXPOSURE:** Sun

LEAVES: Huge, palmate, olive green leaves with petioles 5 to 6 feet long and rounded leaf blades 4 to 6 feet across are striking. Individual leaflet sections are about 2 inches wide and droop at the tips. Note the thumb nail like projection where the leaf blade connects with the petiole. Petioles are green and may or may not have a few pronounced, stout, green spines near the base. The spines tend to decrease in number with age of the plant.

STEM: Large and stout, 10 to 15 inches in diameter and only slightly swollen near the base. The young stem is brown becoming more gray with age. Leaf scars encircle only about one-half of the stem diameter but old fibrous tissue obscures the leaf bases.

FLOWERS: Monoecious. Yellow. Flower stalks may be 4 to 6 feet long and multi-branched.

FRUITS: Elongate, about 3/4 inches long. Dull but attractive, blue-green; darkening with age.

COLOR: Foliage is olive-green. Flowers are yellowish. Fruit is blue-green.

PROPAGATION: Seed.

CULTURE: A very drought-tolerant and moderately salt-tolerant palm that is widely adaptable to soil conditions, from the sands of Florida to the clays of southern California. The drooping tips of the leaflets make it quite distinct. More easily transplanted when young than sabal palms.

PESTS: None serious.

NOTES: A striking landscape palm. Grows quite slowly, thus does not quickly extend upward and out of view. However, a young plant will be 10 to 12 feet or more across, thus requires considerable space. Does best in full sun and becomes more open and less attractive in the shade. Generally not for interior use unless light intensity is quite high.

CULTIVARS: None

RELATED SPECIES: *Livistona australis* Mart., native to north Australia is similarly cold hardy but can reach a height of 40 to 60 feet or more. Leaflets tend to split all the way to the petiole and droop thus giving a more ragged, yet attractive, appearance. Also green spines are more prominent on the petiole bases but with variation among species. A very tough, tolerant, adaptable palm where it is cold hardy.

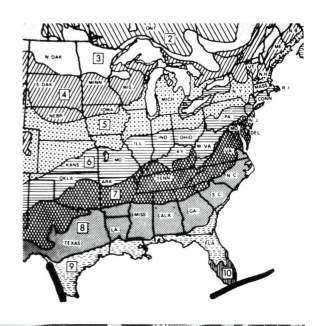

Neodypsis decaryi Jumell.
Palmaceae or Palm Family
Native to Madagascar

Triangle Palm
Hardiness Zone 10

SIZE: 10 to 20 feet tall with triangular spread. Slow to moderate grower.
FORM: Unique, triangular form with fan-like foliage.
TEXTURE: Fine.
EXPOSURE: Sun to partial shade.

LEAVES: Pinnately compound; 8 to 12 feet long and with a hundred or more leaflets that form a distinct "V" down the top of the petiole. The petiole is generally straight for some distance from the trunk, then gracefully arches downward. Some of the basal leaflets may be several feet long, hanging down like long threads. Leaflet color is generally gray- green to blue-green. Areas of brownish red, stiff hairs or scales at the base of young leaves provide another color feature. No spines.

STEM: The wide petiole bases attach to the stem in three distinct vertical rows producing the striking triangular form and make the stem appear much larger. The exposed stem below the leaf bases is distinctly ringed and may be 10 to 16 inches in diameter on a large specimen.

FLOWER: Monoecious. Yellow flowers form along the 3 to 5 foot long, multi-branched inflorescence that arises among the lower leaves.

FRUIT: Yellow to yellow-green; about 3/4 to 1 inch long.

COLOR: Foliage is gray-green to blue-green.

PROPAGATION: Seeds which germinate fairly quickly under warm conditions.

CULTURE: Fairly drought-tolerant in the landscape; however, it requires good moisture maintenance in a container or large planter. Tolerates moderate light intensity and variations in humidity and temperature, as long as freezing does not occur. Good for interior landscape use. Overgrows small containers quickly and needs space to do well indoors. The foliage color and form are striking and may dominate a site.

PESTS: None serious.

NOTES: A spectacular and unusual form for a palm or any other plant. The striking, almost delicate gray-green foliage and brownish red scales at the base of the leaves are real eye-catchers. For years this palm was shunned for indoor landscape use. However, it tolerates the conditions well and where space allows, creates a most notable sight. Remains sufficiently upright so that other complementing or contrasting tropical plants can be grown beneath.

CULTIVARS: None known.

Phoenix canariensis Hort.   Canary Island Date Palm
Palmaceae or Palm Family   Hardiness Zone 9+
Native to Canary Islands
SIZE: 30 to 40 feet tall with a 25- to 40-foot crown diameter.
FORM: A large, lollipop-like crown on a large, single stem
TEXTURE: Fine.   **EXPOSURE:** Sun.

LEAVES: Pinnately compound; 15 to 25 feet long with a very short petiole. Leaflets are dull green; 18 to 24 inches long and about one inch wide. Leaflets near the base have modified into long green spines. Where leaflets are attached to the rachis they are folded upwards into a "V". The leaves make a near perfect sphere at the top of the stem, if left unpruned.

STEM: Largest stem of the Phoenix species, frequently 2.5 to 3 feet in diameter. Solitary. The old leaf scars are quite prominent on young trees and remain readily visible even on very old plants. The stem is very strong and is rarely broken during storms.

FLOWERS: Dioecious. Creamy yellow on densely branched stalks 3 to 4 feet long.

FRUIT: Orange; about 3/4 to 1 inch long. Edible but not tasty.

COLOR: Dull green foliage, brown to gray stem, orange fruits.

PROPAGATION: Seed.

CULTURE: Grows best on deep well drained sandy soils. Quite drought and heat tolerant and performs well even on the west sides of reflective buildings and near parking lots. It is moderate in tolerance to salt spray and salts in soils. Challenging to transplant and slow to recover from transplant stress. Avoid poorly drained soils.

PESTS: Magnesium deficiency frequently causes the older leaves to become yellow and unsightly in much of Florida. Palmetto weevils can damage the bud in times of stress and a leaf skeletonizer can make the foliage unsightly.

NOTES: The huge lollipop-like crown on the large stem dominates the landscape, especially if the leaves have remained healthy; forms a near perfect sphere. When the dead leaves are cut from the tree but the leaf bases remain, various ferns and other plants may establish in the small spaces that collect debris. The fruits can create a mess on sidewalks, patios, or driveways. This is a huge palm and its size should not be under estimated.

CULTIVARS: None. However, hybrids do occur between species providing further variation in plant size and foliage color.

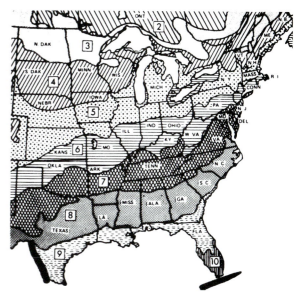

Phoenix dactylifera L.　　　　　　　　Date Palm
Palmaceae or Palm Family　　　　　　Hardiness Zone 9-
Native to North Africa
SIZE: 40 to 60 feet tall with 25- to 35-foot crown diameter. Slow grower.
FORM: A large, lollipop-like crown on a stem but with suckers at the base unless they have been removed.
TEXTURE: Fine.　　　　　　　　　　**EXPOSURE:** Sun.

LEAVES: Pinnately compound; up to 20 feet long with a very short petiole. Leaflets are gray- green to nearly bluish gray-green and glossy about 12 to 18 inches long and about one inch wide. Leaflets near the base have modified into long green spines. Leaflets form an upward "V" where attached to the rachis.

STEM: Unlike *Phoenix sylvestris* which remains as a single stem, this species suckers at a modest rate at the base while it is a young plant. The stem is tall and slender and is covered with old leaf bases or leaf scars.

FLOWERS: White flowers in clusters, on stalks 3 to 4 feet long among the leaves. Dioecious.

FRUIT: One to 3 inches in diameter; deep orange when ripe. Edible and very sweet. The staple food of many in the Middle East and North Africa.

COLOR: Foliage is gray-green to nearly bluish gray-green. Fruits are orange.

PROPAGATION: Seed or suckers from the base of selected cultivars.

CULTURE: Widely adaptable to heat, drought, salt and salt spray. Grows on many soils, even deep, low fertility sands. Grows best in warm, dry climates where it produces lots of fruit. Not well adapted to Florida, so produces few fruits in that humid, high rainfall area. In hardiness Zone 9 the plant grows and is attractive, but produces little or no fruit.

PESTS: Susceptible to lethal yellowing. An assortment of minor pests affect attractiveness and fruit quality.

NOTES: Date palms have been cultivated for centuries in the north Africa and Middle East areas. The plant is grown in nearly all of the dry tropics of the world. Because the crown canopy is more open than *P. canariensis* or *P. sylvestris* it is sometimes shunned as a landscape plant. However, the gray-green foliage and more flexible leaves add interest to many sites. This is the only *Phoenix* species that produces commercial dates. High temperatures are required in the growing and ripening season and rain at harbest time causes problems, thus few fruits are obtained in Florida and only marginal production in Arizona and southern California. The date palm is widely planted as a combination ornamental/fruit-producing tree in the semi-arid tropics and subtropics. Because the plants are dioecious and can be propagated by offshoots, male plants can be obtained to avoid fruit where it is not wanted.

CULTIVARS: Many have been selected for fruit size and taste in its native range; however, none have been selected for landscape use.

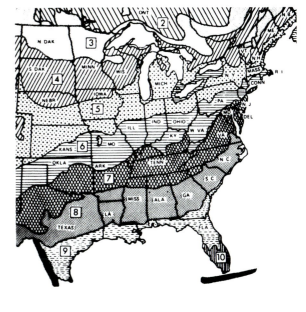

Phoenix reclinata Jacq.   Senegal Date Palm or Reclinata Palm
Palmaceae or Palm Family   Hardiness Zone 9-
Native to tropical Africa
SIZE: 20 to 40 feet tall, 20- to 25-foot crown diameter.
FORM: A large, multi-stemmed, clump palm.
TEXTURE: Medium.   **EXPOSURE:** Sun.

LEAVES: Pinnately compound; 8 to 12 feet long with a longer petiole (spine-covered area) than the larger species. Leaflets are dark green; 12 to 18 inches long and about one inch wide. Spine-like leaflets are especially plentiful. Young leaflets have a whitish scale on undersides.

STEM: Most commonly seen with 6 to 12 or more stems of similar size forming a large clump. If suckers are not removed periodically the mound of vegetation becomes nearly impenetrable. Individual stems are 6 to 8 inches in diameter and covered with brown fiber that appears to have been carefully wrapped around the stem. Outer stems are often gracefully arching.

FLOWERS: Creamy white; in branched clusters 2 to 3 feet long. Dioecious.

FRUIT: Brown or reddish brown; about 3/4 inch long.

COLOR: Foliage is dark green.

PROPAGATION: Seed or division of clumps (very carefully).

CULTURE: Widely adaptable to types of soils, moisture conditions, heat, and drought. The specimen at opposite left is in an island of a large parking lot, yet remains dark green and attractive. Moderately sensitive to magnesium and potassium deficiencies.

PESTS: None serious, yet leaf skeletonizers can make the plant unattractive.

NOTES: Gets too large for many situations. Needs room to become the sprawling green mass that it can achieve. Very attractive when grown with 6 to 12 stems and all suckers are removed. Needs too much room and requires high light, thus is rarely used in interiors. However, a few have been used in large malls with amazing success.

CULTIVARS: None known. However, hybrids between this and other *Phoenix* species probably occur and account for considerable variation.

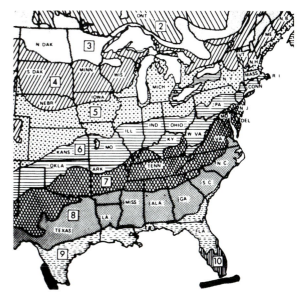

Phoenis roebelenii O'Brien
Palmaceae or Palm Family
Native to Southeast Asia

Pygmy Date Palm
Hardiness Zone 10

SIZE: 6 to 10 feet tall with crown diameter of 6 to 8 feet. Moderate grower.

FORM: A slender solitary stem (mostly) or sometimes planted several together to create a clump; occasionally suckers.

TEXTURE: Fine.   **EXPOSURE**: Partial shade to sun.

LEAVES: Pinnately compound; 3 to 4 feet long; curved and drooping. Leaflets are 10 to 12 inches long, 1/2 inch wide, often drooping at the tip. Petiole is short but armed with several leaflet spines. Color is glossy green above; whitish and scaly below, when young.

STEM: Relatively slender; 3 to 4 inches in diameter and covered with leaf bases or leaf scars which creates a striking pattern. Most plants are single stems yet occasionally a seedling will send up multiple shoots.

FLOWERS: Creamy white; in clusters 10 to 12 inches long among the leaves.

FRUIT: Black; about 1/2 inch long.

COLOR: Foliage is glossy green.

PROPAGATION: Seed.

CULTURE: Of the *Phoenix* species, it is the most adaptable to an array of conditions. Makes an excellent container plant if given sufficient light, good nutrition, and a sufficiently large container. Quite tolerant to drought and low humidity which aids their tolerance of indoor conditions. In the Florida landscape, magnesium, manganese and potassium deficiencies can cause discoloration of the foliage and reduces the attractiveness. If a plant is in a container and two or more feet tall and placed on its side for several weeks, the new growth will turn upward. The plant can then be planted with the arching stem somewhat like occurs naturally with the coconut.

PESTS: None serious, but note the nutritional deficiencies under **Culture**.

NOTES: The fern-like appearance and excellent color of the foliage, adaptability to containers, and moderate light intensity make the plant quite popular for interior landscapes. If several pygmy date palms are planted, one a good crown but little stem, another one with two feet of stem, and one with four feet of stem, the lollipop-like crowns will remain in the stair-stepped position for the life of the plants. (This works for most other palms too and is rarely used, unfortunately, as it can add a great deal more interest to a clump). Also the leaves are more flexible and less hostile to humans and clothing then the other *Phoenix* species. Thus, whether used out-of-doors where it is cold hardy or indoors, there are few negatives about this attractive palm.

CULTIVARS: None. *Phoenix humilis* is probably the same species.

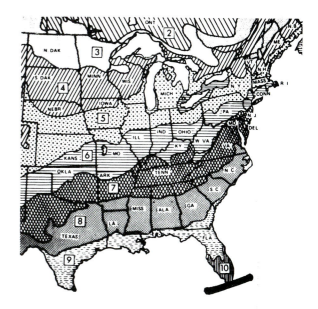

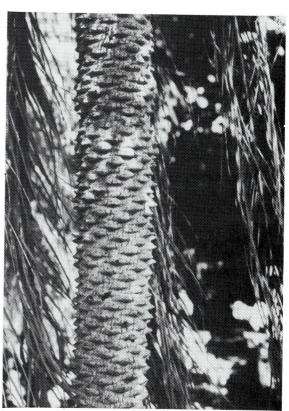

Phoenix sylvestris Roxb.   Wild or Silver Date Palm
Palmaceae or Palm Family   Hardiness Zone 9+
Native to India
SIZE: 30 to 50 feet tall, 20- to 30-foot crown diameter. Moderate grower.
FORM: A large, lollipop-like crown on a single stem
TEXTURE: Fine.   **EXPOSURE:** Sun.

LEAVES: Pinnately compound; 10 to 15 feet long with a very short petiole. Leaflets are dull gray-green to nearly blue-green and 12 to 18 inches long and about one inch wide. Leaflets near the base have modified into long green spines. The leaflets form an upward "V" where attached to the rachis. The leaves make a near perfect sphere atop the tall slender stem.

STEM: Generally 1 1/2 to 2 feet in diameter, distinctly smaller than *P. canariensis*. Leaf bases or leaf base scars are prominent but not as striking as on *P. canariensis*. The stem generally is swollen near the soil surface.

FLOWERS: Creamy white flowers form on flower stalks that are 2 to 3 feet long. Dioecious.

FRUIT: Yellow, turning orange, then reddish purple when ripe. Edible but not good to eat.

COLOR: Foliage is gray-green to nearly blue-green. Fruits are yellow-orange, then reddish purple.

PROPAGATION: Seed.

CULTURE: A very drought-tolerant and widely adaptable palm. Grows well in Florida deep sands as well as heavy marl soils. In Florida, magnesium and potassium deficiencies commonly reduce the appearance by discoloring the older leaves.

PESTS: None serious, yet see under **Culture** the problem with magnesium and potassium deficiency.

NOTES: An attractive palm that is not quite so bold and dominant as the Canary Island date and has a more attractive gray-green to nearly blue-green foliage color. Generally grows faster that *P. canariensis*. Does not sucker at the base so remains as a single stem. General appearance is more similar to *P. dactylifera* the true date palm yet the total crown canopy size is somewhat smaller than *P. dactylifera* and considerably smaller than *P. canariensis*.

CULTIVARS: None. However, hybrids among species provide some variation in size and foliage color.

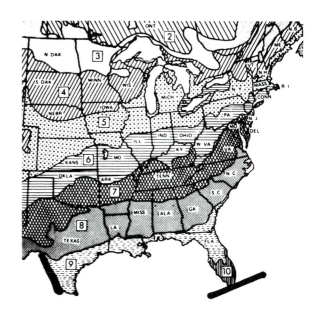

Raphis excelsa A.Henry   Lady Palm
Palmaceae or Palm Family   Hardiness Zone 9
Native to China
SIZE: 6 to 10 feet tall in dense clumps. Moderate grower.
FORM: A large mounding shrub or shrub-like clump.
TEXTURE: Medium   **EXPOSURE:** Partial shade to shade.

LEAVES: Palmately compound; divided into 5 to 10 leaflets, each 8 to 12 inches long and 1/2 to 1 inch wide. Leaves are dark glossy green above, pale below. No spines.

STEM: The multiple stems are slender and covered with leaf bases and matted fiber which is brown when young and turns black with age. No spines.

FLOWERS: Dioecious. The flowers are white- or cream-colored in a multi-branched inflorescence among the youngest leaves.

FRUIT: White; about 1/2 inch oblong.

COLOR: Foliage is dark, glossy green.

PROPAGATION: Mostly division, as few seeds are produced and they are slow to germinate.

CULTURE: Grows well in containers, tubs, or various indoor planters. Grows well in most soils and is moderately drought-tolerant where it can be grown out-of-doors. One of the most shade-tolerant palms and tolerates a wide range of temperatures but grows best in warm conditions.

PESTS: Scales and mealybugs can be problems. Also on alkaline soils, iron and/or magnesium deficiency may mar its appearance.

NOTES: Makes an excellent clump and shrub-like palm for landscape use where it is cold hardy. Because of its tolerance to low light, low humidity, and relatively wide swings in temperatures, it makes an excellent indoor plant. The larger the container or planter, the larger it will grow. The plants below the outdoor restaurant in the photo are along the River Walk in San Antonio, Texas.

CULTIVARS: Some variation exists among plants from various sources but few cultivars have been named. There are a few variegated selections but these are slower to grow and are not common.

RELATED SPECIES: *Raphis humilis*, slender lady palm, generally has more slender stems and grows taller than *R. excelsa*. Similar in appearance, use, and adaptation, and most people cannot tell them apart until they reach considerable age. This may not be a different species but simply the result of slightly different seedlings of *R. excelsa* which for decades have been propagated by division.

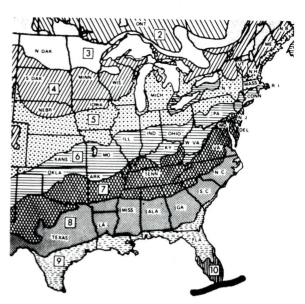

Rhapidophyllum hystrix H. Wendl. & Drude   Needle Palm
Palmaceae or Palm Family   Hardiness Zone 7b
Native to the southeastern United States.
SIZE: 4 to 8 feet tall with spread of 4 to 10 feet. Slow to medium grower.
FORM: Rounded mound shrub.
TEXTURE: Medium to coarse.   EXPOSURE: Sun to shade.

LEAVES: Palmately compound, appearing to be half circles or spokes in a wheel. Individual leaflets are fingers cut nearly to the point of attachment to the petiole. Often appearing torn or jagged at the tips. Generally medium to dark green color above, medium green below. Petiole is smooth, no teeth or saw-like projections are present anywhere on the petiole. The long needles at the base of the petiole arise from the stem.

STEM: Rarely rising more than 2 to 3 feet above the soil surface, appears to be a dense conical mound of long slender, needle-like spines interlaced with fibrous threads, often collecting debris. Individual spines may be 10 to 16 inches long, very slender and sharp-pointed at the tip. Some plants remain single-stemmed while others sucker at the soil surface making the overall plant a broader and denser clump.

FLOWERS: Small, yellow clusters among the spines at the base of the petioles. Not showy.

FRUIT: Small, furry, rounded, about 1/2 inch in diameter; in clusters of 20 or more.

COLOR: Foliage is medium to dark green.

PROPAGATION: By seed.

CULTURE: A very tough, tolerant, adaptable, landscape palm. Native to wet, swampy locations, often in very dense shade. However, when removed to moderate light intensity and given good cultural conditions and fertilization, it will grow rather rapidly into a more compact, mounded, shrub palm.

PESTS: None serious.

NOTES: Often is found growing with *Serenoa repens*, saw palmetto, throughout the Gulf Coast area, particularly in the Southeast. Unfortunately, many people do not recognize that needle palm is a distinct and separate plant from the saw palmetto and both are frequently destroyed. Unlike saw palmetto, which is a questionable landscape plant and difficult to transplant, needle palm is an excellent small shrub, easily transplanted and grown. Tolerates full sun or dense shade once established. When land is cleared, needle palm should be removed from the saw palmetto and utilized in urban landscaping. To distinguish between needle palm and saw palmetto, look for the long needles and the smooth petiole on needle palm, whereas saw palmetto has a very distinct sawtooth margin on the petiole and no spines at the base of the petiole. Should be used more.

CULTIVARS: None, although some authorities have listed the single stem and multiple stem forms as different cultivars or sub-species.

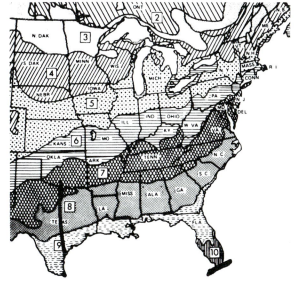

Roystonea regia Cook   Royal Palm
Palmaceae or Palm Family   Hardiness Zone 10
Native to Cuba
SIZE: 50 to 70 feet tall. Slow to moderate grower.
FORM: Fluffy-appearing rounded crown on a single stem.
TEXTURE: Fine.   EXPOSURE: Sun

LEAVES: Pinnately compound; eight to 10 feet or more in length. Hundreds of bright green leaflets two to three feet long and about two inches wide. A distinct, long, smooth, dark green crown shaft (petiole) encompasses the stem. No spines.

STEM: May reach 12 to 18 inches in diameter and more at the base which appears swollen. Solitary stems only, no branches. The stems are very tough, durable, and wind-resistant. Below the crown shaft the stem is distinctly ringed but after a few years the rings mostly disappear and the trunk becomes a grayish white as if made of concrete.

FLOWERS: Monoecious. Yellow flowers occur on a stalk two to three feet long and with multiple branches.

FRUIT: Small, reddish purple, about 1/2 to 1/3 inch oblong.

PROPAGATION: Seed which requires two to four months to germinate.

CULTURE: Royal palms are very sensitive to cold and grow best where conditions are warm much of the year. It is moderately tolerant of drought and salt and responds to fertilizer and supplemental water. Tolerates street and parking lot sites, as long as the soils drain moderately well.

PESTS: Royal palm bug can severely damage foliage. Magnesium and potassium deficiencies can be problems in Florida.

NOTES: Probably the most majestic and stately appearing of the many palms. Large royal palms appear like tufts of delicate foliage on top of concrete or marble pillars. Because of its size and requirement for warmth and high light intensity, it is not suited for indoor use. Good as a street tree since it grows well under those conditions and does not have spines or large fruits that can create hazards which other large palms such as *Washingtonia* and *Cocos*.

CULTIVARS: None. However, some books list four species of royal palms native to South Florida, Cuba, Puerto Rico, and other Caribbean islands. These are most likely ecological races of the same species as they vary only in very subtle ways.

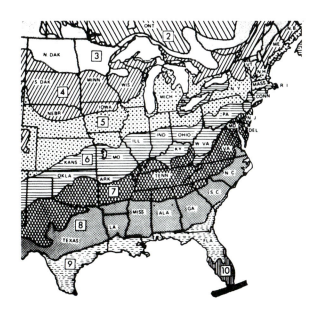

Sabal palmetto (Walt.) Lodd.   Sabal Palm
Palmaceae or Palm Family   Hardiness Zone 8b
Native to the Gulf Coast States and Florida.
SIZE: 20 to 40 feet tall with a 6- to 10-foot rounded crown. Slow grower.
FORM: Lollipop-like crown on a single stem.
TEXTURE: Coarse.   EXPOSURE: Sun or partial shade.

LEAVES: Medium green, 3 to 5 feet long, 2 to 3 feet wide, spiraling around the bud at the tip of the main stem. Leaves are costapalmate, that is, palmately compound with a strong, curving, central stalk or vein that curves or curls to give the leaves a twist or folded appearance, unlike other palms with palmate leaves. The margin of the large compound leaves generally have numerous thread-like hairs.

STEM: A single stem, 6 to 12 inches in diameter. If the old leaf bases have been removed, the stem appears much smaller than if the leaf bases are still present on the trunk. Only rarely does any branching of the stem occur as the only growing point is the very terminal. In addition, like most palms which are monocots or grass family members, the stem is the same diameter from the base to crown because there is no secondary growth capability as in woody deciduous trees.

FLOWERS: In large, loose cluster, extending beyond the foliage. Not showy.

FRUIT: In large, loose cluster, extending beyond the foliage with individual fruits of about 1/2 inch in diameter. Black, maturing in summer.

COLOR: Foliage is medium to dark green.

PROPAGATION: By seed.

CULTURE: Sabal palms are found growing on a variety of soils including poorly drained, wet swamplands along the Gulf Coast and as far north as the Carolinas. Tolerant to a wide range of growing conditions if transplanted and established with care. Larger, older plants, 10 to 15 feet tall, nursery-grown or from the wild, transplant more easily than small young plants. This is due to stored reserves in the main stem for regeneration of new roots. A root ball 3 feet in diameter, 2 to 3 feet deep, is necessary to insure survival. A portion of the leaves of the crown should be carefully removed when transplanting sabal palms and the leaves surrounding the central bud should be tied together to avoid breaking the terminal bud during handling.

PESTS: None serious.

NOTES: Sabal palms are tough, tolerant, landscape plants once established, giving a distinct tropical effect. Often planted in clumps or as groves which represent their natural growing conditions. The terminal bud is sometimes cut from young plants and eaten as palm cabbage, palm salad, or swamp salad. Such disgusting mutilation leads to the rapid death of the plant. When the old leaf bases are left on the palm stem, they present a haven for roaches and other insects.

CULTIVARS: None.

RELATED SPECIES: *Sabal minor* (Jacq.) Pers., bush palmetto, is often found growing on the Gulf Coast in wet lowlands with no trunk or above-ground stem. Only a few palmate leaves can be observed 2 to 6 feet above the soil surface. Zone 8. Not showy.
    Serenoa repens (Bartr.) Small., saw palmetto, is native to the Gulf Coast states and may grow 3 to 8 feet tall with horizontal stems or sometimes growing upright as a small tree, which is rather attractive.

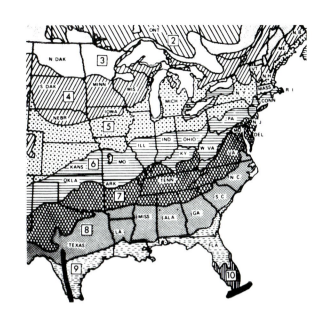

Serenoa repens Small   Saw Palmetto
Palmaceae or Palm Family   Hardiness Zone 8
Native from South Carolina to Florida and across the Gulf Coast.
SIZE: In dense clumps, 4 to 8 feet tall. Slow grower.
FORM: Shrubby, clump palm with almost no distinct stem.
TEXTURE: Medium.   **EXPOSURE:** Sun to partial shade

LEAVES: Palmately compound; 3 to 5 feet long overall. The petiole forms a 2- to 3-foot long handle for the nearly circular "fan". Each leaflet is 18 to 24 inches long and about one inch wide and either shiny green or a distinct blue-gray-green and waxy. Some leaflets may be pointed at the tip while others on the same leaf may be distinctly split. The margin of the petiole is finely toothed, but not as sharp and hazardous as with European fan palm. Leaf base is covered with brown fiber.

STEM: Mostly underground, or partially so, and branches freely. Sometimes grows more erect, becoming almost tree-form. The multiple branches and mostly prostrate stem create an irregular, mounding clump. The stem is covered with leaf bases and brown fibers.

FLOWERS: White; on multi-branched stalks among the leaves. The perfect flowers can be striking and are a source of nectar for bees.

FRUIT: Blue-black; about one inch long.

COLOR: Green or blue-gray-green, depending on seedling. Flowers are white.

PROPAGATION: Seed. Division of clumps is quite difficult.

CULTURE: An extremely tough, drought- and salt-tolerant palm. Grows in nearly any soil, including extremely low fertility sands. Fertilizer response is minimal in most cases. Plants from the wild are very difficult to transplant. Container-grown seedlings transplant and establish easily. From a seedling population, some will have the green foliage while others the blue-gray-green.

PESTS: Palmetto weevils.

NOTES: Makes an attractive shrub form palm that requires little care. The blue-gray-green form is especially contrasting with other vegetation and is quite attractive. Saw palmetto gets its name from the sawtooth margin on the petiole. In some areas of Florida, vast areas beneath pine forests are solid palmetto. In some cases, clumps of saw palmetto have been left during development and form attractive mounds and provide shelter for an assortment of wildlife. In come cases, the stem has been staked or encouraged to grow upright which results in an attractive tree-form palm. Saw palmetto deserves more attention in terms of developing propagation techniques for unique foliage colors and/or growth forms. In much of central and north Florida it is considered too common to be used in landscaping. However, its toughness is amazing and virtually no care is required. More landscape plants of that type are needed.

CULTIVARS: None, yet the seedling color variation is distinct and provides two contrasting colors.

Trachycarpus fortunei (Hook.) Wendl.　　　　Windmill Palm
Palmaceae or Palm Family　　　　　　　　　　Hardiness Zone 8
Native to Burma, Indochina, and Japan.
SIZE: 6 to 20 feet tall with a crown spread of 6 to 8 feet. Moderate grower.
FORM: Rounded mound, shrub-like palm; or with old specimens, a lollipop-shaped, crowned, small palm tree.
TEXTURE: Medium to coarse.　　　　　　　**EXPOSURE:** Sun to shade.

LEAVES: Palmately compound and nearly round, 2 to 4 feet in diameter, deeply slashed through the middle, almost to the base. Fingers of the compound leaf are ribbon-like, often drooping at the ends. Leaves are a rich, dark green, medium green below. Often tipped with yellow on the ends due to magnesium deficiency. Leaves do not form a complete circle as with European fan palm. The petiole is stout, stiff, and green, with many small, saw-like teeth particularly near the base. Sufficiently small to be difficult to see on some specimens, but a useful identification characteristic.

STEM: Single, central leader, does not sucker or sprout at the base as does European fan palm. Eventually develops a tall, slender trunk, covered with hairy black fibers and the remnants of old leaf bases. The stem appears to be wrapped in burlap.

FLOWERS: In small, orange clusters among the leaves. Not showy.

FRUIT: Purplish, about the size of a pea. Maturing during the summer in loose clusters. Not showy.

COLOR: Foliage is a rich, dark green.

PROPAGATION: Seed.

CULTURE: A tough, tolerant palm. Does well in confined locations surrounded by concrete or in tubs, raised planters or in indoor landscaping. Grows best in a light, moist, well-drained soil. Tolerates moderate drought, wind and salt spray. Responds to fertilization and supplemental watering during moisture stress periods.

PESTS: None serious.

NOTES: Windmill palm is one of the showiest of the small palms. Somewhat oriental appearing and often used to create tropical effects along the Gulf Coast. Particularly showy when young as a low mound or shrub form. Tolerates moderate shade and may be used in some solariums or indoor landscaping farther north where moderate light intensity can be maintained. Sometimes confused with European fan palm. However, they can be distinguished by the sawtooth-like base of the petiole, drooping leaflet ends, green undersides of leaves, and no suckers on windmill palm, whereas European fan palm has long needle-like teeth on the base of the petiole, the ends of the leaflets are rigid, the underside of leaves are silvery gray, and many suckers are present at the base.

CULTIVARS: None.

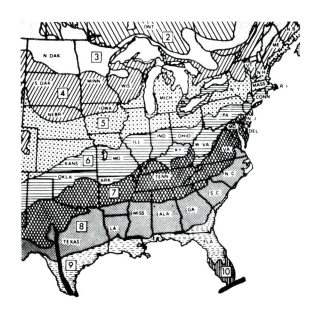

Veitchia merrillii Moore.
(Syn. *Adonidia merrillii*)
Palmaceae or Palm Family
Native to Philippine Islands

Manila, Adonidia, Christmas, or Baby Royal
Palm

Hardiness Zone 10

SIZE: Up to 15 feet tall. Moderate grower.

FORM: Single stem, or occasionally 2, 3, or many stems when many seedlings are allowed to develop in a clump.

TEXTURE: Fine to medium.   **EXPOSURE:** Sun to partial shade.

LEAVES: Pinnately compound, 4 to 6 feet long, rigidly arched. Leaflets are more or less sword-shaped, generally glossy green to dark green. The tips of the leaflets often droop slightly and become somewhat tattered, giving the large compound leaf a slightly feathered appearance on the edge. The petiole is short and smooth with a very prominent, well-developed crown shaft which completely encircles the bases of younger leaves and the growing terminal. Where the leaflets attach to the central leaf stalk they form a downward folded "V".

STEM: Relatively short and stout, generally 4 to 8 inches in diameter with distinct, circular rings where old leaves were attached. Because of the very distinct crown shaft it appears that the trunk is particularly short and is partly gray-brown color and partly green below the leaves.

FLOWERS: The flower stalks originate from the trunk below the crown shaft and have many branches which hold the creamy yellow flowers. Monoecious.

FRUITS: About one inch long, more or less egg-shaped. Bright red; smooth and glossy, very attractive, often maturing in early winter, thus the common name, Christmas palm. The seeds germinate readily in 3 to 4 weeks.

COLOR: Foliage is glossy green to dark green. Flowers are creamy yellow. Fruits are red.

PROPAGATION: Seed.

CULTURE: A very tough, tolerant and easily transplanted palm in terms of growing conditions. However, it is extremely sensitive to cold and is generally less tolerant to low light intensity than others such as *Chrysalidocarpus* or *Raphis* and thus is less adaptable for indoor use except where light intensity is high. The Manila palm is widely planted in south Florida in a variety of soil conditions and exposures and rarely falters. Responds with vigor and improved leaf size and color to liberal applications of fertilizer.

PESTS: Has been found to be susceptible to lethal yellowing. Other pests are minor.

NOTES: *Veitchia* was originally know as *Adonidia*, which is a genus no longer used. However, *Veitchia merrillii* appears to be rather distinctive from the other species now include in the genus. *V. merrillii* is the only species that has been widely planted in South Florida.

Because of its size, absence of spines, excellent foliage color, and prolific, showy fruits, the Manila palm has been widely planted as an accent plant singly or in clusters particularly around single story dwellings. Planted to the extent in South Florida that it is somewhat monotonous. However, this should not take away from the fine qualities of this small, very adaptable palm for outdoor landscape use.

CULTIVARS: None. Other species rarely seen in this country are *V. arecina*, *V. joannis*, *V. montgomeriana* and *V. winim*.

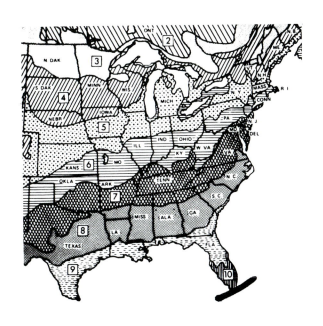

Washingtonia filifera H. Wendl.   Washington Palm
Palmaceae or Palm Family   Hardiness Zone 8
Native to southern California and Mexico.
SIZE: 30 to 50 feet tall with a 12- to 18-foot crown. Slow to moderate grower.
FORM: A large, lollipop-like crown on a single stem.
TEXTURE: Coarse.   EXPOSURE: Sun.

LEAVES: 6 to 9 feet long including leaf blade and petiole. Leaf blade may be as much as 3 to 4 feet wide, palmately compound. Young trees particularly, have many white threads hanging from the margins of leaves, but these are less prominent with age. Generally a gray-green leaf color, remaining green for several years, finally dying and drooping to hang down like a skirt over the stem. The petiole is long and stout with many hard, prominent teeth along the margin of the petiole, particularly near the base. Petiole is generally green with brown or reddish brown teeth.

STEM: Large and stout, sometimes reaching 3 feet in diameter, and distinctly swollen at the base. Generally a rough, vertically furrowed texture if the old leaf bases have been removed. If the leaf bases have not been removed, the stem is covered by old leaves and petioles, giving it a skirt-like appearance, sometimes all the way to the ground. Stems are strong and quite wind resistant. *Washingtonia spp.* have only one growing point at the tip, thus do not branch or sucker.

FLOWERS: Small and white on a large stalk. Upright at first, eventually drooping to hang among the dead leaves. Not showy.

FRUIT: Oval-shaped, 1/2 inch or less in diameter. Black.

COLOR: Foliage is gray-green.

PROPAGATION: By seed.

CULTURE: Tolerates heat and dry conditions but is only slightly cold tolerant. Grows best in a light, moist, well-drained soil. Trees have a dense, fibrous root system and must be transplanted with a considerable root ball to insure survival. Removal of part of the green leaves prior to transplanting, and/or tying the leaves to prevent damage to the bud may also be of assistance.

PESTS: Crown rot occasionally in the Gulf Coast area or in the Southeast where soil drainage may be poor and rainfall is frequent.

NOTES: Large, dominant landscape plants which must be placed carefully in the landscape. Washington palm is better adapted to the area of Texas and westward in Zones 8, 9, and 10.

CULTIVARS: None.

RELATED SPECIES: *Washingtonia robusta*, H. Wendl., Mexican Washington palm, native to northwest Mexico, is better adapted to the Gulf Coast States. Generally has a smaller stem diameter, slightly smaller leaves and petiole and larger, very prominent teeth on the petiole, from the base all the way to the leaf blade. Grows more rapidly and to a much greater height, sometimes reaching 80 to 100 feet and is less cold hardy than Washington palm. Mexican Washington palm belongs no farther north than Zone 9 and seems less sensitive to the wet conditions and poorly drained soils found in the Gulf Coast States and Florida. Both Washington palms are very useful and attractive landscape palms; however, the large petioles with the extremely coarse and hard teeth present a danger any time the leaves fall from the tall trees.

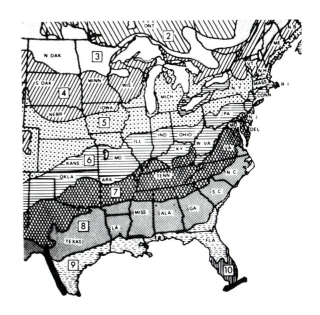

W. robusta

Washingtonia robusta Wendl.   Mexican Fan or Washington Palm
Palmaceae or Palm Family   Hardiness Zone 9
Native to Mexico
SIZE: May reach 80 to 100 feet tall. Moderate grower.
TEXTURE: Coarse.   **EXPOSURE:** Sun

LEAVES: Palmately compound. Bright green and glossy. A leaf may be 5 to 7 feet overall, including a blade with a diameter of 3 feet and a reddish brown petiole which is 2 to 3 feet long. The petiole is heavily spined with brown, spine-like projections. The leaves commonly have an assortment of white hairs or fibers from the margins. When the old leaves die they droop down around the stem giving the effect of a petticoat which is another common name.

STEM: Eighteen to 24 inches in diameter with very little taper up the stem. Somewhat swollen at the base but not as much as *Washingtonia filifera*. The leaf bases form a criss-cross pattern on the stem if the petioles are removed and provide an interesting texture. When the leaf bases are removed the stem is gray with many vertical cracks. The leaf scars are not prominent.

FLOWERS: White; perfect flowers occur on flower stalks that may be 10 feet long or more, erect at first then drooping with the developing fruit.

FRUIT: Brown to near black; about 3/8 inch in diameter.

COLOR: Foliage is bright green and glossy.

CULTURE: This species appears to be more tolerant to the high rainfall areas of the Gulf Coast and Florida, whereas *W. filifera* may be better suited to its native desert habitat of the extreme Southwest U.S. and northern Mexico. Can be grown in containers when small and then transplants easily. Responds to fertilizer and irrigation and appears to be equally at home on the deep sand of central Florida and the heavy clays of the Gulf Coast. The dense, fibrous root system provides good anchorage for the tall crown.

PESTS: None serious.

NOTES: Gets to be a tall, dominant, landscape plant. Attractive when small and of further interest for a number of years if the dead leaves are left on the stem up to a height where their falling becomes dangerous. Because of its slightly smaller size and spread, *W. robusta* is a better choice of the 2 species for small areas. This species is clearly not as cold tolerant as *W. filifera*. The two species may hybridize, creating further confusion in nurseries.

CULTIVARS: None.

Zamia floridana A. Dc.   Zamia or Coontie
Zamiaceae or Zamia Family   Hardiness Zone 8
Native to Florida, Mexico, and the Caribbean Islands.
SIZE: About 3 feet tall with spread of 4 to 6 feet. Slow grower.
FORM: An irregular, rounded mound.
TEXTURE: Fine.   EXPOSURE: Sun to shade.

LEAVES: Pinnately compound, 2 to 3 feet long. Upright or arching, with 20 to 40 long, narrow leaflets that are very hard and leathery, almost as if made of a stiff cardboard. Olive-green to gray-green color contrasts with plants with dark green foliage. The leaflets have an irregular outer end, not serrate, but irregularly pointed. The leaves are in a rosette around the terminal bud on the very short stem.

STEM: Rarely is a stem seen, although an underground stem-like structure exists.

FLOWERS: Dioecious. Both male and female flowers are cone-like structures. The male flowers appear like a blackened corn cob (see photograph). Not showy, but interesting.

FRUIT: Seeds are red-orange; about 3/4 to 1 inch long.

COLOR: Foliage is olive-green to gray-green.

PROPAGATION: Seeds.

CULTURE: Native throughout Florida and west along the Gulf Coast in piney woods. The nitrogen-fixing bacteria associated with the roots allows it to grow on soils of extremely low fertility. Can be easily grown in containers and from there transplants easily into the landscape. However, because of the underground stem, plants collected from the wild have a high mortality rate.

PESTS: Scale insects can be a problem.

NOTES: A striking plant where it can be grown, either outdoors or indoors. Because of the slow growth, it stays in-bounds in the landscape. Somewhat palm-like in appearance. Very drought- and heat-tolerant. Occasionally used in indoor landscape. However, unless used carefully, it appears out-of-place with other tropical plants.

CULTIVARS: None.

RELATED SPECIES: *Zamia pumila* (sometimes listed as *Z. furfuraceae, Z. silvicola,* or *Z. umbrosa*) is slightly smaller in stature but otherwise similar to the species above and native to the same area.

   Zamia latifolia has much broader leaflets giving it a unique appearance as if cut from cardboard and it is less cold-tolerant. Several other species exist.

   All of the related species appear to be similar to *Z. floridana* in adaptation and culture and are worthy of consideration.

 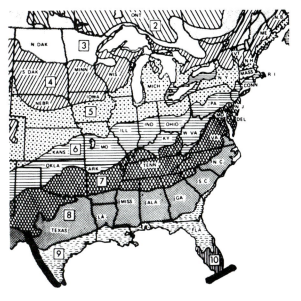

GROUND COVERS

Ground covers play a unique role in modern landscapes. There are areas on many sites that are not suited for growing and maintaining turf, yet something is needed aesthetically and to prevent erosion. Ground covers serve this purpose well, but should be considered for other uses.

A key point to remember, however, is that ground covers often fail because of insufficient maintenance during the first or second growing season. Once established, if the proper ground cover has been selected for the site, little further maintenance will be required. The exception is with ground covers in full sun where Bermudagrass may become a severe pest whereas in the shade, low light intensity reduces its vigor and competitive nature. The herbicide, Roundup, however has the potential to reduce or eliminate the problem of unwanted Bermudagrass.

Aegopodium podogaria L.   Goutweed or Bishop's Weed
Umbelliferae or Carrot Family   Hardiness Zone 4
Native to Europe.
SIZE: 12 to 18 inches tall. Moderate spread laterally.
FORM: A dense ground cover.
TEXTURE: Medium.   **EXPOSURE:** Sun or partial shade.

LEAVES: Compound; with 3 soft and pliable leaflets, 2 to 3 inches long. Dark green above, lighter below, with an irregular, doubly saw-toothed margin. No fall color.

STEM: A weak rhizome spreads at a moderate to rapid rate, depending on exposure and growing conditions. The stems are upright, herbaceous, and succulent, not woody, therefore, if walked on, the stems are readily broken.

FLOWERS: White. At the surface of the foliage, in umbels (clusters). Not very showy, but noticeable.

FRUIT: A small, dry seed; not noticed.

COLOR: Foliage is dark green on top; lighter below.

PROPAGATION: Division of horizontal stems.

CULTURE: An attractive ground cover for the spring, summer, and early fall. Grows in nearly any soil and from full sun to moderate shade. However, foliage is more dense and attractive where full sun is available for a few hours each day. Must be contained either by mowing or edging or by physical structures, as between a sidewalk and a building. Can escape if planted without restraints. Good for controlling erosion since the roots and rhizomes make a dense mat.

PESTS: None serious.

NOTES: Use with care. Where properly located and contained, an excellent ground cover. Becomes sufficiently dense to eliminate most other weeds except for the occasional tree seedling. Because the stem is rather succulent, should not be planted where foot traffic occurs, as each footprint will be noticeable for sometime. Probably most useful where a bright green or variegated ground cover is desired adjacent to outdoor living areas. Not attractive in winter.

CULTIVARS: 'Variegatum': leaves with irregular sections of white along the margins and the green portion of the leaflet is lighter green than the species. Makes a bright and attractive ground cover. Tough and durable; not quite as aggressive as the green form. Others probably exist.

'Variegatum'

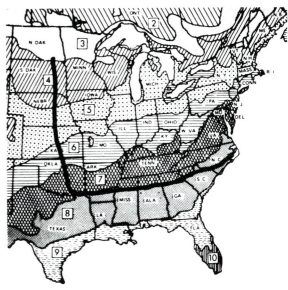

'Variegatum'

'Variegatum'

Ajuga reptans L.　　　　　　　　　　Carpetbugle, Ajuga, or Bugleweed
Labiatae or Mint Family　　　　　　　Hardiness Zone 6
Native to Europe.

SIZE: 6 to 10 inches high, moderate horizontal spread by stolons or runners. Slow to moderate grower.

FORM: Good ground cover or rock garden plant.

TEXTURE: Coarse and irregular.　　　　　**EXPOSURE:** Sun to shade.

LEAVES: Oblong to ovate, 4 to 5 inches long, 1 to 1 1/2 inches wide, with a wavy margin on the outer third, generally a smooth margin near the base. Mostly purplish to green. Shaped somewhat like a ping-pong paddle.

STEM: Appears to have no above-ground stem; however, the horizontal runner is actually a stem. It is soft, not woody, and generally about the color of the leaves.

FLOWERS: Blue, white or rose, depending on cultivar. In terminal spikes generally 3 to 5 inches above the foliage in early to mid spring.

FRUIT: Small seed on old flower spikes.

COLOR: Foliage is purplish green. Flowers are blue, white, or rose.

PROPAGATION: Seed, division, or cuttings. Stems root easily anytime.

CULTURE: Does best with 3 to 4 hours of full sun each day. Also satisfactory in part shade or full sun on northern or eastern exposures. Medium to heavy soils are preferred. Moderately drought resistant but responds to moisture and fertility. Ajuga performs well in some locations and poorly in others, that for all practical purposes are very similar. This has been a continuing frustration to the author and makes one uneasy about recommending ajuga for a particular landscape location.

PESTS: May have nematode problems in light, sandy soils. Spider mites in hot, dry locations. Southern blight in shady, moist locations in the Southeast.

NOTES: Will not tolerate foot traffic as the leaves and stems are soft and easily crushed. Foliage and flower color may not harmonize with other landscape elements due to the purple foliage or the blue to blue-purple flowers. Plantings into or surrounded by light colored stone or bark mulch are very attractive. In the Southeast, ajuga is not a permanent ground cover as plants frequently succumb to southern blight. Better suited to the Southwest. Most attractive during two weeks of flowering and only moderately attractive the rest of the year.

CULTIVARS: 'Alba': white flowers. 'Atropurpurea': blue flowers, bronze foliage. 'Burgundy Lace': rose-white, variegated foliage and rose flowers. 'Rubra': dark purple foliage. Others probably exist.

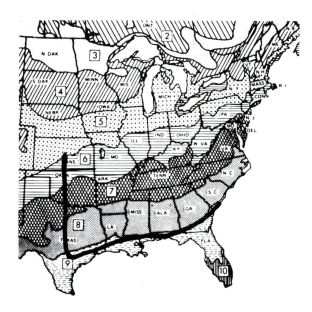

'Rubra'

Aspidistra elatior Blume.
Liliaceae or Lily Family
Native to China and Japan.

Cast Iron Plant
Hardiness Zone 8

SIZE: 18 to 24 inches tall and equally wide. Slow grower.
FORM: Mounding, herbaceous perennial.
TEXTURE: Coarse.   EXPOSURE: Partial shade to shade.

LEAVES: Large, simple; with prominent parallel veins and smooth margins. May reach 18 to 24 inches long, 3 to 5 inches wide with a long, stout petiole arising from a horizontal stem. Dark, glossy green new leaves appear as though they have been shined or polished.

STEM: Not visible above ground, a heavy rhizome just beneath the soil surface. May be divided for propagation. Leaves arise along the upper surface of the stem, forming a dense clump.

FLOWERS: Purple-brown at the soil surface. At first may appear as an indentation in the soil. Neither showy nor attractive. So obscure that few people notice them at all, especially in a landscape situation where the foliage may be quite dense.

FRUIT: A small berry. Inconspicuous.

COLOR: Dark, glossy green leaves of coarse texture.

PROPAGATION: Division of the heavy underground stem (rhizome).

CULTURE: A very tough, durable plant either out-of-doors or in planters or containers indoors. One of the most tolerant plants to low light intensity. Tolerates poor soils, heavy soils, and conditions unsuitable to most other plants. On the other hand, it does best in partial shade with good soil and adequate moisture where it shows off an abundance of glossy green leaves that contrast with most other plants and structures in the landscape. Responds to moderate fertilization and is very drought-tolerant. Remove old leaves periodically to maintain attractive plants.

PESTS: None serious. Occasionally mites in a particularly low humidity location or scale insects.

NOTES: One of the most shade tolerant of all landscape plants. Its closest rival is Japanese aucuba. As a ground cover or edging, the foliage color is excellent and sufficiently dense so as to shade out weeds. Spreads or thickens slowly so does not create a maintenance problem. Should be used more in Zones 8 and 9, especially in very protected areas that offer very little light. Likewise, indoor planters and low humidity are very suitable for this very tough, adaptable plant in any hardiness zone. In the colder climates, atriums or indoor planting areas are frequently filled with tropical plants for visual effects. By using this and similar plants, the temperatures in these planters could be allowed to drop to or slightly below freezing under extreme conditions with no plant damage but substantial fuel savings.

CULTIVARS: 'Variegata': very attractive green and white striped leaves. The white portion is milky white and creates a very striking contrast with the green sections of the leaves. 'Akebono': has white variegation along the leaf margin.

'Variegata'

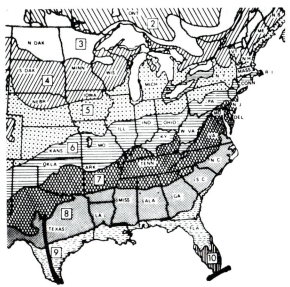

Euonymus fortunei (Turcz.) Hand.-Mazz.   Evergreen Wintercreeper
        (Syn. *Euonymus radicans*)
Celastraceae or Euonymus Family   Hardiness Zone 4
Native to central and west China.
SIZE: Up to 6 feet tall as a shrub, or may reach 20 feet or more as a vine or 12 to 24 inches tall as a ground cover. Variable, depending on cultivar. Medium to rapid grower.
FORM: Irregular, small to medium-sized shrub, ground cover, or vine.
TEXTURE: Medium.   **EXPOSURE:** Sun to shade.

LEAVES: Opposite, simple; elliptical, 1 to 3 inches long and 1/2 to 1 1/2 inch wide, with a short petiole. Margin is smooth to slightly wavy or sawtooth. Several cultivars turn purple to bronze in the fall.

STEM: Shrub-like to vine-like, climbing by rootlets which are very common along all stems in humid locations or within the foliage canopy on most sites. The young stem is green to green-purple, turning gray only with age. During fall and winter the opposite axillary buds are large and sharp pointed. Bud size depends on cultivar.

FLOWERS: Small, greenish, not showy.

FRUIT: A 4-parted capsule which splits in the fall to expose persistent, small, orange fruit. Most cultivars are not consistent fruit producers.

COLOR: Foliage is green to purple-green or bronze in winter. Fruit is orange.

PROPAGATION: Semi-hardwood to hardwood cuttings.

CULTURE: Easily grown. Responds with vigor to fertilizer and grows well in full sun or moderate shade but not for hot, dry, western exposures. Moderately drought-resistant and tolerant to a wide range of soils. One of the easiest broadleaf evergreen shrubs to grow.

PESTS: Euonymus scale may be serious. Nematodes in light soils. Stem gall may be serious on 'Radicans' and 'Sarcoxie'. Mildew in shade with little air movement.

NOTES: The larger cultivars were formerly known as *Euonymus radicans* but are now considered to be the same species. The many cultivars range from about 12 inches to 6 feet tall. The larger cultivar, 'Radicans', bigleaf wintercreeper, is sometimes confused with spreading euonymus which is a larger plant with drooping green leaves on erect stems, rarely if ever, growing strictly horizontal, is a more prolific fruit producer, and only rarely forms aerial roots. Foliage and fruits may be mildly poisonous if eaten in quantity.

CULTIVARS: 'Coloratus': purpleleaf euonymus, leaves are 1 to 1 1/2 inches long. Stems and leaves exposed to moderate light, turn dark deep purple on the upper surface in fall and winter. A good ground cover with few fruits. 'Emerald Cushion': very dwarf, mounding form with dense branching and deep green foliage. 'Emerald Gaiety': small shrub with dense, erect branching and rounded green leaves with white margins. 'Emerald 'n Gold': very low-growing with green leaves that have contrasting gold edges. 'Kewensis' very small, green leaves, 1/2 to 1 inch long and slender stems. A good green ground cover with little color change in winter. 'Radicans', bigleaf wintercreeper, sometimes listed as *E. fortunei* 'Vegetus' and called evergreen bittersweet, due to the production of many bright orange fruit. Will become shrub-like reaching 6 to 7 feet. Leaves are 1 1/2 to 2 inches long with wavy margins and remain green during the winter. Will climb with encouragement as it forms many aerial roots. 'Sarcoxie': more popular north, a hardy, upright, vigorous-grower with glossy green leaves 1 1/2 to 2 1/2 inches long. Similar to 'Radicans'. Many others exist.

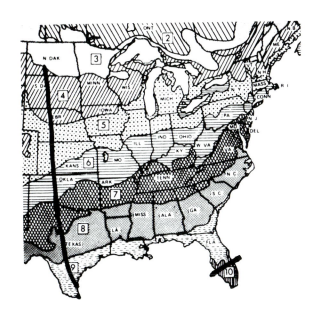

'Sarcoxie'

'Coloratus'

'Coloratus'

'Sarcoxie'

'Sarcoxie'

'Sarcoxie'

'Radicans'

Aerial roots

'Emerald Gaiety'

'Emerald Gaiety'

'Coloratus'

Festuca ovina L.   Sheep's or Blue Fescue
Gramineae or Grass Family   Hardiness Zone 5
Native to Europe and Asia.
SIZE: 6 to 12 inches tall with a spread of 12 to 16 inches. Slow grower.
FORM: Dense, grass-like clumps or mounds.
TEXTURE: Fine.   **EXPOSURE:** Sun to partial shade.

LEAVES: Long, slender, grass-like, 8 to 12 inches long, appearing almost round in cross-section. Green to a very distinct blue-green.

STEM: Inconspicuous. The only stem tissue is in the crown of the clump.

FLOWERS: Narrow panicles, rising above the foliage in late spring or early summer.

FRUIT: In narrow panicles 6 to 10 inches above the foliage. Dead seed heads are objectionable.

COLOR: Foliage is green to a distinct blue-green, depending on seed source or cultivar.

PROPAGATION: By seed or division.

CULTURE: A tough, durable, clump grass for edging, borders, or ground cover in full sun locations or with a slight amount of shade. Will grow in nearly any kind of soil, except where it is extremely wet. Do not plant in irrigated beds or where other plants create a humid condition around plants.

PESTS: None serious in sunny locations; however, crowns die out in wet or very humid locations.

NOTES: A plant for small areas, or borders or as a ground cover. A very low maintenance plant in that no mowing or maintenance is tolerated except to cut off the seed heads in early summer. Will tolerate a wide range of conditions. Will clump to the point that it makes an irregular surface and not a smooth, uniform ground cover. Because it has no spreading or creeping mechanism, it does not bind the soil well on slopes unless planted very thick. It is more effective as a border or line in a sunny location than as a ground cover. In general, ground cover plantings have not proven satisfactory unless the area is reseeded or replanted periodically. If planting is by seed, early fall planting is superior to spring planting.

CULTIVARS: 'Glauca': powdery blue foliage when growing well in full sun. A good blue color for hot, sunny locations. More attractive than the parent. 'Elijah's Blue': has striking blue-gray foliage. May hold its color better in summer.

613

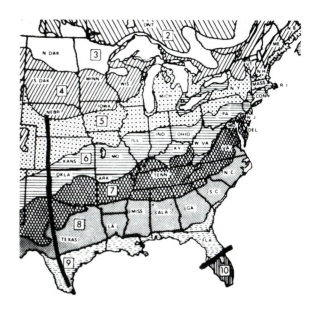

Ficus pumila L.   Creeping Fig
Moraceae or Mulberry Family   Hardiness Zone 8
Native to China and Japan.

SIZE: From a few inches tall as a ground cover, to 40 feet or more. Medium to rapid grower.
FORM: Ground cover or covering on walls or trees.
TEXTURE: Medium to fine.   **EXPOSURE:** Sun or partial shade.

LEAVES: Alternate, simple; on very short petioles. Young leaves are light green, becoming very dark with age. Leaf margin is smooth and slightly heart-shaped at the base. Veins are faint above and prominent below. Juvenile foliage is small, about 1 inch long. Adult foliage is 2 to 4 inches long, not commonly seen except on old plants that have not been pruned for several years.

STEM: Juvenile stems are slender, climbing vines; somewhat zigzag with distinct shoulders or steps with each leaf and axillary bud development. Terminal buds are spear- or heart-shaped. Aerial roots allow the stem to easily attach to wood, masonry or bark of trees. Mature stems are much larger, are not tightly pressed to structures, and support not only larger leaves, but flowers and fruits as well. Stems and leaves of all ficus have milky sap.

FLOWERS: Inconspicuous.

FRUIT: Yellowish, pear-shaped, not edible. Not commonly seen.

COLOR: Leaves are light green, turning very dark with maturity.

PROPAGATION: Cuttings anytime, very easy.

CULTURE: A very tough, durable vine. Frequently wears out its welcome by wearing out the person in charge of maintenance. Too vigorous for many locations. With good soils and moderate sunlight, growth will be many feet per year, making regular maintenance a must.

PESTS: None serious.

NOTES: Very attractive if maintained properly. Creates an interesting contrast to wood or masonry (see photograph). However, growth gets more and more vigorous with age. If removed from wood or masonry, remnants of roots remain, making the surface unsightly. Popular as a houseplant, growing on stakes or small trellises. Useful as a patio tub specimen, either to be grown or left outside in the deep South or moved indoors in more northern climates for winter. Don't be fooled by the innocence of the small stems and leaves on young, juvenile plants. Make sure you understand the maintenance commitment **before** planting.

CULTIVARS: 'Minima': has leaves 1/2 inch long or less, an especially useful houseplant. 'Quercifolia': somewhat oak leaf-shaped leaves. 'Variegata': leaves are green and white. Very attractive, but less cold tolerant than green selections. Other cultivars exist.d551

Hedera helix L.   English Ivy
Araliaceae or Ginseng Family   Hardiness Zone 5
Native to Europe.

SIZE: 6 to 10 inches tall as a ground cover; 60 to 80 feet long as a vine. Rapid grower.

FORM: A spreading vine as a ground cover, trellis cover, planter box, or house plant.

TEXTURE: Medium to coarse, depending on cultivar.   **EXPOSURE:** Sun to shade.

LEAVES: Juvenile leaves are alternate, variously 3- to 5-lobed, somewhat rounded, with smooth margins. Up to 4 inches in diameter, partially enclasping the stem. Leaf color ranges from deep green to almost white, depending on cultivar. Both juvenile and mature leaves exist. Mature leaves are generally less deeply lobed and less attractive. Mature leaves are seen only on very old plants.

STEM: Vine-like with aerial roots. Remains green until very old, finally turning gray.

FLOWERS: Small, greenish. In rounded, loose heads (umbels) but only on mature stems with mature leaves on old plants.

FRUIT: Small and black.

COLOR: Foliage is green to nearly white with some cultivars.

PROPAGATION: Cuttings from juvenile stems root easily but mature stems are difficult to root.

CULTURE: An excellent ground cover for part-shade to shady locations. Can be grown in full sun in protected locations. Does best in fertile, moist, but not excessively wet soils. Withstands city conditions well. Does not damage trees, although it may cover all interior branches. However, the additional wind resistance may increase damage to the tree during high winds.

PESTS: Bacterial leaf spot in humid locations with little air movement. Spider mites in hot, dry locations.

NOTES: Widely known as a house plant. Over 60 cultivars exist which vary by leaf size, leaf shape, and variegation patterns. Cultivars vary a great deal in hardiness and generally the variegated forms are less hardy. ??-POISON-??

CULTIVARS: 'Bulgaria': dark green, hardy to Zone 4. 'Thorndale': another hardy cultivar with somewhat larger leaves. Many others. For a photographic record of many cultivars, see *Exotica III* by Graf. This is an outstanding book of photos of many tropical and a few temperate zone plants.

RELATED SPECIES: *Hedera canariensis* Willd., Algerian ivy, is hardy only in Zones 8b, 9 and 10. Its leaves are larger, frequently reaching 5 to 6 inches in diameter, generally have 3 to 7 shallow lobes and are heart-shaped at the base. Commonly used in the Gulf Coast area and Florida. Foliage and fruits of both species may be mildly poisonous if eaten in quantity.

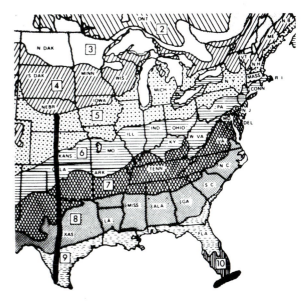

Hedera canariensis

Hosta spp. Hosta or Plantain Lily
Liliaceae or Lily Family Hardiness Zone 5 or 6
Native to Japan.
SIZE: 12 to 18 inches tall, similar spread. Moderate to fast grower.
FORM: Mounding, herbaceous perennial.
TEXTURE: Coarse. EXPOSURE: Partial or full shade.

LEAVES: Simple, tufted, 6 to 10 inches long with long petioles. The leaf surface of most species is dark green and marked by prominent veins which parallel the smooth margin. No fall color since the leaves die following several hard freezes.

STEM: A short, weak rhizome or underground stem that spreads slowly. No above-ground stem.

FLOWERS: White, blue, or lilac; well above the foliage in mid summer, tubular, and fragrant. Very showy.

FRUIT: A 3-valved capsule with many thin-winged seeds.

COLOR: Foliage is dark green. Flowers are white, blue, or lilac.

PROPAGATION: Mostly by division of the clumps.

CULTURE: Excellent plant for shady locations where many other plants will not grow or will grow and become loose, open, and unattractive. Likewise, many plants that will tolerate shady locations flower poorly, if at all. Hostas not only grow well in cool, shady locations, but need these conditions to grow and flower well. Used in the northeastern states more than elsewhere but can be grown in Zones 7, 8, and even 9, if planted in a cool, shady location. Hostas will grow in the Plains States on the north side of buildings or when shaded and given supplemental water during droughts. Not for full sun.

PESTS: None serious, but chewing insects may damage foliage. On heavy clay soils and with excess moisture root and stem rots can be a problem.

NOTES: Attractive and useful plants for creating a dense carpet over the soil surface in part shade or shady locations.

CULTIVARS: Many species and cultivars exist. Leaves range from solid green to variously variegated cream or yellow to nearly all cream-colored. See your favorite nursery and gardening catalogs for those available in your area.

RELATED SPECIES: *Hosta decorata* L.H. Bailey, grows to 2 feet tall with large, ovate leaves with 4 or 5 veins on each side of the midrib and lavender flowers in mid summer.
Hosta fortunei (Bak.) L.H. Bailey, grows 18 to 24 inches tall, with ovate leaves with eight to ten veins on each side of the midrib and flowers that are pale lilac to violet in early summer. 'Marginato-alba' has leaves with broad, white margins: quite striking.
Hosta lancifolia Engl., narrow-leaved plantain lily, grows 18 to 24 iches tall with more elongate leaves and lavender flowers.
Hosta sieboldi J. Ingram, seersucker plantain lily, grows 18 to 24 inches tall with 4 to 5 veins on either side of the midrib. Leaves are flat with a white or yellowish margin. Flowers are violet. 'Alba' has green leaves and white flowers. *The Hosta Book*, by Paul Aden is a good reference or *The Genus Hosta* by W. George Schmid, or *Herbaceous Perennial Plants* by Allan M. Armitage.

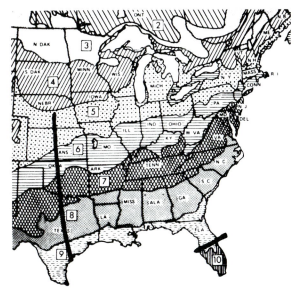

Iberis sempervirens L. Evergreen Candytuft
Cruciferae or Mustard Family Hardiness Zone 5
Native to southern Europe and western Asia.
SIZE: 12 to 14 inches tall with a 12- to 20-inch spread. Slow to moderate grower.
FORM: A low-growing ground cover or edging plant.
TEXTURE: Fine. **EXPOSURE:** Sun, partial shade, shade.

LEAVES: Linear or narrowly oblong, to about 1 1/2 inches long; rounded and rather blunt at the end, with a smooth margin. Leaves are a dull, deep green.

STEM: Upright and spreading growth. Stems are somewhat succulent and generally remain green until of considerable age, finally turning brown.

FLOWERS: White blossoms in elongated heads or racemes during April or May. Very attractive against the evergreen foliage, particularly as an edging plant or border.

FRUIT: None.

COLOR: Foliage is dark green. Flowers are white and showy.

PROPAGATION: Softwood, semi-hardwood, hardwood cuttings or seed.

CULTURE: A durable ground cover or edging plant, particularly for part-shade or shady locations but will grow in full sun if the site is not excessively hot. Grows in a wide range of soil types and moisture conditions. Responds well to pruning immediately after flowering and can be sheared and maintained as a low hedge.

PESTS: None serious, but occasionally grasshopper injury in rural areas.

NOTES: An excellent ground cover and very useful in rock gardens or as a border around other shrubs, especially those that tend to become somewhat leggy or open at the base. A very useful and cold hardy, low evergreen shrub. Blooms about the same time as tulips, narcissus, forsythia, and other spring-flowering plants and can make a spectacular show in masses. A good substitute for sweet alyssum (an annual), thus reducing planting and maintenance costs without giving up the white spring blooms and low, mounding appearance of alyssum. Can be distinguished from common rosemary in that the leaves are flat, whereas, leaves of rosemary are thicker, turn under on the margin and are gray green.

CULTIVARS: 'Nana': more compact than the parent. 'Puree': a very low-spreading mound, neater in appearance without pruning.

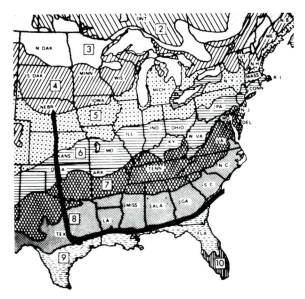

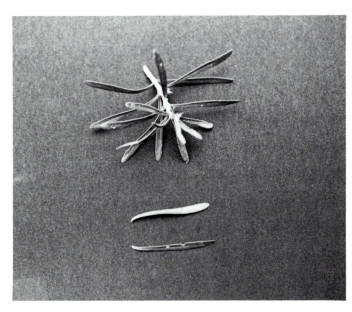

Juniperus conferta Parl.   Shore Juniper
Cupressaceae or Cypress Family   Hardiness Zone 6b to 7
Native to Japan.

SIZE: May reach 24 to 30 inches tall with a spread of 6 to 8 feet, depending on cultivar. Rapid grower.

FORM: Primary horizontal stems have upright secondary branches giving an irregular vertical line effect as a ground cover.

TEXTURE: Fine.   **EXPOSURE:** Sun to slight shade.

LEAVES: Long and slender, longest of the common junipers: 1/2 inch long and needle-like. Gray-green with a white line on top. No scale-like leaves present.

STEM: Primarily stems are horizontal on the ground, rooting down where they contact the soil. Secondary stems develop upright at right angles to the horizontal stem. Frequently the vertical stems fall over during heavy rains or snow, never regaining their upright position and appearing matted down, a disadvantage to the species, but less of a problem with cultivars.

FLOWERS: Inconspicuous.

FRUIT: Rarely seen in the Southeast. Green turning black with a waxy bloom over the surface, about 1/3 inch in diameter.

COLOR: Foliage is gray-green to green to blue-green, depending on cultivar.

PROPAGATION: Semi-hardwood or hardwood cuttings treated with a rooting hormone under mist.

CULTURE: Best grown in full sun but will tolerate light shade or full sun for only a few hours. Will tolerate many soil types, the limitation being only those that are extremely wet. Responds to fertility and is moderately drought resistant.

PESTS: Spider mites, particularly in hot, dry locations such as on the west side of a building. Juniper blight, if planted in humid locations with poor air drainage.

NOTES: Makes a good dense ground cover, works well on beach dunes and tolerates salt. Will trail over walls best of any of the junipers. One of the least hardy junipers, sometimes winter damaged in Zone 7. Can be readily identified from Japanese garden juniper by the horizontal primary stem with the secondary vertical branching and the longer individual needle-like leaves. Japanese garden juniper has shorter leaves and no upright stems or branches.

CULTIVARS: 'Blue Pacific': much like 'Compacta' or 'Dwarf', except bright blue-gray in color, very attractive. Probably the best cultivar for most locations. 'Compacta': gray-green, very dense with little development of secondary upright stems characteristic of the species. Much slower growing, rarely reaching height greater than 8 to 10 inches. 'Emerald Sea': a USDA introduction with compact habit and superior blue-gray foliage color. 'Silver Mist': near silver-blue foliage which is quite dense. 'Blue Tosho': also has silvery blue-green foliage. Other cultivars probably exist.

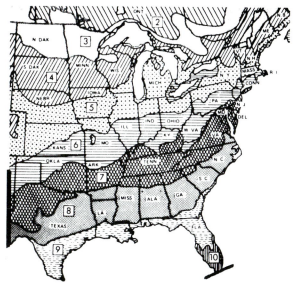

'Blue Pacific'

Juniperus horizontalis Moench.   Creeping Juniper
Cupressaceae or Cypress Family   Hardiness Zone 2
Native to northern United States and Canada.
SIZE: 2 feet tall with a 4- to 6-foot spread, depending on cultivar. Moderate growth rate.
FORM: Irregular, spreading ground cover.
TEXTURE: Fine.   **EXPOSURE:** Sun to slight shade.

LEAVES: Needle-like or scale-like, depending on age and stage of plant development. Both juvenile and mature foliage exists on most plants. Groups of leaves may be arranged in flattened, plate-like or long plume-like clusters, depending on cultivar. May be blue-green to green during summer, many cultivars turn purple in winter.

STEM: Horizontal with secondary branching off the main horizontal stems. May be semi-upright or low and irregular, depending on cultivar. Stems often root when in contact with soil. Main branches are very easily broken where they fork, especially by foot traffic or accumulated ice or snow.

FLOWERS: Inconspicuous.

FRUIT: Rarely seen.

COLOR: Foliage is blue-green to green in summer. Blue-purple to bronze to almost pink in the winter depending on cultivar.

PROPAGATION: Semi-hardwood or hardwood cuttings, easily rooted under mist.

CULTURE: Grows well in a wide range of soil types. Prefers moderately dry to dry conditions; will not tolerate water-logged soils. Does best in full sun.

PESTS: Spider mites are most serious. Juniper blight may be a problem in areas of poor air drainage, high humidity, and dense plantings under irrigation.

NOTES: A questionable ground cover plant. Many cultivars, although attractive as young nursery plants, open up with age, the center dying out exposing central stems. Forks of branches are easily broken by foot traffic or when planting. Can be distinguished from other horizontal junipers in that they have very dominant horizontal-growing stems and both juvenile and mature foliage. Shore juniper has only long, slender, juvenile-like foliage about 1/2 inch long and strong horizontal and upright secondary branches. Japanese garden juniper has only juvenile-like foliage but leaves generally are 1/4 inch long.

CULTIVARS: 'Bar Harbor': plate-like clusters of leaves, blue to blue-gray summer color, blue to blue-purple in winter. Definitely not pinkish as with 'Plumosa'. 'Douglasi', waukegan juniper: an old cultivar with steel blue foliage, tinge of purple and purple-pink in winter; foliage tends to be in flat platelets rather than the plume-like foliage of 'Plumosa'. 'Emerald Spreader': emerald green foliage on plume-like branches. A vigorous spreader with a different leaf color. 'Hughes': often considered a creeping juniper but was selected from Rocky Mountain juniper seed because of greater retention of blue-green foliage color in winter. 'Plumosa', commonly called andorra juniper: more upright, plume-like foliage than other cultivars. Green during the growing season, pinkish to purple-pink during winter. 'Plumosa Compacta' and 'Youngstown' are more compact selections. 'Turquoise Spreader': very dense and attractive blue-green foliage. A vigorous grower with less tendency to mound in the center. 'Webberi': blue-green fine-textured foliage develops a dense mat. 'Wiltoni' or 'Blue Rug': very low-growing, generally can be used interchangeably with 'Bar Harbor', slightly more spreading habit, less plate-like in foliage texture and good winter color. 'Blue Chip': grows to about 12 inches tall with good blue color. Many others exist.

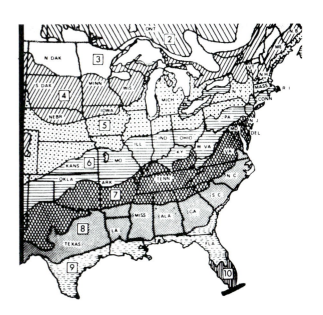

'Plumosa'

'Blue Rug'   'Plumosa Youngstown'

'Blue Rug'

'Webberi'

'Wiltoni'

procumbens

J. conferta

'Turquoise Spreader'

Juniperus procumbens Miq.   Japanese Garden Juniper
    (Syn. *Juniperus chinensis*
Cupressaceae or Cypress Family   Hardiness Zone 4
Native to Japan.

SIZE: Spreading ground cover, rarely reaching a height of more than 20 to 24 inches but may spread 6 to 8 feet. Moderate grower.

FORM: A low-spreading ground cover that will trail over walls of masonry.

TEXTURE: Fine.   **EXPOSURE:** Sun to slight shade.

LEAVES: Needle-like, only somewhat tufted in irregular cluster, about 1/4 inch long. No mature scale-like leaves present. Leaves are slightly blue-green during the growing season and remain green all winter. No purple color as with many creeping juniper cultivars.

STEM: Mostly horizontal, moderate rate of spread as a ground cover or as a rock garden plant. Stems are moderately flexible and stickery to handle. Main branches are easily broken or damaged where they fork. Avoid foot traffic or rough handling.

FLOWERS: Inconspicuous.

FRUIT: Rarely seen.

COLOR: Foliage is slight blue-green depending on the time of year, but generally holds its winter color well.

PROPAGATION: Semi-hardwood to hardwood cuttings in the fall.

CULTURE: Grows well in a wide range of soil types. Will not tolerate water-logged conditions of the root system. Tolerates some shade but tends to become more open in shady locations. Does well in tubs or urns or as a patio specimen in raised planters. Branch forks are eaily broken by foot traffic.

PESTS: Spider mites may be a serious problem in hot, dry locations in late summer, especially on the south or west side of a light colored building.

NOTES: An excellent ground cover plant. Grows denser and taller than creeping juniper cultivars, thus generally does not have the weed problem and thus lower maintenance. Retention of winter color is good and is an advantage. Can be distinguished from creeping juniper cultivars by the longer needle-like leaves present on the stems, denser growth habit, and more stickery foliage somewhat tufted in irregular clusters. Can be distinguished from shore juniper which has longer needle-like leaves frequently reaching 1/2 inch long on horizontal stems with secondary upright branching. *Hortus III* lists Japanese garden juniper and parson's juniper as Chinese juniper cultivars. However, in light of the many differences between either of these species and Chinese juniper, I seriously question this move. Such groupings of unlike plants into one genus only adds confusion for the student and the nursery and landscape industries. Japanese garden juniper develops only needle-like foliage, whereas *Juniperus davurica* 'Parsoni' rarely has all scale-like leaves and these are the same species(?)!

CULTIVARS: 'Nana': very dwarf, compact, with needles slightly shorter than the parent and growth much less vigorous both in height and horizontal spread. Makes an excellent rock garden, bonsai, or patio plant. Does well in raised planters. Less vigorous growth rate can be an advantage in limited space locations. Appears to be less susceptible to mites and blight than the parent. 'Variegata': has bluish green leaves with streaks of cream. 'Green Mound': medium green foliage and slight mounding form. Others may exist.

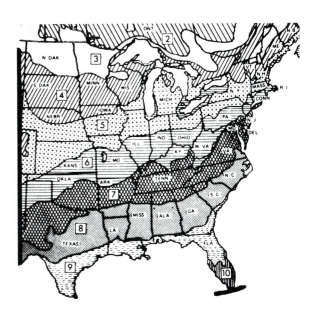

'Nana'

Liriope muscari L.   Lily Turf, Monkey Grass or Liriope
Liliaceae or Lily Family   Hardiness Zone 6b to7
Native to China and Japan.
SIZE: 8 to 20 inches tall, depending on cultivar. Moderate grower.
FORM: Makes a dense, grass-like mat or clump.
TEXTURE: Fine to medium.   EXPOSURE: Partial shade to shade.

LEAVES: Grass-like blades, about 1/2 inch wide and 8 to 20 inches long, depending on cultivar. Deep green on the upper surface; lighter green below. Parallel leaf veins. Many leaves arising from a central crown.

STEM: No above-ground stems showing. However, the plant has a strong rhizome or root stock, which is the primary spreading mechanism. Forms thick tubers that appear something like miniature potatoes.

FLOWERS: Lilac to purple or white, rising above the foliage several inches. Quite showy and very attractive during mid- to late spring.

FRUIT: Small, black berries on the dry flower stalks above the foliage. Unsightly and should be removed.

COLOR: Foliage is dark green. Flowers are lavender to purple. Fruit is black.

PROPAGATION: Division of the clumps, tubers, or seed if the pulp is removed.

CULTURE: Does well in part shade to shady locations or exposed areas not especially hot. Frequently develops a tip burn on the leaves in hot locations. Tolerates moist conditions quite well and is moderately resistant to drought. Grows in any good soil. Has few problems other than the negative response to high temperature. May be pruned to the ground in January or February to remove old, unsightly foliage.

PESTS: None serious, but occasionally grasshoppers may damage foliage.

NOTES: An excellent plant for borders of walkways, paths, or for line effects. Makes a good ground cover in shade to partial shade locations. However, in sunny locations, weeds such as bermuda grass will grow sufficiently well to hamper the development of this plant. In the shady locations, liriope can compete very well with most weeds. Will grow beneath most trees, whereas some ground covers do not. Does not tolerate foot traffic. It puts out one flush of growth per growing season, thus any foot traffic or damage to the top of the plant remains visible until the following spring flush.

CULTIVARS: 'Big Blue': leaves about 1/2 inch wide and may reach height of 18 to 20 inches. Very bold and attractive, large clump or ground cover plant. Attractive flowers. 'Exoflora': very slender leaf, blooms very little. 'Monroe #2': white flowers. 'Variegata': leaves with a yellow stripe on the outer margin. Flowers are paler lavender than the species. Numerous other cultivars exist that have superior flowering characteristics including 'Goldbanded', 'John Birch', 'Christmas Tree', and 'Lilac Beauty'.

RELATED SPECIES: *Ophiopogon japonicus*, mondograss, is very similar to liriope in overall appearance, texture and adaptability. However, mondograss has shorter, narrower leaves creating a finer texture. It is a slower grower than liriope and has small white flowers which do not rise above the foliage and are generally not seen. Makes an excellent soft texture, deep green, grass-like ground cover in partial shade to shady locations. Interestingly rabbit damage is common on mondograss but rarely seen on liriope. Hardy in Zone 7.

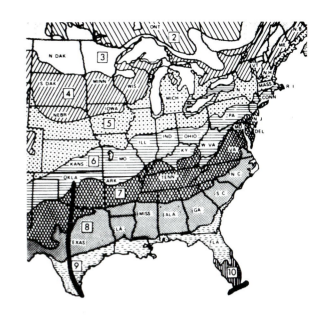

'Big Blue'

'Variegata'

'Silvery Sunproof'

Ophiopogon japonicus

Ophiopogon japonicus

Ophiopogon japonicus

Pachysandra terminalis Sieb. & Zucc.   Pachysandra or Japanese Spurge
Buxaceae or Boxwood Family   Hardiness Zone 4
Native to Japan.
SIZE: 10 to 12 inches tall with a slow rate of spread. Slow grower.
FORM: Stoloniferous, spreading ground cover.
TEXTURE: Medium.   EXPOSURE: Partial shade to shade.

LEAVES: Alternate, wedge-shaped, 2 to 2 1/2 inches long, 1 to 1 1/2 inches broad at the outer end. Serrated or irregularly toothed on the outer portion of the leaf. Rarely are any teeth seen on the lower portion of the leaf blade near the petiole. Leaves tend to be tufted at the tips of the stems. Foliage is a medium to dark green.

STEM: Upright stems arise from the creeping, horizontal stolons. A soft, succulent stem remaining green; very easily damaged by foot traffic.

FLOWERS: Small, creamy white, in the growing terminals. Not showy.

FRUIT: Small, white berries, seldom seen.

COLOR: Foliage is medium to dark green to green-white variegated, depending on cultivar.

PROPAGATION: Cuttings, division, or layering.

CULTURE: An attractive evergreen ground cover for good soils and partial shade or shady locations in the upper South. Does not do well in full sun since growth is slow and foliage is frequently yellow-green. Is not very tolerant to wet areas or drought. Has a fibrous matting root system which transplants easily. Generally does not need pruning once established. For good growing conditions only.

PESTS: Occasionally a scale insect in the upper regions of the South or spider mites in hot locations with poor air movement.

NOTES: A good ground cover around trees where grass does not do well or in shaded courtyards, rock gardens, or planters. Does not do well in the coastal areas or the extreme South below Zone 7. Better adapted to the humid regions of the upper south and northeast portion of the United States. Tolerates no foot traffic since stems are crushed easily and are slow to recover.

CULTIVARS: 'Green Carpet': similar to the parent but with a more compact growth habit. 'Variegata': white, irregularly variegated leaves. The green of the leaves is lighter than that of the parent. Other cultivars probably exist.

RELATED SPECIES: *Pachysandra procumbens* Michx., Allegheny pachysandra, grows about 1 foot high and has broadly ovate leaves about 3 inches long with coarsely toothed margin. Flowers are greenish or purplish in spikes from the base of the stem in spring. Hardy in Zone 5, it is native from eastern Kentucky to Florida and Louisiana. Taller and of a more coarse texture than Japanese spurge, but useful in some situations.

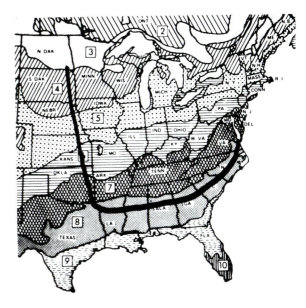

P. procumbens

P. procumbens

Paxistima canbyi A. Gray   Cliff Green or Canby Paxistima
Celastraceae or Staff Tree Family   Hardiness Zone 5
Native to the mountains of West Virginia and Virginia.
SIZE: 12 to 18 inches tall, 3 to 4 feet wide. Slow to moderate grower.
FORM: Low, spreading, evergreen shrub.
TEXTURE: Fine.   EXPOSURE: Sun or partial shade.

LEAVES: Opposite, simple; leathery, narrow-oblong, 1/2 to 1 inch long with few teeth near the tip and a margin that is folded under. Upper surface is glossy dark green, pale below.

STEM: Very slender, spreading horizontally and rooting when in contact with the soil.

FLOWERS: Small, reddish flowers in late spring. Not showy.

FRUIT: A leathery capsule. Not showy.

COLOR: Foliage is glossy, dark green.

PROPAGATION: Cuttings.

CULTURE: A durable shrub for situations with full sun for part of the day but not for hot, dry locations. Intolerant of drought and poorly drained soils. Should have moist, well drained soils for best growth and appearance. Somewhat like flowering dogwood and azaleas in requirements.

PESTS: None serious.

NOTES: A very attractive small shrub or ground cover where the rather specific cultural requirements can be met. Deserves more attention in areas of good soils and moisture or irrigation. Good for raised beds among azaleas and rhododendrons as a ground cover or border plant.

CULTIVARS: None known.

PLANTS OF SIMILAR SIZE: *Alyssum saxatile* L., known as golden alyssum, basket-of-gold, or goldentuft madwort, is now listed as *Aurinia saxatilis* Desv. according to *Hortus III*. This seems like a splitting of hairs and such a name change may never be accepted by the general horticulture trade. Hardy in Zone 5, golden alyssum is a tough, durable, herbaceous perennial for sun or partial shade, with bright yellow to golden flowers and a low, mounding form. Plants rarely exceed 12 to 16 inches tall, growing from the woody roots each spring. Leaves are long and slender and the foliage remains attractive throughout the growing season after the early summer flowers fade. 'Citrina': yellow-orange flowers. 'Compacta': a very compact form with yellow-gold flowers. 'Sulphurea': sulfur yellow flowers. Many others selections exist.
    Phlox subulata L., moss pink or moss phlox, is an evergreen mat or ground cover reaching 6 to 10 inches, hardy in Zone 5, with slender, needle-like leaves about 1 inch long and fine texture. Flowers are pink, lavender, or white; very showy in early spring. Grows well in full sun or part shade in almost any soil. The greatest enemy of moss phlox in sunny spots in the South is bermudagrass, which spreads rapidly and shades out the attractive, needle-like foliage. However, Poast, Fusilade, or Vantage herbicides can be used to kill the bermuda grass with little or no damage to the phlox in most situations. 'Garyi': large, rose-pink flowers. 'Nelsoni': white flowers with rose centers. 'Lilacina': lavender flowers. Many other cultivars exist. Check with your local nurseryman.

Alyssum saxatile

Phlox subulata

Phlox subulata

Rosmarinus officinalis L.   Rosemary
Labiatae or Mint Family   Hardiness Zone 7
Native to the Mediterranean Region.
SIZE: 2 to 6 feet tall with a 3- to 6-foot spread. Variable with growing conditions and age.
Moderate grower.
FORM: Irregular, mounding shrub.
TEXTURE: Fine.   EXPOSURE: Sun to partial shade.

LEAVES: Evergreen, long and slender; 1/2 to 1 1/2 inch long on the same plant. Generally about 1/8 inch wide with rolled edges and a rounded tip. Deep, shining green above, white and wooly underneath. Leaves have a distinct, pleasant odor when crushed.

STEM: A light gray-green when young, becoming light brown and woody with age. Irregular branch development, sometimes twisting or curving irregularly. Responds well to pruning.

FLOWERS: Small, light blue, about 1/2 inch across, in the leaf axils. Generally in April or May, but may bloom irregularly during summer and fall.

FRUIT: Rarely seen.

COLOR: Foliage is a deep, shining green. Flowers are light blue.

PROPAGATION: Softwood, semi-hardwood, or hardwood cuttings. Roots readily with the aid of a rooting hormone.

CULTURE: A very tough shrub. Tolerates drought, exposure, and almost any soil except where very wet. Is used in southern California for hedges along the rocky, dry coastline. Is very salt tolerant. Responds with vigor to fertility and improved growing conditions. Pruning may be needed to make it a more compact shrub, particularly in shaded locations. Becomes open and unattractive in dense shade. Can be trained upright and sheared to make a low tree form or various shapes.

PESTS: None serious.

NOTES: This is the rosemary of folklore and literature. The aromatic leaves are commonly used in cooking and seasoning. The volatile oil is also sold in drugstores. A very attractive, fine-textured, somewhat irregularly mounding shrub. Does well in exposed locations in Zone 7 and southward. Appears to be quite tolerant of any soil conditions and dry locations, especially in exposed situations. Deserves more attention and use, especially in hot, dry, exposed locations without irrigation. Can best be distinguished from gray santolina by the fact that rosemary has long slender leaves and gray-green color, whereas gray santolina has club-shaped, compound leaves which are a gray-white at all times and which, when crushed, have a strong odor, not pleasant as with rosemary.

CULTIVARS: 'Prostrata': a low, spreading form. Looks very much like the parent in other respects. 'Severn Sea': arching growth with prolific, blue flowers. 'Huntington Carpet': grows only about 12 inches tall but a lot horizontally. Leaves are green and flowers are blue. 'Blue Spire': grows more upright and has light blue flowers. Others exist.

 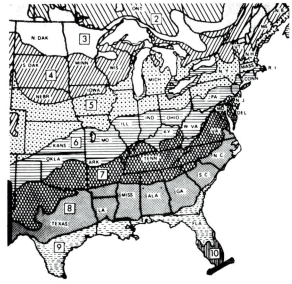

Santolina chamaecyparissus L.   Gray Santolina or Lavender Cotton
Compositae (Asteraceae) or Aster Family   Hardiness Zone 6
Native to southern Europe and the Mediterranean Region.
SIZE: 12 to 18 inches tall, although an individual plant may spread 3 to 5 feet. Moderate to fast grower.
FORM: Asymmetrical, spreading mound.
TEXTURE: Fine.   **EXPOSURE:** Sun.

LEAVES: Pinnately compound with minute segments; the entire leaves appear as small knobby clubs. Evergreen, covered with dense, silvery gray hairs. Very aromatic but not particularly pleasant when crushed.

STEM: Silver-gray, much like the foliage, covered with dense hairs until of considerable age, at which time the stems become hard, woody and a light brown. New branches form readily on the old stems when the plant is pruned back or damaged.

FLOWERS: Yellow clusters rising several inches above the top of the plant during the summer. Somewhat showy.

FRUIT: Dead flowers are unattractive and should be removed immediately.

COLOR: Foliage is a silvery gray. Flowers are yellow.

PROPAGATION: Softwood, semi-hardwood, or hardwood cuttings. Very easy.

CULTURE: A very tough and durable ground cover plant for hot, dry locations. Does not tolerate shade unless it receives several hours of full sun during the day. Will grow in about any soil, from light sand to heavy clay, but does best when the soil is moderately well-drained. Should be pruned back from time to time to make it more compact. Tends to overgrow when under good growing conditions or fertilized and watered regularly, and becomes rather loose; not as compact as when under less desirable growing conditions. Pruning after flowering will make a more compact growth. Pruning may be accomplished with a sharp, rotary lawn mower set about 5 to 6 inches high for a dense mat or ground cover.

PESTS: None serious in full sun. May have a disease problem in moderately shaded locations with high humidity and poor air movement in the South or in areas with heavy soils and irrigation systems applying excess water.

NOTES: An excellent plant for dry, sunny locations where a ground cover is needed. Almost maintenance-free in many locations. Good for borders, foundation planting, edging, as a low shrub or in rock gardens. A good contrast with other plants in the landscape because of the rather unusual silver-gray foliage. Sometimes called cypress lavender cotton. Green santolina is a separate species with 2 inches long, threadlike, dark green leaves. Otherwise similar in form, texture and growth requirements, but cold hardy only in Zone 7. Gray santolina and green santolina work well in sunny beds since they can be managed similarly yet provide a pleasant color contrast.

CULTIVARS: 'Nana': a more dense and compact form.

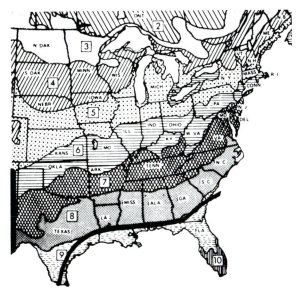
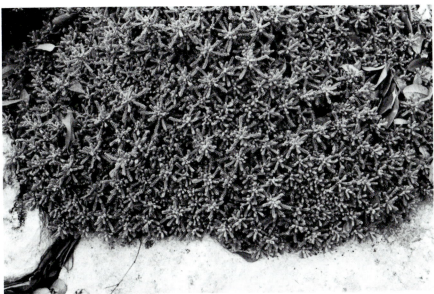

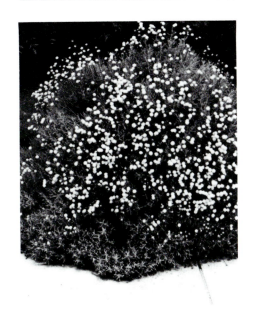

Santolina virens Mill.   Green Santolina
Compositae (Asteraceae) or Aster Family   Hardiness Zone 7
Native to southern Europe and the Mediterranean Region.
SIZE: 12 to 18 inches tall; an individual plant may spread 3 to 5 feet. Moderate to fast grower.
FORM: Asymmetrical, spreading mound.
TEXTURE: Fine.   **EXPOSURE:** Sun.

LEAVES: About 2 inches long, 1/16 inch wide, and finely serrated on the margins. Deep, dark green, turning a rather unsightly brown during severe winters in Zone 7. Aromatic (quite distinctive) when crushed.

STEM: Green, much like the foliage until of considerable age, at which time they become hard, woody, and dark brown. New branches form readily on the old stems when the plant is pruned back or damaged.

FLOWERS: Bright yellow clusters rising several inches above the top of the plant during the summer. Somewhat showy.

FRUIT: Dead flowers are unattractive and should be removed.

COLOR: Foliage is an attractive dark green. Flowers are yellow.

PROPAGATION: Softwood, semi-hardwood or hardwood cuttings. Very easy.

CULTURE: A very tough, durable, ground cover plant for hot, dry locations. Does not tolerate shade unless it receives several hours of full sun during the day. Will grow in about any soil from light sand to heavy clay but does best when soil is moderately well-drained. Should be pruned back from time to time to make it more compact. Tends to overgrow when it is under very good growing conditions or fertilized and watered regularly, thus becoming rather loose and not as compact as under less desirable growing conditions.

PESTS: None serious in full sun if it is not overwatered. May have a disease problem in moderately shaded locations with high humidity and poor air drainage in the Southeast, especially where automatic irrigation systems keep plants excessively wet.

NOTES: An excellent plant for dry, sunny locations where a ground cover is needed. Almost maintenance-free in many instances. Good for borders, foundation planting, low massing, edging, as a shrub, or in rock gardens. Gray santolina is a separate species with gray foliage, pinnately compound, club-shaped leaves divided into minute segments. Otherwise similar in form, texture, and growth requirements.

CULTIVARS: None known.

Sedum acre L.   Gold Moss Stonecrop
Crassulaceae or Stonecrop Family   Hardiness Zone 4
Native to a wide range of Europe and Asia.
SIZE: 4 to 12 inches tall, with variable spread depending on the cultivar. Moderate to fast grower.
FORM: Low, creeping ground cover with thick stems and leaves.
TEXTURE: Fine to medium.   **EXPOSURE:** Sun to shade.

LEAVES: Alternate, somewhat oblong, about 1/4 inch long; thick and fleshy. Light green and more or less triangular.

STEM: Thick, fleshy, and succulent; trailing, rooting at the joints.

FLOWERS: Bright yellow, in terminal clusters. Appearing individually, about 1/2 inch across, in late spring or early summer.

FRUIT: None.

COLOR: Foliage is light green. Flowers are yellow.

PROPAGATION: Cuttings, division or separation of plants.

CULTURE: Does very well in most soil conditions except where soil is very moist and poorly drained. Responds to light applications of fertilizer. The herbicides, Poast, Fusilade, and Vantage can be used over the top to control grassy weeds, generally with liitle or no injury.

PESTS: None serious.

NOTES: A very good, low-growing, maintenance-free plant for rock gardens, in rock walls, or as a ground cover. Develops a dense mat. Will not tolerate foot traffic because of the thick, triangular, succulent leaves and succulent stems which are easily crushed. Slow to recover from any trampling. It should be noted that the genus *Sedum* description takes approximately four pages in Bailey's *Hortus II*. There are many other species that have adaptability for use in many areas, particularly in the upper portion of the South in full sun.

CULTIVARS: 'Aureum': leaves are bright yellow in the spring. 'Majus': 8 to 10 inches tall; larger than the species. 'Minus': a smaller, more compact form. Many others exist.

RELATED SPECIES: *Sedum spectabile* Boreau., grows 10 to 18 inches tall with much larger and thicker leaves and red to pink flowers, depending on cultivar. Similar to gold moss stonecrop in tolerance and adaptability. Many cultivars are available.

Sedum spurium Bieb. 'Dragon's Blood' is a low-growing form with reddish tinted leaves. Foliage becomes more red in winter. Hardy in Zone 3. Many other species of *Sedum* are available.

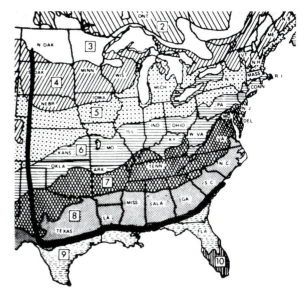

S. spectabile

S. spurium 'Dragon's Blood'

S. spurium 'Dragon's Blood'

Trachelospermum jasminoides (Lindl.) Lem.   Confederate or Star Jasmine
Apocynaceae or Dogbane Family   Hardiness Zone 8
Native to east India through the Orient and Japan.

SIZE: Grows 12 to 16 inches tall as a ground cover or 60 to 80 feet on a tree or other support. Moderate grower.

FORM: Irregular, twining, ground cover, or vine on a tree or trellis.

TEXTURE: Medium.   **EXPOSURE:** Partial shade to shade.

LEAVES: Opposite, oval to ovate, flat, 1 1/2 to 2 inches long, about 1 inch wide, with a smooth margin. Bright, shiny green above and dull, pale green below.

STEM: A thin, wiry, twining vine. Green, changing to dark brown with some age. Mats as a ground cover; wrapping and developing aerial roots in climbing, particularly on trees. Roots where it touches the ground on moist soils.

FLOWERS: Creamy white, about 1 inch across. Very fragrant. Pinwheel-like in appearance. Blooms April or May.

FRUIT: A slender pod about 3 inches long, splitting to expose a small seed with many hairs attached. Generally in clusters of 2 or 3. Not showy. Seeds apparently are not viable under most circumstances and do not become a problem.

COLOR: Foliage is a bright, shiny green. Flowers are creamy white.

PROPAGATION: Hardwood cuttings or layering.

CULTURE: A moderately durable ground cover, trellis or tree plant to grow onto or into various trees in the landscape. Will accept moderately dry conditions and fairly wet conditions in a wide range of soil types. Does only fair in exposed, sunny locations. Does best in partial shade to shady locations. Unlike some shrubs or vines, it also flowers well in shady locations. May be pruned when used as a ground cover to make it more compact. Tolerates only a small amount of foot traffic as a ground cover. Rarely becomes a maintenance problem due to excessive growth.

PESTS: None serious.

NOTES: Frequently planted at the base of tall southern pines or occasionally live oaks. Allowed to grow into the tree for the attractive foliage and the very attractive flowers with their subtle but very pleasing fragrance in the spring. Is readily distinguishable from Japanese honeysuckle in that there are no hairs on the young stem or leaves. Leaves are less flexible, although very similar in size and shape. It has, in many instances, aerial roots where Japanese honeysuckle does not.

CULTIVARS: 'Variegatum': has white/cream blotches on the leaves.

RELATED SPECIES: *Trachelospermum asiaticum* (Sieb. & Zucc.) Nakai, Japanese star jasmine or Asiatic jasmine, seldom flowers and has smaller leaves and stems. Stems are much more slender and wiry. Zone 8. Leaves are a darker green and shiny on the upper surface, generally with the main veins appearing almost white. Mats to a thickness of 12 to 14 inches in some cases and makes an excellent ground cover. May also be used as a ground cover interplanted with narcissus, tulips and other spring flowering bulbs, which rise up through this mass to make a very attractive show. Seldom forms aerial roots, thus does not climb well, but will hang over a wall or out of a planter. 'Nortex' is a cultivar with leaves much more lance- or spear-shaped than the species. Similar in other respects. Sometimes sold as *Trachelospermum jasminoides* 'Nana', particularly in Florida.

T. asiaticum

T. asiaticum 'Nortex'

elongate leaf 'Nortex'

Vinca major L.   Periwinkle
Apocynaceae or Dogbane Family   Hardiness Zone 6
Native to Europe and western Asia.
SIZE: 12 to 18 inches tall, moderate to rapid horizontal spread.
FORM: A dense, irregularly mounding, ground cover.
TEXTURE: Medium to coarse.   **EXPOSURE:** Partial shade to shade.

LEAVES: Opposite, 1 1/2 inches long, 1 to 1 1/2 inches wide, mostly heart-shaped. Leaf margin is smooth. Evergreen, with medium to dark green foliage in Zone 8 and southward but generally suffers considerable winter damage, becoming somewhat unsightly in winter in Zones 6 and 7.

STEM: Remains green; trails, with no aerial roots or clinging mechanisms, thus it does not climb onto other shrubs readily. Roots down at the nodes when in contact with the soil. Dies down in winter below 25 degrees F.

FLOWERS: Bright blue; 1 to 2 inches in diameter. Showy.

FRUIT: Generally not seen.

COLOR: Foliage is medium to dark green or with white patches on the cultivar 'Variegata'. Flowers are bright blue.

PROPAGATION: Stem cuttings anytime, or division.

CULTURE: Does very well in light to heavy shade and will tolerate full sun for a few hours a day, but does not tolerate full sun in hot, dry locations. Tolerates most soils. Moderately tolerant of drought but does best in a moist, shady location.

PESTS: None serious in most locations.

NOTES: An excellent ground cover for shady locations, particularly in the Southwest. May show leaf scorch or desiccation injury in exposed, dry locations. A good rock garden plant. Sometimes used as a ground cover beneath specimen trees or other shady locations. Good for erosion control on shady slopes. Can be used as a hanging basket plant. Does not present a refined appearance for small locations as does *Vinca minor* which has smaller, ovate leaves, a more slender stem, and rarely exceeds 6 inches tall. *Vinca minor* is simply a smaller plant in all respects and has a more refined appearance than *Vinca major*.

CULTIVARS: 'Variegata': irregular, white or cream leaf markings: very attractive in mass plantings. Hardiness and growth requirements similar to the parent.

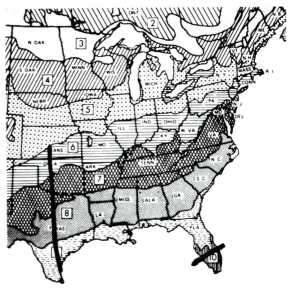

Vinca minor L.   Common Periwinkle
Apocynaceae or Dogbane Family   Hardiness Zone 3
Native to Europe and western Asia.
SIZE: 4 to 6 inches tall; moderate, horizontal spread.
FORM: Dense ground cover.
TEXTURE: Fine to medium.   **EXPOSURE:** Partial shade to shade.

LEAVES: Opposite, 1/2 to 1 1/2 inches long and about 1/2 inch wide. Elliptical to lanceolate with a smooth margin on slender, flexible, arching stems. Upper leaf surface is glossy or waxy, and dark green or sometimes blue-green in shady locations.

STEM: Slender, arching or drooping, remaining green. No tendrils or climbing mechanism; however, roots develop at the nodes when in contact with the soil.

FLOWERS: Bright blue, varying to white and purple depending on cultivar. Singly, 1/2 to 1 inch long, rising slightly above the foliage. Not very showy because the color does not contrast with the foliage except in 'Alba'.

FRUIT: None.

COLOR: Foliage is green to blue-green. Flowers are blue to white or purple.

PROPAGATION: Division or stem cuttings anytime.

CULTURE: Does very well in light to heavy shade and in full sun for brief periods and among other plants. Tolerates most soils without difficulty and is moderately tolerant of drought but does best in a moist, shady location. A good ground cover beneath trees. Not for hot, dry, and exposed locations.

PESTS: None serious in most situations. However, stem rot may be a problem in wet, heavy, clay soils.

NOTES: An excellent ground cover for shady locations. In more sunny locations, grass and weeds can become a severe problem. However, Fusilade or Vantage herbicides can be used to control grasses with little or no injury. A good rock garden, tub, or hanging basket plant. Sometimes used as a ground cover beneath specimen trees.

CULTIVARS: 'Alba': white flowers. 'Multiplex': double, purple flowers. 'Variegata': leaves are green and white. 'Major Bowles': leaves and flowers are slightly larger and leaves are deeper green than those of the parent, under most conditions and may grow slightly faster.

RELATED SPECIES: *Vinca major* has larger leaves, 1 1/2 to 2 inches long, generally more rounded or heart-shaped and lighter green in color. More vine-like, frequently reaching a height of 12 to 18 inches and flowers are blue and 1 to 2 inches in diameter. Hardy in Zone 6. 'Variegata' has white, irregular leaf markings. Cultural conditions and use similar to those of *Vinca minor*.

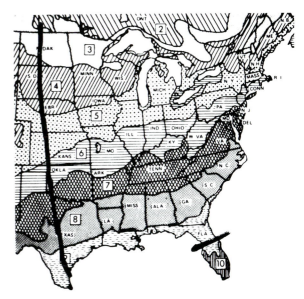

'Major Bowles'

CONIFEROUS EVERGREEN TREES AND SHRUBS

The conifers or cone-bears as a group have a textural feature unique among landscape plants. The small scale-like leaves of Arizona cypress and junipers or the long slender needles of the pines provide a pleasing contrast to the more coarsely textured broadleaf and deciduous plants.

The pines serve well as overstory or canopy trees or to create settings. Their foliage provides a soft, subdued light which enhances many outdoor living areas. In addition, the pleasant sound of a gentle breeze through a pine is a dimension too often neglected by the landscape designer. Perhaps a parallel approach to screening out unwanted sounds in the landscape is to stimulate pleasant natural sounds.

A key point to remember about conifers is that most grow best in full sun or where they receive full sun for a portion of the day. Of the group included here, only podocarpus, yews and American arborvitae are shade tolerant.

Abies concolor (Gord. and Glend.) Lindl.　　　White Fir or Concolor Fir
Pinaceae or Pine Family　　　Hardiness Zone 2
Native to Colorado and New Mexico and northward.

SIZE: 20 to 30 feet tall with a 15- to 20-foot spread.　Grows much larger in its native habitat.

FORM: Formal, perfectly pyramidal tree.　Covered to the ground with branches arranged loosely in tiers.　The upper branches are more upright, the lower ones weeping.

TEXTURE: Fine.　　　**EXPOSURE:** Sun to some shade.

LEAVES: Needles which are 1 to 2 inches long, single, flat, short and stiff, blunt on the end, not sharp to the touch, with a short petiole.　Needles mostly point upwards, densely covering the branches.　Needles on most seedlings are a blue-gray-green.

STEM: The main stem is an upright central leader, with the upper branches angling upward, the mid-branches in horizontal tiers and the lower branches somewhat drooping. Bark is resinous and ash-gray.　Branch development will be poor if shade from adjacent plants becomes heavy.

FLOWERS: Inconspicuous.

FRUIT: A tan-colored cone, 2 to 5 inches long, which stands upright on the branches. Rarely seen outside the native habitat.

COLOR: Foliage is blue-gray-green.　Fruit is tan.

PROPAGATION: Seed.

CULTURE: Tolerates very cold conditions and appears to prefer a deep, rich, well-drained soil.　Does not tolerate heavy clays and wet locations.　Aided by a heavy mulching of the area beneath the tree to reduce soil temperature and increase moisture in the southern and southwestern states.　In areas west of the Mississippi River and east of its native habitat, it is best adapted to northeastern exposures of buildings or other plantings.

PESTS: Mites may be serious in hot locations; twig blight occasionally.

NOTES: A very formal, attractive plant.　Color, form and growth habit vary some with seedlings.　The tiered branches of white fir are very attractive, thus its popularity as a Christmas tree in the West.　Frequently planted in small gardens or confined areas where it overgrows the site.　It must be given proper spacing considerations if used at all.　Not normally recommended for general planting.　*Abies*, the firs, can be distinguished from *Picea*, the spruces, in that firs have blunt-tipped, flat needles whereas spruce have multi-sided needles that are sharp at the tip.　The needles of neither the spruce nor the firs have a papery-like sheath (fascicle) at the base of the needles, which separates both from the pines.

CULTIVARS: 'Compacta': a dwarf shrub with blue needles.　'Candicans': the striking silvery blue needles are amazing.　Growth is upright and narrow.
　　Many other species of fir exist.　Good references include: ***Manual of Cultivated Conifers*** by Den Ouden and Boom and ***Ornamental Conifers*** by Charles Harrison.

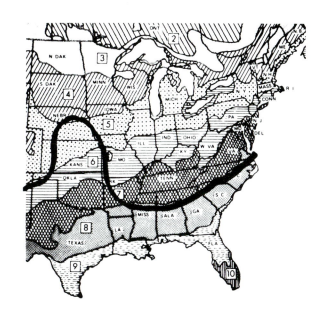

Cedrus atlantica Manetti.　　　　　　　　Atlas Cedar
Pinaceae or Pine Family　　　　　　　　　Hardiness Zone 6b
Native to the Middle East and North Africa.
SIZE: 40 to 60 feet tall with a spread of 30 to 40 feet. Much larger in its native habitat. Moderate to slow grower.
FORM: Irregular, pyramidal tree when young, becoming a large, irregular tree with open growth and a broad, spreading crown at maturity. Branches eventually develop into formal layers or tiers.
TEXTURE: Fine.　　　　　　　　　　**EXPOSURE:** Sun.

LEAVES: Needles are about 1 inch long, stiff, and in clusters on spurs or short shoots or singly on the vigorously growing stems. May be green, yellow-green, or blue-green, depending on seedling variation or cultivar.

STEM: Central leader stem when young with branches mostly at right angles to the main stem until the tree acquires considerable age, at which time it becomes a very informal, asymmetrical tree with a broad, spreading crown. Bark is smooth and gray-brown on young trees, finally becoming rough and dark brown on older specimens. Wood is moderately durable.

FLOWERS: Male flowers appear as miniature cones during late summer.

FRUIT: A cone 2 to 3 inches long, smooth, and egg-shaped; slightly more rounded at the top. Takes two years to mature. Not commonly seen in the United States.

COLOR: Foliage is green, yellow-green, almost pure blue, or blue-gray, depending on cultivar.

PROPAGATION: Seed or grafting of selected cultivars. Roots poorly, if at all, from cuttings.

CULTURE: More difficult to transplant and a somewhat slower growing plant than *Cedrus deodara*. Does well in well-drained soils with moderate nutritional conditions. Responds well to fertilizers, mulching, and supplemental watering during times of drought. Atlas cedar is drought-resistant, growing as far west as western Oklahoma with no irrigation, once established. Grows well in west Texas in an irrigated landscape.

PESTS: None serious under most conditions. However, root rot may be a problem on wet, poorly drained sites.

NOTES: A large, wide-spreading, formal, pyramidal tree with open growth habit with age. Generally an upright central leader with horizontal branching. A most spectacular plant, particularly with some age. Very young trees can be spindly where fertilized heavily.

CULTIVARS: 'Argenta', silver atlas cedar: a silver-blue-gray, almost white, foliage. 'Aurea', golden atlas cedar, has golden new foliage. 'Glauca', blue atlas cedar: a powder-blue foliage. 'Pendula': weeping branches. 'Pendula Glauca' is both weeping and has distinct powder blue foliage. 'Pendula Aurea': golden foliage and weeping branches. Numerous other cultivars exist especially in Europe.

RELATED SPECIES: *Cedrus libani* Loud., cedar of Lebanon, resembles atlas cedar so closely, it is difficult to distinguish between them. Only with considerable age can the two species be readily distinguished. In general, Atlas cedar is preferred. Atlas cedar and cedar of Lebanon can be distinguished from deodar cedar by their shorter needles (about 1 inch) compared to deodar cedar needles which may reach 1 1/2 to 2 inches.

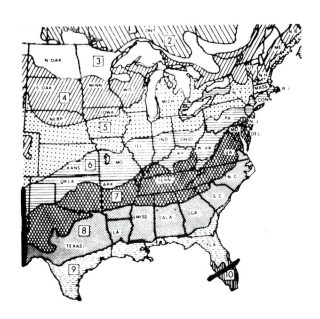

C. *libani*

C. *atlantica*

C. *libani*

C. *a.* 'Pendula'

C. atlantica

C. atlantica

Cedrus spp.

C. atlantica 'Glauca'

C. deodara

C. atlantica 'Glauca'

C. deodara

C. deodara

C. atlantica

C. atlantica 'Glauca'

C. deodara in Lebanon

Cedrus deodara (Roxb.) Loud.   Deodar Cedar
Pinaceae or Pine Family   Hardiness Zone 7b
Native to the Himalayan Mountains.

SIZE: 40 to 60 feet tall with a 20- to 30-foot spread in the South and southwestern United States. Much larger in its native habitat. A rapid grower under good conditions.

FORM: A pyramidal tree with a dense habit and widely spreading branches which droop at the tips when young. Branches will remain close to the ground. As the tree matures, branches become more rigid, making a more flat-topped, asymmetrical tree, but this is rarely seen in the South or Southwest.

TEXTURE: Fine.   **EXPOSURE:** Sun.

LEAVES: Needles; 1 1/2 to 2 inches long in dense clusters on the branches or single on young shoots. Bright green, yellow-green or bluish green, depending on cultivar or seedling. Needle clusters may contain as many as 30 leaves or needles; may be single on rapidly growing branches. When they are single, they have no papery sheath (fascicle) at the base, which distinguishes the genus from that of the pines.

STEM: A central leader with drooping branches throughout the central stem when young, becomes assymetrical with age. Bark is gray and smooth on young trees, brown and deeply furrowed on old trees. Wood is moderately durable.

FLOWERS: Male flowers appear as miniature cones standing upright on the branches during August to October, then dropping.

FRUIT: Cones, more or less egg-shaped but more rounded at the top, 3 to 5 inches long, and about 2 inches wide. Cone surface is much smoother that of a than a pine cone. Takes 2 years to mature; not commonly seen in the United States.

COLOR: Foliage is light green, green, or blue-green, depending on seedling or cultivar.

PROPAGATION: Seed or grafting of selected cultivars. Cuttings root poorly if at all.

CULTURE: Prefers a well-drained loam or clay loam soil. Will tolerate some excess moisture but is also very drought tolerant. It benefits from mulching of the root system, especially around young trees to conserve moisture and reduce soil temperature. Grows best in full sun or with full sun at least half of the day. Becomes open and spindly in shade. Responds vigorously to fertilization and supplemental irrigation during periods of drought. May become more open, loose, and less attractive if made to grow extremely fast.

PESTS: None serious.

NOTES: A magnificent specimen. The pyramidal form and drooping branches are spectacular. Branches emerge from the main stem at near-right angles. Is easy to transplant and responds vigorously to good nutritional conditions and moisture. Most easily distinguished from atlas cedar or cedar of Lebanon by the longer leaves. Deodar cedar leaves are 1 1/2 to 2 inches long, whereas leaves on Atlas cedar or cedar of Lebanon rarely exceed one inch. The least cold hardy of the three species.

CULTIVARS: 'Aurea', golden deodar cedar: pyramidal, 15 to 20 feet tall or more. Leaves are golden yellow in spring, becoming yellow-green in fall. 'Fastigiata': columnar, similar to lombardy poplar in growth with branches ascending. Leaves are unequal in size. 'Pendula': pendulous branches spreading over the ground with ends which turn upright. 'Kashmir': has spectacular silvery blue foliage. 'Shalimar': has blue-green foliage and is said to be more cold-tolerant than seedlings or other cultivars. Numerous other cultivars exist, especially in Europe.

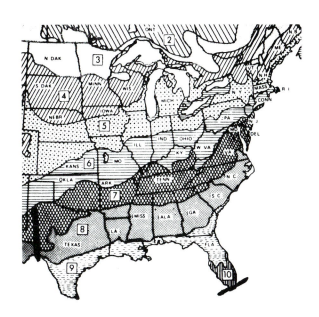

male pollen cones

Cephalotaxus harringtonia C.Koch
Cephalotaxaceae or Plum Yew Family
Native to Japan.

Japanese Plum Yew
Hardiness Zone 6 through 9

SIZE: 4 to 6 feet tall as a spreading shrub or 20 feet tall as a tree form, depending on seedling or cultivar. Slow grower.

FORM: A spreading, mounding shrub or dense, pyramidal tree.

TEXTURE: Fine.
EXPOSURE: Sun to shade.

LEAVES: Narrow, about 1 1/2 inches long, tapering to a point at the tip. Two-ranked, forming a "V" shape down the top of each twig. Glossy, dark green above, with two broad, grayish bands beneath.

STEM: Green when young, turning gray-brown and peeling in long strips with age. Branches are flexible and not easily broken.

FLOWERS: Dioecious. Appearing along the underside of the leaves but formed in the leaf axils. Not showy. Male flowers are shown in the photograph.

FRUIT: Appear in two rows on either side of a twig, beneath the leaves. Ovoid, about one inch long at maturity. Not commonly seen unless several plants and both sexes are present on a site and the plants are quite old.

COLOR: Foliage is dark green.

PROPAGATION: Seeds, or cuttings under mist with difficulty.

CULTURE: One of the more shade-tolerant conifers, thus can be used on the north side of a building and in locations where junipers would slowly die. Grows in most soils as long as drainage is at least moderate. Grows slowly but with few problems in containers and transplants easily. Needs supplemental water the first year but thereafter it becomes quite drought-tolerant.

PESTS: None serious.

NOTES: The cultivar 'Drupaceae' is the most common and is a spreading shrub rarely reaching more than 4 to 6 feet tall. It was grown in southern gardens around the turn of the century, then for whatever reasons lost favor and was mostly ignored for decades. In recent years interest has been renewed and is deserved. This is the best substitute for *Taxus* in the South. Should be used more.

CULTIVARS: 'Drupaceae' (see NOTES), 'Fastigiata': strictly upright with multiple stems and very dark foliage. An extremely slow grower, even under the best conditions; it cannot be rushed. Other cultivars probably exist.

RELATED SPECIES: *Torreya taxifolia*, Florida torreya, is native to northwest Florida and is adapted to moist soils and broken shade. The foliage is similar to plum yew except the tips of the leaves are quite sharp to touch and have an unpleasant odor when crushed. Rarely seen in nurseries but quite attractive.

Taxus floridana, the Florida yew, is a fine textured, mounding shrub or small tree. Leaves are narrow, soft, and rounded at the tip. At first glance it appears like hemlock. Not commonly seen but deserves more attention. Native to a very small ares of northwest Florida.

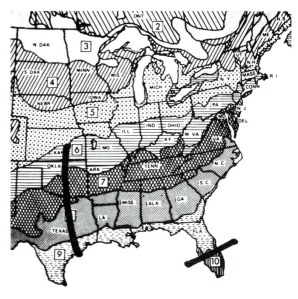

'Fastigiata'

Torreya taxifolia

Torreya taxifolia

Chamaecyparis nootkatensis (D. Don.) Sudw.   Nootka or Alaska Cypress
Pinaceae or Pine Family   Hardiness Zone 4
Native to Alaska and the Oregon and Washington coasts.
SIZE: Variable, depending on cultivar. Slow grower.
FORM: Narrowly pyramidal tree to a rounded or globe-shaped shrub, depending on cultivar.
TEXTURE: Fine.   EXPOSURE: Sun to partial shade.

LEAVES: Scale-like, closely appressed, or somewhat spreading out from vigorously growing stems. Pointed at the tip, not glandular. Medium to dark green, variable with cultivars. Foliage looks very similar in overall texture to oriental arborvitae; however, organization of the branchlets will distinguish the plants.

STEM: Young branches either droop or stand erect. Clusters of branchlets are arranged in more or less vertical plates on the upper part of the plant, reminiscent of oriental arborvitae. The old stem takes on a furry bark which separates into large, thin scales: somewhat similar to the junipers. Wood is moderately tough and durable.

FLOWERS: Not showy.

FRUIT: A small cone about 1/2 inch in diameter. Reddish brown, covered with a powdery bloom. Generally with four to six scales present, often with resinous glands and two to four seeds under each scale. Not commonly seen out of its natural habitat.

COLOR: Foliage is medium to dark green.

PROPAGATION: Seed; selected cultivars are often grafted onto oriental arborvitae root stocks or may be rooted from cuttings with some difficulty.

CULTURE: An interesting geographical misfit. Grows well and functions admirably as a landscape shrub in the Prairie States, which present far different growing conditions than its native Alaskan coastline, where it grows in low-lying areas in moist soils along streams. However, nootka cypress appears to be far more adaptable than has previously been considered and should be used in other areas throughout the United States, particularly as a slow-growing substitute for oriental arborvitae since they are similar in form and texture, particularly when young.

PESTS: None serious although mites may be a problem in hot, dry locations.

NOTES: Several cultivars make spectacular landscape plants, are very cold hardy, and, interestingly, possess a considerable range of drought tolerance. Several old specimens are tolerating heavy clay soils and no irrigation and are functioning very well in central Oklahoma which is much different from the Alaska coastline. Can be propagated from cuttings with difficulty. It may be more advantageous to graft it onto arborvitae root stock. Not common in the nursery trade at the present time, at least not in the South and Southeast, but should be given an opportunity to be used more in these areas. Makes an excellent substitute for oriental arborvitae. Its slower and slightly more refined growth habit, either in the globe or in the weeping forms, make it an outstanding landscape plant.

CULTIVARS: 'Glenmore': may be the same or similar to 'Compacta', a loosely compact, rounded or globular shrub, reaching a height of 5 to 6 feet with similar spread. Foliage is a blue to blue-green during the growing season, slightly off-color green in the winter in full sun. Winter color is superior in locations with a little shade. 'Pendula': spectacular, central leader form with drooping branches: a very showy, eye-catching specimen plant with blue-green foliage and a loose, open habit of growth. Other cultivars exist.

'Pendula'

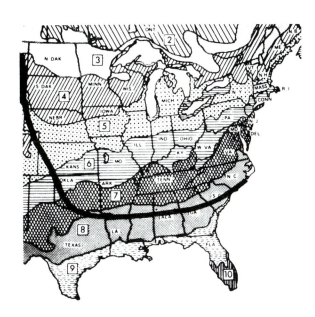

'Pendula'

'Glenmore'

'Glenmore'

Chamaecyparis obtusa (Sieb. & Zucc.) Endl.   Hinoki False Cypress
Pinaceae or Pine Family   Hardiness Zone 5
Native to Japan.
SIZE: 10 to 30 feet tall in cultivation. Slow grower.
FORM: Pyramidal shrub or tree.
TEXTURE: Fine.   EXPOSURE: Sun to partial shade.

LEAVES: Opposite; scale-like, closely pressed to the stem. Dark green above with distinct white lines beneath. Tightly attached to small, plate-like branches.

STEM: Young branches are more or less in plates or tiers; horizontal or nearly so (definitely not strictly vertical like oriental arborvitae). Bark on old stems is reddish brown, rather smooth, peeling off in thin vertical strips. Wood is light-weight but durable.

FLOWERS: Inconspicuous.

FRUIT: A short-stalked, rounded cone with eight to ten scales; not showy. Not commonly seen in the eastern United States.

COLOR: Foliage is dark green.

PROPAGATION: All *Chamaecyparis* can be propagated from semi-hardwood cuttings.

CULTURE: Native to cool, humid climates. Not well adapted to the eastern United States but can be grown there if care is taken to select a suitable site. Best suited to locations with part shade or full sun for a few hours during the day, preferably in the morning. Soil type tolerance is considerable as long as soil is cool, mulched moderately, and not consistently overly wet. Excessive mulch tends to encourage excessive moisture and may be more harmful than beneficial. Somewhat drought-tolerant if not exposed to excessive heat. Grows well under light to medium tree shade on good soils. Numerous species and cultivars are growing well in central Oklahoma, under these conditions. In the northeastern states where summers are milder and rainfall more evenly distributed, *Chamaecyparis* can be grown in more open conditions with success.

PESTS: None serious.

NOTES: Attractive, fine-textured shrubs with a texture distinct from that of the more common conifers. Very useful, especially in locations with some shade or protection.

CULTIVARS: 'Erecta': upright and slender. 'Nana': a compact, low shrub, more rounded in habit. An excellent small shrub form. Many others exist.

RELATED SPECIES: *Chamaecyparis lawsoniana* Parl., Lawson false cypress or port-orford-cedar: pyramidal coniferous evergreen, generally with a dense foliage of scale-like leaves that are often blue-green with white lines beneath, on many slender branches. Of the *Chamaecyparis* described here, least well adapted to the eastern United States. Cool, protected locations with moist, well drained soil seem most suitable. Hardy in Zone 6. Many cultivars exist.

Chamaecyparis pisifera Endl., Japanese false cypress or sawara false cypress: pyramidal evergreens generally with dense foliage and dark green, long, pointed leaves on mostly horizontal branches. Many cultivars exist. 'Squarrosa cyano-viridis': has soft, blue-green juvenile foliage; very striking.

Readers interested in conifers should obtain a copy of *Manual of Cultivated Conifers* by Den Ouden and Boom, Martinus Nijhoff, The Hague, Netherlands. This is a fantastic book with good photographs and many details of cultivars.

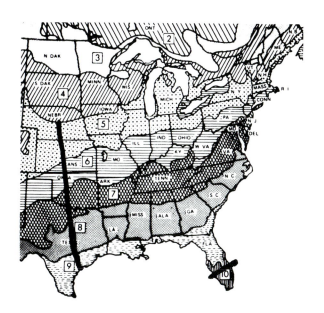

C. *lawsoniana*

C. *pisifera*
'Squarrosa cyano-viridis'

C. *lawsoniana*

C. *pisifera*
'Squarrosa cyano-viridis'

Cryptomeria japonica D. Don.　　　　　　Japanese Cryptomeria
Taxodiaceae or Taxodium Family　　　　Hardiness Zone 6
Native to China and Japan.
SIZE: 30 to 60 feet tall with a 20- to 30-foot spread. Slow to moderate grower.
FORM: Pyramidal tree or large shrub if pruned severely.
TEXTURE: Fine.　　　　　　　　　　　　EXPOSURE: Sun or partial shade.

LEAVES: Spirally arranged on slender stems in five ranks or rows. Individual leaves curve upward and inward. Attachment to the stem makes the leaves and stem appear as though molded from plastic. Dark green in summer but often bronze-green or brown in winter, especially if in a windy, exposed location.

STEM: Young stems are slender and covered with the closely attached leaves. Older limbs develop a shallowly furrowed, reddish brown bark which breaks into vertical strips and becomes gray with age. Wood is stout, aromatic, and decay-resistant.

FLOWERS: Inconspicuous. Monoecious.

FRUIT: Brown. About 1 inch round, and at the tips of the branches.

COLOR: Foliage is dark green; bronze-green in winter.

PROPAGATION: Seed, or cuttings with difficulty.

CULTURE: Adaptable in terms of soils, but not drought- and heat-tolerant. Best used in protected locations or on the north or east side of structures, particularly in the Midwest and central United States. Responds to mulching and restriction of grass competition either by mulching or spraying. Likewise, mulching or the accumulation of natural leaf litter stabilizes soil temperatures and moisture availability.

PESTS: A leaf spot disease, not serious in most locations. Root rot in heavy clay soils.

NOTES: An attractive, coniferous evergreen, especially in protected areas where its winter color is not a dirty brown. Useful as a specimen tree or for screens, since the lower limbs remain in most cases. Best growth appears to be in Zones 6 and 7. In the Deep South, cryptomeria grows poorly for reasons as yet unknown. The compact cultivars are especially useful on north or east exposures where an evergreen shrub is desired and taxus is not the answer.

CULTIVARS: 'Elegans': a juvenile form 10 to 15 feet tall with horizontal branches. 'Globosa Nana': compact, globe form with a maximum height of 3 to 5 feet. Yellow-green in summer, somewhat blue-green in winter. Very attractive. 'Knaptonensis': a dwarf, compact, cushion form with some fine, white leaves. 'Spiralis': very compact, flat, globe form. 'Yoshino': bluish green new foliage, somewhat bronze-green in winter. A rapid, upright grower. Many others exist. The National Arboretum in Washington, D.C., has several cultivars. *Manual of Cultivated Conifers* by DenOuden and Boom, 1965, Martinus Nijhoff, the Hague, Netherlands, lists many cultivars and is an excellent reference book.

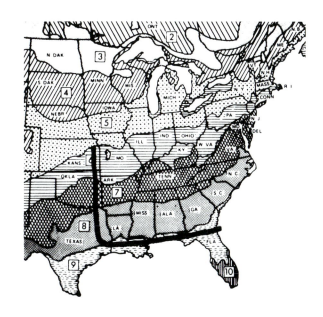

Cunninghamia lanceolata (Lamb.) Hook.   China Fir
Pineaceae or Pine Family   Hardiness Zone 7b
Native to southern and western China.

SIZE: May reach 50 to 60 feet tall with a 20- to 30-foot spread, depending on growing conditions. Moderate to slow grower.

FORM: Pyramidal with branches to the ground when not excessively shaded. Branches are in whorls around the trunk.

TEXTURE: Medium.   **EXPOSURE:** Sun to moderate shade.

LEAVES: 1 to 1 1/2 inches long, about 1/4 inch wide at the base, spirally arranged on the twig. Sharp, stiff, and prickly. Dark, glossy green above with 2 white lines below. In exposed condition, needles take on a purple-brown in winter, especially in Zones 7 and 8. Some dead needles remain on the stem.

STEM: Should be grown as a central leader tree. Lateral branches develop in whorls at near-right angles to the main stem. China fir has a tendency to develop multiple central leader stems. Should be pruned to 1 central leader stem as needed. The terminal winter bud is about the size of a marble or slightly larger, and the spring flush of growth emerges out of the center of that bud. A most unusual growth characteristic. old bark is somewhat shaggy in vertical strips, somewhat like eastern red cedar.

FLOWERS: Inconspicuous.

FRUIT: A 1- to 2-inch round, flattened cone. Rarely seen in the United States.

COLOR: Foliage is deep green to a very attractive blue-green, depending on cultivar or seedling. In full sun in winter, foliage may turn a purple-bronze.

PROPAGATION: Cuttings, with difficulty; or seed.

CULTURE: Grows best in a good, moist, fertile soil but has some tolerance for heavy clay soils. Appears to have minor element deficiencies on sandy soils, particularly in the Gulf Coast area. Where the plant has been damaged from disease or insects, or abused by lawn mowers, suckers may form at the base. Basal suckers should be removed for cuttings.

PESTS: None serious.

NOTES: A very attractive, rather formal evergreen tree during the growing season, particularly when young and allowed to retain branches to the ground. A good southern substitute for Colorado blue spruce, or northern substitute (in Zones 7b, 8, and 9) for monkey puzzle tree, *Araucaria bidwilli* Hook., or Norfolk Island pine, *Araucaria excelsa*. In the extreme southeast Gulf Coast area, China fir can be distinguished by the 2 gray-green lines on the underneath side of the leaves, whereas the leaves of *A. bidwilli* are a uniform green below.

CULTIVARS: 'Glauca': is a blue-gray cultivar which retains winter color well. A good southern substitute for blue spruce but gets large.

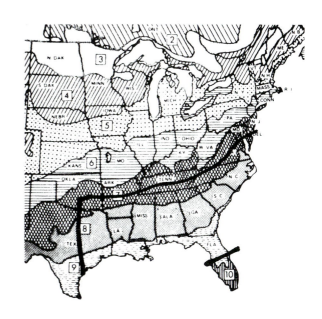

Cupressocyparis X *leylandi* Dall. & Jacks.	Leyland Cypress
Cupressaceae or Cypress Family	Hardiness Zone 6
A hybrid between *Cupressus macrocarpa* and *Chamaecyparis nootkatensis*
SIZE: A 20- to 40-foot tree, depending on growing conditions and age. Rapid grower.
FORM: Pyramidal, graceful, evergreen tree.
TEXTURE: Fine.	EXPOSURE: Sun to partial shade.

LEAVES: Very similar to *C. nootkatensis*: closely pressed to the stem or spreading on vigorous shoots, pointed at the tip, but not prickly like a juniper. Rich green. Aromatic when crushed.

STEM: Branches are flattened, a bit like oriental arborvitae, but only at first glance. Branches are fairly compact. Young shoots are green, turning a distinct red-brown with age, finally becoming a dark brown, with only a faint hint of red. When grown as a central leader tree it is not commonly damaged by wind or ice since the wood is durable and flexible.

FLOWERS: Not showy.

FRUIT: Small cones about 1/2 inch in diameter, with 8 scales and usually 5 seeds.

COLOR: Foliage is a rich green, gray, bluish green or yellowed, depending on cultivar.

PROPAGATION: Terminal branch cuttings under mist in the fall. Avoid poorly drained media or over watering.

CULTURE: A very adaptable conifer that is more cold tolerant and remains more compact than Monterey cypress. Quite drought-tolerant on any reasonable soil. However, roots may be very shallow if the soil is poorly drained. Like many conifers, it does not like wet feet. Can be sheared or pruned to make it more compact or to avoid letting it overgrow a site. Is much more shade-tolerant than junipers and does not have the problem of juniper blight in areas of limited air movement. Useful where a large conifer is desired and where shade prevents the use of junipers.

PESTS: Bagworms occasionally, but not nearly as susceptible as are the junipers and arborvitaes. Root rot on poorly drained sites. Twig and stem blight is becoming serious in many areas.

NOTES: A natural hybrid resulting from seed taken from a Monterey cypress, *Cupressus macrocarpa*, growing adjacent to an Alaska cedar, *Chamaecyparis nootkatensis*, at Leighton Hall, Welshpool, England. A very useful and attractive coniferous tree with good summer and winter color and adaptable to most soils and exposures. Used as a large screen or as a specimen plant over a wide area of the South. Some use as a Christmas tree due to good foliage density, color, and uniformity of cuttings. Requires less shearing than pines.

CULTIVARS: 'Green Spire': columnar with dense, bright green foliage. 'Haggerston Gray': pyramidal tree with distinct gray-green foliage. 'Leighton Green': narrowly columnar with yellow-green, almost chlorotic foliage. 'Naylor's Blue': pyramidal, with blue-gray foliage. 'Castlewellan': golden variegated at the tips but does not hold its color well in winter. 'Silver Dust': new growth is interspersed with stems that are white and small sections of leaves. Good color during the growing season and fair to good winter color. Other cultivars exist.

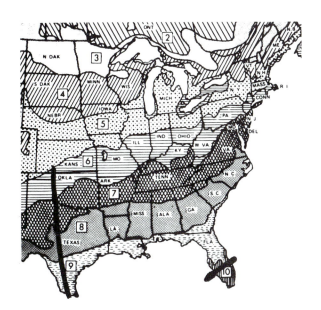

Cupressus arizonica Lemm.   Arizona Cypress
Pinaceae or Pine Family   Hardiness Zone 7
Native to Arizona, New Mexico, and Mexico.
SIZE: 30 to 40 feet tall with a 15- to 25-foot spread. Rapid grower.
FORM: Pyramidal to columnar, depending on cultivar.
TEXTURE: Fine.   EXPOSURE: Sun to some shade.

LEAVES: All leaves are scale-like. Branchlets are at right angles: that is, when looking down at a young branchlet from the very tip, the arrangement of the branches form a "+". Foliage frequently has a silver-gray cast. Foliage is more open and loose than on most species of juniper.

STEM: Young branches are green at first, turning red-brown 6 to 12 inches back from the growing terminal. The old stem is rather smooth with irregular, peeling patches of bark and is rather attractive. Wood is moderately durable.

FLOWERS: Inconspicuous.

FRUIT: A cone, reaching about 1 inch in diameter with various points on the scales or sections of the cones. These cones are generally produced in the upper portion of the plant and retained for a growing season or more before being dropped.

COLOR: Foliage is green to gray-green or silver-gray-green, depending on seedling population or cultivar.

PROPAGATION: Seed or grafting of selected cultivars onto seedlings or oriental arborvitae rootstock. The root system of neither Arizona cypress nor oriental arborvitae rooted from cuttings or grown in containers anchors the plant well.

CULTURE: Grows well on a wide range of soils in dry land conditions throughout the Southwest. Responds to fertilizer and will grow very rapidly. More tolerant to shade than juniper species. However, should not be planted in the shade because of increased susceptibility to juniper blight.

PESTS: Bagworms. Juniper blight in the Southeast. Severity of the disease may limit the planting in many humid locations with poor air movement.

NOTES: A very attractive, blue-gray, pyramidal to conical, upright, large shrub to medium-sized tree. Gets too big for many locations, needs space to develop. Trees on heavy clay soils are very shallowly rooted and frequently blow over during rainy periods. The young twig, a few inches back from the tip of the branch, has a very prominent, varnished, red-brown cast which is useful in identifying Arizona cypress from various juniper species. Also note the fruit, bark, and twig arrangement to distinguish the two genera. The seedling population is hardy only to the lower range of Zone 7. However, the cultivars 'Gareei' and 'Greenwood' are more hardy, surviving as far north as central Zone 6.

CULTIVARS: 'Gareei': silver-blue foliage is very predominant. Hardy throughout Zone 7 and into southern regions of Zone 6. Excellent color retention in winter. 'Greenwood': medium silver-gray-green, otherwise like 'Gareei'. 'Blue Ice': has striking blue-gray foliage that sets it apart in the landscape. Otherwise, growth is typical of the species. Other cultivars probably exist.

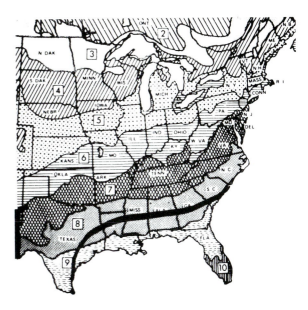

Cupressus sempervirens L.　　　　　　　Italian Cypress
Pineaceae or Pine Family　　　　　　　　Hardiness Zone 8
Native to southern Europe and western Asia.
SIZE: 30 to 40 feet tall with a 3- to 6-foot spread. Rapid grower.
FORM: A strict, vertical column.
TEXTURE: Fine.　　　　　　　　　EXPOSURE: Sun or partial shade.

LEAVES: All leaves are scale-like. Branchlets are at right angles: that is, when looking down at a young branchlet from the very tip, the branches form a "+". Foliage frequently has a dull green cast and is more coarsely textured and loose than that of juniper species.

STEM: Young branches are green at first, turning red-brown 6 to 12 inches back from the growing terminal. The old stem is rather smooth with irregularly peeling patches of bark. Wood is moderately durable and flexible; not commonly broken by wind.

FLOWERS: Inconspicuous.

FRUIT: A cone, reaching about 1 inch in diameter, with various points on the scales of the cones. These cones are green, generally produced mostly in the upper portion of the plant, and retained for a growing season or more before being dropped.

COLOR: Foliage is dull green on most plants.

PROPAGATION: Seed, cuttings or grafting onto seedlings or oriental arborvitae rootstock. The seedling root system of Italian cypress does not anchor the plant well.

CULTURE: Grows well on a wide range of soils thoughout the South. Responds to fertilizer and will grow very rapidly. More tolerant to shade than juniper species. However, should not be planted in the shade because of increased susceptibility to juniper blight.

PESTS: Bagworms. Juniper blight in the Southeast may become so severe that it limits the planting in many humid locations with limited air movement. Mites may be severe in hot locations with poor air movement.

NOTES: A very attractive, vertical column. Gets too tall for many locations. The young twig, a few inches back from the tip of the branch, has a very prominent, varnished, red-brown cast which is useful in distinguishing *Cupressus* from *Juniperus* species. Also note the fruit, bark, and twig arrangement to distinguish the two genera. Italian cypress is often used to accent a line in the landscape; however, caution must be used to insure harmony with other plants. A similar growth form can be obtained from *Juniperus scopulorum* 'Columnaris', which is cold hardy to Zone 3.

CULTIVARS: 'Glauca', blue Italian cypress: has bluish green foliage and a strict vertical growth habit. 'Stricta': the cultivar name often given to the upright seedlings from a population, since the seedlings are moderately diverse. 'Worthiana': cold hardy in Zone 7b; foliage is a dull, deep green. Growth habit is vertical. Very compact, a rapid grower. A yellow-variegated selection exists and is generally sold only as 'Variegata'. 'Swanes Golden': grows like 'Stricta' only has gold-tipped new growth. Other cultivars probably exist.

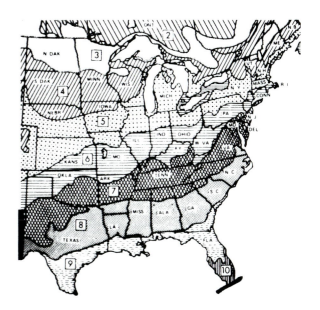

Juniperus chinensis L.   Chinese Juniper
Cupressaceae or Cypress Family   Hardiness Zone 3
Native to China.

SIZE: Uprights reach 30 feet tall. Spreaders reach 6 to 8 feet tall by 15 to 20 feet.
FORM: Upright or spreading shrubs or trees, depending on cultivar.
TEXTURE: Fine.   **EXPOSURE:** Sun.

LEAVES: Scale-like on mature foliage, needle-like on juvenile foliage (see photograph). Most plants will have some juvenile and some mature foliage. The ratio of juvenile to mature foliage will change with growth rate and age and varies among cultivars. Young leaves have a distinct odor when crushed; rather sweet and not sticky.

STEM: Young stems are moderately stout compared to those of other junipers. Bark is rather ragged, almost furry sometimes, and peels in vertical strips.

FLOWERS: Females are inconspicuous; male flowers are not noticed until the yellow pollen can be seen. Male and female flowers are mostly on separate plants.

FRUIT: Green turning bluish to bluish purple, smooth and round. Generally 1/4 inch in diameter. Largest juniper fruit commonly encountered.

COLOR: Foliage color depends on cultivar. Fruit is primarily bluish.

PROPAGATION: Semi-hardwood cuttings of spreaders, grafting of uprights onto 'Hetzi' liners.

CULTURE: Very tough and durable, tolerating dry conditions and poor soils, but sensitive to water-logged conditions. Good scavenger for nutrients and excels in sunny locations. For good growth a few hours of full sun each day is needed. Frequently are not given sufficient space and become a problem after 5 years or more due to excessive growth.

PESTS: Bagworms, spider mites, and root rot in wet, heavy soils.

NOTES: The Chinese juniper cultivars are some of the most durable, sun-loving, narrow-leaved evergreens for hot, dry locations. The major problem, bagworms, is now easily and safely controlled by a spray using the bacteria *Bacillus thuringensis*. Even the compact cultivars need sufficient room to develop. *Hortus III* lists parson's juniper and Japanese garden juniper as Chinese juniper cultivars; however, this author questions the change.

CULTIVARS: 'Blue Vase' or 'Texas Star': blue foliage, branches form a vase-shape; 4 to 6 feet tall with equal spread. 'Hetzi': rapid-grower 8 to 10 feet tall with a spread of 10 to 12 feet. Foliage is blue-green, branch angle of 40 to 45 degrees. Needs plenty of room. 'Keteleeri': common upright "Christmas tree" form. Medium to light green foliage and large powder blue fruits. 'Blue Point': grows like 'Keteleeri', only blue. 'Maneyi': blue foliage, large blue fruit, similar shape to 'Blue Vase' but may reach 6 to 7 feet tall with a 10 to 12 foot spread. Needs room. 'Mint Julip' and 'Sea Green': deep, dark green foliage, summer and winter, similar to 'Hetzi' in branching habit and rate of growth but slightly finer texture. 'Pfitzeriana', common pfitzer juniper: may reach a height of 4 to 6 feet with a spread of 15 to 20 feet. Foliage is green and branching angle is approximately 20 to 25 degrees above the soil surface, in contrast to the higher angle of 'Hetzi'. 'Compact Pfitzer': several trade names: Armstrong, Dwarf Pfitzer, Pfitzer Nana. A much more compact and dwarf form of pfitzer juniper which grows to 3 to 4 feet and spreads 6 to 8 feet, more in scale with single-story dwellings. 'Pfitzeriana Aurea': gold-tipped new growth. 'Pfitzeriana Glauca': blue form of the pfitzer; foliage color much like 'Hetzi' but branch angle is like the more prostrate parent pfitzer. 'Torulosa': asymmetrical, upright, with irregular, bold branching in a number of directions. Deep green color, outstanding specimen plant but eventually may reach 20 feet or more. Many, many more exist.

'Torulosa'

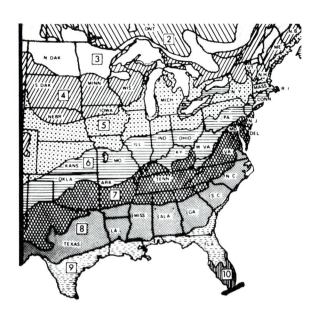

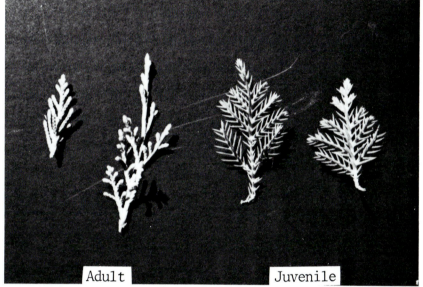

Adult   Juvenile

'Keteleeri'

'Pfitzerana'

'Blue Vase'

'Mint Julep'

'Pfitzerana compacta'

'Pfitzeriana Glauca'

'Torulosa'

'Maneyi'

'Pfitzerana compacta'

'Hetzi'

Juniperus davurica Parl. 'Parsoni'　　　　Parson's Juniper
　　　　(Syn. *Juniperus chinensis*)
Cupressaceae or Cypress Family　　　　Hardiness Zone 5
Native to eastern Asia (probably)
SIZE: 12 to 24 inches tall and spreads to 3 to 4 feet. Moderate to rapid grower.
FORM: Loose, informal ground cover with irregular branches. Characterized by very strong, stiff, dominant, horizontal branches.
TEXTURE: Fine.　　　　**EXPOSURE:** Sun.

LEAVES: Scale-like or needle-like, depending on rate of growth and vigor of plant. Gray-green to dark green; tufted on short, slender stems, rising from the strong, horizontal, primary stem.

STEM: Characterized by very strong, rigid, rapidly tapering, horizontal stems rising 6 to 12 inches above the ground, with moderate branching off this stem but little subsequent development of those branches. The main stem may twist or curl irregularly.

FLOWERS: Inconspicuous.

FRUIT: Not common. When present, nearly round, approximately 1/4 inch in diameter, with multiple seeds.

COLOR: Foliage is gray-green to dark green.

PROPAGATION: Hardwood cuttings with aid of rooting hormone, taken in the fall.

CULTURE: Easily grown, tolerates full sun and hot, dry conditions. Grows in any soil except where excessively wet. Perhaps best suited to raised planters where bermudagrass is less of a problem. Comparable to uses of Savin juniper cultivars but much less sensitive to juniper blight. The herbicides, Fusilade or Vantage do a good job of removing grasses without damaging the junipers.

PESTS: Spider mites in hot, dry locations.

NOTES: Frequently sold as *Juniperus squamata* 'Parsoni' or simply *Juniperus parsoni* or *J. davurica* 'Expansa Parsoni'. *Hortus III* lists *J. davurica* 'Parsoni' as a cultivar of *J. chinensis*: however, I doubt this is correct and prefer to leave it as a separate species. Most readily distinguished from other species by the very rigid, horizontal stem and gray-green to deep green foliage. Plants can be oriented with a strong branch parallel to the edge of a planter to emphasize the line with little or no maintenance. A tough, tolerant juniper that should be used more, particularly as a substitute for creeping juniper cultivars which tend to die out in the center and allow weeds to develop. 'San Jose' Chinese juniper is similar to parson's juniper in overall appearance and may be a closely related cultivar from the same parents. However, it does not have the strong, horizontal branching. It develops a more rounded mound appearance with age. A good plant, far superior to creeping cultivars.

CULTIVARS: 'Variegata': striking cream-colored groups of small twigs among the bluish green foliage. otherwise, the growth, branching, and adaptibility are similar. Appears to be simply a variegated sport of 'Parsoni'.

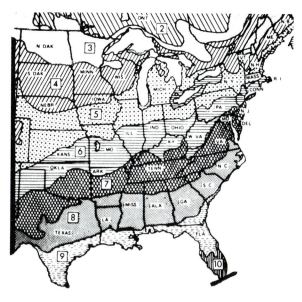

Juniperus excelsa Bied.
Cupressaceae or Cypress Family
Native to the Middle East.

Spiny Greek Juniper
Hardiness Zone 5

SIZE: 10 to 20 feet tall with a 8- to 15-foot spread. Rapid grower.
FORM: Broad, pyramidal, large shrub.
TEXTURE: Fine.   EXPOSURE: Sun.

LEAVES: Gray-green, slender, needle-like; sticking out from the stem, very sharply pointed at the tip and sharp to the touch, thus the common name, spiny Greek. On very old plants the leaves may become scale-like and much less spiny. However, in this country, plants generally die before reaching such an age or size.

STEM: Generally developing multiple stems or multiple-leader stems when young, becoming a loose and weak crown, much like oriental arborvitae, *Thuja orientalis*. Bark is ash-gray, peeling off in vertical strips. Young branches are very slender, gray-green at first, finally turning brown. Wood is rather weak and branches are slender, allowing the tree to open in the center following heavy rains or snows.

FLOWERS: Inconspicuous.

FRUIT: Small and oblong; purplish, with bluish powdery bloom.

COLOR: Foliage is gray-green.

PROPAGATION: Cuttings: unfortunately they root very easily.

CULTURE: Tolerant of a wide range of growing conditions. Grows rapidly under most circumstances and frequently overgrows the site in a very short period of time. Similar to oriental arborvitae in the weakness of the branching, overall growth form, and extremely fast growth. Should not be planted.

PESTS: Very susceptible to juniper blight and bagworms.

NOTES: An extremely fast growing juniper under most circumstances, becoming a nuisance plant in a very short period of time. Also, because of the very spiny or stickery branches, it is very difficult to prune or work around in the landscape. Its extreme susceptibility to juniper blight makes it even more undesirable as it serves as a source of the disease to infect other, ordinarily less susceptible plants. Spiny Greek juniper is often sold as small balled-in-burlap or container grown plants in discount store parking lots or shopping centers. This is a worthless plant and should not be planted anywhere.

CULTIVARS: Several exist but with no particular merit or advantage over the species.

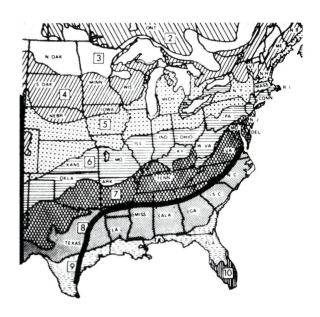

Juniperus sabina L.   Savin Juniper
Cupressaceae or Cypress Family   Hardiness Zone 4
Native from southwestern Europe to Siberia.
SIZE: Dependent on cultivar. Numerous cultivars present: most are the spreading type junipers of varying heights.
FORM: Spreading shrub, depending on cultivar.
TEXTURE: Fine.   **EXPOSURE:** Sun.

LEAVES: Scale-like and needle-like: most plants will have both. Crushed leaves are sticky and have an unpleasant odor in contrast to the sweet-smelling crushed foliage of Chinese junipers. Leaves are mostly light to medium green and are smaller, giving the plant a finer texture than most cultivars of Chinese or Rocky Mountain junipers.

STEM: Spreading horizontally, rather weak and flexible. Generally lacking the stem strength of Chinese juniper cultivars.

FLOWERS: Inconspicuous.

FRUIT: Bluish purple; 1/4 inch in diameter. Not commonly seen on most cultivars.

COLOR: Foliage is light green to medium green, depending on cultivar and time of year.

PROPAGATION: Semi-hardwood to hardwood cuttings under mist in fall and winter.

CULTURE: Tough, durable plant, tolerating dry conditions. Excels in sunny locations in a wide range of soil types. Avoid humid, shady locations because of disease susceptibility.

PESTS: Bagworms, spider mites, and juniper blight. 'Tamariscifolia' is one of the most susceptible juniper cultivars to blight.

NOTES: Desirability depends on cultivar. Many do not hold up well over long periods of time. Some savin juniper cultivars are the most susceptible of all junipers to juniper blight. Avoid planting in cool, shady locations or on north sides of structures. Should not be planted in the humid southeastern United States. In distinguishing savin junipers from other species, the most reliable features are the texture of foliage and the odor and stickiness of crushed young leaves.

CULTIVARS: 'Arcadia': low spreader with lacy, green foliage. 'Broadmoor': a very good, low spreader with dense, mounding form and deep green foliage. May be less susceptible to juniper blight. 'Buffalo': low-spreading cultivar with bright green foliage. Stays lower than 'Tamariscifolia'. 'Scandia': low spreader with dark green foliage. Similar to 'Buffalo' and 'Arcadia'. 'Tamariscifolia', tamarix juniper: once the most popular of the Savin junipers. Very attractive, with dark green foliage when young but opens in the center and becomes unsightly with age. Primary branches rise in the center, then descend horizontally, making a low, mounding form. May reach 4 feet tall with a 5 to 6 foot spread. Useful life span may be 8 to 12 years, depending on location. 'Von Ehron' an old cultivar. In overall form, looks and grows like a green 'Hetzi' Chinese juniper. A more rapid growth than 'Hetzii', frequently reaching 6 to 8 feet tall with a spread of 18 to 20 feet. A huge plant not useful in many locations. Winter color is poor. 'Blue Forest': grows 12 to 16 inches tall with near blue foliage. 'Blue Danube': grows 18 to24 inches, bluish green. 'Calgary Carpet': a selection from 'Arcadia', grows only 8 to 10 inches tall, with green foliage. Many other cultivars are available but few are recommended by this author.

'Tamariscifolia'

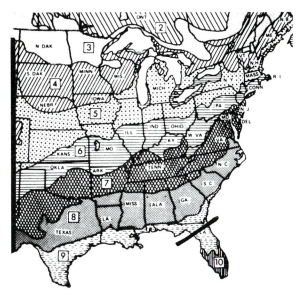

'Tamariscifolia'

'Von Ehron'

'Scandia'

J. sabina 'Buffalo'

J. sabina 'Broadmore'

J. sabina 'Arcadia'

J. scopulorum 'Blue Heaven'

'Blue Heaven'

J. scopulorum 'Columnaris'

Juniperus scopulorum Sarg. Rocky Mountain Juniper
Cupressaceae or Cypress Family Hardiness Zone 4
Native to the Rocky Mountains and western United States.
SIZE: Dependent on cultivar. Upright forms may reach 30 feet or more. Low spreaders exist which are similar to *Juniperus chinensis* and *J. virginiana* cultivars.
FORM: Upright or spreading shrubs or ground covers depending on cultivar.
TEXTURE: Fine. **EXPOSURE:** Sun.

LEAVES: Scale-like or needle-like, but mature foliage (scale-like) nearly always predominates: only occasionally are juvenile leaves seen. Branchlets frequently appear pressed into plume-like, vertical plates. Leaves on most plants are covered by a dense, waxy bloom, giving a blue or blue-gray cast, particularly on rapidly growing plants with young foliage.

STEM: Branches on most upright cultivars grow out and up. Central leader is less dominant than on upright *J. virginiana* cultivars. Bark peels in vertical strips on the older stems.

FLOWERS: Inconspicuous.

FRUIT: Blue-gray. Irregular, 1/8 inch in diameter; somewhat raisin-like.

COLOR: Foliage is blue to gray-green, depending on cultivar.

PROPAGATION: Roots poorly, if at all, from cuttings, thus is grafted onto *Juniperus chinensis* 'Hetzi' or oriental arborvitae rootstocks. Seedlings are variable.

CULTURE: An extremely tough, durable, and drought-tolerant plant. Does well in sunny locations throughout the Great Plains where it is native. Probably the best juniper for western Nebraska, Kansas, and Oklahoma. Intolerant of shade and poor soil drainage. Responds well to fertilizer. Not for humid areas of the Northeast or Southeast.

PESTS: Bagworms and spider mites. Juniper blight in humid areas. Root rot in wet soils.

NOTES: An extremely durable landscape plant for dry, exposed conditions. Many cultivars are available. Most are upright, dense, and blue-green in color. Foliage is very sticky when crushed and has a rather sweet aroma. Fruits are raisin-like.

CULTIVARS: 'Blue Heaven': moderately compact, pyramid form. Foliage is blue in appearance; maintains its color very well throughout the year. Other similar but more compact, upright, blue-gray cultivars include: 'Gray Gleam', 'Cologreen', 'Moonglow', 'Pathfinder', 'Welchi', 'Moffieti', 'Wichita Blue', and 'Erecta Glauca'. 'Columnaris' and 'Skyrocket': strict uprights, may reach height of 20 feet or more while spreading no more than 3 to 3 1/2 feet. Goodd substitutes for Italian cypress in the North and can be distinguished by foliage texture, odor of crushed foliage and young twig color. 'Hughes': often listed as *Juniperus horizontalis* but selected from Rocky Mountain juniper seedlings because of good prostrate growth and blue-green foliage in winter. Similar to *J. horizontalis* 'Wiltoni'. 'Pendula' pyramidal in form but with weeping new branches, 'Tomlinson Weeping': similar to 'Pendula'. Weeping forms can be very soft and attractive in certain landscape situations. 'Tabletop Blue': rich, silver-blue color with loose, oval growth habit. A rather flat-topped, large, vase-like shrub. Very attractive. 'Tollesons Weeping': upright, but drooping branches. Both blue and green selections. Many other cultivars exist.

RELATED SPECIES: *Juniperus virginiana* cultivars have a textural difference, lack any plate-like sections or organization of the foliage and are more horizontally branched, the fruit, although about the same size is rounded, not raisin-like, also the odor of the crushed foliage is different. *Juniperus chinensis* cultivars have much larger, round fruits and crushed new foliage that has a sweet aroma and is not sticky.

691

'Grey Gleam' sheared

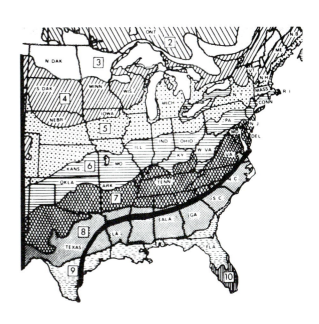

'Tabletop Blue'

'Grey Gleam' not sheared

'Silver King'

Juniperus squamata Buch-Ham 'Meyeri' Rehd.   Meyer or Fishtail Juniper
Cupressaceae or Cypress Family   Hardiness Zone 4
Native to China.

SIZE: Old plants may reach a height of 6 to 8 feet with a 6- to 7-foot spread. Moderate grower.

FORM: Very irregular, asymmetrical, much variation between plants unless sheared.

TEXTURE: Medium.   **EXPOSURE:** Sun.

LEAVES: All needle-like (none scale-like). Grayish to blue-green with 2 white bands on the upper leaf surface. Leaves are generally clustered or tufted on the ends of branches, sometimes creating fishtail-like appearance. Winter color is an unusual blue-purple. A small branch appears similar in leaf size, color, and texture to Japanese garden juniper, *Juniperus procumbens*.

STEM: Irregular, rather rugged and rigid. Generally the main stem branches profusely near the ground to give a dense globe form early, becoming more asymmetrical with age.

FLOWERS: Inconspicuous.

FRUIT: Brown to black in color with a single seed, not commonly seen.

COLOR: Foliage is an unusual blue to blue-green in summer; blue-purple in winter.

PROPAGATION: Semi-hardwood to hardwood cuttings taken in the fall or winter.

CULTURE: A tough, durable, and drought-tolerant plant. Tolerates a variety of growing conditions but not shade, or wet, poorly drained soil. Must have some sun for a portion of the day. Looks best when growing at a moderate to rapid rate. Loses its attractiveness and color when sheared or when growing very slowly. Must be allowed to grow irregularly.

PESTS: Occasionally bagworms, spider mites, juniper scale, or juniper blight, but worth the effort for its unusual effect.

NOTES: A different texture from all other juniper species or cultivars. Must be used with discretion in the landscape; color intensity and form make it rather dominant. Very asymmetrical. Most readily identified by its growth habit, needle-like, blue to blue-purple foliage color and the branch tufting. Some catalogs list 'Parsoni' as being a cultivar of *Juniperus squamata*, but this is incorrect because 'Parsoni' has multiple seeds, whereas *J. squamata* has a single seed. Parson's juniper is rightly *Juniperus davurica* 'Parsoni'.

CULTIVARS: 'Blue Star': a very slow growing, compact plant with a distinct, bluish foliage. 'Blue Alps': may reach 5 feet tall with silver-blue foliage. Striking. 'Blue Carpet' Grows only 8 to 10 inches tall but slowly spread. bluish gray foliage. 'Blue Swede': reminds one of pfitzer juniper, only with blue-green foliage. 'Holger': gray-green foliage and grows about 4 feet tall and may be 5 to 6 feet wide. 'Meyeri': featured here, is striking and different from other junipers. People tend to love it or hate it. I happen to like it. See the photographs and decide for yourself. Others exist.

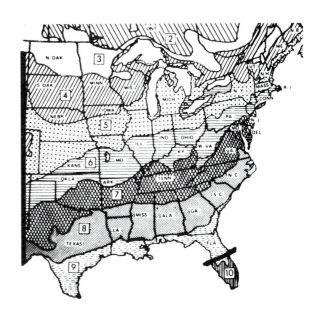

Juniperus virginiana L.   Eastern Redcedar
Cupressaceae or Cypress Family   Hardiness Zone 2
Native to eastern and central United States.
SIZE: Uprights may reach 30 feet or more with a 20-foot spread. Moderate to fast grower.
FORM: Upright or spreading junipers, depending on cultivar.
TEXTURE: Fine.   EXPOSURE: Sun.

LEAVES: Scale-like and needle-like leaves are both present on most plants. Relative amounts of juvenile (needle-like) and mature (scale-like) foliage will change with the growth rate, age, and individual seedlings. Foliage is medium to dark green during the growing season but may become a bronze-brown during the winter. New leaves have a distinct odor when crushed.

STEM: Strong central leaders on upright forms with nearly right angle secondary branching. On old stems, the bark peels in vertical strips; is rather ragged, almost furry in appearance. The main stem and major branches are rarely round in cross section. Wood is hard and decay resistant, used for fence posts and cedar chests.

FLOWERS: Female is inconspicuous; male is a small, yellow-brown cone.

FRUIT: Blue to blue-purple. About 1/4 inch round and smooth. Female trees may be covered with fruit by mid-summer, remaining so until early winter.

COLOR: Foliage is green to blue-green to nearly brown depending on cultivar and time of year. Fruit is blue to blue-purple.

PROPAGATION: Seed or grafting of selected cultivars. Cuttings generally root poorly.

CULTURE: Adapts to a wide range of soil types from hilltops to bottomland, but prefers a good, well drained soil. Growth rate is moderate to rapid, depending on site and fertility. Responds well to fertilization. All varieties respond well to pruning or shearing. Good as far west as western Nebraska, Kansas, and Oklahoma.

PESTS: Bagworms, spider mites, and juniper blight. The most susceptible juniper to cedar apple rust. Should not be planted near apples or hawthorns.

NOTES: A very diverse species. Color, form, and growth habit are variable between seedlings and cultivars. Winter color on most seedlings is a dull green-brown. *Juniperus virginiana* is probably the same plant as *J. silicicola* of the Florida peninsula. To distinguish from *Juniperus scopulorum*, *J. virginiana* has more bluish purple, round fruits, and crushed new foliage has a distinct odor and is not sticky, whereas *J. scopulorum* has fruits which are about the same size but raisin-like and quite blue, and foliage is sticky when crushed and has a distinct odor. A foliage textural difference also exists that can be observed with experience.

CULTIVARS: 'Canaert': upright, very picturesque if not sheared. Irregular, almost horizontal branches off the central leader: similar in appearance to *Juniperus chinensis* 'Torulosa', except the branches on 'Torulosa' tend to grow out and up, whereas 'Canaert' branches tend to be more horizontal. Prolific fruit producer in early fall but generally bare of fruit by mid-winter. It retains deep green color well throughout the winter. One of the best. 'Cupressifolia', hillspire juniper: has medium to dark green foliage, a narrow pyramidal form and finer texture than most cultivars. 'Glauca': sometimes listed as silver redcedar, pyramidal, with silver-gray foliage and an open, windswept appearance. 'Kosteri': slow-growing spreader, getting only 2 to 3 feet tall; dark green foliage. 'Manhattan Blue': pyramidal, upright, similar in appearance to *J. scopulorum* 'Blue Heaven'. Most easily distinguished by the odor of crushed foliage and the size and form of fruit, if present. 'Sky Rocket': narrow columnar form with silvery blue foliage. Many other cultivars exist.

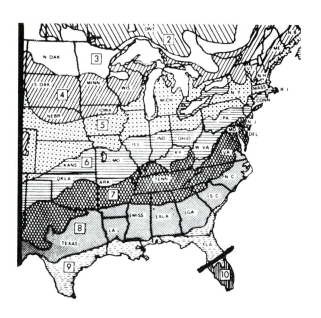

'Canaert'

'Canaert'

cedar-apple rust

Libocedrus decurrens Torr.   California Incense Cedar
    (Syn. *Calocedrus decurrens* Florin)
Pinaceae or Pine Family   Hardiness Zone 5
Native to Oregon and northern California.
SIZE: 30 to 40 feet tall with a 6- to 8-foot spread out of its native habitat. May reach 130 ft. in its native region. A very slow grower.
FORM: Narrowly columnar.
TEXTURE: Medium.   EXPOSURE: Sun.

LEAVES: Evergreen; lustrous, dark green. Foliage has a unique aroma when crushed. Pointed scale leaves only, generally forming a square branchlet (4-ranked), branchlets develop into flattened, vertical, plate-like sections, somewhat resembling an oriental arborvitae. A few inches below the current season's growth a few green leaves appear as an inlay on the older brown stem. Unique.

STEM: A strong central leader tree. Branches are retained to the ground in sunny locations. Older stems have a patchy bark with an irregular vertical line pattern. Wood is durable and wind resistant.

FLOWERS: Inconspicuous.

FRUIT: A small cone, 1 inch long, shaped like a large upside down raindrop. Light reddish brown, only near the tops of old trees.

COLOR: Foliage is a deep, dark green with excellent color retention in winter.

PROPAGATION: Seed or grafting, sometimes grafted onto oriental arborvitae rootstock.

CULTURE: Prefers a fertile, moist soil that is well drained, but is moderately tolerant. Tolerates tight clays fairly well and a wide range of growing conditions. Density of foliage and overall attractiveness will be influenced by growth response to the location. In areas of alkaline soils, it grows better when grafted onto oriental arborvitae rootstock.

PESTS: Bagworms occasionally. Some plants will occasionally lose an isolated branch from an unknown cause.

NOTES: A very attractive, upright, columnar landscape specimen. Excellent substitute for oriental arborvitae in that it is more attractive in the winter, more resistant to disease and insect pests, and slower growing. Should be planted more. Can be distinguished from oriental arborvitae, *Thuja orientalis*, by the deeper green foliage, the more pointed scale-like leaves, and the less regular plate-like sections of the branchlets. Also, California incense cedar has an upright central stem, whereas oriental arborvitae has many stems, no one being a central leader. A very beautiful and formal landscape specimen. One of the best conifers for many areas of Zones 5, 6 and 7 where a neat, upright, slow growing conifer is desired and full or nearly full sun is available.

CULTIVARS: None known.

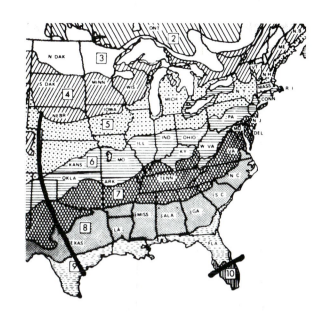

Picea abies (L.) Karst.   Norway Spruce
Pinaceae or Pine Family   Hardiness Zone 3
Native to north and central Europe.
SIZE: To 100 feet tall or more with spread of 20 to 30 feet. Moderate to rapid grower.
FORM: Pyramidal tree with drooping branches.
TEXTURE: Fine.   **EXPOSURE:** Sun to slight shade.

LEAVES: Simple, about 1/2 inch long, needle-like, rather blunt at the tip. Four-sided, thus will roll whereas leaves of fir species are flat. Leaf color is a medium to dark, dull green.

STEM: Young branches are slender and gray-green becoming yellow-brown with age and finally gray-brown and scaly. Main branches are horizontal or slightly upright with distinctly drooping secondary branches. Norway spruce is the only spruce with drooping branches commonly found in the United States. Wood is soft but not especially brittle.

FLOWERS: Inconspicuous.

FRUIT: Drooping, 4- to 6-inch elongated cones, mostly near the top of the tree. Smooth and green, turning brown and opening the thin scales with maturity.

COLOR: Foliage is a medium to dark, dull green.

PROPAGATION: Seed or grafting of selected cultivars.

CULTURE: Norway spruce tolerates an array of soil types and growing conditions, consequently has been planted extensively in Zones 3, 4, and 5. In the Prairie States and Zones 6 and 7, mulching assists establishment and growth, perhaps due to cooler soil temperatures and more favorable moisture conditions since it is rather shallowly rooted. Generally transplants easily.

PESTS: Mites are particularly troublesome in areas of heat build-up due to reflected light on buildings; spruce bud worm.

NOTES: A very attractive, pyramidal conifer, even with age. In most cases, the lower limbs should not be removed to give a full flowing effect. The specimen in the lower left corner of the adjacent page is in southeast Kansas in Zone 6 and adds a much needed effect. On the other hand, in Zones 3, 4, and 5, it may be overplanted, thus contributing to the growth of the problem with spruce mite and bud worms. The cones are useful as Christmas ornaments and many birds nest in the loose branches.

CULTIVARS: 'Acrocona' a semi-dwarf that rarely exceeds 20 feet tall. 'Clanbrassiliana' a low, dense, flat-topped shrub, rarely exceeding 4 feet tall. 'Pendula' all branches are especially drooping. Den Ouden and Boom in the ***Manual of Cultivated Conifers*** list over 60 cultivars. Several of these are present in dwarf conifer collections such as at the National Arboretum in Washington, D.C. and Golden Gate Park in San Francisco, California.

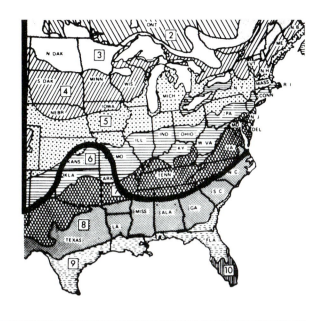

Picea pungens Engelm.　　　　　　　Colorado Blue Spruce
Pinaceae or Pine Family　　　　　　　Hardiness Zone 2
Native to the Rocky Mountains.

SIZE: 80 to 100 feet tall. Rarely reaching more than 30 to 40 feet with a 10- to 20-foot spread in the Midwest and East. Very slow grower.
FORM: Stiffly pyramidal, with horizontal branches in whorls to the ground if not pruned off and the location is sunny.
TEXTURE: Fine.　　　　　　　　　　**EXPOSURE:** Sun to partial shade.

LEAVES: Stiff, sharp-pointed needles, 1 to 1 1/2 inches long with 3 to 4 sides. Needles are single, not in clusters, and may be retained 4 to 6 years. Green to blue-green, covered with a powdery glaucous bloom. Needles are distributed most of the way around the branches.

STEM: A stout, central leader with thick, gray-brown, deeply furrowed bark. Branches are horizontal and stout, smooth and light orange-brown when young. Winter buds are conical, orange-brown, and prominent. Wood is stout and durable.

FLOWERS: Inconspicuous.

FRUIT: A drooping cone, 2 to 4 inches long. Light brown with long, thin, flexible scales, generally only in the very top of old trees.

COLOR: Foliage is green to blue-green to almost bluish white with some cultivars.

PROPAGATION: Seed or grafting of cultivars. Very difficult to root from cuttings.

CULTURE: Adapted to high altitudes generally with cool soil and night temperatures. For best growth in the Great Plains, mulch with 3 to 4 inches of pine bark, pecan hulls, or other suitable material to reduce the soil temperature and retain moisture. Locating the plant on the north or east side of a building or other groupings of plants for protection from the southwesterly winds will also help in Kansas and Nebraska. Somewhat difficult to transplant and establish.

PESTS: None serious, but bud mites or spider mites may be an occasional problem.

NOTES: A very formal attractive plant. Excellent specimen plant, but tends to dominate a landscape with the striking blue foliage color. Very formal appearance and overall attractiveness. Frequently planted in small gardens or confined areas where it overgrows the site. Foliage and branching do not develop well if crowded by another tree or large shrub. On the other hand, branches develop fairly well in the diffused light on the north side of most buildings. *Picea*, spruce, can be distinguished from the firs, *Abies*, in that the spruce have sharply pointed multi-sided needles, whereas firs have flat needles with rounded ends.

CULTIVARS: 'Glauca' leaves are a blue to blue-white. This is a collective name for all blue or blue-gray seedlings or cultivars. 'Koster', Koster blue spruce, a very deep, powdery blue-white cultivar. Dense pyramidal growth. 'Hoopsii' and 'Thompsenii' are similar. 'Fat Albert': a broadly pyramidal grower with flue foliage. Very striking. Numerous other cultivars exist, differing only slightly in the intensity of the blue to blue-gray foliage color.

RELATED SPECIES: *Picea glauca* 'Densata' Bailey, Black Hills spruce, is a compact, slow growing form with deep green foliage and a finer texture than Colorado blue spruce. Similar in adaptability and tolerance.

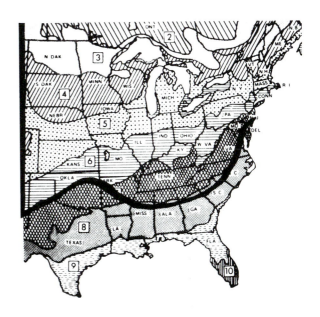

'Koster'

Picea glauca 'Densata'

Picea glauca 'Densata'

Pinus cembroides Zucc. 'Edulus'   Pinyon Pine
Pinaceae or Pine Family   Hardiness Zone 4
Native to the southwestern United States.
SIZE: 20 to 30 feet tall with a 15- to 20-foot spread. Slow grower.
FORM: Pyramidal, upright, central leader, small tree.
TEXTURE: Medium to fine.   **EXPOSURE:** Sun.

LEAVES: Stiff, stout, 1 to 1 1/2 inches long. In bundles of 2, frequently tightly appressed one to the other, looking like only one needle is present. Dark green to blue-green. Naturally occurring varieties of pinyon pine exist with 1 or 3 needles per cluster (fascicle).

STEM: Upright, central leader, pyramidal when young, becoming a round-headed, low tree with age. Bark on mature trees is thin and scaly. Branchlets are dark orange and resinous. Branches tend to be spreading, usually all the way to the ground unless shaded by other vegatation.

FLOWERS: Inconspicuous.

FRUIT: A short-stocked cone, yellowish to red-brown, with very few but large scales, somewhat flattened and irregular. Grotesque looking. Seeds are very large, sometimes 1/4 to 1/2 inch long. Edible.

COLOR: Foliage is dark green to blue-green.

PROPAGATION: Seed.

CULTURE: An extremely tough and drought-resistant, small tree. Tolerates a wide range of soil types and exposures. Well adapted to dry, rocky, poor soils where other plants would grow poorly, if at all. An attractive specimen for a hot, dry location with poor soils and drying winds. However, pinyon pine will not tolerate wet, heavy, clay soils.

PESTS: Pine tip moth may kill some new branches, but in most cases this only tends to make the tree more compact and densely branched since it has a pruning effect.

NOTES: A most attractive, slow growing, compact pine. May be used as a specimen shrub or small tree in hot, dry locations throughout the Midwest. This tree has a great deal of merit and has probably been overlooked as a good, low maintenance landscape shrub or small tree. Primary identification features are the two short needles tightly appressed, slow growth, resinous stem, and if present, the irregular cone.

CULTIVARS: Several cultivars or races exist; however, 'Edulus' is probably the most ornamental.

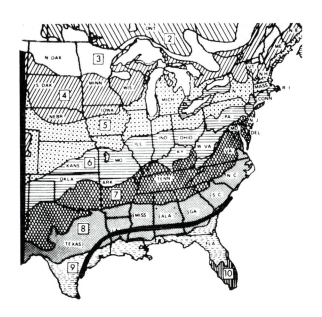

Pinus densiflora Siebold. & Zucc.   Japanese Red Pine
Pinaceae or Pine Family   Hardiness Zone 5
Native to Japan.

SIZE: 60 to 80 feet tall at maturity except 'Umbraculifera' which rarely exceeds 30 feet and forms an umbrella-like crown. Slow to moderate grower.
FORM: Irregular pine with many artistic forms: asymmetrical and attractive.
TEXTURE: Fine.   **EXPOSURE:** Sun.

LEAVES: In clusters of 2, remaining 2 or 3 years. Slender, somewhat twisted but not as much as scotch pine. Leaves are 3 to 5 inches long, bright green, and attractive during the growing season, slightly less attractive during winter.

STEM: Irregularly growing pine; may have a straight stem or may be leaning or irregularly branching to develop many interesting forms. Young stems are smooth, developing a shallowly furrowed and flaky red-orange to orange-brown bark. Winter buds are dark cinnamon-red and fuzzy. Very distinct. Branch color is less intense than on scotch pine. Old stems develop a gray-brown bark with only remnants of the red-orange color where the bark splits. Wood is moderately stout and durable.

FLOWERS: Inconspicuous, monoecious.

FRUIT: A cone about 2 inches long and triangular, broadest at the base. Singly or in clusters, opening the second year and may remain on the tree for an additional year. Cones have a very short spine.

COLOR: Foliage is bright green, young branches are red-orange or orange-brown.

PROPAGATION: Seed, grafting, or cuttings of selected cultivars.

CULTURE: Grows well on a diversity of soils but will not tolerate poorly drained, heavy clays. Responds to fertilizer and good cultural practices with increased foliage density. Easy to transplant either from containers or ball in burlap.

PESTS: Unlike most pines, pine tip moth is rarely a problem. Likewise, few foliage diseases bother Japanese red pine. Scale insects may be a problem in rare instances.

NOTES: A most interesting and informal pine. Does not form the classical Christmas tree, pyramidal pine, especially with age. Not widely planted but should be used more where informal plantings or asymmetrical specimen plants are desired. Sometimes confused with scotch pine, however, scotch pine has shorter and thicker needles that are more twisted, often blue-green, and a more orange bark on young limbs. If all else fails, compare the winter buds: scotch has a small yellow-brown bud, whereas Japanese red pine has a red-brown bud that is quite fuzzy.

CULTIVARS: Tanyosho pine, *Pinus densiflora* 'Umbraculifera' is a multiple-stemmed tree with a broad, umbrella crown and distinctive, rich, bright green leaves. Slow growing but may reach 25 to 30 feet tall with age. One of the finest small ornamental pines, but should be given room to grow. Few evergreen large shrubs or small trees have the grace and grandeur of this plant. Because it must be rooted from cuttings or grafted onto seedlings and grows slowly, it is expensive, but worth the cost. Many other cultivars exist, but are not common in the nursery trade.

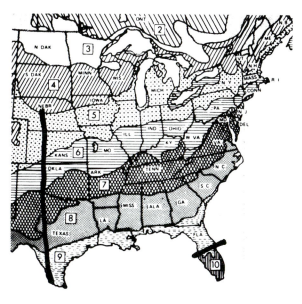

'Umbraculifera'

'Umbraculifera'

Pinus echinata   Shortleaf Pine
Pinaceae or Pine Family   Hardiness Zone 6
Native to southeastern United States west to Texas and Oklahoma.
SIZE: 80 to 100 feet tall on good soils, rarely more than 50 to 70 feet in urban areas.
Moderate to fast grower.
FORM: Pyramidal, upright, slightly irregular.
TEXTURE: Fine.   EXPOSURE: Sun or slight shade.

LEAVES: 3 to 5 inches long, soft, flexible; generally dark green. Not twisted, in clusters of 2, rarely with 3. Good winter color except during severe winters in Zones 6 or 7 when some yellowing may occur. However, better winter color than slash or loblolly pine.

STEM: Young branches are reddish brown to dark brown and soon develop a bark pattern unlike the smooth young branches of spruce pine. The terminal bud is small, sharply pointed and reddish brown. The old stem fissures into large, irregular plates, reddish to gray-brown in color, rather attractive. Wood is fairly stout but brittle.

FLOWERS: Inconspicuous.

FRUIT: A cone, 2 to 3 inches long, rather ovate; armed with a small, sharp spine.

COLOR: Generally dark green except during a severe winter.

PROPAGATION: Seed.

CULTURE: Grows well on wide range of soils including poor rocky or gravelly soils of low fertility. Prefers well drained soils but tolerates all but the heaviest, poorly drained clay. Responds to fertilizers and good cultural practices.

PESTS: Pine tip moth is a serious problem on young trees until 8 to 10 years old. Bark beetles may attack trees under stress. Foliar diseases are generally not a problem.

NOTES: Shortleaf pine makes a good massing or canopy tree, especially when a piney woods effect is desired. Makes an excellent over story canopy for azaleas and other sensitive broadleaf evergreens. Shortleaf pine has received little attention by the nursery trade as it does not grow as straight and tall as loblolly or slash pine. However, in the Upper South it should be considered for many landscape uses. A widely adapted and useful pine. Can be distinguished from spruce pine by the straight needles that are slightly longer and the roughly textured young branches, whereas spruce pine has twisting needles that are slightly shorter and smooth, young branches plus the irregular growth habit.

CULTIVARS: None known.

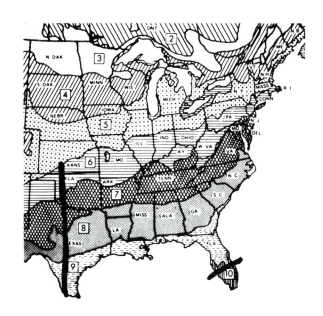

Pinus elliotti Engelm.   Slash Pine
Pinaceae or Pine Family   Hardiness Zone 7
Native to the southeastern United States.
SIZE: 80 to 100 feet tall over most of its range with a 30- to 40-foot spread when grown as a single specimen. Rapid grower.
FORM: Narrowly pyramidal when young to more oval or flat-topped with age.
TEXTURE: Medium.   **EXPOSURE:** Sun.

LEAVES: 8 to 10 inches long, in clusters of 2 and 3; generally light to medium green during the growing season. Winter color is a medium green, slightly darker than loblolly pine. Leaves tend to be clustered at the ends of branches giving a light-textured shade.

STEM: Upright, central leader with nearly right angle secondary branching. Moderately durable wood. Twigs are roughened with spreading scales. Tufts of leaves at the tips of branches give a broom effect. Bark on old stem breaks up into large flat plates.

FLOWERS: Inconspicuous.

FRUIT: Light brown cone, 4 to 6 inches long on a distinct stalk, dropping from the tree by the end of the second year. Each of the scales on the cone has a small recurved spine. The dropping of the cones during the second year and the presence of a distinct stalk on the cone are the best features to distinguish slash pine from loblolly pine which holds its cones for several years in the crown of the tree and cones have very little, if any, stalk.

COLOR: Foliage is light to medium green during the growing season, medium green during winter.

PROPAGATION: Seed.

CULTURE: Native to wet woodlands, swampy areas, shallow ponds, and bays along the Gulf Coast. However, slash pine tolerates a moderate range of soil conditions and some drought. One of the best pines to use in poorly drained areas. By contrast, most species of pine are intolerant of poorly drained soils. Responds to fertilization and cultivation to reduce weed and grass competition. Some of the newer cultivars or seedling strains of slash pine will grow several feet per year in the southeastern states.

PESTS: May be attacked by pine tip moth and fusiform rust in the South.

NOTES: Not very ornamental alone; however, because of its rapid growth and loose crown, it makes an excellent overstory for other shrubs such as azaleas, camellias, and dogwoods. Also serves well as a background plant particularly in areas where excessive moisture may be a problem at times during the year.

CULTIVARS: Several seedling selections exist for rapid growth, primarily used for reforestation in the Southeast.

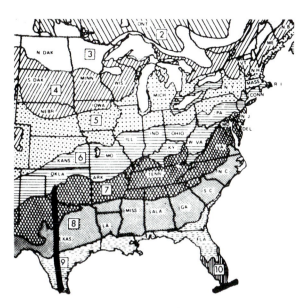

Pinus glabra Walt.   Spruce Pine
Pinaceae or Pine Family   Hardiness Zone 7
Native to the Gulf Coast, Louisiana to South Carolina.
SIZE: 60 to 80 feet tall at maturity, more common as a 30- to 40-foot tree with a 20- to 30-foot spread. Moderate grower.
FORM: Irregular, asymmetrical tree until very old.
TEXTURE: Fine.   **EXPOSURE:** Sun or partial shade.

LEAVES: 3 to 4 inches long, in bundles of 2, slender and twisting. Generally longer and more slender than Scotch pine which twists similarly. Color is bright green in summer with only slight yellowing in winter. Leaf color in winter is superior to slash or loblolly pine.

STEM: Where shading is not a problem, branches are retained to the ground. The main stem is somewhat erratic and may curve or twist unlike most other pines. The young stem is slender and smooth with a very small terminal bud. Bark of the older branches and main stem is shallowly furrowed and flaking, reddish brown to gray-black in color. Wood is moderately stout and flexible, not damaged by ice or winds.

FLOWERS: Not showy. Male catkins are yellow; female flowers are inconspicuous.

FRUIT: A stout-stocked cone; ovoid, about 2 1/2 inches long, without spines.

COLOR: Bright green foliage, very attractive.

PROPAGATION: Seed.

CULTURE: Spruce pine is native to deep, sandy loam soils. However, it does well on the very sandy soils of northern and central Florida as well as moderate to heavy clays elsewhere. Tolerates all but the poorest and most compacted soils or where drainage is very poor. Does not appear to be as susceptible to pine tip moth as most other species. Appears to be resistant to needle blight and other leaf fungus problems observed on some other pines. Responds to supplemental watering, fertilization and elimination of grass competition as do all pines.

PESTS: None serious.

NOTES: A very attractive, asymmetrical pine until age 25 or more. Somewhat reminiscent of the irregular form of hollywood juniper. Foliage is loose and slightly drooping, yet dense enough to make an attractive visual barrier. Unlike the monotonous barriers or screens of many plants, spruce pines add a slight diversity of form with each plant. Not well known in the nursery trade but deserving of much more attention. Reportedly difficult to transplant; however, in studies in Florida and Oklahoma, I have not found this to be the case with either container- or field-grown trees. Hardy to -10 degrees F with desiccating winds and quite drought tolerant in studies in central Oklahoma. Some pines do poorly in shade or on the north side of tall structures; however, spruce pine grows well in moderate shade and lends a texture and color only available from a conifer. An excellent plant.

CULTIVARS: None known.

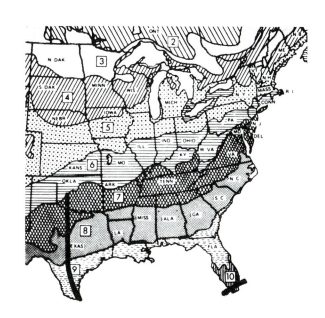

Pinus mugo Turra. 'Mughus'   Mugo Pine
          (Syn. *Pinus mugho*)
Pinaceae or Pine Family   Hardiness Zone 3
Native to Switzerland and Austria (parent plant)
SIZE: Maximum of 6 to 8 feet tall with a spread of 8 to 10 feet. Slow grower.
FORM: An oval or round-topped shrub. One of the few shrub pines available.
TEXTURE: Medium.   EXPOSURE: Sun or slight shade.

LEAVES: In bundles of 2, generally about 1 1/2 to 2 inches long, moderately stiff but **not** twisted. Medium to dark green, attractive.

STEM: Irregular, forming a dense shrub. May be pruned in spring to assist overall form. Winter buds are light brown and small with rounded tips, very similar to scotch pine. However, scotch pine is a tree form with twisted needles and an orange bark on young branches.

FLOWERS: Inconspicuous.

FRUIT: A small ovoid cone; 1 1/2 to 2 inches long, about equally wide. Made somewhat inconspicuous by the dense foliage.

COLOR: Foliage is medium to dark green. Attractive.

PROPAGATION: Seed or grafting of cultivars. Difficult to root from cuttings.

CULTURE: Well adapted to the upper Midwest and northeastern portion of the United States. Does moderately well with some protection either on the north or east side of buildings in Kansas, Missouri, and Oklahoma. Tolerates most soils and some drought but not prolonged wet conditions. Will stand exposure in the northeastern United States. Best suited for Zone 7 and northward. Responds well to pruning in the spring.

PESTS: Pine tip moth may become serious in some locations.

NOTES: An outstanding specimen shrub where it can be grown. It is not well adapted to the deep South and Gulf Coast area as it needs longer days during summer to sustain growth and tolerance to high temperatures. In the western Great Plains, it is best used on northern or eastern exposures which give some protection from the hot, dry, southwest winds. There it will function as an excellent landscape plant.

CULTIVARS: There are numerous cultivars of mugo pine; however, 'Mughus' seedlings as described here are most widely grown in the United States. These dwarf forms are not consistent, but in general, form an oval- or round-topped shrub of good landscape quality. Since cultivars are difficult to root from cuttings or graft, seedlings will probably remain the primary plant form available in the nursery trade.

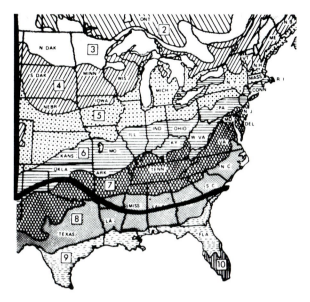

Pinus nigra Arnold.   Austrian Pine
Pinaceae or Pine Family   Hardiness Zone 4
Native to central and southern Europe and Asia.
SIZE: Large tree: 60 to 80 feet tall with a spread of 30 to 40 feet. Slow grower.
FORM: Pyramidal when young, more or less oval after reaching considerable size. May develop a flat top on some sites at maturity.
TEXTURE: Medium.   **EXPOSURE:** Sun.

LEAVES: 3 to 6 inches long, in bundles of 2; often curving or twisting in groups, rarely straight. Generally retained for 2 or 3 years on good sites. Needles are quite stiff and dark, very rich green. Tend to be tufted on the ends of the branches, making the tree somewhat open internally.

STEM: A central leader tree, branches nearly at right angles in whorls or clusters around the main stem. Durable wood, fairly wind and ice resistant. Winter buds are pencil point-shaped, 1/2 to 1 inch long with recurved white bud scale, "star-burst" or "flower-like".

FLOWERS: Female are inconspicuous but male flowers (catkins) are noticeable in spring.

FRUIT: Light brown, woody cone. Borne singly or in clusters, oval, 2 1/2 to 4 inches long. Does not have prickles. Cones fall at maturity each year.

COLOR: Foliage is a rich, dark green. Very attractive. Good contrast to other plants in the landscape since it is among the darkest of foliage colors.

PROPAGATION: Seed.

CULTURE: Rivals all pines in durability under adverse conditions. Will grow in very low rainfall areas and in rather moist soils. Will tolerate salt and wind. Transplants moderately well. The principal concern is to aid its establishment the first 1 or 2 growing seasons. Grows well in the Texas Panhandle, eastern Colorado, and western Nebraska where choices of trees are few.

PESTS: Pine twig blight may be serious some seasons and needle blight. Resistant to pine tip moth. Herbicide vapors are causing a slow decline of Austrian pines over most of the United States. As a result, I no longer recommend the species.

NOTES: An outstanding tree. The deep, dark color makes it a good background tree for general landscape use. Can be used as a specimen when young. Frequently confused with *Pinus thungergiana*, Japanese black pine. The principle difference is Japanese black pine has long, white winter buds with rounded tips and needles that rarely twist or curve. Japanese black pine is less symmetrical and a faster grower than Austrian pine under most conditions with needles that are retained longer, giving a denser internal appearance.

CULTIVARS: Several exist but are not commonly cultivated in this country.

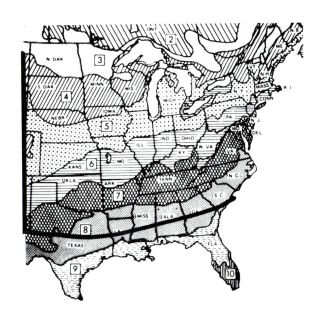

Pinus palustris Mill.   Longleaf Pine
Pinaceae or Pine Family   Hardiness Zone 7
Native to the Gulf Coast Northward to Virginia.

SIZE: 80 to 100 feet tall at maturity. Grows slowly the first few years in the "grass" stage, then grows at a moderate rate under good growing conditions, but never like the fast growth of slash and loblolly pine.

FORM: Straight trunk and oval crown.

TEXTURE: Coarse compared to other pines.   **EXPOSURE:** Sun or slight shade.

LEAVES: 3 per bundle, 8 to 15 inches or more in length. Shorter on mature trees, tufted at the ends of branches. Slender and flexible giving a weeping appearance. Dark green with good winter color except during severe weather near its northern limit.

STEM: Straight, central stem with nearly horizontal branches and foliage tufted at the ends, gives a unique open appearance. Wood is strong and durable. Bark on the main stem is orange-brown to gray-brown, forming large, thin, irregular scales. The dormant bud is silvery white and quite large, often 1/2 inch in diameter.

FLOWERS: Inconspicuous.

FRUIT: A large cone, 6 to 10 inches long. Cylinder-shaped, hanging down, with a small spine at the tip of each scale.

COLOR: Foliage is dark green.

PROPAGATION: Seed.

CULTURE: Native to sandy soils and poor soils throughout the Gulf Coast. Not often planted as an urban tree but tolerates urban conditions fairly well except for very heavy clays that are poorly drained. The slow growing "grass" stage for the first 3 to 5 years makes it unacceptable to nurserymen; however, air-root-pruning and high fertility levels in containers can speed growth substantially.

PESTS: Occasionally bark bettles attack old trees when under stress; however, longleaf pine is resistant to fusiform rust which is a serious problem on slash and loblolly pines.

NOTES: An attractive, large tree with a unique, open crown and drooping leaf character. Provides light, shifting shade for growing tender ornamentals. Tolerates the long, hot summers and reflected heat of urban conditions, once established. Probably should be used more where a light-textured shade is desired over an area. With new nursery techniques of root control and rapid root development following transplanting, longleaf pine may become a more common nursery item.

CULTIVARS: None known.

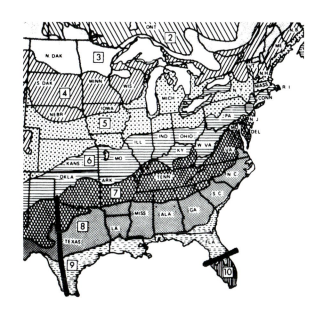

Pinus pinaster Ait.   Cluster or Maritime Pine
Pinaceae or Pine Family   Hardiness Zone 6
Native to the Mediterranean Region.
SIZE: 40 to 80 feet tall with a 20- to 30-foot spread. Moderate to rapid growth rate.
FORM: Oval to pyramidal tree with heavy, dense foliage.
TEXTURE: Medium to coarse.   EXPOSURE: Sun.

LEAVES: Mostly in bundles of 2, 6 to 9 inches long. A bright, light green; stiff, glossy, somewhat twisted. Largest needle diameter of the pines found in the United States. Foliage color stands out in the landscape.

STEM: Central, upright, main stem with nearly right angle branching in whorls. Young branchlets are slightly red-brown. Bark on an older tree is thick, red-gray or red-brown, less striking bark color than scotch pine but very noticeable. Deeply fissured into narrow, vertical ridges covered with small scales. Winter bud is 1 to 2 inches long with the bud scales curved back, making it appear like an ornamental candle. Purple-brown in appearance, very attractive and unique.

FLOWERS: Inconspicuous.

FRUIT: Broad, ovate cone on a short stalk, 3 to 6 inches long, 2 to 3 inches in diameter. Purplish when young, shining light brown when ripe. Sometimes retained several years.

COLOR: Foliage is a bright, light green; glossy, very attractive.

PROPAGATION: Seed or grafting of selected cultivars.

CULTURE: Well adapted to much of Zones 6 and 7. Thrives on well drained soils but tolerates clay soils. Drought-resistant, performing well in western Oklahoma and Texas. Tolerates salt and alkaline soils. Responds with vigor to fertilizer and good cultural practices. Young seedling trees are more sensitive to winter temperatures and drying winds than are larger specimens. Somewhat difficult to transplant as a 6- to 8-foot tree balled-in-burlap. On the other hand, container grown plants transplant well, especially in the spring. Apparently root regeneration is slow following transplanting, especially when the top is dormant.

PESTS: None serious although some damage from pine tip moth may occur while young. However, herbicide vapors cause a slow decline so as to make ti questionable to plant.

NOTES: A very attractive, bold pine in the landscape. Light green color is quite different from the characteristic pine color of other species and cultivars. Useful in the landscape as a background plant, specimen, or for windbreaks. Most easily identified by the delicate purplish winter buds, large diameter needles and the light green color. Not widely grown at the present time but deserves more attention in Zones 6, 7, and 8.

CULTIVARS: Numerous cultivars exist; however, they are not common in the United States.

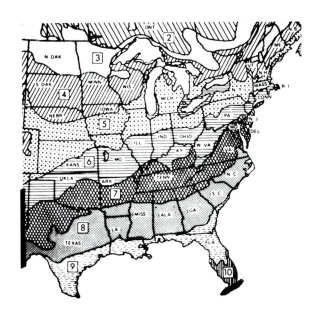

Pinus ponderosa Dougl.　　　　　　　　　Ponderosa or Western Yellow Pine
Pinaceae or Pine Family　　　　　　　　　Hardiness Zone 5
Native to the western U.S.

SIZE: 100 to 125 feet tall in its native range, 40 to 60 feet in most landscape situations. Slow to moderate growth rate.

FORM: Upright, open, somewhat pyramidal tree.

TEXTURE: Coarse, bunchy growth.　　　　　**EXPOSURE:** Sun.

LEAVES: Dark gray-green needles, 6 to 16 inches long, in bundles of 2 or 3. Large in diameter and moderately flexible. Long needles in bunches at the ends of branches give a broom effect.

STEM: A central leader with whorls of branches nearly at right angles to the main stem. Foliage tends to be tufted at the ends of the branches. Young twigs or branches are heavy, dark brown or nearly black. Winter buds are rather oblong, brown, and very resinous, appear as though covered by drops of wax. Bark on older trees is plate-like, gray-brown to black and quite rough. In its native range, bark may be more red, red-orange, to red-brown.

FLOWERS: Female are inconspicuous, male flowers (catkins) are noticeable in spring.

FRUIT: A cone. Ovate to oblong, 3 to 6 inches long on a short stalk. Light red-brown when mature, matures in 2 years. Has a very sharp prickle on each scale.

COLOR: Foliage is dark gray-green.

PROPAGATION: Seed.

CULTURE: Well adapted to dry areas with low humidity and wind. Withstands considerable drought, grows in most soils, even poor rocky soils but will not tolerate excessively wet sites and/or poor soil drainage. Tolerates heat and cold. A very tough, durable pine well adapted to the Great Plains. Not for general use.

PESTS: Heart rot, some insect damage, especially pine tip moth when young. Herbicide vapors may be affecting this species.

NOTES: Not particularly ornamental, but well adapted to a wide range. Works well as background foliage for massing, windbreaks, and to a lesser degree, shade. Best identified by the large diameter, gray-green needles of considerable length, and the heavy dark branches and prickly cone.

CULTIVARS: None commonly grown.

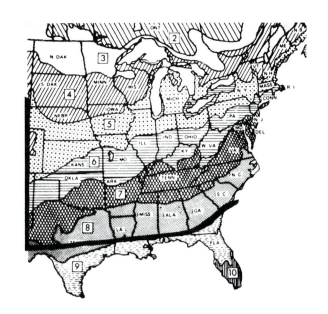

Pinus resinosa Ait.   Red or Norway Pine
Pinaceae or Pine Family   Hardiness Zone 2
Native to northeastern United States and southeastern Canada.
SIZE: 40 to 80 feet tall, 20 to 30 feet wide. Moderate grower.
FORM: Broad, pyramidal tree.
TEXTURE: Fine.   EXPOSURE: Sun.

LEAVES: In clusters of 2, dark green, 4 to 6 inches long. Flexible, dense, remaining for 3 or 4 years. Finely toothed on the margin. Very similar in appearance to Austrian pine; however, an easy way to distinguish the two is that red pine needles will bend then snap, whereas Austrian pine needles will simply continue to bend.

STEM: Young stems are thick and stout, orange-brown, turning reddish brown. The terminal bud is narrowly oval, about 1/2 inch long, resinous, light brown with a few loose scales but nothing like the starburst of bud scales on Austrian pine. Old bark is shallowly furrowed, reddish brown. Wood is light weight but strong, pale reddish brown.

FLOWERS: Generally inconspicuous.

FRUIT: A cone. Oval, 2 to 2 1/2 inches long; singly or in pairs, attached directly to the stem, no stalk, light brown, with no spines on the scales. Opens to release the seed the first year and persists for 2 more years. Sometimes confused with jack pine which has shorter, more slender needles and cones have distinct spines, are curved and persist on the tree for many years.

COLOR: Foliage is dark green.

PROPAGATION: Seed.

CULTURE: Red pine is native to sandy soils in the cool northeast states and southeastern Canada. However, is adaptable to many soils in urban situations and is at least moderately drought tolerant. Specimens in Wichita, Kansas and Tulsa, Oklahoma tolerate drying winds and periodic droughts with no apparent detrimental effects. However, growth is slower in this area than in the Northeast. Not tolerant to "wet feet", poorly drained soils, especially heavy clays. Transplants reasonably well, about like Austrian and scotch pine.

PESTS: Pine tip moth, especially when young.

NOTES: An attractive pine, neat in appearance and striking due to the dense foliage on most specimens. Overall appearance is similar to Austrian pine. See stem and leaf sections for distinguishing features. Austrian bark is gray-brown, whereas red pine has reddish brown bark. A useful landscape tree for the northern states, generally above Zone 6 where growth is faster, especially on sandy loam soils. Can be grown in Zones 6, 7, and 8; however, other species such as Japanese black pine, spruce pine, and cluster pine are better suited to these areas.

CULTIVARS: 'Globosa': shorter needles and rounded form.

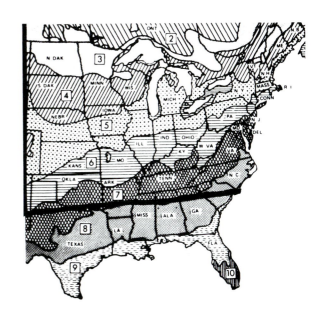

Pinus strobus L.   White Pine
Pinaceae or Pine Family   Hardiness zone 3
Native to the northeastern U.S.

SIZE: 80-120 feet tall in its native habitat; shorter in most urban areas. Moderate to rapid grower.

FORM: Pyramidal when young, becoming more oval-crowned with age.

TEXTURE: Fine.   **EXPOSURE:** Sun to partial shade.

LEAVES: In clusters of 5, very soft, flexible, and slender. Generally with a blue or blue-gray cast to the young needles; medium green to blue-green during the remainder of the year. Tends to be tufted on the outer portions of the branches. Gives a very soft, delicate texture in the landscape.

STEM: Straight, central leader. Secondary branches develop at right angles in whorls. Bark on young trees is thin, smooth, ash gray. On old trees, bark divides into irregular patches or ridges.

FLOWERS: Female are inconspicuous, but male catkins are noticeable in the spring, monoecious.

FRUIT: Long, slender cone, frequently reaching 7 to 8 inches long, 2 to 2 1/2 inches in diameter; with large scales. Has no prickle or spine on the scales.

COLOR: Foliage is a medium green to blue-green.

PROPAGATION: Seed or grafting of selected cultivars.

CULTURE: Does well thoughout a wide range of the northeastern United States. Tolerates climates of eastern Nebraska and Kansas, Missouri, Indiana, Kentucky, Tennessee and mountainous areas of the Carolinas quite well. It is not adapted to the lower regions of the South or the Southwest. Tolerant to a wide range of soils as long as they are moderately well drained. Will not tolerate wet, swampy conditions even for short periods. Somewhat drought tolerant. The limiting factor in the Great Plains region appears to be an intolerance for sustained high temperature and drought unless shaded somewhat. Day length is the limiting factor for growing white pine in the Lower South, where day length has less fluctuation with the seasons.

PESTS: White pine blister rust in the Northeast may be serious some seasons. Occasionally other pests create problems.

NOTES: A very soft-textured pine, very attractive. An excellent background plant or specimen where it can be grown. Very similar in appearance, growth habit, and overall landscape use to *Pinus flexilis* James, the limber pine, and the western white pine, *Pinus strobiformis* Sarg. Limber pine appears to be slightly more tolerant to the dry conditions of the Midwest portions of the United States. Selections of western white pine from New Mexico appear better adapted to the South and Southwest.

CULTIVARS: 'Glauca': leaves are bluer than those of the typical form. Occurs fairly commonly in seed beds. 'Prostrate': prostrate stems, branches at first horizontal and soon spreading over the ground. Original plant found at the Arnold Arboretum in the late 1800s. 'Radiata': dwarf, globular, very compact shrub form, rarely reaching more than 3 feet tall. 'Umbraculifera': broad, umbrella-shaped shrub with crowded branchlets; glabrous, reddish brown, with drooping leaves. Others exist.

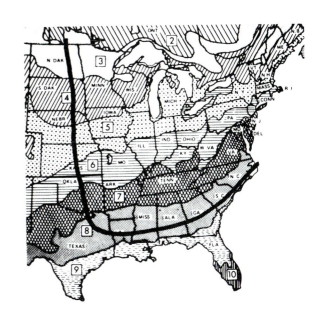

Pinus sylvestris L. Scotch Pine (Scot's Pine)
Pinaceae or Pine Family Hardiness Zone 2
Native to Europe and Asia.
SIZE: 60 to 80 feet tall with a spread of 30 to 40 feet. Moderate grower.
FORM: Pyramidal, formal, upright tree while young; becoming round-topped, quite irregular and picturesque with age.
TEXTURE: Medium. **EXPOSURE:** Sun.

LEAVES: 1 to 3 inches long, in bundles of 2; twisted and stiff. Generally light green to sometimes blue-green on young trees during the growing season, medium green to somewhat yellow-green in winter. Generally 2 seasons of needles are present on the tree at all times.

STEM: Upright, with nearly right-angle branching on most plants. Orange to red-orange bark on limbs from 1 to 6 inches in diameter. Bark color is a useful identification feature. The main stem tends to become irregular with age, frequently becoming a picturesque tree. Winter buds are a light purple-brown, about 1/2 inch long, rounded at the tip. Foliage is very similar to mugo pine, particularly on young plants in the nursery.

FLOWERS: Monoecious. Female are inconspicuous but male catkins are noticeable in spring.

FRUIT: A short-stocked cone without spines, 1 1/2 to 2 inches long, more or less rounded. Rather dull brown; falling at maturity.

COLOR: Foliage is medium green to blue-green to yellow-green, depending on the season, cultivar and exposure.

PROPAGATION: Seed or grafting of selected cultivars.

CULTURE: A tough, durable pine for much of the Midwest and Northeast. Not for extreme western Kansas, Nebraska or Dakotas. Tolerates heavy and light soils, moist conditions, some drought, sun, or light shade. Responds well to pruning and is frequently used in commercial Christmas tree production. Very formal when young, becoming picturesque with age. Responds well to fertilizer and improved growing conditions. Naturalized in some areas of the northeastern United States.

PESTS: None serious, but pine tip moth may damage young trees. Herbicide vapors are damaging scotch pine to the point that I no longer recommend planting it.

NOTES: A good tree for screen or windbreak, background, massing, or for developing shade for growing other plants. Makes a good background tree for contrast for spring flowering shrubs or annuals. Easily transplanted.

Sometimes confused with *Pinus densiflora*, Japanese red pine, which is similar in hardiness and adaptability. However, Japanese red pine has longer needles with less twisting and retains cones longer, tends to be a more open and somewhat more symmetrical tree, particularly at an early age, than is scotch pine.

CULTIVARS: 'Argentia' leaves are a pronounced silvery green. 'Fastigata' columnar form with branches ascending. 'Globosa', sometimes listed as 'Glauca Nana': dwarf, globular, slow growing, more shrub-like, rarely reaching more than 5 to 6 feet tall. Not commonly available. 'French Blue': a seedling-grown selection with more bluish foliage. Numerous others could be selected because of the variability of the common seed; however, difficulty in grafting or rooting from cuttings limits the general practice of separating cultivars.

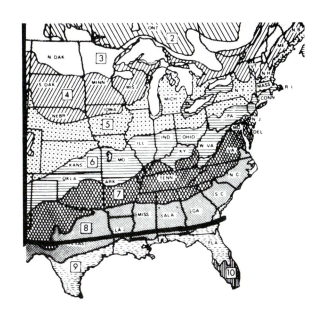

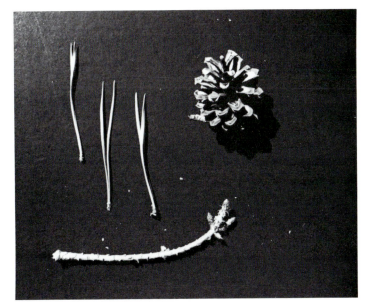

Pinus taeda L.   Loblolly Pine
Pinaceae or Pine Family   Hardiness Zone 6
Native to the southeastern United States.
SIZE: 80 to 100 feet tall over most of its range, with a spread of 30 to 50 feet when competition from other plants is minimal. Moderate to rapid grower.
FORM: Pyramidal when young, becomes more oval with age.
TEXTURE: Medium.   **EXPOSURE:** Sun.

LEAVES: Generally 6 to 9 inches long, rather soft and flexible, in bundles of 3. Generally light green during the growing season. Winter color is a pale green to yellow-brown, depending on severity of the winter, less attractive than many other pines.

STEM: An upright, central leader with nearly right angle secondary branching. Moderately durable wood. Bark on old trees is light red-brown, broken into light, irregular fissures and broad, flat, scaly ridges.

FLOWERS: Inconspicuous.

FRUIT: A light brown cone, generally 2 to 5 in a cluster on short, scaly branches. Ovoid to conical, 3 to 4 inches long, opening irregularly, late in the season. Cones are generally retained for several years, thus the presence of the cones throughout the tree at nearly all times is a useful identification feature, particularly for distinguishing loblolly pine from slash pine, which looks very similar but retains cones only one season in most cases.

COLOR: Foliage is light green during the growing season; yellow-green to brown during the winter.

PROPAGATION: Seed.

CULTURE: Unlike many northern pines, does well on poorly drained soils, wet clays, or swampy lands. Tolerates drought moderately well, performing well in western Oklahoma. Responds to moderate fertilization and cultivation to reduce weed and grass competition.

PESTS: May be attacked by pine tip moth and fusiform rust, particularly in the Southeast.

NOTES: Moderately ornamental when young, becoming somewhat less with age. Winter color is fair to poor. Foliage density is generally poor and retention of cones in the tree also detracts from overall appearance. Perhaps best used as a background plant, particularly in areas where excessive soil moisture may be a problem for other pines. Serves well as an over story tree, providing a light-textured shade for azaleas and other shrubs intolerant of full sun. The aroma from the needles is quite pleasing.

CULTIVARS: 'Nana': grown from "witches brooms" and is globe-formed and grows very slowly. Nice large shrubs. Rapidly growing strains have been developed for reforestation.

RELATED SPECIES: *Pinus ellotti* Engelm., slash pine, is very similar in appearance, growth, and adaptability but is hardy only to Zone 7. The dropping of cones during the second year and the presence of a distinct stalk on the cone are the best features to distinguish slash pine from loblolly pine which holds its cones for several years in the crown of the tree and the cones have a very short stalk.

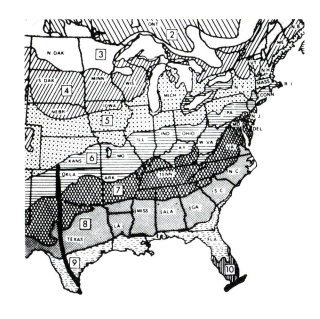

Pinus thunbergiana Franco   Japanese Black Pine
        (Syn. *Pinus thunburgi* Parl.)
Pinaceae or Pine Family   Hardiness Zone 6
Native to Japan, along the seacoast.
SIZE: 40 to 60 feet tall with a 20- to 30-foot spread. Moderate to rapid grower.
FORM: Somewhat pyramidal when young becoming more oval and informal with age.
TEXTURE: Medium.   **EXPOSURE:** Sun.

LEAVES: 3 to 4 inches long, in bundles of 2. Straight, rarely twisting, fairly stiff and harsh to the touch. Excellent summer and winter color. Leaves may be retained 3 years under good growing conditions.

STEM: Strong, upright, central leader with nearly right angle branching in whorls when young. Winter buds, particularly the terminal buds, on either the lateral branches or the main stem, are long, cylindrical, bluntly tapered with a sharp point at the very tip. These buds may be 1 to 4 inches long or more. Bark remains quite dark and blackish gray while the plant is relatively young; becomes fissured into rather elongated plates with age. Wood is only moderately stout.

FLOWERS: Female are inconspicuous, but male catkins are noticeable in spring (monoecious).

FRUIT: A light brown, woody cone, 1 1/2 to 2 1/2 inches long with a very minute prickle on the scales.

COLOR: Foliage is dark green, very similar to Austrian pine.

PROPAGATION: Seed.

CULTURE: A tough, rapidly growing pine. Transplants easily and tolerates a wide range of conditions. Rivals Austrian pine in terms of adaptability to a wide range of soil types, moisture levels, and other growing conditions. May grow 2 to 4 feet per year on good sites.

PESTS: None serious although pine tip moth may be a problem on young trees. The pine nematode may become a serious threat in the East. Herbicide vapors cause a slow decline and have become a serious problem.

NOTES: An outstanding rapidly growing pine. Generally develops irregular angular growth, ideal for Japanese garden effect. When forced to grow very fast, may become somewhat open and loose-branched and lose some of its otherwise very attractive character. Very rapid growth may also decrease resistance to ice or wind damage. Sometimes listed as hardiness Zone 5; however, north of Zone 6, Japanese black pine is somewhat susceptible to early fall or late spring freezes which kill the tops of trees, making them unsightly. Tends to retain its needles longer than Austrian pine, giving it a denser appearance. Can best be distinguished from Austrian pine in that the winter buds of Japanese black pine are longer, blunt on the end with a sharp point in the center and by the fact that the needles tend to be retained longer on the tree, needles are rarely twisted, curved or sickle-shaped If the cones are present, the presence of the small prickle is another identifying feature.

CULTIVARS: Numerous cultivars have been selected in Europe; few are currently being grown in the United States and to my eye offer very little over seedlings.

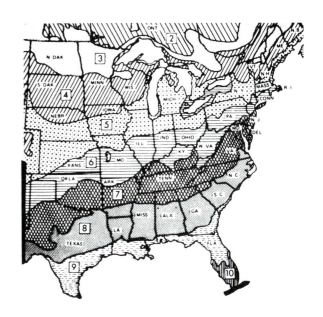

Podocarpus macrophyllus D. Don.   Yew Podocarpus
Podocarpaceae or Podocarpus Family   Hardiness Zone 8
Native to China and Japan.

SIZE: 20 to 40 feet tall with a 5- to 20-foot spread, depending on cultivar. Slow to moderate grower.

FORM: An upright or columnar, large shrub or small tree. Frequently used as a hedge plant.

TEXTURE: Fine to medium.   **EXPOSURE:** Sun to shade.

LEAVES: Long, narrow, and moderately stiff. May reach 3 to 4 inches long and 1/2 inch wide, either pointed or rounded at the tip. Alternate or spirally arranged on the stem. Base narrows into a slightly curved stalk or petiole. Shining bright green above, paler green beneath with the mid vein prominent from above.

STEM: Upright, central leader with gray bark, very shallow furrows in the bark and horizontal, very stout and dense branches. Wood is flexible and durable, wind resistant.

FLOWERS: Inconspicuous.

FRUIT: Red to red-pruple, about 1/2 inch long and 1/4 inch in diameter. Fruit production is quite variable with cultivars or among seedlings. Unlike the similar-appearing fruit of the genus, *Taxus* this fruit is not poisonous, and is frequently eaten or used to make preserves. However, since *Taxus spp.* fruits are poisonous, be sure of the plant's identity before eating.

COLOR: Foliage is dark green and lustrous. Fruits are red to red-purple.

PROPAGATION: Seed or hardwood cuttings. Much variability exists among seedlings. Should be propagated more from cuttings which will root easily as hardwood cuttings, with a very low quantity of mist or without mist in shady, humid conditions.

CULTURE: Easily grown in most soils; however, will not tolerate wet, poorly drained conditions. Tolerates full sun to dense shade, but density and overall attractiveness decrease with increasing shade. May suffer magnesium deficiency on light, sandy or highly organic soils. Correct by using Epsom salts (magnesium sulfate). Transplants easily.

PESTS: Mushroom root rot in wet locations.

NOTES: An excellent shrub or small tree for well drained soils or otherwise dry locations. Very sensitive to poor drainage, even in nursery containers. Tolerates pruning exceptionally well. A good shrub, hedge, or small tree where adapted.

CULTIVARS: 'Maki': small tree or shrub, much like the parent in overall growth habit. Leaves are shorter, 1 1/2 to 3 inches long, about 1/4 inch wide. Thick, leathery and stiff. A more compact, denser foliage than the parent. Commonly in the nursery industry, 'Maki' is considered to have larger, broader, longer leaves than the species. This is an error.

RELATED SPECIES: *Podocarpus gracilior* Pilg., fern podocarpus, is hardy only in Zone 10 and has much softer and shorter leaves. A very soft, delicate shrub or small tree, excellent for indoor landscaping.

Podocarpus nagi (Thunb.) Makino. has broader, more teardrop to ovate-shaped leaves. More coarsely textured than fern podocarpus or yew podocarpus. Hardy in Zones 9 and 10.

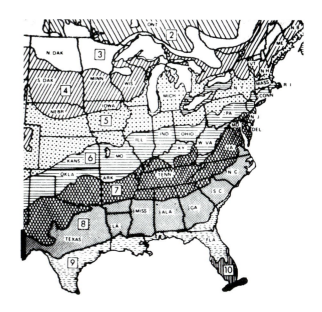

P. nagi

P. gracilior

Pseudotsuga menziesi (Mirb.) Franco   Douglas Fir
Pinaceae or Pine Family   Hardiness Zone 4 to 6
Native to the Rocky Mountains.
SIZE: Up to 100 feet tall or more with a 15- to 30-foot spread. Moderate grower.
FORM: Dense, pyramidal tree when young, becoming more open with age.
TEXTURE: Fine.   **EXPOSURE:** Sun to slight shade.

LEAVES: Simple, spirally arranged, 1 to 1 1/2 inch long, and slender. Needle-like, flattened and rounded at the tip, not stickery. Bluish green above and lighter below with 2 white lines parallel to the smooth margin. Both current season and 1-year-old needles are present at all times and sometimes second year needles. Because the leaves are somewhat shade tolerant, especially on young trees, the foliage remains more dense than on some conifers.

STEM: A strong, central leader tree with soft but durable and decay resistant wood. Branches are horizontal or slightly upright and flexible. Bark on a young tree is thin, smooth, gray with resin pockets but with age becomes deeply furrowed and reddish brown. Young stems are slender and flexible with a distinct sharp-pointed dormant terminal bud.

FLOWERS: Male and female flowers are separate on the same tree (monoecious). Not showy.

FRUIT: A 3- to 4-inch elongated cone, near the top of the tree, with prominent papery bracts that extend beyond the scales.

COLOR: Foliage is blue-green.

PROPAGATION: Seed or cuttings with difficulty.

CULTURE: Douglas fir is native to a broad range of the Rocky Mountains, including the Pacific Northwest. Seedlings from the Pacific Northwest are not as cold hardy (Zone 6) as seedlings from the central and northern Rockies (Zone 4). Grows best on deep, well-drained, moist soil, but tolerates moderate drought in the southern Rockies and Upper Plains states. Grows more slowly on poorer soils with less favorable moisture conditions, but survives reasonably once established. Easy to transplant in its native range and in Zones 4 and 5 but slower to recover from transplanting in Zones 6 and 7. Not recommended below Zone 7 as douglas fir is photoperiod sensitive and therefore grows more slowly. Mulching in Zones 6 and 7 and supplemental moisture during droughts assist young trees.

PESTS: Aphids, leaf blight, bark beetles, especially on trees under stress and other problems. However, these are not everpresent problems and should not discourage planting of this beautiful tree.

NOTES: A magnificent tree when young, with a grandeur all its own. Useful as a specimen tree or screen. In Zones 4 and 5, only seed from the northern Rockies, often sold as 'Glauca', should be used. This the popular seed source for the more intense, blue-green forms popular as Christmas trees.

CULTIVARS: 'Glauca' a term used to describe the more intense blue-green seedlings. 'Fastigiata' a very erect grower. 'Fletcheri': a dwarf that may reach 5 feet tall with blue-green foliage. Others probably exist.

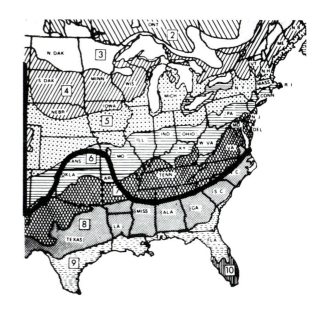

Taxus spp.   Yew
Taxaceae or Taxus Family   Hardiness Zone 4 or 6 depending on species.
Native to England or the Orient.
SIZE: Variable. Low growing shrubs to small trees. Slow growers.
FORM: Irregular, spreading or upright dense shrubs.
TEXTURE: Fine.   EXPOSURE: Partial shade to shade.

LEAVES: Long and slender, often 1 to 1 1/2 inches long, about 1/8 inch wide, with 2 broad, yellowish or gray-green lines on the under surface. Deep dark green above. More or less spirally arranged on the stem.

STEM: Young shoots are green, turning red to red-brown and becoming scaly. Branches are irregular and alternate. Winter terminal buds have many interlacing bud scales.

FLOWERS: Not showy. Male and female plants (dioecious).

FRUIT: A pinkish red, fleshy cup, open at one end containing an oval-shaped seed. Rather showy. Male and female plants are required for fruit production.

COLOR: Foliage is deep, dark green. Fruit is pinkish red.

PROPAGATION: Hardwood cuttings or seed; however, seedlings are variable.

CULTURE: Tolerant to a moderate range of growing conditions as long as a moderate moisture supply is available, soil is well drained, and the location is not extremely hot or exposed. Grows well on north or east sides of structures or under the shade of trees. This slow growing plant makes a superb, low maintenance shrub, hedge, or topiary form in the landscape. Will not tolerate poorly drained soil, even for short periods.

PESTS: None serious.

NOTES: *Taxus* species have the deepest green foliage of the evergreen shrubs commonly grown. Very useful for background or contrast for other shrubs. Best adapted to the central and northeastern states with somewhat limited performance in the Midwest and Prairie States except in selected locations. XX-POISON-XX

SPECIES AND CULTIVARS: *Taxus baccata* L., English yew, hardy in Zone 6, cultivated since early times with many cultivars. In most cases, the English yew is less desirable than cultivars of *Taxus cuspidata* or *Taxus* X *media*.

Taxus cuspidata Sieb. & Zucc., Japanese yew, is hardy through Zone 4 with many cultivars, probably the most common is 'Densa' which is a low shrub about as broad as high, rarely reaching more than 4 to 6 feet with deep green foliage. 'Expansa' has a vase-shaped growth habit, but there may be several variable selections being sold under this name growing 4 to 8 feet tall. 'Capitata' is a single-stemmed, conical, tree-like form when grown from seed. There is much variation in this cultivar throughout the United States. 'Spring Green' retains its color very well in winter and is tolerant of full sun in summer. 'Spreading' is a rather loose, open grower, but very tolerant of summer and winter sun.

Taxus X *media* Rehd. are hybrids between *Taxus cuspidata* and *Taxus baccata*, hardy through Zone 4; many cultivars have been selected from this cross. 'Hatfieldi' grows 10 to 12 feet tall and is a densely pyramidal male. 'Hicksi' is a female, strictly upright, very popular and moderately tolerant to winter and summer sun. 'Densiformis' dense foliage, freely branching without shearing. One of the better cultivars. 'Kelseyi' an upright, moderate grower. Many others exist, check with your local nurseryman. One of the best references on taxus is Ohio State bulletin #1086, A Study of the Genus Taxus, by L. C. Chadwick and R. A. Keen.

Taxus cuspidata

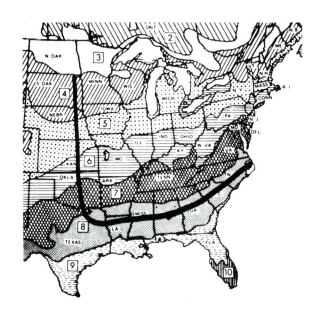

T. media

T. media 'Densiformis'

T. media 'Kelseyi'

T. cuspidata 'Nana'   T. media 'Hatfield'

T. media 'Hicksi'

T. media 'Hicksi'

T. media 'Hicksi'

T. media 'Browni'

T. cuspidata 'Capitata'

T. media 'Densiformis'

T. cuspidata 'Capitata'

T. media 'Densiformis'

T. ? 'Variegata'

Cephalotaxus harringtonia 'Fastigiata'

Thuja occidentalis L.   Eastern Arborvitae or White Cedar
Pinaceae or Pine Family   Hardiness Zone 2
Native to northeast North America.
SIZE: Trees to 60 feet tall or more with variable spread. Many dwarf, upright and globose cultivars. Slow to moderate grower.
FORM: Pyramidal, upright trees or irregular, upright, large shrubs or irregular or oval-formed shrubs, depending on cultivar.
TEXTURE: Fine.   **EXPOSURE:** Sun to shade.

LEAVES: Scale-like, abruptly pointed; those on the main branchlets are glandular. The branchlets are alternate, compressed or flattened into sprays, mostly horizontal. Leaves look somewhat like juniper scale-like leaves only are pressed into flattened platelets. Medium to dark green, depending on cultivar, exposure, and time of year.

STEM: Upright forms generally have a central leader with irregular branching, depending on cultivar. Bark is reddish brown, fissured into narrow, vertical ridges, very similar in appearance to the bark of *Juniperus* species.

FLOWERS: Small, yellow; nearly inconspicuous.

FRUIT: A small, woody cone about 1/2 inch long.

COLOR: Foliage is medium to dark green, depending on cultivar and exposure.

PROPAGATION: Semi-hardwood to hardwood cuttings for selected cultivars.

CULTURE: Does well as far south as Zone 7. Grows in a wide range of soils but responds to good soils and fertility. Prefers considerable moisture but tolerates exposed locations and limited moisture. Transplants easily and responds well to shearing or pruning.

PESTS: Juniper blight may be troublesome on some cultivars, also bagworms and occasionally spider mites.

NOTES: Appears similar to *Thuja orientalis*, oriental arborvitae, however, oriental arborvitae generally has only vertical plate-like sections of leaves, whereas eastern arborvitae has a more regular distribution of plate-like leaves, many of them being horizontal instead of vertical. Not well suited below zone 7. Suffers from exposure, drought, and desiccation by drying winds west of the Mississippi River unless provided some shade or protection, then it does very well. Depending on cultivar, it may discolor considerably in winter becoming rather unsightly.

CULTIVARS: Bailey lists over 60 cultivars with tremendous diversity. 'Alba': upright, pyramidal form, rather free-growing, 6 to 12 feet tall with spreading branches. Leaves are green with a white tip, very prominent, and attractive in winter. 'Aurea': broad, oval shrub with gold-yellow foliage. 'Globosa': dwarf, globular form, 3 feet high, very broad branches somewhat erect and then spreading irregularly. Slightly gray-green in winter. 'Woodward': a dwarf, globe-shaped shrub, 3 to 4 feet tall. Foliage is very dark green. Tolerates more drought and lower humidity than some other cultivars of eastern arborvitae. Should be planted where it will receive winter shade. 'Pyramidalis': a narrow, columnar form. Susceptible to winter burn in the North. 'Techny': a dense, pyramidal form with dark green foliage. One of the better cultivars. 'Emerald': grows 8 to 10 feet tall by 3 to 4 feet wide with dark foliage that retains its color in winter. Relatively new and very nice. Many others exist.

'Pyramidalis'

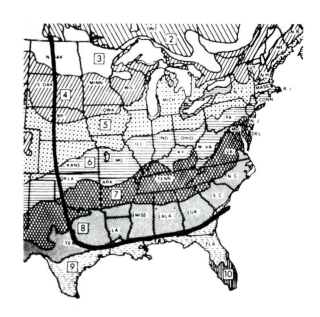

'Woodward'

'Columnaris'

'Woodward'

T. occidentalis 'Techny'

T. occidentalis 'Techny'

T. occidentalis 'Woodward'

T. occidentalis 'Hetz Midget'

T. orientalis

T. orientalis

T. orientalis 'Ruffles Dwarf'

T. orientalis

Thuja orientalis L.   Oriental or Chinese Arborvitae
    (Syn. *Platycladus orientalis* (L.) Franco.)
Pinaceae or Pine Family   Hardiness Zone 3
Native to the northeastern United States and southeastern Canada.
SIZE: 3 to 40 feet tall, depending on cultivar. Slow to very rapid growers.
FORM: Upright, pyramidal to ovate to dense, oval shrub, depending on cultivar.
TEXTURE: Fine.   **EXPOSURE:** Sun to partial shade.

LEAVES: Short and scale-like, tightly appressed onto branchlets which appear as pressed vertical plates. Generally bright green above and yellow-green below unless it is a cultivar with yellow or golden foliage. Winter color is green-brown to yellow-brown and dull with most seedlings and cultivars.

STEM: Upright, without a central leader. The center of the plant is a dense mass of upright-growing branches. This structural weakness of the plant is very obvious after a wet snow or hard wind and rain. However, in most cases, the plant eventually regains its original form. Bark is shallow and splits into vertical strips similar to juniper species.

FLOWERS: Small, yellowish; nearly inconspicuous.

FRUIT: Small, oval, woody cone; 1/2 to 1 inch in diameter. Green when immature, light brown when mature. Tipped with several prominent prickles. Old cones persist.

COLOR: Foliage is medium to light to yellow-green, depending on cultivar.

PROPAGATION: Semi-hardwood to hardwood cuttings under mist.

CULTURE: An exceptionally tough plant, grows anywhere, tolerates heat, drought, and windy exposed conditions, but grows best in a rich, moist, fertile soil. Good in western Kansas and Oklahoma where few evergreens thrive in the dry, open plains.

PESTS: Juniper blight, bagworms, and spider mites. Frequently a continuing source of spider mites and juniper blight fungus, thus contaminates the entire landscape.

NOTES: Extensively over-planted. One of the classic American mistakes in landscaping. This plant is easy to propagate, easy to grow, and easy to transplant and unfortunately, survives very well in nearly all location. Thus it is a common chain store nursery plant that is ill-suited to most landscape situations, both from the standpoint of disease and insect problems, which it creates for other plants, and from its rapid growth in most locations, thus over-growing its usefulness very soon. The tough and extensive root system has merit as an understock for many juniper species and cultivars which do not root from cuttings. Grafted nursery stock shipped north of Zone 5 should be on *Juniperus chinensis* 'Hetzi' rootstocks due to the greater cold hardiness. Sometimes sold as the golden biota. The recent name change to *Platycladus orientalis* is ridiculous for a plant so widely grown and for such minor differences. It will forever be *Thuja orientalis* in the nursery business.

CULTIVARS: Bailey lists over 50 cultivars. Many more probably exist. "Aurea Nana': a slow-growing, dense, globe-shaped shrub with branchlet tips bright golden yellow. 'Baker' a compact-growing, pyramidal arborvitae, bright green. 'Bluecone': upright, pyramidal, compact, green foliage which has a slight blue cast. 'Elegantissimus': upright, columnar, blond-golden green during summer, holds color fairly well in winter. 'Westmont' or 'Ruffles Dwarf': probably the same cultivar. Very compact, slow-growing, pyramidal form with rich, dark green foliage in the summertime; yellow-green in late fall and winter. Rarely reaches height of more then 3 1/2 to 4 feet. Probably the best of the compact arborvitae. Many others exist in England and Europe.

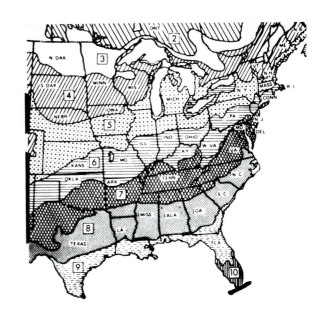

Tsuga canadensis L. Carriere   Canadian or Eastern Hemlock
Pinaceae or Pine Family   Hardiness Zone 3
Native to the northeastern United States and southeastern Canada.
SIZE: 30 to 60 feet tall in most cases, occasionally larger. Slow to moderate grower.
FORM: Pyramidal when young, tall and slender with drooping branches with age.
TEXTURE: Very fine.   **EXPOSURE:** Sun or partial shade.

LEAVES: Simple, 1/2 inch long, flattened needles. Light green when young, dark green with age; with 2 white, narrow bands beneath, rounded or notched at the tip. Two-ranked on slender stems.

STEM: A central leader tree with flexible branches, drooping with age. Wood is light-weight and weak, splits easily and is reddish brown. Bark on the main stem is reddish brown with deep furrows and scaly. Young branches are yellow-brown and hairy, very flexible.

FLOWERS: Male and female separate on the same tree (monoecious). Male cones are small, yellow-green near the tips of branches, noticeable. Female flowers are inconspicuous.

FRUIT: Small, oval cones; about 1/2 inch around with thin, rounded scales. Hang from the young branches. Attractive.

COLOR: New foliage is light green; darker with age.

PROPAGATION: Seed, grafting, or cuttings with difficulty.

CULTURE: Native to mixed stands of trees in cool, moist valleys with dense leaf litter on the soil surface. Hemlocks are neither drought nor heat tolerant and are readily damaged by drying winds. Fortunately, it is moderately shade tolerant and therefore can be grown on the north or east sides of structures or in locations shaded by larger trees. Key factors in growing hemlock are cool soils, stable moisture conditions (neither too wet nor too dry) and limited competition from grass and weeds. The farther west and southwest, the more critical these factors become. For example, there are some beautiful hemlocks in Tulsa, Oklahoma in older residential areas where a tall tree canopy is present. In more northern areas, hemlocks may "winter burn" if exposed to winter sun or drying winds. Easily pruned or sheared as a hedge or dense screen in the Northeast and East. Pick the site carefully and you will be rewarded with a soft, delicate tree unmatched by most trees.

PESTS: Scale insects may be a problem but can be controlled with systemic insecticides. Occasionally mites, leaf blight and rust.

NOTES: One of the most delicate and attractive of all the coniferous trees. A healthy young hemlock is hugable to an avid plantsman. One of the premier landscape plants and worthy of whatever time and attention necessary to find or create a favorable environment. Grows well in the mountainous area of the Upper South but generally should not be planted below Zone 7 as it is photoperiod sensitive and needs the long days of summer for good growth.

CULTIVARS: 'Pendula': a low, weeping selection. Many other cultivars exist especially in England and Europe. Den Ouden and Boom list over 50.

RELATED SPECIES: *Tsuga caroliniana* Engelm., Carolina hemlock, is hardy in Zone 5 and is similar in appearance and adaptability to Canadian hemlock. Leaves are slightly larger and are distributed around the slender branches whereas leaves of Canadian hemlock are in one plane. Less often planted than Canadian hemlock, but equally attractive.

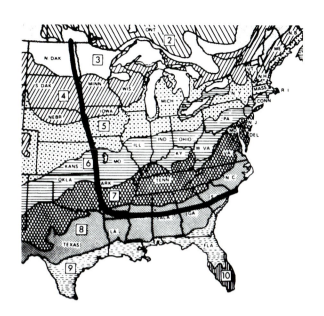

'Minima'

Glossary

Acorn. The fruit of oaks.

Aerial. Parts above the ground or water.

Allergic. Subject to irritation by foreign substances.

Alternate. Placed singly at different levels on the stem. (Ex.: Leaf arrangement of elm trees.)

Alternate host. A situation where a disease organism is on one plant for part of the year and on another plant the rest. (Ex.: cedar-apple rust.)

Apex. The top or termination of a part or organ.

Appendages. Various secondary outgrowths.

Appressed. Closely and flatly pressed against an object such as some of the scale-like leaves on junipers.

Ascending. Growing upward, but not erect.

Asexual. Without sex; reproduction without sexual union, such as by cuttings, buds, bulbs, or grafting.

Asymmetric. Not symmetrical; with no plane of symmetry.

Axil. The upper angle formed by a leaf with the stem.

Axillary. Situated in an axil.

Axis. The center line of a plant' the main stem.

Bark. The dead, corky, outer layer of stems and branches.

Basal. At or near the base.

Berry. A fruit in which the ovary becomes a fleshy or pulp mass enclosing one or more seeds. (Ex.: persimmon)

Blade. The expanded and generally flattened portion of a leaf.

Bract. A more or less modified leaf at the base of a flower or belonging to a cluster of flowers. (Ex.: poinsettia or dogwood.)

Bud. An unexpanded shoot or an unexpanded flower.

Budding. A form of grafting where only a vegetative bud is transferred to the root stock.

Bud scales. Modified leaves protecting a bud, often dry or resinous.

Capsule. A dry fruit composed of more than one section, and splitting when dry.

Catkin. A delicate, scaly-bracted, usually drooping spike of flowers. (Ex.: male flowers on oaks or hickories.)

Clambering. Leaning on other plants or objects; not self-supporting.

Clasping. Enveloping the stem partially or wholly at the base, as leaf bases, bracts, or stipules.

Cleft. cut nearly to the middle. (Ex." white oak leaf)

Climber. Plant seeking support by twining, aerial roots, or tendrils.

Compound leaf. A leaf with the blade divided into two or more leaflets. (Ex.: mimosa or honeylocust)

Compressed. Flattened.

Coniferous. Cone-bearing. (Ex.: pines)

Constricted. Narrowed between wider portions.

Contorted. Twisted.

Creeping. A trailing shoot which strikes roots along most of its length. (Ex.: winter jasmine or creeping junipers)

Crenate. the margin of a leaf with rounded teeth.

Cross-pollination. Transfer of pollen from flower to flower.

Crown. Usually referring to the branches and foliage of a tree; or the thickened bases of stems near the soil line.

Deciduous. Leaves not persistent, generally dropping in the fall; not evergreen.

Deltoid. Triangular.

Descending. Growing or hanging slightly downward, but not weeping.

Desiccate. Drying due to wind and/or low humidity.

Dioecious. With male and female flowers on separate plants. (Ex.: honeylocust, Kentucky coffee tree)

Distinct. Separate, not united.

Diurnal. Opening during the day, closing at night.

Divided. Lobed to near the base.

Division. Separation of a clump, thus propagating a new plant. (Ex.: pampas grass or bamboo)

Dormant. Referring to a period without growth. (Ex.: A maple tree in winter is dormant)

Drupe. A fleshy or pulpy fruit in which the inner portion is hard and stony, enclosing the seed. (Ex.: peach or apricot)

Ecology. The science dealing with plants in relation to their environment.

Ecological race. A unique plant that has evolved or adapted to a somewhat different environment.

Elliptic. Of the form of an ellipse or egg-shaped.

Elongate. Lengthened; drawn out.

Entire. A leaf edge without teeth, notches, or division; smooth.

Epidermis. The surface layer of cells.

Exfoliating. Referring to bark separating into strips or flakes. (Ex.: sycamore or river birch)

Exudate. An excretion of wax, gum, or sap. (Ex.: When a leaf is removed from a Norway maple)

Fascicle. Paper-like sheath at base of needles on pines.

Fastigiate. Having closely set, erect branches.

Fertile. Flowers with pistils capable of producing seeds, or stamens with functional pollen.

Fibrous. Bearing a resemblance to fibers, or possessing fibers, as in fibrous roots. (Ex.: maples)

Fruit. The seed-bearing part of a plant.

Funnelform. Shaped like a funnel. (Ex.: trumpet honeysuckle or morning glory)

Glabrous. Smooth; without hairs or scales.

Glaucous. Covered with a white, waxy bloom. (Ex.: most blue-purple table grapes)

Globose. Globular or spherical in shape.

Grafting. A method of asexual propagation where a top of one plant is united with a root system from a second.

Habitat. The natural environment of a plant.

Heartwood. The oldest wood, enclosing the pith; the hard central, often deeply colored, portion of a tree trunk.

Hybrid. The offspring of genetically dissimilar parents.

Imbricate. Overlapping.

Infertile. Not fertile or viable.

Inflorescence. A flower cluster. (Ex.: lilac or catalpa)

Internode. That portion of stem lying between two successive nodes.

Lanceolate. Shaped like a lance head or spear.

Leaflet. A single division of a compound leaf.

Leaf. The usually thin and expanded portion on the stem.

Leaf scar. Scar left where a leaf was attached to a stem.

Lenticels. Corky growths on young bark. May go around or at right angles to the stem axis.

Lichen. Small plants often found as green or gray irregular patches on tree trunks, rocks, or other objects.

Linear. Long and narrow.

Lobe. Any segment or division of an organ, like fingers on a hand.

Lobed. Divides into lobes, or having lobes.

Longitudinal. Lengthwise.

Microphyllous. Small-leaved.

Midrib. The main rib or vein of a leaf.

Monoecious. With male and female flowers separate, but on the same plant. (Ex.: oaks and hickories)

Node. The joint of a twig; usually a point bearing a leaf or leaf-like structure.

Nut. A hard, one-celled and one-seeded fruit. (Ex.: pecan)

Oblanceolate. Lanceolate with the broadest part toward the tip.

Oblong. Longer than broad and with nearly parallel sides.

Obovate. Inverted ovate.

Opposite. Opposed to each other, such as two opposite leaves at a node. (Ex.: maples or dogwoods)

Organ. A part of a plant with a definite function, as a leaf or flower.

Oval. Broadly elliptical.

Ovate. Egg-shaped, with the broader end closer to the stem.

Palmate or Palmately Compound. A leaf lobed or divided like fingers on a hand. (Ex.: Japanese maple or Virginia creeper)

Panicle. A branched cluster of flowers. (Ex.: crapemyrtle)

Pendulous. More or less hanging.

pH. Referring to the acidity (low) or alkalinity (high) of a soil. High pH often means reduced iron availability to plants.

Perennial. Usually living more than two years.

Persistent. Said of leafs that are evergreen or as in the oaks when the leaves do not drop in the fall.

Petal. The outer appendage of a flower. A modified leaf.

Petiole. the stalk at the base of a leaf. It is part of the leaf.

Pinnate or Pinnately Compound. Compound leaves with the leaflets arranged on opposite sides along a common rachis or axis. (Ex.: honeylocust)

Pistil. The seed-bearing portion of the flower consisting of ovary, stigma, and style.

Pith. The central tissue of a stem.

Pod. Any dry fruit, often long and slender. (Ex.: catalpa)

Pollen. The male germ cells, contained in the anther of the flower.

Pollination. Deposition of pollen upon the stigma or tip of the female flower part.

Prickle. A rigid, straight or hooked, outgrowth of the bark or other plant part.

Procumbent. Lying on the ground.

Prostrate. Flat on the ground.

Pubescence. A covering of short hairs.

Quadrangular. Four-angled.

Raceme. A simple cluster of flowers upon a common, more or less elongated, axis.

Rachis. The central stem of a compound leaf or of a cluster of flowers.

Radial. Developing around a central axis.

Reduced. Not normally or fully developed in size.

Regular. Uniform in shape or distribution of parts; symmetrical.

Revolute. Leaves rolled or turned downward or toward the under surface. (Ex.: live oak leaf)

Rhizome. A prostrate stem under the ground, rooting at the nodes and bearing buds on nodes. (Ex.: iris, bamboo, or nandina)

Rib. A primary vein as in the midrib of a leaf.

Rosette. A cluster or swirl of leaves.

Rotund. Rounded in shape.

Samara. A winged fruit. (Ex.: maples and elms)

Scale. A leaf much reduced in size. (Ex.: junipers or arborvitae)

Secondary. The second division, as in branches or leaf veins.

Seed. A ripened ovule.

Segment. Part of a compound leaf or other organ, especially if the parts are alike.

Self-pollination. Pollination within the flower.

Sepal. A modified leaf found at the base of many flowers.

Serrate. Having sharp teeth pointing forward on the margin of the leaf. (Ex.: American elm)

Sessile. Without a stalk of any kind. The leaf of a crapemyrtle is said to be nearly sessile.

Shoot. A young branch.

Shrub. A woody plant with a number of stems arising from the base, usually smaller than a tree.

Silky. Covered with close-pressed soft and straight hairs.

Simple. In one piece or unit, not compound. (Ex.: American elm leaf)

Spine. A modified stipule, petiole, or branch to form a hard, sharp-pointed structure.

Spike. A cluster of flowers on one central stem. (Ex.: snapdragon)

Stamen. The pollen-bearing organ, usually two or more in each flower.

Standard. A plant grown with a single stem, particularly refers to those regularly having multiple stems.

Stellate. Having the shape of a star; star-like.

Stem. Main axis of the plant.

Sterile. Does not produce fruit or viable seed.

Stigma. That part of the flower (pistil) which receives the pollen.

Stipule. An appendage at the base of a petiole. (Ex.: American sycamore or flowering quince leaves)

Stolon. A branch or shoot growing above ground as opposed to a below-ground rhizome. (Ex.: above-ground stems of Bermudagrass or periwinkle)

Stomates. Minute openings in a leaf, generally in the under surface.

Strict. Erect and straight.

Style. The upward extension of the ovary terminating with the stigma.

Subshrub. Perennial plant with lower portions of stems woody and persistent.

Subtend. Adjacent to an organ, under or supporting; referring to a bract or scale below a flower.

Succulent. Juicy.

Sucker. A stem originating from the roots or lower stem of a plant.

Symmetrical. Divisible into equal and like parts; referring to a regular flower having the same number of parts in whorl or series.

Syn. Synonym: a former scientific name now incorrect.

Taproot. The main or primary root.

Taxonomy. The science of classification.

Tendril. Usually a slender organ for climbing, formed by modification of a leaf, branch, or flower stalk. (Ex.: Virginia creeper)

Terminal. At the end, summit, or apex.

Thorn. A sharp-pointed, modified branch.

Tomentose. Densely hairy with matted wool.

Toothed. Having teeth; serrate.

Torulose. Cylindrical and constricted at intervals.

Toxic. Poisonous.

Trailing. Growing prostrate but not rooting at the nodes.

Transpiration. Passage of water vapor outward, mostly through the stomata of the leaves.

Tri- (prefix). In three parts, as trifoliage (three-leaved), tri-lobate (three-lobed), trifid (three-cleft).

Trichome. A modified hair arising from a epidermal cell. (Ex.: Russian olive or silver-thorn).

Trunk. The main stem or axis of a tree below the branches.

Tuber. A thickened underground stem usually for food storage and bearing buds. (Ex.: liriope or mondograss)

Turgid. Swollen.

Twining. Climbing by means of the main stem or branches winding around an object (without aerial roots or tendrils). Ex.: Japanese honeysuckle)

Unisexual. Of one sex, either male or female only.

Understory. Generally growing beneath larger plants. (Ex.: dogwood)

Vascular. Referring to the conductive tissue in the stems or leaves.

Vegetative. Non-reproductive, as contrasted to seed. As with propagating by cuttings or grafting where no sex is involved. Offspring are identical to the parent.

Veins. Threads of tissue in a leaf, or other flat organ.

Viable. Capable of living or growing.

Whorl. Cyclic arrangement of like plant parts.

Wing. Any thin expansion bordering or surrounding an organ. (Ex.: winged euonymus)

Woolly. Clothed with long, matted hairs.

GOOD BOOKS AND PUBLICATIONS FOR ADDITIONAL INFORMATION

Anonymous. 1967. Handbook on Broad Leaved Evergreens. Plants and Gardens, 12:1-96.

Bailey, L. H. and E.Z. Bailey. 1941. Hortus Second. The Macmillan Co., New York, New York and Hortus III. 1976. Revised and expanded by the staff of the Liberty Hyde Bailey Hortorium. the MacMillan Co., New York, New York.

Chadwick, L.C. and R. A. Keen. 1976. A Study of the Genus Taxus. Ohio Agricultural Research bulletin #1086, Wooster, Ohio.

DenOuden, P. and B.K. Boom. 1965. Manual of Cultivated Conifers. Martinus Nijhoff, The Hague, The Netherlands.

Dirr, Michael A. 1977. Manual of Woody Landscape Plants. Stipes Publishing Co., Champaign, Illinois.

Evers, Robert P. and Roger P. Link. 1972. Poisonous Plants of the Midwest. Special Publication #24, Univ. of Illinois, College of Agriculture, Urbana, Illinois.

Galle, Fred C. 1970. hollies Native to the U.S. Vol. 49 of the American Horticultural Magazine.

Halfacre, R. Gordon. 1971. Carolina Landscape Plants. The Sparks Press, Raleigh, North Carolina.

Hansell, Dorothy E., Editor. 1970. The Handbook of Hollies. Vol. 49 of the American Horticultural Magazine.

Howard, R.A. 1961. Concerning the Registration of Cultivar Names. Arnoldia 21:1-8.

Hume, H. Harold. 1953. Hollies. The MacMillan Co., New York, New York.

Kelsey, Horton P. and William A. Dayton. 1942. Standardized Plant Names, 2nd Ed., J. Horace McFarland Co., Harrisburg, Pennsylvania.

Kingsbury, Hohn M. 1964. Poisonous Plants of the United States and Canada. Prentice-Hall, Inc., Englewood Cliffs, New Jersey.

Kurz, Herman and Robert K. Godfrey. 1962. Trees of Northern Florida. The Univ. of Florida Press, Gainesville, Florida.

Lee, Frederic P., Editor. 1952. The Azalea Handbook. The American Horticultural Society, Washington, D.C.

Maino, Evelyn and Frances Howard. 1972. Ornamental Trees. Univ. of California Press, Berkeley, California.

McClintock, Elizabeth and Andrew Leiser. 1979. An Annotated Checklist of Woody Ornamental Plants of California, Oregon and Washington. Manual 32, Univ. of California, division of Agricultural Sciences, Berkeley, California.

Phillips, Roger. 1978. Trees of North America and Europe. Random House, New York, New York.

Porter, C.L. 1959. Taxonomy of Flowering Plants. W. H. Freeman and Co., San Francisco, California.

Pringle, James S. 1973. The Concept of the Cultivar. The Garden Bulletin of the Royal Botanical Gardens, Hamilton, Ontario, Canada. Vol. 27, no. 3, 13-27.

Rehder, Alfred. 1940. Manual of Cultivated Trees and Shrubs. The MacMillan Co., New York, New York.

Sargent, Charles S. 1926. Manual of the Trees of North America. Houghton Mifflin Co.

Settergren, Carl and R. E. McDermott. 1969. Trees of Missouri. Univ. of Missouri. Agricultural Experiment Station Publication #3767.

Small, John K. 1933. Manual of the Southeastern Flora. Pub. by the author, New York.

Snyder, Leon C. 1980. Trees and Shrubs for Northern Gardens, Univ. of Minnesota Press, Minneapolis, Minnesota.

Stephens, H.A. 1969. Trees, Shrubs, and Woody Vines in Kansas. Univ. of Kansas Press, Lawrence, Kansas.

Swane, Valerie. 1979. The Australian Gardeners' Catalogue. Angus & Robertson Publishers, Sydney, Australia.

Treseder, Neil G. 1978. Magnolias. Faber & Faber Co., Boston, Massachusetts.

Vines, Robert A. 1960. Trees, Shrubs, and Woody Vines of the Southwest. The Univ. of Texas Press, Austin, Texas.

Wilkinson, Gerald. 1978. Epitaph for the Elm. Arrow Books, Ltd. London, England.

Wyman, Donald. 1969. Shrubs and Vines for American Gardens. The MacMillan Co., Toronto, Ontario, Canada.

A Plant Selection Guide

This is a general guide to the adaptation, appearance, tolerance or intolerance of many landscape plants. Use this guide as a general suggestion only. For further details regarding that plant, see the specific page in the main text.

Showy Flowers- Flowers that provide a major landscape effect.

Fragrant Flowers- Noticeable fragrance in most situations.

Showy Fruits- Fruits showy in most cases.

Edible Fruits- Edible, but not necessarily appetizing.

Fall Color- In most areas fall color is distinct and showy.

Litter problem- Dropping of fruits, leaves, twigs or other debris that can become unsightly.

Spines- Spines large enough to pose a hazard to children.

Unusual Foliage- Foliage that contrasts with other plants due to color, texture or size.

For hedge or screen- Plants effective in screening of views or creating hedges.

Poor soils- Plants that tolerate poor soils.

Alkaline soils- Plants that tolerate alkaline or basic soil conditions.

Wet sites- Plants that are tolerant to wet or poorly drained soils.

Drought- Plants that are tolerant of drought.

Intolerant of wet feet- Plants that are killed or damaged by flooding or poorly drained soils.

High heat- Tolerant of high heat, reflected light or other abnormal temperature conditions in the landscape.

Pest problems- Plants with major pest problems that must be considered before planting.

Weak wood- Plants, generally with very rapid growth and weak wood subject to ice and wind damage.

Shade- Plants tolerant to or requiring shade. See text for details.

	Showy Flowers	Fragrant Flowers	Showy Fruits	Edible Fruits	Fall Color	Litter Problems	Spines	Unusual Foliage	For Hedge or Screen	Poor Soils	Alkaline Soils	Wet Sites	Drought	Intolerant of Wet Feet	High Heat	Pest Problems	Weak Wood	Shade
Abelia grandiflora	X	-	-	-	-	-	-	-	X	X	X	-	X	-	-	-	-	-
Abies concolor	-	-	-	-	-	-	-	X	-	-	-	-	-	X	-	-	-	-
Acer barbatum	-	-	-	-	-	-	-	-	-	-	-	-	-	-	-	-	X	-
Acer buergerianum	-	-	-	-	X	-	-	-	-	-	-	-	X	-	-	-	-	-
Acer campestre	-	-	-	-	X	-	-	-	-	-	-	-	X	-	-	-	-	-
Acer cappadocicum	-	-	-	-	X	-	-	-	-	-	-	-	X	X	-	-	-	-
Acer floridanum	-	-	-	-	X	-	-	-	-	-	-	-	X	-	-	-	-	-
Acer ginnala	-	-	-	-	X	-	-	-	-	X	X	-	X	-	-	-	-	-
Acer griseum	-	-	-	-	X	-	-	-	-	-	-	-	-	-	-	-	-	-
Acer grandidentatum	-	-	-	-	X	-	-	-	-	-	-	-	-	-	-	-	-	-
Acer miyabei	-	-	-	-	X	-	-	-	-	-	-	-	X	-	-	-	-	-
Acer negundo	-	-	-	-	-	X	-	-	-	X	X	X	X	-	-	-	X	-
Acer palmatum	-	-	-	-	X	-	-	-	-	-	-	-	X	X	-	-	-	X
Acer platanoides	-	-	-	-	X	-	-	-	-	-	-	-	-	-	-	-	-	-
Acer rubrum	-	-	-	-	X	-	-	-	-	-	-	X	-	-	-	-	X	-
Acer saccharinum	-	-	-	-	-	X	-	-	-	X	X	-	-	-	-	-	X	-
Acer saccharum	-	-	-	-	X	-	-	-	-	-	-	-	-	-	-	-	-	-
Acoelorrhaphe wrightii	-	-	-	-	-	-	X	X	-	X	-	X	-	-	X	-	-	-
Aegopodium podogaria	-	-	-	-	-	-	-	X	-	X	X	-	-	-	-	-	-	-
Aesculus arguta	X	-	-	-	-	-	-	X	-	-	-	-	X	-	-	-	-	X
Aesculus glabra	X	-	-	-	-	-	-	-	-	-	-	-	-	-	-	-	-	-
Aesculus hippocastanum	X	-	-	-	-	-	-	-	-	-	-	-	-	-	-	-	-	-
Aesculus parviflora	X	-	-	-	-	-	-	X	X	-	-	-	-	-	-	-	-	X
Aesculus pavia	X	-	-	-	-	-	-	-	-	-	-	-	-	-	-	-	-	-
Agave spp.	-	-	-	-	-	-	X	X	-	X	X	-	X	X	X	-	-	-
Ailanthus altissima	-	-	-	-	-	X	-	-	-	X	X	X	X	-	X	-	X	-
Ajuga reptans	X	-	-	-	-	-	-	-	-	X	X	-	-	-	-	-	-	-
Albizia julibrissin	X	-	-	-	-	X	-	-	-	X	X	-	X	-	X	X	X	-
Alnus glutinosa	-	-	-	-	-	-	-	-	X	X	X	-	-	-	-	-	-	-
Alyssum saxatile	X	-	-	-	-	-	-	-	-	-	-	-	-	-	-	-	-	X
Amelanchier arborea	-	-	X	X	X	-	-	-	-	-	-	-	-	-	-	-	-	-
Amelanchier grandiflora	-	-	X	X	X	-	-	-	-	-	-	-	-	-	-	-	-	-
Amelanchier laevis	-	-	X	X	X	-	-	-	-	-	-	-	-	-	-	-	-	-
Amorpha glabra	X	-	-	-	-	-	-	X	-	X	X	-	X	-	-	-	-	-
Arecastrum romanzoffiana	-	-	-	-	-	-	-	X	-	X	-	-	-	-	-	-	-	-
Arundinaria variegata	-	-	-	-	-	X	-	-	X	X	X	X	X	-	-	-	-	-
Arundinaria pigmaea	-	-	-	-	-	-	-	X	-	X	X	X	X	-	-	-	-	X
Arundo donax	X	-	-	-	X	-	-	X	-	X	X	X	X	-	X	-	-	-
Aspidistra elatior	-	-	-	-	-	-	-	X	-	X	X	-	X	-	-	-	-	X
Aucuba japonica	-	-	X	-	-	-	-	-	-	X	X	-	X	-	-	-	-	X
Aurinia saxatilis	X	-	-	-	-	-	-	-	-	-	-	-	-	-	-	-	-	-
Azalea obtusum	X	-	-	-	-	-	-	-	-	-	-	-	-	X	-	-	-	X
Bambusa spp.	-	-	-	-	-	X	-	-	X	X	X	X	X	-	-	-	-	X
Bambusa multiplex	-	-	-	-	-	X	-	-	X	X	X	X	X	-	-	-	-	X
Berberis julianae	X	-	X	-	-	-	-	-	X	X	X	-	-	X	-	-	-	X
Berberis X gladwynensis	X	-	-	-	-	-	-	X	X	X	X	-	-	X	-	-	-	X

	Showy Flowers	Fragrant Flowers	Showy Fruits	Edible Fruits	Fall Color	Litter Problems	Spines	Unusual Foliage	For Hedge or Screen	Poor Soils	Alkaline Soils	Wet Sites	Drought	Intolerant of Wet Feet	High Heat	Pest Problems	Weak Wood	Shade
Berberis mentorensis	X	-	X	-	-	-	-	-	X	X	X	-	X	-	-	-	-	-
Betula alba	-	-	-	-	X	-	-	-	-	-	-	X	-	-	-	X	-	-
Betula nigra	-	-	-	-	X	-	-	-	-	-	-	X	-	-	-	-	-	-
Betula papyrifera	-	-	-	-	X	-	-	-	-	-	-	X	-	-	-	X	-	-
Betula pendula	-	-	-	-	X	-	-	-	-	-	-	X	-	-	-	X	-	-
Broussonetia papyrifera	-	-	-	-	-	X	-	-	-	X	X	-	X	-	X	-	X	-
Buddleia davidii	X	X	-	-	-	-	-	-	-	X	-	-	-	-	-	-	-	-
Bumelia lanuginosa	-	-	-	-	-	-	-	-	-	X	X	-	X	-	-	-	-	-
Butia capitata	-	-	-	X	-	-	-	X	-	X	X	-	X	-	X	-	-	-
Buxus harlandi	-	-	-	-	-	-	-	-	X	X	-	-	X	X	-	-	-	X
Buxus microphylla	-	-	-	-	-	-	-	-	X	X	-	-	X	X	-	-	-	X
Buxus sempervirens	-	-	-	-	-	-	-	-	X	X	-	-	X	X	-	-	-	X
Callicarpa americana	-	-	X	-	X	-	-	-	-	X	X	X	-	-	-	-	X	X
Callistemon citrinus	X	-	-	-	-	-	-	-	X	-	X	X	X	-	-	-	-	-
Callistemon rigidus	X	-	-	-	-	-	-	-	X	-	X	X	X	-	-	-	-	-
Calocedrus decurrens	-	-	-	-	-	-	-	X	X	X	X	-	X	X	-	-	-	-
Calycanthus floridus	-	X	-	-	-	-	-	-	-	X	X	-	X	-	-	-	-	-
Camellia japonica	X	-	-	-	-	-	-	-	X	-	-	-	-	X	-	-	-	X
Camellia sasanqua	X	-	-	-	-	-	-	-	X	-	-	-	-	X	-	-	-	X
Campsis grandiflora	X	-	-	-	-	X	-	-	-	X	X	X	X	-	X	-	-	-
Campsis radicans	X	-	-	-	-	X	-	-	-	X	X	X	X	-	X	-	-	-
Carissa grandiflora	X	-	X	X	-	-	X	-	-	X	X	-	X	X	X	-	-	-
Carpinus betulus	-	-	-	-	-	-	-	-	-	X	-	X	-	-	-	-	-	-
Carpinus caroliniana	-	-	-	-	-	-	-	-	-	X	-	X	-	-	-	-	-	-
Caragana arborescens	X	-	-	-	-	-	-	-	X	X	X	-	X	-	-	-	-	-
Caragana frutex	X	-	-	-	-	-	-	-	X	X	X	-	X	-	-	-	-	-
Carya spp.	-	-	-	-	-	X	-	-	-	-	-	-	-	-	-	-	-	-
Carya cordiformis	-	-	-	X	X	-	-	-	-	-	-	-	-	-	-	-	-	-
Carya illinoinensis	-	-	-	X	-	X	-	-	-	X	X	X	X	-	-	-	X	-
Carya ovata	-	-	-	X	X	X	-	-	-	-	-	-	-	-	-	-	-	-
Caryota mitis	-	-	-	-	-	-	-	X	-	X	-	-	X	-	-	-	-	-
Castanea dentata	-	-	-	X	-	-	-	-	-	-	-	X	-	-	-	X	-	-
Castanea mollissima	-	-	-	X	-	X	-	-	-	X	X	X	X	-	-	-	-	-
Catalpa bignonioides	X	-	-	-	-	X	-	X	-	X	X	X	X	-	-	-	-	-
Catalpa speciosa	X	-	-	-	-	X	-	X	-	X	X	X	X	-	-	-	-	-
Cedrus atlantica	-	-	-	-	-	-	-	-	-	X	X	-	X	X	X	-	-	-
Cedrus deodara	-	-	-	-	-	-	-	-	-	X	X	-	X	X	X	-	-	-
Cedrus libani	-	-	-	-	-	-	-	-	-	X	X	-	X	X	X	-	-	-
Celastrus orbiculatus	-	-	X	-	X	-	-	-	-	X	X	X	-	-	-	-	-	-
Celastrus scandens	-	-	X	-	X	-	-	-	-	X	X	X	-	-	-	-	-	-
Celtis laevigata	-	-	-	X	-	-	-	-	-	X	-	X	-	-	-	-	-	-
Celtis occidentalis	-	-	-	X	-	-	-	-	-	X	X	X	X	-	-	-	-	-
Cephalotaxus harringtonia	-	-	-	-	-	-	-	X	X	-	-	-	-	-	X	-	-	X
Cephalotaxus harringtonia 'Fastigata'	-	-	-	-	-	-	-	-	-	-	-	-	-	-	X	-	-	X
Cercidiphyllum japonicum	-	-	-	-	X	-	-	-	-	X	-	X	-	-	-	-	-	-
Cercis canadensis	X	-	-	-	-	-	-	-	-	X	X	-	X	X	-	-	-	-

	Showy Flowers	Fragrant Flowers	Showy Fruits	Edible Fruits	Fall Color	Litter Problems	Spines	Unusual Foliage	For Hedge or Screen	Poor Soils	Alkaline Soils	Wet Sites	Drought	Intolerant of Wet Feet	High Heat	Pest Problems	Weak Wood	Shade
Cercis chinensis	X	-	-	-	-	-	-	-	-	X	X	-	X	X	-	-	-	-
Chaenomeles japonica	X	-	-	-	-	-	X	-	X	X	-	-	X	-	-	-	-	-
Chaenomeles laginaria	X	-	-	X	-	-	X	-	X	X	-	-	X	-	-	-	-	-
Chaenomeles speciosa	X	-	-	X	-	-	X	-	X	X	-	-	X	-	-	-	-	-
Chaenomeles X superba	X	-	-	-	-	-	X	-	X	X	-	-	X	-	-	-	-	-
Chamaecyparis lawsoniana	-	-	-	-	-	-	-	-	X	X	-	-	-	X	-	-	-	-
Chamaecyparis nootkatensis	-	-	-	-	-	-	-	-	X	X	-	-	X	X	-	-	-	-
Chamaecyparis obtusa	-	-	-	-	-	-	-	-	X	X	-	-	-	X	-	-	-	X
Chamaecyparis pisifera	-	-	-	-	-	-	-	-	X	X	-	-	-	X	-	-	-	X
Chamaedorea erumpens	-	-	-	-	-	-	-	X	-	-	-	-	-	-	-	-	-	X
Chamaerops humilis	-	-	-	-	-	-	-	X	-	X	-	-	X	-	X	-	-	-
Chilopsis linearis	X	-	-	-	-	-	-	X	-	X	X	-	X	-	X	-	-	-
Chionanthus retusus	X	-	-	-	-	-	-	-	-	-	-	X	-	-	-	-	-	-
Chionanthus virginicus	X	-	-	-	-	-	-	-	-	-	-	X	-	-	-	-	-	-
Chrysalidocarpus lutescens	-	-	-	-	-	-	-	X	X	X	-	-	-	X	-	-	-	X
Cinnamomum camphora	-	-	-	-	-	X	-	-	-	X	X	-	X	-	X	-	X	-
Cladrastis lutea	-	-	-	-	-	-	-	-	-	X	X	X	X	-	-	-	-	-
Clematis spp.	X	-	-	-	-	-	-	-	-	X	-	-	-	-	-	-	-	-
Clematis X Jackmani	X	-	-	-	-	-	-	-	-	X	-	-	-	-	-	-	-	-
Clematis paniculata	X	-	-	-	-	-	-	-	-	X	-	-	-	-	-	-	-	-
Clematis virginiana	X	-	-	-	-	-	-	-	-	X	-	-	-	-	-	-	-	-
Cleyera japonica	-	-	-	-	-	-	-	X	X	-	-	-	-	-	-	-	-	X
Cocos nucifera	-	-	X	-	-	X	-	-	-	-	X	X	X	-	X	X	-	-
Codiaeum variegatum	-	-	-	-	-	X	-	X	X	X	X	-	-	X	-	X	-	X
Cornus alba	-	-	X	-	-	-	-	-	-	X	X	-	-	-	-	-	-	-
Cornus drummondi	-	-	X	-	-	-	-	-	-	X	X	X	-	X	-	-	-	-
Cornus florida	X	-	X	-	X	-	-	-	-	-	-	-	-	X	-	-	-	-
Cornus kousa	X	-	X	-	X	-	-	-	-	-	-	-	-	X	-	-	-	X
Cornus mas	X	-	X	-	X	-	-	-	-	-	-	-	-	X	-	-	-	X
Cornus sericea	-	-	X	-	-	-	-	-	X	X	-	-	X	-	-	-	-	-
Cornus stolonifera	-	-	X	-	-	-	-	-	-	X	X	-	X	-	-	-	-	-
Cortaderia selloana	X	-	-	-	-	-	X	X	X	X	X	-	X	-	-	-	-	-
Cotinus coggygria	X	-	-	-	X	-	-	-	-	X	X	-	X	X	-	-	-	-
Cotoneaster spp.	-	-	X	-	X	-	-	-	-	X	X	-	-	X	-	X	-	-
Cotoneaster dammeri	-	-	X	-	X	-	-	-	-	X	X	-	-	X	-	X	-	-
Cotoneaster divaricatus	-	-	X	-	X	-	-	-	X	X	X	-	-	X	-	X	-	-
Cotoneaster horizontalis	-	-	X	-	X	-	-	-	-	X	X	-	-	X	-	X	-	-
Cotoneaster lucidus	-	-	X	-	X	-	-	-	X	X	X	-	-	X	-	X	-	-
Cotoneaster multiflorus	-	-	X	-	X	-	-	-	X	X	X	-	-	X	-	X	-	-
Crataegus spp.	X	-	X	-	-	-	X	-	-	X	X	X	X	-	-	X	-	-
Crataegus crus-galli	X	-	X	-	-	-	X	-	-	X	X	X	X	-	-	X	-	-
Crataegus mollis	X	-	X	-	-	-	X	-	-	X	X	X	X	-	-	X	-	-
Crataegus X mordenensis	X	-	X	-	-	-	X	-	-	X	X	X	X	-	-	X	-	-
Crataegus oxyacantha	X	-	X	-	-	-	X	-	-	X	X	X	X	-	-	X	-	-
Crataegus phaenopyrum	X	-	X	-	-	-	X	-	-	X	X	X	X	-	-	X	-	-
Crataegus succulenta	X	-	X	-	-	-	X	-	-	X	X	X	X	-	-	X	-	-
Cryptomeria japonica	-	-	-	-	-	-	-	-	X	-	-	-	-	X	-	-	-	X

	Showy Flowers	Fragrant Flowers	Showy Fruits	Edible Fruits	Fall Color	Litter Problems	Spines	Unusual Foliage	For Hedge or Screen	Poor Soils	Alkaline Soils	Wet Sites	Drought	Intolerant of Wet Feet	High Heat	Pest Problems	Weak Wood	Shade
Cunninghamia lanceolata	-	-	-	-	-	-	X	-	-	-	X	-	-	X	-	-	-	-
Cupressocyparis leylandi	-	-	-	-	-	-	-	-	X	X	X	-	X	X	-	-	-	-
Cupressus arizonica	-	-	-	-	-	-	-	-	X	X	X	-	X	X	-	-	-	-
Cupressus macrocarpa	-	-	-	-	-	-	-	-	X	X	X	-	X	X	-	-	-	-
Cupressus sempervirens	-	-	-	-	-	-	-	-	X	X	X	-	X	X	-	-	-	-
Cycas circinalis	-	-	-	-	-	-	X	X	-	X	-	-	X	-	X	-	-	-
Cycas revoluta	-	-	-	-	-	-	X	X	-	X	-	-	X	-	X	-	-	X
Dasylirion texanum	X	-	-	-	-	-	X	X	-	X	X	-	X	X	-	-	-	-
Deutzia gracilis	X	X	-	-	-	-	-	-	X	X	X	-	-	-	-	-	-	-
Deutzia X lemoinei	X	X	-	-	-	-	-	-	X	X	X	-	-	-	-	-	-	-
Deutzia parviflora	X	X	-	-	-	-	-	-	X	X	X	-	-	-	-	-	-	-
Diospyros kaki	-	-	X	X	-	X	-	-	-	X	X	-	X	-	-	-	-	-
Diospyros virginiana	-	-	X	X	X	X	-	-	-	X	X	-	X	-	-	-	-	-
Elaeagnus angustifolia	-	X	-	-	-	-	-	-	-	X	X	-	X	X	-	-	-	-
Elaeagnus macrophylla	-	X	-	-	-	-	-	X	X	X	X	-	X	X	-	-	-	-
Elaeagnus pungens	-	X	-	-	-	-	-	X	X	X	X	-	X	X	-	-	-	-
Erianthus ravennae	X	-	-	-	-	-	-	X	-	X	X	-	X	X	X	-	-	-
Eriobotrya japonica	-	-	X	X	-	-	-	X	-	-	-	-	X	-	-	X	-	-
Eucommia ulmoides	-	-	-	-	-	-	-	-	-	X	X	-	X	-	-	-	-	-
Euonymus alata	-	-	-	-	X	-	-	-	X	X	X	-	X	-	-	-	-	-
Euonymus bungeana	-	-	-	X	X	-	-	-	X	X	X	-	X	-	-	-	-	-
Euonymus europaea	-	-	-	X	X	-	-	-	X	X	X	-	X	-	-	-	-	-
Euonymus fortunei	-	-	-	X	-	-	-	-	-	X	X	-	X	-	-	-	-	X
Euonymus japonica	-	-	-	X	-	-	-	-	X	X	X	-	X	-	-	X	-	X
Euonymus kiautschovica	-	-	-	X	-	-	-	-	X	X	X	-	X	-	-	-	-	X
Exochorda geraldi	X	-	-	-	-	-	-	-	-	-	-	-	-	-	-	-	-	-
Exochorda racemosa	X	-	-	-	-	-	-	-	X	X	X	-	-	-	-	-	-	-
Fagus grandiflora	-	-	-	-	-	-	-	-	-	-	-	-	-	-	-	-	-	-
Fagus sylvatica	-	-	-	-	-	-	-	-	-	-	-	-	-	-	-	-	-	-
Fatshedera lizei	-	-	-	-	-	-	-	-	-	X	-	-	-	-	-	-	-	-
Fatsia japonica	-	-	-	-	-	-	-	-	-	X	-	-	-	-	-	-	-	-
Feijoa sellowiana	X	-	-	X	-	-	-	-	-	X	-	-	X	-	-	-	-	-
Festuca ovina	-	-	X	-	-	-	-	X	-	X	-	-	X	-	-	-	-	-
Ficus carica	-	-	-	X	-	-	-	-	-	X	-	-	-	-	-	-	-	-
Ficus pumila	-	-	-	-	-	-	-	-	-	X	-	-	-	X	-	-	-	X
Forsythia spp.	X	-	-	-	-	-	-	-	-	-	-	-	-	-	-	-	-	-
Forsythia intermedia	X	-	-	-	-	-	-	-	X	X	-	-	X	-	-	-	-	-
Forsythia japonica	X	-	-	-	-	-	-	-	X	X	-	-	X	-	-	-	-	-
Forsythia suspensa	X	-	-	-	-	-	-	-	X	X	-	-	X	-	-	-	-	-
Forsythia viridissima	X	-	-	-	-	-	-	-	X	X	-	-	X	-	-	-	-	-
Franklinia alatamaha	X	-	-	-	-	-	-	-	-	-	-	-	-	X	-	-	-	-
Fraxinus americana	-	-	-	-	X	-	-	-	-	-	-	X	X	X	-	-	-	-
Fraxinus excelsior	-	-	-	-	X	-	-	-	-	-	-	X	X	X	-	-	-	-
Fraxinus pennsylvanica	-	-	-	-	X	-	-	-	-	-	X	X	X	X	-	-	-	-
Fraxinus quadrangulata	-	-	-	-	X	-	-	-	-	-	-	X	X	-	-	-	-	-
Gardenia jasminoides	X	X	-	-	-	-	-	-	X	-	-	-	-	-	-	-	-	-
Gelsemium sempervirens	X	-	-	-	-	-	-	-	-	-	-	-	-	X	-	-	-	X

	Showy Flowers	Fragrant Flowers	Showy Fruits	Edible Fruits	Fall Color	Litter Problems	Spines	Unusual Foliage	For Hedge or Screen	Poor Soils	Alkaline Soils	Wet Sites	Drought	Intolerant of Wet Feet	High Heat	Pest Problems	Weak Wood	Shade
Ginkgo biloba	-	-	-	-	X	X	-	-	-	-	-	-	X	-	-	-	-	-
Gleditsia triacanthos	-	-	-	-	-	-	-	-	-	X	X	-	X	-	-	-	-	-
Gordonia lasianthus	X	-	-	-	-	-	-	-	-	-	-	X	-	-	-	-	-	-
Gymnocladus dioica	-	-	-	-	-	-	-	-	-	X	X	-	X	-	-	-	-	-
Halesia carolina	X	-	-	-	-	-	-	-	-	-	-	-	-	-	-	-	-	X
Halesia diptera	X	-	-	-	-	-	-	-	-	-	-	-	-	-	-	-	-	X
Halesia monticola	X	-	-	-	-	-	-	-	-	-	-	-	-	-	-	-	-	X
Hamamelis vernalis	X	-	-	-	X	-	-	-	-	X	-	-	-	-	-	-	-	-
Hamamelis virginiana	X	-	-	-	X	-	-	-	-	X	-	-	-	-	-	-	-	-
Hedera canariensis	-	-	-	-	-	-	-	-	-	X	X	-	-	-	-	-	-	X
Hedera helix	-	-	-	-	-	-	-	-	-	X	X	-	-	-	-	-	-	X
Hesperaloe parviflora	X	-	-	-	-	-	-	X	-	X	X	-	X	-	-	-	-	-
Hibiscus rosa-sinensis	X	-	-	-	-	-	-	-	X	X	X	-	-	-	-	-	-	-
Hibiscus syriacus	X	-	-	-	-	-	-	-	X	X	X	-	X	-	-	-	-	-
Hosta spp.	-	-	-	-	-	-	-	X	-	-	-	-	-	-	-	-	-	X
Hosta decorata	-	-	-	-	-	-	-	X	-	-	-	-	-	-	-	-	-	X
Hosta fortunei	-	-	-	-	-	-	-	X	-	-	-	-	-	-	-	-	-	X
Hosta seiboldi	-	-	-	-	-	-	-	X	-	-	-	-	-	-	-	-	-	X
Hydrangea macrophylla	X	-	-	-	-	-	-	-	-	-	-	-	-	-	-	-	-	-
Hydrangea paniculata	X	-	-	-	-	-	-	-	-	-	-	-	-	-	-	-	-	-
Hydrangea quercifolia	X	-	-	-	-	-	-	-	-	-	-	-	-	-	-	-	-	-
Hypericum patulum	X	-	-	-	-	-	-	-	X	X	-	-	-	-	-	-	-	-
Hypericum prolificum	X	-	-	-	-	-	-	-	X	X	-	-	-	-	-	-	-	-
Iberis sempervirens	X	-	-	-	-	-	-	-	-	-	-	-	-	-	-	-	-	X
Ilex altaclarensis	-	-	X	-	-	-	-	-	-	-	-	-	-	-	-	-	-	-
Ilex aquifolium	-	-	X	-	-	-	-	-	-	-	-	-	-	-	-	-	-	-
Ilex cornuta	-	-	X	-	-	-	-	-	X	X	-	-	-	-	-	-	-	-
Ilex crenata	-	-	-	-	-	-	-	-	X	-	-	-	-	-	-	-	-	-
Ilex decidua	-	-	X	-	X	-	-	-	X	X	X	X	X	-	-	-	-	-
Ilex latifolia	-	-	X	-	-	-	-	-	-	-	-	-	-	-	-	-	-	-
Ilex X meserveae	-	-	X	-	-	-	-	-	X	-	-	-	-	-	-	-	-	-
Ilex opaca	-	-	X	-	-	-	-	-	X	-	-	X	-	-	-	-	-	-
Ilex pernyi	-	-	X	-	-	-	-	-	X	X	-	-	-	-	-	-	-	-
Ilex rotunda	-	-	X	-	-	-	-	-	-	-	-	-	-	-	-	-	-	-
Ilex verticillata	-	-	X	-	X	-	-	-	X	-	-	-	-	-	-	-	-	-
Ilex vomitoria	-	-	X	-	-	-	-	-	X	X	-	X	X	-	-	-	-	-
Illicium anisatum	-	-	-	-	-	-	-	-	X	-	-	X	-	-	-	-	-	-
Illicium floridanum	-	-	-	-	-	-	-	-	X	-	-	X	-	-	-	-	-	-
Itea virginica	X	X	-	-	X	-	-	-	X	-	-	X	-	-	-	-	-	X
Jasminum floridum	X	-	-	-	-	-	-	-	X	-	-	X	X	-	-	-	-	-
Jasminum mesnyi	X	-	-	-	-	-	-	-	X	-	-	X	X	-	-	-	-	-
Jasminum nudiflorum	X	-	-	-	-	-	-	-	X	-	-	X	X	-	-	-	-	-
Juglans nigra	-	-	-	X	-	-	-	-	-	X	X	-	X	-	-	X	-	-
Juniperus chinensis	-	-	-	-	-	-	-	-	X	X	-	-	X	X	X	-	-	-
Juniperus conferta	-	-	-	-	-	-	-	-	-	X	-	-	X	X	X	-	-	-
Juniperus davurica	-	-	-	-	-	-	-	-	-	X	-	-	X	X	X	-	-	-
Juniperus excelsa	-	-	-	-	-	-	-	-	-	X	-	-	X	X	X	-	-	-

	Showy Flowers	Fragrant Flowers	Showy Fruits	Edible Fruits	Fall Color	Litter Problems	Spines	Unusual Foliage	For Hedge or Screen	Poor Soils	Alkaline Soils	Wet Sites	Drought	Intolerant of Wet Feet	High Heat	Pest Problems	Weak Wood	Shade
Juniperus horizontalis	-	-	-	-	-	-	-	-	-	X	-	-	X	X	X	-	-	-
Juniperus procumbens	-	-	-	-	-	-	-	-	-	X	-	-	X	X	X	-	-	-
Juniperus sabina	-	-	-	-	-	-	-	-	-	X	-	-	X	X	X	-	-	-
Juniperus scopulorum	-	-	-	-	-	-	-	-	X	X	-	-	X	X	X	-	-	-
Juniperus squamata	-	-	-	-	-	-	-	-	-	X	-	-	X	X	X	-	-	-
Juniperus silicicola	-	-	-	-	-	-	-	-	-	X	-	-	X	X	X	-	-	-
Juniperus virigiana	-	-	-	-	-	-	-	-	X	X	-	-	X	X	X	-	-	-
Kerria japonica	X	-	-	-	-	-	-	-	X	X	X	-	X	-	-	-	-	-
Koelreuteria bipinnata	X	-	X	-	-	-	-	-	-	X	X	-	X	-	-	-	X	-
Koelreuteria elegans	X	-	X	-	X	-	-	-	-	X	X	-	X	-	-	-	X	-
Koelreuteria formosana	X	-	X	-	X	-	-	-	-	X	X	-	X	-	-	-	X	-
Koelreuteria paniculata	X	-	X	-	X	-	-	-	-	X	X	-	X	-	-	-	X	-
Kolkwitzia amabilis	X	-	-	-	-	-	-	-	X	X	X	-	X	-	-	-	-	-
Lagerstroemia fauriei	X	-	-	-	-	-	-	-	-	X	X	-	X	-	-	-	-	-
Lagerstroemia indica	X	-	-	-	X	-	-	-	-	X	X	-	X	-	-	-	-	-
Larix decidua	-	-	-	-	-	-	-	-	-	X	-	X	-	-	-	-	-	-
Larix laricina	-	-	-	-	-	-	-	-	-	X	-	X	-	-	-	-	-	-
Leucophyllum frutescens	X	-	-	-	-	-	-	-	X	X	X	-	X	X	X	-	-	-
Libocedrus decurrens	-	-	-	-	-	-	-	-	-	-	X	-	X	X	-	-	-	-
Ligustrum japonicum	X	X	-	-	-	-	-	-	X	X	X	-	X	-	X	-	-	-
Ligustrum lucidum	X	-	-	-	-	-	-	-	X	X	X	-	X	-	X	-	-	-
Ligustrum obtusifolium	X	-	-	-	-	-	-	-	X	X	X	-	X	-	X	-	-	-
Ligustrum ovalifolium	X	-	-	-	-	-	-	-	X	X	X	-	X	-	X	-	-	-
Ligustrum sinense	X	X	-	-	-	-	-	-	X	X	X	-	X	-	X	-	-	-
Ligustrum texanum	X	X	-	-	-	-	-	-	X	X	X	-	X	-	X	-	-	-
Ligustrum vicaryi	X	X	-	-	-	-	-	-	X	X	X	-	X	-	X	-	-	-
Ligustrum vulgare	X	X	-	-	-	-	-	-	X	X	X	-	X	-	X	-	-	-
Liquidambar formosana	-	-	-	-	X	-	-	-	-	-	-	-	X	-	-	-	-	-
Liquidambar styraciflua	-	-	-	-	X	X	-	-	-	-	-	-	X	-	-	-	-	-
Liriodendron tulipifera	-	-	-	-	X	-	-	-	-	-	-	-	X	-	-	-	X	-
Liriope muscari	X	-	-	-	-	-	-	X	-	X	-	-	-	-	-	-	-	X
Livistona chinensis	-	-	-	-	-	-	X	X	-	X	-	-	-	-	-	X	-	-
Lonicera alpigena	X	-	X	-	-	-	-	-	X	X	X	-	X	-	-	-	-	-
Lonicera fragrantissima	X	X	-	-	-	-	-	-	X	X	X	-	X	-	-	-	-	-
Lonicera japonica	X	-	-	-	-	-	-	-	X	X	X	-	X	-	-	-	-	-
Lonicera maacki	X	-	X	-	-	-	-	-	X	X	X	-	X	-	-	-	-	-
Lonicera morrowi	X	-	X	-	-	-	-	-	X	X	X	-	X	-	X	-	-	-
Lonicera sempervirens	X	-	-	-	-	-	-	-	-	X	X	-	X	-	-	-	-	-
Lonicera tatarica	X	-	X	-	-	-	-	-	X	X	X	-	X	-	X	-	-	-
Lonicera X xylosteoides	X	-	X	-	-	-	-	-	X	X	X	-	X	-	X	-	-	-
Loropetalum chinense	X	-	-	-	-	-	-	X	X	X	-	-	-	-	-	-	-	-
Maclura pomifera	-	-	-	-	X	X	X	-	-	X	X	-	X	-	-	-	-	-
Magnolia acuminata	X	-	-	-	-	-	-	-	-	-	-	X	-	-	-	-	-	-
Magnolia grandiflora	X	X	-	-	X	-	X	-	-	-	-	X	-	-	-	-	-	-
Magnolia macrophylla	X	X	-	-	-	X	-	X	-	-	-	X	-	-	-	-	-	-
Magnolia soulangiana	X	-	-	-	-	-	-	-	-	-	-	-	-	-	-	-	-	-
Magnolia stellata	X	-	-	-	-	-	-	-	-	-	-	-	-	-	-	-	-	-

	Showy Flowers	Fragrant Flowers	Showy Fruits	Edible Fruits	Fall Color	Litter Problems	Spines	Unusual Foliage	For Hedge or Screen	Poor Soils	Alkaline Soils	Wet Sites	Drought	Intolerant of Wet Feet	High Heat	Pest Problems	Weak Wood	Shade
Magnolia tripetala	-	-	-	-	-	X	-	X	-	-	-	X	-	-	-	-	-	-
Magnolia virginiana	X	X	-	-	-	-	-	X	-	-	-	X	-	-	-	-	-	-
Mahonia aquifolium	X	-	X	-	-	-	-	-	X	X	X	-	-	-	-	-	-	X
Mahonia bealei	X	-	X	-	-	-	X	X	X	X	X	-	-	-	-	-	-	X
Mahonia fortunei	X	-	X	-	-	-	-	X	X	X	X	-	-	-	-	-	-	X
Mahonia lamariifolia	X	-	X	-	-	-	X	X	X	X	X	-	-	-	-	-	-	X
Malus spp.	X	X	X	X	X	X	-	-	-	-	-	-	-	-	-	-	-	-
Malus baccata	X	X	X	X	X	X	-	-	-	-	-	-	-	-	-	-	-	-
Malus floribundi	X	X	X	X	X	X	-	-	-	-	-	-	-	-	-	-	-	-
Malus sargenti	X	X	X	X	X	X	-	-	-	-	-	-	-	-	-	-	-	-
Melia azedarach	-	-	-	-	-	X	-	-	-	X	X	-	X	-	-	-	-	-
Metasequoia glyptostroboides	-	-	-	-	-	-	-	-	-	X	X	-	-	X	-	-	-	-
Miscanthus sinensis	X	-	-	-	X	-	-	X	X	X	X	-	X	-	X	-	-	-
Morus alba	-	-	X	-	-	-	-	-	-	X	X	X	X	-	-	-	-	-
Morus rubra	-	-	X	-	-	X	-	-	-	X	X	X	X	-	-	-	-	-
Myrica cerifera	-	-	-	-	-	-	-	-	X	X	X	X	X	-	-	-	-	-
Myrica pensylvanica	-	-	-	-	-	-	-	-	X	X	X	X	X	-	X	-	-	-
Nandina domestica	X	-	X	-	-	-	-	-	-	X	-	-	X	-	-	-	-	X
Neodypsis decaryi	-	-	-	-	-	-	-	X	-	-	-	-	-	-	-	-	-	-
Nerium oleander	X	-	-	-	-	-	-	-	X	X	X	X	X	-	X	-	-	-
Nyssa sylvatica	-	-	-	-	-	-	-	-	-	-	-	X	-	-	-	-	-	-
Ophiopogon japonicus	-	-	-	-	-	-	-	X	X	X	-	-	-	-	-	-	-	-
Opuntia spp.	X	-	X	X	-	-	X	X	-	-	X	-	X	X	X	-	-	-
Opuntia engelmanni	X	-	-	-	-	-	X	X	-	-	X	-	X	X	X	-	-	-
Opuntia imricata	X	-	-	-	-	-	X	X	-	-	X	-	X	X	X	-	-	-
Opuntia lindheimeri	X	-	-	-	-	-	X	X	-	-	X	-	X	X	X	-	-	-
Osmanthus X fortunei	-	-	-	-	-	-	-	-	X	-	-	-	-	-	-	-	-	-
Osmanthus fragrans	-	X	-	-	-	-	-	-	X	-	-	-	-	-	-	-	-	-
Osmanthus hetrophyllus	-	-	-	-	-	-	-	-	X	-	-	-	-	-	-	-	-	X
Osmanthus ilicifolius	-	-	-	-	-	-	-	-	X	-	-	-	-	-	-	-	-	X
Ostrya virginiana	-	-	-	-	-	-	-	-	-	X	X	-	X	-	-	-	-	-
Oxydendrum arboreum	X	-	-	-	-	-	-	-	-	-	-	X	-	-	-	-	-	X
Pachysandra procumbens	-	-	-	-	-	-	-	-	-	-	-	-	-	-	-	-	-	X
Pachysandra terminalis	-	-	-	-	-	-	-	-	-	-	-	-	-	-	-	-	-	X
Parkinsonia aculeata	X	-	-	-	-	-	X	-	-	X	X	-	X	X	-	-	-	-
Parthenocissus quinquefolia	-	-	-	-	-	-	-	-	-	X	-	-	-	-	-	-	-	X
Parthenocissus tricuspidata	-	-	-	-	-	-	-	-	-	X	-	-	-	-	-	-	-	X
Paulownia tomentosa	X	-	-	-	-	-	-	-	-	X	X	-	X	-	-	-	-	-
Paxistima canbyi	X	-	-	-	-	-	-	-	-	-	-	-	-	-	-	-	-	X
Pennisetum alopecuroides	-	-	-	-	-	-	-	-	-	X	X	-	-	-	-	-	-	-
Pennisetum ruppeli	-	-	-	-	-	-	-	-	-	X	X	-	-	-	-	-	-	-
Phellodendron amurense	-	-	-	-	-	-	-	-	-	X	X	-	-	-	-	-	-	-
Phellodendron chinense	-	-	-	-	-	-	-	-	-	X	-	-	-	-	-	-	-	-
Philadelphis coronarius	X	-	-	-	-	-	-	-	X	X	-	-	-	-	-	-	-	-
Philadelphis X lemoinei	X	-	-	-	-	-	-	-	X	X	-	-	-	-	-	-	-	-
Philadelphis microphyllus	X	-	-	-	-	-	-	-	X	X	-	-	-	-	-	-	-	-
Phlox subulata	X	-	-	-	-	-	-	-	-	X	X	-	-	-	-	-	-	X

	Showy Flowers	Fragrant Flowers	Showy Fruits	Edible Fruits	Fall Color	Litter Problems	Spines	Unusual Foliage	For Hedge or Screen	Poor Soils	Alkaline Soils	Wet Sites	Drought	Intolerant of Wet Feet	High Heat	Pest Problems	Weak Wood	Shade
Photinia X 'Fraseri'	X	-	-	-	-	-	-	X	X	X	X	-	X	-	X	-	-	-
Photinia glabra	X	-	-	-	-	-	-	-	X	X	X	-	X	-	-	-	-	-
Photinia serrulata	X	-	-	-	-	-	-	-	X	X	X	-	X	-	-	-	-	-
Phoenix canariensis	-	-	-	-	-	-	X	-	-	X	X	-	X	-	X	-	-	-
Phoenix dactylifera	-	-	-	X	-	-	X	-	-	X	X	-	X	-	X	-	-	-
Phoenix reclinata	-	-	-	-	-	-	X	-	X	X	X	-	X	-	X	-	-	-
Phoenix roebelenii	-	-	-	-	-	-	X	-	X	X	X	-	X	-	-	-	-	-
Phoenix sylvestris	-	-	-	-	-	-	X	-	-	X	X	-	X	-	X	-	-	-
Phyllostachys aureodulcata	-	-	-	-	-	X	-	-	X	-	-	X	-	-	-	-	-	-
Physocarpus monogymus	-	-	-	-	-	-	-	-	X	X	-	-	-	-	-	-	-	-
Physocarpus opulifolius	-	-	-	-	-	-	-	-	X	X	-	-	-	-	-	-	-	-
Picea abies	-	-	-	-	-	-	-	-	X	X	-	X	X	-	-	-	-	-
Picea glauca 'Densata'	-	-	-	-	-	-	-	-	X	X	-	X	X	-	-	-	-	-
Picea pungens	-	-	-	-	-	-	-	-	X	X	-	X	X	-	-	-	-	-
Pieris japonica	X	X	-	-	-	-	-	X	X	-	-	-	-	-	-	X	-	-
Pinus cembroides	-	-	-	-	-	-	-	-	X	X	-	X	X	-	-	-	-	-
Pinus densiflora	-	-	-	-	-	-	-	-	X	X	-	X	X	-	-	-	-	-
Pinus densiflora 'Umbraculifera'	-	-	-	-	-	-	-	-	X	X	-	X	X	-	-	-	-	-
Pinus echinata	-	-	-	-	-	-	-	-	X	X	-	X	X	-	-	-	-	-
Pinus elliotti	-	-	-	-	-	-	-	-	X	X	-	X	X	-	-	-	-	-
Pinus flexilis	-	-	-	-	-	-	-	-	X	X	-	X	X	-	-	-	-	-
Pinus glabra	-	-	-	-	-	-	-	-	X	X	-	X	X	-	-	-	-	-
Pinus mugo	-	-	-	-	-	-	-	-	X	X	-	X	X	-	-	-	-	-
Pinus nigra	-	-	-	-	-	-	-	-	X	X	-	X	X	-	-	-	-	-
Pinus palustris	-	-	-	-	-	-	-	-	X	X	-	X	X	-	-	-	-	-
Pinus pinaster	-	-	-	-	-	-	-	-	X	X	-	X	X	-	-	-	-	-
Pinus ponderosa	-	-	-	-	-	-	-	-	X	X	-	X	X	-	-	-	-	-
Pinus radiata	-	-	-	-	-	-	-	-	X	X	-	X	X	-	-	-	-	-
Pinus resinosa	-	-	-	-	-	-	-	-	X	X	-	X	X	-	-	-	-	-
Pinus strobiformis	-	-	-	-	-	-	-	-	X	X	-	X	X	-	-	-	-	-
Pinus strobus	-	-	-	-	-	-	-	-	X	X	-	X	X	-	-	-	-	-
Pinus sylvestris	-	-	-	-	-	-	-	-	X	X	-	X	X	-	-	-	-	-
Pinus taeda	-	-	-	-	-	-	-	-	X	X	-	X	X	-	-	-	-	-
Pinus thunbergiana	-	-	-	-	-	-	-	-	X	X	-	X	X	-	-	-	-	-
Pistacia chinensis	-	-	-	-	-	-	-	-	X	X	-	-	X	X	-	-	-	-
Pittosporum tobira	-	-	-	-	-	-	-	-	X	X	X	-	-	-	-	-	-	-
Platanus X acerifolia	-	-	-	-	-	-	-	-	-	X	X	X	X	-	-	-	-	-
Platanus occidentalis	-	-	-	-	-	X	-	-	-	X	X	X	X	-	-	-	X	-
Platanus orientalis	-	-	-	-	-	-	-	-	-	-	X	X	X	-	-	-	-	-
Podocarpus gracilior	-	-	-	-	-	-	-	X	X	-	-	-	X	X	-	-	-	-
Podocarpus macrophyllus	-	-	-	-	-	-	-	-	X	-	-	-	X	X	-	-	-	-
Podocarpus nagi	-	-	-	-	-	-	-	-	X	-	-	-	X	X	-	-	-	-
Poncirus trifoliata	-	-	-	X	-	-	X	-	X	X	-	-	X	-	-	-	-	-
Populus alba	-	-	-	-	X	X	-	-	-	X	X	X	X	-	-	-	-	-
Populus deltoides	-	-	-	-	X	-	-	-	-	X	X	X	X	-	-	-	X	-
Populus nigra 'Italica'	-	-	-	-	-	-	-	-	-	X	X	X	X	-	-	-	-	-
Potentilla fruticosa	X	-	-	-	-	-	-	-	X	X	-	-	-	-	-	-	-	-

	Showy Flowers	Fragrant Flowers	Showy Fruits	Edible Fruits	Fall Color	Litter Problems	Spines	Unusual Foliage	For Hedge or Screen	Poor Soils	Alkaline Soils	Wet Sites	Drought	Intolerant of Wet Feet	High Heat	Pest Problems	Weak Wood	Shade
Prosopis juliflora	-	X	-	-	-	-	X	X	-	X	X	-	X	-	X	-	-	-
Prunus armeniaca	X	-	-	X	-	-	-	-	-	X	X	-	X	-	-	-	-	-
Prunus caroliniana	X	-	-	-	-	-	-	-	-	X	X	-	-	-	-	-	-	-
Prunus cerasifera	X	-	-	-	-	-	-	-	-	-	X	-	-	-	-	-	-	-
Prunus X cistena	X	-	-	-	-	-	-	-	-	X	X	-	-	-	-	-	-	-
Prunus glandulosa	X	-	-	-	-	-	-	-	-	X	-	-	-	-	-	-	-	-
Prunus laurocerasus	X	-	-	-	-	-	-	-	-	-	-	-	-	X	-	-	-	-
Prunus persica	X	-	-	X	-	-	-	-	-	-	-	-	-	X	-	-	-	-
Prunus pumila	X	-	-	-	-	-	-	-	-	-	-	-	-	-	-	-	-	-
Prunus serotina	X	-	-	-	-	-	-	-	-	-	-	-	-	-	-	-	-	-
Prunus serrulata	X	-	-	-	-	-	-	-	-	-	-	-	-	-	-	-	-	-
Pseudotsuga menziesi	-	-	-	-	-	-	-	-	X	X	-	-	X	-	-	-	-	-
Punica granatum	X	-	X	X	X	-	-	-	-	X	X	-	X	-	-	-	-	-
Pyracantha coccinea	X	-	X	-	X	-	X	-	X	X	X	-	X	-	-	-	-	-
Pyracantha koidzumi	X	-	X	-	X	-	X	-	X	X	X	-	X	-	-	-	-	-
Pyrus calleryana	X	-	-	-	X	-	-	-	-	X	X	-	X	-	-	-	-	-
Pyrus communis	X	-	-	X	X	-	-	-	-	X	X	-	X	-	-	-	-	-
Quercus acutissima	-	-	-	-	X	-	-	-	-	X	-	-	X	-	-	-	-	-
Quercus alba	-	-	-	-	X	-	-	-	-	-	-	-	-	-	-	-	-	-
Quercus bicolor	-	-	-	-	X	-	-	-	-	-	-	-	-	-	-	-	-	-
Quercus borealis	-	-	-	-	X	-	-	-	-	-	-	-	-	-	-	-	-	-
Quercus falcata	-	-	-	-	X	-	-	-	-	X	-	-	X	-	-	-	-	-
Quercus imbricaria	-	-	-	-	-	-	-	-	-	-	-	X	-	-	-	-	-	-
Quercus laurifolia	-	-	-	-	-	-	-	-	-	X	-	X	-	-	-	-	-	-
Quercus macrocarpa	-	-	-	-	-	X	-	-	-	X	X	-	X	-	-	-	-	-
Quercus marilandica	-	-	-	-	X	-	-	-	-	X	X	-	X	-	-	-	-	-
Quercus muehlenbergi	-	-	-	-	X	-	-	-	-	X	X	-	X	-	-	-	-	-
Quercus nigra	-	-	-	-	-	-	-	-	-	X	-	-	-	-	-	-	-	-
Quercus palustris	-	-	-	-	X	-	-	-	-	-	-	-	-	-	-	-	-	-
Quercus phellos	-	-	-	-	X	-	-	-	-	-	-	-	-	-	-	-	-	-
Quercus robur	-	-	-	-	-	-	-	-	-	-	-	-	-	-	-	-	-	-
Quercus rubra	-	-	-	-	X	-	-	-	-	-	-	-	-	-	-	-	-	-
Quercus shumardi	-	-	-	-	X	-	-	-	-	X	X	-	X	-	-	-	-	-
Quercus stellata	-	-	-	-	X	-	-	-	-	X	X	-	X	-	-	-	-	-
Quercus virginiana	-	-	-	-	-	-	-	-	-	X	-	-	X	-	-	-	-	-
Raphiolepis indica	X	-	X	-	-	-	-	-	X	-	-	-	-	X	-	-	-	-
Raphiolepis umbellata	X	-	X	-	-	-	-	-	X	-	-	-	-	X	-	-	-	-
Raphis excelsa	-	-	-	-	-	-	-	X	X	-	-	-	-	-	-	-	-	X
Rhamnus davurica	-	-	-	-	-	-	-	-	X	X	-	-	-	-	-	-	-	-
Rhamnus frangula	-	-	-	-	-	-	-	-	X	X	-	-	-	-	-	-	-	-
Rhapidophyllum hystrix	-	-	-	-	-	-	X	X	-	-	-	-	-	-	-	-	-	X
Rhododendron spp.	X	-	-	-	-	-	-	-	-	-	-	-	-	X	-	-	-	X
Rhododendron catawbiense	X	-	-	-	-	-	-	-	-	-	-	-	-	X	-	-	-	X
Rhododendron indicum	X	-	-	-	-	-	-	-	-	-	-	-	-	X	-	-	-	X
Rhododendron obtusum	X	-	-	-	-	-	-	-	-	-	-	-	-	X	-	-	-	X
Rhododendron simsii	X	-	-	-	-	-	-	-	-	-	-	-	-	X	-	-	-	X
Rhodotypos scandens	X	-	X	-	-	-	-	-	-	-	-	-	-	X	-	-	-	X

	Showy Flowers	Fragrant Flowers	Showy Fruits	Edible Fruits	Fall Color	Litter Problems	Spines	Unusual Foliage	For Hedge or Screen	Poor Soils	Alkaline Soils	Wet Sites	Drought	Intolerant of Wet Feet	High Heat	Pest Problems	Weak Wood	Shade
Rhus aromatica	-	-	-	-	-	-	-	-	-	X	X	-	X	X	-	-	-	-
Rhus copallina	-	-	X	-	X	-	-	-	-	X	X	-	X	X	-	-	X	-
Rhus glabra	-	-	X	-	X	-	-	-	-	X	X	-	X	X	-	-	X	-
Rhus typhina	-	-	X	-	X	-	-	-	X	X	X	-	X	X	-	-	X	-
Ribes alpinum	X	-	-	X	X	-	X	-	X	X	-	-	-	-	-	-	-	-
Ribes cynosbati	X	-	-	X	-	-	X	-	X	X	-	-	-	-	-	-	-	-
Ribes hirtelloum	X	-	-	X	-	-	X	-	-	X	-	-	-	-	-	-	-	-
Robinia pseudoacacia	X	-	-	-	-	X	X	-	-	X	X	-	X	-	-	-	-	-
Rosa banksiae	X	-	-	-	-	-	-	-	-	X	X	X	-	-	-	-	-	-
Rosa spp.	X	-	-	-	-	-	X	-	-	-	-	-	-	-	X	-	X	-
Rosa rugosa	X	-	-	-	-	-	X	-	-	-	-	-	-	-	X	-	-	-
Rosemarinus officinalis	X	-	-	-	-	-	-	X	-	X	X	-	X	-	X	-	-	-
Roystonea regia	-	-	-	-	-	-	-	X	-	-	-	-	-	-	-	-	-	-
Sabal minor	-	-	-	-	-	-	-	X	-	-	-	X	-	-	-	-	-	-
Sabal palmetto	-	-	-	-	-	-	-	-	-	X	-	X	-	-	X	-	-	-
Salix alba	-	-	-	-	-	X	-	-	-	X	-	X	-	-	-	-	X	-
Salix babylonica	-	-	-	-	-	X	-	-	-	X	-	X	-	-	-	-	X	-
Salix X 'Blanda'	-	-	-	-	-	-	-	-	-	X	-	X	-	-	-	-	X	-
Salix discolor	X	-	-	-	-	-	-	-	-	X	-	X	-	-	-	-	X	-
Salix gracilistyla	-	-	-	-	-	-	-	-	-	X	-	X	-	-	-	-	X	-
Salix matsudana 'Tortuosa'	-	-	-	-	-	-	-	-	-	X	-	X	-	-	-	-	X	-
Salix nigra	-	-	-	-	-	-	-	-	-	X	-	X	-	-	-	-	X	-
Salvia gregii	X	-	-	-	-	-	-	-	-	X	X	-	X	-	X	-	-	-
Santolina chamaecyparissus	X	-	-	-	-	-	-	X	-	X	X	-	X	X	X	-	-	-
Santolina virens	X	-	-	-	-	-	-	X	-	X	X	-	X	X	X	-	-	-
Sapindus drummondi	-	-	X	-	X	X	-	-	-	X	X	-	X	-	-	-	-	-
Sapium sebiferum	-	-	X	-	X	X	-	-	-	X	-	X	X	-	-	-	-	-
Sassafras albidum	-	-	-	-	X	-	-	-	-	-	-	-	-	-	-	-	-	-
Sasa palmata	-	-	-	-	-	-	-	X	-	X	-	X	-	-	-	-	-	X
Sasa pigmaea	-	-	-	-	-	-	-	X	-	X	-	X	-	-	-	-	-	X
Sedum acre	X	-	-	-	-	-	-	-	-	X	X	-	X	-	-	-	-	-
Sedum spectabile	X	-	-	-	-	-	-	-	-	X	X	-	X	-	-	-	-	-
Sedum spurium	X	-	-	-	-	-	-	-	-	X	X	-	X	-	-	-	-	-
Serenoa repens	-	-	-	-	-	-	X	-	-	X	-	-	X	-	X	-	-	-
Sophora japonica	-	-	-	-	-	-	-	-	-	X	-	-	-	-	-	-	-	-
Sophora secundiflora	X	-	-	-	-	-	-	-	X	X	X	-	X	-	X	-	-	-
Sorbus aucuparia	-	-	X	-	X	-	-	-	-	-	-	-	-	-	-	-	-	-
Spiraea X arguta	X	-	-	-	-	-	-	-	-	X	X	-	-	-	-	-	-	-
Spiraea X bumalda	X	-	-	-	-	-	-	-	-	X	X	-	X	-	-	-	-	-
Spiraea cantoniensis	X	-	-	-	-	-	-	-	-	X	X	-	-	-	-	-	-	-
Spiraea japonica	X	-	-	-	-	-	-	-	-	X	X	-	-	-	-	-	-	-
Spiraea prunifolia	X	-	-	-	-	-	-	-	-	X	X	-	-	-	-	-	-	-
Spiraea thunbergi	X	-	-	-	-	-	-	-	-	X	X	X	-	X	-	-	-	-
Spiraea trilobata	X	-	-	-	-	-	-	-	-	X	X	-	-	-	-	-	-	-
Spiraea X vanhouttei	X	-	-	-	-	-	-	-	-	X	X	X	-	X	-	-	-	-
Stewartia pseudocamellia	X	-	-	-	X	-	-	-	-	-	-	-	-	-	-	-	-	-
Syringa amurensis	X	-	-	-	-	-	-	-	-	X	X	-	-	-	-	-	-	-

	Showy Flowers	Fragrant Flowers	Showy Fruits	Edible Fruits	Fall Color	Litter Problems	Spines	Unusual Foliage	For Hedge or Screen	Poor Soils	Alkaline Soils	Wet Sites	Drought	Intolerant of Wet Feet	High Heat	Pest Problems	Weak Wood	Shade
Syringa pekinensis	X	-	-	-	-	-	-	-	-	X	X	-	-	-	-	-	-	-
Syringa persica	X	-	-	-	-	-	-	-	X	X	X	-	X	-	-	-	-	-
Syringa reticulata	X	-	-	-	-	-	-	-	-	X	X	-	-	-	-	-	-	-
Syringa velutina	X	-	-	-	-	-	-	-	X	X	X	-	-	-	-	-	-	-
Syringa vulgaris	X	-	-	-	-	-	-	-	X	X	X	-	X	-	-	-	-	-
Taxodium ascendens	-	-	-	-	X	-	-	X	-	-	-	X	-	-	-	-	-	-
Taxodium distichum	-	-	-	-	X	-	-	X	-	-	-	X	-	-	-	-	-	-
Taxus spp.	-	-	-	-	-	-	-	-	X	-	-	-	-	X	-	-	-	X
Taxus baccata	-	-	-	-	-	-	-	-	X	-	-	-	-	X	-	-	-	X
Taxus capitata	-	-	-	-	-	-	-	-	-	-	-	-	-	X	-	-	-	X
Taxus cuspidata	-	-	-	-	-	-	-	-	X	-	-	-	-	X	-	-	-	X
Taxus media	-	-	-	-	-	-	-	-	X	-	-	-	-	X	-	-	-	X
Ternstroemia japonica	-	-	-	-	-	-	-	-	X	-	-	-	-	-	-	-	-	X
Thuja occidentalis	-	-	-	-	-	-	-	-	X	X	X	-	X	X	-	-	-	-
Thuja orientalis	-	-	-	-	-	-	-	-	X	X	X	-	X	X	-	-	-	-
Tilia americana	-	-	-	-	-	-	-	-	-	-	-	X	-	-	-	-	-	-
Tilia X euchlora 'Redmond'	-	-	-	-	-	-	-	-	-	-	-	X	-	-	-	-	-	-
Tilia cordata	-	-	-	-	-	-	-	-	-	-	-	X	-	-	-	-	-	-
Tilia tomentosa	-	-	-	-	-	-	-	-	-	-	-	X	-	-	-	-	-	-
Tillandsia usneoides	-	-	-	-	-	-	-	X	-	-	-	-	-	-	-	-	-	X
Trachelospermum asiaticum	-	-	-	-	-	-	-	-	-	X	X	-	X	-	-	-	-	X
Trachelospermum jasminoides	X	X	-	-	-	-	-	-	-	X	X	-	X	-	-	-	-	X
Trachycarpus fortunei	-	-	-	-	-	-	-	-	-	X	X	-	-	-	-	-	-	X
Tsuga canadensis	-	-	-	-	-	-	-	-	X	-	-	-	-	X	-	-	-	X
Tsuga caroliniana	-	-	-	-	-	-	-	-	X	-	-	-	-	X	-	-	-	X
Ulmus alata	-	-	-	-	-	-	-	-	-	X	X	-	X	-	-	-	-	-
Ulmus americana	-	-	-	-	X	-	-	-	-	X	X	-	X	-	X	X	-	-
Ulmus crassifolia	-	-	-	-	-	-	-	-	-	X	X	X	X	-	-	-	-	-
Ulmus japonica	-	-	-	-	-	-	-	-	-	X	X	-	-	-	-	X	-	-
Ulmus parvifolia	-	-	-	-	-	-	-	-	-	X	X	X	X	-	X	-	-	-
Ulmus pumila	-	-	-	-	-	-	-	-	-	X	X	X	X	-	-	-	-	-
Uniola latifolia	X	-	X	-	-	-	X	-	-	-	-	X	-	-	-	-	-	X
Veichia merrillii	-	-	X	-	-	-	-	X	-	-	X	-	-	-	-	-	-	-
Viburnum X 'Burkwoodi'	X	-	-	-	-	-	-	-	-	X	-	-	-	-	-	-	-	X
Viburnum carlesi	X	-	-	-	-	-	-	-	-	X	-	-	-	-	-	-	-	X
Viburnum dentatum	X	-	-	-	-	-	-	-	-	X	-	-	-	-	-	-	-	X
Viburnum lantana	X	-	X	-	-	-	-	-	-	X	-	-	-	-	-	-	-	-
Viburnum lentago	X	-	-	-	-	-	-	-	-	X	-	-	-	-	-	-	-	-
Viburnum odoratissimum	X	-	-	-	-	-	-	-	-	X	-	-	-	-	-	-	-	-
Viburnum opulus	X	-	X	-	-	-	-	-	-	-	-	-	-	-	-	-	-	-
Viburnum plicatum	X	-	-	-	-	-	-	-	-	-	-	-	-	-	-	-	-	-
Viburnum rhytidophylloides	X	-	-	-	-	-	-	-	-	-	-	-	-	-	-	-	-	-
Viburnum rhytidophyllum	X	-	-	-	-	-	-	-	-	-	-	-	-	-	-	-	-	-
Viburnum sieboldi	X	-	X	-	-	-	-	-	-	-	-	-	-	-	-	-	-	-
Viburnum suspensum	X	-	-	-	-	-	-	-	-	X	-	-	-	-	-	-	-	-
Viburnum tinus	X	-	X	-	-	-	-	-	-	X	-	-	-	-	-	-	-	-
Viburnum 'Tomentosum'	X	-	-	-	-	-	-	-	-	X	-	-	-	-	-	-	-	-

	Showy Flowers	Fragrant Flowers	Showy Fruits	Edible Fruits	Fall Color	Litter Problems	Spines	Unusual Foliage	For Hedge or Screen	Poor Soils	Alkaline Soils	Wet Sites	Drought	Intolerant of Wet Feet	High Heat	Pest Problems	Weak Wood	Shade
Viburnum trilobum	X	-	X	-	-	-	-	-	-	-	-	-	-	-	-	-	-	-
Viburnum utile	X	-	-	-	-	-	-	-	-	-	-	-	-	-	-	-	-	-
Vinca major	X	-	-	-	-	-	-	-	-	X	X	-	-	-	-	-	-	-
Vinca minor	X	-	-	-	-	-	-	-	-	-	-	-	-	-	-	-	-	-
Vitex agnus-castus	X	-	-	-	-	-	-	-	-	X	X	-	X	X	-	-	X	-
Vitex negundo	X	-	-	-	-	-	-	-	-	X	X	-	X	X	-	-	X	-
Washingtonia filifera	-	-	-	-	-	-	X	-	-	X	X	-	X	-	X	-	-	-
Washingtonia robusta	-	-	-	-	-	-	X	X	-	X	X	-	X	-	X	-	-	-
Weigela florida	X	-	-	-	-	-	-	-	-	-	-	-	-	-	-	-	-	-
Wisteria floribunda	X	-	-	-	-	-	-	-	-	-	-	-	-	-	-	-	-	-
Wisteria sinensis	X	-	-	-	-	-	-	-	-	-	-	-	-	-	-	-	-	-
Xanthoceras sorbifolium	X	-	-	-	-	-	-	-	-	X	X	-	X	X	-	-	-	-
Yucca aloifolia	X	-	-	-	-	-	X	-	-	X	X	-	X	-	X	-	-	-
Yucca elephantiopes	X	-	-	-	-	-	-	-	-	X	X	-	X	-	X	-	-	-
Yucca filamentosa	X	-	-	-	-	-	-	-	-	X	X	-	X	-	X	-	-	-
Yucca gloriosa	X	-	-	-	-	-	-	-	-	X	X	-	X	-	X	-	-	-
Zamia floridana	-	-	-	-	-	-	-	X	-	X	-	-	-	-	-	-	-	-
Zelkova serrata	-	-	-	-	-	-	-	-	-	X	-	-	-	-	-	-	-	-
Ziziphus jujuba	-	-	-	X	-	-	-	-	-	X	X	-	X	X	-	-	-	-

INDEX

In the scientific name index, scientific names are included alphabetically, followed by the correct common name.

In the common name index, common names are included alphabetically followed by the correct scientific name.

Bean,		
Coral	*Sophora secundiflora*	239,240
Mescal	*Sophora secundiflora*	239,240
Beech,		
American	*Fagus grandifolia*	99,100
Blue	*Carpinus caroliniana*	51,52,153
European	*Fagus sylvatica*	99
Birch,		
Canoe	*Betula papyrifera*	43
European	*Betula pendula*	43,44
Paper	*Betula papyrifera*	43
River	*Betula nigra*	41,42
Bishop's Weed	*Aegopodium podogaria*	603,604
Bittersweet,		
American	*Celastrus scandens*	287
Oriental	*Celastrus orbiculatus*	287,288
Black Alder	*Alnus glutinosa*	37,38
Black Alder	*Ilex verticillata*	317,318
Black Jetbead	*Rhodotypos scandens*	359,360
Black Tupelo	*Nyssa sylvatica*	151,152
Blue Beech	*Carpinus caroliniana*	51,52,153
Boston Ivy	*Parthenocissus trisuspidata*	343
Bottlebrush	*Callistemon rigidus*	413,414
Bottlebrush, Citrus-leaved	*Callistemon citrinus*	413
Box,		
Common	*Buxus sempervirens*	411,412
English	*Buxus sempervirens*	411,412
Littleleaf	*Buxus microphylla*	409,410
Korean	*Buxus harlandi*	409,411,412
Boxelder	*Acer negundo*	11,12
Boxwood,		
Japanese	*Buxus microphylla*	409,410
Korean	*Buxus harlandi*	409,411,412
Buckeye,		
Bottlebrush	*Aesculus parviflora*	269,270
Ohio	*Aesculus glabra*	27,28
Red	*Aesculus pavia*	31,32
Texas	*Aesculus arguta*	25,26
Buckthorn,		
Carolina	*Rhamnus caroliniana*	219
Common	*Rhamnus cathartica*	219,220
False	*Bumelia lanuginosa*	47,48
Glossy	*Rhamnus frangula*	219
Bugleweed	*Ajuga reptans*	605,606
Bullbay	*Magnolia grandiflora*	481,482
Bumelia,		
Gum	*Bumelia lanuginosa*	47,48
Wooly Bucket	*Bumelia lanuginosa*	47,48
Burning Bush	*Euonymus alata*	303,304
Bush Cinquefoil	*Potentilla fruticosa*	353,354
Butterfly Bush	*Buddleia davidii*	277,278
Cactus,		
Cholla	*Opuntia spp.*	497,498
Walking Stick Cholla	*Opuntia imbricata*	497

Camellia,		
Japanese	*Camellia japonica*	415,416,418
Sasanqua	*Camellia sasanqua*	417,418
Camphor Tree	*Cinnamomum camphora*	421,422
Canby Paxistima	*Paxistima canbyi*	637,638
Candytuft, Evergreen	*Iberis sempervirens*	621,622
Cape Jasmine	*Gardenia jasminoides*	439,440
Carissa	*Carissa grandiflora*	419,420
Carolina Cherry Laurel	*Prunus caroliniana*	509,510
Carolina Yellow Jessamine	*Gelsemium sempervirens*	441,442
Carpetbugle	*Ajuga reptans*	605,606
Cast Iron Plant	*Aspidistra elatior*	607,608
Catalpa,		
Northern	*Catalpa speciosa*	59
Southern	*Catalpa bignonioides*	59,60
Western	*Catalpa speciosa*	59
Cedar,		
Alaska	*Chamaecypararis nootkatensis*	665,666
Atlas	*Cedrus atlantica*	657,658,659,660
California Incense	*Libocedrus decurrens*	697,698
Deodar	*Cedrus deodara*	660,661,662
Eastern Red	*Juniperus virginiana*	691,695,696
White	*Thuja occidentalis*	741,742,743
Cedar of Lebanon	*Cedrus libani*	657,658
Chaste Tree	*Vitex agnus-castus*	391,392
Cherry,		
Black	*Prunus serotina*	181,182
Autumn Flowering	*Prunus subhirtella*	183
Japanese Flowering	*Prunus serrulata*	183,184
Cherry Laurel	*Prunus laurocerasus*	511,512
Chestnut,		
American	*Castanea dentata*	57
Chinese	*Castanea mollissima*	57,58,191
Chinaberry	*Melia azedarach*	145,146
Chittimwood	*Bumelia lanuginosa*	47,48
Clematis,		
Jackman	*Clematis X Jackmani*	291
Sweetautumn	*Clematis paniculata*	291
Cleyera	*Cleyera japonica*	423,424
Cliff Green	*Paxistima canbyi*	637,638
Coconut	*Cocos nucifera*	551,561,562
Coffee Tree, Kentucky	*Gymnocladus dioica*	115,116
Common Box	*Buxus sempervirens*	411,412
Corktree,		
Amur	*Phellodendron amurense*	161,162
Chinese	*Phellodendron chinense*	161
Cotoneaster,		
Bearberry	*Cotoneaster dammeri*	297,298
Hedge	*Cotoneaster lucidus*	297,298
Many Flowered	*Cotoneaster multiflorus*	297
Rockspray	*Cotoneaster horizontalis*	297,298
Spreading	*Cotoneaster divaricatus*	297

777

Holly Grape	*Mahonia aquifolium*	483,484
Holly Grape, Chinese	*Mahonia lamariifolia*	489,490
Honeylocust	*Gleditsia triacanthos*	113,114
Honeysuckle,		
Alps	*Lonicera alpigena*	335
Amur	*Lonicera maacki*	335,339
'Clavey's Dwarf'	*Lonicera X xylosteoides*	335,339
Japanese	*Lonicera japonica*	477,478
Morrow	*Lonicera morrowi*	333,335,340
Tatarian	*Lonicera tatarica*	333,335,336
Trumpet	*Lonicera sempervirens*	477,478
Winter	*Lonicera fragrantissima*	333,334
Hophornbeam,		
American	*Ostrya virginiana*	153,154
Eastern	*Ostrya virginiana*	153 154
Hornbeam,		
American	*Carpinus caroliniana*	51,52,153
European	*Carpinus betulus*	49,50
Horsechestnut	*Aesculus hippocastanum*	27,29,30
Hosta	*Hosta spp.*	619,620
Hydrangea,		
Garden	*Hydrangea macrophylla*	311
Oakleaf	*Hydrangea quercifolia*	311,312
Peegee	*Hydrangea paniculata*	311,312
Indigo,		
False	*Amorpha fructicosa*	271
Mountain	*Amorpha glabra*	271,272
Ivy,		
Algerian	*Hedera canariensis*	617,618
Boston	*Parthenocissus tricuspidata*	343,344
English	*Hedera helix*	617,618
Poison	*Rhus radicans*	365,366
Jasmine,		
Asiatic	*Trachelospermum asiaticum*	647,648
Cape	*Gardenia jasminoides*	439,440
Carolina Yellow	*Gelsemium sempervirens*	441,442
Confederate	*Trachelospermum jasminoides*	647,648
Japanese Star	*Trachelospermum asiaticum*	647,648
Primrose	*Jasminum mesnyi*	321,322
Star	*Trachelospermum jasminoides*	647,648
Winter	*Jasminum nudiflorum*	321,322
Jerusalem Thorn	*Parkinsonia aculeata*	157,158
Jessamine, Carolina Yellow	*Gelsemium sempervirens*	441,442
Jetbead, Black	*Rhodotypos scandens*	359,360
Jujuba	*Ziziphus jujuba*	265,266
Juniper,		
Chinese	*Juniperus chinensis*	679,680,681,682
Creeping	*Juniperus horizontalis*	625,626,627,628
Fishtail	*Juniperus squamata*	693,694,683
Japanese Garden	*Juniperus procumbens*	629,630
Meyer	*Juniperus squamata*	693,694,683
Parson's	*Juniperus davurica*	683,684

Palm,(contd.)
Coontie	*Zamia floridana*	599,600
Date	*Phoenix dactylifera*	573,574
European Fan	*Chamaerops humilis*	557,558
Everglades	*Acoelorrhaphe wrightii*	547,548
Fishtail	*Caryota mitis*	553,554
Fern	*Cycas circinalis*	563,564
Jelly	*Butia capitata*	551,552
Lady	*Raphis excelsa*	581,582
Manila	*Veitchia merrillii*	593,594
Mexican Fan	*Washingtonia robusta*	597,598
Mexican Washington	*Washingtonia robusta*	597,598
Needle	*Rhapidophyllum hystrix*	583,584
Paurotis	*Acoelorrhaphe wrightii*	547,548
Pindo	*Butia capitata*	551,552
Pygmy Date	*Phoenix roebelenii*	577,578
Queen	*Arecastrum romanzoffiana*	549,550
Queen Sago	*Cycas circinalis*	563,564
Reclinata	*Phoenix reclinata*	575,576
Royal	*Roystonea regia*	585,586
Sabal	*Sabal palmetto*	587,588
Sago	*Cycas revoluta*	565,566
Saw Palmetto	*Serenoa repens*	583,587,589,590
Senegal Date	*Phoenix reclinata*	575,576
Silver Date	*Phoenix sylvestris*	579,580
Triangle	*Neodypsis decaryi*	569,570
Washington	*Washingtonia filifera,robusta*	595,596,597,598
Wild	*Phoenix sylvestris*	579,580
Windmill	*Trachycarpus fortunei*	591,592
Yellow	*Chrysalidocarpus lutescens*	559,560
Zamia	*Zamia floridana*	599,600

Palmetto,
Bush	*Sabal minor*	585
Saw	*Serenoa repens*	583,587,589,590
Pampas Grass	*Cortaderia selloana*	295,296
Parkinsonia	*Parkinsonia aculeata*	157,158
Peach, Common	*Prunus persica*	179,180

Pear,
Callery	*Pyrus calleryana*	185,186
Common	*Pyrus communis*	187,188
Pearlbush	*Exochorda racemosa*	305,306
Peashrub, Russian	*Caragana frutex*	285,286
Peashrub, Siberian	*Caragana arborescens*	285,286
Periwinkle	*Vinca major*	649,650,651
Periwinkle, Common	*Vinca minor*	649,651,652

Persimmon,
Common	*Diospyros virginiana*	91,92

Scholartree, Chinese	*Sophora japonica*	237,238
Screwbean	*Prosopis pubescens*	173
Serviceberry,		
Allegheny	*Amelanchier laevis*	39
Apple	*Amelanchier X grandiflora*	39,40
Downy	*Amelanchier arborea*	39,40
Shrub Althea	*Hibiscus syriacus*	309,310
Silktree	*Albizia julibrissin*	35,36
Silverbell,		
Carolina	*Halesia carolina*	117,118
Mountain	*Halesia monticola*	117,118
Two-winged	*Halesia diptera*	117
Silverberry	*Elaeagnus macrophylla*	427,428
Smoketree	*Cotinus coggygria*	83,84
Smoketree, American	*Cotinus obovatus*	83
Soapberry, Western	*Sapindus drummondi*	145,231,232
Sotol	*Dasylirion texanum*	425,426
Sourwood	*Oxydendrum arboreum*	155,156
Spanish Bayonet	*Yucca aloifolia*	539,540
Spanish Moss	*Tillansia usneoides*	531,532
Spindle Tree, European	*Euonymus europaea*	97,98
Spiraea,		
Bridal Wreath	*Spiraea prunifolia*	375,378
Garland	*Spiraea X arguta*	375,378
Japanese	*Spiraea japonica*	375,377
Thunberg	*Spiraea thunbergi*	375,377
Vanhoutte	*Spiraea X vanhouttei*	375,376,377,378
Spruce,		
Black Hills	*Picea glauca*	701,702
Colorado Blue	*Picea pungens*	701,702
Norway	*Picea abies*	699,700
Spurge, Japanese	*Pachysandra terminalis*	635,636
St. Johns-wort,		
Aaronsbeard	*Hypericum calycinum*	313
Goldcup	*Hypericum patulum*	313,314
Kalm's	*Hypericum kalmianum*	313,314
Shrubby	*Hypericum prolificum*	313,314
Stewartia,		
Chinese	*Stewartia sinensis*	243
Japanese	*Stewartia pseudocamellia*	243,244
Mountain	*Stewartia ovata*	243
Stonecrop,Gold Moss	*Sedum acre*	645,646
Sugarberry	*Celtis laevigata*	61,62,63
Sumac,		
Fragrant	*Rhus aromatica*	361,362,363
Planeleaf	*Rhus copallina*	363
Shining	*Rhus copallina*	363
Smooth	*Rhus glabra*	363,364
Staghorn	*Rhus typhina*	367,368
Velvet	*Rhus typhina*	367,368
Winged	*Rhus copallina*	363

787

SCIENTIFIC NAME INDEX

Abelia grandiflora	Glossy Abelia	401,402
Abelia chinensis	Chinese Abelia	401
Abelia uniflora	Single Flowered Abelia	401
Abies concolor	White or Concolor Fir	655,656
Acer barbatum	Florida Maple	21
Acer buergerianum	Trident Maple	1,2
Acer campestre	Hedge Maple	3,4
Acer cappadocicum	Coloseum Maple	23,24
Acer dasycarpum	Silver, Soft, or River Maple	19,20
Acer floridanum	Florida Maple	21
Acer ginnala	Amur Maple	5,6
Acer griseum	Paperbark Maple	7,8
Acer grandidentatum	Bigtooth Maple	21
Acer miyabei	Miyabe Maple	9,10
Acer negundo	Boxelder	11,12
Acer palmatum	Japanese Maple	13,14
Acer platanoides	Norway Maple	15,16
Acer rubrum	Red or Swamp Maple	17,18
Acer saccharinum	Silver,Soft, or River Maple	19,20
Acer saccarum	Sugar,Hard, or Rock Maple	21,22
Acer truncatum	Shantung Maple	23,24
Acoelorrhaphe wrightii	Paurotis or Everglades Palm	547,548
Aegopodium podogaria	Goutweed or Bishop's Weed	603,604
Aesculus arguta	Texas Buckeye	25,26
Aesculus glabra	Ohio Buckeye	27,28
Aesculus hippocastanum	Horsechestnut	27,29,30
Aesculus parviflora	Bottlebrush Buckeye	269,270
Aesculus pavia	Red Buckeye	31,32
Ailanthus altissima	Tree-of-Heaven	33,34
Ajuga reptans	Carpetbugle, Ajuga, or Bugleweed	605,606
Albizia julibrissin	Mimosa or Silktree	35,36
Alnus glutinosa	Black Alder	37,38
Alyssum saxatile	Golden Alyssum or Basket-of-Gold	635,636
Amelanchier arborea	Downy Serviceberry	39,40
Amelanchier grandiflora	Apple Serviceberry	39,40
Amelanchier laevis	Allegheny Serviceberry	39
Amorpha glabra	Mountain Indigo	271,272
Amorpha fructicosa	False Indigo	271
Amorpha canescens	Lead Plant	271
Aralia japonica	Japanese Fatsia	435,436
Araucaria bidwilli	Monkey Puzzle Tree	671
Araucaria excelsa	Norfolk Island Pine	671
Arecastrum romanzoffiana	Queen Palm	549,550
Arundinaria pigmaea	Dwarf Bamboo	405,406

Arundinaria varigata	Dwarf White Striped Bamboo	405
Arundo donax	Giant Reed Grass	273,274
Aspidistra elatior	Cast Iron Plant	607,608
Aucuba japonica	Japanese Aucuba or Gold Dust Plant	403,404
Aurinia saxatilis	Golden Alyssum	635
Azalea obtusum	Kurume Azalea	525,526
Bambusa spp.	Bamboo	405,406
Bambusa multiplex	Hedge Bamboo	405
Berberis aquifolium	Holly Grape	483,484
Berberis julianae	Wintergreen Barberry	275,407,408
Berberis X gladwynensis	William Penn Barberry	407
Berberis mentorensis	Mentor Barberry	275,276
Berberis thunbergi	Japanese Barberry	275,276,407
Berberis verruculosa	Warty Barberry	407
Betula alba	European Birch	43,44
Betula nigra	River Birch	41,42
Betula papyrifera	Canoe or Paper Birch	43,44
Betual pendula	European Birch	43,44
Betula verrucosa	European Birch	43,44
Broussonetia papyrifera	Paper Mulberry	45,46
Buddleia davidii	Butterfly Bush, Summer Lilac	277,278
Bumelia lanuginosa	Chittimwood	47,48
Butia capitata	Pindo or Jelly Palm	551,552
Buxus harlandi	Korean Box	409,411,412
Buxus microphylla	Japanese or Littleleaf Boxwood	409,410,411
Buxus sempervirens	English or Common Boxwood	411,412
Callicarpa americana	American Beautyberry	279,280
Callicarpa dichotoma	Purple Beautyberry	279
Callistemon citrinus	Citrus-leaved Bottlebrush	413
Callistemon rigidus	Bottlebrush	413,414
Calocedrus decurrens	California Incense Cedar	697,698
Calycanthus floridus	Sweetshrub	281,282
Camellia japonica	Japanese Camelia	415,416,418
Camellia sasanqua	Sasanqua Camellia	417,418
Campsis grandiflora	Chinese Trumpet Creeper	283
Campsis radicans	Trumpet Creeper	283,284
Cannabis sativa	Marijuana	391
Carpinus betulus	European Hornbeam	49,50
Carpinus caroliniana	American Hornbeam or Blue Beech	51,52,153
Caragana arborescens	Siberian Pea Shrub	285,286
Caragana frutex	Russian Pea Shrub	285,286
Carissa grandiflora	Natal Plum, Carissa	419,420
Carya spp.	Hickories	53,54
Carya cordiformis	Bitternut Hickory	54
Carya glabra	Pignut Hickory	53
Carya illinoinensis	Pecan	55,56
Carya laciniosa	Shellbark Hickory	53

Carya ovata	Shagbark Hickory	53,54
Caryota mitis	Fishtail Palm	553,554
Castanea dentata	American Chestnut	57
Castanea mollissima	Chinese Chestnut	57,58,191
Catalpa bignonioides	Southern Catalpa	59,60
Catalpa speciosa	Northern Catalpa	59
Cedrus atlantica	Atlas Cedar	657,658,659,660
Cedrus deodara	Deodar Cedar	660,661,662
Cedrus libani	Cedar of Lebanon	657,658
Celastrus orbiculatus	Oriental Bittersweet	287,288
Celastrus scandens	American Bittersweet	287,288
Celtis laevigata	Sugarberry or Sugar Hackberry	61,62,63
Celtis occidentalis	Hackberry	61,63,64
Cephalotaxus harringtonia	Japanese Plum Yew	663,664
Cephalotaxus harringtonia 'Fastigiata'	Upright Plum Yew	740,663
Cercidiphyllum japonicum	Katsuratree	65,66
Cercis canadensis	Eastern Redbud	67,68
Cercis chinensis	Chinese Redbud	67
Chaenomeles japonica	Japanese Flowering Quince	289,290
Chaenomeles laginaria	Flowering Quince	289,290
Chaenomeles speciosa	Flowering Quince	289,290
Chaenomeles X 'superba'	Flowering Quince	289
Chamaecyparis lawsoniana	Lawson False Cypress	667,668
Chamaecyparis nootkatensis	Nootka or Alaska Cypress	665,666
Chamaecyparis obtusa	Hinoki False Cypress	667,668
Chamaecyparis pisifera	Japanese False Cypress	667,668
Chamaedorea erumpens	Bamboo Palm	555,556
Chamaerops humilis	European Fan Palm	557,558
Chilopsis linearis	Desertwillow	69,70
Chionanthus retusus	Chinese Fringetree	71,72
Chionanthus virginicus	Fringetree or Old Man's Beard	71,72
Chrysalidocarpus lutescens	Cane, Yellow, Butterfly, or Areca Palm	559,560
Cinnamomum camphora	Camphor Tree	421,422
Cladrastis lutea	American Yellowood	73,74
Clematis spp.	Clematis	291,292
Clematis X 'Jackmani'	Jackman Clematis	291
Clematis paniculata	Sweetautumn Clematis	291
Clematis virginiana	Woodbine or Virginsbower	291
Cleyera japonica	Cleyera	423,424
Cocos australis	Pindo or Jelly Palm	551,552
Cocos nucifera	Coconut	551,561,562
Codiaeum variegatum	Croton	403
Cornus alba	Tatarian Dogwood	293,294
Cornus drummondi	Roughleaf Dogwood	293,294
Cornus florida	Flowering Dogwood	75,76,77,78

Cornus kousa	Kousa Dogwood	79,80,81
Cornus mas	Corneliancherry Dogwood	81,82
Cornus sericea	Red-osier Dogwood	293,294
Cornus stononifera	Red-osier Dogwood	293,294
Cortaderia selloana	Pampas Grass	295,296
Cotinus obovatus	American Smoketree	83
Cotinus coggygria	Smoketree	83,84
Cotoneaster spp.	Cotoneaster	297,298
Cotoneaster dammeri	Bearberry Cotoneaster	297,298
Cotoneaster divaricatus	Spreading Cotoneaster	297
Cotoneaster horizontalis	Rockspray Cotoneaster	297,298
Cotoneaster lucidus	Hedge Cotoneaster	297,298
Cotoneaster multiflorus	Many Flowered Cotoneaster	297
Crataegus spp.	Hawthorn	85,86,87,88
Crataegus crus-galli	Cockspur Hawthorn	86,87
Crataegus X lavallei	Lavalle Hawthorn	86
Crataegus mollis	Downy Hawthorn	86,87
Crataegus X mordenensis	Toba Hawthorn	86
Crataegus oxyacantha	Paul's Scarlet Hawthorn	86
Crataegus phaenopyrum	Washington Hawthorn	86,88
Crataegus succulenta	Fleshy Hawthorn	86
Cryptomeria japonica	Japanese Cryptomeria	669,670
Cunninghamia lanceolata	China Fir	671,672
Cupressocyparis leylandi	Leyland Cypress	673,674
Cupressus arizonica	Arizona Cypress	675,676
Cupressus macrocarpa	Monterey Cypress	673
Cupressus sempervirens	Italian Cypress	677,678
Cycas circinalis	Queen Sago, Fern Palm	563,564
Cycas revoluta	Sago Palm	565,566
Dasylirion texanum	Sotol or Bear Grass	425,426
Deutzia gracilis	Slender Deutzia	299
Deutzia X lemoinei	Lemoine Deutzia	299,300
Deutzia parviflora		299
Diospyros kaki	Oriental Persimmon	89,90
Diospyros virginiana	Common Persimmon or Possumwood	91,92
Elaeagnus angustifolia	Russian Olive	93,94
Elaeagnus macrophylla	Silverberry	427,428
Elaeagnus pungens	Thorny Elaeagnus	427,428
Erianthus alopecuroides	Silver Plume Grass	301
Erianthus ravennae	Plume Grass	295,301,302
Eriobotrya japonica	Loquat	429,430
Eucommia ulmoides	Hardy Rubbertree	95,96
Euonymus alata	Winged Euonymus or Burning Bush	303,304
Euonymus americanus	American Euonymus	97
Euonymus bungeana	Winterberry Euonymus	97,98
Euonymus europaea	European Spindle Tree	97,98

Euonymus fortunei	Evergreen Wintercreeper	609,610,611,612
Euonymus japonica	Evergreen Euonymus	431,432,434
Euonymus kiautschovica	Spreading Euonymus	433,434
Euonymus patens	Spreading Euonymus	433,434
Euonymus radicans	Evergreen Wintercreeper	609,610
Exochorda geraldi	Redbud Pearlbush	305
Exochorda racemosa	Pearlbush	305,306
Fagus grandifolia	American Beech	99,100
Fagus sylvatica	European Beech	99,100
Fatshedara lizei	Fatshedera	435,436
Fatsia japonica	Japanese Fatsia	435,436
Feijoa sellowiana	Pineapple Guava or Feijoa	437,438
Festuca ovina	Sheep's or Blue Fescue	613,614
Ficus carica	Common or Edible Fig	101,102
Ficus pumila	Creeping Fig	615,616
Forsythia spp.	Forsythia or Goldenbell	307,308
Forsythia intermedia	Hybrid Forsythia	307
Forsythia japonica	Japanese Forsythia	307
Forsythia suspensa	Weeping Forsythia	307
Forsythia viridissima	Greenstem Forsythia	307
Franklinia alatamaha	Franklin Tree	443
Fraxinus americana	White Ash	103,104,107,109
Fraxinus excelsior	European Ash	105,106
Fraxinus pennsylvanica	Green Ash	103,104,106,107,108,109
Fraxinus quadrangulata	Blue Ash	109,110
Gardenia jasminoides	Gardenia or Cape Jasmine	439,440
Gelseminum sempervirens	Carolina Yellow Jessamine	441,442
Ginkgo biloba	Ginkgo or Maidenhair Tree	111,112
Gleditsia triacanthos	Honeylocust	113,114
Gordonia lasianthus	Gordonia or Loblolly Bay	443,444
Gymnocladus dioica	Kentucky Coffee Tree	115,116
Halesia carolina	Carolina Silverbell	117,118
Halesia diptera	Two-winged Silverbell	117
Halesia monticola	Mountain Silverbell	117,118
Hamamelis vernalis	Vernal Witchhazel	119,120
Hamamelis virginiana	Common Witchhazel	119,120
Hedera canariensis	Algerian Ivy	617,618
Hedera helix	English Ivy	617,618
Hesperaloe parviflora	Red Yucca	445,446
Hibiscus rosa-sinensis	Chinese Hibiscus	309
Hibiscus syriacus	Rose-of-Sharon or Shrub Althea	309,310
Hosta spp.	Hosta or Plantain Lily	619,620
Hosta decorata	Blunt Plantain Lily	619
Hosta fortunei	Tall Cluster Plantain Lily	619
Hosta lancifolia	Narrow-leaved Plantain Lily	619
Hosta seiboldi	Seersucker Plantain Lily	619

Hydrangea macrophylla	Garden Hydrangea	311
Hydrangea paniculata	Peegee Hydrangea	311,312
Hydrangea quercifolia	Oakleaf Hydrangea	311,312
Hypericum calysinum	Aaronsbeard St. Johns-wort	313
Hypericum kalmianum	Kalm's St. Johns-wort	313,314
Hypericum patulum	Goldcup St. Johns-wort	313,314
Hypericum prolificum	Shrubby St. Johns-wort	313,314
Iberis sempervirens	Evergreen Candytuft	621,622
Ilex atlaclarensis	Altaclara Holly Hybrids	447
Ilex aquifolim	English Holly	449,450,451,452
Ilex attenuata	Foster's Hybrid Hollies	462
Ilex cassine	Dahoon Holly	462
Ilex cornuta	Chinese or Horned Holly	453,454,455
Ilex crenata	Japanese Holly	456,457,458
Ilex decidua	Possumhaw or Deciduous Holly	315,316,317,318
Ilex latifolia	Luster Leaf Holly	459,460
Ilex X meserveae	Blue Holly	450
Ilex opaca	American Holly	461,462,463,464
Ilex perado	Perado Holly	449
Ilex pernyi	Pernyi Holly	465,466
Ilex platyphylla		449
Ilex rotunda	Round Holly	467,468
Ilex serrata	Finetooth Holly	317
Ilex verticillata	Winterberry, Black Alder, or Michigan Holly	315,316,317,318
Ilex vomitoria	Yaupon Holly	456,457,458,469,470
Illicium anisatum	Japanese Anise	471
Illicium floridanum	Florida or Purple Anise	471,472
Itea virginica	Sweepspire	319,320
Jasminum floridum		321
Jasminum mesnyi	Primrose Jamine	321,322
Jasminum nudiflorum	Winter Jasmine	321,322
Juglans nigra	Black Walnut	121,122
Juniperus chinensis	Chinese Juniper	679,680,681,682
Juniperus conferta	Shore Juniper	623,624
Juniperus davurica	Parson's Juniper	683,684
Juniperus procumbens	Japanese Garden Juniper	629,630
Juniperus sabina	Savin Juniper	687,688,689
Juniperus scopulorum	Rocky Mountain Juniper	677,690,691,692
Juniperus squamata	Meyer or Fishtail Juniper	683,693,694
Juniperus silicicola	Southern Redcedar	695
Juniperus virginiana	Eastern Redcedar	691,695,696
Kerria japonica	Japanes Kerria	323,324
Koelreuteria bipinnata	Goldenrain Tree	123,124,125,145
Koelreuteria elegans	Formosan Goldenrain Tree or Flamegold	123
Koelreuteria formosana	Goldenrain Tree	123,124
Koelreuteria paniculata	Panicled Goldenrain Tree	123,125,126

Kolkwitzia amabilis	Beautybush	325,326
Lagerstroemia fauriei	Faurei Crapemyrtle	327
Lagerstroemia indica	Crapemyrtle	327,328
Larix decidua	European Larch	127,128
Larix laricina	American Larch or Tamarack	127
Leucophyllum frutescens	Texas Sage	473,474
Libocedrus decurrens	California Incense Cedar	697,698
Ligustrum spp.	Privet	329,330,331,332
Ligustrum japonicum	Japanese or Wax Leaf Ligustrum	475,476
Ligustrum lucidum	Glossy Privet	475,476
Ligustrum obtusifolium	Border Privet	329,331
Ligustrum ovalifolim	California Privet	329
Ligustrum sinense	Chinese Privet	329,332,475
Ligustrum texanum	Wax Leaf Ligustrum	475
Ligustrum vicaryi	Golden Vicary Privet	329,332
Ligustrum vulgare	Common Privet	329,330,331
Liquidambar formosana	Formosan Sweetgum	129,130
Liquidambar styraciflua	Sweetgum	129,130
Liriodendron tulipifera	Tulip Tree or Yellow Poplar	131,132
Liriope muscari	Lily Turf, Monkey Grass, or Liriope	631,632,633
Livistona chinensis	Chinese Fan Palm	567,568
Lonicera alpigena	Alps Honeysuckle	335
Lonicera fragrantissima	Winter Honeysuckle	333,334
Lonicera japonica	Japanese Honeysuckle	477,478
Lonicera maacki	Amur Honeysuckle	335,339
Lonicera morrowi	Morrow Honeysuckle	333,335,340
Lonicera sempervirens	Trumpet Honeysuckle	477,478
Lonicera tatarica	Tatarian Honeysuckle	333,335,336
Lonicera X xylosteoides	Clavey's Dwarf Honeysuckle	335,339
Loropetalum chinense	Loropetalum	479,480
Maclura pomifera	Osage Orange	133,134
Magnolia acuminata	Cucumbertree Magnolia	135,136
Magnolia grandiflora	Southern Magnolia or Bullbay	481,482
Magnolia heptapeta		137
Magnolia macrophylla	Bigleaf Magnolia	139,140
Magnolia quinquepeta		137
Magnolia soulangiana	Saucer Magnolia	137,138
Magnolia stellata	Star Magnolia	137,138
Magnolia tripetala	Umbrella Magnolia	139,140
Magnolia virginiana	Sweetbay or Swamp Magnolia	135,139,140
Mahonia aquifolium	Oregon Grape or Holly Grape Mahonia	483,484
Mahonia bealei	Leatherleaf Mahonia	485,486
Mahonia fortunei	Fernleaf Mahonia	487,488
Mahonia lamariifolia	Chinese Hollygrape	489,490
Malus spp.	Flowering Crabapple	141,142,143,144
Malus baccata	Siberian Crabapple	141

795

Malus floribundi	Japanese Flowering Crabapple	141
Malus sargentii	Sargents Crabapple	141
Melia azedarach	Chinaberry	145,146
Metasequoia glyptostroboides	Dawn Redwood	147,148
Miscanthus sacchariflorus	Giant Miscanthus	339
Miscanthus sinensis	Japanese Silvergrass, Eulalia	339,340
Morus alba	White Mulberry	149,150
Morus rubra	Red Mulberry	149
Myrica cerifera	Southern Wax Myrtle	491,492
Myrica pensylvanica	Bayberry	341,342,491
Nandina domestica	Heavenly Bamboo or Nandina	493,494
Neodypsis decaryi	Triangle Palm	569,570
Nerium oleander	Oleander	495,496
Nyssa aquatica	Water Tupelo	151
Nyssa sylvatica	Black Gum, Sour Gum, or Black Tupelo	151,152
Ophiopogon japonicus	Lily Turf or Mondograss	631,634
Opuntia spp.	Prickly Pear or Cholla Cactus	497,498
Opuntia englemanni	Engleman Prickly Pear	497
Opuntia imbricata	Walking Stick Cholla	497,498
Opuntia lindheimeri	Lindheimer Prickly Pear	497
Osmanthus X fortunei	Fortunes Osmanthus	499
Osmanthus fragrans	Fragrant Tea Olive	499,500
Osmanthus heterophyllus	False Holly	499,500
Osmanthus ilicifolius	False Holly	499,500
Ostrya virginiana	American or Eastern Hophornbeam	153,154
Oxydendrum arboreum	Sourwood	155,156
Pachysandra procumbens	Allegheny Pachysandra	635,636
Pachysandra terminalis	Pachysandra or Japanese Spruge	635,636
Parkinsonia aculeata	Parkinsonia or Jerusalem Thorn	157,158
Parthenocissus quinquefolia	Virginia Creeper	343,344
Parthenocissus tricuspidata	Boston Ivy	343,344
Paulownia tomentosa	Royal Paulownia or Empress Tree	159,160
Paxistima canbyi	Cliff Green or Canby Paxistima	637,638
Pennisetum alopecuroides	Fountain Grass	295,345,346
Pennisetum ruppeli	Crimson Fountain Grass	295
Pennisetum setaceum	Crimson Fountain Grass	345
Phellodendron amurense	Amur Corktree	161,162
Phellodendron chinense	Chinese Corktree	161
Philadelphis coronarius	Sweet Mockorange	347,348
Philadelphis X lemoinei	Lemoine Mockorange	347
Philadelphis microphyllus	Small Leaved Mockorange	347
Phoenix canariensis	Canary Island Date Palm	571,572
Phoenix dactylifera	Date Palm	573,574
Phoenix reclinata	Senegal Date, Reclinata Palm	575,576
Phoenix roebelenii	Pygmy Date Palm	577,578
Phoenix sylvestris	Wild,Silver Date Palm	579,580

Phlox subulata	Moss Pink or Moss Phlox	637,638
Photinia X 'Fraseri'	Fraser's Photinia	501,502,503
Photinia glabra	Japanese Photinia	501,503,504
Photinia serrulata	Chinese Photina	501,503,504
Phyllostachys aureosulcata	Yellowgroove Bamboo	405
Physocarpus monogymus	Mountain Ninebark	349,350
Physocarpus opulifolius	Common Ninebark	349,350
Picea abiea	Norway Spruce	699,700
Picea glauca 'Densata'	Black Hills Spruce	701,702
Picea pungens	Colorado Blue Spruce	701,702
Pieris japonica	Japanese Pieris,Lily-of-the-Valley Shrub	505,506
Pinus cembroides	Pinyon Pine	703,704
Pinus densiflora	Japanese Red Pine	705,706,727
Pinus densiflora 'Umbraculifera'	Tanyosho Pine	705,706
Pinus echinata	Shortleaf Pine	707,708
Pinus elliotti	Slash Pine	709,710,729
Pinus flexilis	Limber Pine	725
Pinus glabra	Spruce Pine	711,712
Pinus mugo	Mugo Pine	713,714
Pinus mugho	Mugo Pine	713,714
Pinus nigra	Austrian Pine	715,716,731
Pinus palustris	Longleaf Pine	717,718
Pinus pinaster	Cluster or Maritime Pine	719,720
Pinus ponderosa	Ponderosa or Western Yellow Pine	721,722
Pinus resinosa	Red or Norway Pine	723,724
Pinus strobiformis	Western White Pine	725
Pinus strobis	White Pine	725,726
Pinus sylvestris	Scotch (Scot's) Pine	727,728
Pinus taeda	Loblolly Pine	729,730
Pinus thunbergi	Japanese Black Pine	715,731,732
Pinus thunbergiana	Japanese Black Pine	715,731,732
Pistacia chinensis	Chinese Pistache	163,164
Pistacia vera	Pistacio	163
Pittosporum tobira	Japanese Pittosporum or Mockorange	347,507,508
Platanus X *acerifolia*	London Planetree	165,166
Platanus occidentalis	Sycamore or American Planetree	165,166
Platanus orientalis	Oriental Planetree	165
Platycladus orientalis	Oriental Arborvitae	744,745,746
Podocarpus gracilior	Fern Podocarpus	733,734
Podocarpus macrophyllus	Yew Podocarpus	733,734
Podocarpus nagi	Broadleaf Podocarpus	733,734
Poncirus trifoliata	Trifoliate Orange	347,351,352
Populus alba	White Poplar	167,168,171
Populus deltoides	Eastern Cottonwood	169,170
Populus nigra 'Italica'	Lombardy Poplar	171,172
Potentilla fruticosa	Potentilla or Bush Cinquefoil	353,354

Prosopis juilflora	Mesquite	173,174
Prosopis pubescens	Screwbean	173
Prunus armeniaca	Apricot	175,176
Prunus caroliniana	Carolina Cherry Laurel	509,510
Prunus cerasifera	Purpleleaf Plum	177,178
Prunus X cistena	Prupleleaf Sand Cherry	177
Prunus glandulosa	Flowering Almond	355,356
Prunus laurocerasus	Cherry Laurel or English Laurel	511,512
Prunus mume	Japanese Apricot	175
Prunus persica	Common Peach	179,180
Prunus pumila	Sand Cherry	177
Prunus serotina	Black Cherry	181,182
Prunus serrulata	Japanese Flowering Cherry	183,184
Prunus subhirtella	Autumn Flowering Cherry	183
Pseudotsuga menziesi	Douglas Fir	735,736
Punica granatum	Pomegranate	357,358
Pyracantha coccinea	Pyracantha or Firethorn	513,514
Pyracantha koidzumi	Formosa Pyracantha	513,515,516
Pyrus calleryana	Callery Pear	185,186
Pyrus communis	Common Pear	187,188
Quercus spp.	Oaks	189
Quercus acutissima	Sawtooth Oak	191,192
Quercus alba	White Oak	193,194
Quercus bicolor	Swamp White Oak	195,196
Quercus borealis	Northern Red Oak	213
Quercus falcata	Southern Red Oak	197,198
Quercus hemisphaerica	Laurel Oak	205
Quercus imbricaria	Shingle Oak	209
Quercus laurifolia	Laurel Oak	205,206
Quercus macrocarpa	Bur Oak	199,200
Quercus marilandica	Blackjack Oak	201,202
Quercus muehlenbergi	Chinquapin Oak, Yellow Chestnut Oak	203,204
Quercus nigra	Water Oak	205,206
Quercus nuttalli	Nuttall Oak	215
Quercus pagodifolia	Cherrybark Oak,Swamp Spanish Oak	197
Quercus palustris	Pin Oak	207,208
Quercus phellos	Willow Oak	209,210
Quercus robur	English Oak	211,212
Quercus rubra	Northern Red Oak	197,213,214,215
Quercus shumardi	Shumard Oak	213,215,216
Quercus stellata	Post Oak	217,218
Quercus texana	Texas Oak	215
Quercus virginiana	Live Oak	517,518
Raphiolepis indica	Indian Hawthorn	519,520
Raphiolepis umbellata	Round Leaf Hawthorn	519,520
Raphis excelsa	Lady Palm	581,582
Rhamnus caroliniana	Carolina Buckthorn	219

Rhamnus cathartica	Common Buckthorn	219,220
Rhamnus davurica	Dahurian Buckthorn	219,220
Rhamnus frangula	Glossy Buckthorn	219
Rhapidophyllum hystrix	Needle Palm	583,584
Rhododendron spp.	Evergreen Rhododendron	521,522
Rhododendron catawbiense	Catawba Rhododendron	521
Rhododendron indicum	Southern or Indica Azalea	523,524
Rhododendron obtusum	Kurume Azalea	525,526
Rhododendron simsii	Southern Azalea	523,524
Rhodotypos scandens	Black Jetbead	359,360
Rhus aromatica	Fragrant Sumac	361,362,363
Rhus copallina	Winged, Shining, or Planeleaf Sumac	363
Rhus glabra	Smooth Sumac	363,364
Rhus radicans	Poison Ivy	365,366
Rhus typhina	Staghorn or Velvet Sumac	367,368
Ribes alpinum	Alpine Currant	369,370
Ribes cynosbati	Prickly Gooseberry	369
Ribes hirtellum	Common Gooseberry	369
Robina pseudoacacia	Black Locust	221,222
Rosa spp.	Rose	371,372
Rosa banksiae	Banks Rose	527,528
Rosa multiflora	Multiflora Rose	527
Rosa rugosa	Rugosa Rose	371,372,527
Rosemarinus officianalis	Rosemary	639,640
Roystonea regia	Royal Palm	585,586
Sabal minor	Bush Palmetto or Dwarf Palm	587
Sabal palmetto	Sabal Palm	587,588
Salix alba	Yellow-stemmed Weeping Willow	223
Salix babylonica	Weeping Willow	223,224
Salix X 'Blanda'	Wisconsin Weeping Willow	223
Salix discolor	Pussy Willow	225,226
Salix gracilistyla	Rosegold Pussy Willow	225
Salix matsudana 'Tortuosa'	Corkscrew Willow	227,228
Salix nigra	Black Willow	229,230
Salvia ballotaeflora	Blue Sage	373
Salvia gregii	Autumn Salvia, Autumn Sage	373,374
Salvia regia	Mountain Sage, Royal Sage	373
Santolina chamaecyparissus	Gray Santolina	641,642
Santolina virens	Green Santolina	643,644
Spindus drummondi	Western Soapberry	145,231,232
Sapium sebiferum	Chinese Tallow Tree	233,234
Sarcococca hookerana	Sweetbox	529,530
Sassafras albidum	Sassafras	235,236
Sasa palmata	Palmate Bamboo	405
Sedum acre	Gold Moss Stonecrop	645,646

Sedum spectabile	Fall Sedum	645,646
Sedum spurium	Dragonsblood Sedum	645,646
Serenoa repens	Saw Palmetto	583,587,589,590
Sophora japonica	Japanese Pagoda Tree	237,238
Sophora secundflora	Texas Mountain Laurel	239,240
Sorbus alnifolia	Korean Mountail Laurel	241
Sorbus aucuparia	European Mountain Ash	241,242
Sorbus tianshanica	Tianshanica Mountain Ash	241
Spiraea albiflora	Japanese White Spiraea	375
Spiraea X arguta	Garland Spiraea	375,378
Spiraea X bumalda	Bumalda Spiraea	375,376
Spiraea cantoniensis	Reeves Spiraea	375
Spiraea japonica	Japanese Spiraea	375,377
Spiraea X multiflora	Garland Spiraea	375
Spiraea prunifolia	Bridal Wreath	375,378
Spiraea thunbergi	Thunberg Spiraea	375,377
Spiraea trilobata	Threelobe Spiraea	375
Spiraea X vanhouttei	Vanhoutte Spiraea	375,376,377,378
Stewartia ovata	Mountain Stewartia	243
Stewartia pseudocamellia	Japanese Stewartia	243,244
Stewartia sinensis	Chinese Stewartia	243
Syringa afghinaca	Afghan Lilac	379
Syringa amurensis	Japanese Tree Lilac	245,246
Syringa X chinensis	Chinese Lilac	382
Syringa lacaniata	Cutleaf Lilac	379
Syringa meyeri	Meyer Lilac	382
Syringa pekinensis	Chinese or Pekin Tree Lilac	245
Syringa persica	Persian Lilac	379,381,382
Syringa reticulata	Japanese Tree Lilac	245,246
Syringa vulgaris	Common Lilac	379,380,381,382
Taxodium ascendens	Pond Cypress	247,248
Taxodium distichum	Bald Cypress	247,248
Taxodium mucronatum	Montezuma Cypress	247
Taxus spp.	Yew	737,738,739,740
Taxus baccata	English Yew	737
Taxus capitata	Japanese Yew	737
Taxus cuspidata	Japanese Yew	737,738,740
Taxus floridana	Florida Yew	663
Taxus media	Hybrid Yews	737,738,739,740
Ternstroemia gymnanthera	Cleyera	423
Ternstroemia japonica	Japanese Cleyera	423,424
Thuja occidentalis	American or Eastern Arborvitae	741,742,743
Thuja orientalis	Oriental or Chinese Arborvitae	697,741,744,745,746
Tilia americana	American Linden or Basswood	249,250
Tilia X euchlora 'Redmond'	Redmond Linden	249,250
Tilia cordata	European Littleleaf Linden	251,252

Tilia tomentosa	Silver Linden	253,254
Tillandsia usneoides	Spanish Moss	531,532
Torreya taxifolia	Florida Torreya	663
Toxicodendron radicans	Poison Ivy	365,366
Trachelospermum asiaticum	Japanese Star Jasmine	647,648
Trachelospermum jasminoides	Confederate or Star Jasmine	647,648
Trachycarpus fortunei	Windmill Palm	591,592
Tsuga canadensis	Canadian or Eastern Hemlock	747,748
Tsuga caroliniana	Carolina Hemlock	747
Ulmus alata	Winged Elm	257,258
Ulmus americana	American Elm	255,256
Ulmus crassifolia	Cedar Elm	257,258
Ulmus japonica	Japanese Elm	255
Ulmus parvifolia	Lacebark or Chinese Elm	257,259,260,261
Ulmus pumila	Siberian Elm	255,257,261,262
Ulmus sempervirens	Lacebark Elm	259
Uniola latifolia	Northern Sea Oats	383,384
Uniola paniculata	Sea Oats	383
Veitchia merrillii	Manila, Adonidia, Chrismas, Baby Royal Palm	593,594
Viburnum spp.	Viburnum	385,386
Viburnum X 'Burkwoodi'	Burkwood Viburnum	385,387
Viburnum carlesi	Koreanspice or Mayflower Viburnum	385,387
Viburnum dentatum	Arrowwood Viburnum	385,387
Viburnum lantana	Wayfaringtree Viburnum	386,388,531
Viburnum lentago	Nannyberry Viburnum	386,388
Viburnum odoratissimum	Sweet Viburnum	533,534,535,536
Viburnum opulus	European Cranberrybush Viburnum	386,389
Viburnum plicatum	Doublefile Viburnum	386,390
Viburnum rhytidophylloides	Hybrid Leatherleaf Viburnum	533,534
Viburnum rhytidophyllum	Leatherleaf Viburnum	533,534
Viburnum sieboldi	Siebold Viburnum	386,390
Viburnum suspensum	Sandanqua Viburnum	535,536
Viburnum tinus	Laurestinus	537,538
Viburnum trilobum	American Cranberrybush Viburnum	386,389
Viburnum utile		385
Vinca major	Periwinkle	649,650,651
Vinca minor	Common Periwinkle	649,651,652
Vitex agnus-castus	Chaste Tree	391,392
Vitex negundo	Chaste Tree	391
Washingtonia filifera	Washington Palm	595,596
Washingtonia robusta	Mexican Washington Palm	597,598
Weigela florida	Weigela	393,394
Wisteria floribunda	Japanese Wisteria	395,399
Wisteria sinensis	Chinese Wisteria	395,396,399
Xanthoceras sorbifolium	Popcorn Shrub	397,398